Preserving Western History

Preserving Western History

Edited by ANDREW GULLIFORD

University of New Mexico Press

Albuquerque

*Dedicated to the next generation
of college students
who will preserve and interpret
the history of the American West*

*And to my wife,
the best muse an historian ever had*

©2005 by the University of New Mexico Press
All rights reserved. Published 2005
Printed in the United States of America
09 08 07 06 05   1 2 3 4 5

LIBRARY OF CONGRESS CATALOGING-IN-PUBLICATION DATA

Preserving Western history / edited by Andrew Gulliford.— 1st ed.
p. cm.
Includes bibliographical references.
ISBN 0-8263-3310-9 (pbk. : alk. paper)
1. Historic sites—Conservation and restoration—West (U.S.)
2. Material culture—Conservation and restoration—West (U.S.)
3. Historic preservation—West (U.S.)
4. West (U.S.)—History, Local. I. Gulliford, Andrew.
F590.7.P74 2005
978—dc22
2005008230

DESIGN AND COMPOSITION: *Mina Yamashita*

Contents

Acknowledgments / vii

Introduction / Personal Reflections

Headnotes / 1

Andrew Gulliford, Old West, New West, Next West: Preserving Western History / 3

William W. Gwaltney, The Lunatic Fringe and Fringed Lunatics: Reenacting Western History in Buckskins / 11

Historical Archaeology

Headnotes / 17

Douglas D. Scott, Interpreting Archaeology at Little Bighorn Battlefield National Monument / 20

Philip Duke, Randall H. McGuire, Dean J. Saitta, Paul E. Reckner, and Mark Walker, The Colorado Coalfield War Archaeological Project: Archaeology Serving Labor / 32

Exhibitions, Museums, and Interpreting Culture

Headnotes / 45

William Wroth, Exhibiting Native American and Hispanic Arts in Cultural Context / 50

Carroll Van West, History and Interpretation at the Western History Museum / 57

Thomas Patin, Western Views and Eastern Visions: National Parks, Manifest Destiny, and American Identity / 66

Raymond W. Rast, Preserving the History of Nikkei Removal on Bainbridge Island, Washington / 74

Hispanic Culture

Headnotes / 89

Lonn Taylor, New Mexican Chests: A Comparative Look / 91

Jon Hunner, Preserving Hispanic Lifeways in New Mexico / 97

Sarah Horton, Where Is the "Mexican" in "New Mexican"?: Enacting History, Enacting Dominance in the Santa Fe Fiesta / 106

Art Gómez, A Memorial to What?: The Vexing Question of Chamizal National Memorial between Texas and Mexico / 117

Native American Preservation Issues

Headnotes / 123

Joseph Weixelman, Interpreting the "Anasazi Myth": How the Pueblo Indians Disappeared from the Story / 128

Amanda Zeman, Preservation and Repatriation: American Indian Sacred Objects and National Historic Landmarks at Grand Canyon National Park / 145

Fred Chapman, The Bighorn Medicine Wheel: Landscape Wars and Negotiating Native American Spirituality in the New West / 159

Sand Creek, Colorado, Case Study

Christine Whitacre, The Search for the Site of the Sand Creek Massacre / 175

U.S. Senator Ben Nighthorse Campbell, Why Preserve a Massacre Site? So the Dead May Rest / 189

Thomas J. Noel, Rewriting the Past for the Present: Public Monuments and Political Correctness, the Colorado State Capitol and Sand Creek / 192

Women in the West

Headnotes / 195

Sally McBeth, Sacagawea: The Making of an American Cultural Icon / 200

Marcia Tremmel Goldstein, "Western Women Wild with Joy!":
History Making, Public Memory, and Women in the American West / 214

Jan MacKell, From the Old Homestead to the Mustang Ranch: Prostitution,
Preservation, and Public History in the American West / 226

Environmental Public History

Headnotes / 235

Andrew Gulliford, Fire on the Mountain: Wildland Firefighter Tragedies and Firefighter Memorials / 239

Patrick Tierney, Ecotourism and Western National Parks: A Case Study in Management
to Protect Natural and Cultural Resources / 253

Jeffrey Nichols, "These Waters Were All Virgin": Finis Mitchell and Wind River Wilderness, Wyoming / 263

Steven C. Schulte, "Where Man Is a Visitor": The Wilderness Act as a Case Study in Western Public History / 272

Historic Preservation and Cultural Landscapes

Headnotes / 283

Ekaterini Vlahos, Colorado Ranch Preservation:
The Twenty-First Century and the Changing American West / 287

Peter Dedek, The Mother Road of Nostalgia: Preservation and Interpretation Along U.S. Route 66 / 298

Jay Price, Making the West Look Western: The Rise of the Old West Revival Architectural Style / 310

Judy Mattivi Morley, Historic Preservation and the Creation of Western Civic Identity:
Case Studies in Albuquerque, Denver, and Seattle / 329

Kara Mariko Miyagishima, From Brothels to Buddhism: A Walking Tour of Denver's Red-Light District / 338

Western Mining Landscapes: Case Studies

Eric L. Clements, For Sale by Owner: Western Tourism and Historic Preservation / 341

Richard Francaviglia, Boomtowns and Ghost Towns: Learning from the West's Preserved Historic Mining Landscapes / 348

David Robertson, Cultural Landscape Preservation and Public History in Cokedale, Colorado / 366

James E. Fell, Jr., Old Mines, New Developments: Preservation, the Environment,
and Public History in the Mining West / 381

Conclusion: A Past Presumed to Be Comfortable and Comfortably Past

Headnotes / 389

Dwight T. Pitcaithley, Being Born Western and the Challenges of Public History / 389

Authors' Biographies / 397

List of Centers in the West / 404

Index / 407

Acknowledgments

Many of these essays and themes were developed at professional conferences, and I would like to thank those program committees who helped these ideas come before the public. Relevant conferences open to public history themes include annual meetings of the American Culture Association, Colorado Preservation, Inc., the National Council on Public History, the National Trust for Historic Preservation, the Organization of American Historians, and the Western History Association. I also appreciate the opportunity I have had to hone public history and preservation ideas during invited lectures at The Colorado College, Northern Arizona University, Southern Methodist University—Taos, Eastern Illinois University, Mesa State College, Belmont University, University of Colorado-Denver, the American Heritage Center of the University of Wyoming, the Buffalo Bill Historical Center, the Colorado Historical Society, the Colorado Springs Fine Arts Center, the Grand Junction Readers Festival, and other venues.

I gratefully acknowledge funding for public history and preservation research, which has helped to produce this book, and appreciate financial support that I have received from the Wayne Aspinall Foundation, the Ballantine Family Foundation, the James Marston Fitch Foundation, the Charles Redd Foundation, the Skaggs Foundation, the Southern Ute Growth Fund, the Colorado Endowment for the Humanities, and the National Endowment for the Humanities.

Some of the essays in this book have been previously published and subsequently updated. I gratefully acknowledge permission to reprint essays from *El Palacio*, *The Journal of American Culture*, *Montana: The Magazine of Western History*, *Prologue: The Journal of the National Archives*, *The Public Historian*, *The Western Historical Quarterly*, and a chapter from John H. Jameson, Jr., ed., *Presenting Archaeology to the Public* (Walnut Creek: AltaMira Press, 1997). I thank the writers who contributed their essays to this volume and wrote new essays just for this book.

Special thanks for ideas and assistance through the years are due to Fred Schroeder, Leslie Fishel, Tom Noel, Carl Scheele, Bill Gwaltney, Patty Limerick (for her wit and verve), Adam Kane, Ken Francis, Bev Rich, Jeff Brown, Jon Hunner, Lorne McWatters, Rebecca Conard, William Grant, Peter Decker, Tom K. Barton, Bruce Craig, Edward Linenthal, Dean May, Rick Ewing, Robert Archibald, Nik Kendziorski, and my Center of Southwest Studies colleagues Todd Ellison, Jeanne Brako, and Catherine Conrad. Larry Gooden, Kim Clawson, and MaryJoy Martin are to be commended for their help with the study questions.

I would also like to thank former students I have taught at Bowling Green State University, Western New Mexico University, Middle Tennessee State University, Mesa State College, and Fort Lewis College, because they helped to shape this reader. I am indebted to Luther Wilson, director of the University of New Mexico Press, for his patience and perseverance, and to my wife, Stephanie Moran, who understands the value of books and how long it takes to craft them.

Editor's Note

A portion of the proceeds from this textbook will be dedicated to scholarships and internships for students from the Center of Southwest Studies at Fort Lewis College and the National Council on Public History.

Introduction / Personal Reflections

Headnotes

Public history is defined as history that is interpreted or taught outside of a school classroom. Examples of public history include historic tours, feature films set in the historical past, and historical sites interpreted by national or state parks. Under contract, each year public historians produce hundreds of documents that define and describe American and Western history, yet these reports are often considered "gray literature," and they are not regularly printed or distributed. Laws requiring historical analysis include the National Historic Preservation Act, the Native American Graves Protection and Repatriation Act, and certain sections of environmental laws. Because there is so much public land in the American West and because tourism and heritage tourism are mainstays of the economy, public history is an increasingly important business. Writing in *CRM Journal* (summer 2004), Michael Kelleher explains that "people seeking cultural or heritage tourism experiences desire authenticity of place and experience." Who better to verify and authenticate those western places than public historians and preservationists? Opportunities exist for public historians in the West and across the nation.

In Washington, D.C., alone there are over 400 historians who work in federal agencies, and "on the ground" in the West, many public land managers require an understanding of the past and changes in the landscape in order to make informed decisions about the present and the future. Public history firms are found from Missoula to Tucson. Public historians help research and describe all manner of celebrations and centennials, and they've recently had a bonanza with the national interest in Lewis and Clark's epic westward journey.

Public history course offerings are becoming more frequent in college curricula, and graduate programs with master's degrees in public history can be found in several western states. Public history tracks and emphases are also now available at the doctoral level in major universities. Public historians not only excel at research and writing, they also interpret the past for the public and must seek the funding to do so through contracts, grants, and other forms of fund-raising, including private patronage. Public historians work in teams, often with anthropologists but occasionally with scriptwriters, filmmakers, musicians, ethnologists, and historic preservation specialists. In her book *Something in the Soil: Legacies and Reckonings in the New West*, University of Colorado historian Patricia Limerick discusses public historians, Western historians, and public intellectuals. She writes about stories and narratives in the West and how "never the simple, pristine, virgin place of the European imagination, the landscape is now knee-deep in stories, many of them forgotten and ready for rediscovery."

Patricia Limerick directs the Center for the American West at the University of Colorado at Boulder, which funds conferences and symposia to present important issues and bring diverse groups together who have different historical perspectives. Trained as an academic historian, she has the attitude and the aptitude to succeed in the public arena. Public history students must choose their profession because they must be entrepreneurial, inventive, and always looking ahead to the next project. They must work well in teams under hard deadlines and be product and goal oriented. An early essay on Western public history by Albert L. Hurtado, "The Significance of Public History in the American West: An Essay and Some Modest Suggestions," appeared in the *Western Historical Quarterly* in August 1988 with detailed analysis and lengthy endnotes. Professor Hurtado wrote a significant essay on public historians, their work, and their employers. The goal of this reader is to unite Western history and public history into one volume, which will inspire the next generation of Western public historians. The book begins with two personal accounts.

In the following essays, historians Andrew Gulliford and William Gwaltney discuss different aspects of public history and how they became public historians. Gulliford, professor of Southwest Studies and History at Fort Lewis College in Durango, Colorado, writes about the circuitous path he took to learn about public history, beginning with a stint as a fourth-grade teacher in Silt, Colorado. While researching and writing numerous Western history topics during summers he came to understand public history, which was a new field not yet being taught at the undergraduate level. He became a public historian while directing projects titled "As Far as the Eye Can See: A High Plains Documentary," "The Years Ahead: Life for the Aging in Northwest Colorado," and the $275,000 eight-state "Country School Legacy: Humanities on the Frontier."

William Gwaltney took a different turn as a public historian with a successful career in the National Park Service. He learned history and interpretive skills in the nation's capital but then moved west to work in a variety of national parks and positions, including interpreter at Bent's Old Fort National Historic Site. Gwaltney honed his skills at buckskinning and re-creating the Black Buffalo Soldiers, or African American troops, who helped settle the Western frontier. His essay describes the ways reenactors succeed as public historians.

Old West, New West, Next West

Preserving Western History

ANDREW GULLIFORD

THERE ARE NUMEROUS MONOGRAPHS on Western history, the new Western history, Indian Wars, settlers, homesteaders, women in the West, and the rise of Western cities. A growing literature also describes public historians who work as archivists, museum curators, historic preservationists, and historians in the employ of federal agencies and corporations.[1] What was missing until now is a book that brings both fields together with selected readings that provide emphasis on public history in the American West.

Many public history books teach about material culture, Chippendale chairs, and curating collections at Colonial Williamsburg.[2] There are also excellent books such as Michael Wallace's *Mickey Mouse History* or Susan Benson's *Presenting the Past*, but they do not address the special issues and historical collections found west of the hundredth meridian.[3] In trying to teach public history in the West to first-generation Hispano and Native American students, I have found it impossible to find one book that presented cogent essays useful to third- and fourth-generation Westerners or Native Americans. So the goal of this book is to provide, through a few previously published articles and mostly new essays, a one-volume introduction to public history in the West.

Of necessity much as been omitted, because the field is too large and growing too fast. Public historians and Western historians have good working relationships with archaeologists and anthropologists, and both groups practice cultural resources management, but this book must be limited to essays and photographs that depict historical archaeology, not prehistoric archaeology. This is a book for the next generation of public historians who will live and work in the West. These authors have generally avoided writing and describing "Western heritage," because all too often "heritage" is perceived as the history that local communities would prefer to have had in contrast to the actual stories that need to be told. David Thelen notes that "memory, private and individual as much as collective and cultural, is constructed not reproduced," and adds that "people reshape their recollections of the past to fit their present needs."[4] Heritage is what people may want to remember as opposed to history, which, if done right, approximates what actually happened on the landscape. My personal path as a public historian in the West has been an interesting journey, and a younger generation can learn from my experience.

I did not begin a career as a public and community historian, but that's the way things evolved. After entering The Colorado College in Colorado Springs as a religion and philosophy major, I dropped out of college after my sophomore year. I moved to San Francisco, worked in a hospital kitchen, wrote a few bad poems, and found the woman who would become my wife. Because I could not take the hustle and bustle of California, after a short stint in a variety of jobs I returned to The Colorado College. I signed up for an accounting class because I thought I wanted to be a hospital manager. I knew that after graduation I would need to "earn a living."

I brought the accounting book home to my apartment, took one look at it, and knew I couldn't possibly enjoy the class. And I made an important decision. I decided if I ever needed an accountant, I would hire one. So I returned the book and instead took a course in European history and loved every minute of it. That was my point of conversion. I knew then that I wanted to be a historian, but public history in its present form did not exist. I became a history major and stayed at The Colorado College to complete a master of arts in teaching degree. I also began to do public history projects for the Plains and Peaks Library System in Colorado Springs, for the Colorado

Centennial-Bicentennial Commission in 1976, and then for the Colorado Endowment for the Humanities in 1977. These were oral history/photography projects documenting rural areas in Colorado.

For the nation's bicentennial Randall Teeuwen and I wrote and produced "As Far as the Eye Can See: A High Plains Documentary," which was a slide/tape show, in those ancient days before PowerPoint presentations. We documented farmers who lived on 50,000 square miles of eastern Colorado between the Platte and Arkansas Rivers. That was a $5,000 project. Then in 1977 we produced "The Years Ahead: Life for the Aging in Northwest Colorado," which involved a similarly large study area but an even more remote part of the state. We had additional sponsors on that $17,000 project. I had moved to Silt, Colorado, and begun teaching fourth grade and working as a historian in the summers.

After those grant-writing successes in 1980, I wrote and directed a $275,000, eight-state National Endowment for the Humanities project titled "Country School Legacy: Humanities on the Frontier," which in 1982 won the Award of Merit from the American Association for State and Local History. For an 18-month project I assembled a dedicated team of 24 historians and librarians who recorded and documented country school experiences and then hosted over 200 public programs. I studied one-room schools in the states of Colorado, Kansas, Utah, Wyoming, Nevada, Nebraska, and North and South Dakota. My partner and I traveled in my 1968 Volkswagen camper bus equipped with beer, film, two sets of 35 mm. cameras, two medium-format cameras, a movie projector, two broadcast-quality tape recorders, and a border collie named Estrella Estrellita. Sleeping in the bus and camping in farmers' fields and city parks, we were on the road and documenting a vanishing part of American culture and education. I still did not know I was "doing" public history, but I was applying my research skills and hosting public programs in small libraries across the Great Plains.

We produced a 26-minute color film and two traveling exhibits for each of eight states. The exhibits

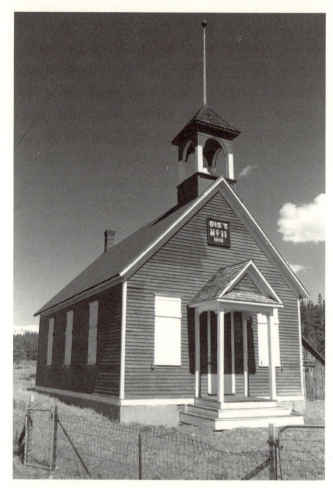

Figure 1. Leadville, Colorado, one-room schoolhouse. Photo by author, 1980.

had to be UPS shippable to be set up in the smallest libraries in South Dakota, which were usually just single-wide trailers. Our team also produced a 50-print photography exhibit, and by 1984 my first book, *America's Country Schools*, was published by the National Trust for Historic Preservation. Finally, at Bowling Green State University in Ohio, I learned about public history and its formal definitions from one of my professors, Dr. Leslie Fishel.

Public history is history for an out-of-school audience, and it involves teamwork and a different kind of delivery instead of class lectures. Other forms of public history include walking tours, historic site interpretation, historic preservation, historic novels and films, archival administration, and museum curation. I came to understand what I wanted to do with my life. I wanted to be a public historian in the West to help

Figures 2 and 3. Old West and new West portraits: the Dodo family at a coal-mining camp in Garfield County, Colorado, circa 1882 and the Johnson family on Silt Mesa, Garfield County, Colorado, ca. 1982. Both photos in possession of the author.

preserve and interpret the West's diverse cultures and landscapes. I finally knew what I wanted to do; now I just had to find someone to pay me to do it!

I hit the job market at the wrong time. Is there ever a right time? And so rather than teach American culture/American history on a college campus, I became a railroad historian in Lima, Ohio, a Rust Belt community with seven railroad lines snaking through town. I interviewed railroad workers. I studied the Lima Locomotive Works, and my office on the town square was a restored five-ton Baltimore & Ohio caboose with the phone number 22-TRAIN. People would call me up to be interviewed and I told them to come on down. Just visit me in my caboose.

It was a good job for a year, but I missed the West and I finally came home to the mountains to Western New Mexico University and the directorship of the WNMU Museum. There I learned about prehistoric Mimbres pottery and archaeological resource issues. In Silver City our second son was born and I edited my dissertation into my second book, *Boomtown Blues: Colorado Oil Shale*. By 1990 we had moved back east to Murfreesboro, Tennessee, where I directed one of the nation's oldest and largest public history and historic preservation graduate programs at Middle Tennessee State University. Though I taught in Tennessee, during the summers I researched tribal historic preservation after working with the Eastern Shoshones on the Wind River Reservation in Wyoming and also as a historian on the Ute Trail in western Colorado. In 2000 I published *Sacred Objects and Sacred Places: Preserving Tribal Traditions*, and I returned to the West, this time for good, to direct the Center of Southwest Studies at Fort Lewis College in

Figure 4. Homestead house on the eastern Colorado plains. Photo by author, 1975.

Durango, Colorado. The Center of Southwest Studies is home to the $2.5 million Durango Collection that features eight centuries of weaving from the Southwest. And now as a college professor, I realize how much we need a public history book that addresses our Western resources and Western themes.

The career path for me has been circuitous, and I want to provide some guideposts for the next generation. Public history has emerged as a definite field in graduate school, and with the explosion of heritage tourism and the tourism industry in the West, it is essential to have accurate historical representations of Western history. This book will steer students toward those goals. Here college students will learn about "doing" public history and historic preservation in the American West.

The concept of Old West, New West, Next West is essential, because the West will change as dramatically in the twenty-first century as it did in the nineteenth century, when Native Americans were pushed off their aboriginal lands because of the notion of Manifest Destiny. Patricia Limerick has defined that time and place in her classic *Legacy of Conquest*.[5] Law professor and historian Charles Wilkinson, in an essay on Ute Indian removal from Colorado, asks hard questions about betrayals. He writes, "Conquerors, as well as the conquered, are diminished when a trust is broken. We know now that we came on too hard and fast for the Ute. We could have accommodated settlement by non-Indians and also allowed for the White River Utes to hold good land."[6] For many Western communities, large and small, who rely on tourism and thus want to make history easy to swallow, their "heritage" and their history are not the same. The sordid side of Indian removals, vigilante justice, racial segregation, and outright theft of land and property is conveniently ignored in favor of pioneer origin stories of hardship and deprivation. Western history, like Southern history, must come to terms with the past. The truth should be told in lieu of a "heritage" that often does not square with the facts.

If the Old West was about cowboys and Indians, cattle herds, gold and silver strikes, and the coming of railroads, it was also about environmental degradation from timber theft, overgrazing by longhorn cattle and merino sheep, and water rights locked into a "doctrine of prior appropriation" and a "use it or lose it" mentality. If we damaged the landscape, almost eliminated the buffalo herds, and shotgunned the passenger pigeon into extinction, we also made big mistakes in human settlement. We put too many homesteaders on marginal land, and despite small waves of successful settlement, there have been and continue to be painful out-migrations of farm and ranch families, particularly on the Great Plains. North Dakota now has fewer people than it did in the 1930s. Eastern Colorado, eastern Montana, and eastern Wyoming represent what cultural geographer Mike Wycoff has called "the waning west."[7] *New York Times* columnist Nicolas Kristof calls it "the failed frontier."[8]

I grew up in eastern Colorado, on the high plains in Prowers County near Lamar. Once home to the Cheyenne and Arapaho and later Bent's Fort, the high plains have seen waves of emigrants as chronicled by Elliott West in his award-winning book *The Contested Plains*.[9] But now there is little opportunity on the prairie. Riding high on the heels of the nineteenth-century West, the twentieth-century West was also a West of resource extraction. It was a West of Phelps

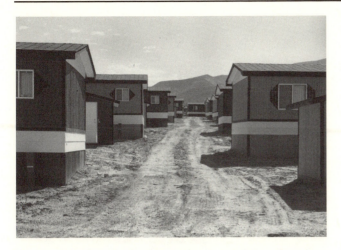

Figure 5. New West worker housing for the oil shale industry at Exxon's Battlement Mesa, Parachute, Colorado. Photo by author, 1982.

Figure 6. The Hippie West: white horse in an abandoned geodesic dome at the site of Drop City, Colorado, near Trinidad. Photo by author, 1978.

Dodge Corporation and a huge open-pit copper mine near Santa Rita, New Mexico; Climax Molybdenum at Leadville, Colorado; and the giant Kennecott open-pit mine in Bingham Canyon near Salt Lake City. The resource West in the twentieth century featured labor strikes, conflict, murder at Ludlow, and mine shafts sunk into deep granite to extract gold and silver. Hardrock miners came from Austria, Tyrolia, and Germany. Coal miners came from Eastern Europe. Basque sheepherders arrived from the Pyrenees, and Mexican migrants resolutely traveled north to work in the mines and on the railroads and in California's fields.

By the end of the twentieth century the rivers had been dammed and the shaft and tunnel mines shut down, but a nineteenth-century conservation ethic emerged into a full-blown environmental movement, with millions of Western acres set aside for national parks, national forests, wilderness areas, and other public lands. Even the General Land Office, whose heritage from the time of Thomas Jefferson had been to give away the West, was finally reorganized into the Bureau of Land Management, with new goals to protect the resources under its charge.

The Old West of gunplay, U.S. cavalry troops, and homesteaders' wagons became the New West of sport utility vehicles, time-share condominiums, and whitewater rafting. What old-timers and homesteaders did because they had to, New Westerners do for fun and recreation. T. K. Whipple summed it up: "All America lies at the end of the wilderness road, and our past is not a dead past, but still lives in us. Our forefathers had civilization inside themselves, the wild outside. We live in the civilization they created, but within us the wilderness still lingers. What they dreamed, we live, and what they lived, we dream."[10]

Thus the Old West of resource extraction, whether for gold, silver, grass, or timber, has given way to the New West of burgeoning metropolitan cities, a huge influx of newcomers along the spine of the Rocky Mountains, and forest trails overcrowded with mountain bikers, hikers, horses and riders, and many "pilgrims" with cell phones and GPS units. This sea change in demographics and culture is best summed up in *The Atlas of the New West*.[11] If the Old West meant settling disputes at the end of a rope, the New West means plenty of time in court with diverse plaintiffs, including savvy sovereign Indian tribes, ready to defend themselves. The old issues are still there—access to land, access to water, and making the most of limited resources. But new issues include how to protect sacred landscapes, where to place microwave towers, and how to keep expensive vacation homes off ridgelines.[12]

Increasingly in the New West, a mining and agriculture economy has been superceded by a service

Figures 7 and 8. Western humor: a photo of a buffalo burger in a café along the Rocky Mountain Front north of Helena, Montana, and entrance to a laundromat at DuBois, Wyoming. Photos by author, 1992.

 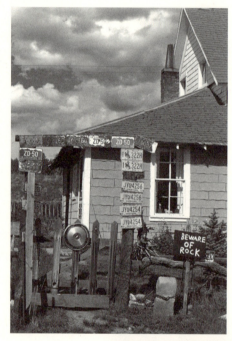

Figures 9 and 10. Homemade stone entrance, Shooks Run, Colorado Springs. Rural entrance gate, El Paso County, Colorado, "Beware of Rock" (note that the rock is chained to the gate to protect visitors). Photos by author, 1974.

Figures 11 and 12. Log V-shaped entrance to San Juan River Ranch, Archuleta County, Colorado. Oversized log entrance gate to the Bootstrap Ranch west of Wolf Creek Pass. Moral: The newer the neighbor, the bigger the gate. Photos by author, 2003.

economy with few good-paying jobs and only minimal benefits.[13] In the Old West fortunes were made off the landscape and dollars flowed East. Now, fortunes are made elsewhere and then spent in the alpine playgrounds of Aspen, Vail, Sun Valley, Telluride, Tahoe, and Park City. From Sierra Vista, Arizona, to Kalispell, Montana, small western towns have become magnets for retirees and "modem cowboys" seeking to relocate close to public lands and dramatic landscapes.

Wallace Stegner, the dean of Western writers, urged us to create "a society to match the scenery." It did not happen in his time, and it might not happen in ours, because there is much income disparity and a crying need for affordable housing at the same time that 4,000-square-foot vacation homes sit idle 10 months out of the year. And yet we may finally have moved beyond Western myth. Rugged individualism has given way to a new sense of community, and there are now innovative attempts to connect people with place (see the appendix for a list of Western centers and institutes).

What will the twenty-first-century West become, and how will it connect the present with the past? How can we both learn from our history and sustain those landscapes that give our lives meaning—those mountain vistas, those expanses of meadow and forest, canyon and prairie, those plateaus that provide, in Edward Geary's words, "the proper edge of the sky"?[14]

Preserving Western History is about just that—not John Wayne's cinematic West or the nouveau ski towns, but the working West of handmade New Mexican chests, high country ranches, controversial ethnic pageants, and linear corridors like Route 66—home of the Mother Road. Some Western counties on the Great Plains have fewer people living there than in 1890, when the frontier officially ended, and some Western counties along the Continental Divide have plenty of new vacation homes, but nobody lives there, either. Frederick Jackson Turner wrote that with the end of the frontier in 1890, "thus has passed the first great age in American history." Now public history in the West has come of age as we seek to record and interpret what once was.

Figure 13. Photo of the book's editor. Note his tie is attached to his shirt by a safety pin to secure it during mountain breezes.

Public historians a decade or two ago were uncertain what we were going to do or where we were going to do it. We loved the West and wanted to understand it, and even, in Edward Abbey's words, "defend it," but how? Thus, the marriage between public history and Western history. We strive to integrate the past with the future and through our work to keep alive the unique Western character, and to preserve and protect our irreplaceable historic artifacts, sites, and landscapes. Enjoy these essays. They were written with the belief that knowing the past gives depth, direction, and meaning to the present and the future.

Notes

1. See Barbara J. Howe and Emory L. Kemp, eds., *Public History: An Introduction* (Malabar, FL: Krieger Publishing, 1988); James B. Gardner and Peter S. LaPaglia, eds., *Public History: Essays from the Field* (Malabar, FL: Krieger Publishing, 1999); and back issues of *History News*, published by the American Association for State and Local History, and *The Public Historian*, published by the National Council on Public History.

2. Thomas J. Schlereth, *Material Culture Studies in America* (Nashville: American Association for State and Local History, 1982), and Thomas Schlereth, *Cultural History and Material Culture: Everyday Life, Landscapes, Museums* (Ann Arbor: UMI Research Press, 1990).

3. Susan Porter Benson, Stephen Brier, and Roy Rosenzweig, eds., *Presenting the Past: Essays on History and the Public* (Philadelphia: Temple University Press, 1986); Mike Wallace, *Mickey Mouse History and Other Essays on American Memory* (Philadelphia: Temple University Press, 1996).

4. David Thelen, ed., *Memory and American History* (Bloomington: Indiana University Press, 1990), ix, xi. See also Robert R. Archibald, *A Place to Remember: Using History to Build Community* (Walnut Creek, CA: AltaMira Press, 1999).

5. Patricia Nelson Limerick, *Legacy of Conquest* (New York: Norton, 1987).

6. Charles Wilkinson, "The Betrayal of Jack," conclusion to Robert Emmitt, *The Last War Trail: Utes and the Settlement of Colorado* (Boulder: University Press of Colorado, 2000).

7. William Wycoff, "Life on the Margin: The Evolution of the Waning West," *Montana: The Magazine of Western History* (autumn 2002): 30–43.

8. Nicolas Kristof, "The Failed Frontier," *New York Times*, September 3, 2002, sec. A:19.

9. Elliott West, *The Contested Plains: Indians, Goldseekers, and the Rush to Colorado* (Lawrence: University Press of Kansas, 1998).

10. T. K. Whipple, "Study Out the Land," from the frontispiece to Larry McMurtry, *Lonesome Dove* (New York: Simon & Schuster, 1985).

11. William Reibesame, ed., *Atlas of the New West* (New York: Norton, 1997).

12. For sacred landscapes see Andrew Gulliford, *Sacred Objects and Sacred Places: Preserving Tribal Traditions* (Boulder: University Press of Colorado, 2000), and the film *In the Light of Reverence*, by Toby McLeod, distributed by Bullfrog Films.

13. See Hal K. Rothman, *Devil's Bargains: Tourism in the Twentieth-Century American West* (Lawrence: University Press of Kansas, 1998).

14. Edward Geary, *The Proper Edge of the Sky: The High Plateau Country of Utah* (Salt Lake City: University of Utah Press, 1992).

Study Questions

1. What is the perceived problem when writing about and describing the concept of "Western heritage"?

2. Define the term *public history*.

3. What is the purpose for compiling the articles in this textbook?

4. Compare and discuss the terms *Old West*, *New West*, and *Next West*.

THE LUNATIC FRINGE AND FRINGED LUNATICS

Reenacting Western History in Buckskins

William W. Gwaltney

Since the publication of Tony Horwitz's *Confederates in the Attic*, there has been a new surge of interest in the hobby of historical reenacting. It's no wonder: Americans find the spectacle of thoroughly modern fellow citizens wearing "funny" clothing on a hot day carrying on with black powder rifles and beaver traps to be almost as entertaining and weird as "reality television." Allegedly the fastest-growing pastime in America, reenacting in the West takes many forms. Enthusiasts of the American fur trade style themselves as "buckskinners" and take to the woods on weekends to recreate and re-create the era of the American fur trade (1807–40). *Western Historical Quarterly* editor Anne Butler asked me to write about these folks and their ways because I know these people. I used to be one of them, and in some ways, I still am.

It would be easy to poke fun at costumed citizens who seem to enjoy not only being on the lunatic fringe, but who, in their buckskin garb, might appear to be fringed lunatics. As it turns out, my long association with these folks and our shared interest in history makes it impossible to dismiss them out of hand. There is more here than meets the eye, and like the trappers of old, we have to be able to read "sign." With a little patience, we can look at the footprints and tell who was here and where they were from.

My interest in the American West started as a child growing up in Washington, D.C. Aided and abetted by my grandfather, I began to visit the Library of Congress, the Smithsonian Institution, and the National Archives. Through high school and college, I maintained my interest in the Old West. I made a set of buckskins and developed an exhibit and an interpretive program. Somewhere along the way, I acquired my first replica black powder rifle.

While a student at the University of Maryland, I had the privilege of having Professor Walter Rundell, once the president of the Western History Association, as a professor of Western history. The teacher's assistant for the course was Anne Butler. Learning of my predilection, Professor Rundell insisted that I come to his classes in my period garb and share the stories I had learned. He also insisted that the university pay me a small stipend.

The day after graduation, I headed for Montana. I hunted coyotes with a muzzle loader and hiked the rimrock country before heading down through Wyoming to Colorado. I had been told about Sam Arnold's restaurant, The Fort, by Professor Rundell, and taking that as a recommendation, I made it my first stop in Colorado. The fort was, and remains, a replica of the fur trading post constructed by Charles and William Bent around 1833. The original fort was built on the edge of United States territory and on the Santa Fe Trail in what would later become southeast Colorado. I was interested in seeing another newly reconstructed version of the same fort used by Sam Arnold as the pattern for his restaurant. "Bent's Old Fort" had been reconstructed the summer before my visit on the original site by the National Park Service.

After traveling to La Junta, Colorado, I spent several days at the reconstructed fort and felt like a kid in a candy store. Someone else shared my interest in history, and it looked like that somebody was the American public. Even better was the fact that the park staff was pleased to find someone interested in the history of the fur trade and who was enthusiastic about working for the National Park Service in a place that was far removed from the scenery of Yellowstone National Park.

My interest in buckskins and black powder, along with the encouragement of Dr. Rundell, did something that was close to impossible in the late 1970s.

The next summer, I was appointed as a seasonal park ranger. When I arrived for duty, I found that the park already had a relationship of sorts with an array of local characters who called themselves "Buckskinners." These folks enjoyed living in a place somewhere between historical fact and historical fiction. As a seasonal ranger, I was introduced to their world and attempted to build bridges with them that could result in public educational programs for the park.

I found that Buckskinning was indeed another world. Fueled by thousands of American men and women, their children, and a handful of Europeans who travel to America to practice their love of Western history, the hobby of "Buckskinning" is a curious mix of primitive camping, fascination with all things American Indian, Western lore, black powder marksmanship, and off-net economy.

It is a subculture in the truest sense. It has its own rules and its own geography. Every summer brings another round of "Rendezvous" and encampments, often in western national forests near where the original trappers held their annual trade fairs in the 1830s. The events are loosely patterned after the mountain trade fairs held from 1825 to 1840 in open mountain parks in present-day southwestern Wyoming and southeastern Utah. The original Rendezvous prevented trappers from having to take their annual catch of furs all the way back to Westport Landing or St. Louis.

It was not only more efficient to keep trappers in the mountains in the nineteenth century, but fur companies found that there was a tremendous profit to be made by centralizing their customers. Indians often outnumbered trappers at these events by a substantial amount. Hundreds of trappers would swap their beaver pelts for blankets, gun parts, traps, soap, coffee, sugar, and raw grain alcohol. The traders could sometimes realize profits of 500 or even 1,000 percent over their original investment.

The scene of pandemonium that was the result of this volatile combination of young men, good credit, and bad alcohol was a sight to behold. Gambling, footraces, horse races, and shooting contests all competed with drunkenness in its many forms for notice. The modern events styled after the original Rendezvous are hosted across the country, including the East, and feature hundreds of people living in canvas tepees, cooking over open fires, and engaging in dozens of improbable contests of skill, including tomahawk throwing, slinging a cast-iron skillet, chili-cooking competitions, and the seemingly inevitable "Liar's Contest," where prevarication, not research, is rewarded.

Some modern Rendezvous feature a "Mountain Man Run," where contestants walk or jog down a trail, having to test their skills by shooting and reloading on the run, starting a fire with flint and steel, or setting a stout beaver trap, all the while knowing that they are working against the clock. The "Mountain Man" with the most points in the shortest time wins.

The participants camp out, sometimes for weeks at a time, in relatively primitive conditions. A few brave the elements to do things the old-fashioned way, but far more succumb to the temptations of modern conveniences. Canvas tepees are often treated with water-resistant finishes, and many a buffalo robe hides a foam mattress. Elaborately carved or painted trunks usually conceal a beer cooler.

While there are rules, they often have little to do with history. Mandates imposed to insist on the wearing of pre-1840 clothes and equipment often results in "looking the other way" at modern cigarettes, sunglasses, cigarette lighters, and wristwatches, none of which would have been in use during the early nineteenth century. Some "Buckskinners," fond of the creature comforts, have gone so far as to construct foam-lined, rawhide beer can covers so as to give an impression completely out of kilter with the version of the past they claim to admire. Here there is no need to confuse the love of history with the knowledge of history. Loving the West, as it was, or as it should have been, is enough.

"Buckskinners" are proud of the sense of instant community that springs up along with several hundred tents and tepees. They boast of the hobby being a safe place for children and that thousands of dollars worth of handcrafted firearms, clothing, and other items are unguarded for hours or even days with nothing being stolen. So far as I can tell, their boasts have some basis in fact.

"Rendezvousing" is mostly recreational in nature. More emphasis is placed on self-enjoyment than on either teaching or learning history. Many of the most common activities are set pieces designed as group maintenance activities that create a sense of continuity and community. Many modern Rendezvous goers create mountain monikers for themselves to the extent that people may have acquaintances for 20 years and not know their actual names. "Grunting Bear" may actually be an accountant in real life, but no one at Rendezvous need know.

While there are many activities designed for the family, alcohol plays a large role in after-hours activities for the adults. Campfire songs are as likely to include twentieth-century songs such as "Puff, the Magic Dragon" as nineteenth-century songs such as "The Boatmen's Dance" or "Green Grow the Rushes, Ho!" Rendezvous provides enthusiasts the chance to really get away from it all. Some of these events are held at such remote locations that they are often the largest cities in some of the counties where they are held.

For men and women living a modern life in the suburbs, Buckskinning creates a distinction that cannot be compared with a bowling league or the Rotary Club. Since many modern fur trade events try to please so many people with different tastes and needs, modern Rendezvous fall somewhere between Boy Scout camp and an Englishman's description of an original Rendezvous in the 1830s: "Maleness Gone Berserk." Grizzled old "gray beards" share their version of the past with whoever will listen and out-of-sorts ne'er-do-wells find a place they have never been before to go back to. "Rendezvousing" has its own brand of commerce. There are dozens of people who make their living supplying old-fashioned clothing, firearms, and services. Some even set up portable bathhouses and restaurants in far-flung places under the western sky to serve the needs of the "Buckskinner."

Over time, I returned to Bent's Old Fort. I was hired as a museum curator and later as chief park ranger. While I continued to participate in summer Rendezvous events, I realized that the park's public interpretive programs needed to be cut from a different cloth than the largely recreational events I had seen across the West. I began to build a network of better-than-average "Buckskinners" from which to form a team of volunteer interpreters. When I began to direct the park's annual Fur Trade Encampment, the cards were quickly laid on the table. There were those who were interested in sharing history with the public and an equal number who were violently opposed to higher clothing standards, restricting the times for alcohol consumption, and the visitor focus that came with the public history responsibilities of the National Park Service.

At the first interpretive event, there were so many "Buckskinners" who wanted to complain about the deviation from the typical, recreational Rendezvous standards that I was forced to designate a "Complaint Tree" where I would meet with unhappy campers.

One Rendezvous participant was disturbed enough that I found myself on the short end of a congressional complaint. I wrote letter after letter explaining the agency's responsibility to the larger public and the damage that could be done to history without standards and evaluation. Luckily, the park has an excellent research library, complete with microfilmed copies of the American Fur Company's trade ledgers. I was able to compile so many kinds of historical proof that my opposition was finally and completely overwhelmed.

In the wake of those difficulties, I began to combine the various points I had made with articles I had written, ledger sheets, and records from Bent, St. Vrain and Company. The final product was bound into a book and was issued to the applicants for the encampment the following year. It was popular enough to be published for sale in the park bookstore.

Out of the maelstrom, I came to discover that the weekend Rendezvous can be contrasted with another costumed pursuit of the history of the fur trade. Another

Figure 14. A Lewis and Clark reenactor stands along the shore of the Missouri River near Great Falls, Montana. Photo by Andrew Gulliford, 2000.

group of costumed weekend warriors rallied to my call at Bent's Old Fort. They are part of a small group of people who treasure history and their days in the wild as cherished learning opportunities to test what has been written down about the history of the fur trade.

Some, like Dan McCrimmon, are real-life educators in their modern lives, while others have become de facto educators, having fallen too far into the past to be really comfortable anyplace else. This brand of enthusiast fancies themselves to be more along the line of "experimental archaeologists." They attempt to adhere to the tenets of historical research and the refinement of period skills and period technology.

The hard core of the lunatic fringe, these men and occasionally women, are often distinguished by their use of horses and mules as opposed to the typically pedestrian "Buckskinner." Their clothing and gear is created with attention to minute detail and their buckskins are often tanned by the wearer with the brains and kidneys of the animal who originally wore the hide. They are gleeful in their lack of comfort, knowing that they are working on a field problem that will take them closer to an understanding of the way things would have been for a small party of trappers. Contrasted with "Buckskinners," they place little focus on food except to ensure its authenticity, regardless of taste.

A story that illustrates this focuses on one of the hardest of the hard core, Dan Muldoon. In the early 1980s, Muldoon was miles from civilization with his "pard" Fred Dixon, headed with a pair of mules and a pair of donkeys from Bent's Old Fort to Taos, New Mexico. When an aggravating tooth demanded removal, Muldoon convinced Dixon to extract it with a brass bullet mold. Without the benefit of anesthetic or sanitized forceps, Dixon was successful in removing the tooth, or at least part of it, leaving Muldoon in greater pain than before. Several days' ride from anywhere, Dixon looked at his pale and pained friend. In the casual spirit of the original mountain men, Dixon asked Muldoon, "If you die . . . can I have your gun?"

Folks like these joined together into a park-based group titled "The Opposition." The name was taken from the term used for all of the smaller trapper-run fur companies that defied the American Fur Company for dominance during the heyday of the trade. "The Opposition" provided outstanding public education programming for park visitors and a new kind of satisfaction for the members themselves. Members of the group were expected to publish annually in scholarly journals as well as participate in public education at the fort. The members had agreed that the group should be made up of people who could be as comfortable in the stacks of a research library as on a weeklong horse trek into the mountains.

As a result of the determination of the members of "The Opposition" and the park staff, interpretive events at Bent's Old Fort took on a new shine during the day and a new spirit at night. Guest historians and curators were invited to share their research with the volunteer interpreters, and the park arranged for period music and dancing in the evenings.

Standards rose to levels previously believed impossible, and interpretive programs were carefully scripted to tell specific stories. Many of the recreational "Buckskinners" stopped participating, but the remaining volunteer interpreters began developing educational programs to be approved by park staff.

A teacher training program titled "Winter Quarters" was developed, which mixed experienced fur trade volunteers with educators from Colorado schools. The four-day program was based on the social stratification of the period and created a depth of experience that still evades description. Several times, the early spring program was enveloped in blizzards. The need for firewood and water was no longer an artifice: we were trapped and had to make do for days at a time on whatever food was available. Park staff found the rules for popular nineteenth-century billiards games and also period card games such as "Spanish Monte" and "Old Sledge," and the participants learned to play those historic games. The "Winter Quarters" programs created a sense of camaraderie, a feeling of adventure, and the fleeting illusion of self-reliance.

My experiences at Bent's Old fort Natural Historic Site and in the world of "Buckskinning" were not without their ups and downs, but there were lessons learned. When I was approached in 1988 to assemble a group of African American reenactors to appear in the motion picture *Glory*, I knew immediately what to do and what not to do. By establishing high standards at the beginning of the project, I was able to help create a volunteer corps of men, Company "B" of the 54th Massachusetts Volunteer Infantry. These men made a commitment to the accurate portrayal of Civil War history as National Park volunteers.

At its best, "living history" can be a useful means of educating the public. For participants, there is the development and practice of those historical skills that can only be learned outside of books. Many a fur trade diary talks of starting a fire with flint and steel. It is, however, a skill that must be mastered on the ground and cannot be learned from reading. At its worst, "living history" can be a cruel joke imposed on the public by well-meaning souls who have failed to recognize the difference between a hobby that provides them with personal satisfaction in a primitive camping lifestyle and the type of public history that is good history shared with the public, often out of doors. The problem is, to the untrained eye, both ends of the spectrum can look like the same thing. What makes a public history professional is a willingness to truly learn from the past, including the recent past.

Lessons Learned

- Public history is a professional, multidisciplinary approach to both research and teaching that allows its practitioners to use historical methods to engage the public outside of the classroom. It is not whatever wanders into view.
- Quality public history requires time and money in planning, execution, and logistical support.

Figure 15. At the recently discovered site of Travelers' Rest near Helena, Montana, a Lewis and Clark interpreter explains the equipment used by the Corps of Discovery. Photo by Andrew Gulliford, 2004.

- The needs of the public must be analyzed and understood in order for public history programs to be fully effective.
- Public history requires professional training at the college and university level and in the field.
- As in any profession, peer review is critical.
- Participation in professional organizations is important. An array of organizations can help to focus your attention on various aspects of public history, including
  - The National Council on Public History
  - The Organization of American Historians
  - The American Association for State and Local History
  - The Association for Living History Farms and Museums
  - The Western History Association
  - The National Association for Interpretation
  - The Midwest Outdoor Museum Coordinating Committee

Public History programs of any size require careful attention to logistics.
- Public historians have to know what is bad in order to produce the good.
- On the ground, public history has an additional set of rules, including
  - You get what you pay for.
  - Public history must be planned.
  - Public history must be managed.
  - Public history must be evaluated.
  - Public history programs cannot be left to run themselves.
  - Close enough "ain't."
- Professionals must be able to recognize the difference between public history as a profession and living history as a hobby.

In learning to bring history enthusiasts to public history, I learned a few things about the skills of the past in the process. Horse packing, flint-and-steel fire starting, muzzle loading, and outdoor cooking are all skills that are second nature to me now. Somewhere along the way, I learned a smattering of Lakota, some Plains Indian sign language, and the difference between a traditional Crow moccasin print and that of the Comanche. When I married, I took my new bride for a week's honeymoon in a tepee on Rowe Mesa near Pecos, New Mexico. I cooked our meals over an open fire and never gave my comfort or that of my wife a second thought. I had lived in this way so many times before that this was just another page in an unending book of outdoor adventures. Maybe all that buckskin and black powder smoke made me a little crazy. Perhaps the same can be said of my Buckskin acquaintances. It is possible that we are all crazy alike—crazy about the history of the American West.

This article appeared in a different form in the *Western History Quarterly* (winter 2001), a publication of the Western History Association, and is used with permission.

Study Questions

1. Who or what are the "Buckskinners," and what is their mission?

2. According to Gwaltney, "what makes a public history professional is a willingness to truly learn from the past, including the recent past." What is meant by this statement?

3. Compare and contrast Sam Arnold's "The Fort" and the NPS's "Bent's Old Fort."

4. Give a brief description of an original Rendezvous from 1825 to 1840.

5. Give a brief description of a "liar's contest" and a "mountain man run."

6. How did the NPS's interpretation at Bent's Old Fort come into conflict with the modern-day Buckskinners' concept of the "Rendezvous"?

7. Explain the mission of the group called "The Opposition" at Bent's Old Fort.

HISTORICAL ARCHAEOLOGY

Headnotes

Archaeology is an important tool to be used in the presentation and interpretation of Western history. Just as public history is an emerging field, so too is the field of public archaeology, which seeks not only to research and document historic sites based on the stratigraphy of artifacts found in the ground, but also to interpret those sites for the keenly interested public, which often finances most of the digs through taxpayer and public support.

Historical archaeology includes a better understanding of Western exploration and settlement through work done at La Purisima Mission by James Deetz; at Sacramento, California, by Peter Schulz and Sherri Gust; and at the mining camp of Silver Reef, Utah, by Robert Schuyler. Formed in 1967, The Society for Historical Archaeology now has over 2,000 members.

Historic archaeological sites of national significance have included the search for Lewis and Clark campgrounds and the exact spot of Fort Clatsop, where the Corps of Discovery spent a long winter near the mouth of the Columbia River. Given the vast expanse of land covered by the Lewis and Clark expedition and the changes wrought by 200 years, tourists are understandably curious about what sites can still be visited. If commemorating the expedition means following its trail, then how can visitors walk in the actual footsteps of the Corps of Discovery? This concern gives special importance to archaeology, because this science can significantly aid interpretation at wayside exhibits, visitor centers, and local, state, and regional museums. Emphasis on the archaeology of Lewis and Clark sites is a recent phenomenon, but it illustrates well some of the special challenges of commemorating the expedition. Unlike a Civil War battlefield or a visit to a historic antebellum house, very little physical evidence remains along the expedition's route. Lewis and Clark campsites have been difficult to validate, because the explorers left few traces. After years of searching, Ken Karzmiski, director of the Columbia River Gorge Discovery Center in Hood River, Oregon, has only found a pin and a wooden stake at Lower Portage Camp, where the corps spent weeks near Great Falls, Montana. The results have been equally dismal along the entire 8,000-mile round-trip route.

One interesting new lead in the hunt for traces of Lewis and Clark is hard to explain in the context of family tourism: it has to do with sex, venereal disease, and the three pewter penis syringes that Lewis bought in Philadelphia and took along on the trip. He used them to inject mercury compounds up the urethra of the enlisted men who found too much delight in women and subsequently caught the clap. Mercury is a deadly heavy metal, and some of the corps probably went to early graves because of their promiscuity. Archaeologically, heavy metals remain deep in stratified soil, so a search has been undertaken to find the latrine at Fort Clatsop and to use that location to identify the fort's actual site. This archaeological strategy assumes the captains followed strict military procedure in building the latrine at a specified distance from the fort. Archaeology may prove the exact location of the 1805–6 winter quarters along the cold and wet Oregon coast.

Searching for those mercury compounds, researchers have recently discovered the Lewis and Clark site near Helena, Montana, known as Travelers'

Rest, which is where the corps stopped both on their outbound and homeward journeys. Thanks to the National Trust for Historic Preservation and other supporters, the site is now a Montana State Park and an essential stop for Lewis and Clark aficionados.

Historical archaeologists think they have found the camping spot for the ill-fated Donner party, whose 181 members, overtaken by early snows in the Sierras, spent four months in the mountains during the winter of 1846–47. Eleven members died of starvation and cannibalism occurred. Adding to work done by Donald Hardesty, University of Oregon historical archaeologist Julie Schablitsky thinks they have found the campsite because archaeologists can perceive where melting snow ran off the tents of the travelers and hit the ground.

The importance of cultural resource laws and a description of the ways in which historical archaeologists and public historians work together can be found in Thomas F. King's *Cultural Resource Laws & Practice: An Introductory Guide*. In 1977 James Deetz wrote a superb book on historical archaeology in colonial America titled *In Small Things Forgotten: An Archaeology of Early American Life*, but so far no single volume has yet encapsulated historical archaeology in the American West. Twenty years later John H. Jameson, Jr., edited *Presenting Archaeology to the Public: Digging for Truths*, which includes important essays on the West such as Douglas D. Scott's essay reprinted here and David T. Kirkpatrick's essay "The Archaeology of Billy the Kid." Billy has been dead for over 100 years, and yet he is still controversial. The latest plan is to dig up his mother's remains in Silver City, New Mexico, and compare her DNA to bones found in the Kid's grave in another part of the state. The public remains fascinated with history, and historical archaeologists play a vital role in interpreting the past.

In this series of essays, authors discuss historical archaeology and the contributions it can make to understanding Western history. Case studies illuminate two important historical sites in the West: the Little Bighorn National Historic Battlefield in Montana (1876) and Ludlow, Colorado, where the Great Colorado Coalfield War (1913–14) became a vicious fight between mine owners and the ethnic laborers who worked for them.

The Little Bighorn Battlefield, known the world over as the site for General George Armstrong Custer's "last stand," was dramatically reinterpreted based on archaeological evidence found after a prairie fire in 1983 left the battlefield scorched and easily accessible to archaeologists. The brushfire did more to upend the legend of Custer's "last stand" than a century of scholarship. Doug Scott of the National Park Service's Omaha, Nebraska, regional office used this opportunity to learn about the battle from hundreds of shell casings left on the ground among almost 5,000 artifacts. Scott's findings punctured the myth of a "last stand" and instead reaffirmed Native American accounts of the battle, which stated that the time it took to kill Custer and his men on "Last Stand Hill" was "the time it took a hungry man to eat his supper." In other words, not long. Scott writes about the tremendous public interest in the archaeological investigations, which resulted in numerous articles, a book, *Archaeological Perspectives on the Battle of the Little Bighorn*, and the subsequent reinterpretation of the site by the National Park Service. Recently the Little Bighorn National Historic Battlefield has been in the news because of the sculpture "Spirit Warriors" recently dedicated at the site to honor native dead who died defending their homeland.

The second case study documents the Great Coalfield War in Ludlow, Colorado, as historical archaeology serving labor. Archaeologists Philip Duke, Randy McGuire, Dean Saitta, Paul Reckner, and Mark Walker explain their philosophical leanings and then describe why the Ludlow site represents a superb synthesis of professional archaeology, public history, and a profound analysis of class warfare. By examining artifacts such as food remains, broken glass, toy fragments, and bullet shell casings as well as tent sites and other historic features on the landscape, the team vividly recreates the tragic winter of 1913–14, when coal miners on strike were repeatedly fired upon by the

Colorado militia in an event that galvanized American unions and helped create the modern labor movement.

The importance of historical archaeology and preserving and interpreting remote historical sites cannot be stressed enough. Recently the Ludlow site, of deep significance to the United Mine Workers of America, was vandalized. The UMW erected a granite statute in 1917 to commemorate the 1914 Ludlow massacre of 18 miners and family members. In May 2003 vandals removed the heads of two figures and hacked the arm off the female statue. The 1,000-pound granite statue of several figures had to be packed for shipment to California for restoration. To prevent such senseless crimes, historical archaeologists and public historians must work together to teach the value of the recent past.

Interpreting Archaeology at Little Bighorn Battlefield National Monument

Douglas D. Scott

The Battle of the Little Bighorn, or Custer's Last Stand, has been an enduring American legend since that fateful day of June 25, 1876, on the prairies of eastern Montana. The near mythological proportions the story has assumed, recently combined with the public popularity of archaeology, has resulted in widespread public attention to the Custer Battlefield Archaeological Project. This attention was focused by an international media blitz that overshadowed the press coverage of the original fight. The overwhelming public interest and how the project attempted to deal with the immediate need for interpretive feedback to the public is the subject of this essay.

Battlefields as a whole are really ceremonial sites where the public can see, touch, and experience an interpreted version of the past. Often battlefields are perceived in very romantic terms. This is especially true at Little Bighorn Battlefield National Monument, where nearly every visitor arrives with a preconceived notion of the story of the Battle of the Little Bighorn. These notions range from those of the truly literate scholar to those of the visitor whose misconceptions are generated from having seen one of the many movies on the subject.

Visitors' attitudes can be classified into one of several very general and overly simplified categories. First are the Custer detractors, who believe that Custer got what he deserved for whatever reason. Second are the Custer apologists, who are convinced that Custer's command was wiped out due to the failure of someone. Often this is the basis for the great cover-up or conspiracy theory. The third category is the "lo, the poor Indian" group, who believe Native Americans were mistreated and this victory was their single greatest triumph, even if it signaled the end of a lifeway.

Obviously no category is exclusively correct or necessarily wrong. The park's interpreters face a real challenge: their oral presentations must be objective and factual, and at the same time, they must be ready to politely dispel myths generated from often uninformed but widely held beliefs. Furthermore, the interpretive story of the Battle of the Little Bighorn and the interpretation of the archaeological data are not exclusive stories. They must be told together, in context, and based on a firm foundation of the documentary resources.

Figure 16. Custer's Last Stand, from the famous Anheuser-Busch, St. Louis, Missouri, print, is a false depiction of what actually happened at the Little Bighorn, based on recently revealed archaeological evidence. There was no last stand. Indian oral tradition also verifies that Custer had no time to rally his men. According to one Lakota warrior, Custer died in "the time it took a hungry man to eat his supper." Western History Collections, Denver Public Library X33630.

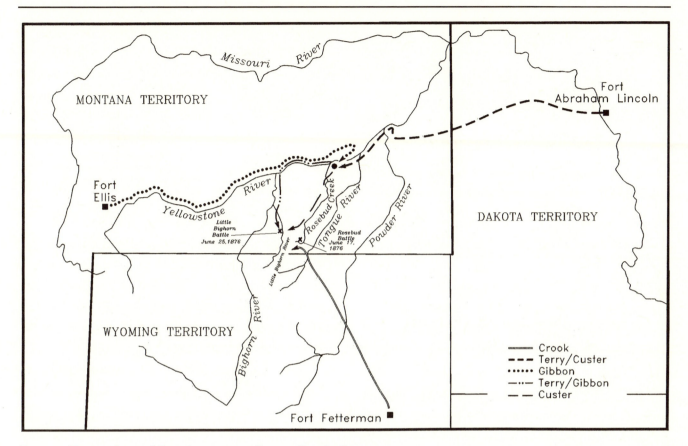

Figure 17. Territorial map of Custer's movement. Courtesy Douglas Scott.

A Brief History

The Little Bighorn story begins in the spring of 1876 with the enforcement of the U.S. government policy to return Sioux and Cheyenne Indians to their reservations. By late June, the army had a good idea of the whereabouts of the Indians but no specific information. General Alfred Terry sent Lieutenant Colonel George Custer and his Seventh Cavalry ahead of two converging columns of soldiers to find the Indians. On the morning of June 25, as they were crossing the divide into the Little Bighorn River valley, Custer let his men rest briefly at a place now known as the Crow's Nest. From here they spotted the Indian camp in the valley below. Custer moved his command into the valley and, in the afternoon, divided his men into three groups. Captain Thomas McDougall and his company guarded the pack train, Captain Frederick Benteen led three companies in a southern arc to cut off a southerly escape route, and Custer took the rest of the men toward the Indian encampment.

Before entering the village, Custer further split his own contingent. Three companies, now assigned to Major Marcus Reno, were to follow the river on the south bank and attack the village, which was situated southwest of the river. Custer, with the remaining five companies, would follow the north bank, cross the river, and attack at the north end of the village. They would thus encircle the Indians while Captain Benteen's men to the south and west would capture those who attempted to escape. Reno and Custer paralleled each other on the opposite sides of the river until Reno reached the village and initiated the attack. As Reno's men began fighting, they saw Custer and his men riding northwest on the bluffs on the opposite side of the river, toward the lower end of the Indian encampment.

After initial confusion in the village, the Indians confronted Reno's men with heavy opposition. The soldiers were forced back, retreating to the woods near the river and then northeast across the river and up

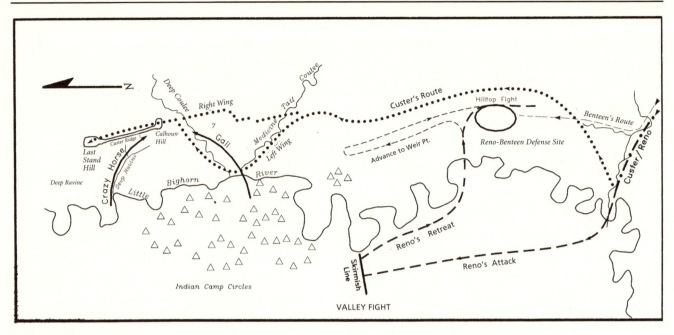

Figure 18. The valley fight map, including Reno's attack and retreat and Custer's route. Courtesy Douglas Scott.

the bluffs. The retreat was confused and disorderly at best. With no skirmishers positioned to defend them, the soldiers crossing the river were easy targets. Many others, who did not hear the retreat call or were not able to move from their positions, were left behind in the woods in the valley. They straggled in over the next 48 hours to rejoin the command.

The men who made it to the top of the bluffs quickly assumed a defensive position and returned the warriors' fire. Custer, meanwhile, had gone north to a ravine now known as Medicine Tail Coulee. From here, he sent trumpeter John Martin back to Benteen with the message, *Benteen come on Big Village. Be Quick. Bring packs. P.S. Bring packs.* Custer was, of course, referring to the ammunition carried by the pack train under McDougall's care.

Martin reached Benteen with the message. Benteen followed Custer's trail and came upon Reno's forces in position on the bluff top. The pack train and McDougall's company trailed Benteen and joined the command a short time later. Reno's men wondered what happened to Custer. They speculated that, like themselves, Custer and his men had assumed a defensive position and were pinned down somewhere to the north. At one point, Captain Thomas Weir led his company to the north in the hopes of finding Custer's men. The rest of the command followed for about a mile to an area known today as Weir's Point before being driven back by Indian fire. Some said that from Weir's Point they could see dust and smoke to the north, where they assumed Custer and his men were fighting.

The Indian fire let up during the night of June 25, and some of the men who had been left in the valley used the cover of darkness to rejoin the command. The attack resumed the next morning. Reno's men were pinned down the entire day but could see a line of Indians leaving the village below them. Twice, when the Indians got too close, Benteen formed his men and charged; the Indians were driven back. Benteen walked the line, encouraging the men and keeping their flagging spirits aloft.

Another blistering Montana June day dawned and, in the intense heat, water became critical for survival, particularly for the wounded. Enlisted men made several trips to the river to fetch water for the injured. Sharpshooters were positioned to draw Indian fire during these forays. When fire again slackened the night of June 26, another foray to the river was made to recover the body of Lieutenant

Benjamin Hodgson, killed while crossing the ford. Individual stories of heroism abound. Some of the sharpshooters and men who went for water were later awarded the Medal of Honor for their gallantry in action.

By the morning of June 27, the Indians were gone. Reno's men observed dust in the distance and then could slowly make out cavalry troops. Several of Reno's officers met General Alfred Terry's and Colonel John Gibbon's commands in the Indian village. All wondered where Custer was. Soon the scouting party brought back the news. Custer and his men lay dead on the slopes beside the Little Bighorn River.

The heat that made water such a critical factor during the battle had not treated the bodies kindly. Reno's men were detailed to quickly bury the dead. The deceased were difficult to identify, even for those who had known them well. The regiment had little in the way of tools; a few shovels and knives and cups from mess kits were used to dig. Meanwhile the dead at Reno's position were also buried, their equipment gathered into a pile and burned so as not to fall into the hands of the Indians. The survivors retreated to the mouth of the Little Bighorn, where the steamer *Far West* was waiting. The steamer made record time to Bismarck, North Dakota, bearing the wounded and the news.

In all, 210 men died on Little Bighorn Battlefield, including Custer and four members of his family. What happened to Custer? how did it happen? and why did it happen? are the three primary questions that have been asked since the battle. None of the questions, even today, are adequately answered to the satisfaction of all.

Archaeology and History Combine to Tell a More Complete Story

Intensive archaeological investigations began in 1983 with an initial assessment of the potential for archaeological work after a significant range fire denuded the Little Bighorn Battlefield of its vegetation. In the succeeding years there have been three major inventories, two major excavations projects, and over a dozen minor projects completed for the park and on the lands surrounding the monument, resulting in reams of documentation and nearly 6,000 artifacts carefully recovered and mapped. The volume of paper generated to document that work is significant, including one master's thesis, one Ph.D. dissertation, four books, three monographs, and 20 short Park Service internal reports. And this does not include the first professional archaeological investigations conducted by Don Rickey and Robert Bray in 1958 nor the work of metal detector hobbyists and collectors who went to the trouble to document their efforts in written form in the years before professional archaeologists became involved in the project.

The amount of paper may be interesting, but it does not begin to convey the whole story of what has been found nor how interpretations of the battle have been altered as a result of the discovery of thousands of pieces of physical evidence documenting the fight between the Lakota and Cheyenne and the U.S. Seventh Cavalry on June 25 and 26, 1876. In the course of the archaeological projects we have had the opportunity to study the Custer fight, the Reno-Benteen defense, movements to and from Weir Point, the fight in Medicine Tail Coulee, the actual remains of some of the soldiers who fought the battle, and one of the Seventh's prebattle camps.

On June 22, 1876, Custer left the Yellowstone River valley and began his fateful march to history. The only Custer column campsite to be investigated to date was done in the fall of 1999.[1] Initial archaeological reconnaissance was conducted at the site of Custer's June 23 camp on Rosebud Creek. Only a handful of artifacts were recovered: a .45–55 cartridge case, the back of a General Service button, a trouser button, a broken mess spoon, a crushed camp boiler, a badly rusted one-gallon can that may have held roasted coffee beans, a Burden horseshoe, and the tips of several horseshoe nails found near a firepit. Taken together, these artifacts are the lost bits of the Seventh's camp equipage from a 13-hour overnight stay by over 600 men.

The next set of archaeological data we have relates to Major Marcus Reno's deployment and attack on the Indian village. In 1993 we mapped battle debris that a local private landowner had found while metal detecting his property. This evidence situated Reno's skirmish line in the valley, elements of the timber fight, and the retreat to the river. Perhaps more exciting, in some ways was the opportunity to see and map finds that relate to Sitting Bull's camp circle.

Archaeologists have not formally investigated the Reno Retreat Crossing, although Retreat Ravine above the crossing, at least that portion within the park fence surrounding the Reno-Benteen defense site, was inventoried in 1985. The 1985 investigations took in the entire Reno-Benteen area owned by the National Park Service, including portions of Sharpshooter Hill. In 1994 and two subsequent years, much of the land between Reno-Benteen and Medicine Tail Coulee was also inventoried with metal detectors.

Evidence for Reno's chaotic retreat up to the defense site was abundantly clear in the archaeological record. Bullets and cartridge cases from both combatant groups were found along the route as well as some lost equipment and personal items. The Reno-Benteen defense is well represented archaeologically with hundreds of bullets, cartridge cases, bits of horse tack, other army equipment, and personal items scattered throughout the defense site. It is not possible to separate the early part of the defense and the movement to Weir Point from the later defense episodes as the artifacts are too intermingled in the defense site proper. Nevertheless, there is evidence of the fight around Weir Point and the retreat back to the defense site. At Weir Point and to the north, cartridge cases and bullets show where the fighting occurred and where men were deployed.

The abundant archaeological evidence of the Reno-Benteen defense shows that was a spirited fight. The Lakota and Cheyenne held positions surrounding the soldiers. Many cartridge cases were found on Sharpshooter Hill and in the swales and behind the knolls that surround the army positions. Among some .44-caliber Henry cartridge cases at one knoll was a brass bracelet, probably lost by one of the warriors. The tip of a gold-painted knife blade that once was part of a war club was found in another location.[2]

Literally hundreds of bullets fired from the Lakota and Cheyenne guns, including many captured from the defeated Custer command, were found imbedded in the Reno-Benteen defense position. Among the more poignant reminders of the power of those missiles are the remains of six of the men who died. One showed dramatic evidence of a gunshot injury to the head. His yet unidentified remains show that a tumbling bullet struck him on the right side of the head and passed through his skull, exiting on the left.[3]

What of Custer and his command; what archaeological evidence is there of that fight? There is essentially no evidence of Custer's movements until he arrives at Medicine Tail Coulee. The archaeological evidence for combat at the mouth of Medicine Tail Coulee is meager but is definitely present.

The archaeological data[4] from Medicine Tail Coulee support the notion that only a light action occurred at the ford. The data also support the contention that some element of Custer's command, probably the left wing, moved from this action at the ford northeast up Deep Coulee to reunite with the right wing at or near Calhoun Hill. Battle debris found on this line as well as debris in line with Nye-Cartwright Ridge suggests the reunion movement was under fire and was contested. The archaeological firearms data and distribution patterns indicate the warriors took possession of this terrain after the soldiers deployed on and near Calhoun Hill. The warriors were certainly on the right, left, and front of the soldiers deployed at this southern end of the field. There is also clear evidence of soldiers returning the warriors' fire in the form of army-caliber bullets associated with Indian-caliber cartridge cases in this area.

Another sobering bit of testimony to the battle's loss of life is a soldier's skeleton found by Frank Bethune in the Deep Coulee area in 1928. Dr. P. Willey examined that skeleton, buried in the national cemetery. He found the remains to be those of a 35-year-old white male about 5' 8" tall. He had a gunshot wound to the head, evidence of blunt force trauma, and at least 98 cut marks on the bones, indicating the victorious Lakota and Cheyenne mutilated him. Evidence of this ritual mutilation was seen on many of the skeletal remains from the Custer battlefield. No identity has yet been established for this soldier.

The Deep Coulee artifact patterning and distribution gives the impression of soldiers moving up Deep Coulee toward Calhoun Hill.[5] The expended army cartridge case distribution indicates there was some firing as the movement took place, but it appears light or at least limited in scope. The distribution of Indian-caliber bullets also gives the distinct impression that the army movement was under fire. Most army bullets were found around the park's boundary fence near Calhoun Hill. The same is true of most of the Indian caliber cartridge cases. This bullet distribution is consistent with firing by Companies C and L after their deployment at the south end of Custer or Battle Ridge. Some army-caliber bullets were also found northeast of the fence corner.

Although the cartridge case and bullet evidence suggests only limited fighting occurred during the movement from Medicine Tail Coulee to Calhoun Hill, the distribution of equipment in the Deep Coulee area indicates it did not occur without some loss. Spurs, picket pins, and the currycomb finds suggest enough haste occurred in the movement to cause the loss of items from the horse equipage or from individual soldiers.

There is no direct evidence for the juncture of the two wings at Calhoun Hill, but there is plenty of evidence for the ensuing fight on the Custer field and the destruction of Custer's immediate command. The archaeological data[6] indicate Custer and the left wing may have moved northwesterly along Custer Ridge after deploying Companies C and L under Lieutenants Calhoun and Crittenden on what became Calhoun Hill. The archaeological evidence in the form of cartridge cases and bullets show the Lakota and Cheyenne warriors poured fire in on the soldiers on Calhoun Hill from the east, west, and south.

Custer most probably advanced beyond Last Stand Hill to a more northerly position just outside the current park boundary, now called Custer Ridge Extension.[7] That movement may have been halted by an advance of warriors associated with a movement around the north end of the battlefield. Custer was pushed back to the vicinity of Last Stand Hill; the warriors took command of the ridge extensions, using these as positions to fire at the soldiers on Last Stand Hill and others who may have been in the vicinity of Cemetery Ridge. Archaeological evidence suggests that when Custer made the movement to Last Stand Hill, numerous warriors gained the Custer Ridge Extension and began firing at the remaining members of the command. They used some Henry and Winchester rifles as well as many army carbines, revolvers, and ammunition just captured from the fallen men of the right wing. Custer's remaining men returned fire until they were overrun and killed. Much of Custer's fire must have come from Last Stand Hill. The bullet orientation strongly suggests this, even though very few corresponding army-caliber cartridge cases were found on Last Stand Hill during the 1984 investigations. It seems likely that one reason cartridge cases were not recovered in corresponding quantity is that they were souvenired from the field in the ensuing decades as this area was heavily visited. The soldiers on Last Stand Hill were not idle, returning fire in quantity until they were finally overrun.

The gross distribution of army-related artifacts[8] provides some idea of the combatant locations during the battle. The positions of cartridge cases, buttons, spurs, equipment, and human bone indicate that soldiers fought and died along the east side of Custer Ridge from Calhoun Hill to the Keogh position and to Last Stand Hill. Fighting also occurred at the northernmost extent of the South Skirmish Line or the Deep Ravine Trail. These troop positions are further corroborated by the presence of impacted bullets from Indian-associated weapons.

At least seven discrete Indian positions can be discerned on the basis of the variety of cartridge case types (representing the variety of weapons used by the Indians) and government bullets impacted around these positions. Two positions are on Greasy Grass Ridge. Another is what we have named Henry Ridge, where numerous .44 Henry cartridge cases were found southwest of Calhoun Hill. Yet another is a knoll 660 feet northeast of Last Stand Hill. In addition to a variety of nongovernment cartridge cases found at the knoll, we also found split .45–.55 government cases, which probably represent captured government ammunition fired from .50-caliber weapons.

The firing must have been intense from both sides. The finds of spent cartridge cases and bullets certainly suggest this. Bullets fired from the soldiers' guns were found embedded in the ground, often within or at the front of the areas where quantities of Indian cartridge cases were found. Bullets in the calibers corresponding to the cartridge cases found at Indian positions were discovered embedded in the army positions. A few were even found in direct association with human remains.

From their positions under cover, and initially at a distance from the soldiers, the Indian fire began to take its toll. As the return fire from the soldiers began to slacken, the Indians moved in closer. The cartridge case data suggest Indian movements along two broad lines. One was from south to north, from Calhoun Hill to Last Stand Hill through the Keogh position; the second was from Calhoun Hill to the South Skirmish Line, joining with the Indian group attacking from the north and west.

The final bit of archaeological evidence relates to the aftermath of the battle. Two separate data sets show what happened after the Indians left the field. First are the remains of the men buried on Custer battlefield, in the valley, and at the Reno-Benteen defense site. They tell the tale of hasty, but not uncaring, burial in the face of uncertainty about when or if the Indians would return. They also tell the tale of the men's lives, the manner of their death, and the burials and reburials those remains have endured.[9]

Second, there is the Reno-Benteen equipment dump, excavated in 1989.[10] It may be one of several equipment disposal areas. It yielded evidence of the deliberate burning and destruction of ammunition and ration crates or boxes, some guns, and a large number of saddles and other horse tack. The army held the field of battle, but they had suffered an ignominious defeat, and they simply destroyed what equipment they could not salvage so as to render it unserviceable to the enemy.

The archaeology of the Battle of the Little Bighorn has yielded thousands of artifacts, reams of notes and other records, and a pile of reports, monographs, and books. We who participated in the project, whether as archaeologist or as volunteer, know that we have not found it all, nor have we learned everything there is to know. But in the years of continuing archaeological investigations, we have found many things that show the historical record is correct on many points, that Native American oral tradition likewise can explain some details better than the army accounts, and archaeological detective work has uncovered artifacts and their patterns of distribution that neither oral tradition nor documentary records mention. The Little Bighorn archaeological record is not better than the others; rather, it should be viewed as another set of information to be compared, contrasted, and correlated with the other information sources. Archaeological data are physical evidence of the battle and as such are the very visible reminder of those past events that have come to play such a role in our lives. The artifacts do not just sit on shelves in the park vault: some of them, and some very poignant ones, are on display in the museum. They and information they convey are a very real part of the interpretation of the Battle of the Little Bighorn.

Methods of Interpreting Archaeology to the Public

In 1879, roughly one square mile of the battlefield near Hardin, Montana, was set aside by the army. At the time, the site reflected the societal values of the era and was a suitable memorial for fallen heroes. Interpretation was primarily based on the available documentary resources—the remembrances of those who fought with Reno, those who buried the dead, and a few Indians who participated in the battle. Interestingly, the accounts of the white survivors and those of the Indians were often at odds. For decades, interpretation of the battle remained virtually unchanged, even when in 1941 the battlefield came under the jurisdiction of the National Park Service as the Custer Battlefield National Monument. In 1992 the name was changed by congressional action to Little Bighorn Battlefield National Monument.

It took a potentially tragic wildfire in August 1983 to bring interpretation for the public in line with ever changing societal values. With vegetation virtually destroyed in the fire, the superintendent of Custer Battlefield National Monument recognized a unique opportunity to commence an archaeological inventory of the battle site. Richard Fox, then a graduate student at the University of Calgary, initially assessed the field for its archaeological potential. His 1983 reconnaissance report was reviewed by the National Park Service, which decided to expand the project to a full-scale inventory with limited excavations. Fox's work had already generated a great deal of interest; undoubtedly there would continue to be widespread public and press attention focused on the project.[11]

Almost all archaeological investigations begin with a research design. The Custer Battlefield Archaeological Project was no different with respect to traditional components—research, logistics, and analytical procedures. However, from its inception, the plan also included a specific element that addressed the need to effectively deal with the public's unflagging interest.

The original plan called for a spokesperson to coordinate activities. Also acting as press contact, this individual would handle members of the public's telephone inquiries and meet with and brief them on the project's status. When field operations actually began in 1984, the park superintendent assumed the duties of coordinator. In response to overwhelming public interest, a literal media blitz descended on the park. Because nearly 40 percent of the superintendent's time was devoted to this special project—time taken away from his normal press of business—a professor of journalism and project volunteer took over as full-time coordinator during the 1985 fieldwork.[12]

Daily early morning briefings were proposed and proved to be very valuable. Each evening, archaeologists reviewed the results of the day's findings, planned the next day's assignments and work areas, and determined what interpretations would be given to the coordinator the next morning. The coordinator thus received the latest details on important discoveries, current project status, and the location of fieldwork. The coordinator in turn prepared press releases, posted information at the entrance of the visitors center, and furnished the park's interpreters and staff with copies of all information for public use. This kept the information fresh and uniform and helped avoid the dangers of off-the-cuff comments and interpretations.

Questions from the public directed to park interpreters and accessible field archaeologists set the tone for the interpretation. The public was most interested in what types of artifacts were being found and how—not if, but how—the archaeological study was changing history. In response to the public's demands, the team implemented several approaches to what was termed field interpretation. First and foremost was the daily briefing posted at the visitors center entrance and distributed to the interpreters. The briefing statements contained information on the types and quantities of artifacts found. We also attempted to ensure that these statements placed the finds in context. If the archaeological work was focusing on the so-called Last Stand Hill, then we included the historical information relevant to that element of the battle. If the archaeological data appeared at odds with the traditional interpretation, we pointed this out. No conclusions were made, but the briefings stressed that future planned, detailed analysis of all the project data would help resolve discrepancies.

A temporary display was also established in the visitors center. The display contained a few traditional archaeology tools, a variety of artifacts found during the investigations, a few photographs of fieldwork in progress, and text to briefly explain the process. This display drew a significant amount of attention and generated numerous questions. The staff interpreters used the display not only as a means to tell the archaeological story, but to generate questions about the varying historical theories on the battle. They could then point out that archaeology could help accept or reject one or more of those opinions.

A third level of interpretation scheduled during the project was small-group tours for in-field interpretation by the archaeologists. At the location, usually the site of an excavation for human remains, the archaeologist would present an overview of the project and a summary of findings. The primary focus of the 15- to 20-minute presentation would be the work going on before the group. Every effort was made to stress the roles of both historical archaeology and analytical laboratory techniques in the study of historic sites. In essence, the presentation was an attempt to inform the public about the process of archaeology.

When the archaeologists were working in accessible areas, visitors tended to congregate to watch the excavations. An archaeologist was assigned to provide impromptu interpretations about the locations and answer the torrents of questions. In numerous cases, the interest was so great that a single interpretive event often ran to nearly an hour.

The staff interpreters were well versed in the event's history, and most had some interest in the material culture of the battle. Thus, a natural feedback system developed between the archaeologists and interpreters, which kept the information flowing in a positive, two-way loop. Archaeological interpretations of specific elements of the battle were literally changing daily, and the interpreters were able to share these changes with the public within 24 hours.

Early in the project a means was devised to help the public understand the archaeological process. The approach, which met with great success, involved comparing the archaeological investigation to a crime scene investigation. Most people could easily relate to the analogy of historians as detectives interviewing victims, suspects, and witnesses, and archaeologists as the forensic personnel gathering the physical evidence for a more detailed analysis. Visitors readily accepted the concept that oral accounts could be suspect—for example, someone did not remember correctly, did not see part of the action, or was opinionated. Archaeological data, or the forensic analyses, provided a more complete picture of the situation than oral accounts could alone. As physical evidence it does not lie. The artifacts were the actual remnants of the battle, although their position and context (provenience) had to be interpreted. It was stressed that the archaeological artifacts, as they were found, were deposited as a result of a decision made in the past. Perhaps neither that decision nor the process of making it could be reconstructed with the artifacts and their provenience, but the result of that decision could be interpreted.

From the archaeologist's point of view, the opportunity to conduct public interpretation was invaluable. On the one hand, it was enlightening to witness first-hand the public's perception of what archaeology is and how it contributes to understanding the past. On the other hand, it gave archaeologists the opportunity to explain field and laboratory techniques to the visitors. Most archaeologist-to-visitor interpretation took place at one of the many marker sites that dot the field and purport to identify where soldiers died in battle. The visitors' fascination with the recovery of human remains at these excavations provided an ideal opportunity to explain why the study of the bones is important and what a variety of detailed scientific and forensic examinations can tell the archaeologist about the people who died in the battle. (In no case did a visitor voice an opinion that the excavation of marker sites was improper. In fact, descendants of the soldiers killed at the battle visited the excavations and expressed their approval of the investigations.)

Figure 19. Four Crow Indians who were Custer's scouts return to grave markers that memorialize the battle of the Little Bighorn. Western History Collections, Denver Public Library X31275.

Follow-up since the completion of the fieldwork has helped maintain a high public profile for the project. Four books,[13] one monograph,[14] and several articles[15] have been published on the archaeological investigations. The books and some of the articles[16] are sold at the park's visitors center. In addition, the results of different aspects of the work are briefly discussed in the Custer Battlefield Historical and Museum Association's annual slick format publication *Greasy Grass*, and the park's handbook or guidebook was revised to add results from the archaeological project. Perhaps the most interest has been generated by four positive identifications of human remains. Ten television programs have also been produced on the archaeological investigations, including shows for PBS, *Scientific American*, and *Archaeology*, two for the Discovery Channel, three for British television, one for German television, one for Italian television, and one video filmed for the park's interpretive program, all done in the years following the field investigations.

There were pitfalls to the interpretive effort, as is the case with any project. First, the amount of time project archaeologists devoted to interpretation was not adequately planned for in the project schedule. Field adjustments had to be made, and a great deal of planning went into maximizing the archaeologists' exposure to the public without jeopardizing the project mission. Second, the public demanded that immediate conclusions be made in the field. It took a great deal of thought and constraint to answer questions when the data required detailed analysis before arriving at conclusions. We also recognized that not all the questions were possible to answer. It was important to help the public realize that much more behind-the-scenes work was required to formulate conclusions.

Just as there were pitfalls, there were benefits. The positive personal interactions among the archaeological team, the staff interpreters, and the visitors, as well as the project's public visibility, are credited with a 20 percent increase in park visitation. A bonus of the increased visitation and project publicity was a 150 percent increase in sales at the Custer Battlefield Historical and Museum Association bookstore. Association membership also trebled in the same time period. Since the association funded the majority of the archaeological investigations, the archaeology was, in a sense, paying for itself. The Custer Battlefield Historical and Museum Association ceased to be a National Park Service cooperating association in 1993. The new cooperating association, South-western Parks and Monuments, has continued the tradition of support for park archaeological investigations with the study of adjacent private lands in 1994, and

Figure 20. In 1886, seven men, four on horseback, visit the Custer monument, which was as yet unfenced. Photo by D. F. Barny. Western History Collections, Denver Public Library B245.

they continue to offer the various archaeological publications in their on-site sales outlet.

Conclusions

While the project is less in the public eye two decades after its inception, communication with the public continues. Publicly oriented articles and other publications are still well received. These publications, while geared to a general audience, do not exclude analytical data nor scholarly interpretations. They are written for the informed but not necessarily scholarly person. These popular publications are perhaps the most important aspect of the work. They have forced us to write in a clear and concise manner and taught us to avoid large and impressive words that often daunt the general reader and obscure the true meaning of the prose. Archaeological interpretation, either for tour groups or through printed matter, is not difficult. It is like any other aspect of a project: it must be planned and organized to be worthwhile and effective.

Notes

1. Archaeological Investigations of Custer's June 23, 1876, Campsite, Rosebud County, Montana. Ms. on file, Midwest Archeological Center, Lincoln, Nebraska.

2. Douglas D. Scott, Richard A. Fox, Jr., Melissa A. Connor, and Dick Harmon, *Archaeological Perspectives on the Battle of the Little Bighorn* (Norman: University of Oklahoma Press, 1989).

3. Douglas D. Scott, P. Willey, and Melissa Connor, *They Died with Custer: Soldiers' Bones from the Battle of the Little Bighorn* (Norman: University of Oklahoma Press, 1998).

4. Douglas D. Scott and Peter Bleed, *A Good Walk Around the Boundary: Archeological Inventory of the Dyck and Other Properties Adjacent to Little Bighorn Battlefield National Monument*. Special Publication of the Nebraska Association of Professional Archaeologists and the Nebraska State Historical Society, Lincoln, 1997.

5. Ibid.

6. Scott et al., *Archaeological Perspectives*.

7. Scott and Bleed, *Archaeological Inventory*.

8. Scott et al., *Archaeological Perspectives*.

9. Scott, Wiley, and Connor, *They Died with Custer*.

10. Douglas D. Scott, ed., "Papers on Little Bighorn Battlefield Archaeology: The Equipment Dump, Marker 7, and the Reno Crossing." *Reprints in Anthropology* 42 (1991).

11. Douglas D. Scott, "Surviving the Second Battle of the Little Bighorn: Methods of Effectively Dealing with a Media Blitz," in *Captivating the Public Through the Media While Digging the Past*, complied by Kristen Peters, Elizabeth Comer, and Roger Kelly. Technical Series No. 1, Baltimore Center for Urban Archaeology, 1987.

12. Warren E. Barnard, "Volunteers Crucial in Custer Battle Dig," *CRM Bulletin* 8, no. 5 (1985): 2–3.

13. Douglas D. Scott and Richard A. Fox, Jr., *Archaeological Insights into the Custer Battle* (Norman: University of Oklahoma Press, 1987); Scott et al., *Archaeological Perspectives*; Richard A. Fox, Jr., *Archaeology, History, and Custer's Last Battle* (Norman: University of Oklahoma Press, 1993); and Scott, Wiley, and Connor, *They Died with Custer*.

14. Scott, *Little Bighorn Battlefield Archaeology*.

15. Douglas D. Scott and Douglas Owsley, "Oh, What Tales Bones Could Tell—and Often Do!" *Greasy Grass* 7 (1991): 33–39; Richard A. Fox, Jr., and Douglas D. Scott, "The Post–Civil War Battlefield Pattern." *Historical Archaeology* 25, no. 2 (1991): 92–103; and R. Glenner, P. Willey, and Douglas D. Scott, "Back to the Little Bighorn: Remains of a 7th Cavalry Trooper Recovered at Little

Bighorn Battlefield in 1903 Provide a Glimpse of 19th Century Dental Practices," *Journal of the American Dental Association* 124, no. 7 (1994): 835–43.

16. Douglas D. Scott and Melissa A. Connor, "Post-Mortem at the Little Bighorn," *Natural History* 95, no. 6 (1986): 46–55; Douglas D. Scott and Dick Harmon, "A Sharps Rifle from the Battle of the Little Bighorn," *Man at Arms* 10, no. 1 (1988): 12–15; Scott et al., *Archaeological Perspectives*; and Scott, *Little Bighorn Battlefield Archaeology*.

Study Questions

1. How has interpreting the facts of the events at Little Bighorn Battlefield been a challenge for the NPS? Which perspective on the battle is most relevant to the facts?

2. What has been the instigation of the "Custer controversy"?

3. Compare the controversies over the Last Stand and Reno-Benteen portions of the battlefield. Why is the Reno-Benteen story not so controversial?

4. What information did the first LBHNM archaeological site yield?

5. Explain the role of cartridge cases in the archaeological investigations and troop movements at Reno-Benteen. Why are they not good for time frame references concerning the defense at Reno-Benteen?

6. How did the archaeological evidence explain the Custer Command's movements during the fight?

7. What do skeletal remains tell us about the individual and Anglo European/Native American warfare?

8. What impact did the archaeological evidence about the fight by Custer's command and the aftermath have on previous NPS public interpretations?

9. How did the Custer Battlefield Archaeological Project include the public? Why?

The Colorado Coalfield War Archaeological Project

Archaeology Serving Labor

PHILIP DUKE, RANDALL H. MCGUIRE,
DEAN J. SAITTA, PAUL E. RECKNER,
AND MARK WALKER

Introduction

Public education should always be one of the primary purposes of academic studies. Nowhere is this basic tenet better showcased than in public history and public archaeology. Both subdisciplines attempt to teach the public the importance of understanding its heritage so that lessons from the past can be learned and a greater appreciation of its importance can be gained. Moreover, since Western time is linear—it proceeds inexorably from past, to present to future—logic requires us, if we wish to make sense of the present, to compare it to the past. That being so, it is obvious that the disciplines of archaeology and history are vital in making sense of the present in that they provide descriptions and interpretations of what happened in the past.

Unfortunately, things are never quite so simple, for each discipline has struggled over how the past is to be (re)constructed. In history, one result of this struggle has resulted in what, in western America at least, is called New Western history.[1] In archaeology, the struggle has manifested itself in a debate between archaeology as objective science[2] and archaeology as a humanity that openly acknowledges the inherent contingency of all archaeological analysis.[3] This debate has been played out in the arenas of feminist archaeology and indigenous archaeology but less so in the arena of what may be termed "classist" archaeology.[4]

The reasons for the paucity of attention to class issues are too complex to be addressed in this essay, but we can at least point out a number of issues that are relevant here. The first is that archaeology—as is the case with history and other academic disciplines—has traditionally been a middle-class endeavor.[5] It speaks to middle-class concerns and is practiced by and large by middle-class professionals (we note anecdotally that the majority of members in local archaeological societies are also middle class). Thus, there is an unconscious bias against "working-class" events and issues (we deliberately avoid a definition of these terms in the interest of brevity). Moreover, we have often found an initial bias against archaeology among working-class audiences.[6]

Augmenting this unconscious bias is the notion that archaeology's big questions concern global phenomena such as the emergence of humans and the rise of civilizations.[7] As important as answering these big questions no doubt is, we maintain that archaeology can answer other, equally important questions. Merriman[8] found from a questionnaire review of museum visitors that while such questions may be of interest to those he called "high status," those of "low status" placed family history as being the most important and world history least important. We conclude from Merriman's study that substantial portions of the population are interested in local events, things in the past that resonate with them at the individual or family level. This is not to say that an interest in the local prevents an interest in more global issues; quite the contrary, for as we shall show below, it is the local that allows us to engage the public in issues of wider concern. It is this acknowledgment that has spurred us to develop the Colorado Coalfield War Archaeological Project.

The Colorado Coalfield War

The southern Colorado coal field is on the east side of the Rocky Mountains, in Las Animas and Huerfano counties. Coal mines were situated in canyons, where the coal seams were exposed by erosion. These fields were a major source of the high-grade bituminous coal that was used to produce coking coal, or coke. Coking coal fueled the new industrial capitalism, especially the steel industry, which supplied rails for the expanding United States transportation network.

Figure 21. On April 20, 1914, laundry hangs in front of the tent camp at Ludlow, Colorado, in Las Animas County, the site of coal strikes and a subsequent massacre. Western History Collections, Denver Public Library Z-193.

In 1913 Colorado was the eighth-largest coal-producing state in the United States.[9] Because of the railroads' need for a steady supply of coking coal, the southern field was heavily industrialized. It was also dominated by a few large-scale corporate operations. The largest of these operations was the Colorado Fuel and Iron Company (CF&I), based in Pueblo. Founded in 1880, by 1892 CF&I produced 75 percent of Colorado's coal. In 1903 CF&I was acquired by the Rockefeller corporate empire. In the early twentieth century CF&I and the other large southern field operators had nearly total control over the economic and political life of Las Animas and Huerfano counties. Most of the miners lived in company towns. They rented company houses, bought food and equipment at company stores, and bought alcohol at company saloons. Many of these expenses were automatically deducted from a miner's wages. Although it was illegal by 1913, scrip, a form of currency redeemable only at the company store, was still in use in the southern Colorado coal towns. Company store prices could be as much as 30 percent higher than those at independent stores outside the coal towns.[10] Doctors, priests, schoolteachers, and law enforcement officers were all company employees. The company selected the contents of town libraries and censored movies, books, and magazines. Entries to the towns were gated and patrolled by armed mine guards.[11] Contemporary accounts described the situation as feudal.[12]

The Colorado mines themselves were notoriously unsafe. They operated in flagrant violation of several state laws that regulated safety and the fair compensation of miners. Miners died in Colorado at over twice the national average.[13] Handpicked coroner's juries absolved the coal companies of responsibility for these deaths almost without exception. For example, in the years from 1904 to 1914, the juries picked by the sheriff of Huerfano County found the coal operators to blame in only one case out of 95.[14] Instead, victims were accused of "negligence" or "carelessness."[15] One of the great ironies of the 1913–14 strike is that workers were probably safer during the period when state militiamen were shooting at them than they would have been had they still been toiling in the mines.

The mine workforce itself was largely "third wave" immigrant labor from southern and eastern Europe, including Sicilians, Tyroleans, Tuscans, Cretans, Macedonians, and others. In America these ethnic groups came to be lumped as "Italians" and "Greeks." Mexicans and African Americans also contributed to the ethnic mix. These workers had been brought into Colorado as strikebreakers in 1903, replacing an earlier, second wave of immigrant miners from Ireland and Wales.[16] In 1912, 61 percent of Colorado's coal miners

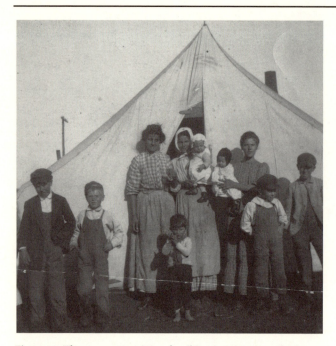

Figure 22. Three women, wives of striking immigrant coal miners, and their children stand outside a tent at the Ludlow colony during the strike. Photo by Ed Doyle. Western History Collections, Denver Public Library Z-217.

were of "non–Western European origin."[17] Before the 1913 strike the United Mine Workers of America, which sought to unionize these workers, counted 24 distinct languages in the southern field coal camps.

This mix of ethnicities obviously had consequences for organizing the miners and maintaining unity during the strike. The CF&I would purposely mix nationalities in the shafts so as to discourage worker communication and solidarity.[18] The ethnic mix also resulted in the strike and its violence being seen—at least in the context of some official histories—as the result of a belligerent Greek and Balkan culture rather than the working conditions that existed in the southern Colorado coal fields.

The United Mine Workers of America was founded in 1890 and in 1903 led a strike in the southern Colorado coal field. This strike failed as operators successfully employed replacement labor and strikebreaking agencies.[19] This defeat did not extinguish the union spirit, however, and organizing continued in a variety of covert ways.

In 1912 the coal companies fired 1,200 southern field miners on suspicion of union activities. In the summer of 1913 the UMWA, spearheaded by national organizers such as Frank Hayes and John Lawson, opened its biggest push yet in the south. In September of that year the UMWA announced a strike when the operators would not meet a list of seven demands:

1. Recognition of the United Mine Workers union.
2. A 10 percent increase in wages on the tonnage rates. Each miner was paid by the ton of coal he mined, not by the hour.
3. An eight-hour workday.
4. Payment for "dead work." Since miners were only paid for the coal they mined, work such as shoring, timbering, and laying track was not paid work.
5. The right to elect their own checkweighmen. Miners suspected, generally with good reason, that they were being cheated at the scales that weighed their coal. They wanted a miner to check the scales.
6. The right to trade in any store, to choose their own boarding places, and to choose their own doctors.
7. Enforcement of Colorado mining laws, some of which already addressed a few of these demands.

Approximately 90 percent of the workforce went on strike, numbering around 10,000 miners and their families. Those who lived in the company towns were evicted, and on September 23, 1913, they hauled their possessions out of the canyons through freezing rain and snow to about a dozen tent sites rented in advance by the UMWA. The tent colonies were placed at strategic locations at the entrances to canyons in order to intercept strikebreakers. Ludlow, with about 150 tents holding 1,200 people, was the largest of the colonies and also served as strike headquarters for Las Animas County. The UMWA supplied tents and ovens and provided the strikers with food, medical attention, and weekly strike relief. This amounted to $3.00 per week for each miner, $1.00 for each wife,

Figure 23. View of the United Mine Workers of America camp for coal miners on strike against John D. Rockefeller's Colorado Fuel & Iron Company in Ludlow. An immigrant woman looks weary after a massive 1914 snowfall during the Ludlow strike. Western History Collections, Denver Public Library X-6035.

and $0.50 for each child. Many important personages in American labor history became involved in the strike on the side of labor, including Mary "Mother" Jones, Upton Sinclair, and John Reed.

The coal operators reacted quickly to the strike. Replacement miners were imported from across the country and abroad. Baldwin-Felts detectives—specialists in breaking coal strikes—were brought in from West Virginia. Violence characterized the strike from the very beginning, with both sides committing shootings and murders.[20] The coal companies soon mounted a campaign of systematic harassment against the strikers. This harassment took the form of high-powered searchlights that played on the tent colonies at night, surveillance from strategically placed machine-gun nests, and use of the "Death Special," an improvised armored car that periodically sprayed the colonies with machine-gun fire. The first exchange of gunfire occurred at Ludlow on October 7.[21] On October 17 the armored car fired into the Forbes tent colony, about five miles south of Ludlow, killing and wounding several people. On October 24 mine guards fired into a group of strikers in Walsenberg, killing four of them.[22] The purpose of this harassment may have been to goad the strikers into violent action, which would provide a pretext for the Colorado governor to call out the state militia. This would shift the financial burden for breaking the strike from the coal companies to the state. With violence escalating and the operators pressing him, Colorado governor Elias Ammons duly called out the militia on October 28, 1913.

Ammons followed this in November with an order allowing militiamen to escort strikebreakers into the coal towns. CF&I billeted militiamen on company property, furnished them with supplies from the company store, and advanced them pay.[23] On a visit to the strike zone, Colorado state senator Helen Ring Robinson observed militiamen entering the offices of CF&I to receive paychecks.[24]

The sympathies of the militia leadership exacerbated the tensions. The militia commander, a Denver ophthalmologist named John Chase, had been involved in suppressing a 1904 miners' strike at Cripple Creek.[25] Following the pattern set at Cripple Creek, Chase essentially declared martial law in the strike zone. This period of unofficial and illegal martial law included mass jailing of strikers, the suspension of habeas corpus, the torture and beating of prisoners, and, on January 22, 1914, a cavalry charge on a demonstration of miners' wives and children in downtown Trinidad. Women and children were important contributors to the miners' cause throughout the strike, specializing in picketing of mine entrances and verbal abuse of militiamen.[26] In this instance they

Figure 24. Ruins of the tent colony after the 1914 fire include tent frames, bed box springs, iron headboards, furniture frames, and stoves. Western History Collections, Denver Public Library Z-199.

were marching to demand the release of Mother Jones, who had been jailed earlier in the month for her organizing activities.

On March 11 the militia tore down tents at the Forbes colony. To one UMWA official this indicated the beginning of a reign of terror designed to drive the miners back to work.[27] By spring 1914, as the cost of supporting a force of 695 enlisted men and 397 officers in the field gradually bankrupted the state, all but two of the militia companies were withdrawn. The mining companies replaced the militiamen with mine guards and private detectives under the command of militia officers. With this move the neutrality of the militia was completely destroyed, and it now became little more than a strikebreaking force.[28]

The climax to this increasing hostility between the two sides came on April 20, 1914, although the exact sequence of events is still unclear. As McGovern and Guttridge[29] point out, little has been written of the events that led to the Ludlow massacre without emotion and distortion. The principals—coal operators, union leaders, militiamen, miners—have been cast in both noble and sinister lights. Much depends on preconceived attitudes about management and workers and the way that one constructs, filters, and relates historical facts.

Rumors of an impending militia attack on the Ludlow tent colony had circulated for some days prior to April 20. The earlier militia attacks on Forbes and at Walsenburg provided a justification for striker paranoia.[30] At 9:00 A.M. on April 20 militia activity increased around a machine-gun nest on Water Tank Hill, approximately 1.5 kilometers south of the Ludlow colony. Those miners who were armed took protected positions in a railway cut and prepared foxholes to draw machine-gun fire away from the colony. Our archaeological excavations at Ludlow indicate that strikers were armed with a variety of weapons, including Winchester rifles and shotguns. The militia detonated two bombs, perhaps as a signal to troops in other positions. Within minutes militiamen and miners were exchanging gunfire.

After a few hours of firing one of the survivors noted that the Ludlow tents were so full of holes that they looked like lace.[31] In the colony there was pandemonium. Some colonists sought refuge in a large walk-in well, where they stood knee deep in freezing water for the rest of the day. Others took refuge behind a steel railroad bridge at the northwest corner of the colony. Many people huddled in the cellars they had dug under their tents. The camp's leaders worked all day to get people to a dry creek bed north of the camp and from there to the home of a sympathetic rancher. Many colonists ultimately bivouacked in the Black Hills to the east of Ludlow.

In the early afternoon a 12-year-old boy named Frank Snyder came up out of his family's cellar and was shot dead. As the day wore on, the force facing the miners grew to almost 200 militiamen and two machine guns. At dusk a train stopped in front of the militia's machine guns and blocked their line of fire. The train crew restarted the train in response to militia threats, but by then most of the people in the colony had fled. By 7:00 P.M. tents were in flames and militiamen were looting the colony.

Toward evening Louis Tikas, the Greek leader of Ludlow tent colony, and two other miners were taken prisoner by the militia and summarily executed. Implicated in the murders was a militia lieutenant named Karl Linderfelt, a professional soldier, Spanish-American War veteran, and former head of mine guards for CF&I. He had also been present at Cripple Creek as a company guard. Linderfelt commanded Company B, which consisted entirely of mine guards and was the most despised of all militia units stationed in the southern coal field.[32]

During the battle four women and 10 children took refuge in a cellar dug beneath a tent. All but two, Mary Petrucci and Alcarita Pedregone, suffocated when the tent above them was burned. The dead included Mary Petrucci's three children and Alcarita Pedregone's two children. This cellar became infamous as the "Death Pit" and is now preserved in concrete at the Ludlow Massacre Memorial. At the end of the day more than 20 people were dead, including three militiamen, one uninvolved passerby, and 11 children.

When news of Ludlow got out, striking miners at the other tent colonies went to war. For 10 days they fought pitched battles with mine guards and militiamen along a 40-mile front between Trinidad and Walsenburg. In largely uncoordinated guerrilla attacks, the strikers destroyed several company towns and killed company employees.

The fighting ended when a desperate Governor Ammons asked for federal intervention. President Woodrow Wilson complied and on April 30 sent

Figure 25. The funeral of Ludlow victims of the United Mine Workers' labor strike against CF&I leaves Trinidad's Catholic church while hundreds of mourners line the streets. Photo by Lewis Dold. Western History Collections, Denver Public Library X60446.

federal troops to Trinidad to restore order. The army confiscated guns from both sides, and gun shops and saloons were closed. The army also had orders not to escort out-of-state strikebreakers into the coal towns. However, CF&I President Jesse Welborn later testified that strikebreakers came freely to Colorado from other states and were protected by the army as they took jobs in the coal towns.[33]

After order was restored, the Ludlow tent colony was rebuilt and the strike dragged on for another seven months. During this time President Wilson sought to broker a settlement between the coal companies and strikers.[34] His efforts were unsuccessful. The strike was eventually terminated by the UMWA on December 10, 1914. With strike funds depleted and new strikes called in other parts of the country, the UMWA could no longer support the Colorado action. Some strikers with families remained on UMWA strike relief until February 1915. Others with families were rehired by CF&I.[35] Many drifted out of state, and still others joined the ranks of the unemployed.

The Ludlow Massacre electrified the nation. Demonstrations and rallies protesting the killing of women and children erupted in cities all across the country.[36] Nearly every newspaper and magazine in the country covered the story, with pro- and anti-company editorials existing side-by-side.[37] John D. Rockefeller, Jr., was excoriated in the national press and demonized in the eyes of the American public by such prominent progressives as Upton Sinclair and John Reed. In early 1915 a spectacular series of congressional hearings exposed Rockefeller's role as a leading strategist in dealing with the Colorado strike.[38]

The widespread national reaction to Ludlow focused attention on living conditions in the Colorado coal towns and on workplace conditions throughout the United States.[39] Rockefeller engaged labor relations expert W. L. Mackenzie King (who later became prime minister of Canada) to develop a plan for a series of reforms in the mines and company towns of southern Colorado. Known as the Colorado Industrial Plan, these reforms called for a worker grievance procedure, infrastructural improvements to company towns (e.g., construction of paved roads and recreational facilities such as YMCAs), enforcement of Colorado mining laws, and the election of worker representatives to serve with management on four standing committees concerned with working conditions, safety, sanitation, and recreation.[40] The plan also forbade discrimination against workers suspected of having been union members in the past. However, it did not provide for recognition of the UMWA or agree to the principle of collective bargaining.[41]

The Colorado Industrial Plan effectively established a company union. Feeling that there was little alternative, Colorado miners accepted the plan. But critics such as UMWA vice-president Frank Hayes condemned the plan as "pure paternalism" and "benevolent feudalism."[42] Mother Jones declared the plan a "fraud" and a "hypocritical and dishonest pretense."[43] Still, the Colorado plan served as the model for many other company unions, which spread across the country and by 1920 covered 1.5 million workers (about 8 percent of the workforce).

It is not clear what direct, practical impacts the Colorado Industrial Plan had on the lives of miners and their families. Some scholars see such industrial-era reforms as little more than corporate welfare or an attempt to control immigrant workers by "Americanizing" them. The conventional wisdom is that the plan produced some real material gains for workers in the company towns.[44] However, more research is required to settle this issue. Certainly the reforms were limited, as indicated by the fact that throughout the 1920s the southern coal fields continued to be embroiled in strikes. Widespread union recognition in southern Colorado only came with New Deal legislation in the 1930s.

The Colorado Coalfield War Archaeological Project

The Colorado Coalfield War Project consists of faculty and students from the University of Denver and Fort Lewis College in Colorado and Binghamton University in New York as well as students from other institutions. The project has received its primary funding from the State Historical Fund of the Colorado Historical Society (funded by taxes on casino gambling). The project was based on the primary assumption that all of its work should serve many communities, such as the traditional communities of the academy and the middle class, but most importantly should serve the communities of unionized labor and the American working class. Initial fieldwork began in 1997.

This project uses archaeology to achieve a number of key goals. First, archaeology's concentration on the mundane objects of material life has enabled us to construct what might be termed a "vernacular history" of the war as opposed to the "official history" to be gleaned from the official government archives and documents of the era (we use these terms as defined by Bodnar).[45]

Official histories of Ludlow, when they address this episode in American industrial relations, focus on famous people, events, and the organizing activities of the UMWA. We have only anecdotal information about the everyday lives and relationships of the population that constituted the labor force. Archaeology can flesh out their side of the story, address official history's blind spots, and help produce a fuller understanding of cultural and historical process.

Specific research questions include the following. To what extent did the shared domestic experience of women and children in the company towns reinforce the class solidarity built up among men in the mine shafts? Once on strike, how did families support themselves, especially given minimal strike relief? How was the considerable ethnic diversity of the tent colonies integrated so as to defuse tension and foster a collective class consciousness that could sustain the strike for 15 months? To what extent did coal camp life really improve following the strike?

To answer these questions, we are taking a comparative perspective on coal camp and tent colony life. The Ludlow excavations provide the strike context, and we are excavating in pre- and poststrike contexts at the Berwind coal camp above Ludlow, from which many of the Ludlow colonists came. We are looking to test documentary and vernacular accounts of life in the coal camps and tent colonies as well as investigate other ways—unrecorded by history—in which miners might have been coping with their circumstances.

The archaeological contexts have good integrity and abundant remains. The assemblages at Ludlow—clothing, jewelry, children's toys, bullets, cartridges—speak to a hurried, catastrophic abandonment. We have only begun to analyze the material, but a few observations provide a sense of how our findings compare to the historical record and the expected responses of labor to strike conditions.

From photos of burned and demolished tents we know that the tents were constructed over wooden joists laid directly on the ground to support a wooden platform and frame. Our excavations have uncovered one of these platforms, defined by stains in the earth and rows of nails that followed the joists. A wide variety of artifacts associated with the floor—men's and women's clothing, toys, diaper pins—indicates occupation by a family. The assemblage also includes a suspender part bearing the inscription (in Italian) *Society of Tyrolean Alpinists* and several Catholic religious medallions. This suggests Italian Catholic ethnicity and provides a reference point for reconstructing the spatial organization of the camp. Future study will attempt to determine the extent to which the spatial organization of ethnic groups in the tent colony duplicated or departed from the ethnic segregation of the company towns.

Historical photos also indicate that cellars were dug beneath the Ludlow tents. Historians suggest that these cellars were used as shelter from gunfire. Excavation of tent cellar locations reveals a variety of uses beyond protection, including storage and possibly habitation. Subfloor features range in size from small pits to "full basements" measuring 2 m by 2.5 m by 2 m deep. They are very well prepared—hard packed and/or fabric lined—with wall niches for storage. Some cellars had wooden floors, suggesting possible habitation use. Thus, the miners were clearly dug in for the long haul.

We are especially interested in what dietary remains at Ludlow can tell us about patterns of local interaction and support, specifically the extent to which strikers may have drawn on local merchants and other sources. Our trash pit and midden excavations reveal an enormous reliance on canned foods, much more than what we see in working-class contexts at Berwind. Some of this canned food is undoubtedly union supplied. At the same time, some features contain evidence for home canning, such as mason jars. This would certainly imply access to local farmers or gardens for fresh vegetables and fruit. Similarly, cow bones showing up in Ludlow deposits may suggest local supply from area ranchers. Further faunal analysis may disclose patterns of meat sharing within the tent colony.

It is interesting to consider the strikers' use of national brands in canned food and milk as a possible *cover* for local support in the form of prepared foods and garden and ranch products. The tent colonies were subject to search, and thus any distinctive, locally produced goods could have been traced to particular merchants. In his work on marginalized households in Annapolis, Mullins[46] shows that African

Americans purchased national name-brand, price-controlled foods as a way to avoid exploitation by local merchants. Strikers at Ludlow may have done the same, but in this instance as a strategy to protect local, striker-friendly merchants from harassment by coal company operatives and state militiamen. This would make sense as part of labor's commitment to using *place*—understood as social ties of kin and community that link workers to family and friends employed in local business, health care, and law enforcement—as a way to offset capital's greater command of *space* through control of markets, telegraph, railroad, and other technologies.[47]

Our most direct evidence of local connections lies in beer and whiskey bottles, whose embossing and labeling reflects Trinidad origins. The frequency of alcohol bottles is higher at Ludlow compared to what we see in the working-class precincts in Berwind. Social drinking is an important part of male working-class culture. Corporate control of the company towns meant control of leisure. Greater alcohol consumption at Ludlow reflects either the greater freedom of workers from company surveillance given their control of place or, alternatively, efforts to relieve boredom and stress under strike conditions. Companies certainly pushed prohibition after the strike, as reflected by the relative paucity of liquor bottles in excavated poststrike assemblages at Berwind.

Comparisons of pre- and poststrike coal camp deposits reveal some interesting changes in household strategy over time. Wood's study[48] of the Berwind remains shows how working-class women in the company towns were able to raise families on miners' wages that would not even feed two people. Trash dating before the strike shows lots of tin cans, large cooking pots, and big serving vessels. Families took in single male miners as boarders to make extra income, and women used canned foods to make stews and soups to feed them. After the strike the companies discouraged boarders, but wages still remained very low. The tin cans and big pots disappear from the trash to be replaced by canning jars and lids and the bones of rabbits and chickens. Women and children who could no longer earn money from boarders instead produced food at home to feed the family. As noted earlier, it remains to be seen whether poststrike contexts suggest an overall improvement in worker living conditions over time.

A second goal of the project has been to show that archaeology can serve the interests of more than just the middle classes. We have encouraged a dialogue between organized labor and scholars. The election of John Sweeny as president of the AFL-CIO in 1995 has led to a revitalization of this organization as a broad-based social movement. We are contributing to this dialogue by studying a history that has meaning for working people and addressing their interests in this history. The Colorado Coalfield War is not exotic or ancient history. It is familiar, close to home, and deals with issues that still confront workers today. We are proud to be invited to speak of our work each year at the annual memorial service held at the Ludlow Massacre site. In June 1999, we twice addressed striking Pueblo steelworkers, who have been on strike to stop forced overtime and thus regain one of the basic rights that the Ludlow strikers died for, the eight-hour day. Groups of interns from the AFL-CIO Union summer program have made visits to the sites, and our field school students have shared their emerging perspectives on labor history with people of their own age who have already committed to labor activism.

Third, archaeology's popular appeal has given us a more immediate access to audiences than might have been the case with other, less "sexy" disciplines. Many of the tourists who regularly pull off I-25 to visit the site still need more explicit information about what happened (many think that it must have been Native Americans who were massacred). During the summer of 1998 over 500 people visited our excavations and through site tours learned what happened. At the memorial service in 1999 we unveiled an interpretive kiosk. The kiosk has three panels, one on the history of the strike and the massacre, a second on our archaeological research, and a third on the relationship of

Figure 26. United Mine Workers of America monument. Photo by Andrew Gulliford, 1997.

Ludlow to current labor struggles. Another component of our educational program is the preparation of school programs and educational packets for the public schools of Colorado. We are currently writing a curriculum for middle school students on the history of labor in Colorado, with the 1913–14 strike as its focus. During the summers of 1999 and 2000 we held Colorado Endowment for the Humanities–sponsored training institutes for teachers at Trinidad State Junior College. The institutes educated teachers on labor history and how to develop classroom materials to use in the teaching of Colorado labor history. We have also prepared a "history trunk" that circulates in Denver-area school districts. This is a box filled with artifacts, photos, and text materials that teachers can use in their classes.

Conclusions

The Colorado Coalfield War Archaeological Project provides an excellent example of how archaeology can make an independent contribution to our understanding of the historical past. Moreover, it presents an example of how a combined study of the past can engage local communities.

The project is also an excellent example of how archaeology and history can be synthesized to provide a much more comprehensive understanding of the past than could be achieved by either discipline alone. The documentary record of the war is extensive and includes primary texts, photographs, and oral histories.[49] These studies have focused on the events, strike leaders, and political consequences of the war and its aftermath. They have emphasized the roles of males in the strike but paid less attention to the importance of women.

Notes

1. Patricia Nelson Limerick, "What on Earth Is the New Western History?" in *Trails: Toward a New Western History* (Lawrence: University Press of Kansas, 1991), 81–88.

2. Lewis R. Binford, *Debating Archaeology* (San Diego: Academic Press, 1989).

3. Ian Hodder, *The Archaeological Process: An Introduction* (Cambridge, MA: Blackwell Publishers, 1999).

4. See Randall H. McGuire, *A Marxist Archaeology* (Orlando: Academic Press, 1992); Michael Shanks and Randall H. McGuire, "The Craft of Archaeology," *American Antiquity* 61 (1996): 75–88; and Phil Duke and Dean Saitta, "An Emancipatory Archaeology for the Working Class," *Assemblage* 4, http://www.shef.ac.uk/~assem/4/4duk_sai.html (accessed March 27, 2000); and L. Wurst and R. Fitts, eds., "Confronting Class," *Historical Archaeology* 33 (1999).

5. Bruce Trigger, *A History of Archaeological Thought* (Cambridge: University of Cambridge Press, 1989).

6. Duke and Saitta, "Emancipatory Archaeology."

7. Lewis R. Binford, *In Pursuit of the Past: Decoding the Archaeological Record* (New York: Thames and Hudson, 1983).

8. Nick Merriman, "Heritage from the Other Side of the Glass Case," *Anthropology Today* 5, no. 2 (1989): 14–15.

9. George S. McGovern and Leonard F. Guttridge, *The*

Great Coalfield War (Boston: Houghton Mifflin, 1972).

10. Priscilla Long, "Women of the Colorado Fuel and Iron Strike, 1913–1914," in *Women, Work, and Protest: A Century of U.S. Women's Labor History*, ed. R. Milkman (London: Routledge & Kegan Paul, 1985).

11. Barron B. Beshoar, *Out of the Depths: The Story of John R. Lawson, A Labor Leader* (Denver: Colorado Historical Commission & Denver Trades & Labor Assembly, 1957), 2; and McGovern and Guttridge, *Great Coalfield War*, 23.

12. Edwin R. Seligman, "The Crisis in Colorado," *The Annalist*, May 4, 1914; and "Colorado's Civil War and Its Lessons," *Leslie's Illustrated Weekly Newspaper*, November 5, 1914.

13. McGovern and Guttridge, *Great Coalfield War*, 6; and James Whiteside, *Regulating Danger: The Struggle for Mine Safety in the Rocky Mountain Coal Industry* (Lincoln: University of Nebraska Press, 1990).

14. Whiteside, *Regulating Danger*, 22.

15. Samuel Yellen, *American Labor Struggles* (New York: Harcourt, Brace, 1936).

16. Beshoar, *Out of the Depths*, 1; and McGovern and Guttridge, *Great Coalfield War*, 50.

17. Whiteside, *Regulating Danger*, 48.

18. "The Voice of the Gun: Colorado's Great Coalfield War of 1913–1914," *Labor's Heritage* 1 (1989): 4–23; and R. Clyne, *Coal People: Life in Southern Colorado's Company Towns, 1890–1930* (Denver: Colorado Historical Society, 1999).

19. M. E. Vallejo, "Recollections of the Colorado Coal Strike, 1913–1914," in *La Gente: Hispano History and Life in Colorado* (Denver: Colorado Historical Society, 1998), 85–104.

20. Beshoar, *Out of the Depths*; McGovern and Guttridge, *Great Coal War*; and Zeese Papanikolas, *Buried Unsung: Louis Tikas and the Ludlow Massacre* (Salt Lake City: University of Utah Press, 1982).

21. Priscilla Long, *Where the Sun Never Shines: A History of America's Bloody Coal Industry* (New York: Paragon House, 1989).

22. Philip Foner, *History of the Labor Movement in the United States, Volume V: The AFL in the Progressive Era, 1910–1915* (New York: International Publishers, 1980); and Vallejo, "Recollections of the Colorado Coal Strike."

23. Graham Adams, *The Age of Industrial Violence, 1910–1915: The Activities and Findings of the U.S. Commission on Industrial Relations* (New York: Columbia University Press, 1966).

24. Long, *Where the Sun Never Shines*, 290.

25. Elizabeth Jameson, *All That Glitters: Class, Conflict, and Community in Cripple Creek* (Urbana, IL: University of Illinois Press, 1998).

26. Long, *Where the Sun Never Shines*.

27. Ibid., "Colorado's Great Coalfield War."

28. A. Sunieseri, *The Ludlow Massacre: A Study in the Mis-employment of the National Militia* (Waterloo, IA: Salvadore Books, 1972).

29. McGovern and Guttridge, *Great Coalfield War*, 344.

30. Yellen, *American Labor Struggles*, 234; and Vallejo, "Recollections of the Colorado Coal Strike," 96.

31. M. T. O'Neal, *Those Damn Foreigners* (Minerva, CA: Hollywood Press, 1971).

32. Papanikolas, *Ludlow Massacre*.

33. Long, *Where the Sun Never Shines*, 249.

34. Yellen, *American Labor Struggles*.

35. H. L. Scamehorn, *Mill & Mine: The CF&I in the Twentieth Century* (Lincoln: University of Nebraska Press, 1992).

36. Long, *Where the Sun Never Shines*, 196.

37. Ibid., 308.

38. Yellen, *American Labor Struggles*, 220; and Foner, *History of the Labor Movement*.

39. Howard Gitelman, *Legacy of the Ludlow Massacre: A Chapter in American Industrial Relations* (Philadelphia: University of Pennsylvania Press, 1988); and Adams, *Age of Industrial Violence*.

40. Gitelman, *Legacy of the Ludlow Massacre*; and Adams, *Age of Industrial Violence*.

41. Adams, *Age of Industrial Violence*.

42. Ibid.

43. Ibid.

44. Margaret Crawford, *Building the Workingman's Paradise: The Design of American Company Towns* (London: Verso, 1995); and L. Roth, "Company Towns in the Western United States," in *The Company Town: Architecture and Society in the Early Industrial Age* (New York: Oxford University Press, 1992), 173–205.

45. John Bodnar, *Remaking America: Public Memory, Commemoration, and Patriotism in the Twentieth Century* (Princeton: Princeton University Press, 1992).

46. Paul Mullins, "A Bold and Gorgeous Front: The Contradictions of African-American Consumer Culture," in *Historical Archaeologies of Capitalism* (New York: Plenum Press, 1999), 169–94.

47. David Harvey, *Justice, Nature and the Geography of Difference* (Oxford: Blackwell, 1996).

48. Margaret Wood, "A House Divided: Changes in

Women's Power Within and Outside the Household, 1900–1930," in *The Dynamics of Power*, ed. M. O. Donovan (Carbondale, IL: Center for Archaeological Investigations, 2002).

49. For example, Beshoar, *Out of the Depths*; McGovern and Guttridge, *Great Coalfield War*; and Papanikolas, *Ludlow Massacre*.

Study Questions

1. Discuss the authors' contention that there is a bias in archaeological analysis against social-economic class. Is this bias reinforced by archaeological investigations?

2. What inspired the Colorado Coalfields War Archaeological Project? What was its goal?

3. How does the project add to our understanding of mining family life in the southern Colorado mining towns?

4. What facts show the control of mine owners/companies and the inhibition of unionization in the southern Colorado mining communities? Did unionism prevail? Explain.

5. What is the significance of Ludlow in the field of labor history?

6. Discuss the paralegal/paramilitary nature of the attacks on the Ludlow colony.

7. What was the purpose of the Colorado Industrial Plan?

8. In the archaeological analysis, what has been determined to be the use(s) for the "cellars" at the Ludlow encampment? How does this compare to traditional historical determinations for the cellars?

9. Discuss the place vs. space evidence at Ludlow and other strike camps.

10. Does the study identify anything about how pre- and poststrike living conditions differ, and is the evidence conclusive?

EXHIBITIONS, MUSEUMS, AND INTERPRETING CULTURE

Headnotes

Henry Ford supposedly remarked that "history is bunk," and yet he spent a fortune re-creating his unique version of the American past without strife and without union workers at Greenfield Village, Michigan, one of the more eclectic museum village sites in the United States. At the beginning of the twentieth century, museums functioned as temples to commerce and civilization and as universities of the common man, though most laborers worked 60-hour weeks Monday through Saturday and could not visit museums to receive enlightenment, moral uplift, and cultivation. Despite good intentions, museums were not for the masses but rather to showcase private collections of the rich.

Beginning with the Victorian impulse to classify and categorize, gentlemen assembled curio cabinets that evolved into marble-halled museums as the Industrial Age created millionaires intrigued by natural and human history. This was the golden age for amassing anthropological collections because everywhere indigenous peoples were perceived to be a "vanishing race." The same colonial impetus that required great nations to have empires assumed those nations would bring back to their museums immense collections of artifacts, bird specimens, reptile skins, wooden masks, totem poles, Indian dwellings, and a wide assortment of everything from human skeletal remains to huge war canoes.

From Ottawa and Toronto to Washington, D.C., Chicago, and Berlin, dedicated curatorial staff gathered cultural items for metropolitan and national museums. Curators put human history into perspective and showcased both the bows and arrows of "primitive" tribesmen and the exploits and pedigrees of the ruling class. Museum staff felt confident in their role to classify and interpret the world around them and to teach visitors their place in the prevailing paradigm, which mandated white Anglo Saxon Protestants on civilization's highest rung and other peoples lower down the ladder depending on the color of their skin and their distance from the northern latitudes.

Curators held enormous sway over their collections and practiced hegemony over their interpretations of people, places, and events. The turn of the century saw the acquisition of some of the great museum collections of the world, including artifacts for the Museum of Man in Berlin, the Heye Foundation in New York City, the Smithsonian Institution in Washington, D.C., and the Canadian Museum of Civilization. The early decades of the twentieth century became an undisputed era for consensus history of the American West. The brave stories of pioneers and the hardships they endured became the origin myth for the American people.

History museums supported that myth, but now we know that the land was not so much virgin as widowed. Millions of North American Indians perished as the tentacles of empire pushed west along the watercourses of rivers paddled by *coureurs de bois*. We had settled a continent. We had proven the evolution of the stages of man from savagery to barbary to civilization, and we had succeeded by divine right and superior technology. Americans labeled it "Manifest Destiny," and the vast collections of Indian artifacts, sacred objects, and human skulls served only as a backdrop for larger triumphs.

As the settlement phase ended, national museums gave way to regional museums intent on collecting the artifacts of pioneering like pistols, rifles, sewing machines, windmills, barbed wire, and buffalo robes. But World War I shook our faith in having established "civilization," and a deepening farm crisis in the 1920s became more acute during the drought of the 1930s. As pioneer farms failed, rural-raised children left for the cities. The pioneer and settlement phase had ended, and now like the Native Americans they themselves had displaced, those pioneer families were history. A few descendants remained to open regional museums and proclaim their fortitude, luck, and pluck.

Another world war and then a "Cold War" in the 1950s and 1960s spawned the rise of social history and a growing environmental movement. These new ideas challenged the social order and context of national histories, and by the 1990s museum directors began to reassess their exhibits' historical interpretations.

Now the collections remain, but how do we honestly interpret the westering movement and the pioneer spirit? Do we address failure as well as success? How do we integrate the story of North America's native peoples? How do we accurately describe the consequences of Western expansion when most history museums cheerfully intone history as celebration and accomplishment?

We have trouble in paradigms. Not only is the ownership of selected artifacts in doubt, but so is the interpretation of artifacts, including sacred Indian objects. Do Blackfoot Indian items belong in Montana or in Alberta? Curatorial authority is contested with every major exhibit, and the people who three decades ago were supposed to come to great museums and learn about their place in civilization now want their own museums to tell their own stories. And they want their artifacts repatriated, as did the Kwakiutl, who finally after lengthy legal struggles received their ancient wooden masks and carved coppers, which they reverently placed in their own U-Mista Cultural Centre at Alert Bay in British Columbia.

In history museums we have gone from consensus to controversy, from undisputed national museums to ecomuseums and community museums telling regional histories. Just as nineteenth-century political empires collapsed, at the end of the twentieth century national history museums lost their centrifugal pull toward a nation's center. What stories should we tell? Today local and regional museums display ethnic pasts and local histories without adequate reference to larger national narratives. At the turn of the century North American history museums focused on progress, technological innovation, and the captains of industry who had harnessed vast natural resources and employed thousands of men. Now we question robber barons and their environmental despoliation. When we describe gold rushes, do we also explain the effects of cyanide leaching on mountain streambeds? As we celebrate cowboys and ranching traditions, do we also focus on overgrazing and the disappearance of native grasses?

Today history is mired in controversy because curators with professional training and graduate degrees have one set of values while their visitors have another set. Hard historical questions do not make for easily digested 50-word captions. Curators learned social history and the 1970s dictum of studying history "from the bottom up," while the public still demands a seamless past and exhibits that celebrate accomplishments and reinforce old truths rather than challenge previous interpretations. Historians feel compelled to rewrite history with each generation, but the public wants the past they learned in school. Recent exhibits point out this poignant impasse.

In 1992 the Smithsonian exhibit "The West as America" at the National Museum of American Art created a storm of protest and indignant letters in part because of renewed patriotism during the Gulf War. Senators threatened a congressional investigation of how the Smithsonian is funded. Curators had used too heavy a hand in writing exhibit labels, and the audience was not prepared to substitute Western myth for Western history.

In 1995, 50 years after the end of World War II, the National Air and Space Museum of the

Smithsonian Institution also came under withering attack because of their proposed exhibit on Hiroshima and the *Enola Gay* airplane, which had dropped the first atomic bomb. Before the exhibit could even be opened, it had been eviscerated by veterans groups and conservative politicians who wanted to "take back their history" from the curators. Major mistakes were made. Mounting such a controversial exhibit on a 50th anniversary was a tactical blunder, and politically correct curatorial interpretation failed to acknowledge two radically different points of view. Curators in their early thirties assumed that dropping the bomb began the Cold War, while aging veterans knew only that the bomb had ended World War II and allowed them to get on with their lives.

The Library of Congress has faced self-censorship from African American employees appalled with a historically correct exhibit on plantation slavery. They found the subject too uncomfortable to be displayed, and it was canceled. An equally controversial exhibit on Sigmund Freud has been postponed.

We enter an age of fragile ethnic egos, bitter contention and political posturing over historical interpretation, and a lack of agreement on major events and personalities affecting our nation's past. And still history needs to be told. If curatorial authority is being undermined and severely questioned, so be it. Perhaps the lessons of social history have finally been heeded and the admonition of "every man his own historian" has new meaning. Flagship museums and exhibit venues may feel under siege, and history museums and historic sites have suffered in attendance because the American demographic is changing. There are over 2,000 historic house museums in the United States, and what may be happening is a profound shift in the definition of acceptable history. The very nature of what constitutes history is in flux.

New museums open daily. Elvis Presley's Graceland is now a world-famous historic house that annually draws over 600,000 people each year to Memphis, Tennessee, for the silver, gold, or platinum tours, which include a walk through his private jet, the *Lisa Marie*.

Louisville, Kentucky, home of the Louisville Slugger baseball bat, has a baseball museum as well as a museum of interdenominational faith in a historic Catholic church. Crowds wait in line for entrance to the Holocaust Museum in Washington, D.C., and in Dallas, Texas, the Sixth Floor Museum of the Texas Schoolbook Depository receives frequent visitors eager to learn about John Fitzgerald Kennedy and theories about his assassination.

Cultural tourism is alive and well, and every small town is assessing its historical assets and trying to uncover long-dead ancestors who may have done something noteworthy. The public loves history, but they want history on their own terms with a dash or two of nostalgia, a pinch of patriotism, and a light topping of gossip and colorful characters. Heartbreaking, contentious history with meaningful analysis does not do well on the exhibit tour circuit. We are enamored of the past, but only if it is noncontroversial and represents civil religion.

Writing in *The Chronicle of Higher Education* on the postponed exhibit on Freud, Michael Roth noted, "There is no simple formula for communicating controversy. The different materials used as evidence for diverse arguments should be included in an exhibition, as should the conflicting arguments that are based on the same evidence." He demanded, "Our cultural institutions must reaffirm their right and their obligation to create programs that challenge, provoke, and teach. Communicating question and controversies is essential to presenting history in a democracy."

The public wants museum exhibits to merely reaffirm what they already know. Curators, on the other hand, understand that museums must combine education, research, exhibition, and curation as essential functions of a proper museum. The issues we are faced with in the museum community are linked both to our success and to our failure. We have been successful creating museums, and so they proliferate in name only. Many museums created today harken back to an earlier nineteenth-century model and are little more than polished private collections with no interpretation and research. They are vanity museums or corporate showpieces devoid of substance and should more accurately be labeled halls of fame. Because museums have been successful, they have been imitated, but with no thought to anything except gate receipts and public relations.

Where we have failed as professionals is in communicating to the public that history museums are not about old things in old buildings, but that history museums are about ideas and concepts and our ever-evolving understanding of an inclusive, complicated past that is not fixed. Our understanding of people and events, of cause and effect, of human foibles and sexuality, of diverse motivations for freedom and independence, of greed and acquisition, and even understanding the paint colors in George Washington's Mount Vernon dining room all change with each new decade of scholarship.

As the editors of *Ideas and Images*, published by the American Association for State and Local History, make clear, all too often our exhibits are artifact driven and not idea driven. Curators look to the strengths of their collections and build exhibits around things rather than the ideas that motivated people in the past. What did immigrants think and feel? Who built the railroads, and what was life like for the laborers? These historical questions can help produce idea-driven exhibits, where we illuminate the past by shedding new light on previous assumptions. Yes, the public wants to be entertained, but they also need to be prodded and provoked. They need to be challenged, and our role should be to carefully and conscientiously confront the public with new scholarly interpretations utilizing artifacts only after clear exhibit themes have been determined.

We have entered another period of uncertainty, conservatism, and nostalgia for a past that never existed. David Lavender has argued that "the past is a foreign country," and many tourists do see the past as a place to go without seeking out the history implicit in their own lives and ancestors. The nineteenth century created some of the world's great museums, but at the beginning of the twenty-first century the hegemony of those national museums is gone, and Americans want museums closer to home to tell their own stories. In the twenty-first century history museums will need multiple voices and broad community involvement. Collections care will remain essential because in a world of laser digital images and CD-ROMs, museums' stock-in-trade will always be the authenticity of real objects and their patina. Two-dimensional computer images convey one thing, but actual objects rich in historical associations like Thomas Jefferson's writing desk, the Wright Brothers' biplane, or Jackie Kennedy's jewels have a meaning and an attraction all their own.

Future curation must be minimal, with balanced historical interpretation and more input from minority curators, who can provide insights into the deeper cultural meanings of artifacts so zealously collected a century ago. To achieve that end, we must vigorously work to recruit more minority museum professionals through internships and degree programs. And finally, the future of our museums is dependent upon our ability to handle difficult historical questions and to challenge the historical status quo while not alienating our audience, who must come to understand that history museums are about ideas and only secondarily about artifacts. As a people we need to know who we were and try to understand our brief moment in time. Only history museums can put the past into perspective and educate as well as entertain. The challenge is before us.

These essays represent an important analysis of exhibitions and museums unique to the American West and how their interpretation helps to define the multicultural identities of the West's diverse population. Curator William Wroth moves beyond artifact analysis to explain the difficulties and opportunities involved in exhibiting Native American and Hispanic arts in their specific cultural contexts. He provides a variety of examples from his own curatorial experience and successful exhibit installations across the Southwest. Historian and historic preservationist Carroll Van West then looks at small local history societies across the West and the museums and living history sites they manage. Van West argues that Western museums seem limited in their representation of Western history and that they have not embraced New West scholarship or all that can be learned from artifacts. He argues that we should spend more time asking research questions of material culture, because original Western artifacts can document history just like newspapers, diaries, and photographs.

Art historian Thomas Patin goes beyond artifacts and exhibitions as cultural constructs to consider Western views in national parks as integral to American identity. Patin believes that the National Park Service, by showcasing natural resources and framing scenery at Yellowstone, Zion, and the Grand Canyon national parks through drives, views, and scenic turnouts, has created cultural icons. Patin believes that scenic views are themselves artifacts. He feels that the National Park Service has shaped American perspectives on the West as surely as any curator or museum director has influenced how we value Western artifacts and Western history.

Raymond Rast describes the complicated preservation issues he encountered while working on a National Historic Landmark application for the Bainbridge Island, Washington, site where Nikkei were forced to congregate prior to removal to inland internment camps. The National Park Service eventually decided not to go forward with the NHL nomination in part because of concerns from the Japanese American community. Rast explains the issues in his award-winning public history essay.

Exhibiting Native American and Hispanic Arts in Cultural Context

William Wroth

Our War Gods are sad and lonely. No one in America, no people walking by them in the museums know their songs, their names, and their prayers. . . . No one cleanses them or prays for them.

The above quote from Zuni elders petitioning the Denver Art Museum in 1978 for the repatriation of their sacred wooden figures called War Gods (Ahayu:da) epitomizes the dichotomy between native peoples and museums when it comes to the presentation of cultural objects.[1] The twin War Gods created by the Sun Father are viewed as living beings, an integral part of Zuni and all life, for they serve to stabilize both the human and natural worlds and prevent chaos and calamities. The traditional Native American view that every created thing is alive and has sacred meaning can only be imperfectly suggested in the museum context, even when sympathetic. In this essay I will explain the origins of this dichotomy, the views of different types of museums toward the collecting and display of indigenous objects, and the changes that have taken place in museums in the last 25 years, with examples from some Southwestern exhibitions of Native American and Hispanic arts and cultures.

The museum is an educational institution using material objects and visual displays as the means of communicating information. Museums collect, preserve, study, and exhibit objects of artistic, cultural, and historical importance. They began as the private "cabinets" of wealthy individuals in the eighteenth century. By the late 1700s the democratization of the museum had begun to take place. They became public institutions making rare objects formerly known only to the rich now available to the public at large. The museum of the late nineteenth century and through much of the twentieth, while accomplishing this admirable goal for the public good, also presented and reinforced the dominant values of the society in which they existed. Even today, these values are reflected in decisions concerning what is to be collected and preserved and what is to be exhibited and how it is to be interpreted.

With regard to ethnographic or indigenous arts in the nineteenth and early twentieth centuries, all of the functions of the museum served to reinforce dominant social views, especially those that stressed the superiority of Western (Euro-American) cultures over non-Western cultures. While the collection, study, and classification of objects might seem to be a neutral "scientific" activity, it actually has been a subtle vehicle for maintaining cultural superiority. Consider the following questions: Who decides what is to be collected and preserved? Who names and defines the meaning and use of the objects to be preserved? Who determines how they will be exhibited, interpreted, and published? These functions have traditionally been carried out by Euro-American art historians, historians, anthropologists, and museum curators, not by members of the indigenous groups under study. Western material and cultural values were, and often still are, taken as an absolute, the norm against which the values of non-Western cultures are measured and often found lacking.

Thus museums displaying artifacts of other cultures often used exhibitions to convey a message of Euro-American superiority. Objects of other cultures were presented for their exotic interest. Members of these cultures were seen as the exotic "other" with strange customs and practices. Objects were often either misinterpreted due to our cultural biases or presented completely out of context.

Four different approaches have historically been taken to the presentation of cultural artifacts, each sharing these limitations in differing ways. Art museums have tended to present objects solely for their aesthetic and formal qualities. The public art museum developed in the late eighteenth century as a secular temple in which the traditional reverence for sacred objects so widespread in earlier times was transmuted into a secular vision of the object in isolation as focus for aesthetic contemplation. The work of art was to be studied and contemplated from a purely aesthetic point of view without reference to its possible sacred and other cultural connotations. To emphasize their aesthetic qualities, this approach displayed indigenous objects in splendid isolation, placing them in a transformed minimalist context determined by Euro-American views of what constitutes quality, beauty, and form. Emphasis was on art historical concerns such as stylistic differences and dating of artifacts. Little or nothing was said about what value or meaning an object has within the culture from which it came.

The approach of the history museum has been to cherish the past and romanticize it from the point of view of the dominant culture. History museums exempted themselves from serious consideration of the history of other cultures, except insofar as these cultures impacted "our" history. From this point of view the history of indigenous peoples begins when they were "discovered" by the Euro-Americans and essentially ends when they have been completely subjugated and presumably assimilated into the dominant culture. In such a presentation the emphasis was on the social and technological achievements of the dominant culture for which the supposed primitivism of indigenous cultures served as a foil. Native peoples were often presented as an obstacle, usually heroically overcome, to Euro-American settlement and the advancement of culture.

Natural history and anthropology museums have shared similarities in their scientific and ethnographic approaches to the presentation of non-Western cultures. Natural history museums often have a propensity to present a simplistic evolutionary model of human culture in which indigenous peoples are depicted at a lower level of development than "advanced" Euro-Americans. They are presented as part of nature, part of the flora and fauna of the natural world, in contrast to Euro-Americans, who are civilized. Indigenous peoples are considered primarily as worthy objects of study by the scientist, just as the biologist might study any aspect of the natural world.

The approach of anthropology or ethnographic museums has shown more interest in the actual cultures of non-Western peoples. However, they have often taken a purely functionalist approach, presenting objects within a cultural context but from a utilitarian point of view, for instance showing procedures for making and using simple domestic objects. This emphasis on utilitarian practices introduces a bias into the presentation because indigenous people are presented as concerned primarily with practical issues, as though they have no culture beyond filling the physical needs of food and shelter, thus dovetailing with the simple-minded evolutionary approach of the natural history museum. The emphasis in anthropology museums has also been on what is called the "ethnographic present"—freezing indigenous people in a mythical precontact or early contact period and not acknowledging them as a living culture. This facilitates the presentation of indigenous people as the "other"—exotic, primitive, and unchanging.

This bias is built into the very terminology of anthropology, for *ethnos*, the root of the words *ethnology* and *ethnography*, means *heathen* (that is, non-Christian, non-Western). Thus ethnology is the study of the heathen nations, by definition, the other. There are several problems with this approach. First, the living humanity of the people is lost—they are merely objects of study. Second, the utilitarian emphasis further obscures both the deeper meaning of objects within the culture and the philosophical and spiritual purposes that these objects might evoke if properly presented and understood. As Joseph Epes Brown has noted: "The so-called arts and crafts of a people, found in such imaginative diversity and aesthetic elegance among Native American peoples, are not just utilitarian, as they are usually treated by art historians [and anthropologists], but represent external projections of a people's inner vision of reality.... It is through both creating and living with such ideas, values, sacred powers made tangible, that people are led to realize who they are in their fullest and deepest potentialities.... In spite of signs of new awareness on the part of some museum curators and art historians, museums and art books continue to present American Indian arts and crafts as *things*, of aesthetic quality perhaps, but extracted out of the ritual and ceremonial context which is essential to full understanding as this was available to those who created, used, and lived with such forms."[2]

In the late twentieth century the shortcomings of this approach have been recognized, part of a dawning realization on the part of many social scientists that their methods lack objectivity and in fact are highly influenced by their own cultural biases. This awakening self-reflection has occurred simultaneously with a renewed awareness by many indigenous people of the values of their own cultures. They are no longer content to accept contemporary Euro-American materialism as the norm toward which they should aspire, nor do they accept the mainstream academic depiction of their culture presented by outsiders who have little real understanding of it. As discussed at the beginning of this essay, the indigenous worldview often conflicts sharply with the implicit or explicit presentation of cultural objects in the museum.

Museums have begun to deal with these concerns, in some cases simply responding to political pressure from Native American and Hispanic groups, as well as those of other ethnic groups. But it is much more than politics that is at issue here: it is a question of redressing a long-standing societal disharmony caused by a history of injustices. A sincere response to Native American and Hispanic concerns will make possible the highest and perhaps most urgent goal of our society: that different peoples can live together in mutual respect and harmony. Here the museum has an exciting role to play because it is so well suited to display and explain the cultural values of other groups. It might seem that the question of past injustices has little to do with the work of the museum, but in fact unresolved injustices are very much alive in the minds and hearts of Native American and Hispanic peoples and thus cannot be separated from the cultural and aesthetic issues with which the museum deals.

Museums in the past and even today often have taken refuge in a false neutrality that is no longer a valid position. Instead it is necessary to take into account the desires, needs, and points of view of the indigenous communities whose culture is being displayed. Community members should be active participants in the planning of exhibitions and in the interpretation of their own objects, cultural practices, and history. Their "voice" must be present, indeed must inform the content of the exhibition. An important role of the museum must be to present the deeper meanings of objects and cultural practices from the community's point of view and not just present aesthetic or scientific information. The primary purpose of an exhibition must be to benefit the indigenous community, which can include, but not be limited to, sparking a new cultural consciousness within the community and increasing understanding outside the community. As Peter Whiteley has astutely noted: "At a basic level, if anthropologists are not interested in the fates of their subjects, then what use can their knowledge have either to the community itself or to any genuine 'science of man'?"[3] This comment applies equally to curators, historians, and everyone involved in the study and presentation of indigenous cultures. The important point here is that a genuine anthropological science cannot be abstracted from the values, needs, and aspirations of the people under study. Science must be human in the real sense of benefiting human beings or it is without value.

Starting in the 1970s, some museums in the West and elsewhere in the country began to listen to the Native American and Hispanic communities whose artifacts and cultures they were collecting and exhibiting. Several welcome steps were taken in the direction of accommodating community values. The first was to establish advisory committees of community members; the second was to incorporate indigenous values and points of view into exhibitions so that the interpretation was not dominated by the point of view of the curators. A final step has been to have indigenous community members actually curate exhibitions. Thus there is a range of accommodation possible from more or less superficial involvement to full involvement. Here I will discuss several exhibitions mounted in Southwestern museums since the mid-1980s to show the degree to which these concerns with community values have been incorporated.

The Museum of International Folk Art (MOIFA) in Santa Fe holds the largest and most complete collection of Hispanic arts of the Southwest in existence. New Mexico has the highest percentage of Hispanic population of any state in the United States, with roots going back to the late sixteenth century. Interest in Hispanic arts in New Mexico dates to the late nineteenth century and really came to the fore in the 1920s, when many Anglo American collectors began to admire and acquire examples of these "Spanish colonial" arts, as they were called by the collectors. MOIFA, as a branch of the state Museum of New Mexico, became the repository for Hispanic arts, and a curator of Spanish colonial arts was hired in the early 1950s who significantly added to the collection. In spite of this extensive collection, the large Hispanic population in the region, and much local interest, no long-term comprehensive exhibition of Hispanic arts and culture was mounted by the museum until the 1980s. In 1985 the MOIFA administration decided to build the Hispanic Heritage Wing, which would be devoted to permanent exhibitions of the collection. The planning of the wing was undertaken from the beginning with an advisory committee of individuals from the local Hispanic community and a Hispanic co-curator who helped to shape its design and the content of the exhibitions. Members of the advisory committee expressed their concern with several important features in the conception and overall planning of the wing. First, they felt it was important to emphasize the present and continuing vitality of Hispanic Southwestern culture and not present it only as something from the past. They also asked that objects selected for the exhibition be presented and interpreted in a dignified manner, that is, within a context of the meaning and value such objects hold within the culture.

The initial plan drawn up by outside design consultants from California was rejected by the committee as being too slick and commercial in appearance. They requested that local and natural materials be used and the work of local Hispanic artisans be incorporated into the plan. The committee also requested that the introductory atrium area of the exhibition be lit with natural light to give the appearance of a courtyard, which was accomplished by the use of a large skylight in place of the ceiling. They asked that performing arts of music, drama, and storytelling be incorporated into the exhibition. This was accomplished by the creation of an ambitious audio program recorded by two New Mexican folklorists, which was continuously available in the atrium area. Hispanic artists were commissioned to make the hand-carved doors leading into the exhibition, to weave fabric in traditional style for the couches and chairs in the atrium area, and to paint a mural for the title panel. Finally, the committee's request for presenting Hispanic New Mexico as a living culture was honored by the installation of a "changing gallery" at the conclusion of the permanent exhibition. Two or three times a year new exhibits of the works of Hispanic artists in many media are displayed in this gallery.

The main exhibition, which opened in 1989 and is still ongoing, is titled "Familia y Fe" (Family and Faith) in acknowledgment of these two important values in the Hispanic community. It focuses first on the remarkable religious folk art of New Mexico, the holy images known as *santos* made by local artist from the mid-eighteenth century until today. These images include a wide array of devotional paintings on wood panels, polychrome wood sculpture, and altar screens. They are presented first from the point of view of their meaning within the culture: their community role, their role within the family, and their meaning for individuals in their personal spiritual practices. Another section of the exhibition explains the history of santo making in New Mexico and the different styles that emerged in the eighteenth and nineteenth centuries. The next section of "Familia y Fe" is devoted to domestic crafts such as weaving, furniture making, jewelry making, tin work, and straw appliqué. These sections show not only the technical and historical aspects of the crafts but also the role they played within domestic life and the local economy. A period room depicts a typical home interior of the early nineteenth century, and an interactive video program keyed to this room gives in-depth information for each craft. Following the main exhibition area a smaller section titled "Agents of Change" shows the impact of outside forces upon Hispanic culture beginning in the late nineteenth century and the revival of Hispanic crafts in the early twentieth century, which led to the present-day flourishing of Hispanic crafts and culture. For the viewer this provides a smooth transition into the changing gallery and its rotating displays of contemporary Hispanic arts.

After the opening the MOIFA staff supplemented the exhibitions with a number of public programs, including demonstrations by Hispanic artisans and musical and dramatic performances, which, along with the changing gallery, provided an ongoing link with the local Hispanic community. The museum also undertook an innovative outreach program in which staff members held informal public gatherings in rural villages to talk about the arts and architecture of the village, showing the residents how their community was part of the larger picture of Hispanic arts and culture. These meetings were followed by museum-sponsored bus trips to Santa Fe, where village participants were greeted by Spanish-speaking docents who led them through the Hispanic Heritage Wing. All of these efforts were intended to make the Hispanic Heritage Wing alive and meaningful to Hispanic New Mexicans and avoid the typical situation in which cultural exhibitions in museums exist in isolation from the culture they represent.

A more specifically focused exhibition of Hispanic arts and culture was "Images of Penance, Images of Mercy," organized by the Taylor Museum of the Colorado Springs Fine Arts Center, which has the most comprehensive collection of late-nineteenth-century santos from New Mexico and southern Colorado in existence. This exhibition opened in Colorado Springs in 1991 and traveled to museums all over the country. It was devoted primarily to the images used by the Catholic lay brotherhood of Our Father Jesus Nazarene, known popularly as the Penitente brotherhood. Among other communal and charitable activities, this lay organization or confraternity is known for its devotion to the suffering of Christ. Each spring during Holy Week members of the brotherhood, using nearly life-size statues, reenact the story of Christ's passion, culminating in His crucifixion on Good Friday. Due to their emphasis on suffering as penance and a means of spiritual purification, the brotherhood has been the source of misunderstanding and controversy since they first came to the notice of incoming Protestant Anglo Americans in the mid-nineteenth century, and they have been reluctant to discuss their spiritual practices with the outside world. As a result little objective information has been available on the Penitentes, and museums have seldom mounted exhibitions dealing with them.

In taking up this subject, the Taylor Museum sought the advice of several members and officers of the brotherhood and their spiritual adviser, Father Jerome Martinez of Santa Fe. These individuals were part of the museum's curatorial advisory committee, which helped develop the content and form of the exhibition, paying special attention to culturally sensitive issues. The guiding principle of the exhibition was a deep sense of respect for the cultural practices in question, combined with clear explanations of these practices and their long history in the Christian tradition as well as their continuing significance within the culture. In particular, their religious statues and paintings were presented as sacred objects with their spiritual meanings rather than their aesthetic qualities emphasized. The result was an exhibition that presented in a straightforward manner the spiritual and communal purposes of the Penitente brotherhood, their ceremonies, and their images. The exhibition was opened in Colorado Springs in March 1991 by a large contingent of members of the brotherhood who came up from New Mexico for the occasion. At the appointed hour they met at the front door of the museum and walked in a formal procession to the gallery of the exhibition, singing traditional *alabados* (hymns) as they went. Upon entering the gallery the brothers sang and prayed before each image on display, then declared the exhibition officially open to the public. It was a remarkable moment in which real life and its artificial representation in a museum exhibition came together in an emotionally and intellectually satisfying manner. The exhibition received numerous positive reviews and comments at the different museums on its traveling tour. Most gratifying to the curators were responses by New Mexican Hispanic people living in other parts of the country who expressed gratitude for the sense of reconnection to their roots they felt when viewing the exhibition.

Two other exhibitions organized by the Taylor Museum in the 1990s used different ways of incorporating meaningful cultural content. "Sacred Land: Indian and Hispanic Cultures of the Southwest" (opened in 1992) was intended as a long-term exhibition of the museum's outstanding Southwestern ethnographic collections. Most museums in the region have historically made a rather false division between Native American and Hispanic cultures and arts, when in fact they have been closely intertwined since the Spanish first arrived in the Southwest in the sixteenth century, and they show many cross-cultural influences.

By featuring Indian and Hispanic arts in the same exhibition in adjoining galleries, the museum accorded them equal status and gave the viewer the opportunity to compare and contrast the rich variety of crafts from different cultures. The curators made a conscious choice to keep their own commentary to a minimum and let the peoples of the Southwest speak for themselves. Each section includes large panels displaying selected statements made by Indian and Hispanic individuals concerning their ideas about art and life, along with historic photographs, which add cultural and environmental context. In addition, a video program without commentary by a narrator is entirely dedicated to the work and words of three artists: Pueblo, Navajo, and Hispanic. The Hispanic section of the exhibition incorporates a careful reproduction of a village chapel with walls and floor actually made of adobe and nineteenth-century folk paintings and statues installed just as they were in the original. Visitors can enter the chapel, which replicates the experience of being in a village church. On several occasions the museum guards have found Catholic visitors leaving offerings or lighting devotional candles and praying before the images.

After seven years of research and planning, the exhibition "Mountain—Family—Spirit: The Arts and Culture of the Ute Indians" opened at the Taylor Museum in July 2000, later traveling to other museums around the country. No comprehensive exhibition devoted entirely to the Ute Indians had ever been mounted by a museum, and in fact they were not well known, even in Colorado, where they are the only Native Americans with tribal lands. In 1993 the Taylor Museum decided it was time to recognize the historical and ongoing contributions of the Utes to Colorado and the Rocky Mountain West. From the beginning the exhibition was conceived as a cooperative venture between the museum and the two Ute tribes in Colorado: the Southern Utes and the Ute Mountain Utes, and also included input from the Northern Utes in Utah. Beginning in 1993, the curators made several visits to Ute headquarters in Ignacio and Towaoc, meeting with tribal officials and with the cultural and elders committees. A curatorial committee was then formed and included five tribal members who took an active part in the selection of materials for the exhibition. They also contributed to and reviewed exhibition label content and contributed text to the exhibition catalog: *Ute Indian Arts & Culture: From Prehistory to the New Millennium*. The exhibition displayed the rich variety of Ute arts and culture both historic and contemporary. Objects and historical photographs were borrowed from museums all over the country, including the Southern Ute Cultural Center in Ignacio.

During the opening of the exhibition in Colorado Springs in July 2000, the museum sponsored a Ute Teachers Institute, which brought schoolteachers from all over Colorado and elsewhere in contact with Ute cultural leaders, artists, and scholars in order to enrich their teaching curricula. This was followed by a symposium at the museum in October 2000. In summer 2001 the exhibition traveled to the Anasazi Heritage Center in Dolores, Colorado, a venue convenient for both the Southern Ute and Ute Mountain Ute reservations. During this showing the Center of Southwest Studies at Fort Lewis College organized another Ute Teachers Institute, which drew a large contingent of educators from the region to learn about Ute arts and culture directly from Ute cultural leaders and artists as well as from scholars involved on the project.

The exhibition was very well received by the Utes themselves and can be counted as a successful instance of cooperation among museums, scholars, and native peoples. The next step in Ute involvement in the exhibition process (and hence in control of the interpretation of their own culture) is already under way. The Southern Ute Cultural Center is planning a large expansion and will be organizing its own comprehensive exhibitions of Ute arts and culture in the near future.

In addition to the above examples of exhibiting Native American and Hispanic arts and culture, several other museums in the Southwest have made serious efforts to involve the local communities in innovative exhibitions of their culture. Among the best have been the Wheelwright Museum and the Museum of Indian Arts and Culture in Santa Fe and the Arizona State Museum in Tucson, as well as the National Hispanic Cultural Center in Albuquerque. Most museums today in the Southwest and elsewhere in the country are trying to actively incorporate indigenous points of view into their ethnographic exhibitions. The sharing of power and decision making in the planning and implementation of the exhibition often adds complexities to the process, but it is a welcome and necessary change in attitude by museums, a serious attempt to bridge that dichotomy between indigenous and Euro-American views so clearly pointed out by the Zuni elders quoted at the beginning of this essay.

Notes

1. Marilyn Youngbird, "The Web That Connects the Heart and Mind," in *American Indian Ritual Object Repatriation Foundation News & Notes* 9, no. 1 (spring–summer 2003): 3.

2. Joseph Epes Brown, *The Spiritual Legacy of the American Indian* (New York: Crossroad, 1982), 127–28, 134.

3. Peter Whiteley, "The End of Anthropology (at Hopi)?" in *Journal of the Southwest* 35, no. 2 (summer 1993): 149.

Study Questions

1. Explain Native American views on cultural objects and the problems this represents for museum exhibitors.

2. How are the ways that museums have collected and displayed objects and artifacts of native peoples changing?

3. Discuss three exhibitions noted in the essay that have made a more sympathetic treatment to their display and interpretation of cultural objects of Southwestern native peoples and Hispanics.

History and Interpretation at the Western History Museum

Carroll Van West

For years, historians and museum professionals have struggled to answer a basic question: Can we learn anything from each other? Collaboration is possible, once both groups learn to negotiate around two roadblocks. The first is history by association: the tendency of history museums to use their artifacts and buildings as merely a stage where history lectures, taken from standard literary texts, are addressed to the public, an interpretive method that enjoys a long history in American history museum practice. The second roadblock is visual illiteracy: the failure of historians and curators to use artifacts and buildings as documentary sources.

The history museum is one of the most pervasive components of the western American landscape. Anyone who travels through the Great Plains, from Texas to North Dakota, cannot escape history museums of one sort or the other. There are local history museums, usually situated in the county seat, where residents have collected and arranged artifacts to speak to their own community accomplishments and sense of worth. Perhaps the most popular museums are those that masquerade as frontier towns, where visitors can experience "firsthand" the life of the pioneers. In fact, travelers entering eastern Colorado on Interstate I-70 first encounter the typical state visitor center and an attached historic village of buildings moved from various eastern Colorado locations to the new frontier village site. Historic sites and historic house museums are found everywhere, magnets for the tourist dollar and reflecting regional preservation efforts. Then there are state historical societies that serve as the major depositories of history in the region; their "formal" history museums become models followed throughout the state.[1]

These four types of history museums—the local museum, the pioneer town/frontier village, the historic site/house, and the state historical society—provide many Westerners, along with a sizable number of other Americans who choose to vacation in the "Old West," with their image of what the West was like, who its significant historical actors were, and which events, people, and places really mattered. Perhaps as much as the Western novel, television, and movies, these institutions have shaped popular perceptions and understanding of Western history.

Yet their influence as teachers of history is problematic, despite the fact that almost every site has a heritage education program of some type. No matter their size, budget, or location, most Western history museums teach history by associating their objects and buildings to historical events and people, an interpretive technique that, more often than not, leaves a legacy of hero worship and elite cultural hegemony. We show the objects we do, we protect the historic buildings we do, and we preserve the historic sites we do because they are associated, in some way or another, with a Great Man or Great Event. The association approach limits the history we take from an artifact, a landscape, or a building; we use artifacts, landscapes, and buildings to illustrate history, not as historical documents in their own right.

Part of this inheritance is directly due to the past interpretations of academic historians. Biographies emphasizing the lives and contributions of Great People have been, and remain, a popular approach to the study of the West. Other historians religiously practiced the "frontier thesis" of Frederick Jackson Turner. In his famous 1893 address to the American Historical Association, Turner spoke of the "perennial rebirth" of the frontier in America as providing "the forces dominating American character." Historians looked to the western frontier for the true meaning of America. While many parts of Turner's thesis have great validity, unfortunately his work led too many scholars to think solely in terms of the "frontier" and the "pioneers" who made it.[2]

As the thesis evolved, the word *frontier* became synonymous with the term *westward expansion*. The frontier was defined as an area where heroic and brave Great Men transformed "savagery" and "wilderness" into a stable, "civilized" society.³ Despite criticism, the "frontier thesis" remained influential, an elaborate historical construct that seemingly proved the march of progress. A large part of the history profession accepted it without question, any nagging doubts overwhelmed by the thesis's alleged ability to explain the totality of the Western experience. Western history museum administrators, educators, and curators embedded the frontier thesis in their presentations of history to such an extent that if the object or place was not associated with the frontier or pioneer experience in some way, it had little significance.⁴

Associating objects and things with the great epic of westward expansion and its heroes has a long tradition in Western history museums. However, an interpretation featuring great events dominated by great men was not invented out west. Westerners inherited this characteristic not only from the way scholars practiced history in the past, but also from the traditions of history museums and historic preservation back east. A desire to deify early American heroes lay behind the first efforts in historic sites and historic house museums. Mount Vernon (Washington), the Hermitage (Jackson), and Monticello (Jefferson) enshrined beloved presidents as godlike heroes. In the late nineteenth century, Americans deified those who died in the Civil War by setting aside battlefields as monuments to valor, courage, and honor. The very monumental nature of the battlefields turned the hallowed ground into military shrines, still visited by hundreds of thousands of pilgrims each year.⁵

Early museum practices established a tradition of historical interpretation best described as a shrine mentality. Museums and sites were not particularly tools for understanding and analyzing history, but they were excellent sources for inspiration and patriotic fervor. More often than not, artifacts, sites, and buildings were preserved and restored because of their association with great men or with great events participated in by great men. The purpose of the history museum or site was to remind everyone of that debt to the past; as shrines, the museums reflected the cultural assumptions of America's economic elite and buttressed the status quo. In each case, the value of the artifact lay in its associative values. Few bothered to see if the artifact itself—through its materials, composition, function, and operation—had a story to tell.⁶

The shrine mentality has lasted well into the twentieth century. The 1920s and 1930s witnessed the restoration of Colonial Williamsburg by John D. Rockefeller II. Rockefeller limited Williamsburg's colonial history to the high-minded days of the revolution, when the "heroes" Jefferson, Washington, Wythe, and Henry walked the streets of the Virginia capital. Rockefeller, and most of the restoration's planners and supporters, perceived the village as a stage where they could "teach the American people about the 'patriotism, high purpose, and unselfish devotion of our forefathers to the common good.'" Later, Rockefeller's sons transformed this vision into a preservation and education project that brought "'forcibly to the people' the values of 'courage, self-reliance, faith, initiative, self-sacrifice, [and] devotion to the common welfare.'" Williamsburg soon became associated with the entire gamut of postwar concerns, particularly the "Cold War" ideological battles of the 1950s and 1960s.⁷

Williamsburg's legacy to the West involved more than the interpretive storyline. Many communities decided they wanted their own Williamsburgs. An excellent example is the 1940s development of Virginia City, Montana. Encouraged by the Williamsburg example, the Bovey family spent its own money and raised funds to restore Virginia City, then largely abandoned and in decay, to its appearance during the years the town served as a major western mining center and the territorial capital of Montana. Like the Williamsburg restoration, which focused on one key story—the revolution—in its depiction of history, the Virginia City restoration also showcased one dramatic event—the vigilante movement for law and order of the late 1860s. Success at Virginia City led the restoration managers to expand their exhibits to the neighboring "ghost town" of Nevada City, where they combined the few remaining original structures with historic buildings moved from several Montana locations to create a "typical" frontier town. The Bovey family lost interest in the project during the 1990s, and at one time it appeared that many of the valuable collections would be sold and dispersed. The State of Montana and thousands of interested citizens stepped forward and raised the money to acquire the property and keep both Virginia City and the re-created Nevada City open to the public.[8]

The development of Nevada City as a re-created frontier village points to another source of inspiration for Western history museums: Henry Ford's Greenfield Village in Dearborn, Michigan. From the late 1920s until his death, Henry Ford molded Greenfield Village as a representative nineteenth-century American village, creating a historical world of fact and fiction. Greenfield Village was the first museum on a massive scale to blend relocated historic buildings with new, reconstructed buildings to re-create an ideal, but totally imaginary, American town, complete with shrines to such nineteenth-century luminaries as Thomas Edison, the Wright Brothers, George Washington Carver, Stephen Foster, and others. Most buildings were important solely for their associative values. Great men had lived in them—or could have lived in something like them. The association with a name or an event made the place important and worthy of exhibition.

Ford's example of moving unrelated buildings to a single site in order to create a history museum of a typical nineteenth-century town has had enormous influence on outdoor Western history museums. Perhaps more importantly, Greenfield Village, despite Ford's rumblings that he wanted an artifact-oriented museum where people could "see" history working, remained a place where associative values largely determined interpretation. Ford admired his industrial heroes like Firestone and Edison, and he wanted all Americans to share in his admiration by seeing places where, once, in some other place, these men had stood, worked, or lived.[9]

How did Western museum professionals adapt the lessons they gained from places like Colonial Williamsburg and Greenfield Village to their own sites? Three examples from the states of Iowa, Kansas, and North Dakota suggest the range.[10] At Living History Farms in Des Moines, Iowa, the museum managers took an existing historic property, the Flynn Farm, featuring a magnificent Italianate-styled brick farmhouse and associated outbuildings, and moved several representative farmhouses from outlying areas to create a living history museum devoted to agricultural history. To round out the museum's interpretation of the farming experience in Iowa, staff at Living History Farms also re-created an imaginary Ioway Indian settlement and built a modern farmhouse of the future. In the 1980s, they decided that even those rural environments were not enough. They chose to broaden their interpretation by re-creating a main street of a typical Midwestern town. The museum lined its street with both relocated historic buildings and copies of other historic structures.

At Living History Farms, patterns of association influence interpretation in interesting ways. No Great Men or Great Events are paraded before the public; rather, the buildings and artifacts are associated with certain periods of agricultural history. While interpreters demonstrate how certain farm tools were used, creating a historical experience that is both alive and real, the buildings often appear as merely historical settings or stages. They are not actively used as physical evidence of historical patterns or developments. As documents of cultural taste, technological adaptations, or the use of locally available materials, the buildings are largely mute.

Cowtown Museum in Wichita, Kansas, exhibits similar patterns. The museum surrounds two relocated dwellings listed in the National Register of Historic Places with a hodgepodge of original historic buildings and newly constructed copies of historic buildings, representing businesses associated with the development of Wichita. To its credit, Cowtown goes far to

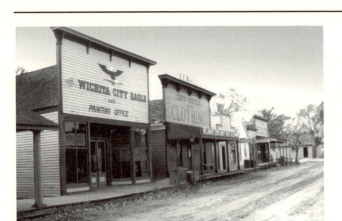

Figure 27. Cowtown Museum, Wichita, Kansas. Photo by Carroll Van West.

Figure 28. The buffalo statue, Pioneer Museum, Jamestown, North Dakota. Photo by Carroll Van West.

suggest the vitality and range of services offered in late-nineteenth-century Western towns, including a graphic depiction of a funeral home, treating themes many museums tend to ignore. But Cowtown does less than Living History Farms in using its artifacts as teaching tools. The entire town, save for two dwellings where stories about the building's owners are told, seems like an elaborate movie set. The interpreters have little information about the buildings as artifacts and the potential for teaching material history is largely wasted.

The Pioneer Village of Jamestown, North Dakota, is not really a museum, but it shows how well-meaning people in a local community can take the frontier village museum to a ridiculous extreme. Originally situated along the major U.S. highway of southern North Dakota, the museum was the classic tourist mecca of the 1950s and 1960s. The complex contains several worthy historic buildings, including the obligatory one-room schoolhouse and the town's Northern Pacific railroad depot, but it features the "world's largest buffalo," which is, of course, a three-story equivalent concrete statue of a buffalo. The statue reflects the Pioneer Village's version of history. Here the romanticized Old West lives in all its glory, and thousands stop by each year to get their dose of Western history.

As these three sites suggest, the untapped potential of many outdoor museums as teachers of history is particularly regrettable because those same buildings and structures actually attract visitors to the property. The physical nature of buildings, structures, and landscapes constitute powerful historical evidence and can be much more than effective historical stages. Remember the noted New England historian John Demos's recounting of his first visit to a colonial site: "The effect was immediate, and visceral, and decidedly mixed: interest alternated with confusion, wonder yielded to acute anxiety. So here is the way it looked and was: no mere words could quite have conveyed the feeling." In the book *American Places: Encounters with History*, edited by William E. Leuchtenburg, several scholars relate similar stories of how their interactions with the physical past caused them to ask new questions and reconsider their own interpretations.[11]

When history museum professionals use the artifacts they have collected, and the buildings in which they display the objects, as mere stage props in front of which an interpreter tells stories about people and events associated with the buildings, they do a great disservice to their collections. It is not that doing history by association is necessarily bad; indeed, associative values are important contributions to our sense of historical identity.[12] But history by association solely limits the type of questions and historical information you can get from artifacts. It certainly is one of the key reasons historians believe museums have little to teach them about history. If artifacts do nothing but illustrate themes taken from historical studies, museums as historical sources are no better than the typical textbook or monograph.

Historians themselves are partly to blame for these regrettable circumstances. Too many are visual illiterates; that is, they have no idea of how to decode and interpret a building or an artifact. Ignorant in general of material history, they train students to do historical research almost exclusively through written and oral documents, thus eliminating a potentially valuable body of evidence from their research. Unfortunately, some of these students will work at the major state history museums or state historical societies, where they will help plan and execute history exhibits that perpetuate their own visual illiteracy. Artifacts remain mere illustrations of history rather than being the things of history itself. Scholars now have criticized "textbooks on the walls" exhibits for more than a decade, but that technique of exhibit development and design may still be found in most history museums across the country.

Thus, history by association and visual illiteracy work together to cause much mischief for the practice of history in Western museums. Historians are uneasy about using artifacts to do history because they do not understand how to interpret these physical manifestations of the past. But they are comfortable in using objects that illustrate, in a three-dimensional form, an abstract idea already worked out on paper. Since artifacts merely had to be associated with great men or great events to produce history exhibits, library work could replace artifact identification and analysis in determining the priorities and direction of museum storylines. Exhibit planning was not collection driven, that is, focused on the artifacts and the information they conveyed, but instead used artifacts as illustrations. Too often, collecting became a matter of merely locating the appropriate artifacts associated with great men and events.

In the 1970s, the museum profession began to change its assumptions and perspectives about artifact study and slowly began to create more collection-driven exhibits. E. McClung Fleming's essay "Artifact Study: A Proposed Model," in the *Winterthur Portfolio*, presented a comprehensive methodology on how to "read" and interpret an artifact.[13] Fleming's model reflected new trends in the history profession, especially the methodological approaches of the "new social history."[14] Scholars of the last generation have looked at buildings as important primary sources of history as never before, attempting to read history out of the artifact rather than merely reading history into a building. The patterns of human behavior inherent in the built environment became an important source of evidence for an increasing number of historians.

Yet in only a relative handful of Western museums have the new directions in material culture studies and in social history worked together. Most Western history museums remained locked in past interpretive messages or are in transition between the old and new. For example, at the Fort Laramie National Historical Site in Wyoming, the National Park Service has broadened its traditional military history emphasis. Visitors see various living history demonstrations, including women who washed clothes and carried out other vital camp functions and soldiers who operated the camp bakery. The buildings, however, remain a vastly underutilized resource about contemporary construction methods, differences in rank, and the living conditions on the northern plains. Artifact interpretation within buildings is usually nonexistent.[15]

Other interesting transitional examples may be viewed at three northern plains and Midwest institutions. The Montana Historical Society in Helena in the late 1980s jettisoned its 1950s history exhibit, which emphasized successive stages of the frontier, for a newly designed and curated exhibit that interprets "how people lived, worked, played, raised families, and built communities." The North Dakota History Center in Bismarck has an exemplary state history exhibit in many ways. Clearly, the concerns of the new social history have influenced its depictions of ethnic contributions to North Dakota and its treatment of popular culture in the twentieth century. The Minnesota Historical Society, which for years occupied cramped quarters near the state capitol, moved into the huge new History Center, which introduced an agricultural history exhibit, complete with a working model of a grain elevator that children and adults could explore.

At a regional level are some of the most interesting new departures. As an example, the Western Heritage Center in Billings, Montana, developed a series of exhibits and programs designed to look at the region's history and culture in new ways. At its signature exhibit, "Our Place in the West: Places, Pasts, and Images of the Yellowstone Valley, 1880 to 1940," curators and designers mounted an ignored artifact from the collections—an irrigation headgate—in the center of the exhibit. The importance of irrigation in the region dates to the Huntley Project, which was the second project of the U.S. Reclamation Service. But this history, and that of agriculture in general, had been forgotten in the latter twentieth century as oil, transportation services, and the health care industry transformed Billings and Yellowstone County into the state's largest urban center.

Research quickly showed one reason why the headgate was in the collection. I. D. O'Donnell, one of the region's leading civic capitalists, had been the first Supervisor of Irrigation for the U.S. Reclamation Service. O'Donnell had even patented a headgate design. If the artifact was to be used, in the old associative way of thinking, then it could logically be mounted on the wall, next to a photograph of O'Donnell, and the "story" would be illustrated and told.

The curators and designers, however, saw beyond the artifact's associative values. Irrigation was the central transformation that the valley experienced in the early twentieth century, an era when men interjected modern technology and machines into the valley in an attempt to maximize water for the production of marketable crops. Thus, they decided to place the headgate at the center of the exhibit and to have it as an actual working headgate. Visitors can turn the wheel and see the valuable water rush forth into the irrigation system. The centrality of agriculture, and water as the region's most precious natural resource, is emphasized by treating the artifact as a functioning part of the exhibit.

Related to the region's irrigation history was the immigration of new migrant agricultural workers, mostly for the sugar beet fields. At another portion of the exhibit, the staff turned to the local Hispanic community to help them rebuild a *colonia* like the types that had once housed Mexican workers. The construction of this exhibit section, which the staff carefully documented, became an object lesson in history and ethnic construction techniques. It also made the local Hispanic residents more comfortable with the museum and its goals, and some residents donated valuable items to the museum.[16]

The recent developments taking place at Billings, Bismarck, and other western locales are important because these state and regional institutions serve as the standard for their respective community museums. Over time, one may see more and more local museums adopt the concepts of new social history, certainly a change for the better. We may also hope for a greater interest in, and concern with, the artifacts as functioning historical documents. For example, instead of the rather standard exhibit caption of "locally made chair," the interpretive panel, or the interpreter, might add more interesting insights, addressing such questions as: Who made the chair? Was it part of a set or made as a single item? Were its materials locally available or imported—or was it a mixture of the two? Why was the chair preserved? Are there any qualities in its design that are unique, or is it similar to many others made at the time? Did one have to be well-to-do to own such a chair? Does the chair mirror contemporary fashions from machine-made chairs, or does it reflect the tastes of its maker and its consumers? Many questions we ask of artifacts are basic ones like these, but if we do not ask them—and try to find the answers—we are left with that same nondescript description: an old locally made chair.

A commitment to artifact analysis, material history, and the information contained in museum collections has the great potential of enriching our understanding of the past and making our exhibits much more than textbooks on the wall. Whenever you are reviewing major new exhibitions, be they in Colorado, Arizona, Montana, Wyoming, or wherever in the West, ask yourself: Are historians still preparing the interpretation and labels and using artifacts to illustrate concepts taken from new social history studies, or are they using their artifact collections to help generate some of the questions and answers?

Western history museums can become important contributors to current historical scholarship when they shift from a sole reliance on traditional written accounts to ideas and concepts taken from material history. Great potential lies in their artifacts, sites, and buildings. Museums can teach new lessons about American history through raising new questions generated by the tons of physical evidence past cultures have left behind. Historians are right: museum professionals sell themselves, and their collections, short when they substitute categorization and association for analysis. But historians can do more to help museums become sources of historical documentation. They must teach themselves and their students about the perils of visual illiteracy. Artifacts convey information about the patterns of social history—that is their greatest value to history. To ignore them eliminates from a historian's arsenal a source of potentially valuable information.

Jules David Prown, a leading student of American material culture, once observed that artifacts allow us "to engage another culture in the first instance not with our minds, the seat of our cultural biases, but with our senses." Artifacts, be they objects, sites, or buildings, contain evidence not found in any written account. The physical nature of the resource makes it a powerful source of information about the patterns of Western history. Merely to associate the resource with a famous event or person or to categorize the resource under such traditional themes that best reflect the literary record of society usually means we have failed to treat the artifact as a historical document of its own merit. We have substituted categorization for historical analysis; we have left historical inquiry out of our history museums.[17]

Notes

1. Useful guides to Western history museums include James B. Gardner and Timothy C. Jacobson, eds., *A Historical Guide to the United States* (Nashville: AASLH Press, 1986), and the various Smithsonian Guides to Historic America, for instance, Suzanne Winckler, *The Smithsonian Guide to Historic America: The Plains States* (New York: Stewart, Tabori, and Chang, 1998).

2. Frederick J. Turner, "The Significance of the Frontier in American History," *Annual Report, American Historical Association, 1893* (Washington; AHA, 1894), 199–227. The continuing popularity of Western biographies is documented through the various volumes of the Oklahoma Western Biographies Series, published by the University of Oklahoma Press, Richard W. Etulain, general editor.

3. Jack D. Forbes, "Frontiers in American History and the Role of the Frontier Historian," *Ethnohistory* 15 (spring 1968): 203–4.

4. Representative critiques include Robert F. Berkhofer, "Space, Time, Culture and the New Frontier," *Agricultural History* 38 (January 1964): 21–30; Gene M. Gressley, "The Turner Thesis—A Problem in Historiography," *Agricultural History* 32 (October 1958): 227–49; Patricia Nelson Limerick, *The Legacy of Conquest: The Unbroken Past of the American West* (New York: Norton, 1987), 17–34; and William Cronon, George Miles, and Jay Gitlin, eds., *Under an Open Sky: Rethinking America's Western Past* (New York: Norton, 1992), 3–27.

5. William J. Murtagh, *Keeping Time: The History and Theory of Preservation in America*, rev. ed. (New York: Wiley, 1997), 30; Marc Leepson, *Saving Monticello: The Levy Family's Epic Quest to Rescue the House that Jefferson Built* (New York: Free Press, 2001); Jessica Foy Donnelly, ed., *Interpreting Historic House Museums* (Walnut Creek, CA: Altamira Press, 2003); Richard W. Sellars, "Vigil of Silence: The Civil War Memorials," *History News* 41 (July/August 1986): 19–24; Edward T. Linenthal, *Sacred Ground: Americans and Their Battlefields*, 2nd ed. (Urbana: University of Illinois Press, 1993); and Cynthia Mills and Pamela H. Simpson, eds., *Monuments to the Lost Cause: Women, Art, and*

Landscapes of Southern Memory (Knoxville: University of Tennessee Press, 2003).

6. James W. Loewen, "Review: E. P. Alexander's *Museums in Motion*," *Winterthur Portfolio* 15 (spring 1980), 66; Loewen's later book, *Lies Across America: What Our Historic Sites Get Wrong* (New York: New Press, 1999), is both insightful and humorous on this theme. Michael Wallace also has written extensively on this theme. See his "Visiting the Past: History Museums in the United States," *Radical History Review* 25 (1981): 63–96, and his *Mickey Mouse History and Other Essays on American Memory* (Philadelphia: Temple University Press, 1996); and David Lowenthal, "Age and Artifact: Dilemmas of Appreciation," in *The Interpretation of Ordinary Landscapes*, ed. D. W. Meinig (New York: Oxford University Press, 1979), 121, and his *Possessed by the Past: The Heritage Crusade and the Spoils of History* (New York: Free Press, 1996).

7. Carroll Van West and Mary S. Hoffschwelle, "'Slumbering on Its Old Foundations': Interpretation at Colonial Williamsburg," *South Atlantic Quarterly* 83 (spring 1984): 161, 165; see also the more recent studies by Richard Handler and Eric Gagle, *The New History in an Old Museum: Creating the Past at Colonial Williamsburg* (Durham: Duke University Press, 1997), and Anders Greenspan, *Creating Colonial Williamsburg* (Washington, D.C.: Smithsonian Institution Press, 2002). Two important Williamsburg pamphlets on the motivation of the restoration in the 1950s and 1960s are *Preserving the Design for Americans* (Williamsburg: Colonial Williamsburg, 1946) and John D. Rockefeller III, *Our Opportunity* (Williamsburg: Colonial Williamsburg, 1948).

8. Al Knauder, "Future Cloudy for Virginia City," *Great Falls Tribune*, August 16, 1993, D-1; Christene C. Meyers, "Stepping into the Past," *Billings Gazette*, June 26, 1994, E-1; Carol Bradley, "Saving the Past," *Great Falls Tribune*, December 1, 1996, 1A, 4A; Carolynn Farley, "Virginia and Nevada City Scrapbook," *Helena Independent Record*, December 8, 1996, C1; and Perry Backus, "Virginia City Turns Unexpected Profit," *Helena Independent Record*, September 7, 1997, 8B; "Virginia City's Future Looks Bright," *Helena Independent Record*, December 28, 1997.

9. Geoffrey C. Upward, *A Home for Our Heritage: The Building and Growth of Greenfield Village and Henry Ford Museum, 1929–1979* (Dearborn: Henry Ford Museum, 1979); William Greenleaf, *From These Beginnings: The Early Philanthropies of Henry and Edsel Ford, 1911* (Detroit: Wayne State University Press, 1964), 89–111; Carroll Van West, "Greenfield Village: A Landscape of the Past, Present, and Mr. Ford," *International Journal of Museum Management and Curatorship* 13 (September 1989): 263–78.

10. The author conducted field visits to these sites between 1987 and 1996.

11. John Demos, "Words and Things: A Review and Discussion of 'New England Begins,'" *William and Mary Quarterly*, 3rd ser., 40 (October 1983): 584; and William E. Leuchtenburg, ed., *American Places: Encounters with History* (New York: Oxford University Press, 2000).

12. Thomas F. King, "Beneath the American Mosaic: The Place of Archaeology," in *The American Mosaic: Preserving a Nation's Heritage*, ed. R. E. Stipe and A. J. Lee (Washington: US/ICOMOS, 1987), 262.

13. E. McClung Fleming, "Artifact Study: A Proposed Model," *Winterthur Portfolio* 9 (1974): 153–73.

14. Fleming's model followed the publication of exciting new scholarship about early American history, studies called then the "new social history." For example, see Summer C. Powell, *Puritan Village: The Formation of a New England Town* (Middleton, CN: Wesleyan University Press, 1963), and John Demos, *A Little Commonwealth: Family Life in Plymouth Colony* (New York: Oxford University Press, 1970). See also Darrett B. Rutman, "Assessing the Little Communities of Early America," *William and Mary Quarterly*, 3rd ser., 43 (April 1986): 163–78, and Thomas Bender, "The New History—Then and Now," *Reviews in American History* 12 (December, 1984): 612–22.

15. Author's field visit, June 1988.

16. "The Evolution of an Exhibit: The New Montana History Museum," *Montana Post* 26 (summer 1988): 4–5; Carroll Van West and Lynda Bourque Moss, "The New Dialogue about Western History," *History News* 48 (March/April 1993): 12–17; and "Life by Comparison" exhibit, Western Heritage Center, Billings, Montana, 2002.

17. Jules David Prown, "Mind in Matter: An Introduction to Material Culture Theory and Method," *Winterthur Portfolio* 17 (spring 1982): 5.

Study Questions

1. What are the "roadblocks" interfering with collaboration between historians and museum professionals?

2. Why was the word *frontier* or the "frontier thesis" so influential?

3. Describe the "shrine mentality."

4. How do living history farms interpret the past? How do you feel about these methods of interpretation? Are they successful?

5. How did the museum profession change its collecting process?

6. Compare the reason the irrigation headgate was collected and how it was actually used. What is the difference?

7. Visit a local museum or think of an exhibit that you have seen in the past. Are the artifacts used to illustrate written labels or are they being used to ask more questions or give answers, integrating new ideas into the exhibits?

8. Describe the four types of history museums and their significance.

9. What are the limitations of history museums as teachers of history?

10. What is the value of using artifacts to illustrate concepts taken from new social history studies?

Western Views and Eastern Visions

National Parks, Manifest Destiny, and American Identity

THOMAS PATIN

Introduction

For some time before the national parks were established, the nineteenth-century American cultural elite suffered an "embarrassment" of the lack, when compared to Europe, of a national cultural identity based on a long and established artistic, architectural, and literary heritage.[1] At the same time, however, it was obvious that what America lacked in cultural treasures it more than made up for in natural wonders. The American landscape became an effective substitute for a missing national tradition and a repository of national pride. By the mid- to late nineteenth century, cultural nationalists saw the western environment, especially places like Yosemite, Yellowstone, and the Grand Canyon in Arizona, as unparalleled, and they looked to scenery as a form of cultural redemption.[2]

This redemption, however, could only be accomplished if parts of the natural world could be converted into cultural heritage. How was such a conversion possible? Only figuratively, of course. That is, this conversion was carried out through the use of a number of rhetorical devices that were so effective that their status as rhetoric was forgotten or missed altogether. I am thinking here especially of figures of speech, painterly rhetoric, and museological techniques that allow for the natural world to be presented as part of a national identity. Certain figures of speech turned natural formations into cultural artifacts. Pictorial rhetoric naturalized historically specific cultural events and social developments. Finally, the use of various museological techniques in the presentation of nature in parks conflated the spaces of museums with the spaces of parks and produced (and still produce) what Barbara Kirshenblatt-Gimblett has called the "museum effect" that shapes the experience of the park visitor.[3]

My primary concern in this essay is with the use of various techniques borrowed from painting and museums used in the presentation of nature in the national parks. Using several national parks as examples, I want to suggest that they are essentially museological institutions, not only because they preserve and conserve, but because they employ many of the techniques of display, exhibition, and presentation—as well as images of the landscape—that have been used by museums to organize and regulate the vision of visitors. The resulting "museum effect" is the result of a strategy that insinuates the museum into the wilderness and produces a so-called vignette of America, furthering the idea that natural wonders are part of America's *cultural* heritage.

Also useful for the conversion of nature into cultural heritage is the implicit attitude that nature, especially in the form of the landscape, is already a natural material that can be shaped into a cultural artifact at will. This can be accomplished, for example, by shaping stone or wood according to a symbolic code. However, there is a more subtle, but no less labor-intensive way to shape nature into cultural forms. According to W. J. T. Mitchell, landscape can be understood as symbolic form, that is, subject matter. Landscape can be represented by painting, but at the same time landscape itself could be "a physical medium" in and through which "cultural meanings and values are encoded," no matter if the landscape in question is a garden, a piece of architecture, or a place we call "nature."[4]

This kind of understanding of landscape is useful for creating an extraordinarily compelling identity for a "civilization," the expansion of which can be partially explained as a "natural" event.[5] In this way it is possible, then, that landscape, understood as a historically specific invention of a new "visual/pictorial medium," is integrally connected with imperialism.[6] To pursue this

Figure 29. Thomas Moran, *Grand Canyon of the Yellowstone*, 1872. National Museum of American Art, Smithsonian Institution.

possibility, Mitchell suggests that we concentrate on what landscape does, on what is done with it, and for whom rather than on what it is.

Ferdinand V. Hayden, when commenting on seeing the Grand Canyon of the Yellowstone, described the pinnacles of stone there as standing out like "Gothic columns . . . with greater variety and more striking colors than ever adorned a work of human art."[7] According to Alfred Runte, one of the most prolific writers on the national parks, everywhere the 1870 Washburn Expedition to Yellowstone turned, they found some geological formation that seemed to suggest architecture to them. One stream, for instance, ran "between a procession of sharp pinnacles, looking like some noble old castle, dismantled and shivered with years, but still erect and defiant."[8] Runte himself seems to succumb to the temptation to describe nature through cultural imagery when he describes Thomas Moran's painting of the Grand Canyon of the Yellowstone. "In the foreground and to the sides of the painting," writes Runte, "the rocks, walls, and trees of the chasm grow progressively bolder and more angular in appearance, as if to suggest that the formations may in fact be thought of as castles, fortresses, or ruins."[9]

According to Runte, the ruins of American Indian dwellings were seen in the late nineteenth and early twentieth centuries as sufficient to make up for the lack of Greek or Roman ruins in the New World.[10] It was especially the natural formations of the western parks that, judging from their names, were reminiscent of architectural ruins, for example, Devil's Tower and Montezuma's Castle. Rufus Steele, remarking about several western parks, described canyons that are "filled with cathedrals and colonnades, ramparts and rooms, terraces and temples, turrets and towers, obelisks and organs."[11] Steele described a journey to Bryce Canyon as a "pilgrimage" to a place where the side walls were "fluted like giant cathedral organs," while other rock forms "tower upward in vast spires and minarets."[12]

In 1996, the Sierra Club published a series of full-page ads on dams on the Colorado River near the Grand Canyon in Arizona. The most famous of these carried the headline "Should we also flood the Sistine Chapel so tourists can get nearer the ceiling?"[13] An Earth First! ad concerning the construction of the Glen Canyon Dam asked whether readers would mind if someone "flooded the Louvre."[14]

Pictorial Rhetoric

Rhetoric has been traditionally regarded as a deliberate exploitation of eloquence for the most persuasive effect in speaking or writing, and the study of rhetoric included the study of the uses of figures of speech, the arts of memory and oratory. For literary critic Terry Eagleton, however, one of the more important uses of rhetorical analysis in our own times is its ability to

Figure 30. Thomas Moran, *Tower Falls and Sulphur Mountain*, 1876 (publication date) chromolithograph. Jefferson National Expansion Memorial, National Park Service.

look upon discourses with an eye to understanding how they produce certain effects, shape understanding, or maintain existing systems of power.[15] Rhetoric is now seen by many critics and theorists as an unavoidable instrument in the establishment of "truth effects." More specifically, a look at the uses of pictorial rhetoric in the representations of nature and national parks allows us to see more clearly how natural wonders can be converted into national heritage.

In the mid-nineteenth century, the very act of observing nature was considered virtuous, and looking at the wonders of nature was thought by some to be an act of devotion.[16] The view beheld by park visitors at Artist Point and Inspiration Point at the Grand Canyon of the Yellowstone is similar to that depicted in Thomas Moran's painting of the canyon. Moran even provides two "staffage figures" or "surrogate viewers" that act as stand-ins for the viewers of the picture, allowing them an imaginary immediacy. The overlooks at the canyon repeat the view depicted by Moran. This happens elsewhere in the park, most obviously at Tower Falls. There the viewing platform includes a reproduction of a Moran painting of the falls with two surrogate viewers.

The elevated point of view made available for viewers of designs such as the ones I have just described produces what art historian Albert Boime has described as the "magisterial gaze." To Boime, this viewpoint "embodies the exaltation of the nineteenth-century American cultural elite before an unlimited horizon that they identified with the destiny of the American nation."[17] Its appearance in the mid-nineteenth century reflects, according to Boime, "the sense of enormous possibility that Americans were beginning to share about the future of their new country and their desire to root out vestiges of the old world."[18] The view from an elevated position has a more worldly function, however. It embodies, says Boime, "like a microcosm, the social and political character of the land, . . . the desire for dominance."[19] It is this gaze of command, or a "commanding view," that is the perspective of the American on the heights searching for new worlds to conquer.[20] The opposite of the magisterial gaze is the reverential gaze: an upward-looking gaze common in European art and exemplified in such parks as Zion National Park, as well as a few others. The magisterial gaze, to Boime, represents not only a visual line of sight but an ideological one as well.[21] The magisterial gaze supports the expansionist desire "by always projecting the vision across the valley as a step ahead of the point where the viewer is located at any given time."[22]

Once Manifest Destiny had been achieved, the government could begin setting aside pockets of wilderness for the enjoyment of the public.[23] The elevated position commonly offered to the park visitor allows for a commanding view of the land, a land that—once seen, claimed, and surveyed—became subject to control and could become part of a national heritage. In the national parks, the magisterial gaze is reenacted millions of times each year through various modes of viewing the scenery in the parks, for example, binoculars, spotting scopes, telescopes, camera lenses, and other devices found onsite.

Literally hundreds of overlooks are designed to present a view from an elevated position. One that offers a commanding view of the countryside is found at Yellowstone National Park at Shoshone Point, on the Grand Loop Road between Old Faithful and West Thumb. From a point on the road at a high elevation this turnout presents the Tetons to the south in a view that is framed by trees to either side (the stumps of trees cleared for the view are visible if you look for them). It is obvious from the symmetrical design of the parking lot and the rock wall where the park visitor should stand to best appreciate the view, and if viewers do stand in the prescribed spot (my unscientific observations found that viewers consistently walked immediately to this spot), they are offered a view of natural beauty as if in a picture painted from an elevated point and put on exhibition.

Many parks also include various devices to aid visitors in viewing and identifying geological features. At Grand Canyon National Park, especially at El Tovar Hotel, Lookout Studio, and the Hopi Watchtower, visitors find high-powered viewing scopes, metal cylinders, and other devices through which they can investigate a small portion of the scenery in detail. On the rim just outside the El Tovar Hotel are a set of viewing tubes that can be rotated around a metal disk and set into notches. Incised on the surface of the disk are the names of various geological features that correspond to the view beheld through the tubes when placed in these notches.

Museological Rhetoric

After F. V. Hayden returned from his expedition to the Yellowstone region in 1871, he arranged for an exhibition of a number of specimens at the Smithsonian and prominently at the Capitol Building in Washington while Congress was still in session. Among the "specimens" were photographs by William Henry Jackson and watercolor sketches by Thomas Moran.[24] Hayden had Jackson print a number of Yellowstone photographs for distribution. Over 400 prints were made and distributed to members of Congress.[25] The lobbying of Congress in 1871 for the establishment of Yellowstone National Park included Hayden's "specimens." These images were more than decoration or pretty scenery. They were more like iconic representations of a nation's heritage. Exhibited in the Smithsonian, effectively functioning both as the nation's curiosity cabinet and art museum, the watercolor sketches, photographs, and geological specimens worked in a supportive interrelationship: natural fact was claimed as cultural heritage through aesthetic convention, while a culturally specific aesthetic was positioned as natural fact. The use of art in justifying the park bill, and in thinking of Yellowstone, was in transforming natural characteristics into artistic wonders/heritage.

After the bill establishing Yellowstone National Park was passed, Moran hung his painting *The Grand Canyon of the Yellowstone*, completed in 1872, "on the West wall of the large room" at the Smithsonian. It was considered massive for American painting at the time, measuring eight by twelve feet. There was great ceremony at its initial unveiling in New York City, attended by Hayden and representatives of the Northern Pacific Railroad. Later, he moved the painting to the Capitol Building, in the old Hall of Representatives.[26] The work was seen by many in Congress, and it was eventually purchased for $10,000 and hung in the Senate wing until 1950, when ownership passed to the Department of the Interior.[27] Moran's paintings of the Yellowstone region were used by brochure designers advertising the "Wonderland Route to the Pacific." By 1890 the idea of the west and of the wilderness as a dark and dangerous place had been replaced with the idea of the west as wonderland.[28]

Of course, nature cannot be enclosed within a museum, no matter how many rocks, photographs, and paintings are used to represent it. It is possible, though, to enclose nature—in a way—within the museum, by using conventional exhibition techniques to present nature. The "Great Picture" convention was a well-established method of exhibiting art in America in the mid-1800s.[29] A light source illuminated a single painting at one end of an otherwise darkened room. The frame surrounding the canvas was usually black or very dark in color and in turn the frame was surrounded by drapes made of dark, light-absorbing fabrics such as velvet.[30]

In the national parks are numerous examples of the incorporation of the Great Picture exhibition

Figure 31. Tunnel View turnout overlooking Yosemite Valley, Yosemite National Park. Photo by author.

convention, such as those I have already described at El Tovar Hotel at the Grand Canyon National Park. Views from inside tunnels or from the exits of tunnels best provide one-to-one parallels to the darkened interior of the Great Picture viewing space. The view from Tunnel View overlook in Yosemite National Park (this is the tunnel on the road between Wawona and Yosemite Valley) as well as the view driving out of the tunnel itself appears before park visitors as if a light has been turned on and shined upon an object. The same can be said of the views from outside and inside the Zion Tunnel (on the Zion–Mt. Carmel Highway in Zion National Park). In this case, the windows inside the tunnel are actually called "galleries," which increases the suggestion of a relationship of the views and art.

The most common similarity between the Great Pictures exhibitions and the parks, however, is the ordinary overlook. The overlook at Tunnel View in Yosemite is an excellent example. The design of the turnout encourages visitors to park their cars and walk toward the guardrail to enjoy the view. There the scenery is framed by the branches and trunks of trees, shrubbery, rocks, guardrails, and information panels. Numerous smaller vignettes of Yosemite Valley are created by the design of the overlook. Visitors can then look through binoculars, camera lenses, and spotting scopes at the details in the landscape that catch their attention. Or, of course, they can look at larger views or read about the formation of the valley on the information panels.

Without a doubt, the most popular form of exhibition in nineteenth-century Europe and America—in fact, one of the most popular forms of entertainment of any kind—was the cyclorama or panorama. In a cyclorama, viewers stood on a raised platform in the center of a circular exhibition space and looked at a 360-degree landscape painting. Spectators typically climbed a spiral stairway around a tower in the center of a rotunda and emerged onto a darkened viewing platform. There they encountered a nearly hidden painting only barely visible by means of a highly controlled skylight.

In the national parks, the cyclorama was reconstituted in the form of the turnout, the view cut, and the observation platform. Trees, rocks, and elevated locations have been used to frame the view and to prescribe contemplation. John T. McCutcheon, upon a visit to the Grand Canyon in 1909, wrote that "the sense of unreality is so strong that one imagines himself standing in the middle of a cyclorama building looking at a painting of highly colored mountains and mysterious gorges, so wonderfully done as to suggest an infinity of space. The silence aids in this delusion, and one half expects to go down some steps out into the noise and reality of a street again."³¹ Mary Colter's Hopi Watchtower, completed in 1932, condenses, simplifies, and separates sections of the canyon for viewing. The hogan-shaped room on the ground floor, called a "kiva" or "view room" in the promotional literature, is almost completely walled with glass. These large windows frame various views of the surrounding desert and canyon as if they were themselves already large pictures. Climbing up the tower itself, the visitor encounters numerous small windows of various shapes and sizes and placed at odd heights through the walls. These small windows also frame views of the scenery just as the windows in the "kiva" do, except that these windows also sometimes compel the viewer to bend, kneel, or get onto tiptoe to see through them. Once on the top floor of the tower, visitors find the most cycloramic viewing space—a room surrounded by windows and a number of viewing scopes available for looking at the canyon and the desert.

In Yellowstone National Park, the cycloramic exhibition technique is commonly found at overlooks, viewing platforms, and view cuts at roadside turnouts, all of which are typically found at the tops of mountains or rises, at cliffs, or at other points that offer views from elevated positions. As early as 1897 platforms and sidings were built for tourists to use to get out of coaches or other vehicles at different points on regularly traveled routes.³² In the teens and twenties, "vista cuts" were made along roads, such as the one on West Thumb Road to allow for a view of Duck Lake and another east of Mammoth Hot Springs to view Wraith Falls.³³ The CCC continued such work into the 1930s, clearing stumps and dead trees, building more guardrails, and creating more turnouts, view cuts, and exhibit shelters like the one at Obsidian Cliff.³⁴ The construction of turnouts and view cuts along the roadways continued through Mission 66, a popular post–World War II Park Service building and roads program, to the present.

The only thing that eclipsed the popularity of the cyclorama in nineteenth-century America was the moving panorama, also called "moving pictures."³⁵ The moving panorama combined the scope of the cyclorama with the more conventional space of theater and added the important element of movement. The audience faced a stage as scenery passed before them painted on a large theatrical backdrop stretched between two rolls of canvas.³⁶ The unrolling of the painting took several hours, and quasi-scientific oral commentaries, anecdotal material, and music of a piano or organ accompanied the images.³⁷ The most popular subject matter for moving panoramas by far was landscape.

The moving panorama was also repeated in the parks, but instead of a landscape unrolling in front of a viewer, it is the visitor that rolls by in front of the landscape on the road systems in the parks. In the early years of Yellowstone National Park, the Northern Pacific Railroad suggested in their promotional literature a sequence for visitors: Mammoth, Obsidian Cliff, Norris Geyser Basin, Gibbon Canyon, Gibbon Falls, Lower and Upper Geyser Basins, Yellowstone Lake, and the Grand Canyon of the Yellowstone.³⁸ Nathaniel Langford, the first superintendent of Yellowstone, also proposed roads in the figure-eight system similar to that scheme and similar to what we now have in the park.³⁹ Philetus Norris, Yellowstone's second superintendent, was concerned with providing visitors with scenic and interesting views along the roads of the park and built the road around the base of Bunsen Peak to provide views of Gardner Canyon.⁴⁰

A 1932 report of landscape architects at Yellowstone National Park included numerous suggestions that would enhance the appreciation of visitors, who were by that time typically touring the park by automobile. These suggestions included the creation of strategically located turnouts and guardrails, removing live trees to create vista cuts, and removing dead trees, which were considered unsightly.⁴¹ The Civilian Conservation Corps (CCC) was involved in roadside cleanup and landscaping projects. Aesthetics remained a major concern of Superintendent Roger Toll, who had conspicuous stumps within 50 feet of the road's edge removed.⁴² In 1951, Frank Mattson, Yellowstone National Park's landscape architect, noted that the plan to provide wider roads and roadside parking areas so tourists could behold the wonders of the park had not yet been achieved.⁴³ Since the 1950s the project of providing visual access to natural wonders from moving vehicles became more directed. In 1958, Conrad Wirth issued his *Handbook of Standards for National Park and Parkway Roads*, in which he states that the purpose of roads in the national park system is "to give the public . . . leisurely access to scenic and other features. Thus [the roads] become principal facilities for presenting and interpreting the inspirational values of a park." Landscape architects and the highway engineer should, Wirth asserted, in all phases of their work, strive "to exercise imagination, ingenuity, and restraint to conserve park values."⁴⁴ Wirth also instructed that roads be fitted to the terrain and that shoulder widths allow for turnouts and overlooks at frequent intervals.⁴⁵ Under Mission 66 new construction included even more turnouts that would allow visitors to stop and enjoy the scenery or picnic or fish.

Techniques borrowed from the Great Picture exhibits, cycloramas, and moving panoramas regulated the vision of park visitors and controlled the physical relationship of visitors to natural wonders. Park visitors were put into positions not unlike those instituted in museums, galleries, and other exhibition spaces. These techniques have been crucial in the conversion of natural wonders into cultural heritage.

Conclusion

The discovery of the American landscape as an effective substitute for a missing national tradition was a springboard for the growing careers of a number of nineteenth-century landscape artists. Through the exhibition of their work, landscape also became a repository of national pride, and the cultivation of the landscape experience was one of the key preoccupations of the age.⁴⁶ The uses of rhetoric, be it verbal, pictorial, or museological, furthered the idea that natural wonders could also be cultural heritage. The use of art in lobbying Congress to pass the first park bill was instrumental since painting conflated the natural wonders of the West and the historically specific culture in nineteenth-century America. In a more general and more theoretical sense this essay seeks to understand how national parks can help to form a sense of individual and national identity through the regulation of vision. The approach to studying the national parks that I have used in this essay may help us to understand how these parks have shaped our understanding of many interrelated things, including nature and the natural world, the development of tourism and sightseeing, and American history and identity.

Notes

1. Alfred Runte, *National Parks: The American Experience* (Lincoln: University of Nebraska Press, 1987), 11.
2. Ibid., 7–8, 18, 41.
3. Barbara Kirshenblatt-Gimblett, "Objects of Ethnography," in *Exhibiting Cultures: The Poetics and Politics of Museum Display*, ed. Ivan Karp and Stephen D. Lavine (Washington, D.C.: Smithsonian Institution Press, 1990), 410.
4. W. J. T. Mitchell, "Imperial Landscape," in *Landscape and Power*, ed. W. J. T. Mitchell (Chicago: Chicago University Press, 1994), 14.
5. Ibid., 17.
6. Ibid., 9.
7. Runte, *National Parks*, 40.
8. Ibid., 38.
9. Ibid., 40.
10. Ibid., 73.
11. Ibid., 113.
12. Ibid.
13. Ibid., 191.
14. Ibid.
15. Terry Eagleton, *Literary Theory: An Introduction* (Minneapolis: Minnesota University Press, 1983), 210.
16. Barbara Novak, *Nature and Culture: American Landscape and Painting 1825–1875* (New York: Oxford University Press, 1980), 196.
17. Albert Boime, *The Magisterial Gaze: Manifest Destiny and American Landscape Painting c. 1830–1865* (Washington, D.C.: Smithsonian Institution, 1991), 38.

18. Ibid.

19. Ibid., 21.

20. Ibid., 20–21.

21. Ibid., 2.

22. Ibid., 138.

23. Ibid., 171.

24. Peter B. Hales, *William Henry Jackson and the Transformation of the American Landscape* (Philadelphia: Temple Univerity Press, 1988), 108.

25. Ibid., 109.

26. Joni Louise Kinsey, *Thomas Moran and the Surveying of the American West* (Washington, D.C.: Smithsonian Institution Press, 1992), 189.

27. Ibid., 65.

28. Ibid., 76–77.

29. Iris Cahn, "The Changing Landscape of Modernity: Early Film and America's 'Great Picture' Tradition," *Wide Angle* 18, no. 3 (1996): 87.

30. Ibid., 89.

31. Marta Weigle and Kathleen L. Howard, "'To Experience the Real Grand Canyon': Santa Fe/Harvey Panopticism, 1901–1935," in *The Great Southwest of the Fred Harvey Company and the Santa Fe Railway*, ed. Marta Weigle and Barbara Babcock (Phoenix: Heard Museum, 1996), 16.

32. Mary Shivers Culpin, *The History of the Construction of the Road System in Yellowstone National Park, 1872–1966* (Denver: Department of Interior, National Park Service, Rocky Mountain Region, 1994), 45.

33. Ibid., 110.

34. Ibid., 195–96.

35. Angela Miller, "The Panorama, the Cinema, and the Emergence of the Spectacular," *Wide Angle* 18, no. 2 (1996): 36.

36. Lee Parry, "Landscape Theatre in America," *Art in America* (November–December 1971): 55–58.

37. Novak, *Nature and Culture*, 23.

38. Judith L. Meyer, *The Spirit of Yellowstone: The Cultural Evolution of a National Park* (Lanham, Boulder, New York: Rowman and Little Field Publishers, 1996), 85.

39. Aubrey L. Haines, *The Yellowstone Story: A History of Our First National Park*, vol. I (Niwot, CO: Colorado Associated University Press, 1977), 192.

40. Culpin, *Road System*, 11.

41. Ibid., 195–96.

42. Ibid., 146–48.

43. Ibid., 142.

44. Ibid., 178.

45. Ibid.

46. Novak, *Nature and Culture*, 20.

Study Questions

1. Why did America want to turn natural scenery into cultural heritage?

2. What are some ways we use nature to represent culture?

3. Why do you think we try to describe natural wonders (caves, rock formations, etc.) in cultural terms, for example, describing tall, thin rock formations as towers or columns?

4. Compare the "magisterial gaze" to the "reverential gaze." How are the many elevated overlooks at national parks adding to the "magisterial gaze" idea?

5. In your opinion, why do museums strive to use the inside of their buildings to exhibit nature?

6. How do tunnel views and cycloramic views give the visitor a different experience from an unobstructed view they discover for themselves?

7. How do you feel about the difference between the audience watching a moving panorama inside a theater and watching the scenery roll by as a park visitor would see it through the windshield of a car?

8. How successful was the attempt to convert "natural wonders" to "cultural heritage" in America?

Preserving the History of Nikkei Removal on Bainbridge Island, Washington

Raymond W. Rast

This essay explores differences between the practices of academic history, public history, and community history. Drawing on my experience as an academic historian making a foray into the field of public history, it examines how a National Historic Landmark (NHL) nomination I coauthored emerged not as a pure product of academic history, public history, or community history, but a mixture of all three.[1] My work on the nomination taught me that effective public historians operate within different parameters than academic historians. Public historians work with and write for multiple groups, each with their attendant agendas, potential contributions, and expectations for the final product. Consequently, public historians are often reminded that the past does not belong to professional historians alone. Such reminders can encourage historians of all stripes to keep the study of history vital, relevant, and thus more likely to be supported by the public.[2]

In agreeing to coauthor the NHL nomination for a site on Bainbridge Island, Washington, related to the removal of the first Japanese American families to be taken to an internment camp during World War II, I joined a faculty member and a fellow graduate student at the University of Washington also involved with the project. After discussing at an early meeting our impressions of the factors that made the experiences of Bainbridge Island's Nikkei community significant, we adopted the working metaphor of the bridge.[3] The rural island's Nikkei residents crossed a bridge (a railroad trestle converted into a ferry dock) on March 30, 1942, when they were forced to leave their homes, board a ferry to Seattle, and continue by train to an internment camp in rural California. But a number of community institutions, including the public schools, the Baptist church, the local Boy Scout troop, and especially the island's newspaper, served as bridges connecting the island's Nikkei and Euro-American residents before, during, and after the three-year period of internment.

The bridge remains a useful metaphor for this essay. What follows is a discussion of the ways in which my coauthors and I conducted archival research, documented the internment embarkation site, collected oral histories, and wrote the nomination. As we completed this work, we attempted to bridge the gaps between the contours of a local history and the broader interests of a national audience; between former internees' commitment to transforming the ferry landing site from a locus of painful memories into a place of reconciliation, on the one hand, and preservationists' concern for protection of the site's physical integrity, on the other; and between the different imperatives of academic history, public history, and community history.

Groundwork

For decades after the end of World War II, older Nikkei seldom talked about their internment experiences. Former internee Mitsuye Yamada explained in a recent essay that she did not indulge in such reflection because she simply was too busy "studying, working for my tuition, getting my degrees, getting married, and taking care of a husband and four children." But she also admits that, like other Nikkei of her generation, she learned from her mother and father that parents should not bring up subjects that would "burden" their children. Her parents' careful silence about their own worries taught Yamada "the parents' role of protecting their children from the unpleasant realities of life. As they were often heard to say, *Kodomo no tame ni* "(for the sake of the children)".[4]

Former internees from Bainbridge Island, like Nikkei elsewhere, had begun by the 1980s to share their stories. Building on the foundation laid by the social movements of the 1960s and 1970s, Japanese Americans throughout the United States also formed a network of associations to press for an official apology from the federal government and compensation for the suffering and material loss caused by internment. Their effort culminated in 1988 when President Ronald Reagan signed an act providing an apology and a payment of $20,000 to each former internee. This victory in turn fueled further interest in gathering and sharing internment histories.[5] Members of the Bainbridge Nikkei community, well organized and committed to teaching younger generations the lessons that older Nikkei had learned from their experiences, decided in the late 1980s to assemble a traveling photo exhibit exploring Nikkei life on the island and in internment camps. They titled the exhibit "*Kodomo No Tame Ni*: For the Sake of the Children."

Two local developments during the 1990s sparked interest in doing even more. First, a company that owned property adjacent to the site from which Nikkei internees left Bainbridge declared bankruptcy in 1993. The company's property, housing a plant that had treated lumber with creosote (a toxic chemical) since the turn of the century, had been classified as a Superfund cleanup site by the Environmental Protection Agency (EPA) in 1987. Ten years later, EPA officials estimated the cleanup would continue for at least two more decades. Nevertheless, community members began talking about how the waterfront property might be redeveloped.[6] Many islanders thought that the internment embarkation site and some of the property next to it would provide a suitable home for efforts to preserve and interpret the history of the island's Nikkei community. Second, the publication in 1994 of David Guterson's novel, *Snow Falling on Cedars*, partially inspired by the traveling photo exhibit and set on an island modeled on Bainbridge, brought heightened attention to the Nikkei community and its history. The release of the movie version in 1999, with many locals cast as extras, fostered interest yet again.[7]

By the beginning of 2000, former internees, their family members, and other supporters decided to form the Bainbridge Island World War Two Internment Memorial Committee. Their goals were to "create a memorial and interpretive site which acknowledges the immeasurable suffering experienced by persons of Japanese ancestry at the hands of the United States government" and to honor "the humble acts of dignity and courage which sustained these persons in their exile . . . [and] the community of beauty and diversity built by all who at any time call[ed] Bainbridge Island their home."[8] In May 2000, the committee invited Stephanie Toothman of the National Park Service and Allyson Brooks of the Washington State Historic Preservation Office to visit Bainbridge and assess the possibilities for preservation and interpretation of the internment embarkation site. Both acknowledged the national historical significance of the events associated with the site, but they discovered that the Eagledale ferry dock—the site's centerpiece—was no longer extant. This loss, of course, compromised the embarkation site's physical integrity.

Despite reservations about the site's integrity, Stephanie concluded that its significance and remaining historic character could be assessed under the National Park Service's guidelines for evaluating cultural landscapes. Stephanie decided to authorize a National Historic Landmark nomination for the site and offered the contract to Gail Dubrow, a University of Washington professor whose specializations in Asian American history and historic preservation planning made her aware of the pressing need to identify and protect Asian American cultural resources—and familiarized her with the challenges of doing so.[9] Gail accepted the contract and recruited myself, a graduate student in history with a focus on the American West, and Connie Walker Gray, a graduate student in urban planning focusing on historic preservation, to join her.

We met for the first time in June 2000 and discussed how to divide the work before us. We decided that Connie would document the Eagledale ferry landing site, determine its boundaries, and write its history. I agreed to review relevant scholarship, conduct

Figures 32 and 33. Nikkei removal from Bainbridge Island, Washington, *Seattle Post Intelligencer* Collection, Seattle Museum of History and Industry 28055 and 28049.

archival research, and write the narrative explaining the site's significance. Gail would coordinate, supplement, and edit our work; set up interviews; and serve as our team's liaison to the NPS and the Bainbridge Island community. We all agreed to conduct and transcribe interviews, to work together on framing our report according to NHL nomination guidelines, and to meet regularly to discuss problems, share ideas, and provide support for each other's work.

Our first tasks included surveying scholarship on Nikkei internment and on the development of Bainbridge Island's Nikkei community. We concluded that works produced by Roger Daniels, Ronald Takaki, and other scholars would provide a sufficient foundation on which to create an interpretive framework for the Bainbridge islanders' internment story.[10] These studies, however, only mentioned the experiences of Bainbridge Island's Nikkei families in passing. Daniels noted in one of his studies that the Bainbridge Nikkei—the first of more than 110,000 Nikkei to be interned during the war—served as "guinea pigs" and that their removal and relocation served as a "kind of dress rehearsal for the full scale evacuation which was to come." Other writers neglected the Bainbridge Island Nikkei experience entirely.[11]

Similarly, scholars had paid little attention to the history of Bainbridge Island's Nikkei community. Historian Stefan Tanaka's master's thesis, written during the late 1970s and based on extensive oral interviews, provided an excellent overview of Nikkei settlement and community development on Bainbridge Island, but Tanaka ended his study with the beginning of World War II.[12] Whenever other studies of Nikkei in the United States discussed the Pacific Northwest, they tended to focus on the Nihonmachis (Japantowns) in Seattle, Portland, and elsewhere. When such studies looked at Bainbridge Island's community, they examined only the 1880s and 1890s, the period during which the island's Port Blakely Mill Company—the largest timber mill on the West Coast during the nineteenth century—helped pull Nikkei laborers to the region.[13] Given the available scholarship on internment and on the Bainbridge Nikkei community, we realized that we would need to turn to archival sources and oral histories in order to recount the events surrounding the removal of the island's Nikkei residents.[14] Archival research and oral interviews also would help us convey a strong sense of this local history's broader significance.

Along with surveying scholarship and gauging our research needs, our initial tasks included making a preliminary survey of the site. Bainbridge Island is a semirural island in Puget Sound eight miles west of Seattle. The site of the Eagledale ferry landing is on the south side of the island's busiest harbor, directly across from the landing where the Washington State Ferries dock today. When we visited the island and met with officials in the local planning department, we learned that the 700-foot stretch of road between the ferry landing and the main thoroughfare on the south side of the harbor remained city property. But even though this section of Taylor Avenue remained undeveloped, the city recently had sunk a well and constructed a well house near the road's northern end.

More important, we confirmed that the ferry dock itself was virtually nonextant, with only a few pilings and several support beams jutting out from the embankment to indicate that the site had been used as a ferry landing. We knew that the physical integrity of the internment embarkation site would be a central factor in determining the success of the NHL nomination.[15] Given the absence of the ferry dock, we found ourselves facing the same challenge and frustration that historian Judith Wellman describes in an essay on the preservation of sites related to the Underground Railroad.[16] As Wellman explains, preservation criteria used by the NPS emphasize the importance of a site's ability to convey its historical significance through its unchanged or little-changed physical features. The problem, Wellman correctly points out, is that "strict definitions of integrity . . . [often exclude] historically important sites relating to economically, politically, or socially marginalized Americans."[17] Sites related to African American history—such as homes, churches, and other buildings that served as stops on the Underground Railroad—have been subject to substantial physical change through neglect (or continued use) over the decades. The dismantling of the Eagledale ferry dock, which we later learned occurred during the late 1950s, reflected a similar failure to appreciate the importance of structures related to the history of a racial minority group.[18]

Despite this obstacle, the NPS support office encouraged us to move forward with the nomination. A promise from the City of Bainbridge Island planning department to consider removing the well on Taylor Avenue buoyed our efforts. So too did a survey of photographs revealing that the landscape and view shed of the entire ferry landing site—which we learned had encompassed parking and waiting areas adjacent to Taylor Avenue on the east side—were much the same as they had been 60 years prior. We remained committed to our research, but we knew that we needed to continue thinking creatively about how to frame the nomination.

A familiarity with the status and integrity of the internment camps and other related sites aided our thinking. As revealed in *Confinement and Ethnicity: An Overview of World War II Japanese American Relocation Sites*, the status of the 10 internment camps (officially known as relocation centers), 17 assembly centers, and eight Department of Justice detention centers varies greatly.[19] All of the internment camps, seven assembly centers, and two detention centers contain some kind of historical marker. Despite the fact that the minimum 50-year criteria for listing has been met, however, only six of the camps and two other sites are on the National Register of Historic Places.[20] Only the Manzanar Relocation Center (California) and the memorial cemetery at the Rowher Relocation Center (Arkansas) have attained National Historical Landmark status, and the central portion of the Manzanar internment camp constitutes the lone National Historic Site.[21]

The integrity of these sites varies as much as their status. As the authors of *Confinement and Ethnicity* conclude, "Although most buildings [in the camps and centers] have been removed or destroyed, there remains a wide range of artifacts and features which evoke the distinct aspects of confinement and ethnicity."[22] At the sites of the Manzanar, Granada (Colorado), Topaz (Utah), and Tule Lake (California) camps, for example, many of the foundations of watchtowers are still in place. Stone sentry posts still stand at Manzanar and Minidoka (Idaho), and perimeter fences at Manzanar and Granada remain mostly intact. Similarly, remnants of features such as landscaping, gardens, ponds, and irrigation systems, all of which reveal internees' maintenance of

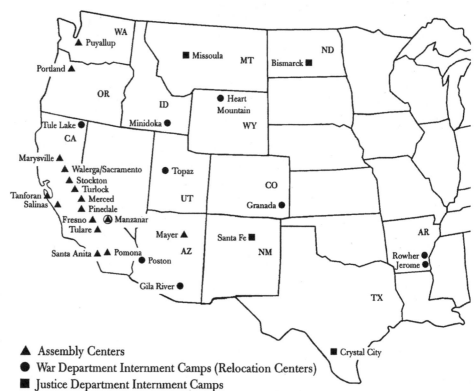

Figure 34. America's concentration camps, from Ruth Okimoto, *Sharing a Desert Home: Life on the Colorado River Indian Reservation—Poston, Arizona, 1942–1945* (Berkeley, CA: Malcolm Margolin, 2001).

Japanese culture, can be found at the Manzanar and Gila River (Arizona) camps and, to lesser degrees, at other sites as well.[23]

The status and integrity of these sites influenced our thinking about how to frame the nomination for the Eagledale ferry landing site in important ways. Scholarship on cultural landscapes had fueled our inclination to focus on the integrity of the ferry landing site as a whole.[24] The findings reported in *Confinement and Ethnicity* confirmed that we did not need to place the integrity of physical structures at the center of our considerations of the site's integrity. If we could demonstrate that the entire ferry landing site— where Nikkei islanders waited for several hours under armed escort for a chartered ferry while other islanders gathered to say goodbye—was significant and that the location, setting, feeling, and association of the site (four categories in which "integrity" is measured) remained evident, then our nomination would be on firmer ground.[25] Moreover, a careful reading of *Confinement and Ethnicity* revealed that the entire focus of efforts to preserve and interpret the history of Nikkei internment had fallen on the sites to which internees were taken. The places that internees left behind had been ignored.[26] Efforts to preserve and interpret internment camps tells an important story, but they do not tell the full story. Only by identifying and protecting sites such as the Eagledale ferry landing on Bainbridge Island, we prepared to argue, would future generations be able to fully appreciate the pain and loss caused by internment policy.

By autumn 2000 our work was well under way. Connie continued collecting historical photographs, conducting research in municipal and county records, and, with the assistance of NPS staff archaeologist Kirstie Haertel, working to document the site and determine its boundaries. I conducted research at the Bainbridge Island Historical Society and at the University of Washington libraries and archives. Drawing on documents generated by officials involved in the implementation of internment policy, local and regional newspapers, contemporary observers' reports, and secondary sources, I worked on preparing a preliminary historical narrative explaining the significance of the Nikkei islanders' removal and the particular significance of their departure from the Eagledale ferry landing.[27] Gail began planning interviews with former internees who had returned to the area after their release. We would conduct the first of these interviews in January 2001 at the Bainbridge Island Nikkei community's *mochi-tsuki*, the traditional gathering of families to make *mochi* (rice cakes) in preparation for the new year.

Creating Oral Histories

When we initiated our interviews with former internees and other island residents, I began to appreciate how the nomination would evolve from a work of academic history, written through collaboration with colleagues, into a work of public history, to be written and revised through cooperation with former internees. I had conducted research and drafted a narrative as my academic training had prepared me to do. However, I had not taken into account the specific memories of former internees, nor their expectations of our work. In other words, I had been writing a history *of* the members of Bainbridge Island's Nikkei community, but not *with* them. Fortunately, Connie, Gail, and I were committed to working with former internees as we prepared the nomination, and we looked forward to creating and incorporating oral histories.

We agreed to finish writing and reviewing preliminary drafts of our historical narrative and our site history and description before proceeding with any interviews. This methodological decision allowed us to devise a series of questions that would parallel our chronologically organized narrative as well as fill in gaps in our research. We also hoped that advanced preparation of a draft narrative and a draft site history and description would enable us to engage in conversational interviews in which we could prompt interviewees on certain points and verify our knowledge on other points. And finally, we expected that our grasp of former internees' historical experiences would help us to cover a lot of ground in a high number of interviews in a short amount of time.

At the mochi-tsuki we spoke with eight former internees in six different interview sessions, each of which lasted close to one hour. After updating each interviewee on the status of the project, we walked through a number of questions. We first discussed each interviewee's family history and memories of daily life on the island during the 1930s and early 1940s. The focus then turned to the weeks and final days leading up to internment, the specific events of March 30, 1942, and finally the internment experience and its aftermath, including the decision to return to Bainbridge Island. We concluded these interviews with the subject of preservation and commemoration, asking former internees what they thought should happen with the Eagledale ferry landing site. Subsequent interviews followed a similar format.[28]

We finished conducting our interviews in February, but the process of creating oral histories was not yet complete. After transcribing the interviews, we mailed transcripts to interviewees for their review and approval. Many interviewees gladly corrected factual errors that they had made and deciphered words and phrases that were unclear on our tape recordings. A few wrote additional comments, and all assented to use of the interviews. This process of creating oral histories continued to reveal to me the importance of the public within the field of public history and demonstrated the value of sharing authorship of the oral histories we had collected. Indeed, I began to see why historian Michael Frisch believes that what is most compelling about public history is its "capacity to redefine and redistribute intellectual authority, so that this might be shared more broadly in historical research and communication."[29] Still, "shared authority" comes at a certain expense. Out of 34 interview participants, only four mentioned personal experiences of racism on Bainbridge Island. One of these four, when given the opportunity to edit the transcript from his interview, removed references to racist hostility that he experienced soon after the bombing of Pearl Harbor. Although the transcript retained allusions to racial tensions, his editing left us with less material from which to draw.

Self-censorship was but one issue that we, like all public historians, had to deal with when creating and using oral histories. Another was the reliability of memory. In one telephone interview, a former internee admitted that his memory was failing and he relied on a scrapbook of newspaper clippings as a crutch. On certain points, therefore, the information he provided came only from his rereading of local newspapers. Other interviewees also admitted that some memories were difficult to recall, and a few former internees explained that because they were too young at the time of internment to form clear memories, they drew from the stories that they had heard from their elders. Despite such challenges, though, our efforts to collect oral histories were worthwhile. Material from the interviews added a personal dimension to the nomination that would not have been there otherwise. Moreover, the process of creating oral histories contributed to the Nikkei community's own mobilization as it continued to work to commemorate Nikkei life on Bainbridge Island and promote public understanding of internment policy and its consequences.

Writing and Revising the Narrative

Our nomination had begun taking shape during autumn 2000. Like all NHL nominations, it was built on two key components: a narrative explaining the site's significance and a physical history and description of the site. During the first few months of 2001, I continued to piece together the former as Connie developed the latter. With our work on the interviews completed by spring 2001, we turned our full attention to finishing the nomination.

When I began preparing a draft of the narrative explaining the Eagledale ferry landing's significance and setting it in its historical context, my colleagues and I concluded that it would not be difficult to make a case for the national significance of internment policy. The internment of Japanese and Japanese Americans is no longer a mere footnote in American history textbooks. As other historians have demonstrated, the history of internment illustrates several important themes that flow through the center of twentieth-century American history: the rising power of the state, the continuing power of racism, the struggles of racial minorities for civil rights and social equality, and the continually contested meaning of "American" identity.[30]

To explain the significance of the internment embarkation site, though, we focused on three key points. First, we pointed out that the Nikkei families on Bainbridge Island were the first in the nation to be taken from their homes by the army and relocated to an internment camp. To be sure, the FBI had taken almost 1,300 Issei individuals into custody immediately after the bombing of Pearl Harbor, and the U.S. Navy forced 3,500 Nikkei residents of Terminal Island, California, to leave the strategically located island in late February.[31] But the removal of the Bainbridge Nikkei—urgently requested by the navy due to the presence of naval facilities in Puget Sound—created the army's first opportunity to relocate an entire community. Under the orders of Lieutenant General John DeWitt, head of the Western Defense Command, officials from the army and several federal agencies gathered in Seattle on March 23 to plan the removal and relocation of the 227 Nikkei still living on Bainbridge Island. As we explained in the nomination, the procedures developed during this planning and the lessons learned from the removal itself informed the evacuation of the other 98 "civilian exclusion areas" identified within Military Area No. 1.[32] The evacuation of Nikkei from Bainbridge Island indeed was a "dress rehearsal" for the full-scale relocation of more than 110,000 Nikkei that followed.[33] But it also was a painful reality for the Bainbridge Islanders, whose anxieties and frustrations were compounded by the lack of well-developed procedures.

Our second point sprang from the highly publicized nature of the Bainbridge Islanders' removal from their homes. On December 7, 1941, Walt and Milly Woodward, publishers of the *Bainbridge Review*, printed a one-page "war extra" in which they warned against and discouraged a "blind, wild, hysterical

Figure 35. Once Japanese Americans had been removed from their homes, the U.S. Army sent them to a variety of camps in the West, including Heart Mountain in Wyoming. Photo by Andrew Gulliford, 1981.

hatred of all persons who can trace their ancestry to Japan."[34] During the next few months the Woodwards repeatedly editorialized against persecution of American citizens of Japanese descent and restrictions of resident alien rights that singled out Japanese but not Germans or Italians. And as federal officials prepared to remove the island's Nikkei residents, the Woodwards publicized the plight of Nikkei islanders who were forced to store or sell their possessions, sell or find caretakers for their farms and businesses, close up their homes, and leave their friends—all within a six-day period. This publicity, we argued, helped to draw a sizable crowd of the island's Euro-American residents to the Eagledale ferry landing on March 30, 1942, despite the army's deliberate selection of that isolated site rather than the more accessible ferry landing on the north side of the harbor. Among the crowd, too, were reporters from regional newspapers and national publications such as *Life* magazine. We concluded that these demonstrations of sympathy and widespread interest were unique and significant. More important, the presence of a large crowd of sympathizers allowed us to focus the nomination on the entire ferry landing rather than just the old ferry dock. The parking and waiting areas of the Eagledale ferry landing—where Nikkei islanders parted from their neighbors—marked the place where the full-scale segregation of Japanese residents and Japanese American citizens, mandated by federal internment policy, began.[35]

Our third point foregrounded the relatively high degree of racial integration on the island, which helped draw the crowd of sympathizers to the ferry landing and helped draw internees *back* to the island after the war. Not surprisingly, Bainbridge Nikkei remained segregated in terms of occupation and social status before the war, and institutions such as the Japanese Language School cultivated Nikkei appreciation for a separate cultural identity. We argued, however, that community institutions such as the public schools, the PTA, the Baptist church, the local Boy Scout troop, Japanese-owned businesses that served the entire community, the local canneries (which bought strawberries from some of the Issei), and especially the *Bainbridge Review* helped tie the island's various racial and ethnic groups together. The weekly newspaper promoted integration by regularly covering Nikkei activities, but it also provided an important bridge between the Bainbridge Nikkei and Euro-American populations during the period of internment. The Woodwards hired a succession of "camp correspondents" to file weekly reports describing internment camp life and sharing news of births, marriages, and enlistments. Likewise, internees received copies of the *Review* and came to see the paper as a vital connection to the island they still considered their home. We concluded that federal internment policy tore apart a remarkably integrated community. Institutions such as the island's newspaper, however, helped piece it back together.[36]

Early drafts of our narrative focused on demonstrating how these areas of significance developed over time and on situating this local history within its national context. Above all, we wanted a narrative that would trace the contours of a local history but still demonstrate how that history reflected and eventually encompassed nationally significant events—as NHL nomination reviewers and a broader national audience would expect us to do. In order to achieve this, we adopted a chronological organization and a narrative structure built on five sets of sections. These sections focused alternatively on local history and its national context as we traced the story up to the last week of March 1942, when the local and larger histories merged into one.

The first two sections discussed historical developments that fueled Japanese migration to the United States during the nineteenth century, including the Meiji government's modernization programs (which displaced thousands of farmers) and the spiraling demand for labor in the American West. These developments brought thousands of Japanese men to the Pacific Northwest, several hundred of whom made their way to Bainbridge Island by the 1880s. This first generation of Nikkei struggled to form a stable community on the island, but an influx of wives and relatives during the 1890s helped. As the "Gentlemen's Agreement" of 1908 officially curtailed the immigration of Japanese laborers and as Bainbridge Nikkei began saving enough money to acquire farmland, members of the island's Nikkei community began to spread out, settle down, and prosper. They would continue to do so through the 1930s.[37]

As we explained in our next pair of sections, the modest success of the Issei in the United States was met with hostility from nativist, agrarian, and working-class interests. Political strikes against the Nikkei, such as laws forbidding citizenship and land ownership, sparked negative reactions in Japan. Tensions between the United States and Japan mounted during the 1930s, and war erupted in 1941. When it did, the progress that the Nikkei on Bainbridge Island had made during the prior decades came to an abrupt halt. The Issei had forged ties with the island community—acquiring land, starting businesses, building homes, and sending their children to the public schools. But their hard work would not be recognized beyond the island. Their integration within the island community would mean nothing to Westerners who demanded the evacuation of all Japanese from the West Coast or to the policy makers who answered those demands.[38]

Our third set of sections emphasized that Californians led the nation in calling for the relocation of all Nikkei. Even though some federal officials had concluded prior to December 1941 that the Nikkei posed no military threat, the *Los Angeles Times* and other vehicles of racist sentiment clamored for internment. Lieutenant General John DeWitt agreed with this sentiment and pursued approval for internment from Secretary of War Henry Stimson and President Franklin Roosevelt. When he received it on February 19, 1942—in the form of Executive Order 9066—the Bainbridge Nikkei realized that their rights as resident aliens or American citizens, along with the fruits of their labor, might be swept away. The Woodwards continued to argue that Nikkei rights should not be curtailed, but the island Nikkei adopted the attitude of *shikata ga nai* ("it cannot be helped") and awaited their fate.[39]

One month later, the Bainbridge Nikkei still faced an uncertain future. Not surprisingly, no one on the island knew that Bainbridge was one of the navy's highest security concerns on the West Coast. Yet the focus of federal internment policy fell on Bainbridge Island during the week leading up to March 30, 1942, and we turned our attention in the penultimate pair of sections to the events unfolding during the six days before removal and the day of removal itself. Drawing on newspaper accounts, observers' reports, and the oral histories we had completed, we examined local reactions to the evacuation order. We then looked at Nikkei efforts to store or sell their possessions, sell or find caretakers for their farms and businesses, and depart from their homes and friends. We presented evidence revealing the unnecessary frustrations confronting Bainbridge Nikkei, such as internment officials' confusion over how the government would take care of personal belongings, and we explained the difficulties faced by those trying to decide which possessions to sell, which to risk in storage, and which to burn or bury. Finally, we looked at the hours leading up to the Nikkei community's departure from the island, as soldiers in army trucks picked up Nikkei islanders and their suitcases, Nikkei families pinned numbered tags on themselves and waited for the ferry near Taylor Avenue, and lifelong friends wept and said goodbye.[40]

The final two sections drew the narrative to a close. We surveyed the ways in which submissions and subscriptions to the *Bainbridge Review*, letters from friends, and even the arrival of high school yearbooks signed by classmates helped internees maintain ties with island residents. We also explored the conditions under which Bainbridge internees decided to return to the island beginning in the spring of 1945. A local resident's efforts in November 1944 to discourage Nikkei from returning revealed that Bainbridge Island still was not a haven from racism. The lack of support for his initiative, the outpouring of letters to the *Review* condemning it, and material from our oral histories, however, confirmed that the majority of Bainbridge residents looked forward to welcoming the Nikkei back to their homes. That return and the longer effort to rebuild lives were not easy, but former internees returned to Bainbridge as old friends and neighbors eager to introduce and meet new babies, fiancés, and spouses—not as unwanted strangers forced to pick up the pieces of their lives by themselves.[41]

The structure of our historical narrative, built on these sets of sections, was in place by the time we began collecting oral histories. At that point, the nomination remained a work of academic history. The oral histories changed the nomination into a work of public history, though, because they added a personal dimension to the nomination. As we revised the narrative we layered in several paragraphs built around material we gained from our interviews. The interviews, for example, helped us understand the tensions that grew within island families after the Nikkei learned of Executive Order 9066. Issei islanders concluded that they would need to demonstrate their loyalty to the United States, and one interviewee remembered that her father did so by cashing in his life insurance policy and purchasing War Bonds. The Issei were torn, though, because most of them still had family members living in Japan. Their children, on the other hand, were more eager to "help beat those guys that bombed *us*," as one Nisei interviewee recalled, but they also had to confront the divides that opened between themselves and their less understanding classmates.[42] They worried, too, about what would happen to their parents in the coming weeks, since they assumed that their own rights as citizens would be recognized.[43]

We also quoted several interviewees at length in order to utilize the emotional power of their words. One Nisei woman, for example, recalled the heartache she experienced as her family destroyed belongings that were too treasured to sell or risk storing:

> I was the first grandchild on my mother's side, so my grandma [in Japan] sent me things all the time. Nice things. Japanese things. Oh, it just made us heartsick to dig a hole and bury them, and all the Japanese records, books, artifacts—anything we had [was] just all burnt. Out on the farm we had an outhouse, so we were dumping a lot of things [too].[44]

Another former internee, whom Walt Woodward hired as his first "camp correspondent," quoted a personal letter from Woodward. The newspaper editor's words revealed his insight and anger:

> When this mess is all over, your people are going to want to come home. You'll be welcomed with open arms by the vast majority of us, but those who don't or won't understand will not feel that way. They may actually try to stir up trouble. But they'll have a hell of a hard time of it if in the meantime you've been creating the impression every week that the Japanese are just down there [in Manzanar] for a short while and that, by being in the *Review* every week, they still consider the island as their home.[45]

These words and others carried a significant amount of emotional weight, but the interview material we used ultimately helped to give the nomination, especially its narrative, an understated tone of sadness rather than anger and of remembrance yet readiness to heal old wounds.

Our strategic inclusion of interview material helped the nomination evolve from a work of academic history into a work of public history. Due to two other factors, the nomination ended up reflecting a mix of academic history, public history, and community history. First, our knowledge that former internees would be reviewing the nomination influenced how we wrote the historical narrative, tugging the narrative toward the realm of community history. Had we been writing for other professional historians, we would have been less rigorous in screening out academic jargon. Although our explanation that the departure of the island's Nikkei community from the ferry landing was a "public spectacle" was informed by recent scholarship on the ways in which marginalized groups exercise agency in public spaces, for example, we avoided specialized language as much as possible. Moreover, because we were writing in part for an audience of Bainbridge residents, we incorporated their perspective on the island's relatively high level of racial integration. We could not deny that racist sentiment existed on the island—it relegated the Nikkei to certain occupations, it fueled a backlash against the Woodwards' newspaper, and it spurred the effort in 1944 to discourage Nikkei from returning to the island. Still, we chose to foreground evidence of racial cooperation and friendship. We pointed out that Nikkei businesses were supported by the community and that Nisei were a integral presence on sports teams, in the Boy Scout troop, and in school plays. Furthermore, we explained that readers of the *Review* wrote letters echoing the Woodwards' editorials and paid for new subscriptions when angry subscribers canceled their own, the PTA collected suitcases for internees to use, many islanders bought Nikkei property for more than its worth, and finally, the movement to prevent the Nikkei from returning collapsed when only 34 people showed up for a second meeting. In short, we strove to write a history of the island that former internees and other community members would recognize as their own.[46]

The second factor that made the nomination a mix

Figure 36. A posed publicity photo of the Ninomiya family, showing their apparent comfort as they wait out the war at Camp Amache, Prowers County, Colorado. Eventually the U.S. Government formally apologized for its treatment of Japanese-American citizens, but financial reparations did not begin to compensate for actual financial losses. The December 9, 1942 photo carried this original caption: "The mother's handiwork in preparing drapes, fashioning furniture out of scrap material, plus the boy's ingenuity in preparing double deck bunks have made this bare brick floored barracks room a fairly comfortable duration home." Western History Collections, Denver Public Library, Photo by Tom Parker, X-6566.

of academic, public, and community history grew from our decision to convey in the narrative's conclusion some of the responses we received when we asked former internees what should happen with the ferry landing site—even though most of those responses clashed with the goals of historic preservation. None of the interviewees preferred to see the site preserved as it was, and only a few suggested that the site be restored and protected. In fact, most interviewees admitted that, although they would be pleased with the recognition garnered by National Historic Landmark status, they planned to explore ways in which the ferry landing site might serve as an anchor for more ambitious efforts to commemorate, interpret, and honor Nikkei experiences in the Pacific Northwest and in internment camps. We called attention to these desires and indicated that the ferry landing site itself might be preserved and property adjacent to it acquired and developed as a companion site housing an interpretive center, a memorial, and a peace park. We joined Bainbridge islanders in arguing that achievement of these goals would transform a place still associated with pain and loss into a site dedicated to remembrance, reconciliation, and vigilance against the repetition of such injustices in the future.⁴⁷

Conclusion: History Connected to Place and Community

The emphasis on connecting history to place—be it to understand, interpret, and preserve or ultimately to transform sites such as the Eagledale ferry landing—is but one of many valuable qualities of public history. Academic historians have begun to pay more attention to place, but public historians, especially historic preservationists, tie their historical studies to specific places as a matter of course. Public historians also seem more likely than academic historians to appreciate the value of cooperative work.⁴⁸ Despite my early anxiety about collaborating with colleagues that stemmed from a lack of exposure to cooperative work during my academic training, our team worked well together and produced a better product than any of us would have individually. Moreover, I learned that collaboration with community historians and other members of the public offers great professional and personal rewards. Former internees and other island residents who participated in interviews and reviewed our work improved the nomination and enriched my experience working on it.

Perhaps the greatest reward—if also, admittedly, the greatest frustration—of working on the NHL nomination sprang from the low level of our influence over the future of the Eagledale ferry landing site. After combining the revised narrative with the physical history and description of the site that Connie had completed, we submitted a final draft of the nomination to the National Park Service in June 2001. As the nomination began circulating through the customary stages of review, Bainbridge community members decided to move forward with more ambitious plans for the site and adjacent property. Island residents began exploring public and private sources of support for the construction of an interpretive center and development of a peace park at the Eagledale ferry landing site. The NPS remained willing to support these efforts and decided to table the NHL nomination until other avenues of achieving the community's goals could be examined. The NPS also worked with Representative Jay Inslee to author a bill that would provide support for a study examining the feasibility of incorporating the ferry landing site as a unit within the Park Service.⁴⁹

These developments reinforced perhaps the most important lesson that I learned from my work on the NHL nomination: the past does not belong to professional historians alone. Community members can and will assert their need for a usable past—a past that they can use to shape the future. In 1942, members of the Bainbridge Island Nikkei community arrived at the Eagledale ferry landing site not knowing what their future would hold. Not surprisingly, the site became associated with this feeling of powerlessness. Sixty years later, Nikkei community members drew on the past to ensure that they would have a voice in deciding the future of the ferry landing site. That future remains undetermined. Yet Nikkei community members' success in shaping that future will create new associations for the site. It will provide a model of civic action for all community members, and it will leave a valuable legacy for generations to come.

Notes

I would like thank Gail Dubrow, Connie Walker Gray, Stephanie Toothman, Brian Casserly, Andrew Gulliford, Andy Kirk, and Veta Schlimgen for reading and commenting on previous versions of this essay.

1. Raymond W. Rast, Connie Walker, and Gail Dubrow, "National Historic Landmark Nomination: Eagledale Ferry Dock" (Seattle: U.S. Department of the Interior, National Park Service, Columbia Cascades Support Office, 2001).

2. Patricia Mooney-Melvin argues that all professional historians should "participate more directly and visibly in

the efforts to present responsible interpretation to visitors at historic sites, museums, historical societies, and monuments. Doing so would allow the public to better see historians as integral players in the definition, preservation, and interpretation of America's historical experience." She quotes Jamil Zainaldin, president of the Federation of State Humanities Councils, to drive her point home: "The more our publics know about us, the more they will come to share our values for our craft and help support the practitioners, the higher education institutions, museums, historical societies, and similar institutions that share our mission." See Patricia Mooney-Melvin, "Professional Historians and the Challenge of Redefinition," in *Public History: Essays from the Field*, ed. James B. Gardner and Peter S. LaPaglia (Malabar, FL: Krieger Publishing Company, 1999), 16–17.

3. *Nikkei* refers to all persons with Japanese ancestry. The term *Issei* refers to first-generation or immigrant Japanese, *Nisei* refers to second-generation Japanese born of Issei parents, and *Sansei* refers to children of Nisei parents. It has become common practice to use these terms without italicization.

4. Mitsuye Yamada, "Legacy of Silence (I)," in *Last Witnesses: Reflections on the Wartime Internment of Japanese Americans*, ed. Erica Harth (New York: Palgrave, 2001), 36.

5. Refer to Robert Sadamu Shimabukuro, *Born in Seattle: The Campaign for Japanese American Redress* (Seattle: University of Washington Press, 2001), and Mitchell T. Maki, Harry H. L. Kitano, and S. Megan Berthold, *Achieving the Impossible Dream: How Japanese Americans Obtained Redress* (Urbana: University of Illinois Press, 1999).

6. See "A Fate Sealed with Creosote," *The Sun* [Bremerton, WA], February 12, 1997, A1, A6–7.

7. David Guterson, *Snow Falling on Cedars* (San Diego: Harcourt Brace, 1994); *Snow Falling on Cedars*, dir. Scott Hicks (Universal Studios, 1999). See also Kery Murakami, "'Snow' Recalls Wartime Bainbridge," *Seattle Post-Intelligencer*, December 6, 1999, A1, A7.

8. See Bainbridge Island World War Two Internment Memorial Committee, "Statement of Purpose" (January 24, 2000), copy in author's possession, and "Honor for displaced citizens," *The Sun* [Bremerton, Wash.], May 2, 2000, A2.

9. See "Scope of Work for Bainbridge Island Embarkation Site NHL Nomination" (contract), May 2000, copy in author's possession. See also Gail Lee Dubrow, "Asian American Imprints on the Western Landscape," in *Preserving Cultural Landscapes in America*, ed. Arnold R. Alanen and Robert Z. Melnick (Baltimore: Johns Hopkins University Press, 2000), 143–68.

10. See, for example, Roger Daniels, *Prisoners Without Trial: Japanese Americans in World War II* (New York: Hill and Wang, 1993); Roger Daniels, *Asian America: Chinese and Japanese in the United States since 1850* (Seattle: University of Washington Press, 1988); Roger Daniels, *Concentration Camps: North American Japanese in the United States and Canada During World War II*, rev. ed. (Malabar, FL: Robert E. Krieger, 1981); Roger Daniels, *The Decision to Relocate the Japanese Americans* (Malabar, FL: Robert E. Krieger, 1975); Ronald Takaki, *Double Victory: A Multicultural History of America in World War II* (New York: Little, Brown, 2000); Ronald Takaki, *Strangers from a Different Shore: A History of Asian Americans* (New York: Little, Brown, 1989); and the Commission on Wartime Relocation and Internment of Civilians, *Personal Justice Denied*, 2nd ed. (Seattle: Civil Liberties Public Education Fund and University of Washington Press, 1997).

11. Daniels, *Decision to Relocate*, 54. Works overlooking the experiences of Bainbridge Island's Nikkei are numerous; see, for example, Page Smith, *Democracy on Trial: The Japanese American Evacuation and Relocation in World War II* (New York: Simon & Schuster, 1995). Another exception, from which Roger Daniels drew, is Audrie Girdner and Anne Loftis, *The Great Betrayal: The Evacuation of the Japanese-Americans During World War II* (New York: Macmillan, 1969).

12. Stefan Akio Tanaka, "The Nikkei on Bainbridge Island, 1883–1942: A Study of Migration and Community Development," Ph.D. diss., University of Washington, 1977.

13. Studies of Nikkei in the United States include David J. O'Brien, *The Japanese American Experience* (Bloomington: Indiana University Press, 1991); H. Brett Melendy, *Chinese and Japanese Americans*, rev. ed. (New York: Hippocrene Books, 1984); and Robert A. Wilson and Bill Hosokawa, *East to America: A History of the Japanese in the U.S.* (New York: Morrow, 1980). See also Takaki, *Strangers from a Different Shore*.

14. Although many NHL nominations can rest on secondary sources, NHL nominations for sites related to the history of racial minorities and other marginalized groups often require primary source research.

15. For National Historic Landmark eligibility guidelines consult National Park Service, *National Register Bulletin: How to Prepare National Historic Landmark Nominations* (Washington, D.C.: Cultural Resources Management, National Park Service, U.S. Department of the Interior, 1999), 11.

16. See Judith Wellman, "The Underground Railroad and the National Register of Historic Places: Historical Importance vs. Architectural Integrity," *The Public Historian* 24 (winter 2002): 11–30.

17. Wellman, "Underground Railroad," 23. On the issue of integrity see also Catherine Howett, "Integrity as a Value in Cultural Landscape Preservation," in *Preserving Cultural Landscapes in America*, ed. Alanen and Melnick, 186–207; and Barbara J. Little, "Archaeology, History, and Material Culture: Grounding Abstractions and Other Imponderables," *International Journal of Historical Archaeology* 1, no. 2 (1997).

18. On this point see also Dubrow, "Asian American Imprints," 163–64.

19. Jeffrey F. Burton, Mary M. Farrell, Florence B. Lord, and Richard W. Lord, *Confinement and Ethnicity: An Overview of World War II Japanese American Relocation Sites* (Tucson, AZ: Western Archaeological and Conservation Center, National Park Service, U.S. Department of the Interior, 1999).

20. The latter two sites are listed for reasons beyond their wartime use for internment.

21. Burton et al., *Confinement and Ethnicity*, 5. On historic preservation efforts at the Manzanar Relocation Center site see "Remembering Manzanar," *National Parks* 67 (May–June 1993): 30–35.

22. Burton et al., *Confinement and Ethnicity*, 12.

23. Ibid., 12–17. The three camps not mentioned are Heart Mountain (Wyoming), Jerome (Arkansas), and Poston (Arizona).

24. This scholarship includes the essays in Alanen and Melnick, eds., *Preserving Cultural Landscapes in America*, and the essays in Paul Groth and Todd W. Bressi, *Understanding Ordinary Landscapes* (New Haven: Yale University Press, 1997). Older works include Melody Webb, "Cultural Landscapes in the National Park Service," *The Public Historian* 9 (spring 1987): 77–89, and Robert Z. Melnick, Daniel Sponn, and Emma Jane Saxe, *Cultural Landscapes: Rural Historic Districts in the National Park System* (Washington, D.C.: Cultural Resources Management, National Park Service, Department of the Interior, 1984).

25. The seven categories in which to measure integrity are location, design, setting, materials, workmanship, feeling, and association; see *National Register Bulletin*, 11.

26. As Gail Dubrow has noted, the focus on internment camps and other related sites "was the result of a congressionally mandated study on that subject. National Historic Landmark Program staff argued for a broader focus that would include Japanese American community life in the prewar period, but their recommendations were not followed." See Alanen and Melnick, eds., *Preserving Cultural Landscapes in America*, 220, n. 58.

27. I discuss drafts and revisions of the narrative below.

28. The interview clips in the documentary *Visible Target* (Seattle: KCTS-9 in cooperation with the Bainbridge Documentary Project, 1985) also provided a valuable resource and point of comparison.

29. Michael Frisch, *A Shared Authority: Essays on the Craft and Meaning of Oral and Public History* (Albany: State University of New York Press, 1990), xx.

30. See for example, Takaki, *Double Victory*; Daniels, *Prisoners Without Trial*; and Smith, *Democracy on Trial*.

31. Consult CWRIC, *Personal Justice Denied*, 55, 108.

32. See Rast, Walker, and Dubrow, "National Historic Landmark Nomination," 12. Military Area No. 1 encompassed the western halves of Washington, Oregon, and California and the southern half of Arizona.

33. Daniels, *Decision*, 54.

34. *Bainbridge Review* (December 8, 1941): 4.

35. See Rast, Walker, and Dubrow, "National Historic Landmark Nomination," 12.

36. Ibid., 12–13.

37. Ibid., 14–15.

38. Ibid., 15–18.

39. Ibid., 18–20. Woodward editorial quoted from *Bainbridge Review* (August 8, 1941): 4.

40. See Rast, Walker, and Dubrow, "National Historic Landmark Nomination," 20–25.

41. Ibid., 25–27.

42. Arthur Koura, in Earl Hanson et al., interview (February 18, 2001), quoted in ibid., 19.

43. See Rast, Walker, and Dubrow, "National Historic Landmark Nomination," 19.

44. Kazuko (Sakai) Nakao interview (January 6, 2001), quoted in ibid., 21.

45. Walt Woodward quoted in Paul Ohtaki interview (February 2, 2001), quoted in ibid., 13.

46. This is not to say that Bainbridge Islanders or other local audiences are not educated and critical readers. As Roy Rosenzweig argues, local audiences often contain some of the most critical readers of written histories in which those locals or people like them appear as subjects. See Roy Rosenzweig, "Afterthoughts: Everyone a Historian," in *The Presence of the Past: Popular Uses of History in American Life*, ed. Roy Rosensweig and David Thelan (New York: Columbia University Press, 1998), 179.

47. See Rast, Walker, and Dubrow, "National Historic Landmark Nomination," 27–28.

48. On this point see also Ann Marie Plane, "On Pulling Together: Historians, Citizens, and Collaboration," *The Public Historian* 24:1 (winter 2002): 8.

49. See H.R. 3747, *Congressional Record: Proceedings and Debates of the 107th Congress* 148 (February 13, 2002): H366.

Study Questions

1. According to the author, why do many Japanese Americans not talk about their experiences in the internment camps? How do they want to interpret the cultural experience of removal?

2. What was the purpose of the Bainbridge Island World War II Internment Memorial Committee?

3. Describe the challenges associated with building a memorial on Bainbridge Island.

4. What is the significance of the ferry landing site?

5. What are some problems with using oral histories and interviews?

6. What did the author's narrative focus on when applying to the NHL?

7. How did the islanders retain ties to their home?

8. How did former internees answer when asked how and if the ferry landing site should be preserved?

Hispanic Culture

Headnotes

The U.S. Congress denied statehood to Arizona and New Mexico until 1912, largely because of their Spanish-speaking populations, their harsh desert environments, and the Spanish, Mexican, and Native American heritage of their inhabitants. Established politicians at the turn of the twentieth century viewed the Southwest's isolation, cultural pluralism, and Catholic hegemony as deterrents to statehood. Yet those same factors that postponed assimilation and statehood produced a rich and unequaled indigenous folk culture. By remaining outside of the American mainstream for three centuries, Arizona and New Mexico evolved their own distinct folkways. Thus today the Southwest is blessed with a rich tricultural mix of Anglos, Hispanos, and American Indians.

Within the last decade the New Western history has begun to place Hispanos into their proper role in the history of the West and Southwest. Books and essays have described everything from new perspectives on the conquistadors, as in John Kessell's *Spain in the Southwest*, to the lives of cannery workers and migrant farmers in California. Museum specialists are defining and describing the Southwest's unique material culture with books such as Marta Weigle and Peter White's *The Lore of New Mexico*, James S. Griffith's *Southern Arizona Folk Arts*, Robert Adams's *The Architecture and Art of Early Hispanic Colorado*, Mary Montaño's *Tradiciones Nuevomexicanos: Hispano Arts and Culture of New Mexico*, and Dexter Cirillo's *Across Frontiers: Hispanic Crafts of New Mexico*. New interest in the Penitentes has resulted in Alberto Lopez Pulido's *The Sacred World of the Penitentes* and Ruben E. Archuleta's *Land of the Penitentes, Land of Tradition* joining Marta Weigle's earlier book *Los Hermanos Penitentes: Historical and Ritual Aspects of Folk Religion in Northern New Mexico & Southern Colorado*. Western historians are rewriting textbooks to reinterpret Spanish and Hispanic contributions, and public historians are intrigued by the complexities of preserving Hispanic identities in the dynamic, multicultural American West. See for instance Vincent C. DeBaca's *La Gente: Hispano History and Life in Colorado* and Charles Montgomery's *The Spanish Redemption: Heritage, Power, and Loss on New Mexico's Upper Rio Grande*.

In this section of *Preserving Western History*, Smithsonian curator Lonn Taylor explains the difficulties two centuries ago of obtaining furniture and craft goods on the long route up the Camino Real from Mexico City to the provincial capital of Santa Fe. Distance and isolation forced New Mexicans to develop their own furniture and craft styles, and they did so with the creation of New Mexican wooden chests. Taylor describes those chests and why they are so valuable today. He is also the author, with Dessa Bokides, of *New Mexican Furniture 1600–1940*. From an essay originally published in *The Public Historian*, Jon Hunner at New Mexico State University describes preserving Hispanic lifeways in New Mexico. A provocative companion essay is anthropologist Sarah Horton's "Where is the 'Mexican' in 'New Mexican'? Enacting History, Enacting Dominance in the Santa Fe Fiesta."

National Park Service Regional Historian Art Gómez discusses Hispanic and Latino politics on an international scale with his insightful analysis of Chamizal National Memorial on the border between El Paso, Texas, and Juárez, Mexico. Gómez explains the difficulties of the international boundary line where the Rio Grande continually changes course and how the radical idea of a peace park along the river was finally accepted by both governments.

New Mexican Chests:
A Comparative Look

Lonn Taylor

One of the great pleasures of working with material culture is that seemingly inanimate objects, when studied properly, can come alive to reveal details about the daily lives and cultural values of the people who made and used them. Traditionally, museum curators have examined such objects individually, tending to treat each one as a unique creation that has something to say about its makers and users. In recent years, however, curators have borrowed a leaf from anthropologists and archaeologists and have begun to view the objects in their care as parts of groups of similar objects or, to be more precise, as members of an ever-widening series of groups, in the same way that one's automobile is not only an individualized vehicle but part of a group of cars of the same make and model, part of a larger group called Fords or Chevrolets, and part of an even larger group called automobiles. Viewed in this way, objects can raise questions that in turn can provide the investigator with new insights or can simply baffle and torment him. Sometimes these questions can be answered by turning to documents that amplify the context of the object; sometimes they must remain, for the present, unanswered.

New Mexican chests, which were the most common item of household furniture in New Mexico for more than two centuries, illustrate this phenomenon perfectly. Examined individually, many of them place the investigator in an almost embarrassing intimacy with their makers and users; looking at them as members of groups of objects with similar characteristics raises questions that, if fully answered, could tell us a great deal about the dynamics of Spanish colonial society in New Mexico.[1]

Documents—in particular the wills and estate inventories filed in the Spanish archives of New Mexico—show that the wooden chest was an object that was common to all New Mexican dwellings, Spanish and Indian, from the beginning of the eighteenth to the beginning of the twentieth centuries. Its widespread use between 1700 and 1845 can be inferred from the 44 estate inventories filed in the Spanish archives that list specific pieces of furniture and thus provide us with detailed glimpses of 44 New Mexican households. Thirty-nine of these contained chests, in numbers ranging from three or four in most homes to 18 in the house of Clemente Gutierrez, a wealthy sheep rancher who died at his home near Isleta in 1785. The inventories give a good deal of detail about these chests, distinguishing, for instance, between chests with locks (*cerraduras*) and without locks, mentioning those that were unpainted or uncarved (*blancos*), and frequently giving the monetary value of each chest listed. Perhaps the most important distinction is made between locally made chests and imported chests (*cajas de tierra afuera* or *cajas de* Michoacán). Of the 150 chests listed on the 44 inventories, exactly one-third are specifically described as being from Michoacán, a cabinetmaking center in central Mexico. Seven more are described as being from "Mexico," presumably meaning the Valley of Mexico, or from "another country." Five are listed as being "from here" (*de este país*). No place of origin is given for the remaining 88.[2]

The inventories also indicate that most of the chests were containers for the long lists of textiles that made up the outward show of wealth and status favored by colonial New Mexicans. Occasionally they held other types of goods. When the Santa Fe merchant Juan de Archibuque was killed by Indians in 1721, the *alcalde* went to his house and was shown several locked chests by the old woman who had been his housekeeper. Two of them proved to be full of textiles, but a third contained 68 bundles of tobacco and a fourth, whose lock had to be forced, held an elk skin bag full of gold and "68 pounds of loose chocolate, of which six pounds were given to the old lady . . .

because she asked for it and was old and infirm."[3] After 1800 another type of chest, the *harinero* (flour chest), began to appear on the inventories. Harineros probably began to emerge as a furniture form at the end of the eighteenth century, when water-powered mills to grind corn and wheat started to appear in New Mexico. They symbolize the New Mexican woman's liberation from the backbreaking daily labor of grinding meal with the mano and metate, since they were large enough to offer rodent-proof storage for an entire winter's supply of mill-ground flour.

The Museum of International Folk Art's New Mexico Furniture History Project has been able to locate and make a detailed examination of 158 wooden chests with a tradition of manufacture or usage in New Mexico before 1900. Establishing an exact date or place of origin for most of these chests has been extremely difficult because, with one extremely important exception, they were collected by museums or individuals through dealers who did not pass on any information about former owners. All of them are made of pine and, with two exceptions, all are fitted with iron hinges of the eyelet, strap, or butt variety. Many show evidence of several generations of hinges or locks. Their measurements indicate that virtually all of them were made according to fixed rules of proportion and that their makers were masters of these sets of rules, which had their origin in the guild systems of Spain and Mexico. They were not made, as has often been suggested, by household members for their own use, but by skilled professional joiners (*carpinteros de lo blanco*), whom the documents and census records show to have been important members of New Mexican society from the time of Oñate's first colony onward.[4]

Examined as a group, the 158 chests fall into several subgroups based on construction and decoration, and these subgroups can be further divided on the basis of further similarities. Many of the chests examined, and many of those with the strongest evidence of New Mexican origin, were joined chests—that is, they were made by grooving wooden panels into a framework of horizontal and vertical wooden members, called rails and stiles, which are joined with pegged mortise-and-tenon joints. This is a very old method of chest construction, reaching back into the Middle Ages and practiced by English cabinetmakers in seventeenth-century New England. A smaller number were board chests: they were made by simply joining the front, back, and two side panels directly with dovetail joints and pegging the bottom to the bottom edges of those four boards—a much simpler and cheaper method of construction.

Curiously, it is the board chests that have been most frequently described as "typically New Mexican." Most of them are decorated with low-relief carvings depicting Spanish heraldic devices such as lions and pomegranates, floral rosettes, and vinelike motifs. On three examples, the front panel has been further divided into seven smaller panels by applied molding, which also borders the two end panels, concealing the dovetail joints. They also all show a skillful use of proportion. An example in the Spanish Colonial Arts Society Collection at the Museum of International Folk Art is laid out on the basis of a square exactly one-half *vara* (42 cm). On a side, one such square forms each of the end panels, and two of them form the front panel, which is one vara wide. The floral design on the front panel was laid out with compasses on the basis of two circles whose radii are one-fourth vara and one-seventh vara. These chests have been dated to the end of the eighteenth century on the basis of the baroque influence on their carved designs and the similarity of these designs to certain motifs found in eighteenth-century New Mexican churches. But no documented history of ownership before the 1920s exists for any of them. They captured the imagination of dealers, collectors, and craft revivalists in the 1920s and 1930s. A drawing of one was the advertising logo of Bruce Cooper's Spanish Chest craft shop in Santa Fe; the low-relief motifs have inspired the designer of the registration desk at the La Fonda Hotel and countless other Spanish colonial revival craftsmen from the 1920s to the present.

The joined chests are much more numerous and have a better-documented New Mexican history.

They fall into three categories: small joined chests on legs, larger harineros, and what might be called false joined chests, or board chests with ornament applied to make them resemble joined chests. The most striking examples of the first category are a group of 17 joined chests that share so many similarities that they must have come from the same shop or at least the same community. They constitute a New Mexican furniture tradition in themselves, and several of them have strong associations with the Taos–Santa Cruz area. All 17 were made by joining two side panels, a back panel, and two front panels into a framework consisting of eight horizontal rails and five vertical stiles, with one of the stiles dividing the two front panels. The surfaces of the stiles and rails in front are heavily chip carved, and the two front panels are carved with geometric designs. The four end stiles are extended to form legs, raising the chest off the floor a distance roughly equivalent to its own height. Two angular braces, also chip carved, join the front bottom rail and the two front legs. On two examples, there is a drawer below the bottom rail, supported by a drawer rail decorated with carved wooden balls. One of these two chests is pictured in a 1915 issue of *El Palacio* over the caption, "An exquisite piece of native wood-carving from the church at Ranchos de Taos."[5] A complex system of grooving, combined with double thickness of the elaborate applied ornament, helps make this harinero rodent-proof. Over 10-feet long, this chest is a monument to the New Mexican carpenter's skill (MNM Collections, on loan to La Cienega Village Museum, Acc. #P.17.52–1).

A much larger example, without the drawer and with a much more complex geometric design on the panels, is in the Harwood Foundation collection at Taos. This piece, which has had its legs cut down and its diagonal braces removed, has a typed label glued to the inside of the lid that reads, *Purchased from Jose Amador Valdez, August 14, 1917. Valdez inherited it from his father Juan de Jesus Valdez, who inherited it from his father Francisco A. Valdez, whose father made it.*

Figure 37. One of a group of joined chests on legs, so similar to one another in construction that they constitute a furniture tradition in themselves. Collection of Fenn Galleries, Ltd., Santa Fe, New Mexico. Photo by Mary Peck. Courtesy Museum of International Folk Art.

Census records show that Juan de Jesús Valdez was born in Rio Arriba in 1805, which, allowing 20 years to a generation, would place his grandfather Valdez's birth about 1765, meaning that this chest and possibly the others that resemble it was made sometime toward the end of the eighteenth century. The Valdezes were a large family in Rio Arriba, the descendants of José Luis Valdez, one of the original (1693) settlers of Santa Cruz. Eighteenth-century documents have not yet revealed any Valdez carpenters, but the first U.S. census of New Mexico (1850) lists five Valdezes who practiced that trade in Rio Arriba County, although none in Taos County.

A third example at the Millicent Rogers Museum in Taos was collected by Millicent Rogers in Taos; it is constructed on the basis of vara squares, with the diagonal braces forming the diagonals of two of those squares. All in all, these chests seem to have strong ties to the Rio Arriba and, if the label in the Harwood chest is correct, to the Valdez family.

The board chests masquerading as framed chests are probably a continuation of this tradition, an attempt to produce a chest in the "accepted" form while saving labor and making use of a new technology: nails. One example in the Spanish Colonial Arts Society Collection at the Museum of International Folk Art, collected by Frank Applegate in the 1920s, is clearly derived from the Taos–Santa Cruz chests: it has the same chip-carved decoration, but it is applied to pieces of wood that are pegged and nailed to the chest rather than to rails, stiles, and panels. This chest is a nailed board chest, possibly an old packing box, with four three-by-threes that have been hollowed out with a chisel to receive its corners, pegged to it to resemble corner stiles. These extend to form legs, while other strips of wood have been nailed to the box to resemble top and bottom rails. The coffered lid, formed by pegging five boards to two gable ends, may indicate the influence of nineteenth-century travel trunks, which had similar lids. A similar chest, also in the Spanish Colonial Arts Society Collection, makes use of molding instead of carved boards to form the false rails and is held together with wood screws and wire nails and painted brown and yellow. Its use in the 1920s is shown by two penciled inscriptions on the inside of the lid, reading, Hoy, *día 20 de Julio 1922, nos fuimos yo E. B. y T. Marquez para a trabajar* and Hoy *dia 27 de Agosto 1923 compre una troca Ford*–colloquial Spanish for "On July 27, 1922, E. B. and T. Marquez and I went to work," and "On August 27, 1923, I bought a Ford truck." The decorations on the end panels, made of lengths of cut molding mitered into square ornaments, have been found on several other chests and even a secretary, all apparently made in northern New Mexico in the late nineteenth or early twentieth century. There are enough other surviving examples of false framed chests to indicate that they were once quite common and that they were chronological successors of the small joined chest in New Mexican households.

The harineros examined by the project reaffirm the importance of the joined chest in the New Mexican cabinetmaking tradition. Of the 22 examined, all but three were joined, many of them quite ingeniously. An example at the Museum's Laboratory of Anthropology has, in addition to the four corner stiles, five additional stiles in front, one on each side, and one in the rear. These vertical stiles are divided by 12 middle rails, each mortised and tenoned into the stiles, framing a total of 24 separate panels. Since the bottom of the chest must bear a tremendous weight, it is not only grooved into all four bottom rails but is given additional support by three slats that are mortised into the front and rear bottom rails below it. As on most harineros, the lid is not a full lid (if it were, its size would make it difficult to lift; it is 190 centimeters wide and 70 deep) but a half lid, hinged to a board that forms the top of the chest. The complex joinery pattern of the front is not repeated on the rear, which is made up of only four panels.

The harinero, with its inherent problems of weight, stress, and security from rodents, was the culmination of the New Mexican joiner's art. Sometimes the panels themselves were ornamented with carving, as in an example in the collection of John Meigs, which has four front panels ornamented with a Maltese cross pattern that is also seen on several other harineros, several *trasteros* (cupboards or china closets), and several doors, one of which has been traced to the town of Manzano, which had an active cabinetmaking industry in the 1870s. Later harineros also show the same tendency toward false joinery that later chests do, with legs nailed on and moldings applied to resemble rails and stiles.

An enormous example from the Museum of International Folk Art collection, on view at Las Golondrinas Museum outside of Santa Fe, is a nailed chest composed of nine boards (three for each side), set on legs that extend upward to the lid and hide the nailed corners, and covered with applied ornament, including curvilinear ornaments cut out with a frame saw, an innovation introduced into New Mexico by Anglo American carpenters and called by Spanish-speaking carpenters a *sierra de moldura* (molding saw). This chest, which is over 10 feet long, is a monument to the New Mexican carpenter's skill. It is subdivided inside into three chests, and the bottom, which had to

Figure 38. Enough examples of false framed chests remain to indicate they were quite common and were the successors of small joined chests. Private collection of Mr. and Mrs. Julian Garcia, Albuquerque, New Mexico. Photo by Mary Peck. Courtesy Museum of International Folk Art.

Figure 39. This harinero is decorated with carving of a Maltese cross pattern that can be traced to the town of Manzano, which had an active cabinetmaking industry in the 1870s. Private collection of Mr. John Meigs, San Patricio, New Mexico. Photo by Mary Peck. Courtesy Museum of International Folk Art.

bear tremendous weight, is made of tightly tongue-and-grooved slats resting on rails nailed to the bottom boards of the front and back of the chest, in the same way that the slats of a bed are secured. The three half lids on top are hinged to boards that are grooved into three rails, which in turn are let into the top boards of the chest's back and front. This system of grooving, combined with double thickness of the elaborate applied ornament, helps make the harinero rodent-proof. The overall impression, however, is of a joined chest.

Clearly, there was an old and long-established New Mexican tradition of joinery that produced joined chests. How, then, do the board chests fit into this tradition, and how could two such dissimilar types of chests be produced in the same isolated region at the same time? For the present, until some documentation is found for the history of the board chests, all answers must be simply informed speculation. The recurrence of heraldic designs on the board chests may mean that they derive from some inexpensive type of Spanish military furniture. Some historians have suggested that there were sharper regional divisions in colonial New Mexico than has been generally assumed; it may be that the board chests have their origin in the Rio Abajo and the joined chests in the Rio Arriba. A third tantalizing possibility is suggested by the presence of the 50 chests from Michoacán on the estate inventories; perhaps the board chests were actually made by the Tarascan Indian cabinetmakers of Michoacán, who were adept in low-relief carving, and found their way into New Mexico through trade. A canvass of Mexican museums for documented examples of eighteenth-century Michoacán chests for comparison has yielded no results, and the occurrence of the same variety of pine in both Michoacán and New Mexico makes wood analysis fruitless. It is fairly certain that in the nineteenth-century painted boxes from the cabinetmaking centers of Michoacán found their way into New Mexico; the board chests could represent the eighteenth-century manifestation of that trade.

One fact does emerge from a comparative examination of New Mexican chests that is certain: colonial New Mexico was a far more complex society, both in internal economic organization and in trade relations with New Spain, than has previously been assumed.

Notes

1. Inventory of the estate of Clemente Gutierrez (1785), Spanish Archives of New Mexico, #371.

2. Tabulation of estate inventories from the Spanish Archives of New Mexico, New Mexico Furniture History Project Files, Museum of International Folk Art, Santa Fe.

3. Inventory of the Estate of Juan de Archibuque (1721), Spanish Archives of New Mexico, #13. Typescript translation at History Library, Museum of New Mexico.

4. George P. Hammond and Agapito Rey, *Don Juan de Oñate, Colonizer of New Mexico, 1595–1628*, 2 vols. (Albuquerque: University of New Mexico Press, 1953), I, 233, 238, 266. The Spanish census of 1790 lists 44 carpenters in New Mexico.

5. *El Palacio*, vol. III, no. 2 (January 1916): 9.

Study Questions

1. What is the value in material culture?

2. Why were harineros so important? What did they mean to New Mexican women?

3. Describe the most typical type of New Mexican chests.

4. How common were wooden chests in a New Mexican household?

5. What happened to the quality of chests as a particular style became more popular?

6. What was the purpose of this study?

Preserving Hispanic Lifeways in New Mexico

Jon Hunner

In March of 1598, settlers from New Spain crossed the Rio Grande near present-day El Paso, Texas, held a thanksgiving mass and feast, and continued north to establish one of the first European colonies in North America. Led by don Juan de Oñate, these 400 settlers included soldiers, priests, miners, and farmers and were of Spanish, Mexican, Native American, and even Moorish heritage. For the next four centuries, the descendants of these and subsequent waves of settlers have created a unique culture and society in an isolated region of North America. Part heirloom tradition, part contemporary creation, the culture of twenty-first-century New Mexico is a rich combination of many peoples in which those of Spanish descent continue to play a major role. A variety of institutions, communities, and individuals in New Mexico collect, preserve, interpret, and exhibit the 400 years of Latino heritage—a heritage that has been a contested ground for generations. The first contested issue that we need to address is what to call New Mexicans of Spanish descent.

New Mexicans of Spanish descent are a diverse group. Most New Mexicans refer to people of Spanish descent as Hispanics. With 400 years of residence, some Hispanic families trace their ancestors back to the original colonists in 1598, while others are more recent immigrants from Mexico and Latin America. Additionally, over the centuries many New Mexicans of Spanish descent married Native Americans, which brought new traditions and cultures into Latino households. Thus, there is no unified culture that identifies people of Spanish descent in New Mexico. Essayist and social commentator Richard Rodriguez observes that there is no one name for people of Spanish descent. Since *Hispanic* is an English name, Rodriguez observes, it aptly illustrates the nature of Spanish descendants in the United States who are a complex minority in an Anglo world.[1] Granted, in other parts of the United States, *Latino* and *Latina* are often the preferred terms to identify people of Spanish descent, but here, the terms *Hispanics* and *Nuevo Mexicanos* will be used to describe New Mexicans of Spanish descent. The route that Oñate and his followers blazed in 1598 is known as El Camino Real de Tierra Adentro (The Royal Road to the Interior Lands).

Opened nine years before the English founded Jamestown, El Camino Real covered 1,500 miles from Mexico City to Santa Fe and took six months to traverse in each direction. It was the first European trail in North America, and for 100 years, it was the longest. El Camino Real was a route of colonization, commerce, and conquest. It also was a route of connection, linking the isolated frontier of New Mexico with the Spanish empire for over 200 years and, after 1821, with the independent nation of Mexico. Settlers, government officials, priests, and businessmen traversed the trail, carrying personal possessions, governmental decrees, and trade goods. El Camino Real brought into New Mexico Spanish language, religion, and culture. Established in the land that don Diego de Vargas in the 1690s called "remote beyond compare," this culture adapted to a place isolated from the rest of the Spanish empire and set among vibrant Native American civilizations. The mixture has created a culture in New Mexico older than and more inclusive of Native Americans than what the English produced in Virginia.

As the oldest European culture in the United States, Hispanic heritage has attracted national attention for several reasons. First, with the civil rights movement attacking the marginalized status of ethnic peoples since the 1960s, Hispanics have renewed the struggle against racism by celebrating their Mexican and Spanish roots. As historian Ignacio M. Garcia has observed: "A political consciousness of being Mexicano in the United States became the impetus for this social upheaval."² Second, as the Hispanic portion of the nation's population grew, New Mexico gained recognition as the oldest center of Latino culture in the United States and as a place to explore those roots. And finally, with Santa Fe as a nucleus of the New West in the 1980s and 1990s, the tourist industry appropriated Hispanic culture for economic development.

New Mexicans preserve Hispanic lifeways for many reasons. For some, Hispanic culture nurtured them in their family of origin, and they preserve it as a way of life. Other people, who were raised in different cultures, find meaning and a kinship with Hispanic culture and incorporate it into their lifeways to fulfill or satisfy something for them. And still others see Hispanic culture as a remnant of a romantic colonial past and appropriate it in order to either revive it (as if it had died with the Mexican-American War), to make it better (as if something is wrong with it), or just to make money.

Hispanic culture sells, which commodifies Hispanic heritage for economic development. Tourists flock to New Mexico to learn of ancient peoples, walk in the footsteps of early Spanish explorers, and see, hear, and taste the manifestations of the Columbian Exchange between Europeans and Native Americans. In New Mexico, the mystification or exoticism of Hispanic culture began with the art colonies in Taos and Santa Fe in the early 1900s. As cultural anthropologist Sylvia Rodríguez notes: "Tourism and the art colony together constituted the means by which this extraordinary transmutation was accomplished. The art colony functioned to convert the disparity between social reality and touristic fiction into a highly marketable set of images."³ Ironically, once Nuevo Mexicanos ceased posing a threat to the United States' hegemony in the late 1800s, their culture was appropriated to attract tourists and advance economic development. To be sure, not everyone who commodifies Hispanic culture is an outsider, since many Nuevo Mexicanos sell their arts and crafts at galleries, gift shops, and the annual Spanish Market in Santa Fe. Preservation, appropriation, and commodification are all part of the complex cultural mosaic of New Mexico.

Preserving Hispanic culture requires more than safeguarding the beliefs of one's parents and grandparents. After all, what does the word *culture* mean? It comes from the Latin word *cult* ("to grow"), as in cultivating a crop or in agriculture. Today culture means a people's beliefs, traditions, and transmitted knowledge; however, culture is not a static set of codes to live by. It is a constantly changing collection of strategies on how to live. Upon the foundation laid by one's family and ethnic background, culture grows with each person's own beliefs acquired through life experiences. As Spanish colonial historian David Weber notes: "Common cultural roots tie most Americans to the history of Western Europe, but culture is a process of never-ending construction and deconstruction rather than a static condition."⁴ In this respect, culture is a verb. Culture changes and adapts to the rapid transformation of our times as individuals add or subtract beliefs and lifeways.

The cultures of the many peoples of New Mexico have intermixed over the last 400 years and have created and continue to create new sets of treasured traditions. Like the activity of cultivating a crop, preserving Hispanic culture means nurturing something that lives, grows, and evolves. What historian George Sánchez observed about Mexican immigrants in Los Angeles holds true for Nuevo Mexicanos: "Ethnicity, therefore, is not a fixed set of customs surviving from life in Mexico, but rather a collective identity that emerged from daily experience in the United States."⁵ Preserving Hispanic lifeways in New Mexico requires not just celebrating a rich past, but also cultivating a vibrant and dynamic present.

Despite efforts to commodify Hispanic culture, people throughout the state are preserving Nuevo Mexicano heritage for reasons besides economic development. From federal and state programs and museums to grassroots historic preservation efforts, Hispanic heritage is nurtured by many people and organizations. The federal government, led by the

Figures 40 and 41. Northern New Mexico and southern Colorado have long been considered part of the same cultural region and are linked by folk traditions. Here is a photo of a classic hand-carved death cart in the collections of the Taylor Museum of the Colorado Springs Fine Arts Center. Photo courtesy Colorado Springs Fine Arts Center. Compare that photo with this modern figure of a skeleton in an old flatbed truck at South Fork, Colorado, along U.S. Highway 160. The truck and its driver represent a modern death cart to traveling tourists. Photo by Andrew Gulliford, 2003.

National Park Service, has initiated several programs both within the state and with Mexico to highlight the importance of Hispanic heritage in the Southwest. New Mexico's state government, through its museums, monuments, and educational institutions, also focuses on both the originating foundation of the Spanish in New Mexico and the current manifestations and evolution of Nuevo Mexicano culture. Nongovernmental organizations work to preserve and interpret Hispanic heritage. Local towns and communities also honor their Hispanic roots through exhibits, neighborhood revitalization projects, and annual celebrations. And individuals throughout New Mexico strive to protect and acknowledge the often centuries-old traditions of their ancestors. The remainder of this essay will explore a number of these innovative initiatives, beginning with federal programs, then exploring state and local government and nongovernmental and grassroots projects. Because of the number of projects under way in New Mexico, the following descriptions are an incomplete listing of the variety of efforts ongoing to preserve Hispanic lifeways.

The United States government has been a partner in the preservation of Hispanic heritage for a long time. During the Great Depression, it targeted Nuevo Mexicano communities for heritage preservation. As historian Suzanne Forrest notes: "A significant proportion of federal funds were channeled into programs designed to assist Hispanic villagers to regain economic independence by augmenting their small-scale agricultural activities with native arts and crafts cottage industries, by modernizing Hispanic village agriculture, and by restoring the fertility of the land."[6] Not all was altruistic with the federal program. According to Forrest, "The more pragmatic economic origins of the Hispanic New Deal derived from a desire to preserve the native cultures as lucrative tourist attractions and prevent the villagers from becoming a rootless, landless population permanently dependent upon federal relief."[7] The New Deal launched many initiatives that put local people to work as woodcarvers and furniture makers and also documented many of the rural villages through Farm Security Administration photographers such as Russell Lee and John Collier, Jr.[8] The federal programs provided some relief, but often a paternalistic attitude prevailed. Public historian Jerrold Hirsch wrote: "The New Deal in Hispanic New Mexico . . . pursued both cultural and economic reform. New Deal policymakers . . . talked about preserving the village (a static notion), when they should have asked Hispanic villagers the more realistic and democratic question: How can we help you conserve and adapt to a changing world that which you value in your cultural heritage?"[9] Today's community public history projects continue to ask this key question.

Since the 1960s, the National Park Service (NPS) has actively preserved Hispanic heritage. On the University of New Mexico campus in Albuquerque, Dr. Joseph Sanchez oversees the Spanish Colonial unit for the NPS, which collects and translates Spanish colonial documents and maps. The U.S.-Mexico Affairs Office of the NPS in Las Cruces conducts cultural exchanges with the Instituto Nacional de Antropología e Historia (INAH) in Mexico and is working on a binational agreement to preserve the remnants of El Camino Real de Tierra Adentro on both sides of the border. The U.S.-Mexico Affairs Office cosponsors with INAH an annual conference on El Camino Real that is forging new ground in innovative ways that the two countries can use to protect and interpret their shared cultural resources. In October 2000, the U.S. Congress added El Camino Real to the National Trails System. The NPS also provides funding to the New Mexico Historic Preservation Division, which helps protect the Hispanic cultural and historic resources of the state.[10]

At the state level, New Mexico has an impressive cabinet-level cultural agency, the Division of Cultural Affairs (DCA). The DCA operates a collection of museums and monuments with major units exhibiting Nuevo Mexicano culture.[11] The Palace of the Governors and the Museum of International Folk Art in Santa Fe, the National Hispanic Cultural Center in Albuquerque, and the New Mexico Farm and Ranch Heritage Museum in Las Cruces all devote at least part and at times all of their exhibition space to celebrating Nuevo Mexicano heritage. As the oldest governmental building in the United States, the Palace of the Governors Museum represents the political and architectural legacy of the 400 years of Hispanic presence in New Mexico. The building that houses the museum was built in 1610, and from then until the 1880s, it served as the capitol of New Mexico. The museum does not limit its exhibitions to just Nuevo Mexicano life, but its exhibits, historical rooms, and interior courtyard do depict the Spanish and Mexican eras.[12]

The Museum of International Folk Art (MOIFA) dedicated a Hispanic Heritage Wing in 1989 to display the rich history and culture of Nuevo Mexicanos. The permanent exhibit, "Familia y Fe" (Family and Faith), focuses on village life, faith, and the syncretism between Nuevo Mexicanos, Native Americans, and Anglo Americans by displaying 5,000 artifacts such as religious art, textiles, furniture, tinwork, household and agricultural items, and jewelry. "Familia y Fe" illustrates that "Family and Faith are the two major sources of strength and continuity in Hispanic New Mexico. Religious faith was the foundation upon which the Spanish colony of New Mexico was established and maintained over several hundred years, while the strong family was the core of colonial and nineteenth-century society. Both continue to have significance in present-day New Mexico."[13] The Hispanic Heritage Wing at MOIFA actively showcases Nuevo Mexicano lifeways and celebrates Hispanic heritage.[14]

The New Mexico Farm and Ranch Heritage Museum in Las Cruces devotes part of its display to the role that Hispanics have played in the state's agricultural history. The permanent exhibit "Generations" describes the contributions that both prominent and ordinary Nuevo Mexicanos have made to ranching and farming. Some of the people featured include Diego de Santandér (1640–67), a priest who brought Spanish farming methods to the pueblo at Gran Quivera; Juana Luján (1684–1762), a woman who farmed and ranched near San Ildefonso Pueblo and acquired porcelain and silk from China and linen and clothing from France; Soloman Luna (1858–1912), a sheep rancher, banker, and politician who helped write New Mexico's constitution, which includes a requirement for all state documents to be bilingual; and Fabián García (1871–1948), who as a professor at what would become New Mexico State University revolutionized the cultivation of chile and pecans. In his will, García bequeathed most of his estate to the college with this warning: "Do not forget poor students with Spanish names. . . . I was a poor boy and I know what hardships are." With this money, NMSU built the García Annex, which today houses among others the Chicano Studies Program.[15]

One of the newest jewels in New Mexico's museum system is the National Hispanic Cultural Center (NHCC) in Albuquerque. Opened in 2000, this facility houses a variety of activities to celebrate not just Nuevo Mexicanos, but Latino heritage throughout the country. With an archive, library, performing arts theater, video production studio, and exhibition space, the NHCC preserves Hispanic heritage through oral and community histories, museum exhibits, publications, dance, music and drama productions, and genealogy records. At its opening, the NHCC launched itself with three main exhibits in its 10,000-square-foot gallery spaces: "Nuevo México Profundo: Rituals of an Indo-Hispano Homeland," a photograph collection by Miguel Gandert; "La Luz: Contemporary Latino Art in the United States," which showcases artists of Hispanic, Puerto Rico, Cuban American, Mexican American, and other Latin American heritages; and "Barelas a Travéz de Los Años: A Pictorial History of Barelas."

As the home neighborhood of the NHCC in south Albuquerque, Barelas is representative of Hispanic life in the state. The introduction to the Barelas exhibit catalog states:

> Barelas has, over the years, been affected by every major social, economic, and cultural trend that Albuquerque has undergone since its founding in 1706. Subsistence agriculture, economic booms, periodic flooding, the impact of the railroad, the arrival of Route 66, the coming of the military bases, suburbanization, structural poverty, urban renewal and dislocation, gentrification, and, more recently, economic and cultural revival are all part of Barelas' history.[16]

Part of the Barelas exhibit includes an interactive computer component where neighbors and the public can identify the 750 photographs on file or submit their names as future interviewees for oral histories. In this way, the community participates in the writing of its own history.[17] The New Mexico Endowment for the Humanities (NMEH) supports preservation efforts through its grants program and *chatauqua* series, which features vivid monologues by actors in historic dress. For example, the NMEH funded "Impact Los Alamos," an oral history project that documented the commuters, mainly Hispanics, who worked at the scientific laboratories of Los Alamos while living in nearby villages. Oral historian Carlos Vásquez, who directed "Impact Los Alamos," observed that many Hispanics who work at Los Alamos National Laboratory live in two worlds (the traditional one of their villages and the high-tech one at the laboratory) and that the high wages earned at Los Alamos support the traditional lifeways. Like many people in New Mexico, Hispanics who work at Los Alamos every day negotiate between very diverse cultures. "Impact Los Alamos" brought new emphasis and analysis to the relationship of Los Alamos and its largely Hispanic neighboring communities in northern New Mexico. The NMEH funds many other projects around the state that preserve and exhibit Hispanic culture and lifeways.[18]

Several programs at New Mexico State University focus on Hispanic heritage. A collection of New Mexican and Mexican *retablos* (paintings on tin of Catholic saints and devotional art) resides at the University Art Gallery at NMSU. From the more than 1,700 items in the collection, an exhibit, "El Favor de Las Santos: The Retablo Collection of NMSU," toured 182 retablos to museums in the United States and Mexico. The cocurators of the exhibit, Elizabeth Zarur and Charles Lovell, published a book from the collection: *Art and Faith in Mexico: The Nineteenth Century Retablo Tradition*.[19] Also at NMSU, the Public History Program has partnered with local organizations, the Division of Cultural Affairs, and the NPS to survey the historic districts of Las Trampas, Columbus, Mesilla, and Las Cruces to record oral histories of Hispanics in New Mexico, to help revitalize historic neighborhoods, and to preserve adobe buildings.[20]

At the University of New Mexico in Albuquerque, the School of Architecture and Planning and its Center for Cultural Landscape Studies are exploring the ways that history, culture, and the physical environment shape and are shaped in the region. In particular, Chris Wilson and his students have worked with communities around the state in developing plans to preserve historic plazas, a direct legacy of Spanish colonial and Mexican times.

In Santa Fe, the Spanish Colonial Arts Society was created in 1925 to preserve the cultural and artistic traditions of northern New Mexico. Since 1950, it has sponsored the Traditional Spanish Market, an open-air celebration held on the Santa Fe plaza every July, which showcases 300 artists and 75 youth artists and attracts over 75,000 visitors. In addition to the Spanish Market, the society has 3,000 objects of Spanish colonial arts and crafts in its collection. Over the decades, the society has shared the collection with the public through loans to the Palace of the Governors, the Museum of International Folk Art, and El Rancho de las Golondrinas. In July 2002, the society opened a new facility in Santa Fe with 5,000 square feet of galleries and another 6,500 square feet that will hold curatorial offices, a research library, a conservation laboratory, and collection storage space.[21]

One final institution completes this incomplete account of those museums that are devoted to exhibiting Hispanic life in New Mexico. El Rancho de las Golondrinas (just south of Santa Fe) is a living history museum that brings alive Spanish colonial times. With its collection of eighteenth- and nineteenth-century haciendas, *molinos* (mills), blacksmith and wheelwright shops, and religious sites such as a *penitente morada* (chapel), *descansos* (roadside crosses), and a *camposanto* (cemetery), El Rancho de las Golondrinas offers an innovative opportunity to experience Spanish colonial life.[22]

Cities, towns, and villages around the state have recognized Hispanic heritage in numerous ways. In the early 1980s, Santa Fe began to aggressively market "Santa Fe style." Touting Santa Fe as a place where Anglos, Hispanics, and Native Americans brew a yeasty cultural concoction of Old and New West, Santa Fe style captured the imagination of national magazines and international tourists. By the early 1990s, readers of *Conde Nast's Traveler* magazine voted Santa Fe as their top tourist destination.[23] Santa Fe's resultant popularity has attracted outsiders, and the increased cost of living has pushed many Santa Feans, including Hispanics whose ancestry goes back generations, out of the core of the city and even out of Santa Fe altogether. Trendy stores, art galleries, and gift shops have replaced local businesses around the plaza, which is no longer a destination for local Santa Feans. In reaction to the transformation of Santa Fe from a capital of Hispanic culture to a trendy "Disney-does-adobe" theme park, El Museo Cultural de Santa Fe was created. At its 16,000-square-foot facility in the railyard west of downtown, El Museo Cultural offers a variety of programs, including art exhibits, guitar and Spanish classes, GED courses, tours of local galleries for young people to acquaint them with gallery owners, and adobe workshops. Despite 400 years of history, until El Museo Cultural came about, no one place dealt with the contemporary Hispanic experience in Santa Fe. With the downtown plaza no longer a central part of Hispanic life in Santa Fe, perhaps El Museo Cultural and other efforts at the railyard will create a new plaza for local residents.[24]

In the southern part of the state, the village of Mesilla continues its efforts to preserve its historic district. Founded in 1849 as a refuge for Mexicans fleeing the annexation of New Mexico by the United States, Mesilla has retained much of its historic characteristics and still holds on to its distinctive Mexican character. To preserve this heritage, Mesilla's activities are twofold: first, the village has acknowledged that its National Historic District is threatened, and second, it has developed a plan to address the decay of its adobe structures. The historic district was placed on New Mexico's Most Endangered Historic Places list in 1999.[25]

To counter the loss of historic structures, residents and the town government of Mesilla are focusing on adobe preservation. For adobe structures, exterior cement stucco (introduced in the 1930s) locks moisture inside the walls. Since adobes are merely sun-dried mud bricks, they erode when in contact with water, and when exposed to water, abode walls melt away. Villages and communities throughout the Southwest are losing historic buildings as well as family residences to the dissolving impact of cement stucco.

Over the last decade, realization about the effect of cement stucco on adobe structures has led to a revival of the ancient art of lime plastering. Mike Taylor, when he was deputy director of the State Monuments of New Mexico, noted: "A renaissance of sorts is taking place in New Mexico with the reintroduction of lime plaster, which was used to protect the surfaces of adobe during the Spanish colonial and Territorial periods. This traditional technique is being reintroduced from Mexico."[26] This reintroduction is led by the Taylor brothers, Mike and Pat, who are collaborating with INAH (Mexico's counterpart to the National Park Service) to bring experts from Mexico to lead workshops teaching the technique of applying lime plaster to exterior walls. Since 1993, TICAL (Taller Internacional Sobre la Cal, or International Lime Plaster Workshop) has brought together adobe preservationists from both sides of the border to help share their knowledge. At TICAL VI, held in October 1999 in Mesilla, 85 people from New Mexico, Arizona, Colorado, Texas, and Mexico learned both the theory and the practicum of lime plastering. Working on a 120-year-old adobe house, participants learned from lime restorers and plaster experts from Mexico and the United States how to prepare adobe walls, mix lime plaster, and apply the plaster to the exterior walls. A video on how to apply lime plaster to adobe structures was created by NMSU's Public History Program, available from the town of Mesilla.[27] Community members continue to work to preserve such adobe structures in Mesilla and southern New Mexico.

Mike and Pat Taylor come from a long line of Nuevo Mexicano heritage preservationists. Their mother and father, Mary and J. Paul Taylor, have donated the family's historic home on Mesilla's plaza to New Mexico State Monuments. In the future, the public will be able to view the historic adobe home along with hundreds of art and artifacts that highlight the Hispanic heritage of the state.

Another organization that combines history with heritage preservation is Cornerstones Community Partnerships. Based in Santa Fe, Cornerstones forms partnerships with communities to strengthen their cultural values by restoring historic buildings, encouraging traditional building practices, and developing skills and leadership among the youth of New Mexico. Since 1986, Cornerstones has forged dynamic links between historic preservationists and the villages and towns of the state. Focusing at first on the small adobe Catholic churches that dot the mountains and valleys of northern New Mexico, Cornerstones has helped over 125 communities repair historic structures and has trained community members in traditional building skills. In 1992, Cornerstones won the National Preservation Honor Award from the National Trust for Historic Preservation for their efforts to restore the historic churches in New Mexico. Despite the appearance

Figure 42. Three Hispanic children, one seven years old, died possibly of the Spanish flu and are buried in the La Garita cemetery in the northern San Luis Valley. Photo by Andrew Gulliford, 2001.

that life is ebbing out of the villages of New Mexico, communities that partner with Cornerstones often illustrate how religious faith and heritage cultivation can revitalize a community and recover lost traditions.[28]

Essential to the revitalization of Hispanic communities through historic preservation is Cornerstones Youth Training Program. In addition to assisting villages in saving historic churches, Cornerstones also provides opportunities for teenagers and young adults to learn traditional building methods. The key to Cornerstones' success is community commitment. As outsiders in these close-knit villages and towns, Cornerstones has learned that it is necessary to "make [its] involvement contingent upon the leadership and ownership from the community. . . . Without the community commitment, we don't come. It must be the responsibility of the community to get people out for work days."[29] In the last five years, Cornerstones has expanded beyond the Hispanic villages of northern New Mexico. Their projects now include a rejuvenation of traditional stone masonry at the Pueblo of Zuni, rehabilitation of Protestant churches, and restoration of churches in southern New Mexico and west Texas.

People who preserve Hispanic lifeways in New Mexico honor their ancestral traditions, revitalize small towns and villages, celebrate a complex culture, and learn about one of the oldest European presences in North America. Preserving Hispanic lifeways also provides opportunities for spiritual, cultural, and economic development. As New Mexico moves toward a majority of its population being either Hispanic or Native American, its Hispanic heritage continues to adapt to our changing times while revitalizing traditional practices and beliefs. From reviving lime plastering to creating and exhibiting Hispanic folk art, from rehabilitating adobe churches to recording life histories, organizations and people from around New Mexico preserve Hispanic lifeways. Today Hispanic and non-Hispanic residents live in Spanish colonial–style houses, eat *carné adovado* (New World red chile with Old World pork), speak Spanish and Spanglish, and observe Cinco de Mayo in May, the Day of the Dead at Halloween, and Las Posadas at Christmas. Throughout the 400 years of Hispanic presence in New Mexico, a dynamic process of change and adaptation has occurred between the peoples of the Land of Enchantment. Nuevo Mexicano heritage in the twenty-first century will continue to nurture both Hispanics and non-Hispanics alike.

Notes

1. Richard Rodriguez, in "Conversations in Latino Identity," Latino USA program, #388/389, National Public Radio, broadcast during the weeks of September 15 and 22, 2000.

2. Ignacio M. García, "Constructing the Chicano Movement: Synthesis of a Militant Ethos," *Perspectives in Mexican-American Studies* 6 (1997): 3.

3. Sylvia Rodriguez, "Art, Tourism, and Race Relations in Taos," in *Discovered Country: Tourism and Survival in the American West*, ed. Scott Norris (Albuquerque: Stone Ladder Press, 1994), 146.

4. David Weber, *The Spanish Frontier in North America* (New York: Oxford University Press, 1997), 10.

5. George Sánchez, *Becoming Mexican-American: Ethnicity, Culture, and Identity in Chicano Los Angeles, 1900–1945* (New York: Oxford University Press, 1993), 11.

6. Suzanne Forrest, *The Preservation of the Village: New Mexico's Hispanics and the New Deal* (Albuquerque: University of New Mexico Press, 1989), 63.

7. Ibid., 16.

8. Russell Lee, *Far from Main Street: Three Photographers in Depression-Era New Mexico*, ed. Russell Lee, John Collier, Jr., and Jack Delano (Santa Fe : Museum of New Mexico Press, 1994).

9. Jerrold Hirsch, "Cherished Values: The New Deal, Cultural Policy and Public History," *The Public Historian* 10 (fall 1990): 78.

10. The web site for the New Mexico Historic Preservation Division is at http://www.museums.state.nm.us/hpd/.

11. To access the Office of Cultural Affairs' web site, go to http://www.nmoca.org/.

12. For the Palace of Governors' web site, go to http://palaceofthegovernors.org/.

13. "Familia Y Fe," exhibit publication, Museum of International Folk Art (Santa Fe: Museum of New Mexico, 1989), 2.

14. The web site for the Hispanic Heritage Wing is at http://www.state.nm.us/MOIFAOnLine/Permanent-Collections/hispanicheritage.html.

15. Text from the "Generations" exhibit at New Mexico Farm and Ranch Heritage Museum. Its web site is at http:/www.frhm.org.

16. Barelas a Travéz de Los Años exhibit catalog (Albuquerque: National Hispanic Cultural Center, 2000), 6.

17. Interview with Carlos Vásquez, September 2000, in Albuquerque and http://www.nmmnh-abq.mus.nm.us/hcc.

18. For NMEH's web site, go to http://www.nmeh.org.

19. Interview with gallery director Charles Lovell, September 2000, in Las Cruces; for the retablos' web site, go to http://crl.nmsu.edu/Research/Projects/retablos/Newretablo.html.

20. For the Public History Program web site, go to http://web.nmsu.edu/~publhist/.

21. Interview with Stuart Ashman, September 2000, in Santa Fe; for the Spanish Colonial Society's web site, go to http://www.spanishcolonial.org.

22. The web site address is http://golondrinas.org/history.html.

23. Alfred Borcover, "Poll Ranks Santa Fe as World's Best Travel Destination," *Albuquerque Journal*, September 27, 1992, C8.

24. Interview in Santa Fe with President Tom Romero and board member Angie Gabaldon Shaffer, September 15, 2000.

25. To see the Most Endangered Historic Places list for New Mexico, go to the New Mexico Heritage Preservation Alliance at http://www.nmheritage.org/.

26. Mike Taylor, "Earthen Architectural Traditions in New Mexico," *CRM* 22, no. 6 (1999): 26.

27. To purchase the video, contact Susan Kruger, Town of Mesilla, PO Box 10, Mesilla, NM 88046.

28. Barbara Zook and Michael Kramer, "Training Youth in Vernacular Earthen Architecture and Associated Cultural Traditions," *CRM* 20, no. 7 (1997), and at http://www.cstones.org/.

29. Karen Nilsson Brandt, "Preservation Program Depends on Community," *Los Alamos Monitor*, April 9, 1995.

Study Questions

1. Why is New Mexico's cultural heritage so unique?

2. Describe how New Mexico was settled. Why was El Camino Real so important?

3. Explain why it is important for New Mexico to preserve Hispanic culture.

4. Why did the federal government help New Mexicans during the Great Depression?

5. What is the significance of the exhibits in the Museum of International Folk Art, the New Mexico Farm and Ranch Heritage Museum, and the National Hispanic Cultural Center (NHCC)? What special part of New Mexican heritage does each exhibit celebrate?

6. Compare the three museums from question 5 to the other four institutions discussed in this essay. Briefly describe how other places in the state are promoting New Mexican heritage.

7. How has Cornerstones Community Partnerships helped New Mexican communities?

8. In your opinion, is there a need for the Cornerstones' Youth Training Program? Why or why not?

Where Is the "Mexican" in "New Mexican"?

Enacting History, Enacting Dominance in the Santa Fe Fiesta

Sarah Horton

Perhaps no other issue of Latino public history has been more inflammatory than the equal inclusion of both Spanish and indigenous heritages in commemorations of Latino history. In the wake of the Columbus Quincentenary and New Mexico's celebration of its colonization by Spanish conquistador don Juan de Oñate, astute public historians should be wary of speaking of any singular "Latino history." In American communities with a Spanish legacy, there appears to be no consensus among public officials or historians on how best to commemorate the history of the Spanish empire. An ethical issue even more difficult than the honoring of a Spanish conquistador is the public staging of historical moments of the Spanish conquest. What are the messages we transmit when we use living actors to enact historical dramas of a conquest whose legacy of inequality still survives? Is the reenactment of the Spanish conquest an innocent commemoration of past Spanish glory, or does it serve as a public sanction of existing racial inequalities?

These questions raise a broader concern in history, that of the partiality of all historical narratives. In attempts to tell history, one group's experience frequently assumes the status of a dominant narrative.[1] In public portrayals of history, these concerns are all the weightier. As Susan Davis has noted in her history of parades in Philadelphia, public actions are always political, illustrating "who should have the right to display themselves collectively in the streets."[2] Some groups are not accorded the right of public display, thus silencing alternative versions of history. Collective action in public spaces implicitly carries the weight of public sanction, she suggests. If we follow analysts of public ceremony in their suggestion that rituals "portray the idealized social relations envisioned by those in power,"[3] then what is the vision of social order sanctioned by the commemoration of the Spanish conquest?

This essay will consider these issues by way of examining the Santa Fe Fiesta, an annual public commemoration of the Spanish reconquest of New Mexico. Revived by Museum of New Mexico officials in the early twentieth century as a lure for tourists and settlers alike, New Mexico's Hispanos[4] have gradually reappropriated the fiesta as a means for the "active preservation of Hispanic heritage in New Mexico."[5] An examination of the history of the fiesta thus illustrates that although it ritually reenacts the Spanish reconquest of New Mexico, it also comments obliquely on another—the Anglo usurpation of Hispanos' former control over the region.

The Santa Fe Fiesta as Conquest Drama

A celebration of Spanish continuity in Santa Fe, the fiesta simultaneously marks a moment in which the Spaniards subdued the Pueblo Indians who had expelled them from Santa Fe in 1680. Incorporating living Pueblo Indians, it dramatizes not only the Spanish reoccupation of the city, but also the conversion of Pueblo Indians to Catholicism. A Catholic ritual giving thanks to Nuestra Señora del Rosario, La Conquistadora, a Marian icon, for the Spaniards' bloodless reoccupation of the city,[6] fiesta rhetoric claims that this shared religion serves as the "ties that bind (three cultures) together in an unbroken bond of unity."[7]

Thus the fiesta may be seen as a variant of a genre of conquest dramas that portray the subjugation of indigenous peoples and their conversion to Christianity, common in mestizo and indigenous communities across Latin America. Such dramas began when the colonizing Spaniards forced indigenous peoples to act out feats of Spanish military prowess and the inevitable triumph of Christianity. The Spaniards initially forced indigenous groups in Latin America to reenact the Spanish victory over the "infidel" Moors and thus their success in unifying a Christian Spain.[8] According to historian Ramón Gutiérrez, as they traveled north, the Spaniards then forced the Pueblo Indians of New Mexico to act out the defeat of the powerful indigenous groups of Mexico as a model for the conquest of New Mexico. Indeed, Gutiérrez notes that don Juan de Oñate not only entered New Mexico with the same Marian icon, "Our Lady of the Remedies," that Cortés had carried into Tenochtitlán in 1519, but also that he made the first Indians he encountered in the Southwest greet him as the Aztec emperor Montezuma had greeted Hernán Cortés 80 years earlier.[9]

Apparently the Spaniards believed in routinized action as a powerful vehicle for bringing about hegemony. Historians of the Spanish conquest have noted that dramatic representations were instrumental in conveying a desired social order to the vanquished and effective both in achieving Spanish military victory and evangelization.[10] Gutiérrez argues that the message of Spanish superiority and indigenous inferiority became internalized through such conquest dramas' repeated reenactment. He writes:

> From the moment the Spaniards reached the banks of the Rio Grande . . . what the Indians saw and heard was but a well-choreographed political drama that was to teach them the meaning of their own defeat, of Spanish sovereignty, and of the social hierarchies that would prevail under Christian rule.[11]

As historians of the Spanish conquest describe them, such rituals or "conquest theaters" had a powerful ideological effect on those reenacting them. Anthropologist Sylvia Rodríguez, for example, describes an "ambivalence" among the Pueblos who continue to perform the *matachines* dance today.[12] Can the reenactment of the Spanish conquest in the Santa Fe Fiesta be anything other than the "conquest theater" that Gutiérrez so disturbingly describes?

There is one important difference between the Santa Fe Fiesta and conquest dramas staged in mestizo and indigenous communities in Latin America, however. In New Mexico, there are two layers of conquest, one atop the other. This racial stratigraphy of New Mexico makes the meaning of the fiesta's conquest drama quite different. In Latin America, conquest dramas appear to perform and enact the dominance of European heritage, perpetuating the existing racial hierarchy. In New Mexico, however, the fiesta is part conquest theater and part theater of resistance to Hispanics' own conquest.

The Santa Fe Fiesta and Spanish Identity

The Santa Fe Fiesta, a civic celebration funded largely by the city and tourism revenues, commemorates Spanish conquistador don Diego de Vargas's 1692 reconquest of the city for the crown of Spain following the Pueblo Revolt of 1680. The Pueblo Revolt was led by Popé, a medicine man from San Juan who had fled to the northernmost pueblo, Taos, to escape Spanish control and plot a rebellion. Resentful of the Spaniards' attempts to stamp out their religious beliefs and disrupt their social organization, the Pueblos had desecrated the symbols of their conversion and forced the Spanish colonists to retreat to El Paso. The surviving Spanish colonists of the revolt— primarily from Santa Fe and from Isleta—gathered in El Paso until don Diego de Vargas led the 1692 attempt to resettle New Mexico for the king of Spain, Carlos II. According to fiesta tradition, don Diego de Vargas made a promise to the Marian icon of La Conquistadora that if he were able to peacefully reoccupy the city, he would hold an annual fiesta in her honor.

The reenactment of this reconquest of Santa Fe forms the heart of the contemporary Santa Fe Fiesta. In this reenactment, also called the "Entrada," a young Hispanic man on horseback, dressed as Don Diego de Vargas and accompanied by a *cuadrilla* of men, negotiates with a Pueblo man dressed as Domingo Naranjo, a Tesuque chief, for the Spaniards' reoccupation of the city. In the script for the 1997 Entrada, don Diego de Vargas tells Domingo Naranjo:

Calm yourselves and be assured that we do not intend to do you any harm whatsoever. . . . Pueblo Indians of New Mexico, I have been sent by the King of Spain to ensure that we all live in peace. . . . I leave it up to you to decide whether we shall settle Santa Fe in peace or whether we shall settle Santa Fe in war.

The Pueblo chief submits and de Vargas calls for the baptism of two Pueblo children as "a sign . . . of our two worlds coming together as one." Then he and his men shout, "Qué viva Carlos Segundo! Qué viva el rey, nuestro señor!" Thus the fiesta clearly is an enactment of Spanish domination, glorifying the reconquest of the region and the long-standing Hispanic presence in the Southwest.

The fiesta may be seen, in part, as but one manifestation of a broader Anglo American fascination with the region's Spanish past. The Spanish heritage of the Southwest, romanticized in the writings of authors such as Helen Hunt Jackson and Charles Lummis, has long proven a powerful draw for tourists.[13] Once native Spanish speakers had all but been dispossessed, it was easier for literati to fondly remember the Spanish era as a "romantic, colorful era of leisurely uncomplicated living."[14] Even today, this romantic portrayal of the Spanish colonial era lingers on in New Mexico's history museums, where one finds a suit of metal armor directly from Spain alongside the more prosaic New Mexican folk crafts such as tinwork and *santos*. As one docent at New Mexico's State Museum, the Palace of the Governors, explained, "We play up the Spanish past here since your average tourist is unaware of the strong Spanish presence in the Southwest. They think the Southwest is Mexican, but they don't always know it was also Spanish." In short, New Mexico emphasizes its Spanish heritage partly because of the images of military glory and idyllic living this history conjures in the minds of Anglo Americans.

Indeed, the public acceptance of this Spanish-dominant version of history in New Mexico is not limited to the history museums. Prior to the fiesta, those involved in the event visit the public schools of Santa Fe in costume to attempt to spread enthusiasm about the event among the city's youths, to demonstrate to them "how proud we should be who we are,"[15] as one fiesta participant put it. At every public school, the young man portraying don Diego de Vargas selects one young Hispanic boy, who dons a conquistador's helmet, to be crowned "de Vargas for the day." The idea, say fiesta participants, is to encourage Hispanic youths to preserve their cultural heritage and to perhaps one day become active in the event themselves. Meanwhile, many public school teachers ask their classes to produce narratives and pictures on the theme of what the fiesta means to Santa Fe, which are then placed on display during the event. Such activities illustrate the degree of public acceptance the state's Spanish past has achieved. Indeed, Spanish heritage has been comfortably enshrined as the dominant narrative of Latino history in the state.

However, what are the implications for other groups—notably Native Americans and Latinos with indigenous heritage—of enshrining this Spanish version of New Mexico's history? An examination of the Santa Fe Fiesta may provide some answers.

First, it is noteworthy that the All Indian Pueblo Council and the state's Eight Northern Pueblos have boycotted the fiesta since the late 1970s. The boycott may be traced to the 1977 decision of a former Fiesta Council president to send a letter to the state's Eight Northern Pueblos requesting that they vacate the plaza area during fiesta. Hoping to reduce the number of tourists at the event and indeed return the celebration to the locals, the letter sent by this former president asked Pueblo vendors not to sell their wares that weekend in their traditional places in the portal of the city's historic Palace of the Governors, across from the fiesta stage. As one former Fiesta Council member remembered of the controversial letter, "It was a slap in the face to the Indians." Angry Pueblo leaders responded by boycotting the event, stating in the daily paper that the letter evinced an "unwillingness to have Indians participate in the Santa Fe Fiesta." In

1980, a nearby Pueblo even held its own commemoration of the history excluded by the fiesta—a celebration of the 1680 revolt against Spanish rule.[16]

The Pueblos' anger at the fiesta's glorification of their defeat led to a decline in the number of Pueblo Indians willing to participate in the event, whether in the leading role of Domingo Naranjo, the Tesuque chief who accepts de Vargas's return, or in the role of Indian princess. When non-Indians were recruited to fill the key role of Naranjo, some Pueblos protested the inaccuracy of the clothing worn by the Anglo actors, which they saw as a denigrating mockery. "I find the [portrayal] insulting to the . . . Pueblo warrior leaders, women and children who fought and died during the time of conquest," one Tesuque woman wrote the Santa Fe newspaper in 1989.[17] "We would appreciate it if our leaders and warriors were not portrayed in the Fiesta celebration." The Pueblos have continued to call for an end to this "celebration of the conquest of their people by Spain" through the 1990s.[18]

Public concern with the fiesta's portrayal of Pueblos peaked again in 1992, when New Mexico folklorist Jeannette De Bouzek captured on film the tears of a young man from Santo Domingo Pueblo who had agreed to portray the role of Domingo Naranjo.[19] As the other "Indians" portrayed by young Anglo and Hispanic men assemble onstage in burlap sacks, red and black war paint, and large headdresses,[20] Randy, the Pueblo man portraying chief Naranjo, wavers in his resolve. "It looks like everyone else looks pretty savage, more savage than me," he comments. One "Indian" asks Randy if he too would like to put on a headdress, and Randy declines with discomfort. This moment cannot help but uncomfortably recall Gutiérrez's description of the Pueblos' involvement in the conquest dramas. He writes of the Pueblos:

> They continually relived their own defeat, their own humiliation and dishonor, and openly mocked themselves with those caricatures of Indian culture the conquistadores so fancied.[21]

Reflecting on this moment later, Randy says, "If I stopped to take a hard look at the reason [the fiesta is] being celebrated, I probably wouldn't have done it."[22] With her portrayal of this young Santo Domingo Pueblo man, De Bouzek captures a rare moment in which the hegemonic power of the fiesta's conquest drama unravels. As Randy watches the portrayal of the Pueblos through these Anglo actors' eyes, the fiesta is seen for what it is—a glorification of the subjugation of the region's Pueblo Indians.

The Fiesta Council has taken steps to appease the event's critics. After the screening of the De Bouzek video, the 1992 fiesta reflected attempts to emphasize peaceful coexistence rather than heroic reconquest. The 1992 Entrada began with the new introduction, "Spanish and Indians have lived in harmony as a direct result of the reconquest by Don Diego de Vargas."[23] The council added a "Mass of Reconciliation," which then-president Rick Berardinelli described as "to help heal old wounds between Pueblos and Hispanics."[24] For the first time in the event's history, the young man portraying Don Diego de Vargas performed the Entrada with a crucifix rather than a sword. Council members also changed the portrayal of Native Americans in the event, attempting to make their attire culturally appropriate and to present them as "equals" in the event along with the members of the de Vargas staff.[25] Finally, in subsequent fiestas, the council also made the script for the Entrada subject to the approval of the governor of Tesuque Pueblo, the home of Domingo Naranjo, with whom de Vargas negotiated the Spaniards' return.[26] While one Santa Fe newspaper called the 1993 fiesta a "model for the future,"[27] Pueblo leaders still claimed the fiesta "smacks of oppression" and "should be done away with."[28]

Where Is the "Mexican" in "New Mexican"?

The fiesta also serves to exalt Spanish culture over other forms of Latino heritage. While other forms of Latino culture are featured throughout the fiesta weekend—particularly in the form of Mexican mariachi singers and dancers—the core of the event continues to glorify a Spanish heritage. This may be seen in the

Fiesta Council's selection of youths to portray the key roles of de Vargas and Fiesta Queen in the event. The requirements for such youths—a Hispanic surname, nativity in New Mexico, residency in the county for the past five years, and proficiency in the Spanish language—select for a very particular kind of Latino background.[29] For example, one young man who had been selected as de Vargas remarked of a fluent Spanish speaker who had been his competitor, "[He] spoke Spanish really well, but he spoke more of a *mocho* Spanish. I believe that if you're going to speak Spanish in public, it is important it be standard and correct."[30] Thus though this contestant had a fluent command of Spanish, his delivery may have been too distinctively marked with ethnic and class connotations to play the role. The council may select against candidates who appear to have a more "Chicano" or "Mexican" background in their search for a person deemed appropriate to portray this conquistador.

The specter of the council's elimination of other forms of Latino heritage reared its head again in 1999 when Monica Maestas, a young woman with mixed heritage who had competed for the role of Fiesta Queen, withdrew from the event, charging racism.[31] The candidate, whose father is from Isleta del Sur Pueblo and who herself was an active member of both Mecha and the Native American Students' Association at college, identified herself strongly as a person of mixed heritage. "I'm of Isleta Indian blood and of Spanish and Mexican surnames," she told the council during the competition for queen. A devout Catholic, this candidate's competition speech had ironically emphasized the importance of La Conquistadora and of Catholicism in unifying Pueblo and Spanish worlds.

According to Maestas, what had sparked her resignation was the council's tacit message that her mixed heritage had made her an inappropriate candidate for queen and even perhaps for the queen's court. According to the council's selection guidelines, unsuccessful contestants for the role of queen are traditionally invited to be Spanish *princesas* on the queen's court; however,

Maestas reports that council members had asked her to be an Indian *princesa* instead. Calling her participation in the event a "humiliation," she told the newspaper: "I went into the [competition] thinking, 'It will be based on my merit, it will be based on the speech,' but really, that's not the way it is."[32] Thus Maestas's experience in running for the role of Fiesta Queen led her to believe that there is no place for participants of indigenous, "Mexican," or mixed heritage in this celebration of conquistador glory.

The fiesta's selection of youths with a particular kind of Latino heritage—particularly of youths who can trace their heritage to the first Spanish settlers of the region—raises the additional issue of New Mexico's Hispanos' "cultural distinctiveness." The native Spanish speakers of New Mexico have long been the center of a simmering controversy over whether they, to a greater degree than other Latinos in the Southwest, share a closer affinity to "Spanish" than to "Mexican" culture. The propensity of many native New Mexicans toward a self-identification in English as "Hispano" or as "Spanish American" is well documented in the sociological literature,[33] making native New Mexicans something of an anomaly in a greater Mexican American–identified Southwest. This controversy recently came to a head in the *Annals of the Association of American Geographers*, in whose pages geographer Richard Nostrand argued that due to the relative isolation of Spanish settlements in New Mexico and the lack of "dilution"[34] of this Spanish culture by Mexican immigrant influence over the generations, New Mexican culture has remained relatively "*distinctively* Spanish in a cultural sense."[35]

Although academic disputes over whether Hispanos are ethnically more "Spanish" or "Mexican" have frequently probed New Mexicans' culture content and even bloodlines, the more relevant question appears to be *why* Hispanos have clung to an identification as "Spanish American." As opposed to an identification as "Spanish American," an identification as "Chicano"—a term originally denoting working-class

Mexican Americans—embraces Latinos' indigenous heritage and finds within it a source of resistance to Anglo oppression. Thus many Chicano-identified scholars argue that the claim to Spanish descent is an ideological strategy, or "myth" (perpetrated by both Anglos and Hispanos themselves), that more closely affiliates Hispanos with the European heritage of Anglos rather than with the mixed heritage of their forebears. They further charge that a "Spanish American" identification is an affectation adopted by a Hispano elite wishing to distance itself from its working-class, and less fortunate, "Chicano" brethren. Thus for such esteemed scholars who helped elaborate a Southwest-wide Chicano identity, Hispanos' emphasis on their Spanish descent is not merely a form of false pretense, but a form of "false consciousness" that serves to divide Latinos in their common struggle against Anglo oppression.[36]

However, New Mexican scholars caution that close attention to the historical circumstances surrounding the formation of a Hispano identity reveals otherwise. Sociologist Phillip B. Gonzales has argued that a "Spanish American" identification first arose at the turn of the century in response to increasing Anglo immigration as New Mexicans sought to remind incoming Anglos of their proud heritage. Such an identification was of further use during New Mexico's drive for statehood because it served to distance New Mexico's Hispanos from the turbulence of the Mexican Revolution and to claim "Spanish Americans" as a population deserving of the rights of citizenship.[37] Thus Gonzales makes a convincing case for "Spanish American" being a "protest-motivated" rather than accommodationist identification "applied in direct action confrontations with Anglo racism and social domination."[38]

However, a "Spanish American" identification may be applied in new circumstances for new purposes. For what purposes is Hispanos' identification with their Spanish heritage being deployed today? If, as social constructionist theories of ethnic relations suggest,[39] the assertion of an ethnic identity is simultaneously the drawing of an ethnic boundary, then the question becomes whether the assertion of a "Spanish American" identity includes or excludes Mexican elements. We have seen that the fiesta clearly draws ethnic boundaries between "Hispanos" and "Pueblos." If we take seriously the experience of former Fiesta Queen candidate Monica Maestas, it would appear that the fiesta also serves to distinguish New Mexicans with a "Spanish" background from those with mixed heritage and indeed to privilege the former. Though the fiesta speaks intimately to Hispanos' history, its portrayal of a distinctively "Spanish" version of history may indeed alienate, and exclude, other perspectives.

Thus the fiesta does serve to portray a very partial version of history as New Mexico's Hispanos would like it to be told: that of descent from Spanish, rather than mixed, bloodlines. As Antonio Ríos-Bustamante and J. M. Blaut argue in their refutation of Nostrand's "distinctiveness thesis," this "myth" of Spanish heritage "is a variant of a larger myth, the belief on the part of elites in many areas of Latin America that they are descendants of the Spanish colonizers and are not, therefore, Indian or Black or *mestizo* or *mulatto*."[40] Thus the fiesta may indeed be said to uphold a racial hierarchy in New Mexico that privileges "Spanish" ancestry over a mixed background; similar to the Latin American conquest dramas it may be said to "legitimate [Spanish] right to rule through language and ceremony."[41]

The Fiesta and Hispano Pride

Clearly, then, the fiesta's glorification of Spanish heritage has been a point of contention with the region's Pueblo Indians and Chicanos for decades. However, this is only half of the story. Though offensive to some, it remains an important commemoration of the long-standing presence of Latino settlement in the Southwest, and one particularly significant to New Mexico's native Hispanos. In fiesta promotional literature, the event bills itself as "the oldest community celebration in the U.S.," honoring "the return of Spanish culture to Santa Fe."[42] Thus an analysis of the

Figure 43. Religious motifs abound in Hispanic New Mexico, even on pickup truck tailgates. Here Jesus and the Virgin Mary are airbrushed on to a black tailgate below the truck's rear air spoiler. Photo by Andrew Gulliford, 1997.

fiesta would not be complete without consideration of its importance for Hispanos in Santa Fe.

Santa Fe's Hispanos emphasize the festival's celebration as a source of Hispano pride and as a public recognition of their presence in what was once northern New Spain before Anglo Americans occupied it in 1848. As one native New Mexican who said he could trace "twelve generations" back to the settlers of the region proudly stated, "It's a tradition that's been going on for 400 years." As a celebration of the retaking of Santa Fe, the capital of what was formerly this northern province of New Spain, the fiesta also serves as public recognition that "Santa Fe was the first capital of the U.S.," he said. Indeed, participants in the event echo its importance as an illustration of the longevity of Hispano settlement in the region and of the continuity of Hispano culture. "My heritage is deep in Spanish traditions and stuff," said Marcos Andreas Tapia, a former Don Diego de Vargas. "The minute that you hear those mariachis and you see La Conquistadora your religion just comes out. And then you start thinking about your ancestors and what they went through to make [Santa Fe] what it is today."[43]

Indeed, popular tradition holds that the fiesta has been celebrated continuously since a 1712 proclamation issued by the Marqués de Peñuela that de Vargas's reoccupation of the city be "celebrated with Vespers, Mass, Sermons, and Processions through the Main Plaza."[44] The city's early commemorations of this historical event in fact bore little resemblance to today's fiesta: they consisted solely of solemn processions carrying La Conquistadora from her shrine to her permanent home in the St. Francis Cathedral.[45] Regional historians instead trace the origins of the contemporary fiesta to commercial fairs held by territorial officials in the late nineteenth century to promote the developing region for settlement and tourism.[46] These early fiestas played up the region's Spanish and Indian heritages for tourists' entertainment, staging "mock battles" between Spanish and Pueblo forces[47] and including tributes to Spanish explorers Cabeza de Vaca and Coronado.[48] These early commercial fairs were sporadic and lacked a formal organizing body. Shortly after New Mexico became a state in 1912, however, Museum of New Mexico director Edgar Lee Hewett and the city's chamber of commerce decided to revive such commercial fairs in the form of a citywide fiesta in order to boost a flagging economy.[49] As Wilson describes them, these early fiestas were animated by a modernist yearning for a preindustrial sense of community, a desire that had rekindled a fascination with historical pageants across the nation.[50] Thus the fiesta's early history clearly illustrates the role of Anglos and Museum of New Mexico officials in promoting a "Spanish" version of Latino history in the state.

Though originally created as a tourist attraction, however, New Mexico's Hispanos have steadily reclaimed the event as a celebration of Hispano culture by and for Hispanos. By 1927, the event that had formerly displayed New Mexico's history as a "pageant of three cultures"[51]—Pueblo, Spanish, and Anglo—had begun focusing exclusively on the Spaniards' resettlement of the city.[52] During the 1920s, the fiesta also incorporated a Catholic mass to commemorate New Spain's Franciscan friars killed by Pueblo Indians during the Pueblo Revolt, further imbued with a Hispano Catholic overtone.[53] Nor has it only been the subject matter of the fiesta that has become more Hispano: in the 1940s, a Hispano was first elected president of the formerly predominantly Anglo Fiesta

Council, the body that organizes and directs the fiesta.⁵⁴ By the 1960s and 1970s, Hispanos constituted a majority of members, and today roughly 90 percent of the council is Hispano. As one public official proclaimed in a recent fiesta program, the contemporary fiesta is a "tribute to the active preservation of Hispanic heritage in New Mexico."⁵⁵

Finally, Hispanos have also reappropriated the role of historical personages in the fiesta, roles once routinely filled by Anglos. For example, until 1929, when Colonel José D. Sena usurped the role from John H. DeHuff, most men portraying the role of Don Diego de Vargas in the fiesta had been Anglo.⁵⁶ Indeed, in 1937, one Santa Fe newspaper opined:

> The native people should be encouraged to have their annual Fiesta with all of its religious and historical significance as it was originally intended.... The natives would be the participants, the Anglos from near and far would be in their rightful place of spectators.⁵⁷

Soon thereafter Anglos were indeed spectators alone. By 1940, in a fitting move of symbolic reappropriation, New Mexican Hispanos had once and for all reclaimed the role of conquistador for themselves.⁵⁸

With Hispano Santa Feans' taking back the role of conquistador, they have simultaneously reclaimed the glory attributed to their Hispano past. Dean Rehberger notes that at the time of the first wave of art colonists to Taos and Santa Fe, Anglo-directed New Mexican theater continued to rely upon metaphors of Spanish conquest to naturalize the new social hierarchy. In these dramas, Anglos, rather than Hispanos, played the role of Spanish "don" and "patron" to the Hispano masses, or "peons." Here the patron-peon relationship was extended to the new racial order, implicitly sanctioning Anglo stewardship of Hispano lives.⁵⁹ Hispanos' reappropriation of the heroic role of conquistador fittingly resists this ideological strategy, reclaiming the glory of their past for themselves. Thus the fiesta cannot be reduced solely to a glorification of Pueblo subjugation; clearly it also reminds Anglos who, as one fiesta observer put it, "was here before them."

Thus we have come full circle to the third layer of racial stratigraphy in New Mexico: that of the Anglo conquest. Though similar to the conquest dramas of Latin America, the fiesta's celebration of Spanish glory assumes an altogether different significance in an Anglo-dominated context. For many New Mexicans, the celebration allows them to display a sense of ethnic solidarity and unity even as they steadily lose demographic ground in the city to Anglos.

For example, the 1990 census revealed that Anglos outnumbered Hispanos for the first time in the city's history.⁶⁰ In many ways, the fiesta serves as a form of resistance to Anglo gentrification, a trend that has become more pronounced since the popularization of "Santa Fe style" in the 1980s. Indeed, one community activist could not refrain from comparing the Spanish reconquest of Santa Fe in 1692 to what he called the "continuing conquest" of the city by Anglos. Whereas the fiesta commemorates Pueblos and Spaniards' negotiation of a means of sharing the land, the "newest of conquistadors" are not interested in partnership but rather "ownership," he said. "And today that very situation of land is what brings us into conflict with the newest of arrivals, the newest of conquistadors, because they *do* come to conquer, they come to conquer our way of life, they come to conquer our land, they come to make a profit," he told New Mexico folklorist Jeanette De Bouzek.⁶¹

As a conquest drama of sorts, then, the fiesta's message of Spanish dominance may be read two ways. Though conquerors of New Mexico's Pueblo Indians, Hispanos have since been usurped by Anglos as the region's "newest conquistadors." For many Hispano New Mexicans, the fiesta serves as a display of Hispano unity and of the "preservation of Hispanic culture"⁶² despite the dominance of the region by its most recent colonizers.

Notes

1. For essays concerning the partiality of historical narratives in Chicano historiography, see in particular Tomás Almaguér, "Ideological Distortions in Recent Chicano Historiography: The Internal Model and Chicano Historical Interpretation," *Aztlán* 18, no. 1 (1989); Alex M. Saragoza, "Recent Chicano Historiography: An Interpretive Essay," *Aztlán* 19, no. 1 (1990).

2. Susan Davis, *Parades and Power* (Philadelphia: University of Pennsylvania Press, 1986), 13.

3. William H. Beezley, Cheryl English Martin, and William E. French, *Rituals of Rule, Rituals of Resistance: Public Celebrations and Popular Culture in Mexico* (Wilmington, DE: Scholarly Resources, 1994), xv.

4. The term *Hispano* denotes a regional subgrouping of Spanish speakers concentrated in northern New Mexico and southern Colorado. These Hispanos, some of whom also refer to themselves as "Spanish Americans," trace their descent from the colonists sent north from New Spain to the new colony of Nuevo México beginning in the sixteenth century.

5. Mayor Debbie Jaramillo, "Proclamations," *The 285th Annual Santa Fe Fiesta: The Official Fiesta Program*, *The Santa Fe New Mexican*, September 1997, 28.

6. The reoccupation of Santa Fe the following year, however, involved bloodshed and the execution of 70 Pueblo Indians. See Ramón Gutiérrez, *When Jesus Came, the Corn Mothers Went Away: Marriage, Sexuality, and Power in New Mexico, 1500–1846* (Stanford: Stanford University Press, 1991), 145.

7. According to the script of the Entrada from the 1997 Santa Fe Fiesta.

8. Sylvia Rodríguez, *The Matachines Dance: Ritual Symbolism and Interethnic Relations in the Upper Rio Grande Valley* (Albuquerque: University of New Mexico Press, 1996), 145.

9. Gutiérrez, *When Jesus Came, the Corn Mothers Went Away*, 48.

10. See especially Beezley, Martin, and French, *Rituals of Rule, Rituals of Resistance*.

11. Gutiérrez, *When Jesus Came, the Corn Mothers Went Away*, 47.

12. Rodríguez, *The Matachines Dance*, 18.

13. See especially Carey McWilliams, "The Fantasy Heritage," in *North from Mexico: The Spanish-Speaking People of the United States* (1948; reprint, New York: Greenwood Publishers, 1968), 41–53. David J. Weber, "The Spanish Legacy in North America and the Historical Imagination," *The Western Historical Quarterly* (February 1992); David J. Weber, *The Spanish Frontier in North America* (New Haven: Yale University Press, 1992).

14. Tom Cameron, *Los Angeles Times*, August 29, 1947, as quoted in Carey McWilliams, *North from Mexico*, 45.

15. Erika Davila, "Qué Viva Las Fiestas?: The Annual Commemoration of Santa Fe's Origins and Its Spanish Heritage Appear to Be on Divergent Paths," *The Santa Fe New Mexican*, September 7, 1999, A2.

16. "Enjoy Fiesta," *The Santa Fe New Mexican*, September 15, 1977; "Pueblo Participation Uncertain for Fiesta," *The Santa Fe New Mexican*, September 16, 1977; "Drive Continues to Bring Indians Back to Fiesta," *The Santa Fe New Mexican*, September 31, 1981.

17. "Letter to the Editor," *The Santa Fe New Mexican*, September 21, 1989.

18. "Pueblo Leaders Call Fiesta Offensive," *The Santa Fe New Mexican*, September 12, 1993, A1.

19. See Larry Calloway, "Danger: Ethnic Harmony Discussion in Progress," *The Albuquerque Journal*, July 16, 1992; Sharon Niederman, "'Gathering Up Again: Fiesta in Santa Fe': Making a Video That Made Waves," *The Santa Fe Reporter*, September 9–15, 1992, 21; Charlene Sewady, "Conquest Means Conquest: Commentary from a Fiesta Resister," *The Santa Fe Reporter*, September 12–18, 1994.

20. The Anglos' portrayal of Indians in the fiesta recalls stereotypes of Plains Indians. Pueblos do not wear war paint nor headresses, and traditional male attire bears no resemblance to burlap sacks.

21. Gutiérrez, *When Jesus Came, the Corn Mothers Went Away*, 48.

22. Jeanette De Bouzek, "Gathering Up Again: Fiestas in Santa Fe" (Santa Fe: Independent Documentary Research, 1992).

23. Kay Bird, "A Kinder, Gentler *Entrada*," *The Santa Fe New Mexican*, September 12, 1992, A1.

24. Rick Berardinelli, Fiesta Council President, *The Santa Fe New Mexican*, August 26, 1992.

25. Bird, "A Kinder, Gentler, *Entrada*," A1.

26. "Fiesta 1993: Model for the Future," *The Santa Fe New Mexican*, September 14, 1993, A8.

27. Ibid., A8.

28. "Pueblo Leaders Call Fiesta Offensive," *The Santa Fe New Mexican*, A1.

29. When anthropologist Ronald Grimes did his study of the fiesta in 1973, he stated that the residency requirement was only one year at the time. However, since the 1970s, this requirement has been strengthened. See Ronald Grimes,

Symbol and Conquest: Public Ritual and Drama in Santa Fe (Albuquerque: University of New Mexico Press, 1976).

30. *Mocho* is a term to denote Spanish that is slang rather than standard. It is more common among urbanized or assimilated Hispanics.

31. Erika Davila, "La Reina Candidate Leaves Court, Saying Competition Is Fixed," *The Santa Fe New Mexican*, September 7, 1999, A1.

32. Ibid., A1.

33. See in particular Phillip B. Gonzales, "The Hispano Homeland Debate: New Lessons," in *Perspectives on Mexican American History* (Albuquerque: University of New Mexico Press, 1997); also Phillip B. Gonzales, "The Political Construction of Latino Nomenclature in Twentieth Century New Mexico," *Journal of the Southwest* 35, no. 2 (summer 1993): 158–85; and Nancie González, *The Spanish Americans of New Mexico: A Heritage of Pride* (Albuquerque: University of New Mexico Press, 1969).

34. Richard Nostrand, "The Hispano Homeland in 1900," *Annals of the Association of American Geographers* 70 (1980): 396.

35. Richard Nostrand, "Comment in Reply," *Annals of the Association of American Geographers* 71 (1981): 283.

36. See in particular Rodolfo Acuña, *Occupied America: The Chicano's Struggle Against Liberation* (San Francisco: Canfield Press, 1972): 55–77; and McWilliams, *North from Mexico*, 41–53. Blaut and Bustamante also present this argument in J. M. Blaut and Antonio Ríos Bustamante, "Commentary on New Mexico's 'Hispanos' and Their 'Homeland,'" *Annals of the Association of American Geographers* 74, no. 1 (March 1984).

37. Gonzales, "Hispano Homeland Debate," 128; Gonzales, "Latino Nomenclatures," 161, 166.

38. See Gonzales, "Hispano Homeland Debate," 135. For further elaboration on the protest-motivated political underpinnings of the formation of a Hispano/Spanish American identity, see Gonzales's discussion of Hispanos' popular protests of Anglo racism and social and political exclusionary tactics: Phillip B. Gonzales, "*La Junta de Indignación*: Hispano Repertoire of Collective Protest in New Mexico, 1884–1933," *Western Historical Quarterly* 31 (summer 2000): 161–86.

39. See in particular Fredrik Barth, ed., *Ethnic Groups and Boundaries* (Boston: Little, Brown, 1969).

40. Blaut and Bustamante, "New Mexico's 'Hispanos' and Their 'Homeland,'" 158.

41. Beezley, Martin, and French, *Rituals of Rule, Rituals of Rebellion*, xiii.

42. See in particular Mayor Debbie Jaramillo, "Proclamations," *The 284th Annual Fiesta: The Official Fiesta Program*, *The Santa Fe New Mexican*, September 1996, 22.

43. Quoted in De Bouzek, "Gathering Up Again," 1992.

44. Fray Angélico Chávez, "The First Santa Fe Fiesta Council, 1712," *New Mexico Historical Review* (July 1953): 183.

45. See Chris Wilson, *The Myth of Santa Fe: Creating a Modern Regional Tradition* (Albuquerque: University of New Mexico, 1997), 184.

46. See Rita Younis, "Early Days of La Fiesta de Santa Fe," *La Herencia del Norte* XI (fall 1996): 24. See also Chávez, "The First Santa Fe Fiesta Council, 1712," 190; DeHuff, "The Santa Fe Fiesta," 324; Hal Rothman, *Devil's Bargains: Tourism in the Twentieth-Century American West* (Lawrence, KS: University Press of Kansas, 1998), 102; and Chris Wilson, *The Myth of Santa Fe*, 205.

47. Younis, "Early Days of La Fiesta de Santa Fe," 24.

48. Wilson, *The Myth of Santa Fe*, 207.

49. See Chávez, "The First Santa Fe Fiesta Council, 1712." See also Suzanne Forrest, *The Preservation of the Village: New Mexico's Hispanics and the New Deal* (Albuquerque: University of New Mexico Press, 1989), 51; and Chris Wilson, *The Myth of Santa Fe*, 192.

50. Wilson, *Myth of Santa Fe*, 195.

51. Forrest, *Preservation of the Village*, 51.

52. Wilson, *Myth of Santa Fe*, 207.

53. Ibid., 209.

54. Wilson, *Myth of Santa Fe*, 226.

55. Jaramillo, "Proclamations," 28.

56. See "Caballeros de Vargas Roster: Those That Have Enacted the Role of General Don Diego de Vargas for Fiesta," Archives of the Santa Fe Fiesta Council, Santa Fe, New Mexico. See also Chris Wilson, *Myth of Santa Fe*, 226.

57. "The Fiesta," *The Santa Fe Examiner*, September 9, 1937, as quoted in Wilson, *Myth of Santa Fe*, 219.

58. Wilson, *Myth of Santa Fe*, 226.

59. Dean Rehberger, "Visions of the New Mexican in Public Pageants and Dramas of Santa Fe and Taos, 1918–1940," *Journal of the Southwest* 37, no. 3, 453.

60. Wilson, *Myth of Santa Fe*, 165.

61. Community activist Erwin Rivera, as quoted in Jeanette De Bouzek, "Gathering Up Again."

62. "Proclamations," September 1997, 28.

Study Questions

1. Describe the Santa Fe Fiesta. What are the organizers dramatizing?

2. What is involved in the Entrada portion of the fiesta?

3. How did the Pueblo Indians react to the Santa Fe Fiesta?

4. How does the Fiesta Council choose the participants?

5. What does it mean to be a "Spanish American"?

6. Why is the Santa Fe Fiesta a source of pride for Hispanos in New Mexico?

7. Where do Anglo Americans fit into the fiesta?

8. What is the real reason for the Santa Fe Fiesta (in the eyes of the participants)?

A Memorial to What?

The Vexing Question of Chamizal National Memorial between Texas and Mexico

Art Gómez

As for the Rio Grande, it didn't divide the land and peoples on either side of it any more than a zipper divides a pair of pants.
—Statement by Elliot West,
Western History Association Conference, 2002

In May 2002, 40 years after he coauthored the text for the Chamizal Treaty, which resolved a 100-year-old territorial dispute between Mexico and the United States, former ambassador Frank V. Ortiz returned to the El Paso–Juárez region for only the second time. Apologizing for his prolonged absence, the now graying yet remarkably poised former diplomat delighted the audience with reminiscences of his personal experiences on the international border during the height of the Chamizal Treaty negotiations. Although the diplomatic accord authorized the transfer of a mere 467 acres from the United States to Mexico, the exchange of sovereign territory between the two nations was unprecedented. In fact, at no time since it became an independent republic had the United States conceded territory to another foreign nation. The diplomatic world heralded the peaceful resolution of the lingering and often contentious contravention between bordering communities. Delicate negotiations, in which Ambassador Ortiz became intimately involved, transformed the so-called Chamizal Zone of west Texas from a flash point of hostility and political dissension to a testimonial for cultural understanding and mutual respect. The path that led to the diplomatic metamorphosis was understandably not an easy one.

Many late night debates between negotiators centered around one question: How would Mexico use the land once ownership officially transferred? No one doubted that the urban-industrial milieu of Ciudad Juárez, Mexico's most robust border community, would quickly absorb the minuscule parcel of former U.S. territory into the city's labyrinth of concrete and steel. For this reason, Ortiz and his fellow diplomats agreed that at least some portion of the land be set aside in tribute to the remarkable outcome resulting from determined negotiation in lieu of military intimidation. The two nations agreed that Cordova Island, an outcropping of Mexican territory residing on the north bank of the Rio Grande, the result of centuries of whimsical meanderings along the river's course, be divided equally between Mexico and the United States. Negotiators further agreed that each nation build a memorial as testimony to the diplomatic accord. Forty years later, Ortiz summarized the enormous feeling of accomplishment among his fellow diplomats: "The Chamizal settlement was really an extraordinary event. It is now enshrined . . . in two national memorials to remind new generations of what good will and hard effort can accomplish."[1]

When the foreign ministries of both nations signed the Chamizal Treaty in August 1963, both considered the historical event worthy of recognition; therefore a "memorial" to the momentous occasion seemed not only an appropriate gesture but more a diplomatic imperative. Accordingly, on June 30, 1966, Congress authorized the establishment of Chamizal National Memorial. The original title for the park as introduced to the House and Senate was the Chamizal Treaty National Memorial, a name that in my judgement correctly assumed the importance of the historic event and not the geographic locality. In a personal interview several years later with Frank Smith, the park's first and longest-tenured superintendent, he assured me that the name change was "not accidental." Many of those in government at the time, Smith included, firmly held that the Chamizal story often transcended the much celebrated—and in his opinion—sometimes overstated legal proceedings.

Of more enduring value, Smith affirmed, is the story of two multicultural communities, independent republics in large measure because historical events dictated that a politically imposed boundary—the Rio Grande—forever separate them. History has proven the international border to be mercurial, contentious, and in recent years hopelessly ineffective in isolating both nations from each other. The border culture in particular functions more or less as a single entity. People cross the Rio Grande at will to enter the respective countries. Neither Spanish nor English is the dominant spoken language; instead, bilingualism prevails. The international boundary imposes no discernable obstruction to cultural interaction. Food, music, and daily activity are amazingly similar on either side of the international border. One startling exception to the region's sameness is the obvious economic disparity between Mexico and the United States. Prosperity is readily apparent on the north bank of the Rio Grande as evidenced by enormous shopping malls, a well-defined skyline, attractively engineered transportation networks, and abundant productivity. Conversely, the south bank projects sustained poverty, a conspicuous lack of modernity, and a subsistence economy. For these reasons, Smith intoned, "The story of the Chamizal should emphasize two disparate nations working in cooperation to resolve their political differences and to promote mutual understanding."

To the dismay of the visiting public, however, the omission of the word *treaty* from the enabling legislation appears over time to have caused some confusion. The average park visitor tends to deal in absolutes; therefore a border region or community extending for hundreds of miles parallel to the Rio Grande is too nebulous and too cumbersome a concept to fully comprehend. Geographical designations are best understood when defined by well-established boundaries. National battlefields are a good example. When one visits Gettysburg, Lexington, Palo Alto, or Little Bighorn battlefields, the actual battle site is generally clearly delineated, although the cumulative acreage of the historic landscape may vary considerably from place to place. In most instances, there are recognizable—and in the case of national parks—legally established parameters that define the parameters of the historical event so far as it has been determined. Thus, park visitors neither readily understand nor do they entirely appreciate unfamiliar geographic entities such as the "Chamizal Zone" within the El Paso–Ciudad Juárez metropolitan area. In short, without sufficient explanation the term is meaningless.

More vexing still to the general public is the designation "national memorial." Since the tragic chain of terrorist events that began with the bombing of the Alfred P. Murrah Federal Building in Oklahoma City on April 19, 1995, and recently continued with the demolition of the World Trade Center on September 11, 2001, the subject of "memorials" weighs heavily on the minds of the American public. How do we remind future generations of Americans about the unanticipated tragedies that shook the nation to its core in only six years? How do we prevent complacency among the nation's citizens or caution national leaders to never forget that the United States is no longer invulnerable to international terrorism? The creation of an acceptable memorial has been the standard response. The USS *Arizona* Memorial at Pearl Harbor, for example, is not only an emotional tribute to the thousands of servicemen and women who died on December 7, 1941, but also serves as an ominous reminder to the federal government to maintain constant military vigilance, especially in the absence of a clearly defined enemy.

We live in an age where historical events worthy of memorialization—be they tragic or triumphal—occur almost routinely. Since the detonation of the world's first nuclear device that ended World War II in August 1945, this nation has either celebrated or commiserated historic events of unequaled importance. The eradication of life-threatening, communicable diseases such as polio and smallpox, the advent of television, the lunar landing, the civil rights movement, and the routine application of laser technology are just a few of the truly life-altering events of our time. On the other hand, the highly publicized assassinations of John and

Robert Kennedy, Mahatma Gandhi, and Martin Luther King; the military debacle in Vietnam; two space shuttle catastrophes; and the terrorist assaults in Oklahoma City and New York City have left an indelible sadness on the inhabitants of the United States—if not the world. Memorials, understandably, have become as common a feature of the American landscape as the interstate highway.

Although memorials have certainly proliferated in recent decades, they have always occupied an important place in the American consciousness. Since the birth of the nation in the late eighteenth century, Americans have erected memorials to their most outstanding leaders, including venerated political figures—Washington, Lincoln, Jefferson—and celebrated war heroes, whether they were officers of outstanding repute such as Robert E. Lee, George Armstrong Custer, or Douglas MacArthur. Even lesser-known combatants have enjoyed a certain immortality. The all-black 54th Massachusetts Regiment, the arrow-riddled troopers of the Seventh Cavalry, the unsuspecting marines who planted the American flag atop Mount Suribachi on Iwo Jima, and the 56,000 American casualties whose names are inscribed into the highly polished yet solemn black granite of the Vietnam Veterans Memorial have been so honored.

More important than the memorial itself is the process of memorialization. In the case of the impending World Trade Center Memorial, what will we memorialize? Do we want to remember for all time the extreme heroism of policemen, clergy, city officials, firefighters, military servicemen, and ordinary citizens who simply showed up to work on that fateful day? What about the unsung heroes of September 11, those average individuals who gave their lives on American Airlines Flight 93 to prevent even greater disaster? Will a grateful American population care enough about the crew and passengers of that ill-fated flight to visit the remote site in Somerset County, Pennsylvania, designed to honor their unselfish personal sacrifice? Apparently, our congressional leadership believes it will. On September 24, 2002, the U.S. Congress enacted legislation (PL 107–226) to establish the country's 29th national memorial under the familiar care and supervision of the National Park Service.

National memorials held a place in the federal bureaucracy long before the appearance of the National Park Service in August 1916. Previous to the Revolutionary War, the Continental Congress authorized the fledgling nation's first known memorial in honor of General Richard Montgomery, who died during an assault against French troops on the heights of Quebec. The death of George Washington on December 14, 1799, prompted a resolution in the U.S. Congress to erect a marble monument honoring the young nation's first chief executive. The Washington Monument, as we know it today, was not dedicated, however, until February 1885. On the occasion of America's first centennial in 1876, France presented the Statue of Liberty as a gift to the American people. Today the National Park Service preserves and protects the Washington Monument, the Statue of Liberty, and the numerous other celebrated memorials that accentuate our nation's capital.

Although national memorials need not necessarily be sites or structures historically associated with their subjects, they are primarily commemorative. There is no standard size or design for a memorial. They may range in size from a small cross or headstone to denote where someone has died, similar to those scattered across the valley of the Little Bighorn, or they may assume the stature of Mount Rushmore, the massive sculpture in South Dakota dedicated to four former American presidents. Their design may be as simple as the "eternal flame" that graces John F. Kennedy's grave in Arlington National Cemetery. Others, like the Vietnam Veterans Memorial in Washington, D.C., are elaborate architectural designs as well as artistic creations.

The process of memorialization is equally varied. Since 1916, the number of national memorials that have come under the auspices of the National Park Service has increased from six to 29. Typically, early memorials commemorated either outstanding individuals or significant episodes in history: Theodore

Roosevelt National Memorial, Mount Rushmore, Wright Brothers National Memorial, and more recently Jefferson National Expansion Memorial are a few notable examples. Beginning with the Reorganization Act of 1933, commemorative sites, certainly the majority of those whose maintenance and preservation transferred from the War Department to the National Park Service, have tended to commemorate personal tragedies and cataclysmic events in regional, state, and national history. Gettysburg, Shiloh, Antietam, Little Bighorn, the USS *Arizona* Memorial—all remnants of war; Ford's Theatre, the site of Abraham Lincoln's assassination, and the Petersen House, where doctors labored in vain to save the gunshot president; the Confederate-operated prison camp at Andersonville, Georgia, and the Japanese American detention center at Manzanar in northern California are monuments to human misery. The site of Pennsylvania's Johnstown Flood, Kent State University, where Ohio National Guardsmen gunned down antiwar demonstrators; or Wounded Knee, Sand Creek, and other so-called sites of shame, where American soldiers annihilated virtually defenseless Indian encampments; Dealey Plaza in downtown Dallas and the infamous Texas School Book Depository, the presumed source of the gunshots that killed John F. Kennedy, or the Lorraine Motel in Memphis, where James Earl Ray abruptly shattered Martin Luther King, Jr.'s, dreams of equality and civil rights; and, of course, the gaping void evident today in downtown Oklahoma City and lower Manhattan, where tangled vestiges of wanton destruction once stood; all are disturbing reminders of America's "landscapes of violence and tragedy."

The prevalence of so many memorials consciously scattered throughout the country to remind us of our war-ridden and all too often antagonistic past begs the questions: Do we as a nation memorialize acts of belligerence and violence more so than we do those of peaceful resolution and harmonious coexistence? Can others be reminded of America's finest hour without the invariant emphasis on conflict or human catastrophe? This is not to suggest that the tumultuous events that have disrupted our lives—in some instances have irrevocably altered them—are not deserving of recognition or remembrance. Rather, it is a statement of fact that the informed American bears witness to few examples of memorialization that commemorate a positive or uplifting historical experience. We as a so-called peace-loving people need to be reminded that America is the same nation that rebuilt Germany and Japan after the unequivocal yet nonetheless horrendous end to World War II; airlifted precious food and medical supplies to desperate Europeans in their time of need; discovered a preventative vaccine—if not the cure—for polio; opened its doors to homeless immigrants from Europe, Asia, and more recently Latin America; landed the first human on the moon; and invited the Beatles to perform on American television. These were especially meaningful yet intoxicating events.

While most assuredly not a historic benchmark to equal the lunar landing, the peaceful resolution of the nagging Chamizal issue in 1963 through the mutual cooperation of a handful of dedicated public servants is also worthy of commemoration. In effect, the Chamizal Treaty was a diplomatic triumph for Mexico, a nation the United States overshadowed politically and militarily since 1821. As for the Americans, the diplomatic accord demonstrated the willingness of a traditionally domineering neighbor to make concessions in the cause of international goodwill. True, the transfer of territory amounted to only 467 acres of land, a paltry sum by anyone's measure. But that particular parcel of land encompassed a significant portion of El Paso's industrial core. More impressive, the United States spent the astronomical sum of $49 million to repatriate the disputed territory to Mexico, its rightful owner.

What manner of memorial adequately conveys the importance of this event? Not surprisingly, both governments agreed that "memorial parks" seemed appropriate. Mexico forged ahead with an ambitious plan to rival Chapultepec Park in Mexico City. The United States, on the other hand, floundered for nearly a decade before dedicating Chamizal National

Memorial to the public. As the two memorials evolved, their physical disparity in many respects mirrored the significance of the Chamizal Treaty to the respective nations. The Mexican park reflected national pride and thus became a symbol of territorial sovereignty and diplomatic perseverance. The American counterpart, on the other hand, fulfilled a legal commitment to Mexico, but some—especially Texas "sacred soilers," ardent champions of states rights—viewed Chamizal National Memorial as a persistent reminder of judicial frustration. Only through the combined effort of El Paso civic leaders and a handful of "innovators" representing the Southwest Region of the National Park Service did the national park become a "living testimonial" to cultural understanding along the Rio Grande corridor. Park-sponsored activities—the Border Folk Festival, the Siglo de Oro Drama Festival, and Symphony Under the Stars—are in effect kinetic expressions of memorialization to the peaceful coexistence between two nations as defined in the Chamizal Treaty.

Nevertheless, the conspicuous absence of a formal memorial at Chamizal has over the past three decades resulted in an "identity crisis" within the park. During its formative years, Park Service administrators reluctantly endorsed Chamizal for inclusion into the national park system. Unlike other national parks, which are authorized through congressional legislation, or national monuments, which are created by executive order, Chamizal was the stepchild of an international agreement promulgated by the U.S. State Department and the Mexican Foreign Ministry. To complicate matters further, it was virtually impossible to associate the Chamizal settlement with a single, fixed geographic location; the legal ramifications affected the entire Mexico–U.S. border region. The immediate problem at hand for Park Service consultants was to assign historic and national significance to a featureless landscape (Cordova Island) devoid of any particularly outstanding characteristics. Former Southwest Regional Historian Robert Utley, to whom fell the unenviable responsibility of justifying the historical importance of the proposed national park, lamented: "I had to come up with some kind of conceptual framework in which this hunk of barren land could stand for a great nationally significant story." "The whole question of what was the legitimate role of the National Park Service was very much at the forefront," Utley added. "Of course, Chamizal was so far out there that it would inevitably provoke opposition." Despite detractors in Washington, D.C., to the proposed Texas park, Utley's justification prevailed. He turned to the seldom used designation of national memorial "as a way of compromising professional rectitude with political necessity."

The park's original concept development plan called for a 33-foot reflection pond to accent an artistically designed monument to the Chamizal Treaty. The consistently arid climate and water-depleted environment of west Texas precluded the construction of the proposed aquatic feature and monolith. To this day, there exists no obvious memorial feature or conventional monument in recognition of the historic event directly responsible for the park's creation. For this reason, perhaps, local residents and curious visitors have over the years perceived Chamizal more as an urban and recreational park than a national memorial. Unquestionably, the reflection pool would have been impractical—if not irresponsibly incompatible—with El Paso's astringent surroundings. Yet one wonders if the concept of a small, neatly landscaped contemplative area within the park's boundary might be an appropriate tribute to the Chamizal Treaty and the ideals of friendship and international cooperation. Former park superintendent Cordell Roy recently summarized his thoughts on the matter: "Memorialization could be very effective here. It could be inviting. We have the landscape that can portray the entire border at large."

The debate to memorialize or not to memorialize will be ongoing at Chamizal for years to come. Regardless of the outcome, the fact remains that this unassuming national park, only 55 acres in its entirety, stands in testimony to an amicable conclusion between two contesting nations through the purposeful negotiation of seemingly unresolvable issues. In that respect, Chamizal National Memorial is unique within the global political community. It is, in my judgment, a small park with a huge story to tell. In his mesmerizing presentation to El Paso residents in May 2002, former ambassador Ortiz reminded the audience that one of the volatile issues between Palestine and its non-Islamic neighbors today centers around the use of the waters of the river Jordan. Not unlike the Rio Grande, Colorado River users in the American Southwest are routinely engaged in legal jousting over its use. The states of California, Arizona, and Nevada are especially protective and unforgiving in matters concerning the distribution of Colorado's water. These issues are not likely to subside as the population of the West enlarges to the point that available water resources become totally exhausted.

The formal agreement concluded between Mexico and the United States in 1963 to channelize the Rio Grande so that it never again violates the sometimes illusory international border should serve as an example to other nations engaged in seemingly irreconcilable legal and territorial disputes. Ambassador Ortiz's optimism that the inhabitants of the Rio Grande border region represent "beacons of hope and inspiration for those suffering in northern Ireland, Palestine, Chechnya, Kashmir, Bosnia, Kosovo, and all of the places where there are cultural, religious, and economic differences, land disputes, and hate dominates" should not be viewed lightly. One day, perhaps, Chamizal National Memorial may serve as a neutral meeting ground for nations to resolve their longstanding enmity.

Notes

1. "Former Ambassador Recalls Settlement of Chamizal Dispute," *El Paso Inc.*, May 12, 2002, 30a; "Reminiscences on the Chamizal—Forty Years Later," Ambassador Frank V. Ortiz, speech, Millennium Lecture Series, University of Texas at El Paso, May 1, 2002, El Paso, TX.

2. Quotes as cited in Frank Smith interview with Art Gómez, September 12, 1998, El Paso, TX, 1; Elliot West, "Reconstructing Race," *Western Historical Quarterly*, xxxiv (spring 2003): 13.

3. Edward Tabor Linenthal, *Sacred Ground: Americans and Their Battlefields* (Urbana: University of Illinois Press, 1991), especially 1–6; see also Edward T. Linenthal, *The Unfinished Bombing: Oklahoma City in the American Memory* (New York: Oxford Press, 2001).

4. Richard West Sellars, "On Memorials," National Park Service e-mail circular, September 26, 2002; "Flight 93 National Memorial Act" (H.R. 3917), http://thomas.loc.gov, November 13, 2002.

5. Harry Butowsky, "History and Definition of the Names of Historical Units Within the National Park System" (Washington, D.C., National Park Service, Division of History, 1980), 9, 10; Catherine M. Howett, "The Vietnam Veterans Memorial: Public Art and Politics," *Landscape* 28 (November 2, 1985): 1–9.

6. Kenneth E. Foote, *Shadowed Ground: America's Landscapes of Violence and Tragedy* (Austin: University of Texas Press), 1997.

7. Robert M. Utley, interview with Art Gómez, Moose, WY, July 25, 1995.

8. Cordell Roy, interview with Art Gómez, El Paso, TX, September 27, 2002.

9. "Reminiscences on the Chamizal," 2, 10.

Study Questions

1. What was the reason for building the memorial?

2. What is the major difference between people living on either side of the Rio Grande? Was it successful in separating the United States and Mexico?

3. According to the author, why are national memorials important?

4. What was the nation's first memorial?

5. What is the difference between early memorials and more modern memorials in America? Why do you think this is the case?

6. How did the United States and Mexico each view the challenge of building a national memorial to commemorate the Chamizal Treaty?

7. How does the actual use of the Chamizal Memorial, not its intent, represent the fluidity of Hispanic culture on both sides of the border?

Native American Preservation Issues

Headnotes

All too often Western history textbooks have a riveting chapter on the Sand Creek Massacre (1864) or the Wounded Knee Massacre (1890) and then go on to describe the settlement of the West with little notice of living tribal peoples and the issues they face. Yes, there are numerous statistics on Native American poverty, disease, and unemployment in books on the twentieth-century West, but what historians have missed and what public historians are now describing is a major Indian renaissance focused on the return of human remains, the preservation of cultural artifacts, and the protection of sacred sites. Having survived a population nadir in 1900, when American Indians appeared to be a "vanishing race," and having also survived the 500th anniversary of Christopher Columbus's arrival, Native Americans are more determined than ever to strengthen and maintain their cultural traditions.

The growing literature on tribal preservation issues includes Klara Bonsack Kelly and Harris Francis's *Navajo Sacred Places*, Kelli Carmean's *Spider Woman Walks This Land: Traditional Cultural Properties and the Navajo Nation*, Andrew Gulliford's *Sacred Objects and Sacred Places: Preserving Tribal Traditions*, and Keith Basso's award-winning *Wisdom Sits in Places* about Apache mapmaking. In fall 1996 *The Public Historian* printed a special issue titled *Representing Native American History*.

In 2000 CRM published a thematic issue titled *Beyond Compliance: Tribes of the Southwest*, and sacred site issues continue to take center stage in Nat Stone's "The Spirit of Zuni Lake," in *Preservation*, May–June 2004. Tribal concerns over sacred sites vary from Indian Pass Wilderness in California, where "The Trail of Dreams" crosses the pass, to climbing bans at Cave Rock near Zephyr Cove, Nevada. At that site the Access Fund is suing the U.S. Forest Service over climbing restrictions despite the Washoe Tribe's spiritual connections to the site. *Essays in Native Americans and Archaeologists: Stepping Stones to Common Ground*, edited by Nina Swidler et al. points to new understandings and accommodations among tribal peoples and federal agencies and their professional staff. The literature on repatriation and sacred objects also continues to grow.

Protecting sacred sites and sacred landscapes is a key concern among native peoples. Repetition and tradition, unbroken continuity over time—these elements are essential to native religion whether it is a young man at a remote vision quest site, a tribe like the Shoshones or the Utes at their annual sun dances, or Miwok leaders on a pilgrimage to collect plants for religious purposes as they visit sacred shrines in California. Native religion is intricately bound to a tight web of place and an intimate, subtle, even secret understanding of landscape. Protecting and preserving native sacred sites depends upon using the stories of native peoples and the skills of ethnographers, public historians, and geographers.

When land is lost to native peoples, federal laws can help preserve and protect sites that indigenous peoples no longer own. Applicable federal laws mentioned in the following essays include the Antiquities Act of 1906; the National Historic Preservation Act (1966 and amended 1992); the American Indian

Religious Freedom Act (1978); the Archaeological Resources and Protection Act (1979 and amended 1989); and the Native American Graves Protection and Repatriation Act (1990), which continues to spur ongoing legal controversy, specifically the disposition of the 9,600-year-old human remains of Kennewick Man. Presidential Executive Order 13007, Protecting Native American Sacred Sites (1996), also has significance for federal land managers though it represents guidelines instead of judicial action. Relevant references include National Register Bulletin #38, which defines traditional cultural properties, and articles in CRM, in particular the special issue *What You Do and How We Think*. Because Native Americans, Native Alaskans, and Native Hawaiians all have cultural claims to former tribal lands now included in national parks, important references include Robert Keller and Michael Turek, *American Indians & National Parks*; Mark David Spence, *Dispossessing the Wilderness: Indian Removal and the Making of the National Parks*; and a special issue of *Practicing Anthropology* (winter 2004), with the focus "Miki Crespi and the Applied Ethnography Program of the National Park Service."

Native Americans continue to gain pride in their tribal roots. Cultural goals include protecting sacred objects and sacred places, but other pressing needs are health care, full employment, adequate housing, and educational opportunities on and off reservations. Although over half of all American Indians today live in urban settings or away from reservation lands, Indian culture thrives and evolves within the framework of fixed traditions and the revival of ancient ceremonies. A younger generation now recognizes elders as tradition bearers, and maintaining culture has become essential to the health of tribal peoples.

Demographically, native peoples enjoy high birthrates and a very young population compared to the rest of the United States. At Zuni, New Mexico, over half the tribal population is now under the age of 30, making the transfer of cultural traditions and values a critical issue. To prevent the theft of cultural information, the Hopis have closed their kachina dances on First Mesa in Arizona to all visitors except for in-laws who may be nonnatives. The Zunis have previously closed their winter Shalako house blessing ceremonies to non-Indians. New Age religious believers who have rejected mainstream churches and seek Indian spirituality do so without proper initiation and without tribal permission, and they sometimes steal authentic offerings left by tribal peoples. Indian religion is private and closely held. Some knowledge of sacred objects and access to sacred sites is confidential information not to be shared with outsiders or even with tribal members from different clans or medicine societies.

A legal researcher in the Hopi Cultural Preservation Office, Yvonne Hoosava, says people telephone her because they want to give their business or their boat a Hopi name. They want phone numbers for traditional Hopi healers, and they want to know all about the Hopi religion in a few short minutes over the telephone. She sighs and explains, "To know our culture one must grow up in it. You have to live it on a daily basis. We continue to learn every day." On the Hopi reservation, New Agers have left offerings, granules of salt, and strung materials up in trees. In the Coconino National Forest near Sedona, Arizona, New Agers rearrange rocks, cut boughs from trees, and make their own miniature medicine wheels, all to the chagrin of local Forest Service employees, who must repair the woods and take down the pseudoshrines.

In Colorado, New Agers have damaged Ute Indian sacred sites by moving stones aligned centuries ago at high elevations in Rocky Mountain National Park. An intruder on the White River National Forest near Aspen, Colorado, created a fake medicine wheel to stop expansion of a ski area. Tribal sacred sites are beset by vandals as well as misguided religious enthusiasts who seek to participate in Medicine Wheel ceremonies, sweat lodges, and vision quests. At Chaco Culture National Historic Park in New Mexico, a World Heritage site, New Agers during a "Harmonic Convergence" scattered the ashes of one of their friends in a great kiva. Navajo workers refused to go near the site to do any maintenance, and finally the National Park Service had to remove two inches of topsoil from the kiva before stabilization and preservation could continue.

At the Hopi Preservation Office in Kykotsmovi, Arizona, Yvonne Hoosava explains, "We have been taught that if you see something that you leave it alone. You do not pick it up. The term is *kyaptsi*. It means respect for all mankind, insects, and animals. One of our main teachings is respect." Whereas Indians understand these implicit and explicit cultural boundaries and do not cross kiva lines or ask about the affairs of other medicine societies, nonnatives, Hoosava says, "want to know because it is secret. The more secretive it is, the more they want to know. Outsiders do not understand." She tries to explain to them on the telephone. "I tell them that your people had spirituality years ago. Go back to them. You will never learn our culture in a day or two or a week. It takes a lifetime, and even then you do not know it all."

Consequently, the Hopis, like other tribes, express concern over their intellectual property, their names, songs, dances, sacred teachings, and their shrines. They insist research protocols be followed by legitimate students and scholars. Each village can decide which of the many dances to open or close, but the snake dances are now closed, and First Mesa is off-limits entirely for photography, audio recording, or sketching of any kind, though villagers permit walking tours. There is no fee, only a donation box. At the community center on First Mesa, where the tours originate, signs proclaim "No Cameras" in six different languages.

Hopi Cultural Officer Leigh Kuwanwisiwma explains, "There are over 300 books on the Hopi and none of them have been written by a Hopi member. Much of the material is false or has been misinterpreted." Like the Hopi, Apache tribes seek exclusive control over Apache cultural property, including "all images, texts, ceremonies, music, songs, stories, symbols, beliefs, customs, ideas, and other physical and spiritual objects and concepts" related to Apache life including representations of Apache culture by non-Apaches. In an article titled "Can Culture Be Copyrighted?" Michael Brown explains that native peoples seek their fair share of any profits from "the acquisition of native crop varieties for the genetic improvement of seeds, the transformation of traditional herbal medicines into marketable drugs by pharmaceutical firms [and] the incorporation of indigenous graphic designs into commercial products." Brown calls for "urgently needed public discussion about mutual respect and the fragility of Native cultures in mass societies."

At Zuni the tribe has initiated its own publishing department, and former publications director Anne Beckett says, "The square peg of Zuni tradition and philosophy is trying to place itself in the round hole of Western intellectual property. Zuni tradition is predicated upon collective rights, and intellectual property is based on individual rights never conceived of by Zunis." She adds, "Conversely, Zuni traditions are collectively owned in ways never conceived of by law." The issue of trademarks and copyrights creates conflicts. Anne Beckett, a non-Indian, says, "We are forcing them to have concepts of ownership and we are breeding dissent. This is splitting families and tribes." She cautions, "In forcing people to adapt to Western ways, we are in the process of destroying something ancient and irreplaceable." Bemoaning white infatuation with Indian ideas and perspectives, she says, "We must temper our fascination with the need to know. We really don't need to know everything about everybody. Somewhere along the line our curiosity got lethal."

Tribal intellectual property issues include the right to plant, harvest, and distribute Indian corn. Over millennia Pueblo peoples have grown corn, just as in the Northwest tribes have caught salmon or harvested huckleberries, but now the rare Hopi and Zuni species of drought-resistant corn in colorful colors, including blue, are being coveted and used by others. One company boldly received a Certificate of Plant Variety Protection for "Hopi blue popcorn," without Hopi tribal authorization or consent. As a result the rights of farmers, especially Hopis, to sell the seed are limited. A

Phoenix factory manufactures Hopi Blue Corn pancake mix, and in San Francisco, Hopi Blue Corn Flakes contain a box top history of the Hopi agricultural way of life and the statement, "Made from the blue corn that the Hopi ate for strength." Says Leigh Kuwanwisiwma, "Hopi society has always been an open society based on our philosophy of promoting brotherhood, sisterhood, and universal community," but those shared values may not withstand the surge of interest from outsiders (see also Tom Greaves's *Intellectual Property Rights for Indigenous Peoples: A Sourcebook*).

From reburying their ancestors to writing preservation ordinances to preserving sacred geography and rebuilding ceremonial houses, native peoples are reclaiming hegemony over their cultural practices. In the future, native peoples will have tremendous impact not only on the maintenance and preservation of their own cultural heritage, but also in helping other Americans develop a parallel preservation movement that does not just focus on bricks and mortar and historic structures, but also on landscapes, sacred sites, ceremonies, pilgrimages, and respect for elders. As native peoples demand protection of their sacred geography, laws and procedures will change and evolve. All Americans will benefit as the values and traditions of native peoples reshape the historic preservation movement.

The following essays speak to those complex issues involving Native Americans who tell their own stories and preserve and interpret their diverse pasts, especially at important sites such as Mesa Verde, the Grand Canyon, the Medicine Wheel, and the Sand Creek Massacre site. Historian Joseph Weixelman, in consultation with the Hopi, begins with interpreting the myth of Anasazi disappearance that for almost four decades negated a cultural connection between the Ancestral Puebloans of the Four Corners and Mesa Verde region and living Pueblo peoples along the Rio Grande river valley. For years National Park Service rangers taught that the Anasazi left the Four Corners because of drought. Visitors assumed that the prehistoric Indians had disappeared, when in fact they had migrated south and east. The Hopi figure prominently in Weixelman's essay as they do in the writing of National Park Service historic preservationist Amanda Zeaman, who describes complicated issues of historic preservation and repatriation at Hopi House.

Designed by Mary Colter, Hopi House, on the south rim of the Grand Canyon in Arizona, has been a successful gift and curio shop for almost a century. The building is a National Historic Landmark built by Hopi craftsmen, who secretly included sacred shrines within portions of the structure. Can the shrines be repatriated without damaging the landmark? In Zeaman's essay this and other issues are elaborated with careful attention to federal law and a concise analysis of the Native American Graves Protection and Repatriation Act (1990).

One of the most powerful sites in North America is the Medicine Wheel, in northern Wyoming, which is aligned to both the summer solstice and the rise of summer stars Aldebaran, Rigel, and Sirius. The Medicine Wheel is an entire religious complex, including vision quest sites, sacred trails, and even stone cairns in the shape of an arrow pointing to the site from over 40 miles away across the Big Horn Basin. According to Fred Chapman, Native American liaison with the Wyoming State Historic Preservation Office, the Medicine Wheel represents an "archetypal form of religious architecture." At 1,500 years old, the Medicine Wheel is so powerful that Shoshone medicine men make a pilgrimage to it only once or twice in their lifetimes. Archaeologist Chapman explains difficulties in managing the wheel to meet the expectations of Indian peoples and federal land managers.

Although Colonel John M. Chivington's infamous predawn attack at Sand Creek resulted in a congressional investigation and a major shift in nineteenth-century Indian policy, the exact location of the massacre site and the placement of the Cheyenne and Arapaho village remained unknown. National Park Service historian Christine Whitacre describes the painstaking process of specifically locating the massacre site, which was essential for its inclusion as a new unit of the National Park Service. Former U.S. Senator Ben Nighthorse Campbell, a Northern Cheyenne, eloquently describes the importance of the site. He authored federal legislation to have Sand Creek included as a national monument. Historian Tom Noel concludes in "Rewriting the Past for the Present: Political Monuments and Political Correctness" that altering a nineteenth-century Civil War monument on the steps of the Colorado state capitol in Denver may not be the best way to reinterpret the past.

Interpreting the "Anasazi Myth"
How the Pueblo Indians Disappeared from the Story

Joseph Weixelman

Public historians often interpret a culture other than their own, leading to confusion in the perception of American minorities. Nowhere is this more true than in the representation of the history and culture of native peoples. Unfortunately, the National Park Service (NPS) has often been a participant in such misinterpretations. For example, most literature about Yellowstone National Park claimed the tribes of that region feared the geysers, leaving visitors with the popular image of "savages" cowering before natural forces.[1] The national parks and monuments that most directly affect the public perception of native peoples are those in the Southwest that preserve the remains of ancestral Pueblo Indians. These parks include Mesa Verde, with its impressive cliff dwellings, Chaco Canyon, with its imposing community houses, and many other national monuments of the Four Corners.

The public associates these ruins with the "Anasazi," an archaeological term borrowed from the Navajo, which refers to Ancestral Puebloans.[2] However, most people do not understand that this term refers to the ancestors of today's Pueblo Indians. Instead, the common perception is that those who inhabited the cliff dwellings and canyon villages mysteriously disappeared, leaving scientists baffled. American Romanticism and the inability of scholars to adequately convey their ideas to the public gave birth to the myth that the "Anasazi" vanished.[3] The economics of tourism and popular novels perpetuated the myth. The NPS indirectly contributed to the public's misunderstanding by using interpretive methods emphasizing a compelling story. The ultimate effect of perpetuating the myth was to deny Pueblo Indians their historical and cultural heritage, to alienate them from academic discussions of their past, and to make interpretation by public historians confusing.

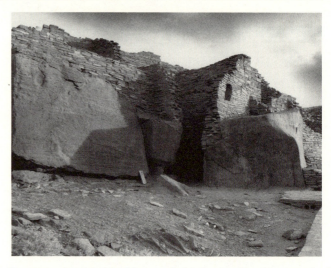

Figure 44. Ancestral Puebloan walls built around boulders stand at Wupatki National Monument, Arizona. Photo by Andrew Gulliford, 1997.

For Pueblo Indians there was never a question about the builders of the ancient villages of the Four Corners.[4] However, after enduring more than 450 years of persecution for trying to preserve their culture and traditions, under both Spain and the United States, they are reticent to discuss their culture unless it is necessary to fend off a legal attack.[5] Every pueblo has traditions telling of migrations that brought them to the places they reside today. Joe Sando of Jemez Pueblo, the historian of the All Indian Pueblo Council, recorded that the Pueblos "settled in the Four Corners area, where they developed their civilization and settled for some hundreds of years before moving to their present homelands."[6] The Hopi speak of these ancient sites, and everything associated with them, as their "footprints."[7] Zia Pueblo recounts its migration story at an annual observance that takes four hours and includes specific references to Chaco Canyon and Mesa Verde.[8] They do not forget their ancestors; neither do their traditions require the sanction of Anglo scientists and historians. They know their history.

The Origins of the Myth

The idea of a "forgotten race" or "vanished civilization" inhabiting North America before Columbus is an old European concept. As American pioneers poured over the Alleghenies and stumbled upon the earthen mounds of ancient Native Americans, they could not believe that the ancestors of the "savage" Indians they knew could have built such sophisticated structures. Some discoverers claimed the Toltecs built the mounds on their way to Mexico. A more popular version suggested that a race of white men built the mounds and that the "savage" Indians then invaded and drove them away.[9] This popular theory justified the appropriation of Indian lands—the white man was only taking back what had belonged to his people before.[10]

As Americans encountered the ruins of large Pueblo buildings in the Southwest on their western migration, they applied similar theories to explain them. The ruins of Pecos Pueblo, an important village during Spanish colonial times, were the first such site Americans found because of its proximity to the Santa Fe Trail. Until 1838, when disease and warfare forced the last of the Pecos population to move to Jemez, it had been an animated pueblo.[11]

In 1843, William Prescott suggested the Aztecs came from the American Southwest in his popular book, *The Conquest of Mexico*. More familiar with Prescott's book than Jemez traditions, riders on the Santa Fe Trail generated stories of Montezuma at Pecos.[12] Josiah Gregg told such a story in 1844. He related that Montezuma decreed that the pueblo should keep a "sacred fire." He further claimed their watch was so severe that many died from exhaustion and their bodies were fed to a gigantic snake subsisting "entirely upon the flesh of his devotees; live infants, however, seemed to suit his palate best."[13] One can imagine this yarn passing among travelers as a late night ghost story. Unwilling to credit the Pueblos, Gregg noted that there was "sufficient evidence in the ruins that still exist to show that those regions were once inhabited by a far more enlightened people than are now to be found among the aborigines."[14] As this misperception grew prominent, Southwestern ruins were increasingly identified as "Aztec ruins."

As "Manifest Destiny" moved America west, a variant of Romanticism derived from the European artistic movement permeated American culture. In particular, Romantic artists were enamored of the past and of distant cultures. Their interest in antiquities moved the American painter Thomas Cole to paint ruins to elicit the "vestiges of antiquity, whose associations so strongly affect the mind."[15] Pioneers carried such notions westward. Susan Shelby Magoffin, who visited the Pecos ruins in 1846, wrote this melancholy reflection:

> It created sad thoughts when I found myself riding almost heedlessly over the work of these once mighty people. There perhaps was pride, power and wealth, carried to its utter most limit, for here tis said the great Montezuma once lived.[16]

When Lieutenant James H. Simpson accompanied Colonel John Washington's expedition against the Navajos in 1849, he wrote the first official report on Chaco Canyon. He discounted the idea that Pueblo Indians built the structures there by derisively stating that they displayed "a condition of architectural excellence beyond the power of the Indians or New Mexicans of the present day to exhibit."[17] Instead, he romanticized that these were the ancient habitations of the Aztecs. With Simpson's soldier escort was frontier artist Richard H. Kern, who sketched Pueblo Pintado in the Romantic tradition with diminutive explorers examining it while clouds brooded overhead.

Not every explorer believed the ancient ruins of the Southwest were Aztecan. When Professor John S. Newberry visited the "Aztec ruins" on the Animas River with the Macomb Expedition in 1859, he dismissed claims that the Aztecs built them, asserting "the people who built ... these structures belonged to the common aboriginal race of this region, now generally known as the Pueblo Indians."[18] Ten years later, when John Wesley Powell floated the Colorado River, he recorded various Puebloan ruins. When he passed a three-story cliff dwelling, he was quick to perceive that the Hopi were "of the same race as the former inhabitants of these ruins."[19] Later that day, he watched the sunset from a ledge and waxed poetic. "Here I stand, where these now lost people stood centuries ago, and look over this strange country . . . disappearing under cover of the night."[20] With these comments, the Hopi ancestors became a "lost people."

Other scientist-explorers vacillated like Powell in the reports of the great surveys of the 1800s. After asserting that a ruin was Puebloan, they romanticized the scene and the people became "forgotten." William Henry Jackson, who in 1874 was the first to photograph the cliff dwellings of Mancos Canyon and record the ruins of Yucca House and Hovenweep, wrapped them with the atmosphere of "romance and charm of legendary association."[21] At a ruin in McElmo Canyon that he christened Battle Rock, his guide told him of a Hopi legend that here they "made their last stand before being dispossessed & driven out of the country by the northern bands."[22] Although he saw the resemblance between these dwellings and modern pueblos, and even though he noted that "from here they went to their present habitations in New Mexico," Jackson still referred to the builders in his official report as "a forgotten race."[23]

More important to the public than the official reports of these explorers and scientists were articles by newspapermen who tagged along on these expeditions. Ernest Ingersoll, a reporter from the *New York Tribune*, accompanied Jackson and romanticized the West for its readers. As he described it, they were exploring remote canyons because they had "vaguely heard of marvelous relics of a bygone civilization."[24] He used romantic descriptions freely, referring to "forlorn cedars" and describing one site as a "haunted Castle."[25] When he recounted the legend of Battle Rock, he gave the story all the makings of a romantic drama with "peaceful" people, "merciless" foes, and a struggle leaving the rocks stained with their

Figure 45. A "museum rock" with Ancestral Puebloan sherds from broken pots lies near a small Pueblo site at Canyons of the Ancients National Monument. Well-meaning tourists place shards on a "museum rock" for others to see. This is not recommended. The recommendation is to scatter or hide sherds rather than to collect them in one place. Photo by Andrew Gulliford, 2002.

"mingled blood."[26] A few years later, Richard Hinton, writing for *Harper's Weekly*, created an equally Romantic piece on Casa Grande, which he likened to a "fortress" and a "castle," while asserting that the builders could not possibly be related to Pueblo Indians.[27]

In 1879, Emma Hardacre wrote "The Cliff Dwellers" for *Scribner's Monthly*, introducing the average American to Southwestern archaeology. Illustrated by Thomas Moran, the whole article exuded romantic sentiments that are hard to take seriously today. Hardacre described one tower waiting "through the centuries the coming of the dead braves to light again its signalfires."[28] To prove the cliff dwellers were peaceful, she presented the remarkable evidence that "all the arrows lie with their points toward the ruins."[29] Dreamily, she reflected, "who knows but from this eyrie, some dusky bride watched for her lover, when the evening shades settled dark in the canyon lane."[30] Moran's accompanying illustrations are equally sentimental. In one drawing, a warrior with his arms crossed over his chest gazes out from a watchtower. His most dramatic picture, *An Attack on a Village of Cave-Dwellers*, shows a savage mob clambering to a cliff house where villagers prepare their defense as the

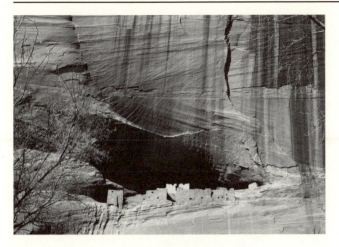

Figure 46. The most photographed Ancestral Puebloan site, and an icon in the Southwest, is the Figure of White House Ruin at Canyon de Chelly National Monument on the Navajo Reservation. Photo by Andrew Gulliford, 1980.

sun sets in the west. The meaning is clear: they are "vanishing" into history.[31]

In this atmosphere, Jackson displayed his photographs at the 1876 Centennial Exhibition in Philadelphia, acquainting thousands with the antiquities of the Southwest.[32] Most visitors were members of the working class, not scholars, and were not far removed from homesteaders on the frontier. A prime example is Sherman Howe's family, who settled in the lower Animas valley. Years later, Howe recalled his father's response when he asked about the nearby ruins. "Nobody knows when they lived here or where they came from or what became of them."[33] This family remained unaware of Dr. Newberry's report linking these same ruins to Pueblo Indians.

In a similar way, when Richard Wetherill and Charley Mason first saw Cliff Palace at Mesa Verde, they did not credit the site to Ancestral Puebloans. Instead, Wetherill and his brothers spent the winter of 1888–89 digging for relics, trying to understand for themselves what happened to the people who lived there. They put these artifacts on display the next year in Durango, Pueblo, and Denver, Colorado, and sold their first collection to the Colorado Historical Society for $3,000. They sold their second collection to the H. Jay Smith Exploring Company and the third to Baron Gustaf Nordenskiöld, a scientist from Sweden.[34]

Nordenskiöld heard of the Mesa Verde cliff dwellings in 1891 while traveling through the region to recover from tuberculosis. He hired the Wetherills to assist with the first scientific excavations on Mesa Verde. Afterward, Alfred Wetherill guided him to Hopi to study a modern Pueblo group. He compared their methods of construction, kivas, pottery, and trade to build analogies with the cliff dwellers.[35] Still, he would only state that for "greater or less reason" they were "supposed to be the descendents of the people that built the ruined structures."[36] When Nordenskiöld left the area with his extensive collection, the local populace was in an uproar. A schoolteacher wrote a newspaper article deploring his "vandalism" and an editor suggested "he ought to be lynched."[37] Coloradoans were up in arms against this "foreigner . . . destroying some of the most beautiful ruins." Nordenskiöld complained that "Americans would rather that cowboys, miners, etc., dig amongst their antiquities than foreigners."[38]

He was correct. Local pioneers, like Charles McLoyd and Howard Graham, went into the market of relic hunting, and other homesteaders living near ruins did the same. Aaron and Jake Gold exemplified the trade with their Santa Fe business—Gold's Old Curiosity Shop. They advertised in the *Santa Fe New Mexican*, offering Indian pottery from Acoma and Santa Clara alongside "Aztec idols and curios" and "pottery, etc., etc., from the Cliff Dwellers."[39] By 1891, Eastern visitors like Dr. William Birdsall could remark that many locals were "recognizing their commercial value" and making "a business of forming collections for exhibitions or sale."[40]

Richard Wetherill's biggest contribution to the public understanding of the Ancestral Puebloans was his interpretation of their relics at the Chicago Columbian Exposition of 1893 for the Colorado State Historical Society. Mummified remains of Ancestral Puebloans attracted the most attention while Wetherill explained that nobody knew who built the

Figure 47. Ancestral Puebloan site in Mancos Canyon in Ute Mountain Ute Tribal Park, on the southern border of Mesa Verde National Park. Photo by Andrew Gulliford, 1997.

cliff dwellings. He used the word *Anasazi* publicly for the first time, explaining that they "vanished."[41] The H. Jay Smith Exploring Company also exhibited its collection of artifacts at the Chicago Fair. In a re-creation of Battle Rock, they displayed the artifacts in artificial caves with models of the most famous cliff dwellings. Besides pottery and tools, they exhibited a "collection of mummies" including "men, women, children, skulls and hair, burial robes, and wrappings."[42] The company produced a brochure describing the cliff dwellers as "an extinct race, leaving no history" who left "an interesting and puzzling subject of conjecture for ethnologists, fascinating for its illusiveness."[43] This brochure painted them as a "mythical race . . . at variance with the common idea of aborigines" whose architecture was "peculiarly advanced for such primitive people." The brochure created a mystery by stating, "How and why they became extinct is a puzzle to all explorers."[44]

The effect of all this publicity at the Chicago Exposition was to popularize knowledge of Puebloan antiquities in the Southwest. However, what the public understood was that these were the remains of a "vanished people" and that their ruins were open to appropriation. The American flag flying over the re-created Battle Butte made this last point clear.

The Creation of the Pueblo Heritage National Parks

The relic hunting, not the desecration of Puebloan burials, worried the scientific community in the late 1800s as a nascent movement for antiquities legislation began. The preservation movement followed two paths. Some sought congressional action to set apart certain ancient ruins as national parks. Its first success came with the Hemenway Expedition in 1887–88, organized by Frank Cushing with the philanthropic assistance of Mary Hemenway, a wealthy Bostonian. In 1889, the expedition petitioned Congress and won an appropriation of $2,000 to stabilize and preserve the Casa Grande ruins. The act also authorized the president to set aside the first archaeological reserve, which President Harrison did when he created the Casa Grande Preserve in 1892.[45] By 1900, Virginia McClurg and the Colorado Cliff Dwellings Association (CCDA) had chosen this route to fight for the preservation of Mesa Verde.[46]

The other path pursued sweeping legislation to preserve all archaeological sites. The Association for the Advancement of Science backed a measure in 1899 allowing the president to preserve "cliff dwellings, cemeteries, graves, mounds, forts, or any other work of prehistoric, primitive, aboriginal man."[47] The bill did not pass then, but when the CCDA introduced a bill for Mesa Verde National Park in 1901, Reverend Henry Mason Baum and his Records of the Past Exploration Society sponsored another bill for preserving all antiquities.[48] With Progressives arguing nationwide for better management of the nation's lands and Teddy Roosevelt in the "bully pulpit," prospects looked good. John Lacey, a well-known conservationist heading the House Committee on Public Lands, joined Edgar Lee Hewett in guiding a revised bill through Congress, which passed both the Antiquities Act and legislation creating Mesa Verde National Park in 1906.

Hewett was the energetic leader of the Santa Fe Archaeological Society. He encouraged the *Santa Fe New Mexican* to criticize Wetherill's excavation of Pueblo Bonito and produced a report on the archaeology of the Pueblo region for the General Land Office in 1903 that became an appendix to congressional reports dealing with antiquities preservation.[49] His stance on the identity of the ancient builders was typical of the scientists of his day. In a 1906 report, he stated that "the ruins herein described were the ancient habitations of Indian tribes some descendents of which are doubtless now living in the adjacent valley of the Rio Grande and its tributaries, but most of whom are probably dispersed widely over the southwest."[50]

While asserting that the ruins were Puebloan, Hewett and other scientists tried to distance the ruins from Pueblo Indians. Hewett's doctoral dissertation, an expanded version of his 1903 report, asserted, "We have found no trace of most of the San Juan . . . groups. Their disappearance is as complete as that of the Lost Tribes of Israel."[51] Quite possibly, he vacillated on this point because New Mexico was trying for statehood and many opposed it on the grounds that the Hispanic and Indian population could not be assimilated. Hewett knew the public would more favorably receive theories that distanced the ruins from modern populations. At the same time, New Mexico would benefit from the exploitation of ancient ruins as a national heritage.[52]

As antiquities legislation wound through Congress, there was one expert witness who stood up for the Puebloan heritage: S. J. Holsinger. In a 1905 report on the proposed Pajarito Cliff Dwellers National Park, he expressed concern because "the prehistoric structures to be preserved and embraced within a national park are the ancient homes of the Santa Clara and San Ildefonso Pueblo Indians." He alone among those giving testimony considered this fact. He advocated expanding the Santa Clara reservation and recommended that as these lands "contain their burial mounds . . . these Indians should therefore be considered and their rights respected."[53]

In the 1906 Antiquities Act, which Hewett authored, he inserted wording to allow the president to withdraw lands that held significant "historic landmarks, historic and prehistoric structures, and other objects of historic or scientific interest."[54] His term, "National Monument," created a new category of government lands, and over the next decade, national monuments proliferated, encompassing many of the sites Hewett listed in his 1903 report. As presidents created them, the wording of the proclamations revealed much about public perceptions of ancient people. When Chaco Canyon became a national monument in March 1907, the proclamation only mentioned the "extraordinary interest" of "a prehistoric people."55 In December, the proclamation setting aside the Tonto Cliff Dwellings identified them as the "relics of a vanished people."56 When the cliff dwellings of Betatakin and Keet Seel were set aside as Navajo National Monument, the official proclamation was more explicit still, stating "the public interest would be promoted by reserving these extraordinary ruins of an unknown people."57 When Woodrow Wilson created Bandelier National Monument out of lands slated for Pajarito Cliff Dwellers National Park, he again referred to the "relics of a vanished people."58 These proclamations incorporated the myth into the laws of the nation.

The Perpetuation of the Myth

Once the government preserved these archaeological wonders as national parks and monuments, the government entered the field of historical interpretation. In a pamphlet published by the Railroad Administration, promoters continued the romantic portrayal of ancient ruins and encouraged tourists to create their own explanations.

> There is always a fascination about the unexplainable—and the attraction becomes greater if we are enabled to come in contact with the mysterious object and endeavor to conjure up an explanation. In Mesa Verde National Park opportunities for such speculation are offered lavishly.59

The brochure commented on the architects by saying, "These people are supposed to have been the ancestors of the Pueblo Indians."60 The myth that the Ancestral Puebloans "vanished" was perpetuated by vague statements.

In 1915, the secretary of the interior placed Stephen Mather in charge of the National Parks with Horace Albright as his assistant. Their first task was to establish a National Park Service to coordinate the administration of all national parks and monuments. Mather hired Robert Sterling Yard, of the *New York Herald*, to promote these sites. That year, he published *Glimpses of Our National Parks*, which boasted of the Pueblo Indian heritage, a close second to the cultures of Mexico and Peru, by claiming that "city planning" began at Mesa Verde.61 He alluded to the fact that a "few of [the] modern descendents still live."62 His 1916 *National Parks Portfolio* went through six editions. It referred to the builders of most Southwestern monuments as simply "prehistoric" but said the ruins at Wupatki were "built by the ancestors of the Hopi."63 At Mesa Verde, however, it related only that the Indians thereabouts shunned the spirit-ridden ruins and refused to believe the spirits were "their own ancestors."64 But the Indians thereabouts are Utes, not Pueblo Indians, and thus the spirits were not their ancestors. With no other explanation, Mesa Verde must have appeared mysterious to potential visitors.

To create the NPS, Mather and Albright relied on key conservation organizations to assist them in winning congressional approval. One ally in their struggle was Gilbert S. Grosvenor, director of the National Geographic Society. He devoted the entire April 1916 edition of *National Geographic* to national wonders. The article had a profound effect on the nation because Grosvenor presented a copy to every congressman. The text described Mesa Verde as hiding "in its barren canyons the well-preserved ruins of a civilization which passed out of existence so many centuries ago that not even tradition recalls its people."65

This description of a "lost race" became the staple in literary works during the 1920s. Zane Grey emerged as the propagandist of the Western genre. His biographer, Erwin Bauer, estimated that more people read him than almost any other American author.66 Grey chose Southwestern landscapes as the settings for many novels, popularizing what had been uninteresting scenery.

He peppered his novels with exotic descriptions of the desert, its "purple sage," and mysterious cliff dwellings of a "vanished" people. They helped create an ambience of mystery in novels like *The Vanishing American* (1925).[67] In other novels, like *Lost Pueblo* (1927), where an archaeologist searches for an undiscovered ruin, the cliff dwellings are more prominent. Yet Grey never identifies the builders of the Lost Pueblo except to say that they were "cliff dwellers."[68] However, it was *Riders of the Purple Sage* (1912), selling more than 1.2 million copies, that most Americans remember best. In it, a cliff dwelling forms the background to a love story. Bern, a heroic cowboy, saves Bess's life by carrying her to a cliff dwelling. Upon seeing it, Bern reflects that cliff dwellings "left him with haunting memory of age and solitude."[69] Discussing the identity of the cliff dwellers, Bern teaches her that they had all "vanished," leaving the area "full of old houses and ruins."[70]

Once created, the NPS began a program of interpretation at the national parks during the 1920s and 1930s. Mesa Verde was in the forefront, under the influence of Jesse Nusbaum, the first superintendent trained as an archaeologist.[71] He conceived of an educational program with three components.[72] The first was a professional corps of rangers to guide tourists through the cliff dwellings and explain their history. He personally selected and trained the rangers and did not allow tourists in the cliff dwellings without them.[73] The second facet was the expansion of the Mesa Verde museum, the first in any national park. The Civilian Conservation Corps built five dioramas depicting the evolution of Pueblo culture and brought the ancient culture to life. However, they left out the final stage, which would have linked the cliff dwellers to modern Pueblo Indians.

The final component was the popular evening campfire program, in which Navajo crewmen joined the program by singing traditional Yeibeichai songs after a ranger talk.[74] Similarly, the Navajos participated in the dramatic productions Nusbaum's wife, Aileen, staged in the ruins of Spruce Tree House between 1924 and 1926. In the evening, visitors watched from across the canyon as red and green railroad flares lit the scene. Zuni and Navajo mythology inspired her first play, *The Eagle Woman*, but her second play, *Fire*, she based entirely on a Navajo story. *Fire* was a love story written around Navajo dances in an attempt to reproduce the ceremonial life of the cliff dwellers.[75] Claims it was authentic confused most visitors, who did not understand the differences between Navajo and Pueblo cultures.[76]

Nusbaum received his archaeological training at the School of American Research under the direction of Dr. Hewett along with Alfred V. Kidder and other well-known archaeologists. In 1927, he attended the first Pecos Conference, called by Kidder, which outlined a chronology for Southwestern archeology.[77] These scientists did not question that these ancient villages were linked to the Pueblos. Yet when Nusbaum explained why he used a Pueblo revival architectural style for building the Mesa Verde administrative district, he stated he was following the design of the present Hopi Indians, "the presumable descendants of the cliff dwellers."[78] This hesitation was typical during most of the century. Western science required written evidence to prove that the ancestors of the Pueblos built these antiquities. In part, this was because of the conservative nature of science: science teaches probabilities more than certainties.[79]

In the national monuments, the interpretive story was similar to that of Mesa Verde, but the monuments never had the budgets of the parks.[80] The man most responsible for interpretation at national monuments during these formative years was Frank Pinkley, Casa Grande custodian. He lobbied for a museum and a library to benefit Southwestern monuments, but there was no money. He personally guided visitors through the ruins and bombarded Washington with advice. The NPS rewarded him by appointing him superintendent of the 14 Southwestern monuments.[81] Pinkley offered counsel and tried to instill professionalism in his volunteer staff. He also attended the first Pecos Conference and hesitated to affirm the Puebloan connection. In an article his wife wrote, published after her death, the builders of Casa Grande were referred to only as "an extinct race."[82]

One of the custodians Pinkley appointed was Gus Griffin, a trader at Chaco Canyon. In charge of Chaco Canyon from 1922 into the Depression, he and his wife, Ramona, provided lodging and refreshment as well as interpretation. Ramona described Chaco Canyon as "the home of an ancient people and their descendents today—the Pueblo and Navajo tribes of Indians."[83] Yet she also wrote that "this departed race" left no trace as to "where they went. No record has been left other than the efforts of indefatigable toil."[84] The lack of written records prohibited park managers from making an explicit connection between Ancestral Puebloans and modern Pueblo Indians.

During the 1950s, Freeman Tilden encapsulated the concept of interpretation for the NPS in his well-known handbook, *Interpreting Our Heritage*. The essence of his thought was the need for rangers to involve the audience on an emotional level, to draw them in with a compelling story.[85] While this is an admirable sentiment, interpreters must also remember his advice to research their story, for Tilden repeated the mistake of asserting that a "vanished race" lived in the Southwestern parks and monuments. In his 1968 introduction to the national parks, he says that "the Chaco people began to leave for parts unknown."[86] People had repeated the story so often, it went unquestioned.

The institution that benefited the most from the efforts of the NPS to interpret the Puebloan past was the emerging tourist industry. Since the days of the Wetherills, guiding visitors to the ruins had been a profitable activity for pioneers. Al Wetherill estimated that over a thousand tourists came to be guided to the cliff dwellings in the 1890s.[87] However, they lost business to Charles B. Kelly, a Mancos liveryman, who broke into the trade by adding the amenity of a rustic cabin overlooking Spruce Tree House. When the government offered concessionaire privileges in 1913, he was quick to secure the transportation concession.[88] Superintendent Thomas Rickner's daughter, Oddie Jeep, held the campground concession and expanded it to include a hotel. How these early tourist facilities interpreted the archaeology is hard to tell. Rickner provided no ranger guides to the ruins, so his eight-year-old grandson and his friends provided this service for a fee. Nusbaum observed that the interpretive story these children told was "out of this world," but gave no specifics.[89]

A controversy developed after Mesa Verde became a national park when McClurg joined Texas entrepreneur Harold Ashenhurst, who wanted to build a model cliff dwelling nearer the urban populations of the Front Range. His Ashenhurst Amusement Company dismantled an Ancestral Puebloan site in the McElmo drainage and conveyed it to Phantom Cliff Canyon above Manitou Springs, rebuilding it to resemble the cliff dwellings in an artificial alcove near the popular resort.[90] Other CCDA members sharply disagreed with the plan.[91] Hewett stated "nothing but disapproval for it."[92] The *Rocky Mountain News* called it "an anachronism of the age."[93] Regardless of the opposition, the Manitou Cliff Dwellings opened for business in 1907.

The interpretation at Manitou Cliff Dwellings was interesting from the start. Their brochures first called the reconstructed cliff dwelling "an *exact* and *scientific* reproduction."[94] Later, they wrote that their "preserve demonstrates the architectural perfections achieved by the Indians of the Southwest."[95] By 2003, their brochure was calling them "actual ruins."[96] Perhaps because the Manitou Cliff Dwellings were not authentic, their creator had reason to deny the link between the Ancestral Puebloans and their modern descendents. In a 25-cent pamphlet produced in 1907, the company argued vociferously against such a connection. Quoting Cecil A. Dean, identified as a Denver archaeologist, they tried to prove that Pueblo Indians were not descended from the cliff dwellers. Dean asserted that "this race passed from the earth" due to a volcanic eruption and cited examples where lava flows and their "fiery breath must have been the cause of [their] destruction." Because the Pueblo Indians he knew lacked knowledge of his imagined catastrophe, he maintained they were not related to those who perished in the conflagration.[97] Another version of this pamphlet quotes Hewett: "Undoubtedly all of the Pueblos of today . . . have an infusion of Cliff Dwellers' blood."[98] This double talk was probably more than a little confusing for the average tourist.

Tours to Ancestral Puebloan sites picked up in the 1920s with the advent of the automobile and good roads. In New Mexico, Erna Ferguson ran Koshare Tours, taking tourists to Chaco Canyon and other national monuments along with visits to the modern Pueblos. Her brochures draw the link explicitly, calling Chaco Canyon "the ancient home of the modern Zuni Indians."[99] The Fred Harvey Company bought Koshare Tours in 1926, but Ferguson stayed to train young women as couriers for the Fred Harvey Indian Detours.[100] Mary Jane Colter also helped with their training, producing a manual for guides at the Grand Canyon. Though advertisements spoke of "ancient races" and their brochures stated "the tribe completely vanished more than six centuries ago," Colter's manual stated that "Pueblo Indians are the acknowledged descendants of the so-called Cliff-dwellers."[101] In this confusion, what the visitor understood was a matter of personal choice.

In 1929, the Mesa Verde Park Company (MVPC), a subsidiary of the Denver and Rio Grande Railroad, bought the concessionaire privileges at Mesa Verde from Oddie Jeep. The railroad produced a brochure on Mesa Verde declaring, "Mystery—all is mystery!"[102] When the depression reduced railroad travel and the MVPC declared bankruptcy, Nusbaum invited Ansel Hall to come to Mesa Verde National Park to takeover the concessions. Hall had a long history of National Park service, having studied forestry at Berkeley and worked at Yosemite National Park. Rising quickly in the new NPS, Hall became chief naturalist in 1923. Asked to come to Washington, D.C., in 1939, he chose to leave the NPS and accepted Nusbaum's suggestion of taking over the bankrupt MVPC.[103] Hall believed he should promote his business like any other businessman.[104] To this end, he produced interpretive aids aimed at the average tourist, including *Mesa Verde: A Brief Guide*, available for a dime. Besides information on concessionaire facilities, the booklet explained the park was established "to preserve and exhibit the cities left by a vanished race."[105] A later photographic portfolio tried to capitalize on the mystery by asking provocative questions like,

> What happened to the people when they deserted their cliff cities during the great drought? . . . What mystic ceremonies took place in the underground chambers we call kivas—and were they, perhaps, the direct ancestral pattern for the Hopi, Zuni, and other Pueblo dances and chants of today?[106]

In the 1950s, the MVCP began publishing a brochure that with minor variations continued until 1976. The brochure emphasized the "restful atmosphere," "spectacular scenery," and "intriguing prehistoric ruins." Visitors could expect "the thrill of exploring enormous ruins left by a prehistoric people that vanished almost a thousand years ago."[107] Though the layout changed over the years, the words *exploring* and *vanished* remained. The intent seems clear—to use mystery to draw potential tourists to the Four Corners.

The Mesa Verde Company sold to ARAMARK in 1976. Its current brochure continues the Hall legacy of building a "mystery" around the ruins. Emphasizing "exploration and intrigue," it states that the "Mesa Verde inhabitants left everything they couldn't carry . . . and moved on," without telling where they moved. In conformity with modern NPS practice, the authors refer to the "Ancestral Puebloan people" rather than the "Anasazi," but the sense of mystery is there.[108]

The Effect of the Myth

The 1915 Mesa Verde pamphlet invited the public to "conjure up an explanation" for the "vanished" peoples of the Southwest. Many tourists have done just that, ignoring the pleas of the Pueblo Indians to respect their heritage. In 1995, the NPS commissioned

Martha Lee and Douglas Stephens to study visitation patterns at three Pueblo heritage sites: Mesa Verde, Chaco Canyon, and Wupatki. They asked visitors what motivated them to visit. The answers reveal how the public perceives these monuments. One person answered, "The atmosphere of mystery and magic," another cited his "continuous pursuit of the Anasazi," and another, to "feel the spirits that linger here."[109] Few cited understanding and appreciating modern Puebloan culture.

Since these sites lack a connection to a contemporary people, many feel they can be appropriated for other purposes. Given the spiritual emptiness many Americans feel and the perceived emphasis on spirituality by the Ancestral Puebloans, it is not surprising that many travelers seek to emulate the religious heritage of the Puebloan past. In the above study, one respondent said he came to perform his "own personal ceremony in Casa Rinconada," the largest great kiva at Chaco Canyon.[110] In fact, Casa Rinconada has drawn many New Age practitioners there as a kind of New Age Mecca. In 1987, New Age participants gathered in the kiva for the Harmonic Convergence. By 1996, they were leaving over 100 "offerings" in the great kiva each year, severely damaging the provenance for archaeological research and eventually leading to its closure.[111] For many Pueblo Indians, the problem is deeper; it is the disrespect accorded their religion. As Peter Pino, a tribal official at Zia Pueblo, explained, "we are offended—they are practicing a religion they do not understand."[112]

One writer who encapsulates much of the New Age sentiment toward the Ancestral Puebloans is Mary Summer Rain. Her book, *Ancient Echoes: The Anasazi Book of Chants*, purports to be a nonfictional account of "Anasazi" spiritual practices. In fact, it disregards Pueblo traditions and revels in the belief that she found the truth that escaped the scholarly community. She defines her methodology as "spirit memory recall," a process that involves no systematic study but simply the writing of what one feels moved to record.[113] Her "chants" show no relation to religious practices among the Pueblos and her description of "Anasazi" society contradicts all that scientists know about the Ancestral Puebloans. She intuits that the "Anasazi" could program crystals "with information equivalent to a modern encyclopedia," that they traveled in "star vehicles," and that they needed "to remain undetected in this new and strange land." They met this exigency by confusing archaeologists.[114]

Although Mary Summer Rain represents the extreme position, many visitors influenced by her or Erich von Daniken come to the Pueblo Heritage Parks more willing to accept an outer space connection than a Native American one.[115] It is not uncommon for rangers at Mesa Verde and Chaco Canyon to have visitors tell them that aliens abducted the Ancestral Puebloans.[116] The thought is so entrenched in popular culture that the 1990s television show *The X-Files* even exploited the alien abduction theory. In a 1995 episode titled "Anasazi," Agent Mulder spoke to a Navajo elder who asserted:

> There was a tribe of Indians who lived here more than 600 years ago; their name was Anasazi. It means "the Ancient Aliens." No evidence of their fate exists. Historians say they disappeared without a trace. They say that because they will not sacrifice to the truth.

When Mulder asked, "You think they were abducted?" he replied, "By visitors who come here still."[117] The episode had an impact on park visitors. In 2002, two young boys following a ranger told him they knew about the "Anasazi" being abducted from the *X-Files*.[118] The word "Anasazi" itself is part of the problem. Many visitors confuse the term with an actual tribe and assume they disappeared because there is no "Anasazi" reservation.

The final irony in this case came about in the implementation of the Native American Graves Protection and Repatriation Act of 1990 (NAGPRA). The federal law mandates that institutions receiving federal funds determine the affiliated tribes for their human remains and the funerary and sacred objects in their collections. In other words, it requires the NPS to determine the cultural affiliation of "shared group identity which can be traced . . . between a present day Indian tribe . . . and an identifiable earlier group," thus precluding the possibility of a "vanished race."[119] Three Pueblo heritage parks, Mesa Verde National Park, Chaco Culture National Historical Park, and Aztec National Monument, identified the Pueblos as affiliated. As other national monuments began the process, an unexpected surprise appeared when the Navajo stepped forward to claim cultural affiliation as well. This set off a firestorm of controversy all because the NPS had wavered in their twentieth-century interpretation and encouraged the concept of a "vanished race." It allowed the NPS to accept a Navajo connection where most anthropologists and archaeologists did not see one.[120] While the NPS determination provoked all Pueblo Indians, the Hopi tribe initiated proceedings to require the NPS to comply with the law and its definitions as set forth by NAGPRA. This entire legal wrangling could have been avoided if public historians had been clear about Ancestral Puebloan identity from the start.

This is the duty of public historians. They should tell compelling stories and involve their audience. However, they *must* research their subjects and set the facts straight first. The reality in this case was that nobody "vanished." Ignoring this obvious fact, early historians helped create a mystery romanticizing the Southwest at the expense of modern Pueblo Indians. It robbed them of their heritage and denied them the respect due their ancestors. Public historians must work to ensure they accord other cultures the credit that is theirs.

Figure 48. The Ancestral Puebloans did not vanish. By 1300 they simply moved from the Four Corners region to the Rio Grande Valley. One of the earliest Pueblo communities there is Taos Pueblo, a World Heritage Site. Photo by Andrew Gulliford, 1997.

Notes

1. For information on the portrayal of Native Americans at Yellowstone National Park, see the author's article, "Fear or Reverence?: Native Americans and the Geysers of Yellowstone," *Yellowstone Science* 9, no. 4 (fall 2001): 2–11.

2. The word *Anasazi* does not simply mean "ancient ones" as many believe. A better translation is "enemy ancestors" (Gary Matlock, *Enemy Ancestors: The Anasazi World with a Guide to Sites* [Flagstaff, AZ: Northland Publishing, 1988], ix). A compound Navajo word from two other terms, *ana*, meaning "other than us," and *sazi*, meaning "ancient," another translation would be "ancestors of those other than us." Clyde Benally, interview with author at Chapin Mesa Archaeological Museum, December 16, 1995). The Navajo used the word to refer to the ancestors of the modern Pueblos, a people with whom the Navajo warred, traded, visited, and married.

The word *Anasazi* was first disseminated by Richard Wetherill at the Chicago World's Columbian Exposition in 1893. Knowing it was a Navajo term for those who lived in the cliff dwellings, he used it when he exhibited his artifact collection for the Colorado Historical Society. However, it was the eminent Southwestern archaeologist Alfred V. Kidder who chose the term for the emerging science of Southwestern archaeology. Kidder called the first Pecos Conference in 1927, when distinguished archaeologists throughout the Southwest adopted a classification sequence that defined the chronology for Southwestern archaeology—eight periods based on the stratigraphic record, three in the pre-Pueblo, or Basketmaker, period, and five in the Pueblo stage, the contemporary period. Thus, there was no question among these scientists that the pueblos were tied to the ancient villages.

In 1936, Kidder was looking for a convenient word to refer to the ancestors of today's Pueblo Indians, incorporating those who built pueblos—the compact, multistoried villages common to the sedentary indigenous peoples of the Southwest—and those who came before them and built pit-houses—single-room dwellings, dug into the earth, with four posts supporting a roof. He suggested the term *Anasazi* to replace the cumbersome Basketmaker-Pueblo then in use, knowing only that it was an Indian word that he thought meant "Old People" (Alfred V. Kidder, "Speculations on New World Prehistry," in *Essays in Anthropology presented to Alfred L. Kroeber*, ed. Robert H. Lowie [Berkeley: University of California, Press, 1936], 152). He put forth this word as a "trial balloon" rather hesitatingly, but the term was soon accepted by all Southwestern archaeologists. As they wrote up their reports, "Anasazi" became ingrained in Southwestern scientific literature.

Unfortunately, the term carries more meaning than these early archaeologists realized. Pueblo Indians see it as derogatory. For most, it is an insulting term that dishonors their ancestors. In addition, "Anasazi" came to be misunderstood by a public that did not comprehend what archaeologists meant by the term and loaded it with their own definitions, including the perception of a "vanished race."

3. For the purposes of this essay, "myth" can be defined as "an unproved collective belief that is accepted uncritically and used to justify a social institution" (*Webster's Encyclopedic Unabridged Dictionary*, new rev. ed. [1996]). As tourism has become institutionalized, the definition is particularly poignant for the Southwest.

4. The word *Pueblo* refers to those Native Americans of the Southwest who were living in compact stone and adobe villages and practicing maize agriculture when Europeans invaded their world. The first invaders were the Spanish, who named them *indios pueblos*, meaning "village Indians," for their lifestyle was more akin to European lifestyles than the *indios barbaros* ("wild Indians"—Utes, Apaches, Navajos, and Comanches), whose nomadic way of life they considered inferior. The Pueblo Indians still live in the towns the Spanish found them in, although their population has been drastically reduced due to warfare and the introduction of European diseases. The last four centuries of history have also brought change to their lives, as they have to all people. They should not be conceived of as a tribe, but rather as autonomous villages that share a common culture.

There are 19 pueblos in New Mexico today, along the middle Rio Grande and west between Albuquerque and Gallup. In addition, there are a dozen Hopi villages in northeastern Arizona that share the same pattern of Pueblo culture. The Pueblos speak four distinct languages. The pueblos of the northern Rio Grande speak Tanoan, which can be further divided into three dialects: Tewa, spoken at San Juan, Santa Clara, San Ildefonso, Nambe, Tesuque, and Pojoaque; Tiwa, spoken at Taos and Picuris, north of Santa Fe, and Sandia and Isleta, near Albuquerque; and Towa, spoken only at Jemez. Between Santa Fe and Albuquerque there are also five pueblos speaking Keresan languages: Cochiti, Santo Domingo, San Felipe, Zia, and Santa Ana. Keresan is also spoken at Laguna and Acoma, west of Albuquerque. Zuni, near Gallup, speaks its own unique language. Eleven of the 12 Hopi villages speak Hopi, a Uto-Aztecan language. The twelfth speaks Tewa, as it was settled by immigrants from the Rio Grande valley after the arrival of the Spanish.

5. As late as 1932, the U.S. government outlawed their religious dances. See Joe S. Sando, *Pueblo Nations: Eight Centuries of Pueblo Indian History* (Santa Fe: Clear Light Publishers, 1992), 92–96.

6. Ibid., 22.

7. Hopi Cultural Advisory Task Force, interview with author, June 20, 2002.

8. Peter Pino, interview with author, April 18, 2002.

9. For the story of the myth of the Mound Builders, see Robert Silverberg, *Mound Builders of Ancient America: The Archaeology of a Myth* (Greenwich, CT: New York Graphic Society, 1968). For a discussion of the ways Americans have stereotyped Indians, see Robert F. Berkhofer, Jr., *The White Man's Indian: Images of the American Indian from Columbus to the Present* (New York: Vintage Books, 1979).

10. Silverberg, *Mound Builders of Ancient America*, 57–58.

11. For the story of Pecos Pueblo, see John L. Kessell's book *Kiva, Cross, and Crown: The Pecos Indians and New Mexico, 1540–1840* (Tucson: Southwest Parks and Monuments, 1987).

12. William Prescott, *The Conquest of Mexico*, vol. 2 (London: Everyman's Library, 1909), 390.

13. Josiah Gregg, *Commerce of the Prairies*, ed. Max L. Moorhead (Norman: University of Oklahoma Press, 1954), 188–89.

14. Ibid., 197.

15. *Thomas Cole: Landscape into History*, ed. William H. Truettner and Alan Wallach (New Haven: Yale University Press, 1994), 64.

16. Susan Shelby Magoffin, *Down the Santa Fe Trail and into Mexico*, ed. Stella M. Drumm (Lincoln: University of Nebraska Press, 1982), 99–100.

17. Lieutenant James H. Simpson, *Navaho Expedition: Journal of a Military Reconnaissance from Santa Fe, New Mexico, to the Navaho Country Made in 1849 by Lieutenant James H. Simpson*, ed. Frank McNitt (Norman: University of Oklahoma Press, 1964), 54.

18. John S. Newberry, *Report of the Exploring Expedition from Santa Fe, New Mexico, to the Junction of the Grand and Green Rivers of the Great Colorado of the West in 1859* (Washington, D.C.: Government Printing Office, 1876), 80.

19. John Wesley Powell, *The Exploration of the Colorado River and Its Canyons* (New York: Dover Publications, 1961), 227–28.

20. Ibid., 229.

21. William Henry Jackson, "Ancient Ruins in Southwestern Colorado," in Ferdinand V. Hayden, *The United States Geological and Geographical Survey of the Territories, Embracing Colorado and Parts of Adjacent Territories; Being a Report of Progress of the Exploration for the Year 1874* (Washington, D.C.: Government Printing Office, 1876), 380.

22. William Henry Jackson, *The Diaries of William Henry Jackson: Frontier Photographer*, ed. LeRoy R. Hafen and Ann W. Hafen (Glendale, CA: Arthur H. Clark, 1959), 316. This rock is now called Castle Rock.

23. Ibid., 319, and Jackson, "Ancient Ruins," 377.

24. Ernest Ingersoll, *The Crest of the Continent: A Record of a Summer's Ramble in the Rocky Mountains and Beyond* (Chicago: R. R. Donnelley and Sons, 1885), 156.

25. Ibid., 158 and 162.

26. *New York Tribune*, November 3, 1874, as quoted in Jackson, "Ancient Ruins," 380.

27. Richard J. Hinton, "The Great House of Montezuma," *Harper's Weekly* (May 18, 1889), 398.

28. Emma C. Hardacre, "The Cliff Dwellers," *Scribner's Monthly: An Illustrated Magazine for the People*, 17 (November 1878–April 1879): 269.

29. Ibid., 270.

30. Ibid., 274.

31. For a discussion of the artistic portrayal of Indians as "vanishing" from the continent, see Brian W. Dippie, *The Vanishing American: White Attitudes and U.S. Indian Policy* (Lawrence, KS: University Press of Kansas, 1982).

32. James M. Aton and Robert S. McPherson, *River Flowing from the Sunrise: An Environmental History of the Lower San Juan* (Logan, UT: Utah State University Press, 2000), 51.

33. Sherman Howe, *My Story of the Aztec Ruins* (Farmington, N.Mex.: Times Hustler Press, 1947), 6.

34. Frank McNitt, *Richard Wetherill, Anasazi* (Albuquerque: University of New Mexico Press, 1974), 24–33.

35. Gustaf Nordenskiöld, *The Cliff Dwellers of the Mesa Verde, Southwestern Colorado: Their Pottery and Implements*, trans. D. Lloyd Morgan (Glorieta, N.Mex.: Rio Grande Press, 1979), 135–44.

36. Ibid., 134.

37. Gustaf Nordenskiöld, *Letters of Gustaf Nordenskiöld: Written in the Year 1891 and Articles from the Journals* Ymer *and the* Photographic Times, ed. Irving L. Diamond and Daniel M. Olson, trans. Daniel M. Olson (Mesa Verde National Park, CO: Mesa Verde Museum Association, 1991), 52, 63.

38. Ibid., 45, 53.

39. For the history of the relic-hunting business, see James E. Snead, *Ruins and Rivals: The Making of Southwest Archaeology* (Tucson: University of Arizona Press, 2001), 12–21. For an example of Gold's advertising, see *The Santa Fe New Mexican*, November 16 and 19, 1901.

40. William R. Birdsall, "The Cliff Dwellings of the Canon of the Mesa Verde," *Bulletin of the American Geographical Society* 23, no. 4 (December 1891): 611.

41. McNitt, *Richard Wetherill, Anasazi*, 57.

42. The H. Jay Smith Exploring Company, *The Cliff Dwellers* (Chicago: World's Colombian Exposition, 1893), 17.

43. Ibid., 1.

44. Ibid., 1–2, 9.

45. Hal Rothman, *America's National Monuments: The Politics of Preservation* (Lawrence: University Press of Kansas, 1989), 11–12.

46. Duane A. Smith, *Mesa Verde National Park: Shadows of the Centuries* (Lawrence: University Press of Kansas, 1988), 43–47.

47. Ronald Freeman Lee, "The Antiquities Act of 1906," ed. Raymond Harris Thompson, *Journal of the Southwest* 42, no. 2 (2000): 224.

48. Smith, *Mesa Verde National Park*, 43–47, and Lee, "The Antiquities Act," 230–31.

49. *The Santa Fe New Mexican*, April 30, 1900, and Edgar Lee Hewett, *A General View of the Pueblo Region* (Washington, D.C.: Government Printing Office, 1905), 585.

50. Edgar Lee Hewett, *Antiquities of the Jemez Plateau, New Mexico* (Washington, D.C.: Government Printing Office, 1906), 12.

51. Edgar L. Hewett, *Ancient Communities in the American Desert*, ed. Albert H. Schroeder, *Archaeological Society of*

New Mexico Monograph Series: 1 (Albuquerque: Archaeological Society of New Mexico, 1993), 102.

52. Snead, *Ruins and Rivals*, 126–27.

53. U.S. Congress, House of Representatives, Hearings before the Committee on the Public Lands, "Preservation of Prehistoric Ruins on the Public Lands" 58th Cong., 3rd sess., January 11, 1905, 30.

54. *The Antiquities Act*, 34 Stat. 225 (1906).

55. President Theodore Roosevelt, proclamation, "Chaco Canyon National Monument," in *Proclamations and Orders Relating to the NPS Up to January 1, 1945*, comp. Thomas Alan Sullivan (Washington, D.C.: Government Printing Office, 1947), 148.

56. President Theodore Roosevelt, proclamation, "Tonto National Monument," in *Proclamations and Orders Relating*, 306.

57. President William Taft, proclamation, "Navajo National Monument," in *Proclamations and Orders*, 252.

58. President Woodrow Wilson, proclamation, "Bandelier National Monument," in *Proclamations and Orders*, 121.

59. *Mesa Verde National Park* (Washington, D.C.: Government Printing Office, n.d.), 4, copy available at the Laboratory of Anthropology Archives, Santa Fe [hereafter LAA], #89 ELH.058.

60. Ibid.

61. Robert Sterling Yard, *Glimpses of Our National Parks* (Washington, D.C.: Government Printing Office, 1916), 30.

62. Ibid., 31, 34.

63. Robert Sterling Yard, *The National Parks Portfolio* (Washington, D.C.: Government Printing Office, 1928), 133, 264, 266, 268, 269.

64. Ibid., 144.

65. Gilbert H. Grosvenor, "The Land of the Best—Tribute to the Scenic Grandeur and Unsurpassed Resources of Our Own Country," *National Geographic* 19, no. 4 (April 1916): 411.

66. Erwin A. Bauer, "Zane Grey: Ohio's Writer of the Purple Sage," in *Blue Feather and Other Stories* (New York: Walter J. Black, 1961), 229–30.

67. Zane Grey, *The Vanishing American* (New York: Black's Readers Service, 1925).

68. Ibid., *Lost Pueblo* (New York: Harper and Brothers, 1954), 47, 52, 120. Originally this book was published as *The Water Hole* (n.p.: P. F. Collier and Sons, 1927).

69. Ibid., *Riders of the Purple Sage*, ed. Lee Clark Mitchell (Oxford: Oxford University Press, 1998), 95.

70. Ibid., 83, 106.

71. Barry Mackintosh, *Interpretation in the National Park Service: A Historical Perspective* (Washington, D.C.: National Park Service, 1986), 6. See also the author's article "Jesse Nusbaum and the Re-creation of Mesa Verde National Park," *Colorado Heritage* (spring 2000): 26–27.

72. Jesse Nusbaum, "Mesa Verde National Park," in "Annual Report of the Director of the National Park Service to the Secretary of the Interior, 1929" (Washington, D.C.: Government Printing Office, 1929), 103.

73. Jesse and Rosemary Nusbaum, *Tierra Dulce: Reminiscences from the Jesse Nusbaum Papers* (Santa Fe: Sunstone Press, 1980), 75.

74. Jesse Nusbaum, "Report to the Superintendent" (1924), 126.

75. *Mancos Times*, July 23, 1926, and *Rocky Mountain News*, July 13, 1925.

76. Philip Burnham, *Indian Country, God's Country: Native Americans and the National Parks* (Washington, DC: Island Press, 2000), 64.

77. Florence C. and Robert H. Lister, *Earl Morris and Southwestern Archaeology* (Albuquerque: University of New Mexico Press, 1968), 85–87.

78. Nusbaum, "Report to the Superintendent" (1921), 85.

79. I owe this discussion of science to ideas discussed at the Annual Conference of the Center for the Southwest at the University of New Mexico on April 12, 2003, titled "Heating Up: Coping with Climate Change in the Southwest."

80. For a discussion of the problems faced by national monuments during these years, see Hal Rothman, *America's National Monuments*, 74–116.

81. Ibid., 121.

82. Edna Townsley Pinkley, "Preserving American Antiquities," *The Santa Fe Magazine* (September 1930): 46.

83. Ramona Rollins-Griffin, *Chaco Canyon Ruins: Ancient Spirits Were Our Neighbors* (Flagstaff, AZ: Northland Press, 1971), 6, 19–21.

84. Ibid., 24.

85. Freemen Tilden, *Interpreting Our Heritage* (Chapel Hill: University of North Carolina Press, 1957).

86. Ibid., *The National Parks* (New York: Alfred A. Knopf, 1968), 426.

87. Benjamin Alfred Wetherill, *The Wetherills of the Mesa Verde: Autobiography of Benjamin Alfred Wetherill*, ed. Maurine S. Fletcher (Lincoln: University of Nebraska Press, 1977), 181.

88. Smith, *Mesa Verde National Park*, 93.

89. Jesse Nusbaum as quoted in Smith, *Mesa Verde National Park*, 97.

90. Smith, *Mesa Verde National Park*, 68–69, and *Rocky*

Mountain News, October 25, 1906.

91. Lucy E. Peabody, letter to Dr. Edgar Lee Hewett, February 17 and April 26, 1907, Hewett Collection: AC 105-Box 1-File 5: "Correspondence 1907," Fray Angélico Chávez History Library, Palace of the Governors, Santa Fe [hereafter HC].

92. Edgar L. Hewett, letter to Dr. A. Noyes, February 15, 1907, HC.

93. *Rocky Mountain News*, October 25, 1906, 11.

94. *The Manitou Cliff Dwellings: "The Educational Trip,"* Cliff Dwellings file, Colorado Springs Public Library.

95. *Manitou Cliff Dwellings Museum*, Cliff Dwellings file, Colorado Springs Public Library.

96. *Manitou Cliff Dwellings Preserve and Museums*, brochure handed out at the entrance.

97. Cecil A. Dean, *Historical Facts of the Ancient Cliff Dwellers and a Glimpse of the Ruins and Canon at Manitou* (Colorado Springs, CO: Manitou Cliff Dwellers' Ruins Co., 1907).

98. J. A. Jeancon, "The Southwest of Yesterday," in *Historical Facts of the Ancient Cliff Dwellers and a Glimpse of the Ruins and Canon at Manitou* (Colorado Springs, CO: Manitou Cliff Dwellers' Ruins Co., n.d.), 3.

99. Ethel Hickey and Erna Ferguson, *The Koshare Tours* (Albuquerque: Koshare Tours, n.d.), 42, copy available at the Center for Southwest Research at the University of New Mexico, Albuquerque, and New Mexico Pamphlet Collection (MSS 112 BC, Box 1, Folder 4A).

100. Kathleen L. Howard and Diana F. Pardue, *Inventing the Southwest: The Fred Harvey Company and Native American Art* (Flagstaff, AZ: Northland Publishing, 1996), 124.

101. "Indian Tour Advertisements," RC 39 (9A), 35; *Indian Country of the Southwest* (n.p.: Santa Fe Railway, n.d.), 13–14, RC 39 (9B), 11, "Fred Harvey Company Association Files," Heard Museum, Phoenix, AZ [hereafter HM]; and Mary Jane Colter, *Manual for Drivers and Guides* (Grand Canyon National Park: Fred Harvey, 1933), 27, HM.

102. Joseph Emerson Smith, *The Story of Mesa Verde National Park* (n.p.: Denver and Rio Grande Railroad, n.d.), 1, copy available at LAA, #89 ELH.058.

103. Biographical information on Ansel Hall can be found in Smith, *Mesa Verde National Park*, 143, Mackintosh, *Interpretation*, 4–5, and Olga Curtis, "The Winklers of Mesa Verde," *Empire Magazine*, November 26, 1978, 14–19.

104. Smith, *Mesa Verde National Park*, 163.

105. Ansel F. Hall, *Mesa Verde: A Brief Guide*, in "Mesa Verde Printed Materials," Collection MO 32, Box 2, Folder 11, Series 2, Center of Southwest Studies, Fort Lewis College, Durango, CO [hereafter CSWS].

106. Ansel Hall, *Mesa Verde National Park* (Denver: Smith-Brooks, n.d.), in Mesa Verde Printed Materials Collection MO 82, Box 2, Folder 15, Series 2, CSWS.

107. *Map and Guide to Mesa Verde National Park* (Mesa Verde National Park: Mesa Verde Company, 1955), copy available at Colorado Historical Society, Denver, CO, VF 978.84 "Mesa Verde Brochures," CHS Stephen Hart Library, Denver, Colorado.

108. *Mesa Verde National Park*, Mancos, CO, ARAMARK, n.d.

109. Martha E. Lee and Douglas Stephens, *Anasazi Cultural Parks Study: Assessment of Visitor Experiences at Three Cultural Parks* (Flagstaff, AZ: Colorado Plateau Research Station for the NPS, 1995), 97 and 99.

110. Ibid.

111. "Protection of Casa Rinconada Interior Environmental Assessment" (Chaco Culture National Historic Park, N.Mex.: NPS, 1996), 1.

112. Peter Pino, interview with author.

113. Mary Summer Rain, *Ancient Echoes: The Anasazi Book of Chants* (Charlottesville, VA: Hampton Roads Publishing, 1993), i.

114. Ibid., 118, 144, 188.

115. Erich von Daniken, *Chariots of the Gods?* (New York: Berkley Books, 1968). Von Daniken put forth a popular theory that beings from outer space created many of the unexplained archaeological mysteries around the earth. Although his book has problems with the evidence, as pointed out by Clifford A. Wilson in *Crash Go the Chariots: An Alternative to "Chariots of the Gods"* (n.p.: Master Books, 1986), it was still popular with large segments of the public. In his book, Von Daniken does not mention any Puebloan heritage site directly. Still, his theories can easily be applied to them and many people have tried to do it.

116. During the summers of 2000–2, I asked rangers at Mesa Verde and Chaco Canyon to record comments visitors made concerning the "vanishing Anasazi." I was surprised afterward by the high percentage of comments that somehow dealt with beings from outer space being responsible for their "vanishing" (ranger notes in author's possession).

117. Chris Carter, "Anasazi," *The X-Files*, directed by R. W. Goodman, May 19, 1995.

118. The tour in question was on July 17, 2002, and the author was the ranger. A journal entry recorded afterward is in the author's possession.

119. *Native American Graves and Repatriation Act*, 104 Stat. 3048 (1990).

120. Matlock, *Enemy Ancestors*, 16, and Burnham, *Indian Country, God's Country*, 63. For a discussion of the Navajo arrival in the Southwest and its timing, see David Brugge, "Navajo Prehistory and History to 1850," in *Handbook of North American Indians*, vol. 10, *Southwest*, ed. Alfonso Ortiz (Washington, D.C.: Smithsonian Institution, 1983), 489.

Study Questions

1. Give a complete description of the word *Anasaszi*.
2. Who was Professor John S. Newberry?
3. Who was S. J. Holsinger?
4. What institution benefited the most from the efforts of the National Park Service to interpret the Puebloan past?
5. Who was Erna Ferguson?
6. Two examples are given of New Age insertions into Pueblo traditional religion and sites. Describe one and include your own response.
7. Why did the National Park Service promote the idea that the Ancestral Puebloans had disappeared?

Preservation and Repatriation

American Indian Sacred Objects and National Historic Landmarks at Grand Canyon National Park

AMANDA ZEMAN

The preservation community became aware of American Indians' concern for the protection of sacred sites in 1990, when *National Register Bulletin: Guidelines for Evaluating and Documenting Traditional Cultural Property* was written (last revised in 1998).[1] It caused historic preservationists to begin thinking about the unique task of nominating American Indian traditional cultural properties and sacred sites to the National Register of Historic Places as part of our collective American heritage. Following passage of the Native American Graves Protection and Repatriation Act (U.S. Code 25, §§ 3001–3013) in 1990, all federally funded agencies and institutions are required to inventory American Indian unassociated funerary objects, sacred objects, and objects of cultural patrimony in their possession and return requested items to their respective tribes. Throughout the nation, objects of sacred significance are being returned to the tribes from which they were originally taken, purchased, or acquired by any other means as a result of the Native American Graves Protection and Repatriation Act (NAGPRA). In 1996, Executive Order 13007 was passed, requiring federal agencies to consult with American Indians regarding the protection of sacred sites on federal land. This became a more important issue for historic preservationists in 2001, when the Section 106 process of the National Historic Preservation Act (U.S. Code 16, 470) was revised to ensure that tribal governments and tribal historic preservation offices were included in the consultation process.[2] How to justify these two processes in a potentially conflicting situation in order to establish a communally beneficial result for all involved parties is the theme of this essay.[3]

The issue at hand involves two buildings at Grand Canyon National Park, Hopi House and the Watchtower at Desert View, both designed by Mary Elizabeth Jane Colter during the early twentieth century.[4] The buildings and the American Indian objects within them were identified as nationally significant under NHPA in 1987 as part of the M. E. J. Colter National Historic Landmark (NHL) district. Because the Indian objects within these buildings were described as significant contributing elements, repatriation of these objects under NAGPRA triggers Section 106 of NHPA. The purpose of this essay is to analyze the application and integration of NHPA and NAGPRA with regard to NHL properties. This is an important issue, one that affects any NHL that houses American Indian objects of sacred significance, because at first glance, repatriation may be viewed as an adverse effect. To understand the complex issues surrounding the repatriation of significant objects from Hopi House and the Watchtower first requires an understanding of the history and development of Grand Canyon National Park and the Fred Harvey Company.

In 1916, the National Park Service, and thereby the National Park system, was established to protect and preserve the natural and cultural wonders of this country.[5] As a result of the 1916 Organic Act, the National Park Service inherited several national parks and monuments that had previously been set aside by Congress or the president for their natural and/or cultural significance. The national importance of these areas was recognized not only by Congress, but also by many entrepreneurs, including railroad companies, who sought to capture the burgeoning tourism market by establishing food and lodging facilities in and among these great wonders. By and large, many concessionaires were present well before the National Park Service was even established, as was the case at Grand Canyon.

With the arrival of the Atchison, Topeka & Santa Fe Railroad (ATSF) at Grand Canyon in 1901 came the Fred Harvey Company, a food service and hostelry operation, which was founded in 1878 and established the most well-known hospitality business west of the Mississippi River.[6] Although the ATSF transported people to the Grand Canyon, it was Fred Harvey's hospitality that persuaded them to stay for weeks at a time and return again and again to enjoy the majesty of the canyon.

In 1902, the Fred Harvey Company Indian Department, a division of the Fred Harvey Company, was founded in order to generate an American Indian ethnological collection for sale and display in Harvey Houses throughout the Southwest. Over the years, the Harvey Company relied heavily on the American Indian artistic tradition for promotional material and decorative inspiration. During the early twentieth century, many scholars believed that the American Indian was a dying race, as did the Fred Harvey Company's staff. As a result, much of the Harvey Company Indian Department's work during the early twentieth century was conducted in response to this mythic threat of cultural extinction.

One person more than any other emerged as a significant contributor to the Fred Harvey Company's quest to develop a distinct Southwestern/Indian ambiance. Mary Colter grew up in Minnesota and studied art and architecture at the California School of Design, graduating in 1890.[7] After graduation Colter returned to Minnesota but was hired by the Fred Harvey Company in 1902 to design Hopi House, her first of several buildings at Grand Canyon. Her proven success led to almost 50 years of experience with the Harvey Company, for which she traveled throughout the Atchison, Topeka and Santa Fe Railway system designing Harvey Houses.

In an effort to provide comfortable lodging and enjoyable food service for visitors to Grand Canyon during the early twentieth century, the Fred Harvey Company designed and ATSF financed the construction of the grand El Tovar Hotel, which opened to the public in 1905. That same year, they also completed construction of the Hopi House, a curio shop and museum designed by Mary Colter to house a portion of the Fred Harvey Company's Indian collection. Mary Colter generated her design for Hopi House having first visited Old Oraibi, one of 12 villages on the Hopi Reservation. She designed the exterior of Hopi House to look like a building near the plaza in Old Oraibi,[8] but her replication of an existing building's exterior was not purely based on aesthetics. Colter believed the Hopi were a vanishing race, and thus she wanted to closely mimic a Hopi building as a tribute to Hopi artistic and architectural traditions. The interior of Hopi House was, however, designed to meet modern uses and was not intended in any way to replicate the interior spaces present in the original building at Old Oraibi.

Colter did not typically draft the plans for her own buildings. She generally came up with an idea, sketched it, modeled it, and then passed the technical aspects of design to the ATSF architects, who would prepare the architectural drawings for the construction crews to follow. Nevertheless, Colter remained on-site during construction to ensure that the building was constructed according to her vision. For Hopi House, however, Colter was not the only one overseeing construction. Mennonite ethnographer Henry R. Voth (1855–1931[9]) arrived at Grand Canyon in October 1904, remaining until Hopi House was fully complete in February 1905.[10] Voth served as the resident Hopi expert because he had by this point spent almost 10 years living with the Hopi as a missionary. He spoke their language and was familiar with many of their customs and ceremonies.[11]

While living among the Hopi, Voth began collecting Hopi-made objects and studying tribal life and culture for the Columbia Museum, later to be known as the Field Columbian Museum (1894) and still later renamed the Field Museum of Natural History in Chicago.[12] Obviously, Voth's work would not have gone unnoticed by the Fred Harvey Company, since the Harvey Company was beginning to collect Indian art at the same time as Voth was generating his own collection. So in 1902, Voth was approached by the

Harvey Company, who requested that he re-create a Hopi altar for the new Indian Building in Albuquerque. Voth complied, and the altar was displayed on the walkway outside the Alvarado Hotel.[13] Almost immediately, several Hopis protested the installation of the altar, calling it "sacrilegious."[14] Nevertheless, Voth was invited to assist with the construction and decoration of Hopi House in August 1904. In addition, the Fred Harvey Company requested that he assemble and display a large ethnographic collection and two Hopi altars in Hopi House.[15] Most of this collection was limited to three cases on the first floor and the two altars on the second floor.

Voth meant no intentional disrespect to the Hopi for his ethnographic explorations. He merely wanted to collect and display their history and culture for all to see. Nevertheless, he was a controversial figure for the Hopi, some willingly selling sacred objects and inviting him to participate in ceremonies, while others staunchly opposed his actions.[16]

After completing numerous other projects, Colter returned to Grand Canyon in 1930, when she was asked to design a rest area at the terminus of Cameron Road (now called East Rim Drive).[17] Noted historians have remarked that the Watchtower is the most important of Colter's later projects.[18] In 1930, Mary Colter was 61 but still actively pursuing her architectural career with the Fred Harvey Company. In fulfillment of her duties as a Harvey Company architect, she devoted a lot of time to creating a realistic design for the Watchtower, which captured the spirit of an indigenous architectural tradition.[19] She not only incorporated traditional Indian architectural design elements (as she did with Hopi House), but also consolidated these different elements into a complete unit, thereby designing a unique building (unlike Hopi House, which is largely a duplicate of an existing building) reminiscent, but not an exact copy, of the Anasazi tower tradition.

Colter's design for the Watchtower consisted of a 70-foot-tall stone tower, 30 feet wide at the base, accompanied by a large aboveground Kiva Room and tower "ruin."[20] On the exterior, Colter added details, which she observed during her trip through the Four Corners region. For instance, she incorporated a large protruding rock she found at Grand Canyon because it resembled Balolookong, the great plumed serpent of Hopi legend. Similarly, she inserted stones that possessed real petroglyphs taken from Ash Fork, Arizona.[21]

Hopi craftsmen and artisans were also involved with the construction and decoration of the Watchtower, in particular, a young artist named Fred Kabotie (1900–1986),[22] who came to Grand Canyon to paint the Watchtower murals at the request of the Fred Harvey Company. Fred Kabotie was born in 1900 at Shungopavi on Second Mesa in Arizona and was initiated into the Wuwuchima society when he was a teenager.[23] From an early age he showed artistic promise, but it was not until he was taken to the Indian boarding school in Santa Fe, New Mexico, in 1918 that he received formal training and encouragement to develop his artistic talent.

Fred Kabotie came to the attention of Mary Colter and the Fred Harvey Company sometime in the late 1920s. Colter explains in the *Manual for Drivers and Guides Descriptive of the Indian Watchtower at Desert View and Its Relation, Architecturally, to the Prehistory Ruins of the Southwest* that she asked Fred Kabotie to contribute to the Watchtower because he was recognized as one of the three great modern Indian artists of his time.[24] Colter thought it pertinent to employ the skills of a Hopi artist, rather than an artist from any other tribe, because of the deep-seated association Hopis have with Grand Canyon. "[Hopis] claim that they originated in the Canyon itself, their ancestors emerging through the Sipapu, a mythical small opening somewhere in the deepest depths of the Canyon."[25] By the 1930s, Kabotie had proven himself an outstanding artist versed in Hopi ceremony and culture. "At no time has he surrendered his integrity to the demands of popular art . . . his role as a guardian of traditional Hopi culture has never been compromised."[26]

Between 1901 and 1968, the Fred Harvey Company invested heavily at Grand Canyon, constructing numerous hotels, restaurants, and curio stores, and to this day, the Fred Harvey Company's successor reaps the benefits. Unfortunately, the Harvey Company suffered financially as a result of World War II and was sold to Amfac, Inc., in 1968.[27]

The value and importance of Hopi House and the Watchtower at Desert View to the history and development of Grand Canyon is of undoubted importance to this analysis. If it were not for visionaries like Fred Harvey and Mary Colter, Grand Canyon National Park would not be what it is today. The Atchison, Topeka and Santa Fe Railroad brought people to Grand Canyon in 1901, but it was the Fred Harvey Company that kept them coming back for over 100 years. Moreover, Mary Colter complemented Fred Harvey's vision for a memorialized indigenous experience by bringing her architectural expertise and appreciation of American Indian art and culture to the Fred Harvey Company in 1902. This illustrious relationship, lasting almost 50 years, helped to shape the American Southwest. Never before had there been such motivation and desire for Easterners to see the Southwest and Grand Canyon. Together, Mary Colter and the Fred Harvey Company Indian Department developed a vision of the Southwest that was both alluring and exhilarating. Borrowing from the Arts and Crafts eclectic tradition, Mary Colter and the Fred Harvey Company focused their efforts on a level of authenticity so precise that it created some strife among local Indian tribes. There are, for example, numerous reports of Hopis contributing to the embellishment of Harvey Houses, including Hopi House and the Watchtower, which often caused conflict within the tribe among those who viewed these buildings and their decorations as sacrilegious. Even then, many Indians believed selling and/or trading sacred objects and objects of cultural patrimony was inappropriate. Only there were no laws prohibiting such actions at the turn of the twentieth century.[28]

Preservation and Repatriation: Conflict or Complement?

The National Historic Preservation Act of 1966 and the Native American Graves Protection and Repatriation Act of 1990 generally work in tandem, each attempting to protect important resources, for different reasons and in different ways, but there is at least one instance where the features of these laws are not complementary. When NAGPRA was conceived, legislators and supporters probably never envisioned a situation in which NHPA and NAGPRA would diverge, but in the case of Hopi House and the Watchtower at Desert View, these two laws are potentially at odds. Under NHPA, no federal undertaking is to adversely affect a National Historic Landmark without first considering, to the maximum extent possible, the ways in which the federal agency may minimize harm to the property.[29] Undertakings include activities directly carried out by a federal agency, projects funded by a federal agency but performed by others, activities requiring a federal permit or license, and regulatory actions delegated by a federal agency to a state or local government.[30] In the legislation, an "undertaking" is defined as "a project, activity, or program funded in whole or in part under the direct or indirect jurisdiction of a Federal agency."[31] For all intents and purposes, when repatriation of NAGPRA-eligible objects is carried out by a federally recognized tribe,[32] it can be loosely defined as a federal undertaking and thus should be subject to Section 106 review, or at least presented to the Advisory Council on Historic Preservation for comment.[33]

When the Fred Harvey Company sold its assets to Amfac in 1968,[34] it included not only the Grand Canyon concession contract, but also all the buildings that the Harvey Company and the Santa Fe Railway constructed during the first half of the twentieth century. To this day, Amfac owns all of the Colter-designed buildings at Grand Canyon, including Hopi House and the Watchtower at Desert View. In essence, Colter's buildings are neither publicly owned nor federal property, which becomes an important distinction when applying NHPA and NAGPRA. However, in Amfac's contract with Grand Canyon National Park, it states, "The Concessioner must comply with all Applicable

Laws in fulfilling its obligations under this Contract at the Concessioner's sole cost and expense."[35] Under this contract, "Applicable Laws" are defined as "federal, state and local laws, rules, regulations, requirements and policies governing nondiscrimination, protection of the environment and protection of public health and safety."[36] Thus, under this contract, Amfac is required to abide by all "Applicable Laws," which naturally includes both NHPA and NAGPRA. In fact, NHPA is specifically mentioned in the South Rim Accommodations, Facilities, and Services Concession contract: "Certain structures are listed on, or may be nominated to, the National Register of Historic Places. . . . The Concessioner must comply with all Applicable Laws in repair and maintenance activities affecting any of these."[37] Even though there will always be some differences between the National Park Service and Amfac with regard to management policies, Amfac has maintained good relations with the NPS staff at Grand Canyon, and they have worked together on all restoration projects. When Amfac's concession contract was up for renewal in 2000, Grand Canyon explored the possibility of hiring another concessionaire. As part of this renegotiation, all of Amfac's Grand Canyon assets were assessed. Based on this assessment, Amfac's property value at Grand Canyon is estimated to be approximately $165,000,000.[38] In order for NPS to replace Amfac, NPS must first purchase all of Amfac's investments at Grand Canyon, an absolute economic infeasibility for the foreseeable future. Thus, Hopi House and the Watchtower remain the property of Amfac.

Hopi Tribe has been pursuing repatriation of certain objects since the early part of the twentieth century. When Henry R. Voth installed a re-creation altar in the Albuquerque Indian Building in 1913, several Hopis voiced their concerns since it appeared so authentic. Twenty years later, when several Third Mesa Hopis were taken to the Century of Progress exhibition in Chicago, they discovered more Hopi altars and other Voth-created exhibits. Upon first inspection, the Hopis believed that the altars had been stolen, since they appeared so authentic and since there was a tradition of authentic ritual items being sold to Voth in the early twentieth century.[39] Nevertheless, this discovery at the Field Museum sparked the initial wave of Hopi repatriation requests. The first such request was for a ceremonial mask from the Heard Museum, which was returned to Hopi in 1936.[40] Similarly in 1958, the Fred Harvey Company returned five masks to Hopi Tribe from the Henry R. Voth collection.[41] These included two masks believed to be the property of the Shungopovi Kachina and Cloud clans, a stone fox used to bring luck to hunters, and a gourd ceremonial vessel.[42]

The Hopi House altars represent a similar circumstance. Sometime in the 1960s, Hopi requested the return of the Hopi House altars. At approximately the same time, Hopi Tribe also requested the return of a ceremonial mask that Colter used in decorating Hopi House.[43] Unfortunately, much of the documentary evidence is unavailable, but it appears that Amfac, probably at NPS's suggestion, returned the mask in 1968 when the Voth collection of Hopi objects was removed from Hopi House.[44] It is suspected that the Fred Harvey Company, instead of returning the altars, locked the Hopi House's Altar Room door, preventing all but authorized personnel from gaining access to the room. Following passage of NAGPRA in 1990, the Hopi Cultural Preservation Office (HCPO) requested that the Hopi House altars (and the Watchtower altar) be repatriated, and at that time, NAGPRA consultation between NPS and HCPO began regarding repatriation of the Hopi House altars.[45] Finally, in October 2001, the Hopi House altars were repatriated.[46]

Hopi House and the Watchtower are NHLs, which make all projects regarding these buildings subject to NHPA regulation. Under NHPA, the buildings are defined as significant, but so too are the objects within them, including the altars. When nominating properties to the National Register of Historic Places, the exterior and/or interior of a building may be designated. Both the exteriors and interiors of Hopi House and the Watchtower are designated as part of the NHL nomination.[47] In the 1987 nomination for Colter's buildings, the Hopi House altars are specifically identified and it says, "Included in this landmark nomination are all of the historic furnishings and ceremonial objects."[48] This means that all of the decorative features Colter added to her design of Hopi House, including the altars, are integrally tied to the historic integrity of the building. Though the Watchtower altar is not specifically mentioned in the 1987 Colter nomination, it is without a doubt a contributing element to the overall significance of the building. The Watchtower altar serves as the centerpiece for understanding the interpretive message of the tower. First of all, the altar is centrally located, making it visible from all points in the tower (except the top floor). From the upper stories, all attention is focused toward to the altar through an open well. The altar is also integrally tied to the tower's decorative motif. In the main room, the altar is prominently situated near a mural that depicts the Legend of the Snake Clan, and above the altar is a depiction of a feathered serpent, a mythic beast from Hopi legend, which winds itself around the opening in the ceiling. For these reasons, the Hopi House and Watchtower altars are significant contributing elements to the overall significance of the buildings, thus requiring that any "impact" to these altars be evaluated for their overall effect on the integrity of the buildings.

Although NAGPRA primarily deals with the repatriation of human remains,[49] several provisions within NAGPRA refer to unassociated funerary objects, sacred objects, and objects of cultural patrimony, which are unrelated to human remains. In the language of the legislation, these objects are defined as follows:

Unassociated funerary objects means those funerary objects with which they were placed intentionally are not in the possession or control of a museum or federal agency.

Sacred objects means items that are specific ceremonial objects needed by traditional Native American religious leaders for the practice of traditional Native American religions by their present-day adherents. . . . These regulations are specifically limited to objects that were devoted to a traditional Native American religious ceremony or ritual and that have religious significance or function in the continued observance or renewal of such ceremony.

Objects of cultural patrimony means items having ongoing historical, traditional, or cultural importance central to the Indian tribe or Native Hawaiian organization itself, rather than property owned by an individual tribal or organization member. These objects are of such central importance that they may not be alienated, appropriated, or conveyed by any individual tribal or organizational member.[50]

Based on these definitions, if the altars in Hopi House and the Watchtower were original (that is, not re-creations), they would without a doubt be considered "sacred objects," because they are specific to particular religious ceremonies and contribute to the continued and/or renewed observance of those ceremonies.

When dealing with unassociated funerary objects, sacred objects, and objects of cultural patrimony, NAGPRA requires tribes and holding institutions to complete a four-step repatriation process. First, the onus is on the tribes to identify the objects as unassociated funerary objects, sacred objects, or objects of cultural patrimony based on the definitions and criteria set forth by NAGPRA. Second, the tribes must prove cultural affiliation through geographical, kinship, biological, archaeological, linguistic, folklore, oral tradition, or historical association to the area from which the objects were taken or the object itself. Establishing cultural affiliation is often a lengthy process, delaying repatriation for months or even years. After cultural affiliation has been determined, information must be presented, which provides a preponderance of evidence demonstrating that a particular object belongs to a particular tribe or individual. Because most objects were taken from tribes prior to written record, oral histories and historical knowledge often suffice for evidence.⁵¹ Once these three steps have been completed by an Indian tribe; it then becomes the holding institutions' responsibility to prove "right of possession," which means that it is on the onus of the institution to prove that it acquired the object by legal means; that is, "possession [was] obtained with the voluntary consent of an individual or group that had the authority of alienation."⁵² This process becomes a point of some contention for Indian tribes and holding institutions, because it is often difficult, if not impossible, for a tribal member to divulge ceremonial or sacred "evidence" about an object. Likewise, it is often difficult for museums and federal agencies to prove "right of possession," because their records are not always complete, up-to-date, or accurate.

When considering NAGPRA compliance, a complication arises regarding the question of possession. Under normal circumstances, a private museum, institution, or individual is not required to abide by NAGPRA,⁵³ even though some private institutions have willingly participated in the repatriation process, because they feel morally obligated. In the case at hand, Amfac is a private company that would not normally be responsible for NAGPRA compliance, but as a concessionaire, Amfac acts in concert with NPS, which makes Amfac subject to the same regulatory controls as a federal agency.⁵⁴

A few nagging questions remain with regard to NAGPRA and this case. Under normal circumstances, reproduced American Indian objects would not be subject to NAGPRA, and Indian tribes rarely, if ever, show an interest in such nonauthentic material. Here the notion of "authenticity" becomes an issue. What qualifies something as "authentic"? Is "originality" the minimum requirement for "authenticity?" Voth's altars may be reproductions, but because they are so accurately constructed and decorated, they may be considered "authentic."

The Indian Arts and Crafts Act of 1990 defines "Indian products" as any art work or craft that is made by an Indian in a traditional or nontraditional Indian style.⁵⁵ As was previously described, Hopi elders using traditional techniques, colors, and materials made most of Voth's reproduction altars. Thus, under strict interpretation of the Indian Arts and Crafts Act, should we consider Voth's altars to be "Indian products," which in turn grants them a considerable level of authenticity? In William J. Hapiuk, Jr.'s, *Stanford Law Review* article, he explains six ways in which the Indian Arts and Crafts Board should interpret the Indian Arts and Crafts Act's implied definition of *genuine* Indian products.⁵⁶ He begins with a literal interpretation of the act: an authentic Indian object is an object that is made by an authentic Indian.⁵⁷ In other words, if the object's creator is a member of a federally recognized tribe, then the person, and likewise the object, is authentically Indian. Hapiuk goes on to suggest that this definition should be broadened to define authentic Indian products according to their methods of production, materials, symbolism and imagery, use, and quality.⁵⁸ He even proposes that certain replicas be included as authentic Indian objects if their use justifies them as such. According to these proposed definitions, Voth's reproduction altars are authentic Indian products, because they were produced using traditional methods and materials, include the appropriate symbolism and imagery, may be used in traditional ceremonies, and possess a high quality of workmanship. Thus, according to Hapiuk's critical analysis of the Indian Arts and Crafts Act, Voth's altars should be declared authentic Indian products; however, the Indian Arts and Crafts Act specifically states that its definitions and provisions do not apply to objects made before 1935, and of course, all of Voth's altars were constructed prior to his death in 1931.

Aside from determining if Voth's reproduction altars are authentic or not, we must also determine if the altars are "sacred objects" according to NAGPRA's definition. In other words, are they needed for the practice of a traditional Indian religion or necessary for the continued observance of that religion? In cases where an original altar no longer exists, Voth's altars may, in fact, allow for the continuance of a religious ceremony, thus suggesting that Voth's altars meet NAGPRA's definition of "sacred objects."⁵⁹ There is at least one reported instance of an original Hopi altar being taken from its traditional resting place by military personnel in the late nineteenth century.⁶⁰ The religious society from which this altar was taken is unknown, but it is conceivable that a Voth altar may be used in place of the original.

Where an original altar does still exist, we may question whether it is appropriate to repatriate a reproduction altar, which in essence would be a duplicate. According to this author's understanding of Hopi religious practices, each religious society possesses and uses one altar.⁶¹ There does not appear to be any case where a duplicate would meet NAGPRA's definition of "allowing for the continued observance of the religion,"⁶² since only one altar is required for religious ceremonies.

Another important question that must be reviewed is whether or not repatriation is to be considered an adverse effect under NHPA. The statute defines an adverse effect as follows: "An undertaking is considered to have an adverse effect when the effect on a historic property may diminish the integrity of the property's location, design, materials, workmanship, feeling, or association."⁶³ When it is determined that an action may cause an adverse effect, the agency must initiate consultation with the State Historic Preservation Office (SHPO) and other interested parties, which in this case would include HCPO and Amfac. Through consultation, all parties are to consider ways in which the potential effect may be mitigated. In some cases, "acceptable loss" is the only solution, which means that the benefits of the undertaking outweigh the significance of the property.⁶⁴ Section 110(f) of NHPA requires federal agencies to pay special attention to the potential effect their actions will have on NHLs,⁶⁵ which means that if repatriation were determined an adverse effect, then the federal agency (NPS and HCPO) must, to the greatest extent possible, consider other alternatives. Based on this definition of "adverse effect," we must first determine if repatriation of the altars will "diminish the integrity" of Hopi House and the Watchtower. After that is determined, the effect repatriation will have on the overall eligibility of the properties can be evaluated.

It can be safely assumed that the altars originally contributed to the overall significance of the building, but for more than 30 years they have not been integral to the public use and interpretation of the building, as they originally were, and so their recent "loss" does not adversely affect Hopi House's integrity.⁶⁶ This cannot, however, be said for the Watchtower, because the altar is so integrally tied to the function and understanding and public use of the tower. In this case, the altar is not specifically described as a significant contributing element in the nomination, but its loss will certainly diminish the integrity of the building, thereby requiring Section 106 review. The problems surrounding repatriation of the Watchtower altar are complex, and there is no easy answer.

Because the altars were described as significant contributing elements to the historic significance of Hopi House, repatriation of the altars should have gone through Section 106 review, even though NPS personnel believed that removing the Hopi House altars would not wholly affect the building's historic integrity.⁶⁷ Regardless, the National Park Service has an obligation to protect and maintain National Historic Landmarks to the "greatest extent possible," which at the very least means that repatriation should be subject to Section 106 review, even if a determination of adverse effect will still result in repatriation.

Like NAGPRA,⁶⁸ there are four basic steps to the Section 106 process: identification, assessment, consultation, and comment. In most cases, the NAGPRA and Section 106 processes work in tandem to protect the resource. They both require that the item(s) be identified, then assessed for historic or cultural significance/affiliation, which is then followed by consultation, during which the adverse effect is mitigated and/or the right of possession is established.

Section 106 first requires that historic properties be identified and evaluated. This is established by first determining whether or not the proposed action is a

Figure 49. A view of the Grand Canyon from the South Rim shows the immensity of the canyon carved by the Colorado River. Photo by Andrew Gulliford, 1997.

federal undertaking, then the area of potential effect (APE) must be established, and finally, historic properties are identified. With regard to the repatriation from Hopi House and the Watchtower, it has been determined by this author that the proposed action constitutes a federal undertaking. It has also been established by this author that the APE is limited to the interior of Hopi House and the Watchtower, as these are the only buildings or objects directly or indirectly affected by the undertaking. And finally, it is well known that Hopi House and the Watchtower are National Historic Landmarks; therefore the historic significance and eligibility of the properties is established. Thus, step one is complete.

In step two of the Section 106 process, the effect of the federal undertaking upon historic properties is assessed. Section 800.9(a) of NHPA establishes the criterion of effect:

> An undertaking has an effect on a historic property when the undertaking may alter characteristics of the property that may qualify the property for inclusion in the National Register. For the purpose of determining effect, alteration to features of a property's location, setting, or use may be relevant depending on a property's significant characteristics and should be considered.[69]

All federal undertakings subject to Section 106 will be analyzed to determine if there is "no effect," "no adverse effect," or an "adverse effect" on historic properties. When it is determined that the undertaking will have no effect or no adverse effect, the agency must notify the State Historic Preservation Office, and possibly the Advisory Council on Historic Preservation, of their determination.[70] Following the SHPOs and/or Advisory Council's concurrence with the assessment of effects, the project is permitted to proceed. If, however, it is determined that the undertaking will have an adverse effect on historic properties, then the federal agency and SHPO (and maybe the Advisory Council) initiate consultation (step three), including all interested parties. With regard to the Watchtower,[71] it should be determined that repatriation of the altar constitutes an adverse effect, which means that NPS, Amfac, HCPO, and the SHPO must initiate consultation.

Step three of Section 106 involves consultation among the federal agency, SHPO, and all interested

Figure 50. B-24 bombers below the South Rim of the Grand Canyon practiced aerial photography in 1943. Later this group, VMD 254, would be assigned to photo reconnaissance in the South Pacific. They valued their time over the canyon, and the pilots and crew returned to visit the National Park after World War II. Photo by David O. Gulliford, Andrew Gulliford Collection, Center of Southwest Studies, Fort Lewis College.

parties. The Advisory Council may also become involved at its discretion. The purpose of consultation is to "mitigate the adverse effects of the undertaking on historic properties."[72] This is accomplished by discussing the effect of the undertaking with the SHPO and all interested parties in an attempt to determine how best to accomplish the undertaking while still protecting the integrity of the resource in a manner that best serves the public interest.[73] In consultation, the following alternatives may be considered: limitation, modification, repair, rehabilitation, restoration, preservation, documentation, relocation, and salvage.[74] Any of these are acceptable alternatives if all parties agree to their methods and implementation. Of course, "acceptable loss" is sometimes also considered an appropriate alternative.[75]

Conclusion

In 2001, the Hopi House altars were repatriated without undergoing Section 106 review, primarily because no precedence existed for such application of Section 106 and because no method had been established that might apply Section 106 to NAGPRA. The innate connection between Hopi and other American Indian tribes to the Grand Canyon qualifies Hopi's claim for repatriation of the Hopi House and Watchtower altars under the Native American Graves Protection and Repatriation Act. Hopi maintains rightful claim to the altars under NAGPRA, even though the altars are reproductions created by Henry R. Voth and in the possession of a private corporation. National Park Service concession law requires that all concessionaires abide by federal regulations.

In this essay, the inherent conflict between preservation and repatriation with regard to National Historic Landmark buildings with NAGPRA-eligible objects was addressed. There is no precedence for this, as there are no other reported cases of NAGPRA-eligible objects contributing to the historic significance and/or integrity of National Historic Landmarks.[76] This situation presents a conundrum, particularly for historic preservationists, but also for Tribal Preservation Offices, park managers, and park interpreters, because it challenges every previously established resource management standard. The innate difference of opinion and approach to cultural resource standards by Indians and non-Indians adds additional complication, because each group is applying NHPA and NAGPRA to the same situation, but because of differing interpretations, the laws are being implemented in slightly different ways. The issues surrounding repatriation of the Hopi House and Watchtower altars present a lot of questions and no easy answers, but as long as we take the time to understand all sides of this issue and consider the effect repatriation may have on the historic integrity of these buildings, we should be able to come to an agreement that is satisfactory to all parties.

This essay was made possible by the generous support and endorsement of Grand Canyon National Park and the Hopi Cultural Preservation Office. HCPO granted the author research privileges in 2001 after undergoing a lengthy permit process. The resulting study is authorized under HCPO Research Permit, License No. 01–016. However, HCPO does not necessarily accept or endorse the positions stated or the recommendations made in this report.

Notes

1. Patricia L. Parker and Thomas F. King, *National Register Bulletin: Guidelines for Evaluating and Documenting Traditional Cultural Property* (Washington, D.C.: U.S. Department of the Interior, National Park Service, 1990; rev. 1992; 1998).

2. Section 106 is the review and compliance section of NHPA, requiring that federal agencies take into account the impact their undertakings will have on historic properties. (Advisory Council on Historic Preservation, "Section 106 Regulations Changes," *Working with Section 106*, April, 26, 2002, May 21, 2002, <http://www.achp.gov/106changes.html#2>.)

3. The full results of this study are included in Amanda Zeman, *Preservation and Repatriation: American Indian Sacred Objects and National Historic Landmarks at Grand Canyon National Park* (master's thesis, Ithaca: Cornell University, 2003).

4. Hopi House was completed in 1905, and the Watchtower at Desert View was completed in 1932.

5. The National Park Service was established under the National Park Service Organic Act of 1916 (U.S. Code 16, 1). Hawaii Volcanoes National Park was the first park created under this legislation, although Yellowstone and 12 others had been set aside as "national parks" prior to 1916. Grand Canyon National Park was established under this act in 1919.

6. William Patrick Armstrong, *Fred Harvey: Creator of Western Hospitality* (Bellemont, AZ: Canyonlands Publications, 2000), 11.

7. Unfortunately the California School of Design was destroyed in the 1906 San Francisco earthquake, obliterating all records of Colter's attendance and financial assistance. It is unknown if Colter received a scholarship to attend the California School of Design (Arnold Berke, *Mary Colter: Architect of the Southwest* [New York: Princeton Architectural Press, 2002], 294).

8. Ibid., 64.

9. Barton Wright, *Hopi Material Culture: Artifacts Gathered by H. R. Voth in the Fred Harvey Collection* (Flagstaff, AZ: Northland Press, 1979), 1.

10. Hopi House opened to the public on January 1, 1905, but it was not fully complete until February, at which time 14 Hopi artisans moved in (Field Museum, Department correspondence, H. R. Voth [1893–1935] and letter from H. R. Voth to Dr. Dorsey in Chicago on February 3, 1905. [Field Museum, Department Correspondence (1895–1935), H. R. Voth, 1905]).

11. Harry C. James, *Pages from Hopi History* (Tucson: University of Arizona Press, 1974), 157.

12. "Annual Report of the Director to the Board of Trustees, 1899–1900," publication 52, vol. 1, no. 6 (Chicago: Field Columbian Museum, October 1900), 499.

13. Barton Wright, *Hopi Material Culture: Artifacts Gathered by H. R. Voth in the Fred Harvey Collection* (Flagstaff, AZ: Northland Press, 1979), xiv.

14. Richard O. Clemmer, *Roads in the Sky: Hopi Indians in a Century of Change* (Boulder, CO: Westview Press, 1995), 99.

15. Wright, *Hopi Material Culture*, 4. As per the author's agreement with the Hopi Cultural Preservation Office, the clan affiliation and/or religious significance of the Hopi House and Watchtower altars will not be revealed in this essay, nor will the altars be described or identified (Hopi Cultural Preservation Office Research Permit, License No. 01–016, issued December 7, 2001).

16. If Voth were attempting the same thing today, he would never succeed.

17. East Rim Drive was not completed until 1931, at which time Harvey Company tour buses began offering

tours to Desert View, called such because it offered fantastic views of the Painted Desert to the east (Berke, *Mary Colter*, 188).

18. Marta Weigle and Barbara A. Babcock, *The Great Southwest of the Fred Harvey Company and the Santa Fe Railway* (Phoenix: Heard Museum, 1996), 31.

19. Colter spent six months researching her design for the Watchtower (Virginia Grattan, *Mary Colter: Builder Upon the Red Earth* [Grand Canyon: Grand Canyon Natural History Association, 1992], 69).

20. The Watchtower at Desert View is listed on the National Register of Historic Places as a National Historic Landmark. It is included in the M. E. J. Colter Buildings Historic District, along with Hopi House, Lookout Studio, and Hermit's Rest, listed on the National Register on May 28, 1987. The Watchtower and accompanying structures are also included in the Desert View Watchtower National Historic Landmark District, listed on the National Register on January 3, 1995.

21. The Desert View Watchtower Historic District is listed on the National Register under Criterion A for entertainment/recreation and Criterion C for architecture (Jamie M. Donahoe, "The Desert View Watchtower Historic District," January 3, 1995, and Laura Soulliere Harrison, "M. E. J. Colter Buildings Historic District," May 28, 1987).

22. Berke, *Mary Colter*, 196, 303. "Harvesting" of this type is now prohibited under the Archaeological Resources Protection Act of 1979. Removing archaeological remains from federal land was prohibited under the Antiquities Act of 1906, backed by similar state legislation in 1927.

23. Heard Museum finding aid for Fred Harvey.

24. Fred Kabotie with Bill Belknap, *Fred Kabotie: Hopi Indian Artist: An Autobiography Told with Bill Belknap* (Flagstaff, AZ: Museum of Northern Arizona and Northland Press, 1977), 48.

25. Mary Colter, *Manual for Drivers and Guides Descriptive of the Indian Watchtower at Desert View and Its Relation, Architecturally, to the Prehistory Ruins of the Southwest* (Grand Canyon National Park: Fred Harvey Company, 1933), 27–28.

26. Colter, *Indian Watchtower*, 28. The Sipapu is a real feature within Grand Canyon; its existence is not mythical.

27. Frederick J. Dockstader, "Fred Kabotie" (UNM MSS.99 [BC] Box 7, folder 25).

28. Even though the Fred Harvey Company, as a distinct entity, no longer exists, the name is still used in association with Grand Canyon Lodges, a division of Amfac, which purchased the Fred Harvey Company in 1968. In 2002, Amfac was renamed Xanterra.

29. The Antiquities Act of 1906 only prevented removal of archaeological remains from federal land. It did not prevent the purchase or absconding with American Indian sacred objects.

30. This requires that federal agencies are to do everything reasonably possible to ensure that an undertaking will not adversely affect an NHL.

31. Cultural Resources Programs, *Federal Historic Preservation Laws* (Washington, D.C.: U.S. Department of the Interior, National Park Service, 1993), 32–33.

32. Ibid., 32.

33. A federally recognized tribe is an "Indian or Alaska Native tribe, band, nation, pueblo, village, or community that the Secretary of the Interior acknowledges to exist as an Indian tribe pursuant to the Federally Recognized Indian Tribe List Act of 1994, 25 U.S.C. § 479a" (Office of American Indian Trust, *Federal Indian Policies, 1993–1998* [Washington, D.C.: U.S. Department of the Interior, 1998], 7–8). The list of federally recognized tribes was established in 1994 but is amended as needed when additional Indian groups "prove" they are an established Indian group with historical ties to precontact native organizations. In the 1950s, the federal government "terminated" 109 legitimate Indian groups as part of the termination program supported by the Truman and Eisenhower administrations. The end result was a smaller number of tribes entitled to federal Indian programs and protective acts, like NAGPRA (Sherene Baugher, "Who Determines the Significance of American Indian Sacred Sites and Burial Grounds?") *Of What for Whom?: A Critical Look at Significance*, ed. Michael Tomlan [Ithaca: National Council for Preservation Education, 1998], 100.

34. When a federally recognized tribe wishes to repatriate human remains, repatriation will not necessarily be viewed as a federal undertaking.

35. When Amfac purchased Fred Harvey, Grand Canyon Park Lodges became the division of Amfac that manages Fred Harvey's former holdings at Grand Canyon National Park (interview with Bill Johnston, October 3, 2001). However, for ease of understanding, all references to Grand Canyon Park Lodges will be generically referred to as "Amfac."

36. Personal correspondence with Laura Shearin, Concession Contracting Analyst, Grand Canyon National Park, Arizona, May 22, 2002.

37. Ibid.

38. Ibid.
39. Ibid.
40. Wright, *Hopi Material Culture*, 6.
41. Clemmer, *Roads in the Sky*, 302.
42. Personal interview with Jan Balsom, January 8, 2002.
43. Weigel and Babcock, *Great Southwest*, 72.
44. Joe Ernst, manager of the Hopi House between 1926 and 1970, said Hopis laid claim to a mask sometime during his tenure. "[Hopis] asserted that it should not be there. There was no hesitation on the part of Colter and Fred Harvey Company officials in returning it to the Hopis."
45. Wright, *Hopi Material Culture*, xiii.
46. Personal interview with Jan Balsom, January 8, 2002.
47. The Hopi House altars were repatriated to Hopi without Section 106 review or consultation with the Arizona SHPO.
48. Laura Soulliere Harrison, "Colter Buildings Historic District."
49. Ibid., Section 7, 2.
50. Thomas F. King, *Cultural Resource Laws and Practice: An Introductory Guide* (Walnut Creek, CA: AltaMira Press, 1998), 150.
51. 43 CFR Subtitle A, § 10.2.
52. Under certain circumstances, however, oral histories and tribal knowledge may be rejected by the holding institution as insufficient evidence of cultural affiliation.
53. Devon A. Michesuah, ed., *Repatriation Reader: Who Owns American Indian Remains?* (Lincoln: University of Nebraska Press, 2000), 143–45, and 43 CFR § 10.10.
54. Except in the case of human remains and associated funerary objects in the state of Arizona. Arizona's A.R.S. §41–844 and §41–865 requires that human remains and associated objects on private land be reported to the Arizona State Museum (A.R.S. §41–844, §41–865).
55. Concession Program Management, *South Rim Accommodations, Facilities, and Services Concession Contract (CC-GRCA001-01)* (Grand Canyon: Grand Canyon National Park, 2001).
56. Indian Arts and Crafts Act of 1990, 25 CFR § 309.
57. William J. Hapiuk, Jr., "Of Kitsch and Kachinas: A Critical Analysis of the Indian Arts and Crafts Act of 1990," *Stanford Law Review* (April 2001).
58. Indian Arts and Crafts Act of 1990, 25 CFR § 309.2d.
59. Hapiuk, "Of Kitsch and Kachinas."
60. 43 CFR Subtitle A § 10.2. and interview with Lee Wayne Lomyestewa, October 5, 2001.
61. Interview with Lee Wayne Lomyestewa, October 5, 2001.
62. However, Hopi will not necessarily be required to reveal whether or not they possess an original copy of the altar they wish to repatriate as part of the NAGPRA consultation process.
63. 43 CFR Subtitle A § 10.2
64. Advisory Council on Historic Preservation, *Section 106, Step-by-Step* (Washington, D.C.: Advisory Council on Historic Preservation, 1986), 25.
65. "Acceptable loss" is a term used by the Advisory Council to describe the tolerable and/or agreed upon removal of significant features or buildings from historic properties or districts following Section 106 review (Advisory Council on Historic Preservation, *Section 106, Step-by-Step*, 36–37).
66. Advisory Council, *Section 106*, 47.
67. Interview with Jan Balsom, on January 8, 2002.
68. It is possible that HCPO filed a determination of "no adverse effect" in order to minimally satisfy their responsibilities under NHPA, but it is very unlikely, since this author has no knowledge of such a document being submitted to the Arizona SHPO, Grand Canyon, or ACHP.
69. The four-step NAGPRA process: identification, cultural affiliation, tribal right of possession, museum right of possession (*Mending the Circle*, 1996), 13–14.
70. Advisory Council, *Section 106*, 25.
71. In most cases, the Tribal Historic Preservation Office (THPO) is not required to inform a SHPO of its Section 106 determinations, since the THPO effectively assumes all SHPO responsibilities under the 1992 amendment to NHPA, but like SHPOs, THPOs must inform ACHP when an NHL will be adversely affected by a federal undertaking. In fulfillment of Section 106, tribes often assume the responsibilities of a federal agency, but tribes may also participate in the Section 106 consultation process as "interested parties" (National Park Service, *Keepers of the Treasures: Protecting Historic Properties and Cultural Traditions on Indian Lands* (Washington, D.C.: U.S. Department of the Interior, May 1990), 84.
72. Since the Hopi House altars were repatriated without first completing the Section 106 process, the effect of this undertaking was not determined. We do, however, have an opportunity to determine the impact repatriation will have on the historic integrity of the Watchtower at Desert View.
73. Advisory Council, *Section 106*, 36.
74. Ibid.
75. Ibid.
76. The full results of this study are included in Amanda Zeman, *Preservation and Repatriation: American Indian Sacred Objects and National Historic Landmarks at Grand Canyon*

National Park (master's thesis, Cornell University, 2003).

In general, this also applies to National Register eligible properties (interview with Jane Crisler at Advisory Council on Historic Preservation, March 26, 2002, and Interview with Frank McManamon at NPS Department of Archeology and Ethnography, October 12, 2001).

Study Questions

1. In this essay, how is the word *protection* used for sites and buildings of religious and historical significance?

2. Define the word *undertaking* and how it is connected to Section 106 review.

3. What three types of objects are referred to in NAGPRA other than human remains?

4. Describe the four-step repatriation process required under NAGPRA.

5. In your opinion, are the altars that were constructed and decorated by Henry R. Voth authentic?

6. Define and explain the term *acceptable loss* in connection to the term *adverse effect* under the National Historic Preservation Act.

7. What is the future of NAGPRA, given recent court decisions?

The Bighorn Medicine Wheel

Landscape Wars and Negotiating Native American Spirituality in the New West

Fred Chapman

Over the past three decades, Native American sacred sites on public land in the western United States have become frequent venues for contentious debate between native practitioners and the dominant Euro-American culture and bureaucracy.[1] Increasingly, the contending parties focus on the issue of establishing defensible boundaries intended to define the geographical extent of native sacred sites and site complexes. The debate is commonly formatted in terms of (1) the procedural requirements of Section 106 of the National Historic Preservation Act (36 CFR 800), which obligate federal agencies to consider the effects of land management decisions on cultural resources, and (2) the documentation standards for listing important historic and prehistoric sites on the National Register of Historic Places (36 CFR 60), which is the federal government's list of the most significant cultural resource localities in the United States.

Profoundly dissimilar ideological and cultural differences underlie this debate. To Native Americans, sacred sites are often components of a much larger landscape consisting of related traditional use areas and natural features whose expansive boundaries are frequently amorphous. Euro-Americans tend to regard these same sacred sites as smaller, discrete loci with well-defined boundaries. Government agencies, particularly federal land management authorities, are challenged to mediate these widely divergent viewpoints in ways that accommodate Native American religious freedom prerogatives while also promoting multiple land use policies shaped by a bewildering array of sometimes contradictory statutory authorities, congressional resolutions, and executive orders regarding natural and cultural resource management. The negotiations that lead to accommodation, if accommodation is even possible, are frequently protracted and excruciating but ultimately contribute to the broader multicultural discourse that is redefining a postmodern America in which previous, familiar interpretations of cultural geography must now share intellectual space with competing narratives of significance and meaning.

The negotiations and discourse I refer to concern the human dimensions of what has been called the "New West" by Patricia Limerick and others since the early 1990s. The "New West" is a physical and psychological landscape in which the traditional, mythical characterizations of the solitary, resourceful cowboy and stoic Indian locked in honorable combat comes face-to-face with the contemporary realities of corporate ranching, public/private land management disputes, the hegemony of powerful extractive industries, the influx of "outsiders" who want to live in this land of dreams and enduring legends, and the modern reservation Indian afflicted by an epidemic of poverty, alcoholism, and diabetes. As the proceeding narrative will show, a resurgent Indian nativistic and tribal sovereignty movement is also characteristic of the New West.

It probably all began with the G-O Road, an acronym for Gasquet-Orleans Road, intended to provide loggers in northwestern California with a convenient route to remove virgin timber from U.S. Forest Service land. The project involved plans to construct a logging haul road through a landscape considered sacred by the Hupa, Karok, Tolowa, and Yurok tribes. In a document (published in 1979) that represents one of the earliest attempts to comprehensively integrate archaeological and Native American ethnographic data pursuant to the National Historic Preservation Act, a consortium of anthropological researchers suggested that the multiple sacred sites, pathways, and archaeological localities described in the report constituted an "entire site system [that] needs to be included in any nomination of sites to the National Register."[2] To the dismay of local political and economic interest groups, the consultants recommended that the most important sites occupied approximately 24 square miles that should be protected from future development projects.

The study was subsequently challenged in court in 1988 (*Lyng v. Northwest Indian Cemetery Protective Association*). Thomas King's review of the case is sardonic but accurate. He states, "The Court found . . . that the construction of the road through the District didn't actually prohibit the tribes from exercising their freedom of religion. They could still go up there and pray, they'd just have to dodge the trucks."[3] Ironically, the haul road was never completed because the project area was designated a Wilderness Area before legal proceedings were completed. The Wilderness Area designation meant that logging within the contested project area was no longer permitted.

Another high-profile, contested Native American sacred landscape is Devil's Tower in northeastern Wyoming. In the early 1990s, various Plains Indian tribes, but particularly the Gray Eagle Society of the Lakota Sioux, protested the right of recreationalists to climb the tower. The dark underbelly of this episode in the century-long history of Devil's Tower involves how the National Park Service, in my opinion, methodically manipulated the public consultation process in order to promulgate a climbing management plan unpopular to both the mountaineering industry and the local community.

At Mount Shasta in northern California, efforts to list 150,000 acres on the National Register as a Native American traditional cultural property based on careful ethnographic research were vigorously opposed by local citizens and a prominent California congressman. The congressman subsequently threatened to amend the National Historic Preservation Act to circumvent the listing. Personnel from the Keeper of the Register, the federal authority responsible for processing all National Register nominations, toured the study area in 1994 and appeared to support the recommended boundaries. Soon thereafter, however, they bowed to political pressure and withdrew their active support of the original boundaries.

The Sweetgrass Hills, a geologically anomalous remnant of ancient volcanic activity in north-central Montana, constitute an important sacred area to the Blackfeet and five other Northern Plains tribes. The Bureau of Land Management (BLM) intended to lease the Sweetgrass Hills for gold exploration in accordance with the Mining Act of 1872 as well as the multiple land use provisions of the Federal Land Policy Management Act. A broad and almost unprecedented coalition of Indian tribes, ranchers, land developers, recreationalists, and environmentalists opposed the lease. The Montana State Historic Preservation Office (SHPO) spent several years in the late 1980s and early 1990s assembling voluminous documentation in support of a Native American traditional cultural property district in the Sweetgrass Hills of north-central Montana. Once again, government authorities balked at actually listing the Sweetgrass Hills on the National Register, not because the ethnographic documentation was deficient, but because of the highly charged political situation.

There are many other examples of disputed Native American sacred sites and landscapes throughout the American West, such as Mount Graham in Arizona, Bear Butte in South Dakota, Garden of the Gods in Colorado, and closer to home here in Wyoming, Inyan Kara Mountain south of Sundance, Foote Creek Rim near Arlington, the Sandstone Reservoir area south of Rawlins, and the Bighorn Medicine Wheel east of Lovell. All of these important sacred locales share a common set of almost scripted attributes: intransigent opposition by the local public to any form of additional commemoration, skepticism that contemporary Native American ethnography is objectively valid, fear that the recognition of expansive sacred landscapes may lead to public access and other land use prohibitions, government agency ambivalence concerning land management decisions that may result in public criticism or legal actions, and the customary bureaucratic habit of responding to potential political threats at the expense of statutory obligations—what government officials call "risk management."

Figure 51. Crow Indian "Cut Ear" at the Medicine Wheel, looking northwest. This 1916 photograph may be the oldest figure of the Wheel. Photo by H. H. Thompson. Courtesy Wyoming Division of Cultural Resources.

This chapter will feature a case study involving the administrative history of the Bighorn Medicine Wheel National Historic Landmark, a narrative that encapsulates a debate that has become a fixture of many land management issues involving Native American sacred sites and traditional use areas in the western United States. In this larger context, the Wheel is one of several possible prototypes for interracial, public, and governmental conflict in the contemporary New West, as well as a possible subset of the Sagebrush Rebellion of the late 1970s and early 1980s, in which local opposition to federal land policies gave rise to confrontational environmental politics. These historical events appear to share a common origin involving distrust of government authorities and a reluctance to let go of the invented traditions that created and continue to define the mythical American West. The Euro-American interpretation of the vast, natural landscapes of the northwestern United States, perhaps first conveyed to a receptive Eastern audience by Lewis and Clark, is an important feature of the psychological landscape that informs the collective national identity. The imagery of national identity clearly includes Native Americans, but not, perhaps, the contemporary reservation Indian, who is no longer the autonomous equestrian warrior of the plains.

The Bighorn Medicine Wheel is precedent setting in the revisionist history of the New West. In combination with the surrounding alpine landscape, the Wheel is recognized as one of the most important Native American sacred site complexes in North America, as well as Wyoming's most long-standing and contentious historic preservation issue, involving death threats to federal and state personnel. The 1999 Medicine Wheel nomination became the first in the United States to be submitted for review by the general public. The Medicine Wheel will also be the first National Historic Landmark nominated as a Native American traditional cultural property. And finally, the strenuous negotiations, which involved six government agencies and 16 Indian tribes over a period of 15 years, established protocols for conducting Native American consultation that are today in common use throughout the Rocky Mountain West and adjacent regions.

In the late 1980s and throughout the 1990s, knowledgeable Indian religious practitioners—some representing the highest traditional authorities for their respective tribes—disclosed that the Medicine Wheel is an essential but secondary component of a much larger spiritual landscape composed of the surrounding alpine forests and mountain peaks. In contrast, the

Figure 52. Early photo of the Medicine Wheel showing distinct spokes, cairns, and a square stone wall. Photo courtesy American Heritage Center, University of Wyoming.

local Euro-American community, for whom the Medicine Wheel and vicinity has served as a recreational destination, mining district, and commercial timber source over the past century, feels that Native American ties to the Wheel are spurious, unsupported, and therefore illegitimate. These conflicting narratives of significance and meaning contain deeply embedded geosophical[4] considerations and, while not the focus of this chapter, deserve brief mention.

Several authors have shown persuasively that historians of the late 1800s and very early 1900s characterized the Great Plains as the successful subjugation of an endlessly desolate and often hostile environment by intrepid Anglo-Saxon settlers and stalwart frontiersmen.[5] Although there was some acknowledgment that various Indian tribes occupied the region, this admission was decisively subordinated by a EuroAmerican historical view that emphasize the favored industry of valiant pioneers who set about to transform a marginal environment and unconstructed landscape into a state of agricultural productivity. These historical landscapes of Euro-American national identity are different than the landscapes known to traditional Native Americans. It is probably safe to say that landscape features have been very deeply encoded into the social and religious structures of some tribes indigenous to the Rocky Mountains and Northwestern Plains.

When noted Cheyenne elder William Tallbull speaks of the abundant spirit life in the Tongue River Valley of south-central Montana, he is telling us about an integrated set of spiritual reference points that are indivisible from the larger Tongue River Valley landscape.[6] Tallbull used these points, as well as physical reference points in the vicinity of the Bighorn Medicine Wheel,[7] as mnemonic devices to help him reconnect and in some cases rediscover the spirituality inherent in a landscape unencumbered by boundaries of ownership. His relationship to spiritual landscapes was deeply personal and conditioned by the oral religious traditions of his tribe. Similarly, Curly Bear Wagner, a Blackfeet elder and tribal preservation representative, relates that "Blackfeet people have resided near the Sweetgrass Hills [the island mountain range in northern Montana mentioned above] for many centuries. During that time we have developed a spiritual relationship with the Hills and their plants, rocks, tree, and animals that is profound to our culture. As they have been for thousands of years, the Sweetgrass Hills continue to be a place for vision quests, fasting, offerings, and other traditional Blackfeet activities that are impossible to translate into the non-Native language but are the essence of who we are as a people."[8] Like Tallbull and the Tongue River Valley, Curly Bear closely identifies with the entire Sweetgrass Hills landscape not as a casual recreationalist in search of nature, but as an individual whose tribal identity is intimately linked to the landforms, flora, and fauna that occupy the Hills.

Case Study: The Medicine Wheel National Historic Landmark

At an elevation of 9,642 feet near the crest of the Bighorn Mountains of north-central Wyoming, the Medicine Wheel National Historic Landmark occupies a high, alpine plateau about 30 miles east of Lovell, Wyoming. The Medicine Wheel is the type site for medicine wheels in North America. Between 70 and 150 medicine wheels have been identified in South Dakota, Wyoming, Montana, Alberta, and Saskatchewan. Most are found in southern Alberta and Saskatchewan.[9] The oldest medicine wheel is the 5,500-year-old Majorville Cairn in southern Alberta.

The Medicine Wheel occupies the northern periphery of a culture area that encompasses the Rocky Mountain and Northwestern Plains[10] of the United States, which includes the evocative Western landscapes painted by Bierstadt and Moran, as well as the sacred visionary landscapes of the Lakota medicine man Black Elk and the Cheyenne prophet Sweet Medicine. This region, which was inhabited by indigenous peoples for at least the past 12,000 years, comprises an area of approximately 200,000 square miles in Wyoming, southern Montana, eastern Idaho, and smaller, adjacent portions of Colorado, Nebraska, and the Dakotas. With the possible exception of the Numic-speaking antecedents of the Shoshone and Bannock, who may have been residents of the central Rocky Mountain cordillera for millennia, current archaeological and ethnohistoric evidence suggests that the Indian tribes encountered by Euro-American trappers, miners, stockmen, and emigrants over the past 200 years migrated into the region from elsewhere.

The most conspicuous feature of the Landmark is a circular alignment of limestone boulders that measures about 80 feet in diameter and contains 28 rock "spokes" that radiate from a prominent central cairn.

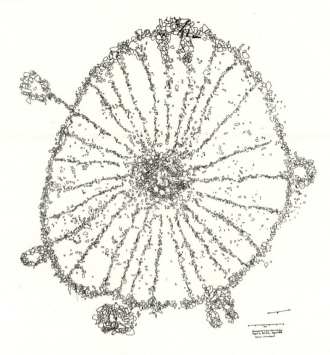

Figure 53. Medicine Wheel drawing, mapped by Don Grey, August 1958. Drawing courtesy of the Wyoming State Historic Preservation Office.

Five smaller stone enclosures are connected to the outer circumference of the Wheel. A sixth and westernmost enclosure is exterior to the Medicine Wheel but is clearly linked to the central cairn by one of the "spokes." The enclosures closely resemble Northern and Northwestern Plains vision quest structures described by several researchers over the past 30 years.[11] The surrounding 23,000-acre landscape contains over 50 discrete historic and prehistoric sites that include tepee rings, lithic scatters, buried archaeological sites, and a system of relict prehistoric Indian trails all superimposed by a century of nonnative use by loggers, ranchers, miners, and recreationalists.

The study area also contains numerous contemporary Native American traditional use areas and features. These include ceremonial staging areas, medicinal and ceremonial plant gathering areas, sweat lodge sites, altars, offering locales, and vision quest enclosures. Many of these traditional use areas coincide with prehistoric sites containing problematic rock alignments that probably relate to early ceremonial or spiritual use. An accumulating body of ethnographic evidence

Figure 54. Wide-angle view of the Medicine Wheel surrounded by a barbed-wire fence that the U.S. Forest Service has since removed. Photo courtesy Wyoming State Historic Preservation Office.

collected over the past decade demonstrates that the Medicine Wheel and the surrounding landscape is and has been a major ceremonial and traditional use area for many regional Indian tribes. Contemporary traditional Arapaho, Bannock, Blackfeet, Cheyenne, Crow, Kootenai-Salish, Plains Cree, Shoshone, and Sioux generally venerate the Medicine Wheel because it embodies uniquely important and powerful spiritual principles that figure prominently in tribal, family, and band-specific oral and ceremonial traditions. To many Native Americans, the rock alignments and cairns that make up the Medicine Wheel represent religious architecture rather than archaeological data. Most knowledgeable Indian religious practitioners regard the Medicine Wheel as an essential but secondary component of a much larger spiritual landscape composed of the surrounding alpine forests and mountain peaks.

Professional researchers generally believe that the Medicine Wheel is a Late Prehistoric composite feature that was constructed over a period of several hundred years. Twelve ceramic sherds from early Shoshone and Crow pottery vessels were recovered from the eastern half of the Medicine Wheel during fieldwork conducted by the Sheridan Chapter of the Wyoming Archaeological Society in 1958. The 1958 fieldwork project also produced nine early-nineteenth-century glass beads found near the central cairn, a wood sample from one of the cairns that was tentatively dated to AD 1760 by means of dendrochronological techniques, and a 4,400-year-old projectile point that was reportedly encountered beneath the central cairn structure.[12] Four hearth charcoal samples recovered from within 400 yards of the Medicine Wheel have produced dates ranging from the modern era (post-1950) to 6650 BP. Although these diagnostic artifacts and radiocarbon dates fail to decisively explain the construction and use of the Medicine Wheel, the evidence clearly indicates that the study area was used by prehistoric Native Americans for nearly 7,000 years. Whether or not this prehistoric occupation and use was predominantly oriented toward ceremonial or spiritual use—with the Medicine Wheel landscape as the central focus—is a speculative issue that archaeological data probably won't be able to resolve. In this regard, Brian Wilson's comments are especially pertinent. He suggested that to fully comprehend a site like the Medicine Wheel "probably requires a world view in which the secular/religious dichotomy simply does not exist."[13]

In the fall of 1988, the Bighorn National Forest introduced plans for access road and facility improvements at the Medicine Wheel National Historic Landmark in the Bighorn Mountains of north-central Wyoming in order to accommodate increasing tourism. During a field consultation with Forest Service personnel, Northern Arapaho traditional elders expressed concerns that the proposed construction would disturb or possibly destroy the spiritual life residing in the vast subalpine landscape that surrounds the Medicine Wheel. The elders later recounted how a federal official advised them that the Forest Service could "bulldoze the Medicine Wheel" as long as the agency followed certain undisclosed regulatory procedures.[14] The incident marked the beginning of years of intricate negotiations and chronic acrimony between federal, state, and local government agencies, the general public, and Native American traditional elders from the region.

The Native American community subsequently circulated a petition that asked the Forest Service to recognize the Bighorn Medicine Wheel as an important Native American religious locality, allow Indian people to conduct ceremonies at and near the Wheel, and prohibit new construction within half a mile of the Landmark. A total of 659 signed petitions were eventually submitted to the Forest Service. Commentary from the local community was sometimes racist in nature and tended to vilify Native American involvement and motives. An influential former state senator from Big Horn County stated publicly that "the ceremonies conducted by Indians might be an attraction for tourists." Others were alarmed by what was obviously a "land grab" supported by powerful Indian advocacy lawyers from the East Coast. Most Indians, they insisted, had never even heard of the Medicine Wheel. A growing assembly of agencies and organizations uniformly opposed the planned construction activity on the grounds that it would seriously impact the values that contributed to the significance of the cultural landscape that included the Wheel. The Forest Service was dismissive, and in a public comment analysis published by the Forest Service in 1989, the 659 Indian petitions (which represented 85 percent of all public comment) were counted as a single response.

By 1990 it had become apparent to most interested parties that the Forest Service's inability to reach a public consensus for managing the Medicine Wheel was profoundly influenced by the fact that the archaeological and ethnohistoric parameters of the Medicine Wheel were not well known. Although the Medicine Wheel had been studied by numerous professional researchers, beginning in 1903 with S. C. Simms of the Chicago Field Museum, no comprehensive effort had ever been made to synthesize the existing data. Based on fieldwork conducted by several prominent archaeologists, it was clear that the Medicine Wheel was merely part of a much larger cultural landscape containing numerous archaeological and ethnographic localities. Although initially opposed by the Forest Service, the involved government agencies eventually agreed to cooperatively sponsor and produce a study designed to establish boundaries encompassing all historic, ethnographic, and archaeological sites associated with the cultural landscape that included the Medicine Wheel. Efforts to collect ethnographic information from Indian practitioners proved extremely difficult due to the disinclination of a wary Native American consultancy to reveal highly discretionary sacred knowledge.

Throughout the early 1990s, the Forest Service committed a number of miscues that severely undercut their credibility in the eyes of the Native American community. The Forest Service scheduled a series of open-house events intended to solicit public input concerning various management proposals for the Medicine Wheel. An open house was scheduled for Riverton, Wyoming, which adjoins the Wind River Indian Reservation, home to the Northern Arapaho and Eastern Shoshone tribes. Forest Service officials expressed disappointment that no Native Americans attended the Riverton open house and concluded that there was little real interest in the Medicine Wheel within the Indian community. Only later did the Forest Service discover they had scheduled the open

Figure. 55. Close-up view of an active vision quest site within the Medicine Wheel. Photo by Andrew Gulliford, 1992.

house during the Arapaho and Shoshone sun dances—a time when traditional Native Americans are least likely to participate in any event not related to this important ceremonial event.

By 1993, increasing visitation—which rose from 2,100 visitors in 1967 to approximately 70,000 visitors in 1992—was noticeably impacting the Medicine Wheel. In this regard it is important to point out that the Medicine Wheel is inaccessible to normal traffic for eight or nine months of the year due to snow cover. Consequently, visitation is concentrated during the three summer months. Vandalism accelerated. Rocks and other artifacts were removed from the area. In an apparent effort to emulate the Native American religious custom of leaving prayer flags and other religious offerings on the fence surrounding the Medicine Wheel, non-Indian visitors decorated the fence with condoms, tampons, used cigarette lighters, fish hooks, belt buckles, and other inappropriate items.

In 1994, the consulting parties began work on a Historic Preservation Plan for the Medicine Wheel and vicinity. This difficult work proceded slowly due to endless revisions, internecine warfare between contending tribal factions, and a deliberate strategy of delay later openly acknowledged by federal managers. The resulting agreement documents, executed in September 1996, were compromise documents that reflected the diverse and contending interests of the consulting parties. Most significantly, the document established a 23,000-acre "area of consultation" that encompassed all cultural resources associated with the Medicine Wheel. The Preservation Plan also facilitated traditional cultural use by Native American practitioners by providing for scheduled ceremonial use and allowing plant gathering in support of religious activities. Additionally, the 1.5-mile-long road leading up to the Wheel was closed to most vehicular traffic.

By the mid-1990s, federal land management officials had accepted the fact that the Medicine Wheel represented only a small part of a much more extensive cultural landscape, but a politically energetic faction of the local Euro-American community strenuously resisted all attempts to change the original National Historic Landmark boundaries. There were other developments. The children of a Forest Service manager were harassed by schoolmates because of their "Indian-loving" father. He was later reassigned after receiving multiple anonymous death threats by phone. The Medicine Wheel boundary revision study, which was intended to establish Landmark boundaries that objectively reflect both archaeological and ethnographic values, was vigorously attacked by the local logging industry, conservative advocacy organizations, and local citizens who did not believe Native Americans had any legitimate spiritual ties to the Medicine Wheel. These dissenting factions were able to influence members of the Wyoming congressional delegation, who subsequently expressed their disapproval in a variety of ways. For instance, the Casper *Star-Tribune* (October 22, 1999) reported:

> Citing the more than 100-fold proposed expansion of the Medicine Wheel National Historic Landmark in the Bighorn National Forest, U.S. Senator Craig Thomas, R-Wyo., said Thursday that historic-preservation laws are being abused. At a hearing of the National Parks, Historic Preservation and Recreation Subcommittee that he chairs, Thomas told National Park Service Director Robert Stanton he is "concerned that the National Historic

Preservation Act is being used to lock up more federal land in the West."

Thomas subsequently used his influence to convince state and federal officials to submit for public review the draft National Register nomination for the Medicine Mountain Cultural Landscape. Professional staff from the Wyoming State Historic Preservation Office (SHPO) objected on the grounds that the nomination contained vast amounts of highly sensitive information explicitly protected from public disclosure by Section 304 of the National Historic Preservation Act. Further, federal regulations governing review procedures for National Register nominations did not include provisions for public review. Notwithstanding the legal ramifications of doing so, the document[15] was subsequently made available to any requesting citizen. The Medicine Mountain National Register nomination remains the first and only nomination in the United States to be reviewed publicly in this manner.

The public review generated over 300 individual responses. While a few individuals provided review commentary on the factual contents of the nomination, most public reviewers expressed concern over the land management implications of the document. Many reviewers objected strenuously to the increased size of the proposed National Historic Landmark boundaries but failed to articulate why they thought the boundaries were too large. Commentary from local government entities was particularly strident, as in the following example from the town of Lovell.

The factual information such as climate, geology, environment, and administrative history that has been documented by either the Forest Service or other individuals outlined in the narrative description, appears to be interesting and accurate. From that point, the document lacks in its ability to give one the comfort of fact rather than historic fiction.... The slanted and sometimes inaccurate statements in this document lead us to believe that a lot of people will go to any length to enhance the cause of the 15,230 acre land grab.[16]

In late 1996, Wyoming Sawmills, Inc., appealed the Historic Properties Plan (HPP) to the Forest Service Rocky Mountain Regional Office in Denver, Colorado. Federal agency reviewers denied the appeal in January 1997 by affirming the administrative decisions of the Bighorn National Forest supervisor. In February 1999, Mountain States Legal Foundation filed suit against the U.S. Forest Service on behalf of Wyoming Sawmills. The secretary of agriculture, chief of the Forest Service, regional forester (Region II), and Bighorn National Forest supervisor were named as defendants. The plaintiff alleged that (1) the Medicine Wheel HPP was "undertaken for the sole purpose of furthering Native American religions" and is therefore unconstitutional because it violates the Establishment Clause of the First Amendment, (2) the terms of the historic preservation plan unlawfully prevent timber harvest in the vicinity of the Medicine Wheel, and (3) the establishment of the HPP and subsequent amendment of the Forest Plan violated a host of federal laws and regulatory procedures.

Wyoming SHPO personnel enlisted the assistance of several highly experienced researchers and set about to revise the nomination document in response to the professional and public comments. The work proceded slowly throughout most of 2000 due to the political necessity of carefully sifting through the considerable tonnage of review commentary in order to address all possible information concerns. Additional ethnographic interviews were conducted and the professional literature was scoured, one last time, for references to the Medicine Wheel. In January 2001, a meticulously crafted final draft nomination was submitted by the Wyoming SHPO to the Bighorn National Forest. Soon thereafter, State of Wyoming officials informed the Forest Service that the SHPO would no longer be involved in revisions to the Medicine Mountain nomination. This action completed a process of disengagement by state officials begun in 1995, when the Wyoming SHPO formally withdrew from active participation in the Medicine Wheel negotiations but retained observer status.

The fate of the National Register document was now fully in the hands of the Bighorn National Forest, which immediately forwarded the draft nomination to the Keeper of the National Register in Washington, D.C., for informal review. The Keeper's review, issued in March 2001, identified a number of technical problems and substantive issues that needed to be addressed in the final version of the nomination. It was abundantly clear that federal authorities were not yet prepared to endorse the document, even though many experienced cultural resource specialists regard it as the most comprehensive and finely detailed National Register nomination ever produced in Wyoming. The Forest Service subsequently drafted their own version of the nomination. They reduced the proposed boundaries from 15,230 acres (originally recommended by Forest Service archaeologists who contributed to early versions of the nomination) to 2,650 acres. Most of the ethnographic narratives contained in the January 2001 nomination were either removed or substantially summarized. The Administrative History section, which was factual but not particularly flattering to either the Forest Service or the local Euro-American community, was almost entirely omitted. The Forest Service version of the nomination was crafted in ways that addressed many of the concerns of the local Euro-American community to the general exclusion of the involved Native American organizations and historic preservation interests. The National Historic Landmark nomination is currently under review by the involved government agencies and Indian community.

Finally, in December 2001 and after nearly three years of deliberation, the U.S. Federal District Court dismissed the suit filed against the Forest Service by the Mountain States Legal Foundation. Mountain States immediately filed an appeal with the 10th Circuit Court of Appeals in Denver. Legal experts

Figure 56. A Native American offering on the fence surrounding the Bighorn Medicine Wheel in Wyoming. Native Americans have made pilgrimages to Medicine Mountain for centuries if not millennia, and they leave offerings at the site. Photo by Andrew Gulliford, 1992.

familiar with the case believe the suit will end up in the U.S. Supreme Court.

Conclusions: Interpretive Dissonance on the High Plains

One is tempted to view the Bighorn Medicine Wheel, and the deeply encoded cultural landscape that surrounds it, as a predominantly anthropological expression due to the clear archaeological and ethnological dimensions by which the Wheel is conventionally understood. I have tried to show, however, that the story of Native American landscapes involves a web of interdisciplinary connections to anthropology, historical geography, environmental studies, sociology, political science, public history, and public administration. To see the broader picture and not be distracted by the details, we must adjust our vantage point slightly. Most, if not all, of the regional conflicts involving Native American traditional use areas, sacred sites, and sacred landscapes are accompanied by a suite of disturbing questions concerning social ethics, veiled racism, and the parameters of legitimate scientific inquiry. These conflicts—individually and collectively—are essentially studies of postmodern change in a multicultural America.

The scientific and public narratives associated with sites important to Native Americans are often subject to diverse interpretations. To the professional archaeologist, the Wheel is the type site for all North American medicine wheels. As such, it embodies important research values and knowledge that can be articulated by means of archaeological survey and excavation and the careful collection of ethnohistoric and ethnographic information from informed Native American traditional elders. To cultural anthropologists, the Medicine Wheel also represents a rare opportunity to study a prehistoric site complex in the context of contemporary traditional use by numerous Indian tribes. Ethnographic interviews conducted with traditional Native Americans, and culture history interviews conducted with elderly Euro-Americans who live nearby, provide an important opportunity to systematically collect and curate knowledge that might otherwise be lost to subsequent generations.

To many long-term residents of the northern Bighorn Basin, the Medicine Wheel represents a popular and highly valued recreational locus for camping, hunting, fishing, and picnicking. The first documentary reference to the Wheel occurred in 1895, when Paul Francke described his hunting exploits in an article published in *Forest and Stream*. This recreational emphasis, which has a time depth of a little over 100 years, has been documented by means of recent oral interviews conducted with elderly residents of the area and by reviewing local area newspapers going back to about 1920.

At one time the site locale contributed significantly to the local economy. At the turn of the century, miners and loggers exploited the natural resources near the Medicine Wheel, and the resident bighorn sheep were soon hunted to extinction. Later, the area served as an important summer range for domestic sheep and cattle. The historic imagery of the resourceful logger, miner, and rancher living close to the land in a wilderness setting remains a powerful image to local Euro-Americans. Local residents have a proprietary interest in the Medicine Wheel strongly reinforced by interconnected family historical narratives that relate to the commercial and recreational use of the area. The residents who have frequented the Medicine Wheel claim they have never seen Native Americans at the Landmark until quite recently. They generally reject out of hand the abundant evidence contained in Forest Service archives, the professional literature, and photographic archives that clearly shows Native Americans knew about and used the Wheel before and after the settlement of the basin by predominantly Mormon immigrants during the early twentieth century. For these residents, the Medicine Wheel is a simulacrum[17] representing Native American spiritual use that never actually occurred. They resent what they regard as the recent intrusion by Native Americans and feel that unwanted change is being forced on them by federal land management agencies and various external government entities.

The fact that the available documentary and photographic evidence is dismissed by the local Euro-American community is not perhaps as dishonest and wrongheaded as it seems. I argue that this pervasive attitude accurately reflects the cultural insularity of the region and long history of proprietary concern for Medicine Mountain as a valued recreational destination and symbol of economic development traditions such as ranching, timber harvesting, and tourism. It was, after all, the local citizens and their politicians who pressed the issue of commemorating the Wheel first as a National Monument and later as a National Historic Landmark. There are many informal historical accounts of how the local Boy Scout troop or other concerned citizen groups periodically maintained the Wheel. In sum, scientific and Native American accounts of the Medicine Wheel are clearly exterior to the closely guarded, local oral traditions that have over the past century achieved a kind of inviolable sacredness that spans the entire history of Euro-American occupation in the Big Horn Basin. In this context, the Medicine Wheel is connected to memories of family outings, making a living from the wilderness, and to the magic of a mysterious stone alignment of unknowable origins.

The Native American agenda was complex. On the surface, the Indian traditional community wanted access to the Medicine Wheel in order to conduct personal and group ceremonial activities. None of the involved tribes advocated exclusion of non-Indian visitors, except during important ceremonial events. Tribes argued internally and with other tribes concerning the proper spiritual use of the Medicine Wheel, and it became clear that there was much variation in the spiritual use traditions associated with Medicine Mountain. Several prominent and influential Native American traditional elders removed themselves from the ongoing negotiations because of the increasingly strident and acrimonious debate. Due to the significance of the Medicine Wheel and the surrounding sacred landscape, it was considered culturally inappropriate and spiritually perilous to engage in arguments concerning the Medicine Wheel. To some Native American representatives, the Medicine Wheel engendered issues of tribal sovereignty and religious freedom, and to these individuals Medicine Mountain assumed spiritual *and* political importance.

To cultural resource management professionals and the government agencies they represent, Medicine Mountain epitomizes new consultation partners with unfamiliar agendas. At first, government agencies tended to ignore the Indian tribes and the preservation community in deference to the customary pro-development stance of the local Euro-American community. Cultural resource specialists attempted to inform their managers that there were statutory requirements mandating the inclusion of all interested parties in land management decisions concerning the Medicine Wheel. Federal and state administrators responded by systematically removing cultural resource specialists from engagement in Medicine Wheel issues, which resulted in a kind of internecine warfare within and between the involved government agencies. Government agencies were also placed in the difficult position of having to mediate a settlement among groups representing mutually incompatible agendas within the broader context of a substantial and often contradictory body of federal laws, statutes, guidelines, and protocols.

Let me conclude with several observations about the contemporary status of Native American consultation in the western United States. Although cultural resource management specialists and their administrators have accepted the inevitability of consultation with tribal members in the historic preservation venue, there remains a strong undercurrent of "why in the hell are we doing this?" Of perhaps greater significance is the impatient industrial land developer, who, under current federal regulations, receives a lease from the federal government, with implied consent to exercise that lease, in advance of any comprehensive resource analysis. In the western United States, this situation carries with it a broad range of problems for land development projects subject to National Environmental Policy Agency (NEPA) and NHPA because the consultations and technical analysis mandated by these two statutes intended to identify project impacts to natural and cultural resources almost always occurs *after* a commercial lease has been issued. Potential impacts to important historic sites or Native American sacred sites are consequently often identified after a company has made substantial project investments in terms of time and money. Federal agencies have developed a wide array of techniques to alleviate impediments to land developers, most notoriously, in my opinion, the Finding of No Significant Impact (FONSI) following an Environmental Assessment (EA), which is really nothing more than an abbreviated resource synthesis. The FONSI nearly always obligates the involved federal agency to comply with existing resource laws and regulations but assumes that (1) all resource impacts can be acceptably mitigated and (2) land development activities can proceed concurrently with regulatory compliance procedures, which include public consultation as well as conducting technical field studies.

There are no easy solutions to this interconnected series of problems, but let me suggest a couple of possibilities. First of all, the federal government should always strive to engage in good-faith negotiations with the Native American community. This isn't happening when federal managers have already decided that a project with the potential to impact a sacred site will be authorized regardless of the resource impacts identified during the consultation process. Second, there needs to be some way to monitor and restrict the abusive practice of relying on FONSIs in order to create project environments favorable to land development. Today advocacy organizations or individuals who oppose a land development action must resort to time-consuming administrative appeals and formal court proceedings. While legal settlements have helped refine and standardize the interpretation of pertinent laws and regulations intended to guide land management decisions, legal actions (I think everyone can agree) have become too numerous and should be avoided. Implementing regulations that create clear thresholds for improper federal project authorizations should be developed.

Native American consultation is further complicated by federal laws and procedures that mandate and support the creation of Tribal Historic Preservation Offices (THPOs) without providing adequate training to the tribal officials who supervise the THPOs or to the THPO personnel who are actually "on the ground." The net result is an ineffective THPO populated by employees who don't have sufficient professional experience to work constructively with their federal and state government counterparts. Recent negotiations between the Wyoming SHPO and Northern Arapaho tribal authorities point the way to a better way of creating a proficient THPO. In a recent application for an Historic Preservation Fund (HPF) grant, the Arapaho tribe has explicitly requested formal training by SHPO personnel regarding the procedures and techniques of cultural resource management. In doing so, the Arapaho have acknowledged that tribal historic preservation interests at the present time are best realized with the close cooperation of highly experienced non-Indian preservation specialists. The National Park Service, who is responsible for administering HPF grants to qualifiying THPOs, should promulgate regulations or guidelines that mandate professional assistance in the establishment of any prospective THPO. Strong and credible THPOs are really in everyone's best interest.

The Native American community is not blameless. Embracing yet another short-term economic development opportunity and applying it to their extended family members, elected tribal officials have developed a penchant for appointing their unqualified sons, uncles, and cousins to act as tribal historic preservation consultants to federal agencies and land development interests. These are often native people who know very little about tribal oral traditions and ethnohistory. This job should be returned to the appropriate traditional authorities who are the true experts in such matters.

The National Register of Historic Places program should be overhauled in ways that make it less liable to political influence and more inclusive of tribal perspectives of site significance and meaning. Originally intended to commemorate the most significant historic properties in the United States by means of a common set of documentation standards, the National Register has not really changed much since it was authorized as a component of the National Historic Preservation Act of 1966. Although documentation standards for historic and prehistoric sites have been upgraded over the years and in 1994 *National Register Bulletin* 38 ("Guideline for Evaluating and Documenting Traditional Cultural Properties") provided researchers with guidelines for documenting Indian traditional sites and landscapes for inclusion in the National Register, in reality Native American traditional cultural properties are often held to a much higher standard of documentation than other kinds of eligible sites. This is particularly true if the prospective National Register designation is politically charged or opposed by the local Euro-American community. Typically, Native American sacred landscapes such as Mount Shasta in California, the Sweetgrass Hills in Montana, and the Bighorn

Medicine Wheel, all of which have been opposed by a very vocal Euro-American minority, have failed to achieve National Register listing due to federal reviewers[18] who are overly concerned with political fallout. The quality and quantity of data presented in support of listing does not seem to be a factor, although these factors are often used to deny listing. For instance, the most recent iteration of the unsuccessful Medicine Mountain Cultural Landscape nomination is about 120 pages long, a third of which contains highly detailed and scrupulously researched ethnohistoric and ethnographic data. In contrast, federal reviewers concurred that the noncontroversial Torrey Canyon Petroglyph District in northwestern Wyoming was eligible for the National Register of Historic Places as a Native American traditional cultural property based on ethnographic data that occupied a total of two paragraphs.

There are several problematic issues involved in the process of documenting Native American traditional cultural properties for the purposes of the National Register. First, the information sets required in any nomination are founded on the empirical principles of the contemporary practice of history, historic architecture, and archaeology. Cultural anthropology (specifically ethnohistory and ethnography) and ethnoarchaeology are fairly recent additions to the disciplinary backdrop that underlies the systematic collection of information used to support National Register eligibility. These are Eurocentric disciplines unfamiliar and often irrelevant to the traditional Native American community, which relies on systems of knowledge that hinge on the communication of oral traditions and that can change incrementally—but not fundamentally—through time.

A good example of this phenomenon has been discussed by James Boggs[19] with reference to the Bighorn Medicine Wheel. In the course of his ethnographic investigations, he noted that the Crow Indians now commonly use for ceremonial purposes a stone foundation that likely represents the extant remains of a Civilian Conservation Corps (CCC) camp dating to the 1930s. The foundation has been incorporated into sacred protocols involving vision questing (fasting) on Medicine Mountain in ways that demonstrate not only the dynamic nature of nativistic religion, but also the way traditions of use can change through time. To the Crow, the foundation is an integral part of the entire landscape that includes the Medicine Wheel, and its use is therefore sanctioned by its inclusion in the sacred landscape. The Euro-American history of the foundation, so important to the compilation of National Register nomination documents, is irrelevant to the Crow, whose ceremonial use traditions involving the locale now supercede all other historical interpretations.

To some Euro-American observers, particularly those who oppose efforts to expand the existing National Historic Landmark boundaries, the use of the CCC foundation by the Crow is an invented tradition of very recent vintage that undercuts Indian claims of having conducted ceremonies at Medicine Mountain continuously for centuries. To the Crow, the foundation is an adaptive reuse of a convenient historic feature that occupies a landscape they have used for centuries. To further complicate matters, National Register guidelines categorically exclude from consideration historic properties less than 50 years old. Federal reviewers, including Forest Service archaeologists, have suggested that the foundation should be considered a "noncontributing" property because its use as a traditional ceremonial locale is quite recent. This dismissive attitude obscures a greater truth—that the CCC foundation is an example of the evolving occupation and use of Medicine Mountain by native people, whose archaeological record unequivocally shows they have been present in the immediate area for seven millennia.

Finally, I should mention the discretionary nature of Native American sacred knowledge. The story of the Medicine Mountain as an Indian sacred site, as presented in this essay, is only a fraction of the information total involving the Medicine Wheel and the surrounding landscape. To most tribal representatives, sacred knowledge is not merely confidential, its disclosure has the potential to cause great personal harm and produce a powerful state of cosmic imbalance that can adversely affect not just the tribe, but human society in general. In many instances, the disclosure of sacred knowledge about the Wheel by native consultants was preceded by ceremonial events in which the participants sought assistance from nativistic spirits regarding what information could be shared and what could not. The Wyoming SHPO project files contain documents in which sensitive ethnographic testimony has been redacted at the request of tribal traditional authorities. The most recent version of the Medicine Mountain Cultural Landscape National Register nomination submitted to Forest Service authorities by the Wyoming SHPO contains several individual paragraphs and sentences that took months and sometimes years to write due to the extreme cultural sensitivity of the material to certain Indian tribes. One information stream, a highly detailed and well-documented account of ancient ceremonial use of the Medicine Wheel by the Northern Cheyenne, was negotiated over a period of nearly two years. In the end, tribal elders decided it would be spiritually inappropriate to divulge the information for use in the nomination. Although they were well aware the account would establish, beyond any reasonable doubt, Tsistsista use rights to Medicine Mountain, the elders concluded the custody of the account could not be violated. It could not be shared with either trusted Euro-American bureaucrats or other tribes, not as a issue of mistrust, but as a matter of tribal custom and community safety.

In the end, I believe our western states bureaucracies will gradually come to accept, if not understand and appreciate, the value of Native American perceptions of the landscape as a cultural preservation issue. Landscape archaeology, practiced today by Australian and New Zealand heritage resource specialists and managers, has yet to catch on in North America, although the recent establishment of expansive First Nation reserves in northern Canada suggests that our neighbors to the north understand cultural landscapes, and how to define them, better than we do. Although the National Park Service first published "Guidelines for Evaluating and Documenting Rural Historic Landscapes" in 1989, the guidelines are today mostly applied to historic period farming and ranching communities, and Native American sites that occur in these rural landscapes are often treated as subsidiary resources. Hundreds of Euro-American historic landscapes have been listed in the National Register, ranging from Civil War battle sites to landscaped gardens. Although *Bulletin* 38 clearly states that "a location associated with the traditional beliefs of a Native American group about its origins, its cultural history, or the nature of the world" may possess sufficient significance to be listed in the National Register of Historic Places, relatively few Native American sacred sites have actually attained listing. And it's not because no one has tried. There is clearly something amiss in the practice of cultural resource management in the United States with regard to Native American traditional use areas. Euro-American landscapes are clearly privileged in ways that Native American sacred landscapes are not. It's time for a change.

Notes

1. See Elizabeth Eddy and William L. Partridge, eds., *Applied Anthropology in America* (New York: Columbia University Press, 1978); Robert M. Laidlaw, "Federal Agency Management and Native American Heritage Values," *CRM* 14 (1991); Brian O. K. Reeves and Margaret A. Kennedy, eds., *Kunaitupii: Coming Together on Native Sacred Sites: Their Sacredness, Conservation & Interpretation* (Calgary: Archaeological Society of Alberta, 1993); Jack Trope, "Existing Federal Law and the Protection of Sacred Sites—Possibilities and Limitations," *Cultural Survival Quarterly*, 19 (1996): 30–35; Thomas F. King, *Cultural Resource Laws & Practice: An Introductory Guide* (Walnut Creek, CA: AltaMira Press, 1998), 97–101, 149–162; and Andrew Gulliford, *Sacred Objects and Sacred Places: Preserving Tribal Traditions*, (Boulder, CO: University Press of Colorado, 2000).

2. Dorothea J. Theodoratus, Joseph L. Chartoff, and Kerry K. Chartoff, *Cultural Resources of the Chimney Rock Section, Gasquet-Orleans Road, Six Rivers National Forest* (Fair Oaks, CA: U.S. Department of Agriculture, U.S.

Forest Service, Six Rivers National Forest, 1979), 410.

3. King, *Cultural Resource Laws & Practice*, 161–62.

4. Geosophy is the study of how different cultures conceptualize the geography they inhabit.

5. See, for example, Martyn J. Bowden, "The Great American Desert in the American Mind: The Historiography of a Geographical Notion, in *Geographies of the Mind: Essays in Historical Geosophy in Honor of John Kirtland Wright*, ed. David Lowenthal and Martyn J. Bowden (New York: Oxford University Press, 1975), 119–47.

6. William Tall Bull and Nicol Price, *The Battle for the Bighorn Medicine Wheel in Kunaitupii: Coming Together on Native Sacred Sites, Their Sacredness, Conservation and Interpretation, A Native and Non-Native Forum*, ed. B. O. K. Reeves and M. A. Kennedy (Calgary: Archaeological Society of Alberta, 1993), 96–101.

7. James P. Boggs, Robert York, and Fred Chapman, Medicine Mountain Cultural Landscape National Register of Historic Places Nomination (Cheyenne, 2001), 48.

8. Gulliford, *Sacred Objects and Sacred Places*, 150.

9. J. M. Calder in "The Majorville Cairn and Medicine Wheel Site, Alberta," *National Museum of Man Mercury Series Paper* 62 (1977).

10. Although Fenneman (in his classic monograph *Physical Divisions of the United States*) does not separate the Great Plains into direction components, several prehistorians have done so since the late 1950s based on cultural and environmental commonalities.

11. Stuart W. Connor, "Archaeology of the Crow Indian Vision Quest," *Archaeology in Montana* 23 (1982): 85–127.

12. For a more complete report of findings, see Don Grey, "Summary Report of the Medicine Wheel Investigation," in *Symposium on Early Cretaceous Rocks of Wyoming and Adjacent Areas*, ed. R. L. Enyert and W. H. Curry (Laramie, WY: Wyoming Geologic Survey, 1962), 316–17.

13. Michael Wilson, "A Test of the Stone Circle Size-Age Hypothesis: Alberta and Wyoming," in "From Microcosm to Macrocosm: Advances in Tipi Ring Investigation and Interpretation," ed. L. B. Davis, *Plains Anthropologist Memoir* 19 (1981): 113–37.

14. Anthony Sitting Eagle, Northern Arapaho traditional elder, personal communication, 1989.

15. The names of Native American consultants and all site locational information was blacked out in the National Register nomination submitted for public review.

16. K. Jameson et al., To Whom It May Concern, letter, September 22, 1999, Wyoming SHPO Project Files, Cheyenne.

17. A simulacrum, as defined by Jameson, is an "identical copy for which no original has ever existed."

18. The Keeper of the National Register, an adjunct of the National Park Service, is the highest review authority for National Register nominations and is responsible for listing historic properties on the National Register of Historic Places.

19. James Boggs, "Anthropological Knowledge and Native American Cultural Practice in the Liberal Polity," *American Anthropologist* 104, no. 2 (June 2002): 599–610.

Study Questions

1. Discuss the results of the Bighorn Medicine Wheel National Historic Landmark on today's Native American consultations involving land use management.

2. What evidence indicates that the Medicine Wheel and its surroundings have a long traditional use for ceremonies and spiritual matters?

3. How did the Forest Service react to native concerns about the Medicine Wheel when contemplating nearby construction? How did native peoples respond?

4. What was the reasoning for expanding the boundary of the Medicine Wheel?

5. How did the National Historic Landmark designation for the Medicine Wheel deviate from the normal nomination process? Why?

6. How do native peoples and government agencies view cultural resources and their locations when considering land management policies?

7. Discuss the G-O Road's significance in understanding land management vs. Native American concepts about archaeological investigation. Did the NHPA stop lumber interests in the G-O Road case?

8. How do local non-Indian communities feel about the Medicine Wheel and native claims to ceremonial and sacred site status? Whose argument is stronger?

9. How did various Native American groups and tribes disagree over the use of the Medicine Wheel site?

Sand Creek, Colorado, Case Study

The Search for the Site of the Sand Creek Massacre

CHRISTINE WHITACRE

On November 29, 1864, approximately 700 soldiers led by Colonel John Chivington attacked a Cheyenne and Arapaho village in what is now southeastern Colorado. The village, made up of around 100 lodges, was on the banks of a meandering, intermittent stream known as Sand Creek. Under the leadership of Cheyenne chief Black Kettle, about 500 Cheyenne and Arapaho people were camped at the site, believing that they were not only at peace with the U.S. government but also under its protection. Nevertheless, Chivington's troops, made up of volunteers from the Colorado First and Third Cavalry, launched a surprise dawn attack that left at least 150 Cheyennes and Arapahos dead—mostly women, children, and the elderly. During that afternoon and the following day, the soldiers followed up the massacre by committing atrocities on the dead before withdrawing from the field. Upon their return to Denver, the soldiers received a heroes' welcome, which included a display of scalps and body parts that had been taken from the Indian victims. Soon, however, the Sand Creek Massacre was recognized for what it was: a national disgrace that was condemned by three separate federal investigations.[1]

Nearly 135 years after the event, Senator Ben Nighthorse Campbell (R-CO), the only Native American member of Congress and a Cheyenne descendant of survivors of the Sand Creek Massacre, sponsored legislation that began the process of memorializing the massacre site. Senator Campbell introduced Senate Bill 1695, which was signed by President Bill Clinton on October 6, 1998, as Public Law 105–243. Known as the Sand Creek Massacre National Historic Site Study Act of 1998, the legislation directed the National Park Service (NPS)—in consultation with the Cheyenne and Arapaho tribes of Oklahoma, the Northern Cheyenne Tribe, the Northern Arapaho Tribe, and the State of Colorado—to complete two tasks. First, the National Park Service was to verify the location and extent of the Sand Creek Massacre site. Indeed, a lack of conclusive evidence as to the site's location had been the major obstacle to earlier efforts to designate the site. Second, the NPS was to evaluate a range of management alternatives for the site, including the feasibility of making the Sand Creek Massacre site a unit of the National Park System. Congress also mandated that the project be completed within 18 months.

The National Park Service Sand Creek Massacre project team took a wide-ranging multidisciplinary approach to finding the massacre site. As part of the site location effort, Cheyenne and Arapaho descendants of the Sand Creek Massacre, a number of whom were members of the project team, told stories of the massacre that had been handed down to them through the generations. Historians researched maps, diaries, reminiscences, and congressional and military investigative reports for information that might shed light on the location of the massacre. The National Park Service also held public open houses in southeastern Colorado, encouraging local residents to come forward with information, including artifacts found on their land that might be evidence of the massacre. Historical aerial photographs, the earliest dating from the 1930s, were examined for evidence of trails leading to and from the massacre site. Before the archaeological survey got going in May 1999, the NPS team conducted a geomorphological assessment of Sand

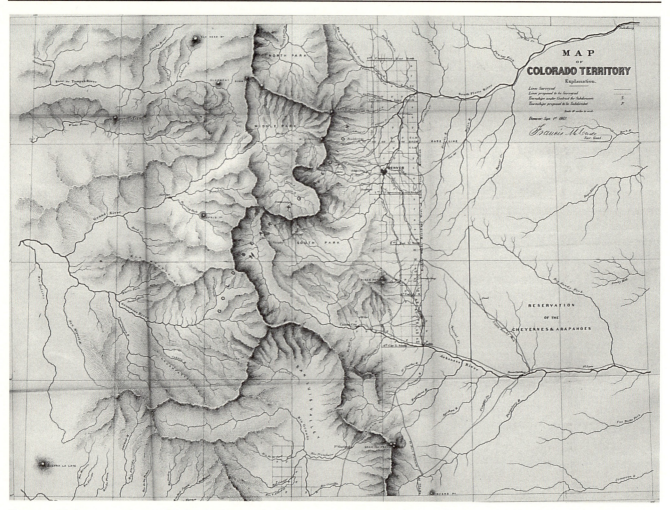

Figure 57. Early territorial map of Colorado showing the location of the Cheyenne and Arapaho Reservation on the eastern plains.

Creek that identified, through an analysis of soil samples, those specific landforms from which 1864-era artifacts might be recovered.

Archival documentation at the National Archives played a significant role in the successful completion of the Sand Creek Massacre project—which led, ultimately, to Sand Creek's authorization as a national historic site in November 2000. A map drawn by U.S. Army lieutenant Samuel Bonsall in 1868 that was found by archivist Scott Forsythe in the National Archives and Record Administration–Great Lakes Region, was integral to the discovery of the Sand Creek Massacre site. Jerome Greene, NPS lead historian for the site location study, called the map "the most important document yet located to convincingly posit the site of the Sand Creek Massacre."[2]

Historical Background

The Sand Creek Massacre is one of the most emotionally charged and controversial events in American history; it is also, as Jerome Greene has noted, "a tragedy reflective of its time and place."[3] Although army reports of the massacre are grouped with the official records of the Civil War, Sand Creek more closely reflects the vast cultural, social, and political changes that were taking place in the West during the mid-nineteenth century, far removed from the battlefields of Gettysburg and Manassas. The tragedy at Sand Creek was the culmination of several forces, including the Colorado Gold Rush, the ambitions of local politicians and military leaders, the clash of cultures on the western plains, and the claims of different groups of people to the same land.

By the time the Civil War had begun, the Cheyenne and Arapaho people had been on the western plains for decades. Under the terms of the 1851 Treaty of Fort Laramie, Cheyenne and Arapaho territory included much of the front range of Colorado. But major gold strikes in the mountains west of Denver in 1858 and 1859 precipitated a tide of Euro-American immigration. In 1859 William Bent, the well-known trader who also served as the Colorado and Arapaho agent in Colorado, called upon the U.S. government to better define the territorial rights of the Indians in the area. The result was the 1861 Treaty of Fort Wise, by which the Cheyennes and Arapahos surrendered most of their land and received instead a much smaller, triangular-shaped tract along and north of the upper Arkansas River in southeastern Colorado. Sand Creek, also known as Big Sandy Creek, formed the eastern border of this reservation.

But not all Cheyennes and Arapahos recognized the Treaty of Fort Wise, and many refused to abide by it. By the summer of 1864, a number of conflicts between Euro-Americans and Indians heightened an already tense situation within Colorado Territory. Colorado's territorial governor, John Evans, as well as Colonel John Chivington, who headed the U.S. Army military district in Colorado, interpreted the attacks upon white settlers as proof that the Indians were preparing for war, even though evidence indicates that they were the actions of warriors acting beyond the control of their chiefs. On June 11, 1864, Arapaho warriors attacked and murdered the Hungate family, 30 miles from Denver. The public display of the family's bodies, which included two young children, terrified Colorado's citizens, many of whom left their ranches to seek protection within the walls of Denver's mint. Two weeks later on June 27, Governor Evans issued a proclamation to all "Friendly Indians of the Plains" to present themselves to assigned military posts. The Cheyennes and Arapahos who wanted to be at peace with the government were told to go to the military authorities at Fort Lyon, which was along the Arkansas River near present-day Lamar,

Colorado. Meanwhile, Governor Evans began preparing for military action. On August 11, Evans received permission from federal authorities to raise a regiment of 100-day U.S. Army volunteers, designated the Third Colorado Cavalry under the command of Colonel Chivington. Also in August, Evans issued a proclamation that contradicted his earlier one to the "Friendly Indians of the Plains," now calling upon citizens to kill all Indians and seize their property.

At the same time that Evans and Chivington were assembling military forces, Cheyenne and Arapaho chiefs were attempting to negotiate a peace settlement. Cheyenne chief Black Kettle contacted Major Edward Wynkoop, the commander at Fort Lyon, about his desire for peace. In response, Wynkoop led his command of First Colorado Cavalry to meet Black Kettle and the Arapaho leader, Left Hand, at the big timbers of the Smoky Hill River near Fort Wallace, Kansas. Here the Cheyenne and Arapaho chiefs turned over several white captives and consented to meet with Evans and Chivington. That meeting took place on September 28 at Camp Weld, outside of Denver. Although the Indians departed Camp Weld believing that they had negotiated a peace settlement, Governor Evans soon notified officials in Washington of the tribes' continued hostilities and noted that "the winter . . . is the most favorable time for their chastisement."[4]

In late October and early November, the Arapahos and Cheyennes began arriving at Fort Lyon to comply with what they believed were the conditions of the peace settlement. Major Scott Anthony, the fort's new commander, instructed the Indians to camp at an area approximately 40 miles north-northeast of the fort. Simultaneously, however, the army was already initiating its attack. On November 14, Chivington's troops began marching out of Denver. The troops reached Fort Lyon midday on November 28. At approximately 8 P.M., now joined by troops from Fort Lyon, Chivington's men began an all-night ride toward the Cheyenne and Arapaho encampment on Sand Creek, following an old Indian trail that led to the site.

At dawn on November 29, Chivington's forces,

equipped with four 12-pounder mountain howitzer guns, attacked the village. Many of the villagers who survived the initial attack fled upstream to the north. Approximately one mile above the village, according to most accounts, the Indians sheltered themselves in hastily dug trenches along the banks of the creek. The soldiers followed the Indians to this area, known as the "sandpits," bringing with them at least two mountain howitzers. By day's end, at least 150 Indians had been killed. On the army's side, 10 soldiers died. Afterward, Chivington ordered his men to plunder and burn the village. After the massacre, Cheyenne and Arapaho survivors began making their way northeast to the camps of their kinsmen along the forks of the Smoky Hill River.

Previous Efforts to Locate the Sand Creek Massacre Site

Although most historic accounts of the Sand Creek Massacre placed it at the "Big South Bend" of Sand Creek, its exact location became obscured over time. As Mildred Red Cherries of the Northern Cheyenne noted at project meetings, the Sand Creek Massacre became "lost," even to the descendants of those who had survived the attack. The massacre site was left unmarked and, by the turn of the century, there was little evidence of the terrible events of November 29, 1864. In 1908, army veterans who had participated in the massacre planned a reunion at the site. However, upon reaching the banks of Sand Creek, even they could not agree on its location.

On August 6, 1950, the Colorado Historical Society erected a Sand Creek Massacre historical marker on State Highway 96 near the town of Chivington, Colorado. On that same day, the historical society participated in a second dedication ceremony approximately 15 miles to the north, on property now owned by Bill and Tootie Dawson. Here, overlooking an approximate 90-degree bend of Sand Creek, the local community placed a second marker, designating it as the site of the massacre. Tribal members also returned to the area, using their traditional tribal knowledge and oral histories to identify the massacre site. In 1978 the Arrow Keeper of the Cheyenne Tribe recognized what is now referred to as the Dawson South Bend as the Sand Creek Massacre site when he blessed it as "Cheyenne earth."

Still, there were those who disagreed that the site had been found. Many observers were troubled by the lack of physical evidence of either the village site or the military's ammunition. In particular, critics questioned why no evidence of Civil War–era ammunition, including 12-pounder mountain howitzer ordnance, had been found at the Dawson South Bend. The Sand Creek Massacre was the only Civil War–era event in Colorado in which the army used such guns, and many believed that the discovery of howitzer-related artifacts would offer significant proof of the site location.

In the early 1990s, amateur archaeologists and metal detector hobbyists who had surveyed the Dawson South Bend, but had not found artifacts associated with the Sand Creek Massacre, approached the Colorado Historical Society with their findings. In response, the Colorado Historical Society initiated a project to identify the location of the massacre. In 1994 the society asked Richard Ellis of Fort Lewis College, Durango, Colorado, to develop a project to verify the location of the Sand Creek Massacre. As an important first step, Ellis and the Colorado Historical Society began consulting with descendants of Cheyenne victims of the Sand Creek Massacre. In 1997 Ellis also asked archaeologists Douglas Scott of the National Park Service, William Lees of the Oklahoma Historical Society, and Anne Bond of the Colorado Historical Society, in cooperation with other volunteers and metal detector organizations, to conduct reconnaissance-level archaeological surveys of two possible Sand Creek Massacre sites. The team surveyed the "vee" of the Dawson South Bend as well as another large bend of Sand Creek, often referred to as the "North Bend," which was approximately 10 miles north of the Dawson South Bend. But the state-funded Fort Lewis College project was unable to conclusively identify the location of the Sand Creek

Massacre site. No 1864-era artifacts were found in the North Bend, and only 12 1864-era items were found in the Dawson South Bend, either through the 1997 survey or later by the landowner. As a result, although there was now growing interest in designating the Sand Creek Massacre as a national historic site, there was still no definitive physical evidence, or consensus, regarding its location.

National Park Service Efforts to Locate the Site

Following the passage of the Sand Creek Massacre National Historic Site Study Act in October 1998, the responsibility for the Sand Creek Massacre project was delegated to the Intermountain Regional Office of the National Park Service, headquartered in Denver. A project team was assembled that included historians, ethnographers, archaeologists, geomorphologists, and other disciplines.[5]

As mandated by Congress, the major goal of the Sand Creek Massacre site location study was to map the "location and extent" of the Sand Creek Massacre. One of the team's first tasks was to identify all potential locations of the massacre. The methodology was based on two basic principles. First, all possible sites would be evaluated according to the evidence; there was no presumption as to the "right" location of the massacre site. Second, the project team would follow four major lines of evidence: (1) historical research, (2) oral histories, (3) traditional tribal knowledge, and (4) physical evidence of the site, as determined by a reconnaissance-level archaeological survey.

The archaeological survey was scheduled for May 1999. Evaluation of oral histories, traditional tribal methods, aerial photographs, historical research, and geomorphology was to be completed first. The archaeological survey could then focus on those areas that were the most likely locations of the Sand Creek Massacre and that were most likely to have physical evidence of the massacre.

Historical Research

Historical research efforts involved examination of a large number of published and manuscript historical maps for information about streams, trails, roads, land use, ownership, and other data that might help pinpoint the site. Among the most important sources of information were four maps drawn or annotated by George Bent, a mixed-blood Cheyenne survivor of the massacre. One of the maps, drawn by George Hyde and annotated by George Bent, places the Sand Creek Massacre in the North Bend of Sand Creek. As noted earlier, the 1997 state-funded archaeological survey of this area uncovered no massacre-related artifacts.[6] The second map, also drawn by Hyde and annotated by Bent, places the massacre site below the confluence of Rush and Sand Creeks, approximately 20 miles south of the Dawson South Bend.[7] The remaining two maps, which were drawn by George Bent approximately 40 years after the Sand Creek Massacre, focus on the massacre site itself. These maps show the placement of Indian encampments within the village, the location of the sandpits area in relationship to the village, and the troop movements. These two maps, one of which is in the collection of the Oklahoma Historical Society and the other in the archives at the University of Colorado Library at Boulder, also show that the massacre occurred near a 90-degree bend of Sand Creek, a configuration that greatly resembles the Dawson South Bend.[8]

In addition to the Bent maps, a manuscript map drawn by U.S. Army lieutenant Samuel Bonsall in 1868 also contained significant information that pertained directly to the location of the Sand Creek Massacre.[9] In 1992, while processing records associated with nineteenth-century military activities in the Trans-Mississippi West, archivist Scott Forsythe found the Bonsall map in Record Group 77, Records of the Army Corps of Engineers, in the National Archives and Records Administration–Great Lakes Region in Chicago. "It is unusual that records such as the engineering officer records of the Department of the Platte would have found their way into a regional archives facility but, through unknown circumstances, these records ended up with the Chicago district of the Corps of Engineers and were transferred into the holdings of the Great Lakes Region," noted Forsythe. The discovery of the Bonsall map was memorable for Forsythe, because he was well acquainted with Sand Creek and understood the map's reference to "Chivingtons Massacre." A few years after finding the Bonsall map, Forsythe learned of the upcoming State of Colorado–Fort Lewis College project to locate the site of the Sand Creek Massacre. Forsythe subsequently contacted the Colorado Historical Society and, in 1996, sent them a copy of the Bonsall map.[10] In 1998, when the National Park Service efforts to locate the Sand Creek Massacre site began, Colorado state historian David Halaas gave a copy of the map to NPS historian Jerome Greene.

The Bonsall map was drawn by Second Lieutenant Samuel W. Bonsall, Third Infantry, who was stationed at Fort Lyon in 1868; the map documents the route of Bonsall's detachment of 11 infantry soldiers from Fort Lyon to Cheyenne Wells, Colorado. Bonsall and his men were escorting Lieutenant General William T. Sherman east following a tour of frontier sites. The map was prepared in June 1868, within four years of the Sand Creek Massacre, in accordance with U.S. Army regulations. Rendered in the form of a strip map and journal, the map is graphically detailed with regard to landmarks and place names, including time and mileage readings. The map shows the site of "Chivingtons Massacre" in relative placement to two landmarks. Bonsall placed "Chivingtons Massacre" between a point, south of the massacre site, where the road from Fort Lyon crossed Sand Creek, and a point approximately six miles north from it, where that same road branched into "three forks." Between these points, the lieutenant drew a bold line, approximately two miles long, representing the extent of the massacre site.

The significance of the Bonsall map became even more apparent when it was compared to historical aerial photographs of the massacre site. Art Ireland, an NPS archaeologist on the project team, examined a series of historical and contemporary aerial photographs for evidence of landmarks that had been delineated on the Bonsall map. In particular, Ireland searched for segments of the historic trail that the army may have traveled between Fort Lyon and the massacre site, including the point at which it crossed Sand Creek. Ireland also examined the photographs for evidence of "three forks," that point six miles north of the massacre at which the trail branched into three separate routes.

The earliest aerial photographs of the Sand Creek area were taken in 1936–37 by the Soil Conservation Service.[11] These photographs, taken nearly 70 years after the massacre, precisely confirm the "three forks" point as delineated on Bonsall's map. The photographs, which indicate that the area had changed relatively little since the time of the account, also clearly show a road leading to and from Fort Lyon. Thus, prior to the archaeological survey of the Sand Creek Massacre site, Greene—primarily based on an analysis of the Bonsall map and its comparison to the 1936–37 aerial photographs—concluded that the village attacked by Chivington's troops on November 29, 1864, was approximately one mile north of the "vee" of the Dawson South Bend, the site traditionally believed to be the massacre site.

Oral Histories

The oral histories of descendants of the Cheyenne and Arapaho survivors of the massacre were significant sources of information. From the beginning of the project, the National Park Service had been committed to the collection of oral historical data as one of the primary lines of evidence in locating the Sand Creek Massacre site. Between April 1999 and February 2000, 32 Cheyenne and Arapaho descendants of survivors of the Sand Creek Massacre gave oral history accounts, which they permitted to be recorded and transcribed.[12]

The Sand Creek Massacre oral history project specifically focused on information that would help identify the location of the massacre site. In particular, descendants were asked specific questions about topics such as geographic landforms, physical descriptions of the size and extent of the Indian encampment, and information on trails that led to the site. Several geographic elements recurred in the oral history interviews. Among these was the often-stated need for the campsite to have been close to water, both for the people and for their horses. In particular, a number of interviewees said that Cheyennes always followed watercourses and always camped by water. Many said that there was no flowing water in Sand Creek at the time of the massacre. While horses could have drunk from the standing pools, oral history accounts indicated that people would have dug for water or used spring water. Several people emphasized the importance of an available spring as a source of drinking water, noting that it is against traditional Cheyenne belief to drink from a source of water that had been standing overnight. The information on the water source was of particular significance because an extant spring is approximately two miles east of the Dawson South Bend. The proximity of this spring supported the Cheyenne belief that the Dawson South Bend was the area of the Indian encampment.

Interviewees also revealed information on the proximity of the sandpits area to the village site. Several people recounted that the majority of people in the village were women, children, and the elderly, who could not have run very far from their lodges before seeking out hiding places. Other stories noted the presence of rocky hiding places. In particular, Northern Arapaho interviewees gave accounts of limestone outcroppings in the area, which survivors had used as shelter. Several people mentioned the presence of hills and trees near the massacre site. Interviewees also provided details about the size of the encampment, in terms of both geographic space and number of lodges. Many also discussed the makeup of the encampment, particularly the relative placement of the Cheyenne and Arapaho groups. However, with important exceptions—such as the description of the massacre site provided by Southern Cheyenne descendant Laird Cometsevah—geographic details of the massacre site were generally nonspecific as to exact location. (Some interviewees expressed a reluctance to provide more detail because of the often-stated fear of government retribution, extreme emotion, or the belief that the stories belong to the families only.) As NPS ethnographer Alexa Roberts observed, geographic details in the oral histories of the Sand Creek Massacre were peripheral to the descriptions of the atrocities committed during that event. Overwhelmingly, the oral histories provided powerful testimony to the horrors of the events of November 29, 1864, and the devastating effects of the massacre on families and the tribes that linger to this day. Although accounts of physical features associated with the site varied among the oral history accounts, every story shared "the sense of chaos, running, scattering, horror, fear, and blood."[13]

Traditional Tribal Methods

As part of the site location study, Cheyenne and Arapaho spiritual leaders and elders also agreed to employ traditional tribal methods to help determine the location of the massacre. Descendants of survivors of the Sand Creek Massacre had often stated that there are ways other than oral histories or written accounts by which they know of the location of the massacre site. Among the traditional ways mentioned most frequently is sensing a spiritual presence or hearing the voices of women, children, horses, or other animals while present on the site. The National Park Service understood that these methods were often private in nature and could not be used effectively in the presence of non-Indians but agreed to assist in these investigations to whatever extent possible.

The Sand Creek Massacre, Volume One: Site Location Study includes an account given by Robert Toahty, a descendant of an Arapaho survivor of Sand Creek. Based on visions that he saw at the site, Toahty believes that the people killed at Sand Creek are scattered for about two miles in the creek bed north of the stone monument in the vicinity of the Dawson South Bend. Other descendants noted hearing the voices of both people and horses. Southern Cheyenne descendant Laird Cometsevah described hearing voices in the Dawson South Bend while on-site during both the 1997 and 1999 archaeological field sessions. And, as noted earlier, the Cheyenne Arrow Keeper blessed the Dawson South Bend as "Cheyenne earth" in 1978, thereby designating it as the Sand Creek Massacre site.

Archaeological Survey

By the time the archaeological survey began in May 1999, a number of draft reports—including the historical documentation report by Jerome Greene—had been completed. The results of these efforts, as well as preliminary information from the oral history interviews and traditional tribal methods, indicated five areas as potential sites of the Sand Creek Massacre. The research also indicated that the massacre did not take place in a small isolated area. According to a variety of accounts, the massacre was a running engagement that occurred along a stretch of Sand Creek approximately five to six miles in length. Encompassed within this area were the Indian village site, the sandpits, and areas of Indian and troop movements.

An underlying assumption of the site location study was that the Cheyenne and Arapaho village site, and possibly the sandpits area, might contain enough intact archaeological remains to identify the massacre site. Historical archaeology has been very successful in verifying the location of various battle sites throughout the Trans-Mississippi West. The investigations at Sand Creek used metal detecting and other remote-sensing applications to identify cultural material associated with the Indian village and the military. Remote-sensing equipment minimized disturbance to the landowners' pastures and fields and to any human remains below.

In preparation for the archaeological investigations, the National Park Service commissioned a geomorphological survey of the Sand Creek area. Geomorphologists analyzed soil samples to determine if a site was likely to contain physical evidence of the 1864 massacre and if it contained a layer of soil dating from the 1864 era. Dating the soil layers was particularly important along Sand Creek, as many people speculated that the layer that contained the Sand Creek Massacre artifacts might have been lost to flooding and wind erosion. Test results indicated that the alignment of Sand Creek had not changed substantially over time, eliminating that as a factor in locating the site. In addition, the geomorphologists concluded that the area in the vicinity of the Dawson South Bend had not been substantially disturbed by erosion or agricultural practices, at least not to the extent that such activities would have destroyed all archaeological evidence of the Sand Creek Massacre.

In May 1999, NPS archaeologist Douglas D. Scott oversaw the archaeological reconnaissance survey of several areas along Sand Creek. The investigation, which included NPS staff, volunteers, landowners, and several members of the Cheyenne and Arapaho tribes, resulted in the collection of nearly 400 artifacts that, according to archaeological analysis, confirmed the location of Black Kettle's village in the area projected by Jerome Greene's historical research. The greatest numbers of artifacts were concentrated in Section 24, Township 17 South, Range 46 West, at the northern edge of the Dawson South Bend. Found here were Civil War–era tin cups, cans, horseshoes, horseshoe nails, plates, bowls, knives, fork, spoons, barrel hoops, a coffee grinder, a coffeepot, iron arrowheads, bullets, and case shot fragments.

As archaeologist Douglas Scott observed, the majority of the artifacts are objects typical of Native American encampments of the nineteenth century and, when compared to lists of trade and annuity goods known or requested for distribution to the Cheyennes and Arapahos in southern Colorado, "demonstrate a striking degree of concordance."[14] The team also found a variety of iron objects modified for Native American uses. These artifacts include knives altered to awls, iron wire altered to awls, fleshers or hide scrapers, strap iron altered by filed serrations as hide preparation devices, and several iron objects altered by filing to serve an as-yet unidentified cutting or scraping purpose. Cheyenne and Arapaho members of the archaeological team identified many of these artifacts. Among them was a crescent-shaped object identified as a Cheyenne man's breast ornament.[15]

Many of the artifacts showed evidence that they had been intentionally broken, a pattern of destruction typical of U.S. Army actions of the period. The arms and ammunition that were found are likewise consistent with those carried by the cavalry units that participated in the massacre. In particular, the archaeological fieldwork uncovered fragments of 12-pounder mountain howitzer shells.

Identification of the Location and Extent of the Sand Creek Massacre Site

By fall of 1999, the end of the first project year, the National Park Service believed that the first task mandated by the Sand Creek Massacre National Historic Site Study Act—identifying the location and extent of the massacre site—had been accomplished. Jerome Greene's review of historical documents, primarily the 1868 Bonsall map, had indicated that Section 24, Township 17 South, Range 46 West was the likely site of the village. And, indeed, the archaeological survey uncovered approximately 400 artifacts in a concentrated area within this section, the type and distribution of which are consistent with an Indian village of approximately 500 people. Also within this artifact concentration—among the shattered plates, utensils, hide scrapers, awls, and trade items that had once been part of the daily lives of the Cheyennes and Arapahos who had camped here—the survey team found evidence of the ammunition and weapons used to attack and kill them. Although no conclusive evidence of the sandpits was found during the 1999 archaeological survey, historical accounts indicate they were anywhere from 300 yards to two-plus miles upstream of the village, but most likely at around one-quarter mile to one mile. As such, Greene concluded that the probable location of the sandpits is in Sections 13 and 14, Township 17 South, Range 46 West. Among the artifacts that had been found in

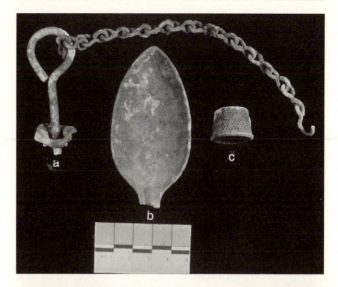

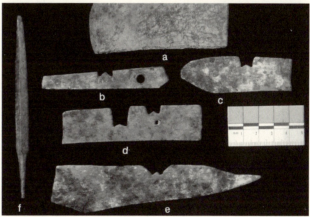

Figures 58 and 59. Scrapers, a spoon, a thimble, and a military canteen stopper chain are archaeological artifacts found during the search for the Sand Creek massacre site. Metal detecting and other remote-sensing applications were used to find the physical evidence. Photos courtesy of the National Park Service.

this area were shell fragments from 12-pounder mountain howitzers, which were known to have been used in the sandpits area.[16]

However, at an October 1999 project meeting, the Cheyenne tribal representatives to the project team, as well as the representative of the State of Colorado, disagreed with the conclusions of the National Park Service as to the location of the village and the sandpits. As noted earlier, Cheyenne tradition held that the village lay within the "vee" of the Dawson South Bend, not at its northern edge, where the artifact concentration was found. Cheyenne representatives and Colorado state historian David Halaas also pointed to the two sketch maps drawn by George Bent that showed the Indian encampment as being within the "vee" of the bend. While NPS historians found the Bent maps to be valuable tools in terms of placing the relative locations of specific encampments, they also believed that they lacked scale and immediacy to the event. Moreover, while the National Park Service believes that the placement of the village at the northern edge of the Dawson South Bend does not conflict with most oral history accounts of the massacre, that view is not shared by all of the tribal representatives to the project. The Cheyenne and Arapaho tribes of Oklahoma and the Northern Cheyenne Tribe believe that the oral histories are strong evidence that the village is in the "vee" of the Dawson South Bend.

If, as the representatives of those tribes believe, the village was in the "vee" of the Dawson South Bend, then what is the concentration of artifacts approximately one mile north in Section 24? Laird Cometsevah, great-grandson of Cometsevah, who was a survivor of the Sand Creek Massacre, believes the artifacts may be evidence of the sandpits, or perhaps a later Euro-American settlement in the area. Others believe the artifacts may be the northern edge of the village, the area where the soldiers bivouacked after the massacre, or both.

The Northern Arapaho representatives of the project team concur with the conclusions drawn by the National Park Service with regard to the location of the village site and the sandpits. However, the Cheyenne and Arapaho tribes of Oklahoma and the Northern Cheyenne Tribe maintain that additional archaeological survey work will provide proof that the village was, indeed, within the crux of the Dawson South Bend. While the distance between these two contested village locations is less than one mile—and are both situated within the Dawson South Bend—they also reflect a much wider gulf between interpretations of "truth" and of scientific evidence versus cultural knowledge. They also represent, in a broader sense, a continuing distrust of the U.S. government by tribal members, a relationship at least partially rooted in the Sand Creek Massacre itself.

While there was no consensus regarding these issues, all members of the project team also recognized the importance of the larger effort to memorialize and protect the Sand Creek Massacre site. Ultimately, the entire team—the National Park Service, the Cheyenne and Arapaho tibes of Oklahoma, the Northern Arapaho Tribe, the Northern Cheyenne Tribe, and the State of Colorado—agreed on a map that delineated the boundaries of the Sand Creek Massacre site (which extends approximately five and a half miles in length and two miles in width). All parties agreed that all the significant events of the massacre—including the Cheyenne and Arapaho village site, the sandpits, the area of Indian flight, and the point from which Chivington and his troops launched their attack—are within that boundary. Senator Ben Nighthorse Campbell concurred that this map met the intent of the Sand Creek Massacre National Historic Site Study Act to define the "location and extent" of the massacre site, which allowed the project to move forward. The final site location study includes the various viewpoints, including interpretive maps, as to the locations of the components of the massacre site. The study also notes that while there is no consensus regarding the exact location of some elements of the massacre, project team members believe that additional archaeological work may resolve some of these issues.

Authorization to Establish the Sand Creek Massacre Site as a National Historic Site

The final task of the project team was to develop management alternatives for the Sand Creek Massacre, including an assessment as to whether or not the Sand Creek Massacre site would be a feasible and suitable addition to the National Park Service. Under Alternative 1, the "no action alternative," the site would remain under private ownership. Alternative 2 proposed the creation of a Sand Creek Massacre memorial on a small portion of the site, approximately 1,500 acres of land. Visitors would be able to visit a memorial that would stand on a bluff overlooking the

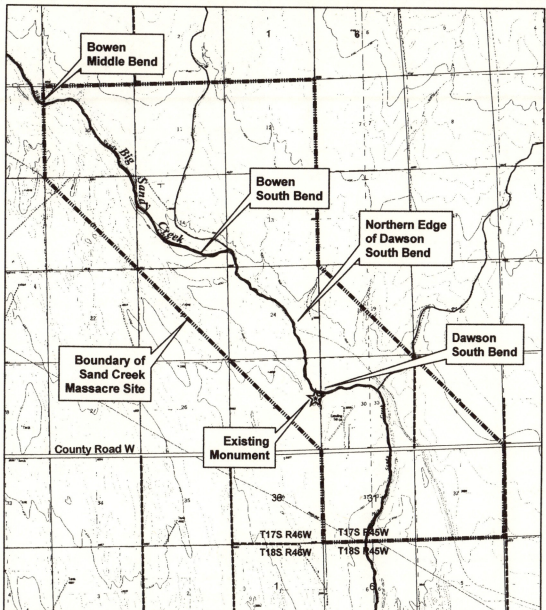

Figure 60. Despite disagreement over the exact location of the village, all parties could agree that the major events of the Sand Creek Massacre were situated within the boundaries shown on the National Park Service map.

Figure 61. Sand Creek site of Cheyenne encampment, Sand Creek Battle Ground, November 29 and 30, 1864, as it looked November 29, 1995. Photo © Hal Gould, the Camera Obscura Gallery, Denver. Photo courtesy Center of Southwest Studies, Fort Lewis College.

Figure 62. Legislation has authorized the establishment of a National Park Service Historic Site at Sand Creek once a sufficient land base is acquired. Modern photo of Sand Creek, courtesy National Park Service.

massacre site, but they would not have access to most of the site. Alternative 3 proposed the establishment of a Sand Creek Massacre Historic Site, which would provide the greatest protection for the site while allowing for visitor access. The historic site boundary would include the entire massacre site, as well as additional land to provide for visitor facilities and to protect critical view sheds, encompassing approximately 12,480 acres of land. In July 2000 the National Park Service submitted to Congress the results of the site location study, the three proposed management alternatives, and the public response to them. Soon thereafter, Senator Campbell introduced Senate Bill 2950, the Sand Creek Massacre National Historic Site Establishment Act of 2000, which supported the establishment of a 12,480-acre national historic site as described in Alternative 3.

On November 7, 2000, President Bill Clinton signed the Sand Creek Massacre National Historic Site Establishment Act, which became Public Law 106–465. The law recognizes the importance of the Sand Creek Massacre as "a nationally significant element of frontier military and Native American history; and a symbol of the struggles of Native American tribes to maintain their way of life on ancestral land." It also authorizes the secretary of the interior—upon the acquisition of sufficient land that will "provide for the preservation, memorialization, commemoration, and interpretation of the Sand Creek Massacre"—to establish the site as a national historic site. Moreover, the law provides "opportunities for the tribes and the State to be involved in the formulation of general management plans and educational programs for the national historic site." Public Law 106–465 also supports special rights of access within the site for the Indian tribes. It specifically states that all land within the historic site is to be acquired from willing sellers only.

Postscript

Since the time that this essay was first published in summer 2001, there have been new developments regarding the Sand Creek Massacre National Historic Site. Thanks to The Conservation Fund and a grant from the State of Colorado, the National Park Service is currently acquiring property within the boundaries of the authorized Sand Creek Massacre National Historic Site. The National Park Service recently acquired 40 acres of land at the site, bringing the total federal property within the authorized site boundaries to 920 acres. The 1,465-acre property formerly belonging to William F. and Tootie Dawson has been purchased by Southwest Entertainment, Inc., which intends to convey it to the Cheyenne and Arapaho tribes of Oklahoma. The tribes will, in turn, enter into an agreement with the National Park Service for the land to be managed as part of the Sand Creek Massacre National Historic Site. The National Park Service and its partners anticipate that with the conveyance of this property to the tribes and with the mechanisms in place for it to be included in the management of the National Historic Site, the formal establishment of the Sand Creek Massacre National Historic Site will follow shortly. In the meantime, The Conservation Fund continues the process of assembling additional properties for inclusion in the National Historic Site, and the National Park Service is working closely with neighboring landowners, Kiowa County, and the associated Cheyenne and Arapaho tribes to appropriately care for the land and resources under NPS administration.

Notes

An earlier version of this essay appeared in the summer 2001 issue of *Prologue*, published by the National Archives.

1. U.S. Senate, 38th Cong., 2nd sess., Report of the Joint Committee on the Conduct of the War, Massacre of the Cheyenne Indians, Report No. 142 (1865); U.S. Senate, 39th Cong., 2nd sess., Report of the Joint Special Committee, Condition of the Indian Tribes with Appendix (The Chivington Massacre), Report No. 156 (1867); and U.S. Senate, 39th Cong., 2nd sess., Report of the Secretary of the War, Communicating . . . a Copy of the Evidence Taken at Denver and Fort Lyon, Colorado Territory, by a Military Commission Ordered to Inquire into the Sand Creek Massacre, November 29, 1864, Ex. Doc. No. 26 (1867).

2. Jerome Greene, *Sand Creek Massacre Project*, vol. one: *Site Location Study* (2000), 44.

3. Ibid., vol. two: *Special Resource Study and Environmental Assessment* (2000), 24.

4. Alvin M. Josephy, Jr., *The Civil War in the American West* (1991), 307, cited in Sand Creek Massacre Project, volume two, 33–34.

5. The project manager was Rick Frost, assistant regional director, communications, for the NPS Intermountain Region; historian Christine Whitacre was team captain; and Barbara Sutteer of the Intermountain Regional Office of American Indian Trust Responsibilities served as Indian liaison. Other key NPS personnel included Jerome A. Greene, the project's lead historian; Douglas D. Scott, who oversaw the archaeological fieldwork; and ethnographer Alexa Roberts, who assisted the Cheyennes and Arapahos in recording their oral histories and traditional tribal knowledge of the massacre site. The team also included representatives of the State of Colorado and the Cheyenne and Arapaho tribes. David Halaas, historian of the Colorado Historical Society, served as the state representative. Indian participants in the project included Southern Cheyenne representatives Laird Cometsevah, Joe Big Medicine, Eugene Black Bear, Jr., Edward Starr, Jr., and Edward White Skunk; Northern Cheyenne representatives Mildred Red Cherries, Steve Brady, Otto Braided Hair, Steve Chestnut, Lee Lonebear, Conrad Fisher, Norma Gourneau, Reginald Killsnight, Sr., Holda Roundstone, and Joe Walks Along; Southern Arapaho representatives William "Lee" Pedro and Alonzo Sankey; and Northern Arapaho representatives Eugene J. Ridgely, Sr., Gail J. Ridgely, Ben S. Ridgely, William J. C'Hair, Anthony A. Addison, Sr., Hubert N. Friday, Burton Hutchinson, Joseph Oldman, and Nelson P. White, Sr. Also participating in the project were private property owners of areas that were identified as possible sites of the Sand Creek Massacre, including Mr. and Mrs. Bill Dawson and members of the Charles Bowen, Sr., family.

6. George Bent, map of "Sand Creek Area," prepared ca. 1905–14, folder 10, Bent-Hyde Collection, Western History Collections, University of Colorado Library, Boulder.

7. George Bent, map of Arkansas River, Sand Creek, and western Kansas, showing the massacre site below the confluence of Rush and Sand creeks, prepared ca. 1905–14, folder 3, Bent-Hyde Collection, Western History Collections, University of Colorado, Boulder.

8. George Bent, untitled map of the Cheyenne Village and Sand Creek Massacre, Indian Archives Division, Cheyenne/Arapaho Agency File, "Warfare," 1864–85, microfilm roll 24, Oklahoma Historical Society, Oklahoma City; and map of Sand Creek Massacre showing Cheyenne village, prepared ca. 1905–14, folder 1, Bent-Hyde Collection, Western History Collections, University of Colorado, Boulder.

9. Samuel W. Bonsall, map accompanying "Journal of the march of the men belonging to the Garrison of Fort Lyon, C.T., under the command of Lieut. S. W. Bonsall 3rd Infantry, from Old Fort Lyon C.T., to Cheyenne Wells, pursuant to S.O. No 66 Hdqrs Fort Lyon C.T. June 12, 1868," Letters, Reports and Graphic Materials Received,

1868–1903, Department of the Platte, Omaha, Nebraska, Records of Topographical Engineer Departments, Chicago District, Record Group (RG) 77, Records of the Office of the Chief of Engineers, National Archives and Records Administration–Great Lakes Region (Chicago).

10. Scott Forsythe, interview with author, February 13, 2001.

11. Soil Conservation Service aerial photographs, Kiowa County, CO, roll AG 298, frames 31, 32, 33, 46, 47, 48, and roll AG 299, frames 05, 06, 07, 08, taken October 17, 1936, and roll YO 56, frame 56, and roll YO 55, frame 68, taken October 27, 1937, Records of the Soil Conservation Service, RG 114, National Archives at College Park, Maryland.

12. National Park Service ethnographer Alexa Roberts coordinated this recordation effort; her report on the project, which includes transcripts of the oral history interviews, is published in the *Sand Creek Massacre Project*, vol. one: *Site Location Study* (2000). Also contributing to this oral history effort were Carolyn Sandlin, Laird and Colleen Cometsevah, Luke Brady, Otto Braided Hair, Patsy Riddle, Gail Ridgely, Eugene Ridgely, Sr., Tom Meier, John C'Hair, and Joe Waterman.

13. Roberts, "The Sand Creek Massacre Site Location Study Oral History Project," *Sand Creek Massacre Project*, vol. one: *Site Location Study* (2000), 281.

14. Douglas D. Scott, *Sand Creek Massacre Project*, vol. one: *Site Location Study* (2000), 133.

15. The Cheyenne man's breast ornament was identified by Luke Brady of the Northern Cheyenne Tribe.

16. These 12-pounder mountain howitzer case fragments were found by Chuck Bowen, the son of landowner Charles Bowen, Sr., prior to the National Park Service archaeological survey. For a complete discussion of Bowen's discovery, see Scott, "Identifying the 1864 Sand Creek Massacre Site Through Archeological Reconnaissance," *Sand Creek Massacre Project*, vol. one: *Site Location Study* (2000).

Study Questions

1. Who is Ben Nighthorse Campbell, and what was his role in the memorial to the Sand Creek Massacre?

2. What was the NPS required to do under the Sand Creek Massacre National Historic Sites Study Act of 1998?

3. Discuss NPS efforts to locate the site of the Sand Creek Massacre. Why was this such a difficult task?

4. What evidence finally identified the location of the massacre site?

5. What factors led to the attack on the Cheyenne encampment at Sand Creek in 1864?

6. Why were the Cheyenne and Arapaho at Sand Creek not afraid of the Colorado Volunteer soldiers?

7. What type of artifacts would provide evidence signifying the potential site of the massacre?

8. What evidence convinced the NPS about the site's location?

9. How did Cheyenne oral history add to the geographical evidence of the site's location?

10. What was the objection to the NPS's 1999 archaeological investigation that determined the site of the massacre and village, and how is it unresolved?

11. What three proposals were suggested to commemorate the site and manage it? Which was chosen and why?

Why Preserve a Massacre Site? So the Dead May Rest

U.S. Senator Ben Nighthorse Campbell

The morning of November 29, 1864, dawned much like the winter mornings we are used to waking up to east of the Rocky Mountains. At the Big Bend of Sandy Creek, the low sun crested the horizon with glints of bright light reflecting off the frosted stalks of buffalo grass and rabbitbush. Thin snow lingered on the north side of the cottonwood trees, their lonely leaves flittering in the breeze on the mostly barren trees. Dry twigs snapped and leaves rustled underfoot as dogs rooted and horses began to forage. By sunrise, most of the Cheyenne and Arapaho people were still in their lodges, waiting for the sun to rise high enough in the sky to warm the early winter chill on the village. They rested peacefully under the white flag of truce and the American flag hanging from Chief Black Kettle's lodge.

A mile away, five battalions of soldiers were approaching hard and fast from Fort Lyon, led by Colonel John M. Chivington, a former Methodist preacher. He and his troops marched for five days through some tough weather from Denver at the order of Colorado territorial governor John Evans. The governor believed that ridding the territory of Indians would assist his efforts to gain statehood for Colorado, then a territory of Kansas, and for the transcontinental railroad to proceed through Colorado. Chivington had previously fought Confederate troops on Glorieta Pass in New Mexico and was anxious to rid his new Colorado militia of the derogatory designation as "the Bloodless Third Regiment," a moniker earned due to a lack of battle with either Confederates or Indians.

Governor Evans had earlier invited leaders of the Cheyenne and Arapaho to a council east of Denver in the hope they would agree to adhere to a treaty that surrendered their lands and granted them instead a triangular-shaped tract north of the Upper Arkansas in eastern Colorado. The tribes were not at all interested, as the buffalo and most of the game were no longer available on the tract. The tribes' snub and the fact that settlers' livestock was turning up in Cheyenne camps—combined with Evans's worry that the tribes would align with the Confederacy—pushed the situation on Colorado's eastern plains to a bloody conflict. The killing of the Hungates, a white family of four settlers earlier in the year, gave Chivington and Evans all the reason they needed to carry out Chivington's order to "kill Cheyennes wherever they are found."

Evans met again with tribal leaders two months before the massacre and told them to quit hunting and instead rely on government assistance for sustenance. He told Black Kettle that his people could be saved from fighting if they surrendered to military authority, at the time being meted out by Chivington.

Black Kettle believed he had made his peace by going to Fort Lyon earlier in the year. He, his people, and the Arapahos believed camping at Sand Creek was agreeable and flew both the U.S. and the white flag at the encampment with that understanding. The commander of Fort Lyons didn't make any effort to bring the tribes in from Sand Creek because he didn't have the provisions available to give them. Tribal misunderstanding and a lack of preparedness by local military authorities was quickly becoming a breach of any agreement and a pretext to battle.

Adding to the volatility of the situation were the passions being whipped up in Denver. Pro-Union sympathies, a general hatred of Indians coupled with the desire for statehood, and rhetoric from *The Rocky Mountain News* demanded Chivington act, and he was more than willing to. *The News'* first reports of the massacre called it "among the brilliant feats of arms in Indian warfare."

Those howitzer rounds exploding over the lodges ripped open the cool, quiet dawn that November morning along with rifle reports, the rolling thunder of 500 mounted calvary at full charge, and the attendant buglers.

Figure 63. After the massacre, soldiers committed atrocities on the dead Indians, including cutting off their heads. Sets of Cheyenne human remains from the Sand Creek Massacre are wrapped in blankets and packed with cedar chips in cedar boxes by three leaders of the Southern Cheyenne. Left to right: Moses Star, Jr., Nathan Hart, and Lucien Twins. The handmade boxes then made the journey to Oklahoma for tribal burial. Photo by Laurie Minor-Penland, National Museum of the American Indian.

The militia cut off the Indians' horses. Those Indians who could fought standing against the charge. Others fled along the dry creek bed. Still others dug pits in the low cliffs above the village, some hoping to fight, others hoping to hide, others waiting to die.

By 11 A.M., the bulk of the fighting was over. More than 150 Cheyenne and Arapaho lay dead, including women and children. Black Kettle died under the flags on his lodge that he thought would protect him and his people. It was not enough to kill the Indians at Sand Creek. Many of the soldiers, including officers, spent the balance of that day and the next scalping and mutilating the dead. Women's privates were cut out and stretched over militia saddle horns, triumphantly paraded through the streets of Denver on December 22 by the "victors" of the massacre. Other women's breasts were cut off and used for tobacco pouches. Such was the ferocity of the times that even death was not good enough for Indian people, my people.

As descriptions of the savagery of the massacre came to light, Evans, Chivington, and others were summoned before Congress to try and explain their bloodlust. Chivington had mustered out of military service and could not be tried for any crimes by the time attempts were made to make him accountable.

Evans became governor and had one of the highest mountain peaks in the state named after him. The tribes were left with yet another massacre to fill their last free days on the plains.

It has taken more than a century for the truth about Sand Creek to be separated from the popular version of history recorded by the conquering culture, which proclaimed this a "battle." But my relatives always knew what happened that day, and we passed our history along from generation to generation by word of mouth. We never doubted a massacre occurred that day.

When I learned that Bill and Tootie Dawson, the owners of the property on which the massacre occurred, were anxious to sell their ranch, I moved to secure the property for all Americans so that we can forever honor the spirits of those who died there that day. We are all indebted to the massacre descendants, the National Park Service, and many others for their tireless work to create the Sand Creek Massacre National Historic Site. It is a holy place, and the restless spirits of those who died are heard today in the wind through the trees and seen in the owls that guard the stands of trees and in the deer who quietly graze.

While we have the boundaries of the monument established on paper, the effort continues to secure the

Figure 64. Native Americans, particularly the Cheyenne, want the Sand Creek site acquired by the National Park Service and interpreted as a site of shame. Sand Creek Descendants Association members left to right: Joe Big Medicine (sun dance priest), Longdale, OK; Laird Cometsevah (traditional chief), Southern Cheyenne, Clinton, Oklahoma; George Black Owl, Southern Cheyenne artist, Clinton, Oklahoma; Colleen Cometsevah (genealogist); Arly Rhoades (director, Cheyenne Arapaho Senior Center), Clinton, Oklahoma; and "Little Joe," son of Joe Big Medicine. Photo © by Hal Gould, Camera Obscura Gallery, Denver. Photo courtesy Center of Southwest Studies, Fort Lewis College.

affected property from willing sellers. I believe firmly that one day we will be able to visit the ground on which so much blood was spilled that day in 1864. My intent is for this place to be a living memorial, like Gettysburg, to our intolerance of others. I believe that as Americans we are blessed with the courage to be able to honestly view our past, to be proud of our accomplishments and honest enough to admit and learn from our shortcomings. History is littered with the lost lessons of intolerance and hate. A dear friend of mine, Laird Cometsevah, is a Spiritual Leader of the Cheyenne and Arapahos of Oklahoma and a massacre descendant. He and his wife, Colleen, have dedicated their lives to the memory of the people killed at Sand Creek. In his wisdom, Laird once said: "Sand Creek means a lot to people. It will never disappear. Only the people will." We can never silence the screams of the women and children killed that cold day in November 1864, nor the cheers of the Denver citizenry upon learning of the massacre. But we must constantly work to find ways to be better human beings. Our ancestors and our children both demand this place become a memorial so the dead may rest.

Study Questions

1. What is the author's perspective on the Sand Creek Massacre, and why should it be commemorated?

2. How does Senator Campbell explain the need for and the goals of establishing a National Historic Site at Sand Creek?

3. Senator Campbell refers to Sand Creek as a "holy place." What does he mean by that? Holy for which group of people? Is it a sacred site?

4. Senator Campbell encourages the reader that "we must constantly work to find ways to be better human beings." Do you agree with him? How can public history help to achieve that goal?

Rewriting the Past for the Present

Public Monuments and Political Correctness, the Colorado State Capitol and Sand Creek

Thomas J. Noel

One of the worst slaughters by the U.S. military of peaceful Indians—mostly women and children—took place at Sand Creek, Colorado, in 1864. The Indians were camped on Sand Creek, where the army had told them to stay under American and white flags. There an estimated 150 Cheyenne and Arapaho—mostly women and children—were slaughtered by the U.S. Army. Babies were shot and their mothers raped and mutilated by soldiers who took their private parts back to Denver as trophies.

The Sand Creek Massacre is continually refought in books, articles, and public monuments and proclamations. In 1998 the Colorado legislature passed a bill to chisel the words *Sand Creek* off the 1909 list of *Battles* on a pedestal under the bronze soldier guarding the Colorado State Capitol in Denver. Other legislatures have also expressed horror about Sand Creek's human tragedy. The U.S. Congress stopped in the middle of the Civil War to investigate Sand Creek and condemn Colonel John M. Chivington and the Colorado Volunteers for being far more savage than the so-called savages they exterminated. Chivington was relieved of his command, as was John Evans, the territorial governor officially in charge of Indian affairs.

Although Washington, D.C., called it a massacre, many Coloradoans did not. Understandably alarmed by Indian raids and atrocities, white Coloradoans cheered Chivington. The monument in front of the capitol reflects that time and sentiment. To erase the two words would not undo Sand Creek; it would erase a painful lesson that each generation needs to relearn.

The story of Sand Creek, with all its various interpretations, needs to be left open for public discussion and reflection. Cheyenne Indians provided an interesting perspective on the massacre. Tribal members, including Sand Creek Massacre descendants, argued that too much of their history has already been erased. They suggested that it would be more to the point to add another interpretative marker providing a more Indian-friendly view.

Many citizens regarded Major John M. Chivington as a hero. As a Methodist minister, he helped found churches and a pioneer Sunday school in Denver. He heroically defeated Texans at the Battle of Glorieta Pass in 1862—the last time anyone stopped Texans from invading Colorado. A town in Kiowa County near Sand Creek is named for Chivington. Grateful Denverites elected him their county coroner in 1891. A large crowd attended his funeral and burial at Fairmount Cemetery in 1894. Defenders decorate his grave with flowers every November, calling him Colorado's most neglected hero.

As the Sand Creek case proves, Native Americans present a tremendous challenge to Western historians. Indians have generally been treated either with too much sympathy or with too much contempt, with bitter racism or romantic fawning. Even "Indian lovers" tend to treat Native Americans as victims rather than as courageous survivors of a group that is growing and still making American history.

"Sand Creek" should not be erased from history in the well-intentioned but misguided interests of political correctness. The Colorado legislature's 1998 move resembled other efforts to erase or ignore awkward reminders of national atrocities in the past. Fortunately, the legislature belatedly came to its senses and rescinded its plan after the public, the Colorado Historical Society, and Indians asked that Sand Creek not be erased.

Sand Creek is not the only political correctness battle brewing in Colorado. At Mesa Verde National Park, visitors experience a positive, flattering look at prehistoric Indians who used to be called Anasazi.

Recently, however, the politically correct banned the word Anasazi and decreed that henceforth these Indians are to be called Ancestral Puebloan or Pre-Puebloan Peoples. Pueblo Indians in New Mexico and Arizona, who are thought to be descendants of the prehistoric Indians of Mesa Verde, have objected to the word *Anasazi*. They point out that it is not their word but a Navajo term meaning "ancient ones" or "ancient enemies."

Further clouding a once pretty picture at Mesa Verde National Park is nauseating new research from Professor Christy Turner. Turner, a cultural anthropologist, contends in *Man Corn: Cannibalism and Violence in the Prehistoric American Southwest* (Salt Lake City: University of Utah Press, 1999) that ritualistic cannibalism and terrorism by their own people helped drive Pre-Puebloans from what is now Mesa Verde National Park and other southwestern settlements. The National Park Service, however, is not in any hurry to try to reinterpret their many southwestern parks with such an unflattering perspective on a prehistoric Indian culture long praised as the most advanced society north of Mexico.

The United States has also been very slow to erect public monuments and interpret World War II Japanese internment camps. In its most shameful twentieth-century action, the United States interred all Japanese, even grandmothers and day-old babies who were U.S. citizens, on the same racial guidelines used by Adolf Hitler.

The tricky issues of political correctness have sent Confederate flags into hiding and have probably led more than one community to hide statues of its pale-faced Indian War heroes. In New London, Connecticut, for instance, the monument to Pequot War hero John Mason was removed and replaced by a flower garden to avoid offending Native Americans.

A few scholars have addressed the issue of political correctness and public monuments. Michael Kammen, in his book *In the Past Lane: Historical Perspectives on American Culture* (New York: Oxford University Press, 1997), argues that heritage and public monuments are different from history in celebrating only those happy aspects of history appealing to diverse groups. Such public history manifestations focus on a past time of innocence, consensus, and happy days—on a mythical golden age. Historical monuments use symbols that often ignore problematic facts—or politically incorrect individuals or events.

David Lowenthal, in *Possessed by the Past: The Heritage Crusade and the Spoils of History* (New York: Free Press, 1996), argues that public heritage monuments and celebrations are comparable to religious faith. They celebrate heroes and ideals and golden ages without demanding hard proof and historical evidence. They honor people, events, and eras based more on faith and feeling than on hard historical analysis. If this mythical heritage is not true, supporters contend, it should be. Ethnic histories celebrating the accomplishments of certain groups probably fall into this category more often than historians admit.

Why not hold history and heritage monuments to higher standards? Public monuments do not always need to be happy, harmless, and Walt Disneyish. We have monuments at Auschwitz, Pearl Harbor, and Wounded Knee. We need monuments that recall and present varying perspectives on conflict, tragedy, and terrible events. Memorializing the darker moments in history is perhaps the best way to prevent their reoccurrence. Erasing politically incorrect monuments is a dangerous business. Better to place beside them markers with new and different perspectives.

Each generation must learn and revise history for itself. Ours should not be the generation to destroy evidence that future revisionists will want to see for themselves. If each generation censors the monuments and topples the heroes of it predecessors, history becomes hopelessly short sighted.

The "battle" over Denver's Sand Creek monument showed that monuments can be compromised without compromising history. The 1909 Civil War Soldier and the list of "battles" on his pedestal in front of the Colorado State Capitol survived the political correctness wars. Unlike many of his similarly incorrect

Figure 65. Civil War monument, Colorado State Capitol, Denver, Colorado. Photo by Andrew Gulliford, 2002.

colleagues, this handsome bronze soldier has not been toppled, desecrated, or put into secret storage. Staring toward the West with two howitzers at his feet, he has been preserved in a process that was conciliatory: on November 29, 2002, exactly 138 years after the massacre, the Colorado Historical Society, the State Capitol Building Advisory Committee, and the Colorado Department of Transportation unveiled on the 138th anniversary of the massacre a new Sand Creek Interpretive plaque. It was installed on the pedestal of that same solder at the west steps of the capitol. Among the dignitaries present were spokespersons for the Cheyenne and Arapaho, including descendants of Sand Creek survivors. State Senator Robert Martinez, who had introduced the resolution to erase Sand Creek from the plaque five years earlier, also spoke expressing approval at what had been, for all concerned, an instructive process in historical revisionism. What follows is the wording for the recently installed plaque:

The controversy surrounding this Civil War Monument has become a symbol of Coloradoans' struggle to understand and take responsibility for our past. On November 29, 1864, Colorado's First and Third Cavalry, commanded by Colonel John Chivington, attacked Chief Black Kettle's peaceful camp of Cheyenne and Arapaho Indians on the banks of Sand Creek, about 180 miles southeast of here. In the surprise attack, soldiers killed more than 150 of the village's 500 inhabitants. Most of the victims were elderly men, women, and children.

Though some civilians and military personnel immediately denounced the attack as a massacre, others claimed the village was a legitimate target. This Civil War Monument, paid for by funds from the Pioneers' Association and the State, was erected on July 24, 1909, to honor all Colorado soldiers who had fought in battles of the Civil War in Colorado and elsewhere. By designating Sand Creek a battle, the monument's designers mischaracterized the actual events. Protests led by some Sand Creek descendants and others throughout the twentieth century have since led to the widespread recognition of the tragedy as the Sand Creek Massacre.

This plaque was authorized by Senate Joint Resolution 99–017.

Study Question

1. How do you evaluate the controversy over the Sand Creek inclusions in the Civil War soldier monument at the Colorado State Capitol building? Is this just an issue over political correctness?

2. What other examples of political correctness does the author note, and what are the controversies over them?

3. How does the author interpret the role of public monuments as heritage?

4. Was the Colorado State Capitol Civil War soldier monument issue resolved? If so, how, and do you agree with the outcome?

Women in the West

Headnotes

Over 77,000 historic sites are listed on the National Register of Historic Places by the Keeper of the Register, who works for the National Park Service in Washington, D.C. Yet despite the fact that women represent half of the American population, historic sites related to women constitute less than 10 percent of the historic sites and historic districts listed on the National Register. Far more listings are devoted to the homes of Great White Men (GWM) and battlefields. Western historians have much work to do to place women back into the history of the American West, but the movement has begun. Western history and public history have come a long way since Dee Brown's *The Gentle Tamers*, and there is even a digital museum of Western women's history—the WOW Museum, or "Women of the West." Historical scholarship on Western women has mushroomed, but more applicable public history projects are needed. Relevant history books include Lilian Schlissel, *Women's Diaries of the Westward Journey*; Glenda Riley and Richard Etulain, *By Grit & Grace: Eleven Women Who Shaped the American West*; Lesley Poling-Kempes, *The Harvey Girls: Women Who Opened the West*; and Sharon Niederman, *A Quilt of Words: Women's Diaries, Letters & Original Accounts of Life in the Southwest, 1860–1960*. Pioneer women are interpreted at historical societies and museums, and there is some interpretation of the Harvey Girls at Bright Angel Lodge on the rim of the Grand Canyon, but much more Western women's history needs to be available to the public.

For recent anthologies see Susan Armitage and Elizabeth Jameson, eds., *The Women's West*, and Lillian Schlissel et al., *Western Women: Their Land, Their Lives*. For historic preservation see Mona Demosh and Joni Seager, *Putting Women in Place*; Polly Welts Kaufman and Katharine T. Corbett, eds., *Her Past Around Us: Interpreting Sites for Women's History*; and Gail Lee Dubrow and Jennifer Goodman, eds., *Restoring Women's History through Historic Preservation*.

Perhaps one of the most interesting women in Western and public history is a young Indian mother. We are not sure how to pronounce her name, we are not sure where she was from, we cannot positively identify her tribe; we are not certain where and when she died, and there are no photos of her. Despite such historical anonymity, much has been written about Sacagawea. There are more statues of her than any other American woman and possibly more statues of her than any other American. The most recent Sacagawea statue was installed in National Statuary Hall on Capitol Hill in Washington, D.C., in 2003, and it is the first statue of a native woman in the hall.

By far the most important native individual to assist the Lewis and Clark expedition was Sacagawea, the Shoshone (some say Hidatsa) woman who joined the expedition in the spring of 1805. Not surprisingly, Sacagawea elicits a great deal of conversation on the Lewis and Clark tourist trail. Some of this reflects the influence of romantic novels like Anna Lee Waldo's *Sacajawea* (1984), some pulls from debates among historians, and some comes from unclear or inconclusive passages in the expedition journals. Invariably, questions arise about the pronunciation and spelling of her name—is it *Sacajawea*, *Sacagawea*, or *Sakakawea*? The answer is never definitive, but it is usually *Sacagawea*, with a hard *g*. The question, and the answer, is less important than the continuing fascination that surrounds the historical figure. Although each generation wants to see a different symbol in Sacagawea, she remains central to how people understand the Lewis and Clark expedition and its significance. Of course, there is always deep fascination about her personal and psychic survival as the only female among more than two dozen men. In the early twentieth century, this made her a key symbol for the women's suffrage movement. At other times, her position within the expedition has led to more personal reflection—for artists, writers, and tourists alike.

The expedition journals provide some dramatic scenes that have piqued the imaginations of many. In the freezing Bitterroot Mountains of Idaho, facing starvation, Sacagawea offered to share with Captain William Clark a crust of bread that she had kept hidden on her person to feed her baby, Jean Baptiste. And during that cold, wet Christmas at Fort Clatsop in Oregon she presented Captain Clark with a stunning gift of two dozen white weasel tails—the most valued fur from the Rocky Mountains. Did she admire Clark because he was such a contrast to her lout of a husband, Charbonneau, or was there more to their relationship? Historians and Lewis and Clark aficionados lightly pass over such questions, but many tourists following the Lewis and Clark Trail still wonder. After all, for months, Lewis, Clark, Charbonneau, Sacagawea, and the baby stayed together in the same quarters, whether it was tepees or wooden huts.

Feminists have yet to write about Lewis and Clark, and until very recently no one has dealt with the complex issues of female representation surrounding Sacagawea. The height of Sacagawea representation came at the turn of the twentieth century as the Daughters of the American Revolution and other women's groups sought to create a female heroine to take her rightful place in American history. Sacagawea succeeded as a female symbol of bravery and personal independence, yet she also represented stoicism, loyalty, motherhood, and native participation in the expedition. What does that say about us as Americans, and what does that say about her? The Sacagawea dollar is doing so well that the coins can hardly be found in circulation. In this trio of essays on Western women's public history, anthropologist Sally McBeth describes and defines Sacagawea in her timely essay "Sacagawea: The Making of an American Cultural Icon."

Historian Marcia Tremmel Goldstein helps place women in the history of the West by focusing on the right to vote, when women suffragists successfully campaigned for equality at the voting booths in 1893. In Colorado, how they achieved that equality is carefully detailed in Goldstein's essay. She also chronicles Colorado's Suffrage Centennial in 1993 and the modern-day campaign to bring the past to the public in the present. Women historians of Colorado gained even deeper respect for their historical counterparts as they sought to host a year-long series of events and symposia to discuss the unique role Western women played in American voting history.

The last essay focuses on an area of Western history much known but little discussed: the issue of prostitution and the preservation of bordellos. Throughout the West in the 1890s, especially in mining camps and on cattle ranches, the ratio of men to women was seven to one. This gender imbalance resulted in the almost universal acceptance of prostitution in the nineteenth-century West, yet rarely are brothels preserved as part of Western women's history. Scholarly books on the topic include Anne Butler's *Daughters of Joy, Sisters of Misery: Prostitution in the American West 1865–90* and Jeffrey Nichols's *Prostitution, Polygamy and Power.*

In the absence of other diversions, the "sporting culture" of most mining camps and boomtowns meant getting drunk and visiting a house of ill repute. In Virginia City, Nevada, only months after the Washoe Rush, residents numbered 2,379 men and 147 women. Across the West there are innumerable stories, some fact and some fiction, of the flourishing red-light districts, of madams who married well, of high-priced whores in fancy houses and poor working girls in two-room cribs or living unprotected on the street. Realize that in the prudish Victorian era women did not go barefooted or bare armed. Ankles were not to be seen. The average middle-class housewife left the front steps wearing 22 pounds of clothing. Sexual inhibitions abounded, and rarely did husbands and wives see each other naked. The golden age of parlor houses spanned the 1870s to World War I, but in the West, prostitution remained legal in Laramie, Wyoming, through the 1950s and in Silver City, New Mexico, until the late 1960s, when the law finally closed Silver City Millie's famous Hudson Street houses. Truly, she was one of the last of the frontier madams as described in Max Evans's book *Madam Millie*.

The extent of prostitution in the American West can only be imagined. In Cripple Creek, Colorado, in the 1890s, when Cripple Creek gold helped to bring the entire nation out of the 1893 depression, the red-light district stretched five miles long and included women of every color. Rawhide, Nevada's, Stingaree Gulch from 1907 to 1908 stretched a fourth of a mile long with between 500 and 600 women of every race and nation. What were the employment opportunities for single women in the West? Teaching? Clerking? Dressmaking? Max Evans tells the story of rural Oklahoma teachers who were astounded to learn that ladies of the night made as many dollars in an evening as they made all month; for that reason at least three teachers chose to forsake their ABCs.

Julia Bulette, a crib girl in Virginia City, Nevada, worked on her own and became very popular with the local fire department. The only known photo of her shows her attired in a fireman's front shirt with belt and helmet that have the insignia of Virginia Engine Company No. 1, of which she was an honorary member. Cockeyed Liz from Buena Vista, Colorado, received an eye injury in a drunken brawl. Despite the fight, she trained her magpie to mimic words that sounded like, "Come in, boys, come in."

Madams moved west as entrepreneurs, and though the New Western history has touched on many topics, the business end of frontier prostitution remains virgin territory, so to speak. Knowledgeable madams first tried the cow towns of Kansas and then moved west into the mining camps of Colorado. Moving east from San Francisco into the uproar of Virginia City, Nevada, madams issued tokens worth from 5 to 50 cents. In the brawling, bustling Western mining camps, according to Mark Twain in his classic book *Roughing It*, full jails and hordes of prostitutes were signs of prosperity. He wrote, "Vice flourished luxuriantly during the heyday of our 'flush times.' The saloons were overburdened with custom; so were the police courts, the gambling dens, the brothels and the jails—unfailing signs of prosperity in a mining region—in any region for that matter."

Why did women seek out the sporting life? Many had been abused or abandoned as children and could not maintain stable relationships, but some women simply wanted a gayer, more exciting life than being a farm wife and mother or being married to the factory floor back east. Prostitutes wore fine clothes and make-up, which other women did not; hence the phrase "painted ladies." Ladies of the night had intriguing nicknames. For instance, in the notorious Blair Street district of Silverton, Colorado, prostitutes answered to Nigger Lola, Sheeny Pearl, Denver Kate, Gipsy Brown, Diamond Tooth Leona, 21 Pearl, Dutch Lena, Blonde Peggy, Minnie "the Baby Jumbo," and Oregon Shortline. Historical accounts of prostitution are interesting, such as the 1872 charge against Mary Brady, who lived north of Laramie, Wyoming, and who was hauled into court for "keeping a common, ill-governed and disorderly house to the encouragement of idleness, drinking and fornication." Clearly in Wyoming in the 1870s the Protestant ethic was in danger.

The language of the demimonde included phrases such as bawdy house, tenderloin district, dance hall girls, brothel dwellers, saloon workers, crib women, streetwalker, camp followers, fallen women, and simply "working girls." Youth was their number-one asset. Most prostitutes lived hard and died young, frequently of a drug overdose, because laudanum, a liquid derivative of opium, was easily available on the frontier. On the Comstock in Nevada in 1875, of 307 prostitutes 88 were white, 75 Oriental, 55 Irish, and 35 were 18 or younger. Soiled doves settled in as part of the social fabric in the hastily constructed mining camps. Women may have turned tricks at night, but during the day they did laundry, and in a medical emergency such as a smallpox or flu epidemic they aided their communities.

A Colorado legend is the story of Silver Heels, who was an attractive young dance hall girl in Alma who received silver heels as a gift from appreciative miners. During a smallpox epidemic she risked her life to minister to the sick. Because of her close contact with infected miners she caught the disease and became horribly disfigured, losing her attractiveness as a dancer and prostitute. Her career ruined, she left the mining camp, though miners begged her not to go. An itinerant artist painted her beautiful face on a local barroom floor, and a nearby mountain was named in her honor.

Across the West, the tenderloin districts had their own geographical parameters, such as Market Street, paralleling Larimer Street in Denver, Myers Avenue in Cripple Creek, and State Street in Leadville. In Telluride cribs were situated close to the San Miguel River. In Nevada an ordinance against the proximity of whorehouses and churches stipulated that brothels must be at least 400 yards from a house of worship. So lest they be found guilty of violating a town ordinance, city fathers in one Nevada mining boomtown recruited the necessary laborers and equipment and moved a local church!

In parlor houses like those run by Silver City Millie, women felt safe, ate well, were protected, and knew they were part of a sorority of sisters. A nineteenth-century maxim was, "A parlor house is where girls go to look for a husband and husbands go to look for a girl." In sparse, two-room cribs, women entertained men alone and were subject to rough beatings by drunks and other kinds of abuse. Rates varied, but during the 1849 gold rush, depending upon the sexual favors, brothels charged between 25 cents and $2. In the first part of the twentieth century $5 answered for a quick date and $15 to $30 allowed the amorous cowboy to spend the night—and a month's wages. Exotic sexual favors cost more.

Women promoted their wares or marketed themselves in a variety of ways. Girls would display their bosom by leaning out upstairs windows in tight dresses or showing off their upper arms. They would come down to the dance hall floors in low-cut, short-skirted dresses. As a marketing tool, girls had full-length photographs taken of themselves handsomely attired to give to their best customers as a fond remembrance. If found in a man's personal effects, these stately portraits bore no hint of scandal. Such *carte de vistes* were inscribed with the girl's name.

In various red-light districts girls would "take an airing in the afternoon" to show off. Jennie Rogers in Denver kept a high four-in-hand coach and toured her girls through Denver's streets. When scandalized city fathers insisted that prostitutes wear yellow ribbons, she had all new yellow outfits made for her ladies and proudly paraded them through Denver. Silver City Millie's technique was to let her women, particularly her new girls, walk Millie's poodle downtown while the dog wore a special cocked hat. This simple gesture signaled to any interested males that a new working girl had arrived and that she would be available that evening.

Working men understood working girls. Soiled doves averaged 20 minutes of "bed" time with a client and usually engaged four to six men per night. Girls did piecework, and men who were paid by the pound of beef or by the ton of ore understood the ladies' working conditions. In the copper mining town of Butte, Montana, the prostitutes' wages rose and sank with the wage scale of the miners. The men understood. They knew all about exploitation.

Madams made fortunes not only by taking half of the wages their girls made each night, but also by selling vast amounts of liquor. In 1880 in Denver, Jennie Rogers and Mattie Silks made fortunes by charging $1 for a bottle of beer and $5 for a split of champagne. Against a $300 monthly liquor bill, alcohol sales averaged $3,000 per month. Working girls drank colored water but got a cut of the profits from drinks their patrons bought and a percentage of the tips. The ladies also paid for their room and board, which included handsomely furnished bedrooms with enamel or brass beds, dressers, commodes, slop jars, rockers, straight chairs, rugs, lamps, lace curtains, and even writing desks.

Madams expected their girls to dress in the very latest styles, haute couture, and keep extensive and expensive wardrobes. Girls had their own trunks with seven or eight evening dresses and two or three afternoon costumes. Frequently they charged their clothing against the madam's account, and she would get a kickback from the seamstresses. Plus, women from the tenderloin had their clothing prices marked up higher than the same dresses sewed for "good" women.

Ladies entertained their customers with singing, dancing, and games, and their favorite card game was *panguingui*, because you could leave and come back to it later in the night. A madam's share of the take was used to buy off police and pay fees and fines, to keep the house running, and to hire servants, piano players, and bouncers as needed. The very best houses across the West would get cowboys drunk, laid, and back in the saddle by dawn without robbing them, or "pinching their poke." Fallen women worked sundown to sunup and had to worry about angry men, potential rivals, and the uninitiated who kept falling in love with them. As for the painted ladies, the lucky ones married their customers, became madams, or turned respectable. The others died young. But what about their bordellos? What has happened to their houses of ill repute?

In her lively essay "From the Old Homestead to the Mustang Ranch: Prostitution, Preservation, and Public History in the American West," archivist Jan MacKell dispels old myths and traverses the West from Cripple Creek, Colorado, to Butte, Montana, where the International Sex Worker Foundation for Art, Culture and Education (ISWFACE) sought to preserve the famous Dumas Bordello. Perhaps her most amazing find is that the Bureau of Land Management in Nevada owned a brothel. What federal land managers did with their historic structures is part of MacKell's intriguing essay.

Sacagawea

The Making of an American Cultural Icon

SALLY MCBETH

It is said that there are more monuments erected to honor Sacagawea and more geographical features (lakes, peaks, valleys) named after her than *any other* person in the United States. There is even a crater on Venus (all of the features are named for women) named after Sacagawea. What in the world does all this mean? How did this teenage Indian mother, wed to a man three times her age, gain such renown? Admittedly she accompanied Lewis and Clark from what is today western-central North Dakota to the Oregon coastline and back (about 3,000 miles) and she acted as interpreter for the "Corps of Discovery" (1804–6) but she was with them for only 17 months, not a long time!

Most historians would agree that all that we really know of this young woman is recorded in the journals of Lewis, Clark, and other expedition members who may have mentioned her in their record. Most readers of these journals would also agree that very little is revealed about her in these thousands of pages of journaling. Sacagawea, simply, is a mystery. We don't know what she looked like, we don't know much about her personality, and what little we do know is revealed through a male lens. To begin, the reader needs to be familiar with the debates about Sacagawea, as these disagreements capture the essence of the enigma that surrounds the story of this young woman.

Background
Name

The name Sacagawea or Sacajawea evokes the image of a young Indian woman—her infant strapped to a cradleboard—pressing westward, pointing out the way to the Pacific for the famed Lewis and Clark Expedition of the early 1800s. Knowledge of her role in the expedition and the controversies surrounding her later life are critical to an understanding of the creation of Sacagawea as an American cultural and historical icon.

A note on the spelling and meaning of the name is in order. I have chosen to use the *Sacagawea* spelling in this essay because it is currently preferred by most historians. Many readers will be more familiar with the *Sacajawea* spelling (depending on where you grew up). Both Lewis and Clark wrote her name variously as *Sah ca gah we ah*, *Sah-kah-gar-wea*, *Sar kah gah We a*, *Sah-cah-gar-weah*, and so forth. Over the years, writers have employed numerous spellings and pronunciations, including *Sacajawea*, *Sakajawea*, *Sacagawea*, *Sakakawea*, *Tsakakawea*, *Sacajowa*, *Saykijawee*, and recently *Saca tzah we yaa*. There is a great deal of controversy surrounding this woman's name and two major theories relating to its proper spelling, pronunciation, and meaning.

One theory is that the name is of Hidatsa origin and means "Bird Woman," from *tsakaka* or *sacaga* (bird) and *wiis* or *wea* (woman). Since the Hidatsa language does not contain the hard *j* sound, the name should be spelled and pronounced *Sacagawea* (or *Sakakawea*). Lewis's journal entry of May 20, 1805, appears to support the Hidatsa derivation. He writes: "The mouth of shell river a handsome river of about fifty yards in width discharged itself into the shell river on the Stard or upper side; this stream we called Sâh-câ-gar me-âh or bird woman's River, after our interpreter the Snake [another name for Shoshone] woman."[1]

The other theory says that the name is Shoshone and means "boat launcher," from *sac* (boat or canoe) and *jaw-e* (to throw, cast, or launch). It is debatable whether the name *is* a Shoshone name since the Shoshone language does not include the hard *j* sound, and indeed some linguists do not believe it has a comprehensible Shoshone meaning; some Lemhi Shoshone of Idaho hold that her Shoshone name was Saca tzah we yaa, which translates to "one who carries a heavy burden." The first publication of the Lewis and Clark journals in 1814 by Biddle and Allen[2] used the Sacajawea spelling and likely influenced future generations to retain that spelling. Historians are not sure why Biddle and Allen chose this configuration rather than Sacagawea, which is more common in the journals. Irving Anderson suggests that Clark sometimes formed his handwritten g's like j's. His careless penmanship may have created the confusion.[3] I question whether it will ever be determined how her name was actually pronounced (or spelled) since professional linguists of the Hidatsa and Shoshone language differ considerably in their conclusions about the meaning and spelling of her name.

Roles

There is also little agreement about the roles that Sacagawea played in the Lewis and Clark Expedition. While it is beyond the scope of this essay to rearticulate the debates (and supporting evidence from the notes of the journalists) as to whether Sacagawea was central or merely peripheral to the success of the expedition, it is important to outline these briefly.

Sacagawea was, of course, the only woman who accompanied Lewis and Clark in their expedition across the newly acquired Louisiana Purchase. She joined the expedition on April 7, 1805, and left it on August 17, 1806. Little is known of Sacagawea's childhood. Two entries in Captain Lewis's journal of July 28 and August 19, 1805,[4] historical reconstruction, and Shoshone oral traditions are the only sources of this limited information. Sacagawea was probably born around 1788 in a Shoshone village in the Lemhi River Valley (also known as Shoshone Cove) in what is today Idaho. It is likely that she was a member of the Agaideka or Salmon Eater band of the Shoshone tribe. When Sacagawea was between 12 and 14 years old, she was captured and taken prisoner near what is today Three Forks, Montana. Most historians believe that the Hidatsa Indians from the Knife River village of Metaharta (in present-day North Dakota) were her captors. Sometime between 1800 and 1804, she and another Shoshone girl were purchased by Toussaint Charbonneau, a French Canadian fur trapper and trader. Charbonneau was eventually hired by Lewis and Clark to be their interpreter, and he was instructed to bring one of his wives with him to act as interpreter among the Shoshone Indians.

Figure 66. This grandfather tree at the top of Lemhi Pass on the Idaho and Montana border may date from the time of the Lewis and Clark expedition. Photo by Andrew Gulliford, 2000.

Sacagawea was chosen, although no mention is made at this time that this teen would be carrying a young child across the Rocky Mountains and westward. Sacagawea had given birth to a son, Jean Baptiste Charbonneau, on February 11, 1805, at Fort Mandan. The infant became the youngest member of the expedition, which left Fort Mandan on April 7, 1805. Sacagawea's most important role, then, was likely that of interpreter. Clark mentions that she functioned as translator four times; Lewis mentions it on three occasions.

A much-debated second role is that of Sacagawea as expedition guide. Sacagawea has been described by many as the guide and pilot of the Lewis and Clark Expedition; however, there is little information in the journals of Lewis and Clark to support this contention. She was unfamiliar with most of the terrain through which the expedition traveled and so could not have directed Lewis and Clark to the Pacific Ocean. Her geographical knowledge was limited to the region near her homeland in the Three Forks area of the Upper Missouri River. In and around this area she recognized landmarks and provided some direction to Lewis and Clark, and this is recorded on two occasions, but otherwise she did not routinely point out the trail. There are two recorded occasions when Sacagawea did act as a guide. One was in late July–early August 1805, while trekking toward the Pacific, and the other on the return trip in 1806. In the summer of 1805, she recognized landmarks in the area of her homeland and reassured Lewis and Clark that they were on the right path. On the homeward journey, Sacagawea recommended passage through the Bozeman Pass. Clark writes on July 13, 1806: "The Indian woman who has been of great Service to me as a pilot through this Country recommends a gap in the mountain more South which I shall cross."[5] Many refute Sacagawea's role as guide. One's position in this particular debate depends on how the term "guide" is defined. Lewis and Clark both acknowledged that Sacagawea acted as guide on occasion; Clark refers to her as "pilot," supporting her role as guide.

A third role that Sacagawea played was that of emissary. Meriwether Lewis knew that if he did not find Sacagawea's tribe of Shoshone people in August 1805 as he descended the western slopes of the Rockies that the Corps of Discovery might not survive the winter. Not only did the expedition connect with Sacagawea's own Shoshone band, but her brother, Cameahwait, had become a chief of the Shoshone Indians during her absence. Sacagawea, both as sister and as emissary, was instrumental in convincing her brother to provide horses and guides for the westward journey across the Bitterroot Mountains and through the Salmon River country to the navigable waters of the Clearwater and Columbia rivers.

Equally significant in terms of her role as diplomat was her presence as an Indian woman with child. Clark twice noted the reactions of Indian groups upon

Figure 67. When Sacagawea became deathly ill, probably because of complications from giving birth, Captain Meriwether Lewis gave her water from this sulfurous spring along the Upper Missouri River near Great Falls, Montana. She recovered, probably because she was only dehydrated. Photo by Andrew Gulliford, 2000.

seeing Sacagawea and her son. For example, on October 13, 1805, Clark records: "The wife of Shabono our interpetr we find reconsiles all the Indians, as to our friendly intentions a woman with a party of men is a token of peace."[6] While some disparage this "role" as due only to the "accident" of her female sex,[7] it was nonetheless a wise diplomatic decision for Lewis and Clark to have included Sacagawea and Jean Baptiste in their expedition, whether or not they knew the full implications at the time they made their decision. Her presence and her connections made her role as expedition emissary a natural one.

In addition, Sacagawea collected wild foods to supplement the expedition's rations, and she boosted morale when the members were cold and weary. She even saved valuable instruments and records from being lost overboard in a storm when the expedition was traveling on the Missouri River. Captain Lewis (who was not nearly as fond of Sacagawea as Captain Clark) writes in his journal entry of May 16, 1805, of this near catastrophe: "The Indian woman to whom I ascribe equal fortitude and resolution, with any person onboard at the time of the accedent, caught and preserved most of the light articles which were washed overboard."[8] Clark was particularly impressed by

Figure 68. This is an actual segment of the Lewis and Clark Trail in the Bitterroot Mountains. Crossing this trail during an early and unexpected wet snowfall proved to be a formidable test of the Corps of Discovery. Captain William Clark stated that he had never been as cold and as wet in his life. Sacagawea had hidden some bread on her person for her baby, but along this trail she gave the bread to Captain Clark. Photo by Andrew Gulliford, 2000.

Sacagawea's service and strength, and he nicknamed her "Janey" in his expedition journals. The explorers had a lot of affection for her son, Jean Baptiste. William Clark nicknamed him "Pomp" or "Pompy," called him his "little dancing boy," and offered to educate him and raise him as his own child.

Perhaps the most important tribute to Sacagawea comes from a letter from Clark to Charbonneau dated August 20, 1806 (only six days after he and Sacagawea left the expedition): "Your woman who accompanied you that long dangerous and fatigueing rout to the Pacific Ocian and back diserved a greater reward for her attention and services on that rout than we had in our power to give her at the Mandans."[9] Sacagawea's services certainly seem to have contributed to the success of the expedition, as indicated in the final journal entry in which she was mentioned. On August 17, 1806, Clark's brief entry does not even use her name; he says, "We also took our leave of T. Chabono, his Snake Indian wife and their Son Child who had accompanied us on our rout to the pacific Ocean in the Capacity of interpreter and interpretes."[10] She and Charbonneau and their one-and-a-half-year-old baby left the expedition at Fort Mandan, the same place where they had joined the expedition 17 months earlier.

Death Date

An understanding of the dispute over where and when Sacagawea died is also central to an understanding of the controversies surrounding this woman. This dispute is significant because whether Sacagawea died in her midtwenties or in her midnineties leaves 70 years of room for speculation. Most non-Indian academic historians writing today believe that Sacagawea died at Fort Manuel Lisa, in present-day South Dakota, on December 20, 1812. Historical records suggest that Charbonneau, Sacagawea, and Jean Baptiste went east to St. Louis, Missouri, around 1810 to accept Clark's offer of 320 acres of land and additional pay for services rendered and financial assistance for the education of their son. City life, however, did not agree with Toussaint Charbonneau, and both he and Sacagawea (presumably) left St. Louis to return to the Upper Missouri to work for Manuel Lisa, a famous Missouri Fur Company trader. Jean Baptiste Charbonneau probably remained in St. Louis to begin his education under the patronage of William Clark. Sacagawea is believed to have been ill and to have died of a fever shortly after returning to the Missouri River country. This story refutes claims made by many Eastern Shoshone that she was a contemporary of Chief Washakie (who died in 1900). In this view she was reunited with her Shoshone people only once since her abduction from them—and this was en route to the Pacific Ocean with Lewis and Clark in 1805.

Three important documents support the position of an 1812 death date. The first of these comes from the journal of Henry Brackenridge (author, statesman, lawyer) of Pittsburgh, who was on board a trading boat in the vicinity of Fort Manuel in 1811. His journal entry of April 2, 1811, records that a wife of Charbonneau was on the Missouri River in 1811 and that her health was poor. He says:

> We had on board a Frenchman named Charboneau, with his wife, an Indian woman of the Snake nation, both of whom had accompanied Lewis and Clark to the Pacific, and were of

great service. The woman, a good creature of a mild and gentle disposition, greatly attached to the whites, whose manners and dress she tries to imitate, but she had become sickly, and longed to visit her native country; her husband, also, who had spent many years among the Indians, had become weary of civilized life."[11]

The second piece of evidence (not published until 1920) comes from the journal of John Luttig, who was the head clerk of Fort Manuel Lisa. He wrote the following journal entry on December 20, 1812, one year and eight months after Brackenridge's document: "This Evening the Wife of Charbonneau a Snake Squaw, died of a putrid fever she was a good and the best Woman in the fort, aged about 25 years she left a fine infant girl."[12] Most historians (and the Lemhi Shoshone) believe this entry provides conclusive evidence of Sacagawea's death in 1812; she would have been around 24 years old. There are records that make reference to an infant girl, Lisette, but her whereabouts after 1812 are unknown. It is likely that Luttig took her to St. Louis, Missouri, where William Clark eventually officially adopted her and her brother, Jean Baptiste.

The reader should take special note that neither Brackenridge nor Luttig refer to Sacagawea by her name; they call her wife of Charbonneau (who had many wives). Not only is this revealing about women's (especially Indian women's) relative status, but it also introduces an air of uncertainty. Could these men have gotten it wrong? Some new evidence that came to light in 1962 seems more conclusive. Donald Jackson had heard of an account book belonging to William Clark that listed on the cover the whereabouts of the expedition members.[13] This account book is currently in the Graff collections of the Newberry Library in Chicago. On the cover Clark wrote: *Se car ja we au Dead*. (Clark clearly spelled her name on the cover of this cashbook with a *j*, not a *g*). This cashbook is dated 1825–28; it is not known exactly when Clark wrote his infamous note on the cover. Historians thus rest their case with what they

Figure 69. Sacagawea Cemetery, Wind River Reservation, Wyoming. Most Wind River Shoshone believe Sacagawea was buried here in 1884. Scholars and historians feel she was buried along the bank of the Missouri River near the South Dakota/North Dakota border several decades earlier. The other two monuments memorialize her sons, though Jean Baptiste is actually buried in eastern Oregon. Photo by Sally McBeth.

believe is fairly conclusive evidence that Sacagawea died in 1812. The negative evidence that her name is not recorded (written) anywhere after this date is also cited as proof of her death in 1812.

An alternative version of Sacagawea's later life, however, persists. Oral traditions of the Wind River Shoshone, Comanche, Mandan, Hidatsa, Yakima, and others maintain that Sacagawea lived to be an old woman; the Wind River Shoshone insist she died on April 9, 1884, and is buried on their reservation.[14] The various oral histories record her name as Sacagawea (Bird Woman in Hidatsa), Sacajawea (Boat Pusher or One Who Carries a Heavy Burden in Shoshone), Porivo (Chief Woman), Wadze Wipe (Lost Woman), and Bo-i-naiv (Grass Woman).

According to these oral traditions, Sacagawea left Charbonneau in the St. Louis area and headed west, perhaps around 1810. It is said that she wandered from tribe to tribe in what are now the states of Kansas, Oklahoma, and possibly Texas, finally settling with the Comanche. There she married a man called Jerk Meat and had children with him. Upon the death of her Comanche husband, she traveled up the Missouri River in search of her own people. Reunited with her son, Jean Baptiste (now known simply as Baptiste), and an adopted nephew, Bazil (adopted while she was with her tribe in 1805), she settled in the Fort Washakie area of Wyoming. She was now called Porivo and arrived back in time to be present at the negotiations for the treaty of 1868, which ceded Shoshone lands to the government and created the Wind River Reservation.[15]

Some say that Sacagawea helped her Wind River Shoshone people in their transition to life on their newly created reservation and that she was venerated by her tribe and buried on the Wyoming Reservation in 1884. Others maintain that the assistance she provided to Lewis and Clark (and the subsequent opening of the Louisiana Purchase) left her only marginally accepted by her Wind River people. She lived her later life out on the reservation, but not as a central historical figure. And what of the "conclusive" 1820s cashbook on which Clark stated that "Se car ja we au" was dead? Interestingly, Clark also writes that expedition member Patrick Gass was dead. Gass lived to be 99 years old; he did not pass away until 1870 and was the last known survivor of the expedition.

Suffragist Movement

The evolution of interest in Sacagawea and the subsequent debate concerning the year of her death may have begun with the woman's suffragist movement. In 1902, Eva Emery Dye, Clackamas County chairman for the Oregon Equal Suffrage Association, wrote a historical novel: *The Conquest: The True Story of Lewis and Clark*. In this book Dye portrays Sacagawea as the guide of the Lewis and Clark expedition. In book II, chapter 27, "The Home Stretch," Dye writes:

> Sacajawea, modest princess of the Shoshones, heroine of the great expedition, stood with her babe in her arms and smiled upon them [the members of the departing expedition] from the shore. So had she stood in the Rocky Mountains pointing out the gates. So had she followed the great rivers, navigating the continent. Sacajawea's hair was neatly braided, her nose was fine and straight, and her skin pure copper like the statue in some old Florentine gallery. Madonna of her race, she had led the way to a new time. To the hands of this girl, not yet eighteen, had been intrusted the key that unlocked the road to Asia.[16]

It has been suggested that she and others created this heroine for their cause. Eva Emery Dye, in fact, admitted that she was in search of a strong woman of the past with whom suffragettes could identify. She writes:

> My thoughts were turned to that memorable Lewis and Clark expedition and I was persuaded by my publishers to weave a story about that.... I struggled along as best I could with the information I could get, trying to find a heroine.... I traced down every old book and scrap of paper, but still was without a real heroine. Finally, I came upon the name of Sacajawea and I screamed, "I have found my heroine."
>
> I then hunted up every fact I could about Sacajawea. Out of a few dry bones I found in the old tales of the trip I created Sacajawea and made her a real living entity. For months I dug and scraped for accurate information about this wonderful Indian maid.
>
> The world snatched at my heroine, Sacajawea.... The beauty of that faithful Indian woman with her baby on her back, leading those stalwart mountaineers and explorers through the strange land, appealed to the world.[17]

It is clear that some aspects of Sacagawea's life *have* been embellished and that many of the creative legendary components of Sacagawea's life emerge from Dye's early writings. For example, Sacagawea's role as singular expedition guide and the hint of a romantic relationship with Clark have become a part of the legend that surrounds this heroine's life. Dye was one of the first to mythologize Sacagawea. She did so to create a heroine for the Portland Centennial Lewis and

Clark Exposition and for the annual meeting of the National American Woman's Suffrage Association, both held in the summer of 1905 in Portland, Oregon. Suffragists used stories of Indian women to serve their cause because these women seemed to offer an alternative to American patriarchy. It was also the case that women like Sacagawea and Pocahontas were suitable candidates because they mediated between white and Indian cultures. They are perceived as having assisted America in "civilizing" the land and its indigenous populations. The citizens of this country may also have been more accepting of these historical Indian figures because they could be seen as exonerating the notion of Manifest Destiny.

In her *History of Woman Suffrage*, Ida Husted Harper[18] quotes Dr. Anna Howard Shaw:

> May we, the daughters of an alien race who slew and usurped your country, learn the lessons of calm endurance, of patient persistence and unfaltering courage exemplified in your [Sacagawea's] life, in our efforts to lead men through the Pass of justice, which goes over the mountains of prejudice and conservatism to the broad land of the perfect freedom of a true republic; one in which men and women together shall in perfect equality solve the problems of a nation that knows no caste, no race, no sex in opportunity, in responsibility or in justice!

The suffragists were not arbitrary in their selection of Sacagawea as their paragon of feminine and feminist ideals. In their eyes this Indian woman integrated many of the ambiguities of what "being a woman" meant. In this abiding national myth, issues of miscegenation and ownership of women combine with the more acceptable traits of "calm endurance and patient persistence." These issues certainly rang as true for women at the turn of the twentieth century just as they do for women at the turn of the twenty-first.

Political science professor at the University of Wyoming and suffragist Grace Raymond Hebard

Figure 70. This is the famous Sacagawea statue in Forest Park, Portland, Oregon, which helped inspire the suffragette movement. Photo by Andrew Gulliford, 2001.

(1861–1936) took a consequent step in keeping Dye's legends alive. Hebard's first article, printed in 1907, was titled "Pilot of First White Men to Cross the American Continent."[19] In this article Hebard says that a member of the Wyoming legislature informed her that he actually knew Sacagawea and her offspring. This Sacagawea obviously could not have died in 1812. Hebard continued research, which culminated in the publication of her 1933 book, *Sacajawea* (subtitled "A Guide and Interpreter of the Lewis and Clark Expedition, with an Account of the Travels of Toussaint Charbonneau, and of Jean Baptiste, the Expedition Papoose").[20] Hebard wove stories collected from informants at Wind River and in Oklahoma with other pieces of evidence that suggest "Sacajawea" (also known as Porivo) lived to be an old woman of about 100 years and was buried on the

Wind River Reservation in 1884. This book went on to become the standard reference despite much criticism of its controversial stand that Sacagawea lived to be a woman of nearly 100 years old and that she had traveled west from St. Louis around 1810, spent time with the Comanche tribe in the southern plains, and then made her way back "home" to the newly created (1868) Wind River Reservation in what is today Wyoming. Hebard's research and convictions influenced the writings of many subsequent scholars and popular writers.

Historians have documented that some of the oral testimonies presented as fact in Hebard's book are suspect.[21] But what were Hebard's motives for creating a Sacagawea who lived to be nearly 100 years old? Her detractors cite a threefold explanation. The first (following Dye) was to enliven the strong image of Sacagawea for the woman's suffrage movement. The notion that Hebard was misguided and confused because of her fanatic dedication to the women's movement emerges frequently in the historical writings about Hebard's Sacagawea research. The second reasoning is that Hebard wanted to glorify her home state of Wyoming by situating Sacagawea's final resting place in that state rather than South Dakota. The third possible motive is that Hebard simply wanted to make a name for herself. If these above-cited assessments of Hebard are correct, the story of Sacagawea's life from 1812 to 1884 did not begin with the Indians themselves but was the result of Hebard's amateur scholarship and tall tales. Certainly, however, not all of Hebard's research can be discounted.[22] The question is: Which sections are valid and reflect the testimony of her Indian informants, and which have been elaborated to serve Hebard's agenda? The answers to these questions are unlikely ever to be unraveled.

Many reputable ethnographies of the Eastern Shoshone make reference to Bazil and an aged Sacagawea. Äke Hultkrantz, for example, says, "There is no doubt that the woman who died this year [1884] on the Wind River Reservation and who was called 'Bazil's mother' was Sacajawea."[23] Anthropologists Milford Chandler, Frederick Hodge, Robert Lowie, Demitri Shimkin, and Judith Vander all refer to "Sacajawea's" presence on the Wind River Reservation in the 1880s. Historians might argue that these ethnographers were misled by Hebard, her informants, and revisionist histories. Still, perhaps these references should not be dismissed in their entirety, and each should be examined on an individual basis.[24]

The debate over when and where Sacagawea died and was buried became so heated in the early part of this century that the commissioner of Indian Affairs requested that Charles Eastman, a noted Sioux physician and graduate of Dartmouth College and Boston University, make an official investigation to end the speculation once and for all. Eastman's task was to resolve the squabbles between the states of South Dakota and Wyoming over the final resting place of the now famous "guide" of the Lewis and Clark Expedition.

Eastman arrived at his conclusions eight years before Hebard's book was published. It is, however, not clear if his investigations were independent of Hebard's. Eastman's 1925 report was based on the oral traditions of the Shoshone of Wyoming, the Comanche of Oklahoma, and the Hidatsa of North Dakota.[25] It contends that Sacagawea died in 1884 and was buried at the "Sacajawea" Cemetery in Fort Washakie, Wyoming. His report, completed 40 years after one Sacagawea died and 112 years after the death of the "other," only added fuel to the fire. Historians argue that as an Indian person, Eastman may have had an agenda of his own and that his historical scholarship is questionable. Many native people, of course, disagree with this derogatory assessment.

Contested Pasts

As if there wasn't enough disagreement among historians about the roles that Sacagawea played in the expedition and how the early influences of suffragists created the legend of where and when she died, native people themselves insist that their tribal oral histories should also be included in our understanding of who Sacagawea was. These tribal perspectives are not in agreement with one another (nor do they necessarily agree with the historical record), but they may be understood as gateways to an understanding of alternative constructions of reality. This section on "contested pasts" will consider the Lemhi Shoshone (Idaho), the Wind River Shoshone (Wyoming), and the Hidatsa (North Dakota) oral traditions.

Lemhi Shoshone

The Lemhi Shoshone are a fusion of the Shoshone Agaideka (Salmon Eaters), Tukudeka (Sheep Eaters), and Kucundika (Buffalo Eaters) bands, which occurred by around 1855. This federally unrecognized tribe currently resides on the Fort Hall (Shoshone-Bannock) reservation near Blackfoot, Idaho. The Lemhi Shoshone traditions surrounding Sacagawea (they insist that the Sacajawea spelling is correct) are most closely in accord with the written historical and archival record. The Lemhi Shoshone hold that Sacagawea was born in a Northern Shoshone village in the vicinity of the Lemhi River Valley, in what is today Idaho. The tribe also holds that she was a member of the Agaideka, or Salmon Eater, band of the Shoshone. Around 1800, while her tribe was engaged in a hunting expedition east of their home territory, in the Three Forks area of the Missouri River in Montana, the Hidatsa of the Knife River Village of Metaharta (North Dakota) captured her. At the time of her capture, Sacagawea was about 12 years old. By 1804, she had become the property of Toussaint Charbonneau, a French Canadian trader.

In the winter of 1804–5, Captains Meriwether Lewis and William Clark stayed at Fort Mandan on the Missouri River, in what is today North Dakota. There they encountered Charbonneau and Sacagawea. Before leaving Fort Mandan in April 1805 to continue their westward journey, Lewis and Clark hired Charbonneau as an interpreter, requesting that he bring one of his Shoshone wives with him. Charbonneau brought Sacagawea, who had given birth to their son, Jean Baptiste, on February 11, 1805. The infant became the youngest member of the expedition. Lemhi Shoshone stress the importance of Sacajawea's knowledge of and identification with her Shoshone heritage as characteristics that were crucial to the successful completion of the Lewis and Clark Expedition

On August 13, 1805, Lewis and some members of the expedition came into contact with a band of Shoshone people with whom they were able to communicate through sign language. Two days later, on August 17, Charbonneau and Sacagawea met the party that was indeed Sacagawea's own Shoshone band. She was overjoyed at seeing her people again, and her unexpected reunion with her brother is one of the most touching and emotional entries of the expedition journal. She had, of course, not seen her sibling since her abduction years earlier. As she sat and stared at Cameahwait, recognizing him as her brother, "She jumped up, ran & embraced him, & threw her blanket over him and cried profusely.... After some talk between them she resumed her seat & attempted to interpret for us, but was frequently interrupted by her tears."[26]

During her absence, her brother, Cameahwait, had become a chief of the Shoshone Indians. Sacagawea was instrumental in convincing him to provide horses and guides for Lewis and Clark's westward journey across the Bitterroot Mountains and through the Salmon River country to the navigable waters of the Clearwater and Columbia. The Lemhi Shoshone trace their lineage from Sacajawea's brother, Cameahwait, to her nephew, Chief Tendoy. They also hold that Sacajawea died in 1812.

Wind River Shoshone

Another Shoshone tradition also exists. The traditions of the Wind River Shoshone of present-day Wyoming are similar to those of the Shoshone of Idaho in a number of ways. The Wind River Shoshone Reservation was created in 1868. In 1878 the Northern Arapaho were moved to the Wind River Reservation; it remains a shared reservation today. Like the Lemhi Shoshone, the Wyoming Shoshone attribute the success of the expedition to Sacagawea's Shoshone, rather than Hidatsa, cultural knowledge. They also note her reunion with her brother, Cameahwait, in present-day Idaho. However, the similarities end here. Most Wind River Shoshone do not believe that Sacagawea died in 1812. They add 72 years to her life.

Many Wind River Shoshone claim that an aged Sacagawea (also known as Porivo) returned home to her Wind River people. This woman recounted stories of traveling west with a group of white men, of seeing a gigantic fish as big as a house (Sacagawea did see a beached whale on the Pacific coast), and of being abused by her husband (Clark records that he chastised Charbonneau for striking Sacagawea). Rather than returning up the Missouri River with Charbonneau around 1810, the Wind River story recounts that Sacagawea left Charbonneau in St. Louis because he continued to be abusive and had also taken another Indian wife. Then she began her migration back home to her Shoshone people. She wandered through many states on her westward journey. When she got to Indian Territory, in what is today Oklahoma, she passed through Comanche country. Comanche and Shoshone are closely related languages and cultures, and the oral tradition of both tribes concur that she settled there for a while, married a Comanche man by the name of Jerk Meat, bore him some children, and then moved on after their children were grown and her husband had died. She left Comanche country in search of her other sons. Wind River Shoshone tradition holds that Sacagawea had two sons: Jean Baptiste (now Baptiste) and Bazil (an adopted nephew), both of whom she thought might have eventually traveled west and north to their Shoshone homelands in their adult years. Wind River tradition has it that after many years of travel, at about the age of 80, Sacagawea returned home to her people in what later (1890) became the state of Wyoming.

According to the Wind River traditions, Sacagawea worked with Chief Washakie to help her people in their transition to reservation life. She had traveled extensively and had acquired an in-depth knowledge of the emerging American culture. It would have been unusual for a woman to speak in council, but as an elder, her tribe sought out Sacagawea's expertise. She assumed an important and unusual position for a woman when she acted as liaison to Chief Washakie.

A Sacagawea who was dead at 24 years of age is disempowered; the prestige that is associated with women who have reached old age has been denied to her. Most historians do not accept the Wind River story and attribute it to the (some would say inaccurate) early works and influences of Grace Raymond Hebard, whose influence on the creation of the legend of Sacagawea has been discussed. It is important to note, however, that Comanche oral history supports the Wind River claim that Sacagawea spent time with the Comanche in the southern plains. But the Lemhi Shoshone also raise the pertinent question, "Why would Sacajawea return to the Wyoming Shoshone rather than her Idaho Shoshone people?"

Hidatsa

A third tradition about Sacagawea is current among some Hidatsa people of present-day North Dakota. The Three Affiliated Tribes, the Mandan, Hidatsa, and Arikara, share the Fort Berthold Reservation, established in 1870 and situated along the northern Missouri River. This version of the story asserts that Sacagawea was not Shoshone, but Hidatsa. In their journals, both Lewis and Clark clearly document that they believe Sacagawea was Shoshone, as do the journals of expedition members Patrick Gass, John Whitehouse, and John Ordway.

The Hidatsa insist on the *Sacagawea* spelling, as the name is clearly translatable into Hidatsa; *Sacaga* means "bird"; *wea* means "woman." The Hidatsa invert the kidnapping story and claim that the Shoshone captured her from her Hidatsa village and home and that with the intervention of wolf allies, she was able to escape her Shoshone captors and return to her Hidatsa village: Twilight Walker or Nightwalker village. The Hidatsa explain that Cameahwait, her brother, was also a captive, but because of his abduction at a young age he felt a deeper connection with the Idaho Shoshone and decided to stay rather than return with her. Their story also reinforces the claim that her

Hidatsa identity (as settled horticulturists) in the northern plains is of central importance to the success of the Lewis and Clark Expedition.

The Hidatsa acknowledge that this version of the Sacagawea story clearly contradicts the information contained in the Lewis and Clark journals that Sacagawea was Shoshone. Lewis and Clark repeatedly refer to Sacagawea as Snake or Shoshone. An excerpt from Clark's field notes of November 4, 1804, provides a clear example. He states, "A french man by Name Chabonah, who Speaks the Big Belley [Gros Ventre, Hidatsa] language visit us, he wished to hire and informed us his 2 Squars were Snake [Shoshone] Indians, we enga[ge] him to go on with us and take one of his wives to intepret the Snake language."[27]

Many Hidatsa believe that translation problems account for the misunderstanding as to which tribe Sacagawea belonged. Lewis and Clark relied on translators for their information; they spoke neither Hidatsa nor Shoshone and simply got the story wrong. Furthermore, Hidatsa ask: If the Shoshone were her people, why didn't she stay there with them instead of continuing on with Lewis and Clark? By staying with Charbonneau and the expedition, she knew she might one day return to her Hidatsa people and to the horticultural Knife River villages. Recently (2003), the Fort Berthold Tribal Council issued a proclamation titled: "The Mandan, Hidatsa, and Arikara Nation Proclaims the Oral History of the *Hidatsa Origin* [emphasis added] of Sakakawea to be the Official Position of the Tribes." They do not want to leave any question about where they stand on the issue of Sacagawea's tribal identity.

Analyses and Questions

Perhaps the preceding discussion begs the question introduced in the first paragraph of this essay: What in the world does all this mean? How did this teenage Indian mother, wed to a man three times her age, gain such renown? Sacagawea's story is not as opaque as it might first appear. If we imagine the various "legends" about Sacagawea as windows into personal, feminist, and tribal identities, we may come closer to an understanding of

Figure 71. Leonard Crumelle created the Sacagawea sculpture (1910) in Bismarck, North Dakota. Photo by Sally McBeth.

how all histories are constructed and to comprehend how these constructions distill and clearly establish the worldviews of native people, Western historians, suffragists, and others. As complex constructions of social histories, these stories reveal connections between the past and the present. They are potent and they will (I hope) remain permanently ambiguous.

There are acute differences between Western conceptions of the past and American Indian ways of envisioning and interpreting their worlds. Native American history, like all history, is not static but represents a dynamic ongoing relationship between past events and the present. It is also primarily an oral history, unlike Western history, which is almost exclusively written. Without oral history, however, cultures that continue to rely (at least in part) on the oral passage of traditions

Figure 72. The Daughters of the American Revolution sponsored many Sacagawea memorials, such as this large granite boulder and plaque (1914) at Three Forks, Montana. The plaque reads: In patriotic memory of Sacagawea, an Indian woman whose heroic courage, steadfast devotion and splendid loyalty in acting as guide across the Rocky Mountains made it possible for the Lewis and Clark Expedition 1804–1806 to occupy so important a place in the history of this republic. Photo by Andrew Gulliford, 2000.

could lose all relationship with past traditions. This loss would weaken and seriously erode current tribal and collective identities.

These competing narratives have come to be deeply entrenched in the collective memories of the suffragists, the Lemhi Shoshone of Idaho, the Wind River Shoshone of Wyoming, and the Hidatsa of North Dakota. I believe that the reason these narratives have ultimately come to be accepted is twofold. First, these stories reveal key elements of identity and consequently provide an important lens into cultures. By claiming (some would say creating) a connection to Sacagawea, specific tribes as well as suffragists revive and reinforce an ethnic or feminist identity not only for this generation, but for the next. So while these pasts (including the suffragist interpretation) may appear to stand in a segmented relationship to one another, they still share certain patterns and themes.

Second, and perhaps more importantly, these stories integrate underlying components of specific worldviews into the narratives that compose them. In this way they are different from more commonly accepted Western conceptions of the past. Keith Basso suggests that "remembering often provides a basis for imagining."[28] Following his thoughts on the topic, the reader may be led to consider issues such as how and why we construct, deconstruct, and reconstruct the histories that help us make sense of the present.

Conclusions

What conclusions can a reader draw from these contradictory but richly complex stories about Sacagawea? In an insightful essay on history and narrative, historian William Cronon says, "We cannot escape confronting the challenge of multiple competing narratives in our efforts to understand the human past."[29] Cronon further reflects that this vision of history (which includes narratives that may be at odds with one another) is not very reassuring to historians; we must nonetheless listen to and consider what is being expressed in alternative interpretations of the same events.

Native people question why oral histories are discounted as subjective while what is written is not, although it is filtered through personal, historical, and cultural lenses. I believe that the dispute over when Sacagawea died or which band or tribe she belonged to will never be resolved to the satisfaction of all. Therefore, I seek metaphorical significance in the roles attributed to Sacagawea as preserved in tribal oral traditions and suffragist philosophies. She is traitor and heroine; she is an Indian woman abused by her white spouse and a fiercely independent woman who assisted her people in their accommodation to reservation life. She is a wanderer, a mother, a captive, an elder. All of these roles speak to the question of how people appropriate oral tradition and stories to talk about their past, to understand their present, and to survive into the future. While some scholars might call what has been included here an invention of tradition,[30] it is really much more than a convenient creation or story meant to establish cohesion. These stories are complex constructions of social histories that reflect both past and current concerns.

In an Internet-based interview, Lewis and Clark historian James Ronda says, "If ever there was a person in the expedition's history who was displaced, who was [a] person out of time, [a] person out of the world, [a] person who belonged nowhere, it's Sacagawea."[31] I would argue that precisely the opposite is true. Sacagawea belongs to us all. She belongs to the suffragists, to the Lemhi and Wind River Shoshone, to the Comanche, and to the Hidatsa. Recent stories suggest she may also belong to the Sioux. Certainly she belongs to all of America.

Notes

This essay was excerpted from *Essie's Story* (E. Horne and S. McBeth, University of Nebraska Press, 1998) and from "Memory, History, and Contested Pasts: Reimagining Sacagawea/Sacajawea" (*American Indian Culture and Research Journal* 27, no. 1 [2003]: 1–32).

1. Gary Moulton, *The Journals of the Lewis and Clark Expedition*, vol. 4, April 7–July 27, 1805 (Lincoln: University of Nebraska Press, 1987), 171.

2. Nicholas Biddle and Paul Allen, *History of the Expedition Under the Command of Captains Lewis and Clark . . . 1804-5-6*, ed. James K. Hosmer. 2 vols. (1814; Chicago: A. C. McClurg, 1902).

3. Irving W. Anderson, "Sacajawea, Sacagawea, Sakakawea?", *South Dakota History* 8, no. 4 (1978): 303–11.

4. Moulton, *Journals*, vol. 5, November 2, 1805–March 22, 1806 (1988), 8–9, 120.

5. Moulton, *Journals*, vol. 8, June 10–September 26, 1806 (1988), 180.

6. Moulton, *Journals*, vol. 5, July 28–November 1, 1805 (1983), 268.

7. David Lavender, *Land of Giants* (Garden City, NY: Doubleday, 1958), 67.

8. Moulton, *Journals*, vol. 4, April 7–July 27, 1805 (1987), 157. See also Clay Jenkinson, *The Character of Lewis: Completely Metamorphosed in the West* (Reno: Marmarth, 2000), 92–93, for an insightful overview of the differences between Lewis's and Clark's perspectives on Sacag/jawea.

9. Donald Jackson, ed., *Letters of the Lewis and Clark Expedition and Related Documents, 1783–1854*, 2 vols. (Urbana: University of Illinois Press, 1962), 315.

10. Moulton, *Journals*, vol. 8, June 10–September 26, 1806 (1983), 305.

11. Henry M. Brackenridge, *Journal of a Voyage Up the River Missouri Performed in Eighteen Hundred and Eleven*, 2nd ed. (Baltimore: Coale and Maxwell, 1816), 10.

12. John C. Luttig, *Journal of a Fur-Trading Expedition on the Upper Missouri, 1812–1813*, ed. Stella Drumm (St. Louis: Missouri Historical Society, 1920), 138.

13. Jackson, *Letter*, 638.

14. Charles Eastman, *Report to the Commissioner of Indian Affairs (Investigation of Sacajawea's Final Burial Place)*, letter dated March 2, 1925 (Washington, D.C.: U.S. Department of the Interior, Office of Indian Affairs, 1925); Grace Raymond Hebard, *Sacajawea* (Glendale, CA: Arthur H. Clark, 1933); and Harold P. Howard, *Sacajawea* (Norman: University of Oklahoma Press, 1971), 175–92.

15. Hebard, *Sacajawea*, 153–201.

16. Eva Emery Dye, *The Conquest: The True Story of Lewis and Clark* (Chicago: C. McClurg, 1902), 290.

17. Alfred Powers, *History of Oregon Literature* (Portland, OR: Metropolitan Press, 1935), 410.

18. Ida Husted, *History of Woman Suffrage*, vol. 5 of 6 vols. (New York: Source Book Press, 1922), 124.

19. Grace Raymond Hebard, "Pilot of First White Men to Cross the American Continent," *Journal of American History* 1 (1907): 467–84.

20. Hebard, *Sacajawea*.

21. Irving W. Anderson, "J. B. Charbonneau, Son of Sacajawea," *Oregon Historical Quarterly* 71, no. 3 (1970): 247–64; Irving W. Anderson, "Probing the Riddle of the Bird Woman," *Montana* 23, no. 4 (1973): 2–17; Anderson, "Fort Manuel: Its Historical Significance," *South Dakota History* 6, no. 2 (1976): 131–51; Anderson, *Sacajawea*; Anderson, "A Charbonneau Family Portrait," *The American West* 17, no. 2 (1980): 4–13; Helen Crawford, "Sakakawea," *North Dakota Historical Quarterly* 1, no. 3 (1927): 2–15; Bernard De Voto, "Sacajawea: Inspirational Indian Maid," *Montana* 4, no. 4 (1954): 61; Howard, *Sacajawea*, 155–74; Helen Addison

Howard, "The Mystery of Sacagawea's Death," *Pacific Northwest Quarterly* 58, no. 1 (1967): 1–6; Jackson, *Letters*, 638; Donna Kessler, *The Making of Sacagawea* (Tuscaloosa: University of Alabama Press, 1996), 100–2; David Reed Miller, "Review of Sacagawea of the Lewis and Clark Expedition, Ella Clark and Margot Edmonds," *Western Historical Quarterly* 12, no. 2 (1981): 186–87; Russell Reid, *Saka'kawe'a: The Bird Woman* (Bismarck: State Historical Society of North Dakota, 1950); James P. Ronda, *Lewis and Clark among the Indians* (Lincoln: University of Nebraska Press, 1984), 256–59; Blanche Schroer, "Sacajawea: The Legend and the Truth," *Yesterday in Wyoming* (winter 1978): 22–28, 37–43; and Blanche Schroer, "Boat-Pusher or Bird Woman? Sacagawea or Sacajawea?," *Annals of Wyoming* 52, no. 1 (1980): 46–54.

22. B. Miles Gilbert, "Sacajawea: A Problem in Plains Anthropology," *Plains Anthropologist* 17, no. 56 (1972): 156–60; Ella E. Clark and Margot Edmonds, *Sacagawea of the Lewis and Clark Expedition* (Berkeley: University of California Press, 1979); and Anderson, "Probing the Riddle."

23. Äke Hultkrantz, "Yellow Hand, Chief and Medicineman among the Eastern Shoshone," *Proceedings of the 38th International Congress of Americanists* 2 (1971): 294, n. 6.

24. Milford Chandler, "Sidelights on Sacajawea," *The Masterkey* 43, no. 2 (1969): 58–66; Frederick Hodge, *Handbook of American Indians North of Mexico* (Washington, D.C.: Smithsonian Institution, Bureau of American Ethnology Bulletin 30, vol. 2 [1910]), 401; Robert Lowie, "Notes on Shoshonean Ethnography," *Anthropological Papers of the American Museum of Natural History* 20, no. 3 (1924): 223; Demitri Shimkin, "Wind River Shoshone Ethnography," *University of California Anthropological Records* 5, no. 4 (1947): 316; and Judith Vander, *Songprints: The Musical Experience of Five Shoshone Women* (Urbana, University of Illinois Press, 1988).

25. Eastman, *Report*.

26. Jackson, *Letters*, 519.

27. Ernest Osgood Staples, ed., *The Fieldnotes of Captain William Clark, 1803–1805* (New Haven, CT: Yale University Press, 1964), 174.

28. Keith Basso, "'Stalking with Stories': Names, Places, and Moral Narratives among the Western Apache," in *Text, Play, and Story*, ed. Edward M. Bruner (Prospect Heights, IL: Waveland Press, 1984), 19–55.

29. William Cronon, "A Place for Stories: Nature, History, and Narrative," *The Journal of American History* 8, no. 4 (1992): 1347–76.

30. Eric Hobsbawm and Terence Ranger, eds., *The Invention of Tradition* (Cambridge: Cambridge University Press, 1983).

31. James Ronda, "What Happened to Sacagawea?" Internet-based interview http://www.pbs.org/lewisandclark/living/4.html, July 26, 1997.

Study Questions

1. Why is Sacagawea a mystery, yet she is still a cultural and historic icon despite the relatively short time she spent with the Corps of Discovery?

2. What does Sacagawea's name, its origins, and spelling tell us of the historical status of women in this period?

3. What was Sacagawea's role in the expedition? What other roles attributed to her are in dispute? Why?

4. How much of Sacagawea's story and her veneration is attributable to the women's suffrage movement?

5. What do the oral histories and documents tell us of this woman's life? Compare two of the oral traditions that involve her contested past.

6. What conclusion does the author draw from the history, oral traditions, and contending narrations on Sacagawea's life? Are native people's oral histories and traditions as valid as the recorded, documentary evidence of the West? Why or why not?

7. How many Indian women can you name? How many Indian men can you name? What do your answers say about gender? About the disciplines of anthropology and history? About your limited knowledge of Indian women's roles and positions?

8. What is so appealing about Sacagawea? What is it about her that captures the imagination of Indian and non-Indian alike? Why is her role as "guide" so evocative?

9. Discuss the various roles that Sacagawea played in the Lewis and Clark Expedition. What benefits did she provide? What drawbacks would a young teenage woman (remember, she was the only female) present in an otherwise all-male group?

10. Define Manifest Destiny. How does it relate to the Lewis and Clark Expedition as well as to Sacagawea's role? How do the quotes by Dye (from *The Conquest*) and Shaw also relate to the concept of Manifest Destiny?

"Western Women Wild with Joy!"

History Making, Public Memory, and Women in the American West

MARCIA TREMMEL GOLDSTEIN

When Colorado women realized their hard-won suffrage victory at the polls on November 7, 1893, Denver's most flamboyant suffragist and editor of *The Queen Bee*, Caroline Nichols Churchill, preserved the exuberance of the decades-long campaign in a tiny headline: "Western Women Wild with Joy over the Election in Colorado!"[1] A new generation of Colorado women rediscovered the phrase on a scratchy piece of microfilm 100 years later. "Wild with Joy" best describes the enthusiastic spirit of Colorado's Suffrage Centennial celebration in 1993. That year, a statewide grassroots coalition of historians, museums, libraries, women's organizations, politicians, youth groups, and educators successfully revived the public's historical memory of this landmark event, which had almost disappeared from the published historical record. Colorado's year-long suffrage centennial celebration was a prime example of what public historian Lois Silverman defines as "history making," or defining "how people understand, present, and use" the past.[2] The "history-making" framework explains how a suffrage centennial project could *create* a public memory where none existed before and in the process change the public's attitude about Western women's history and women's rights.

This essay will first explore the current status of women's "history making" with regard to interpretation of historic sites in the American West. The second section will discuss two case studies of women's public history projects that expand beyond "site-based" history into the area of historic reenactment and cyberspace: the Colorado Suffrage Centennial and the Women of the West Museum.

Women and Historic Preservation: The State of the Western Field

Exciting groundwork has been laid by several decades of work by public historians and preservationists who have focused upon interpreting and reinterpreting American women's history, such as the Women's Rights National Historic Park, Susan B. Anthony's home, Clara Barton's field hospitals, or the Lowell textile mills in eastern locales like Washington, D.C., New York, and Boston.[3] But the history of women in the American West should provide equally fruitful new ground for a myriad of public history projects. The field has emerged as one of the fastest-growing arenas of academic inquiry during the last several decades. Historians of the "New Western history," such as Patricia Limerick and Richard White, have emphasized the importance of viewing the western region as a geographic place, a "meeting ground" where people of both genders and a myriad of ethnicities, races, and economic stations converged, confronted, competed, as well as cooperated in the struggle to survive on the western landscape.[4]

Western women's historians were among the first to take up the challenge to interpret the West as a complex, multicultural meeting place.[5] These scholars have expanded our inquiry well beyond the stereotypes: the slavish but noble "savage" Indian woman, the white "prairie madonna" perched bravely on the covered wagon, Annie "Get Your Gun" Oakley, tragic and triumphant romantic heroines such as Baby Doe Tabor and the "Unsinkable" Molly Brown, and *Gunsmoke*'s barmaid "Kitty," who put a TV-friendly, innocent face on Western prostitution. Research now centers on more realistic, inclusive, and complex topics such as the social and political interactions between white middle-class missionaries and Chinese immigrant women in San Francisco Chinatown's "rescue" missions, cultural relations between anthropologists and Native American women, interracial marriages between white fur traders and Indian and Hispanic women who formed business partnerships essential to the success of early Western economic ventures, and the raw world of one of the West's largest occupations of women: prostitution.⁶

One must not forget that activist women began the movement for historic preservation and national parks in the American West and Southwest in our public lands during the late nineteenth and early twentieth centuries. Tenacious female lobbyists, such as Virginia McClurg from Colorado, helped secure passage of the Federal Antiquities Act of 1906, which has protected the Ancestral Puebloan cliff dwellings and artifacts of Mesa Verde National Park and countless other precious remains of our earliest civilizations from unscrupulous artifact profiteers and insensitive developers alike for a century.⁷

Western women's history abounds in many existing historic sites, including those primarily associated with powerful Western men. In fact, women architects created some of our most treasured Western landmarks. One remarkable example is the famous "Hearst Castle" in San Simeon, California—one of the most popular and extravagant tourist attractions in the West. The elaborate and eclectic mansion and grounds were built by newspaper tycoon William Randolph Hearst, a name recognized far and wide through film and legend as a ruthless, wealthy power monger. But how many visitors are aware that this magnificent architectural landmark was designed from top to bottom by Julia Morgan, perhaps America's first and finest world-class woman architect? When visitors travel up the coast of California, they can also explore Julia Morgan's lesser-known architectural landmarks. These include many private homes in Oakland and Berkeley, California, as well as Asilomar, the historic conference grounds of the Young Women's Christian Association (YWCA), near Monterey, California. Morgan's restored buildings at the historic still-used conference center reflect an intense relationship with the Western coastal environment, and like her more well-known male contemporary, Frank Lloyd Wright, she utilized building materials of wood and stone that seamlessly blend with the surrounding natural landscape.⁸ The peaceful, restful seaside site also reflects Morgan's sensitivity to the needs of the YWCA, long one of America's leading women's organizations, which brought women from around the country to Asilomar to develop spiritual awareness and programs for uplift and social change for women and girls of all races.

The National Park Service should be credited with an early appreciation and careful preservation of the work of another innovative, environmentally oriented woman architect: Mary Elizabeth Jane Colter. Millions of visitors to Grand Canyon National Park have come away with vivid memories of Colter's historic stone and log tourist buildings: Hopi House (1905), Hermit's Rest (1914), the Watchtower (1932), the Bright Angel Lodge (1935), and other delightful rustic stone buildings that perch on the South Rim as though they were built soon after the canyon was formed.⁹ Colter got her start as a landscape architect designing hotel interiors and grounds and eventually buildings for hotel proprietor Fred Harvey and the Santa Fe Railroad Company from 1902 to 1948 throughout the Southwest. Perhaps the most well preserved of Colter's hotels is now a thriving historic inn—La Posada Hotel, a Spanish-colonial-style masterpiece built in 1930 in Winslow, Arizona. La Posada and other historic "Harvey Hotels" house another significant episode of Western women's history awaiting interpretation by public historians—the "Harvey Girls"—a unique population of Western women workers made up of young, single, Midwestern farm girls recruited by Fred Harvey to staff his hotels and restaurants.¹⁰

While Mary Colter memorialized the cultural and design legacy of Indians and Hispanics in popular tourist-oriented structures, the written historical record of Hispanic and Native American women in the American Southwest remains scanty. Archaeologists and public historians are literally breaking new ground by finding these women among the ruins of early village and town sites. The Rancho Camulos Museum in Ventura County, California, encompasses portions of an 1839 Mexican land grant and the De Valle family ranch, established by this well-known family of "Californios" in 1853.[11] Also known as "the Home of Ramona," Rancho Camulos interprets a significant chapter of Western literary folklore as well. The buildings and grounds served as the fictional setting for Helen Hunt Jackson's famous 1884 romantic novel, *Ramona*. Hunt's novel about the love between a mixed-blood Mexican girl and an Indian slave on a California rancho awakened the nation to the plight of impoverished Native Americans, just as Harriet Beecher Stowe's *Uncle Tom's Cabin* had popularized the movement against slavery a generation before. The Rancho Camulos site builds upon the romantic notoriety of Jackson and *Ramona* to more closely interpret the real lives of the Hispanic and Indian residents of the ranch through living history, restoration of the ranch buildings, and educational exhibits.[12]

The early cattle-ranching town of Boggsville along the Santa Fe Trail in southeastern Colorado provides another rich but hidden source of Hispanic and Native American women's history, but in a site primarily noted for its Anglo male founders and residents, cattle baron John Prowers and trader/military agent Kit Carson. University of Denver anthropologist Dr. Bonnie Clark has uncovered "tangible history"—artifacts, building sites, and landscapes—significant evidence that points to the central role of Amache Ochinee Prowers, the Cheyenne wife of John Prowers, in designing the orientation and layout of the town in keeping with her native cultural and religious practices.[13] The presence of Mexican American women, such as Kit Carson's wife, Josepha Jaramillo Carson, and her sister, Rumalda Boggs, has been uncovered as well at Boggsville, as the historical town site is within the boundaries of a Mexican land grant of millions of acres in Colorado and New Mexico. Through place-based history, Clark has demonstrated that women of color often *lived* along the Santa Fe Trail, acting as cultural mediators and innovators (whereas more well-known Anglo women such as Susan Magoffin observed life along the "trail" as outsiders traveling through).[14]

Although scholarly research focusing on women has blossomed, Western women's experiences still too often take a backseat in public interpretations of our region's past in favor of more "popular" male-oriented Western themes: soldiers, miners, railroaders, cowboys, and outlaws.[15] Fortunately, we are beginning to catch up. Historical societies and house museums are more carefully highlighting women's role in Western community building. Western libraries are now aggressively identifying, accessioning, and cataloging archival collections and artifacts relevant to Western women and their institutions that might have been shunned just a couple of decades ago. The National Park Service has focused new attention on interpreting existing and newly acquired western parks and historical sites, such as Mary Colter's Grand Canyon tourist buildings, from the viewpoint of women's history.[16] And historic preservation organizations are creating tours and publications that interpret sites on the basis of historical relevance to women's experience rather than architectural significance alone.[17] All of these efforts are aimed at "history making" and often require rebuilding a more accurate, multidimensional "public memory" of Western women's past.

What are the basic elements of "history-making" projects that successfully expand the public's interest in new and different Western themes (such as women's roles) in site-based public places? National Park Service historian Heather Huyck offers the following recommendations for interpreting historical sites: (1) "Assume that women were there—and find them—*all* of them"; (2) "tell the whole story" and invite everybody; (3) "Ask new questions of "traditional" sources and utilize all the sources available: documentary, archaeological, material culture, landscapes, etc.[18] To that I would add: build grassroots community support. Whether organizing a series of public events, a women's history tour, an exhibit, the preservation of a historic site, or an archival collection, public historians are sure to succeed if they start with grassroots community support beyond the traditional historical community and expand the work from that base. The Women of the West Museum and the Colorado Suffrage Centennial are two excellent case studies of community-oriented projects upon which to model other projects.

Case Study: The Women of the West Museum and Western Suffrage Online

The Women of the West Museum (WOW) is a fine example of expanding women's public history from a narrow localized effort to regional, national, and even international exposure. The WOW Museum constitutes a major outgrowth of the public interest in Western women's history generated by recent scholarship and literary works about the lives of Western women as well as public history projects such as the Colorado Suffrage Centennial. Originally organized in the late 1980s by a core of high-powered women business leaders and leading Western women's historians, the Women of the West Museum was originally conceived as a multi-million-dollar state-of-the-art museum and archive, housed in a new building to be in Boulder, Colorado. But several years of fund-raising among a small community of wealthy donors still had not produced a building or a museum. The Museum board of directors determined that they needed to reach out to the public at large and produce actual women's history projects despite the lack of a physical space. Thus was launched WOW Museum's innovative "online" museum, which utilized the latest technology and the growing popularity of the Web to graphically depict the historical experiences and cultural contributions of Western American women to the widest of audiences—the world! The Women of the West Museum has enjoyed so much success that it has now merged with one of our region's premier Western heritage centers, the Autry Museum of Western Heritage, in Los Angeles, California.[19]

Several of WOW Museum's projects stand out as exemplary efforts to elevate public awareness of the contributions of women in the Western past. "Walk a Mile in Her Shoes" is a creative, award-winning online exhibit that was created by a team of historians, elementary school children, teachers, parents, and neighborhood families. The project centered on historic women in the neighborhood of Denver's oldest extant public school building and historic landmark, Dora Moore School. Students researched the lives of such notable former female students as former first lady Mamie Dowd Eisenhower, internationally acclaimed recording artist Judy Collins, and pioneering public health advocate Dr. Florence Sabin. With the help of their teachers, the children then found and identified the childhood homes of these notable women who had grown up in their own neighborhood, took photographs, then placed the images, biographies, and historical information online in an exhibit they designed. The result is a charming and accessible educational tool, as well as a recognition of local women as significant makers of history. The project has been replicated in other local communities in California, Arizona, and elsewhere.

"This Shall Be the Land for Women: The Struggle for Suffrage in the American West, 1860–1920" [http://www.autry-museum.org/explore/exhibits/suffrage/] traces the Western suffrage movement through the stories of 10 different western states, each emphasizing the diversity of experiences, ethnicities, races, social, and political cultures in the West. New research into the myth and reality of political "opportunity" in the history of the West has revealed the essential role played by women in forming and changing political institutions that incorporated the interests of the community at large. Western women took advantage of new, relatively open Western political institutions to carve out unprecedented equal opportunities for their gender in voting rights, office holding, and law making. Indeed, Western American women were the first in the world to win full suffrage rights, beginning with Wyoming in 1869, then moving to the other Rocky Mountain states of Colorado, Utah, and Idaho in the 1890s. In 1911 California's male voters approved full suffrage equality before any state east of the Mississippi River had done the same. Jeannette Rankin of Montana won the first woman's seat in Congress in 1918, when the majority of American women still could not vote for president or most state offices prior to the passage of the Nineteenth Amendment in 1920. These "pioneering" accomplishments still resonate with the American public in our time, when women have made great headway in gaining positions of political power and leadership but still lack full equality with men.[20]

Building on WOW Museum's previous innovative, interactive online projects, the Western women's suffrage exhibit is organized around a map of the American West, clearly marking the West as the birthplace of women's voting rights throughout the nation and world. Visitors to the exhibit may click on their choice of location, from the first victory in Wyoming, to the popular movements in Colorado, Utah, and California, to the more disappointing, less successful campaigns in New Mexico, Texas, and Hawaii. Rich in photographs, timelines, historical and biographical narratives, bibliographies, and other source material, the exhibit has proven a valuable and unique educational tool for students and educators at all levels. The exhibit is perhaps the only centralized source for the Western women's suffrage movement in existence today.

Case Study: The Colorado Suffrage Centennial, 1893–1993—A Holistic Approach to Women's History Making

Like public historians today, Colorado suffragists over a century ago had to create in the minds of sometimes apathetic constituents (i.e., male voters) a sense that women's concerns were important. "The idea was to create a sentiment in every part of the city, and trust to its leavening powers," recalled Denver journalist and suffrage leader Ellis Meredith.[21] In early 1893, a newly elected Populist governor and legislature agreed to place the issue on the ballot as a referendum for that year's November election. Like modern political candidates, suffragists had to organize their battalions and raise lots of money fast! *They determined to get organized and make a spectacle of themselves!* The women handed out thousands of flyers and leaflets on street corners and soup lines, linking women's voting rights to political demands of desperate unemployed miners in the midst of the economic cataclysm of the silver crisis known as the Panic of 1893. Suffragists buttonholed politicians, wrote inflammatory editorials, held elaborate conventions, and addressed packed meeting halls bedecked with suffrage banners and bouquets of yellow flowers. Once registered to vote, the men had to be convinced to stay sober, get to the polls, and mark the X next to *Woman suffrage approved* on the ballot. "Let the women vote!," became the rallying cry among disgruntled male voters, "they can't do any worse than the men have!"

The sense of urgency and laserlike focus exhibited by Colorado's original suffragists provided inspiration to modern-day organizers of the suffrage centennial in 1993. When the Colorado Coalition for Women's History spearheaded a planning committee, we realized that the number of Coloradoans, even among academics and public history professionals, who knew when or how women got the vote would have fit around a small conference table. One of those who would have been at the table was Congresswoman Pat Schroeder, who in 1976 had placed a plaque in Denver to commemorate the centennial of the first Colorado Woman Suffrage Association when Colorado became a state in 1876. Schroeder, a master at invoking the lessons of history to win modern reforms for women, was perhaps our centennial committee's earliest, most ardent and visible supporter. Colorado history professors Dr. Tom Noel of the University of Colorado at Denver and Dr. Steve Leonard of Metropolitan State College of Denver urged our committee to pursue the project with gusto, as did Dr. Patricia Limerick of the Center for the American West at the University of Colorado at Boulder.

Despite encouragement from high places, our idealistic Suffrage Centennial Committee faced a daunting task: How could we bring this significant landmark suffrage victory back to life for everyone living in the state today? We needed to raise our battalions and lots of money in just a few months! We had to sustain the organization, events, and projects of the centennial for an entire year! *In short, we had to get organized and make a spectacle of ourselves!*

One of the first tasks of the centennial committee was to define the reasons why Colorado's suffrage story was important to celebrate—we needed to make it relevant to today's citizens. The group came up with several reasons. First, the suffrage victory was a major event in the history of women in the West and their struggle for equality. Colorado was the first state to win suffrage by *popular election* (Wyoming women were the first female voters in the world in 1869, thanks to their territorial legislature—which numbered less than 20 men!). Our project could highlight both the historical and the current contributions of women in general to our state and region. Second, like all of today's political campaigners, Colorado suffragists had to mobilize tens of thousands of voters. They had to build nonpartisan political alliances of Democrats, Republicans, and Populists; businessmen and labor unions; native-born whites, blacks and the foreign born; farmers and city dwellers; miners and mine owners; housemaids and society women; socialists and Methodists! Our celebration would therefore educate the public about the importance of building political coalitions that break down divisions of party, race, geography, and gender. Third, Colorado's 1893 suffrage campaign was among the earliest *public* campaigns for women's rights in the world. Prior to the late nineteenth century, American and European culture frowned upon women speaking or even appearing in public in more than a decorative role. We could show the emergence of women breaking through the confines of the private "domestic" realm to which they had often been relegated and encourage modern-day women and girls to do the same. Fourth, women's right to vote helped change the focus of Colorado politics from the economic concerns of corporate mining and railroads to a more humane, community-minded agenda: schools, libraries, social welfare laws and institutions, electoral reforms, child labor laws, legal protections for workers, improvements in environmental health, and historic preservation all emerged as soon as women voters joined the state's electorate! Our centennial celebration would therefore call attention to the importance of citizenship and encouraging both women and men, young and old, to exercise their right to vote today in order to improve their own community.

Now that we had plenty of reasons to celebrate Colorado women's suffrage, we turned to the next question: How would we make that celebration a reality without any financing or backing from any major institution? Again we looked to history as a guide. As with most successful popular movements, the Colorado suffrage campaign began with a small core of committed activists who built a broadly based movement by reaching out and appealing to people from almost every walk of life. In the same vein 100 years later, a small handful of public historians and activists came together and vowed to meet again in two weeks, each bringing a new person who wanted to help. Our coalition building bore fruit, and before long we had over 25 regular activists and the official endorsements of over 50 women's and historical organizations statewide. We formed grant-writing and fund-raising committees, which quickly produced propaganda and publicized our cause.

The next step was to get the history right. We set up a research committee to explore the literature, interpret the findings, and condense the highlights into usable formats, such as a traveling exhibit, popular publications, and public events. We started with master's theses and articles in local historical journals, such as Billie Barnes Jensen's articles in the 1960s, which painstakingly traced the facts and events.[22] Colorado historians Steve Leonard, Tom Noel, and others included short sections on the suffrage campaigns in Colorado and Denver history texts.[23] Our research committee then perused national suffrage histories and found that most of these works ignored the Colorado and Western suffrage story. Although Western women voted first in state after state, the American suffrage story was an "Eastern" one, according to national histories. The West was important only because that was where Wyoming was. End of story.

A breakthrough came when we studied a more recent work by women's historian Carolyn Stefanco,

"Networking on the Frontier: The Colorado Woman Suffrage Movement, 1876–1893."[24] Stefanco's work helped us formulate the interpretation of Colorado's suffrage history as well as providing a strategy for organizing the centennial commemoration itself—*networking!* The article also brought to light the powerful role that *women played themselves* in winning the right to vote in Colorado, asserting that "Colorado women had created a social reform movement unique for the period.... [They had] demonstrated the 'powerful potential' of organized women."[25]

Historian Susan Marilley's 1985 political science dissertation revealed that Colorado suffragists were extraordinarily savvy in developing the strategy and tactics of their campaign.[26] Looking around them, they saw a state in the midst of a devastating economic depression, accompanied by a rising tide of Populism and discontent with the established political order. When they believed the time was right, they had the essential elements of a winning political campaign strategy in place: (1) a strong, committed, activist core, (2) a network of organizations and resources statewide, and (3) political connections in all three political parties. Both Stefanco and Marilley described a dedicated, sophisticated suffrage leadership that cleverly determined when to abandon the polite, quiet approach and begin to make a spectacle. Submerging all doubts and differences, they declared that "clearly this was the time to strike!" in early 1893.[27]

Our research led us to our final destination—the primary sources: the fragile, leather-bound pen-and-ink constitution, bylaws, and minutes of the original Colorado Woman Suffrage Association formed in 1876 at the time Colorado became a state. These women had launched an unsuccessful campaign to write woman suffrage into the original state constitution, in which voters rejected the idea by a two-to-one majority. Susan B. Anthony herself endured the rigors of train travel, rough mining towns, and hostile audiences in her sweep through the state in 1877. Anthony's lonely and frustrating experiences were recorded in diary pages located at the Women's Rights National Historic Park in Seneca Falls, New York.

Our search for 1893 material was rewarded when we began to inspect the letters and papers of journalist and Colorado suffrage leader Ellis Meredith, also known as the "Susan B. Anthony of Colorado." Meredith saved original handwritten letters from Lucy Stone, Susan B. Anthony, and Carrie Chapman Catt as well as the typewritten carbons of her responses. These provided almost a conversational record of campaign strategy and tactics throughout 1893. Campaign flyers, newspaper clippings, rare women's journals, scrapbooks, a few photos, and other documents filled two boxes of Meredith's collection, located at the Colorado Historical Society archives.[28] Our scouting team rescued fragile disintegrating copies of more 1893 campaign flyers and news articles in a brown manila "clippings" envelope at the Denver Public Library Western History Department. When the word got out about our research project, local researchers sent photographs, drawings, and other documentary resources from all over the state.

All of our research led us to conclude that our commemorative activities should reflect women as proactive participants. Women were not "given" the right to vote by Colorado men, as progressive and democratic as they might have been. According to suffrage leader Ellis Meredith, suffrage was won only through a great deal of "toil and anxiety and heart-burning" on the part of the women themselves.[29]

Now we needed money! Leaping out of these documentary sources were the words *Traveling Exhibit! Publications! Slide Lectures! Video Documentary! Teacher Packets! Endowment for the Humanities! Grant Proposals!* We felt like the suffragists must have felt in early 1893 when their entire treasury held $25. We had won the moral support of Pat Schroeder and other politicians, local museums and libraries, history and women's studies departments at the university level, statewide women's organizations such as the League of Women Voters, Young Women's Christian Association, Coalition of Labor Union Women, American Association of University Women, and many others. But we still had no major financial or organizational backing.

A small planning grant from the Colorado Endowment for the Humanities (CEH) got us started on the traveling exhibit by financing a trip around the state to generate contacts, ideas, and enthusiasm. Local committees popped up in Fort Collins, Aspen, Pueblo, and other Colorado towns. We held a strategy session with the chairs of each major university history department in Denver and Boulder. Several months later and hours of grant proposal writing later, we learned to our disappointment that funding for our proposed $50,000 project had been turned down by the CEH, which feared a committee headed by graduate students and volunteers lacked the stamina and institutional backing to pull the project off.

Rejection of our project reminded us of when Ellis Meredith met with Susan B. Anthony at the Chicago World's Fair in the summer of 1893 to ask for money and organizational backing for the Colorado campaign. She argued, "Probably you will think us maniacs, but we feel that we have twice as much show as Kansas to get suffrage.... There is not a single particle of organized opposition in the state."[30] Imagine her shock and disappointment when she received a curt reply from Anthony: "Why was your campaign precipitated when our hands are so full?"[31] "The whole case is at a disadvantage!" Lucy Stone wrote to Ellis Meredith.[32] But local activists vowed to raise the necessary funds despite Colorado's hopeless entanglement in the most severe economic depression and crisis in the nation's history to that time—the Panic of 1893. The Suffrage Association looked at the $25 in their treasury and assigned the fund-raising task to their treasurer, African American club member Elizabeth Ensley, and press secretary, society page editor, and Populist Party activist Minnie Reynolds. The Women's Christian Temperance Union and other charity groups vowed to find a way to feed the hungry and house the homeless while simultaneously launching a massive statewide political campaign.

While the centennial committee certainly did not face the life-threatening hardships that the suffragists and unemployed faced in 1893, we learned from their experience in the face of our own financial void. We could underwrite our exhibit and other projects by soliciting small membership dues, individual donations, and small grants from local institutions and businesses. We also took the risk of investing in commemorative T-shirts and mugs, hoping to sell them at a profit. With a $1,000 grant from the Federal Women's Bureau, we held a Women's History Month fund-raising banquet. Those proceeds and a $2,000 check from the Friends of the Auraria Library financed the first copy of the traveling exhibit. Curator Rebecca Hunt masterminded the project, which was completed in less than a month from beginning to end. The traveling exhibit was so well received that additional donations yielded a second copy, and dozens of bookings at schools, libraries, churches, and city halls followed in the months and years ahead. From that point on we were financially self-sufficient, and to this day we have a fund for ongoing women's history projects.

What else could we learn from Colorado suffragists' knack for "making a spectacle"? Like them, we wished to bring our message to the masses. In 1893, Colorado suffragists gained the editorial support of three-fourths of the state's newspapers, allowing them to reach voters in every small corner of the state. Our centennial committee could not afford to publish our own propaganda and educational materials, but perhaps we could pique the interest of local print media. Woman reporters and editors at the *Rocky Mountain News* thus became our valued partners and published a year-long series depicting the lives and issues that faced women from all walks of life at the time of the suffrage campaign 100 years ago. The series was capped by a special section during November highlighting "100 Women Who Made History in Colorado."[33] Local newspapers around Colorado published feature articles as well. The Colorado Historical Society's popular quarterly magazine, *Colorado Heritage*, published a special issue commemorating the suffrage centennial with scholarly articles and a photo essay depicting a range of women's suffrage and day-to-day life experiences.[34] A commemorative booklet authored by committee members was published by the Institute for Women's Studies at Metropolitan State College and other campus groups from Denver's Auraria Higher Education Center.[35]

One of our proudest moments came when over 100 women and girls, garbed in vintage 1890s costumes, assembled from all over the state to re-create an old-fashioned suffrage march at Denver's St. Patrick's Day Parade in March 1993. Suffrage parades in other cities and towns caught on quickly, including the Potato Days Parade in the mountain town of Carbondale and the State Fair Parade in Pueblo. As the parade crowds cheered or jeered the suffrage marchers, we realized that the historic suffrage campaign was becoming a living reality to thousands of everyday people! Just as Susan B. Anthony must have felt when she was jeered out of a Leadville saloon in 1877, it was hard for us not to take those male jeers seriously enough to hit them with our banners. This brought up a frightening prospect: In reenacting an historical movement for women's rights, how could it be that so many men (who we believed had no public memory of the events of 100 years ago) could latch on to the antisuffrage scoffing and male affirmations of superiority with such ease and familiarity? Our modern-day suffragists re-created the shock and indignation that their foremothers must have felt, careful not to anger or alienate the good-natured audience. Perhaps there was more "public memory" about the women's suffrage movement than we had realized.

No event brought out these real and emotional reflections of historical gender roles in more vivid detail than our great suffrage debate reenactment called "Shall Women Vote?" Over 600 men and women of all ages filled Denver's historic Central Presbyterian Church to hear over 20 historical personalities, from Buffalo Bill to Molly Brown to Horace Tabor, debate the pros and cons of women's right to vote as they might have been presented 100 years ago in the Colorado state legislature. Our centennial committee teamed up with the Colorado History Group, a popular assemblage known for creative Colorado history "happenings." Susan B. Anthony herself (Congresswoman Patricia Schroeder) traveled all the way from Washington, D.C., to debate "Reverend NO!" of Colorado Springs (our state's modern hotbed of conservatism!), who argued against "special rights" for women. Archbishop Joseph Machebeuf, who had traveled the state in 1877 vehemently opposing suffragists as "tired old-maids, disappointed in love," proved a formidable opponent to Anthony and her supporters.

Finally, in November 1993, the centennial committee teamed up with the League of Women Voters to mark 100 years of Colorado women serving in the Colorado state legislature with a "high tea" at the governor's mansion. We invited every living woman who had served in state public office and secured a proclamation from Governor Roy Romer declaring 1993 the year of official suffrage centennial commemoration. We followed the model of the Non-Partisan Equal Suffrage Association of 1893, making this a truly bipartisan event honoring women in politics.

After a year of literally living and breathing Colorado woman suffrage, our committee was ready for a rest! We knew how Colorado suffragists felt at the end of 1893—jubilant and exhausted. The agenda of the historical women's movement is not so different from that of the women's movement today, and commemorations of past victories can point the way for future progress. Further, like political campaigns, historic commemorations that combine the efforts of academics, teachers, politicians, journalists, union members, businesspeople, and schoolchildren make more waves than any one group could achieve alone. In the case of Colorado, we attempted a "holistic" approach to women's history and public memory, and we believe it was a great success.

Conclusion

Western women's history has come alive in a myriad of museums, libraries, historic sites, and community-based historical societies in our region. Caroline Churchill wanted all Americans to discover for themselves what Western women had won in 1893: "Come ye disconsolates wherever you languish, come to Colorado and cast in your lot, here the sun shines brightest and there is hope for all women. . . . Come ye sinners poor and needy, come to Colorado now, *this shall be the land for women, this shall be the land I trow.*"[36] Public historians throughout the American West are proving that our region's women's history can be a significant focal point that inspires our communities to broaden their "public memory" with an appreciation of the West as a meeting ground of men and women from many walks of life—as a "land for women" as well as a land for men.

Notes

1. *The Queen Bee*, Denver, Colorado, November 29, 1893, 1.

2. Lois Silverman, quoted in Otis L. Graham, Jr., "No Tabla Rasa—Varieties of Public Memories and Mindsets," *The Public Historian* 17, no. 1 (winter 1995): 12.

3. Polly Welts Kaufman and Katharine T. Corbett, eds., *Her Past Around Us: Interpreting Sites for Women's History* (Krieger Publishing Company, 2003); Gail Lee Dubrow and Jennifer Goodman, eds., *Restoring Women's History through Historic Preservation* (Johns Hopkins University Press, 2003); and Mona Domosh and Joni Seager, *Putting Women in Place* (New York: Guilford Press, 2001).

4. Patricia Nelson Limerick, *The Legacy of Conquest: The Unbroken Past of the American West* (New York: Norton, 1987); and Richard White, *"It's Your Misfortune and None of My Own": A New History of the American West* (Norman: University of Oklahoma Press, 1991).

5. For excellent collections of scholarly articles on various topics, see Susan Armitage and Elizabeth Jameson, eds., *The Women's West* (Norman: University of Oklahoma Press, 1987), Elizabeth Jameson and Susan Armitage, eds., *Writing the Range: Race, Class, and Culture in the Women's West* (Norman: University of Oklahoma Press, 1997); and Lillian Schlissel, Vicki L. Ruiz, and Janice Monk, eds., *Western Women: Their Land, Their Lives* (Albuquerque: University of New Mexico Press, 1988). For an overview of issues in Western women's history, see Peggy Pascoe, "Western Women at the Cultural Crossroads," in *Trails: Towards a New Western History*, ed. Patricia Nelson Limerick, Clyde A. Rankin, and Charles E. Milner (Lawrence, KS: University of Kansas Press, 1991).

6. Peggy Pascoe, *Relations of Rescue: The Search for Female Moral Authority in the American West, 1874–1939* (New York: Oxford University Press, 1990); Vicki L. Ruiz, *Cannery Women, Cannery Lives: Mexican Women, Unionization, and the California Food Processing Industry, 1930–1950* (Albuquerque: University of New Mexico Press, 1987); Judy Yung, *Unbound Feet: A Social History of Chinese Women in San Francisco* (Berkeley: University of California Press, 1995); and Sarah Deutsch, *No Separate Refuge: Culture, Class, and Gender on the Anglo-Hispanic Frontier in the American Southwest, 1880–1940* (New York: Oxford University Press, 1987).

7. Janet Robertson, "The Women's Park: Virginia Donaghe McClurg and Lucy Peabody," in *The Magnificent Mountain Women: Adventures in the Colorado Rockies* (Lincoln, NE: University of Nebraska Press, 1990), 61–72; Duane Smith, *Mesa Verde National Park: Shadows of the Centuries* (Norman: University of Oklahoma Press, 2003); and Polly Welts Kaufman, *National Parks and the Woman's Voice* (Albuquerque: University of New Mexico Press, 1998).

8. Nancy E. Loe, *Hearst Castle: An Interpretive History of W. R. Hearst's San Simeon Estate* (San Simeon, CA: Aramark Leisure Services and Hearst San Simeon State Historical Monument, 1994); and Ginger Wadsworth, *Julia Morgan: Architect of Dreams* (Minneapolis: Lerner Publications, 1990).

9. National Park Service, Women's History Month 2003, Mary Colter sites: http://www.cr.nps.gov/nr/feature/wom/2001/colter.htm.

10. Virginia L. Grattan, *Mary Colter: Builder Upon the Red Earth* (Flagstaff, AZ: Grand Canyon Natural History Association, 1992); Arnold Berke, *Mary Colter: Architect of the Southwest* (New York: Princeton Architectural Press, 2002); and Lesley Poling-Kempes, *The Harvey Girls: The Women Who Opened the West* (St. Paul, MN: Paragon House, 1991). The "Harvey Girls" were romantically memorialized in a popular 1950s film as well.

11. The term *Californios* refers to landholding families of Mexican/Spanish decent who retained their land after the U.S. conquest of California from Mexico in 1848.

12. Phil Brigandi, "The Rancho and the Romance—Rancho Camulos: The Home of Ramona," and Dydia DeLyser, "Through Ramona's Country: A Work of Fiction & the Landscape of Southern California," *The Ventura*

County Historical Society Quarterly vol. 42, nos. 3, 4 (1998).

13. Bonnie Clark, paper presented at the panel titled "Women's History, Preserving the Past" (National Preservation Conference: New Frontiers in Preservation, National Trust for Historic Preservation, Denver, Colorado, October 2, 2003). See also Clark's master's thesis, "Amache Ochinee Prowers: The Archaeobiography of a Cheyenne Woman" (University of Denver, Department of Anthropology, 1996).

14. Stella M. Drumm and Howard Lamar, eds., *Susan Magoffin, Down the Santa Fe Trail and into Mexico: Diary of Susan Shelby Magoffin 1846–1847* (New Haven: Yale University Press, 1963).

15. Heather Huyck, "Beyond John Wayne: Using Historic Sites to Interpret Women's History," in *Western Women: Their Lands, Their Lives*, ed. Lillian Schlissel, Vicki L. Ruiz, and Janice Monk (Albuquerque: University of New Mexico Press, 1988).

16. Page Putnam Miller et al., "Exploring a Common Past: Interpreting Women's History in the National Park Service," National Park Service pamphlet, 1996. http://www.cr.nps.gov/history/hisnps/NPSHistory/womenshistory.htm.

17. See, for example, Marcia Tremmel Goldstein, *Denver Women in Their Places: A Guide to Women's History Sites* (Denver: Historic Denver, Inc., 2002), which has formed the basis for local women's history bus and walking tours.

18. Dr. Heather Huyck, moderator's introductory remarks and outline for panel presentation, "Women's History: Preserving the Past" (National Preservation Conference: New Frontiers in Preservation, National Trust for Historic Preservation, Denver, Colorado, October 2, 2003).

19. Marsha L. Semmel (former president and CEO of Women of the West Museum), paper titled "Reaching Out: Women's History in the Neighborhood" presented at the panel titled "Women's History, Preserving the Past" (National Preservation Conference: New Frontiers in Preservation, National Trust for Historic Preservation, Denver, Colorado, October 2, 2003).

20. See, for example, Elisabeth Clemens, *The People's Lobby: Organizational Innovation and the Rise of Interest Group Politics in the United States, 1890–1925* (Chicago: University of Chicago Press, 1997); Carolyn Stefanco, "Networking on the Frontier: the Colorado Women's Suffrage Movement, 1876–1893," *The Women's West*, ed. Susan Armitage and Elizabeth Jameson (Norman: University of Oklahoma Press, 1987); Suzanne M. Marilley, "An Exceptional Victory: The Colorado Campaign of 1893," chapter 5 in *Woman Suffrage and the Origins of Liberal Feminism in the United States, 1820–1920* (Cambridge: Harvard University Press, 1996), 124–58; Carol Cornwall Madsen, ed., *Battle for the Ballot: Essays on Woman Suffrage in Utah, 1870–1896* (Logan: University of Utah Press, 1997); Gayle Gullett, "Constructing the Woman Citizen and Struggling for the Vote in California, 1896–1911"; and "A 'Test of Chiffon Politics:' Gender Politics in Seattle, 1897–1917," *Pacific Historical Review* vol. 69, no. 4 (November 2000); Michael Goldberg, "Nonpartisan and All-partisan: Rethinking Women's Suffrage and Party Politics in Gilded Age Kansas," *Western Historical Quarterly* 25 (spring 1994): 21–44; Joan Jensen, "'Disfranchisement Is a Disgrace': Women and Politics in New Mexico, 1900–1940," in *History of Women in the United States*, ed. Nancy F. Cott, vol. 19, part 1, "Woman Suffrage" (Munich: K. G. Saur, 1994).

21. Ellis Meredith, "Women Citizens of Colorado," *The Great Divide* (February 1894): 53.

22. Jensen, Billie Barnes, "Let the Women Vote," *Colorado Magazine* 41 (winter 1964), and "Colorado Women Suffrage Campaigns of the 1870s," *Journal of the West* (April 1973).

23. See Carl Abbott, Stephen J. Leonard, and David McComb, *Colorado: A History of the Centennial State* (Boulder: Colorado Associated University Press, 1976), and Stephen J. Leonard and Thomas J. Noel, *Denver: Mining Camp to Metropolis* (Niwot: University Press of Colorado, 1990).

24. Carolyn Stefanco, "Networking on the Frontier."

25. Ibid., 273.

26. Susan Marilley, "Why the Vote: Woman Suffrage and the Politics of Democratic Development in the United States" (Ph.D. diss., Harvard University, 1985).

27. Joseph G. Brown, *History of Equal Suffrage in Colorado* (Denver: News Job Printing, 1898), 19–20.

28. Ellis Meredith Collection, Colorado Historical Society, Denver, Colorado.

29. Anna Wolcott Vaile and Ellis Meredith, "Women's Contribution," vol. 3, *History of Colorado*, 5 vols., ed. James H. Baker and LeRoy Hafen (Denver: Linderman, 1927), 1121.

30. Ellis Meredith to Carrie Chapman, dated June 30, 1893, Meredith Papers, Colorado Historical Society, Denver, CO.

31. Susan B. Anthony to Ellis Meredith, Meredith Papers.

32. Lucy Stone to Ellis Meredith, June 12, 1893, Meredith Papers.

33. *Rocky Mountain News*, November 8, 1993, Spotlight section, 1, 3–5, 9.

34. Lee Chambers Schiller, "Colorado Women Get the Vote," Stephen J. Leonard, "Bristling for Their Rights," Carolyn Stefanco, "Harvest of Discontent," Rosemary Fetter and Thomas J. Noel, "Putting Women in the Picture," and Marcia T. Goldstein and Rebecca Hunt, "From Suffrage to Centennial: A Research Guide to Colorado and National Women's Suffrage Sources," *Colorado Heritage*, Colorado Historical Society (spring 1993).

35. Rosemary Fetter and Marcia T. Goldstein, *The Colorado Suffrage Centennial: 1893–1993*, commemorative booklet (Denver: Colorado Committee for Women's History, 1993).

36. Churchill, *The Queen Bee*, November 15, 1893.

Study Questions

1. What are recent researchers studying regarding women and public history?

2. Who was Julia Morgan?

3. How are Western historians "catching up" and recognizing women in Western history?

4. How did the WOW Museum include the public in projects researching women's history in the West?

5. Describe the method used by women to convince men they should have the right to vote.

6. Name three things that happened as soon as women won the right to vote.

7. Who was the "Susan B. Anthony of the West" and why was she so important?

8. According to the author, how did she find out how men feel, even today, about women's suffrage?

9. In your opinion, have today's women achieved full equality with men? Why or why not?

From the Old Homestead to the Mustang Ranch

Prostitution, Preservation, and Public History in the American West

Jan MacKell

Figure 73. Unpainted, vintage Telluride, Colorado, "cribs," or tiny whorehouses, for a single prostitute. The buildings, common in mining camps, had two rooms and two doors. On busy nights after a payday, a miner could be arriving in the front door and another one leaving out the back almost at the same time. Older, weary prostitutes sank to the level of working in cribs, which were frequently owned by the town's wealthy gentlemen, who charged high rents. Photo by Andrew Gulliford, 1978.

Prostitution has been among the most shunned and detested of all career choices, and it is only recently that this integral part of any city economy has begun wrenching itself free of Hollywood clichés. A movement throughout America has worked to create monuments to the lucrative, if socially unacceptable, industry of prostitution. While literally thousands of former bordellos have been torn down or converted to other uses, a healthy handful of museums and businesses acknowledging their shady pasts are preserved or at least in the process of becoming landmarks. These include Fanny Ann's Saloon and Restaurant in Old Sacramento, California. At Mattie Silk's Restaurant in Denver, employees relish telling about its former occupant. The Monte Carlo in Trinidad, Colorado, retains its former glory in the form of a bar. Likewise, the Pioneer Bar, former brothel of Madam Hazel Brown in Leadville, is under renovation. In 1997 the National Park Service also acquired two additional alley structures in Skagway, Alaska, that were former houses of ill repute and restored them as rental properties.

The Old Homestead Museum in Cripple Creek, Colorado, is probably the oldest continuously operating brothel museum in the United States. Converted for public tours in 1958, the Old Homestead experienced much success—at least until gambling was legalized in Cripple Creek in 1991. Unfortunately, the Old Homestead lies in an area zoned for gaming. In 1995, due to exorbitant taxes, the house was sold by Harold and Lodi Hern, owners since 1964. Although the property was initially offered to the city of Cripple Creek, officials declined the offer and the property instead fell into the hands of a lodging and gaming conglomerate.

Within eight months of the purchase, the new owners claimed the museum was not making enough money and announced plans to close it to the public. Ironically, just a year before, the company had completed construction of the Jubilee Casino, which butted directly up against the Homestead. In a town booming with gaming proceeds, tourism, and an economic boost unlike anything seen in decades, the reason behind the closure seemed driven more by greed for valuable commercial casino property than anything else. Equally upsetting was the city of Cripple Creek's decision not to purchase the museum.

Public outcry ultimately prevented the closure, but there were still issues at hand. The owners would, on occasion, insist that the insurance liability was too much at the Homestead and would order it closed. Staff at the museum were alarmed when a suspicious number of antique dealers began taking tours of the museum and asking detailed questions about specific items, only to learn that an auction was planned to sell off the furnishings. Then in 1998 the Jubilee Casino closed its head office because of financial troubles.

With the casino closed, the Old Homestead staff worked quickly to form the Old Homestead House Museum, Inc., and vowed to purchase the structure for $250,000. But financial difficulties between the bank and the owner held up the sale. "I'll never totally relax until it's bought and in our hands," said Charlotte Bumgarner, who began spearheading efforts to save the Homestead in 1998. "I'll sure feel a lot more comfortable when it's done."[1] In fact, Bumgarner applied for several grants. Most came on the condition that more local support be offered. In addition, the building has needed a new roof for some time, and utility bills typically run $350 to 400 per month. The museum has successfully appealed to the city of Cripple Creek for funding to see them through the winter months, but it's not enough.

When Walsh Rivera Investment Partners of Illinois next purchased the building in 2002, talk resurfaced about the Old Homestead's uncertain future. In addition, the company purchased most of the north 300 block of Myers Avenue, where the Old Homestead reposes, as well as property across the street. Over time, there had already been much speculation and loose talk regarding the Old Homestead. Various developers and city officials considered building over or around the building. As for Walsh Rivera, plans were immediately in the works to open the Wild Horse Casino in the former Jubilee building. Early plans also included knocking a hole in the wall to the Old Homestead, using the building as office or casino space, and closing the museum—that is, until the women involved with Walsh Rivera went on a tour and stopped all thoughts of such nonsense.

In a rare act of benevolence, Walsh Rivera next announced plans to take an active part in the Annual Pearl's Follies, established to raise funds to save the Homestead, by sponsoring the event in March 2003. Indeed, from all appearances the Wild Horse seemed to be very interested in preserving the Homestead's fascinating history. It was a refreshing course of action for those concerned about the museum's future.

In October 2003, however, the museum took another downswing as Walsh Rivera took on another new partner—one that saw the Homestead as nothing more than additional square footage for slot machines. As of this writing, the remaining partners and others were working to educate Walsh Rivera's new manager while the Old Homestead House Museum, Inc., continues to vie for its purchase. Once the building is secured, Charlotte Bumgarner plans to continue the museum's Buy-a-Brick program, in which donors of $100 can have a brick in the historic building commemorated for them. Sadly, the city of Cripple Creek has continued to be apathetic over the Old Homestead's fate, while local historians and other fans of the Homestead may soon be rounded up to join in the fight to save one of Colorado's most historic structures. "We just need more local support," says Bumgarner. "Pearl needs a place to live."[2]

Another bawdy house of contention has been the Dumas Brothel in Butte, Montana, home to one of the nation's largest national landmarks. The Dumas is situated along Venus Alley, the city's large red-light district, and bordered by Galena, Main, Mercury, and Wyoming streets. The six-block, fortresslike alley was specially designed so that customers could not exit easily. For some reason, pimps here were actually referred to as "secretaries." Thousands of women plied their trade in Venus Alley. In his autobiography, actor Charlie Chaplin noted the women of the alley were some of the most beautiful in the world.

Many of the cribs in Venus Alley featured phones, a rare amenity, so that orders could be placed for liquor or food. Women such as Dirty Mouth Jean Sorenson reigned supreme in Venus Alley. It was said that Sorenson, who had the "foulest mouth of any madam west of Paris," kept a petrified walrus penis behind the bar to quell trouble-causing customers.[3]

The Dumas, built in 1890, operated until 1982—nearly 100 years. It was an imposing, two-story brick affair with a whopping 43 rooms. Over time the building even included cribs in the basement, with an outside stairway leading down to them. A door in this basement led to tunnels within the red-light district.

An additional tunnel could be accessed from a main floor hallway, which opened into larger rooms separated by pocket doors. Upstairs were suites with skylights and a large balcony. A 1913 one-story addition on the back of the building housed eight more cribs. These cribs, along with the basement cribs, were likely used to service customers of less wealth than those allowed in the fancier upstairs rooms.

The Dumas was open 24 hours a day, with several girls working three different shifts. Although it is portrayed as a high-class parlor house, the prices were much less than in other known parlor houses across America. The fee varied over the years, from 50 cents to a dollar at the turn of the century, to $2 in the 1940s, to $5 during the 1950s. When the Dumas closed in 1982, the price was $20. Throughout this time, the girls were paid roughly 40 percent of the fee. Famous madams of the Dumas included the brothel's first owner, Delia Nadeau. By 1922, Delia and her husband, Joseph, owned several buildings in the red-light district. Elenore or Elinore Knott was another famous madam who committed suicide in the bordello in 1955.

In 1970, the Dumas Brothel was successfully nominated to the National Register of Historic Places and listed as an active house of prostitution. Its style is actually classified as "Victorian Brothel," said to be the last of its kind in the United States. Inside, aside from lowered ceilings and added paneling, the interior remained intact. In 1989, the Dumas was purchased by antique dealer Rudy Giecek from the brothel's last madam, Ruby Garrett. Ruby ran the Dumas from 1971 to 1982, with her business succumbing to the recession via nonpayment of back taxes. When Giecek offered to buy it, Ruby sold it to him on the condition he would keep it in its original condition. Accordingly, Giecek studied the building's history with much zeal, relishing its bawdy history. Based on a diary he allegedly found in one of the cribs under the Dumas, Giecek penned his own graphic story, told in present tense and first person and inspired by the "ghost of Madam Elinore Knott."[4]

In fact, Giecek and others maintain that the

Figure 74. Photo of Silverton, Colorado, ladies of the night. Courtesy of the San Juan County, Colorado, Historical Society, J1A32d.

Dumas is indeed haunted. The Dumas Brothel web site contains a number of photographs of people and rooms in the building showing ghostly "orbs," fogs, mists, and a few bona-fide-appearing apparitions. Visitors have reported seeing the spirits of both men and women, including Elinore Knott. By the early 1990s, Butte's former red-light district had already lost the famed Copper Block, a brick saloon and hotel that was also once home to many prostitutes and gamblers. Venus Alley was no more than a brick alley, with the other houses of prostitution long gone. Under Giecek's ownership, the Dumas was and still is successfully maintained as a brothel museum, with city officials recently dedicating a park across from the house in memory of the red-light ladies of that town.

In 1998, Giecek ran into financial trouble and was looking to sell the Dumas. Almost immediately, the International Sex Worker Foundation for Art, Culture and Education (ISWFACE) expressed an interest in saving the brothel. The organization planned to reopen the structure as a museum, art gallery, and convention center. Letters of support for saving the Dumas included one from Dr. Ellen Baumier, National Register of Historic Places Sign Program coordinator, and Lon Johnson, National Register of Historic Places coordinator. "The Dumas is not only significant as the last standing parlor house in this area of Butte," Baumier wrote in her correspondence to the Montana Historical Society in 1999, "but also because of its length of operation and as a rare, intact commentary on social history."[5]

In addition to Baumier's letter, Giecek also successfully lobbied to have a number of articles written about the Dumas. Such articles circulated as far away as New York, Boston, Los Angeles, Seattle, and Baltimore. Even *USA Today* ran a story. In Montana, according to Giecek, the Montana *Standard* ran no less than 12 stories between 1991 and 1999, with additional articles appearing in the Missoula *Independent* and the Billings *Gazette*. Radio and television features followed, and a number of magazines have also followed the story of the Dumas's survival.

With all the national attention flowing its way, the Dumas inevitably ran up against folks who failed to appreciate its past as a house of ill fame. A 1999 article in the Montana *Standard* reported on comments made by individuals, including two former working girls, who opposed restoration of the brothel. "It's not the innocent entertainment that I thought it was," stated former stripper Karyn Shados. "It's not the innocent entertainment that most men think it is."[6] Shados, who had witnessed violent scenes during her employment in Missoula and Billings, predicted that Butte would soon be filled with sexual predators and even pedophiles. Further comments by others insinuated that volunteers at the Dumas might actually strive to operate the brothel as something other than a museum. Especially in question was the ISWFACE and its president, Norma Jean Almodovar. A former Los Angeles police officer, Almodovar called the Los Angeles Police Department the "blue Mafia" and chose instead to become a prostitute: "Being a prostitute was the best job I ever had." She later recalled becoming a prostitute in 1972 and stated, "As a person who enjoys sex and giving pleasure, I believe that if murder is the worst thing you can do to a person, giving them an orgasm has to be one of the best things."[7]

Almodovar, who had just recently arrived to take over operations, immediately assured the public that not only would volunteers at the Dumas not be engaging in prostitution, but that they would also not tolerate any illegal activities at the former brothel. Rather, according to Almodovar, her organization hoped to use the Dumas to educate and change the general public's outlook on prostitutes and strippers. Besides, the ISWFACE had already made a down payment towards the brothel's $95,000 asking price.

Unfortunately, the ISWFACE's happy business relationship with Giecek soon took an unhappy turn. Beginning in September 2000, Giecek claimed the ISWFACE owed him $52,000 in wages for work performed starting in May 1998, when the organization took over the Dumas. ISWFACE was ultimately ordered by Montana courts to pay Giecek his wages plus penalties. Today the ISWFACE web site warns viewers that the organization is no longer associated with the Dumas in any way.

In 2001 and again in 2003, news of the Dumas surfaced once more when the brothel was put up for auction on eBay. " I did have it on eBay for a while, and I had plenty of people interested," said Giecek, "but they didn't have any money."[8] Giecek is still very concerned about the Dumas's uncertain future. Among other things, he said, the building still needs a new roof or it will cave in on itself. He even tried to apply for grants through the Montana Historical Society. The problem? The grants require a cash match, and Rudy doesn't have it.

SILVERTON

Miss Louesa Crawford...

Aided by eleven charming assistants, extend to yourself and friends a cordial and standing invitation to make your headquarters (while in the City) at her house

———————— 557 Blair Street

FREMONT PASS.

ARCH ROCK—DEER CREEK.

SILVERTON

MISS CORA LIVINGSTON

With her five assistants are entertaining friends and callers at the Big House, cor. 13th and Blair Streets.

Will be pleased to number yourself as one.

TELLURIDE

Call at the Big House.
Gussie Grant, Prop.
Cor. Pine St. and Pacific Ave.

SILVERTON

STELLA ALLISON,
——————————— BLAIR STREET.

EXAMINATION CERTIFICATE

_____
Examined

_____ 193___
Expires

_____ 193___

_____
Health Officer.

Examination Certificate

This is to Certify That _____
has been examined this _____ day of _____ 193___
and found to be free of evidences of venereal disease.
This certificate expires on the _____ day of _____ 193___
_____
_____
Health Officer.

Figure 75. These were ads placed in railroad brochures for visiting tourists. Courtesy the San Juan County, Colorado, Historical Society. Also from the town of Silverton, see the certificate doctors would fill out stating that ladies of the evening were free of venereal disease.

For now, the Dumas is still open for summer tours, and the admission price is moderate at $5. The Dumas Brothel web site still explains that the brothel is for sale, while Giecek continues to hang on to it. The purchase includes original artifacts on display and other antiques. "It would cost $100,000 just to clear the title," Giecek said, adding that in the meantime, he hopes to publish his fictionalized manuscript about the brothel's history to help promote it. Also, Giecek anticipated that property values may go up in Butte soon, a turn of events that could save—or be a further detriment—to the historic building.

As in the case of the Dumas Brothel, historic preservation battles include a fair share of people and organizations that believe it is wrong to commemorate the illicit business of prostitution. Other public history efforts have stooped to conquer and won their cause. In Alaska, Ketchikan's Creek Street includes Dolly's House, once owned by Madam Dolly Arthur and touted as the city's most famous brothel beginning in 1919. The second floor at the Red Onion Saloon in Skagway includes a restored bordello, and in Dawson City, visitors may also tour restored houses of ill fame.

Naturally, the state of Nevada with its legalized prostitution has had a number of brothels still in operation, as well as a few places commemorating prostitutes of the past. Among them was the Brothel Art Museum near the Crystal Springs Bar and Restaurant, located "minutes from Las Vegas." Even now, their web site advertises such tourist temptations as "sexy souvenirs, easy truck turnaround, restaurant and bar, adult magazines, games, paved roads, acres of parking, package liquor, adult T-shirts." The brothel was closed for renovations in 2001 but was opened in 2002. The phone number to the museum has been disconnected, and so its fate is unknown. Better known is the Julia C. Bulette Red Light Museum in Virginia City. Brutally murdered in 1867, the generous and kind Bulette survives as one of the heroines of Nevada's heyday. Visitors to the museum may view medical and brothel artifacts, contraceptives, and a display of authentic patent medicines guaranteed to cure all ills.

Photographs and dioramas educate visitors about Ms. Bulette herself.

In Wallace, Idaho, a bordello that operated as recently as 1988 is now a museum offering guided tours of its second-floor rooms. Called the Oasis Museum, the structure was built in 1895 as a bar and hotel with female entertainment upstairs. According to docent Jack Mayfield, the business became a full-time brothel beginning in 1903. The last madam, known only as Ginger, purchased the Oasis in 1963 or 1964 and operated it until its last day. Visitors to the Oasis may view the brothel just as it was the day it closed, "from lipstick on the dressers to the groceries on the shelves," according to Mayfield.[9] Eleven rooms, five of them once reserved for the working girls, are on display. Like the Dumas, the Oasis charges only $5 for a guided tour and closes during the winter months.

San Angelo, Texas, also has a brothel museum in the form of Miss Hattie's Bordello. There guests can visit Hattie's house of ill fame complete with lace curtains, velvet drapes, ornate furnishings, tin ceilings, and a kitchen. The rooms are named for the ladies who worked there and include beds that are said to squeak quite loudly if you wiggle the frames. The brothel was closed in 1946 by the Texas Rangers. Tours of Miss Hattie's are available year-round.

Still other museums have small portions of their facilities dedicated to the shady ladies of the town. Tombstone, Arizona's, Silver Nugget Museum replicates both a gambling den and a brothel complete with Victorian furniture. Likewise, Cripple Creek, Colorado's, District Museum dedicates a room to gambling, prostitution, and taverns, complete with the original tombstone of Madam Pearl DeVere and a dress replicating the garment she was buried in. Deadwood, South Dakota's, Adams Museum also developed its own brothel exhibit, titled "Prostitution and Deadwood's Badlands District." The stories of such bad girls as Calamity Jane, Madam Mustachio, and Dirty Em are told, along with displays of photographs of madams, drug paraphernalia, gambling items, and a pocketbook belonging to Poker Alice Tubb. A 1995 walking guide in Belle Fouche, Montana, also directs visitors down "Saloon Street," now known as Fifth Street, pointing out former saloons and houses of ill repute.

There are many more brothels whose futures still lie in the balance. They include the infamous Mustang Ranch, 15 miles from Reno. The Mustang is famous for becoming Nevada's first legal brothel in 1971, four years after it opened. As a willing prototype, the bordello led to the legalization of prostitution in 12 other counties. It is also unique in its design, with six "wings" extending off an octagonal main room. The brothel closed in 1999, seized by the government for a $13 million tax debt. Owner Joseph Conforte was fondly remembered for giving turkeys to the poor and providing free service to veterans of Desert Storm. These days, Conforte is wanted for tax evasion and was last seen in Brazil, where some speculate he opened more brothels.

The Mustang Ranch's decor and furnishings, from keys to "menus of pleasure" to a three-foot-wide disco ball, were auctioned off in December 2002. Much of the memorabilia was purchased by Dennis Hof, owner of the nearby Moonlite Bunny Ranch. Then in February 2003, the Bureau of Land Management (BLM) acquired the 340-acre property and announced plans to demolish the house and several other buildings because of their location in a floodplain and safety code violations. Several former employees, however, wanted to save the building from demolition. "I really think it would be a big tourist draw if they turned it into a museum," said former worker Sharnel Silvey, madam of the Mustang from 1986 to 1999. "It's world famous. People still drive by to see it and they would pay to go inside."[10] The madam also cited emotional ties to the girls who worked there, such as a row of trees that were planted for each woman who worked at the ranch and who passed away.

The BLM acquiesced by offering to let Mustang supporters move the buildings if they could come up with the money. Alternatives included moving the buildings to nearby Virginia City. Ms. Silvey quickly established the Mustang Ranch Museum, Inc., and began her battle by accusing the BLM of failing to fully comply with Section 106 of the National Historic Preservation Act. "Although the Mustang Ranch was built in 1975 and is therefore less than 50 years old," wrote Silvey, "we believe that the building qualifies for National Register listing through Criteria Consideration G, Exceptional Significance, because it was the first brothel constructed following the legalization of prostitution in Nevada."[11]

As the Mustang Ranch Museum, Inc., rallied for support and funding, the BLM put the historic ranch buildings up for sale on eBay. The purchase included structures and interior components such as the bar, plumbing, spas, sauna, the surrounding fence, and a guard tower—everything but the land itself. The buildings were to be moved upon purchase. Naturally, conditions of the sale came with listings of dangerous materials and appliances that might be present, with stipulations that bonds and insurance must be obtained upon purchase. A first attempt in June 2003 to sell the Mustang ended below the BLM's reserve price.

A second auction on October 16, 2003, however, netted $145,100 for the ranch's main building. Twenty-nine bidders vied for the Mustang. On October 28 Lance Gilman, owner of the newly opened, $5-million Wild Horse Resort & Spa in Sparks, stepped forward as the new owner and wired the payment in full. As it happened, the Wild Horse's grand opening in June 2003 coincided with Dennis Hof's announcement of plans to build his own brothel museum and include the items he purchased from the Mustang. But Hof also scored a piece of the Mustang's history by successfully bidding on its annex on October 12 and vowing to proceed with his brothel museum on land east of Carson City. The purchase totaled $8,101. Both buyers were given 90 days to move the buildings from the site. In the aftermath of the sale, questions surfaced as to who owned the rights to the Mustang Ranch name. Hof claimed he had applied with the federal government in 2002 to purchase the rights to the trademark, including the logo.

Figure 76. Prostitution continues in the New West in parts of rural Nevada, where the nineteenth-century custom of fancy parlor houses in business districts has given way to modern double-wide trailers out among the sagebrush. One wonders why Billie had to add the line "men only" to her sign. Perhaps gender equity has yet to come to certain service industries in the Silver State. Photo by Andrew Gulliford, 1981.

According to BLM attorneys, the bureau retained those rights until the property was sold. As of this writing, Hof had pledged to fight for the name, while the BLM planned to rehabilitate the land and use it for recreation as well as flood control.

Pros and cons aside, the American West continues to acknowledge its shady past in many small ways. The occasional plaque on a wall in an historic district might reveal some clues to a neighborhood's shady past, but efforts to remember our soiled doves of yesterday are underappreciated and need more recognition. An entire class of Western women has been forgotten. Many died knowing that once in their graves, their existence would be forgotten, but their actions shaped societal rules and regulations that we know today. Parlor house girls contributed to the towns they inhabited, no matter how small, and helped make those towns what they were and what they are. Indeed, it is hard to imagine a history of the American West without our ladies of lost virtue.

Notes

1. Jan MacKell, "Pearl's Follies to Benefit the Old Homestead," *Colorado Gambler* (March 2001). See also MacKell, *Brothels, Bordellos and Bad Girls: Prostitution in Colorado, 1860–1930* (Albuquerque: University of New Mexico Press, 2004).

2. Charlotte Bumgarner, interviews with author, January–October, 2003.

3. Letter from George Everett to Susan Schwerer, May 14 1997, http://www.h-net.msu.edu/~women/threads/disc-prostwestexhib.html.

4. Dumas Brothel web site, http://www.thedumasbrothel.com/

5. Ibid.

6. Diana Setterberg, "Dumas Foes Warn Against Restoration," *Montana Standard Magazine* (June 19, 1999); http://www.angelfire.com/mn/fjc/montana.htm

7. Mark Egan, "Wild West Brothel to Become Museum," Reuter News Service, http://www.iswface.org/reuters.html.

8. Rudy Giecek, interview with author, October 21, 2003.

9. Jack Mayfield, interview with author, Oasis Bordello Museum, October 22, 2003.

10. Former Prostitutes Want to Turn Brothel into Museum, http://www.cnn.com/2003/US/West/03/26/mustang.ranch.museum.ap/.

11. www.mustangranch.com.

Study Questions

1. What industry almost succeeded in closing the Old Homestead Museum in Cripple Creek, Colorado? How?

2. Briefly describe the history of the Dumas Brothel in Butte, Montana, up to its closure in 1982.

3. What steps have been/are being taken to preserve the Dumas Brothel, and what is one of the roadblocks encountered?

4. How do various cities (Wallace, Idaho; San Angelo, Texas; Tombstone, Arizona; etc.) commemorate female prostitution?

5. What is the Mustang Ranch famous for? Where is it?

6. The sale of the Mustang Ranch included everything but what? Why?

- Tisalder
- Hollydog

Environmental Public History

Headnotes

Since the publication of Rachel Carson's *Silent Spring* (1962), Terry and Renny Russell's *On the Loose* (1967), Edward Abbey's *Desert Solitaire* (1968), and the creation of the Environmental Protection Agency in 1970, American environmental history has come of age. Standard texts include *American Environmentalism: Readings in Conservation History*, edited by Roderick Nash; Hal Rothman's *Greening of a Nation*, Benjamin Kline's *First Along the River*; and Philip Shabecoff's *A Fierce Green Fire*. For a radical perspective see Susan Zakin, *Coyotes and Town Dogs: EARTH FIRST! and the Environmental Movement*. Other books include Carolyn Merchant, ed., *Major Problems in American Environmental History*. In 2004 the American Society of Environmental History met with the National Council on Public History, and the two professional groups have much in common. The winter 2004 issue of *The Public Historian* is devoted to "Public History and the Environment/ Environmental History and the Public" with excellent case studies and notes from the field. For students of Western history more books are needed to help define and describe environmental issues unique to the West, such as water and dams, grazing, mining, fire and timber, and themes germane to Western urban development and sustainable communities beyond the 100th meridian. Public historians need to help Westerners, especially the thousands of new retirees who have moved to the intermountain West, to understand the historical contexts for a host of pressing environmental issues.

Two useful books include Charles Wilkinson's *Crossing the Next Meridian: Land, Water and the Future of the West* and James E. Sherow, ed., *A Sense of the American West: An Environmental History Anthology*, which is a reader on Western environmental history. See also Hal Rothman, ed., *Re-opening the American West*, developed in partnership with the Arizona Humanities Council. Donald Worster remains the dean of environmental history, and among his many writings two selected books are *The Wealth of Nature: Environmental History and the Ecological Imagination* and *An Unsettled Country: Changing Landscapes of the American West*.

The following series of essays in *Preserving Western History* helps to address the common ground of Western environmental history by focusing on wildland fire memorials, ecotourism and national parks, and wilderness areas. These are important themes for public history students studying environmental history in the West. Environmental historians quip that only God can make a tree, but only Congress can designate a national park or a wilderness area.

Andrew Gulliford, in "Fire on the Mountain: Wildland Firefighter Tragedies and Firefighter Memorials," describes how a community reacts when firefighters die defending a small town. He argues that statues and a memorial trail near Glenwood Springs, Colorado, may represent the West's first environmental memorial. Books are emerging on wildland fire, including Hal Rothman, ed., *"I'll Never Fight Fire with My Bare Hands Again,"* which features edited oral histories from firefighters in the Northwest, and Christopher J. Huggard and Arthur R. Gómez, eds., *Forests Under Fire: A Century of Ecosystem Mismanagement in the Southwest*. Other essays in this section focus on the environmental impacts of tourism in national parks. Guide, outfitter, and outdoor recreation professor Patrick Tierney writes from experience in his essay "Ecotourism and Western National Parks: A Case Study in Management to Protect Natural and Cultural Resources." Tierney owns Adrift Adventures and leads raft trips on the Green, Yampa, and Gunnison rivers. For a perspective on park tourism see Alfred Runte, *National Parks: The American Experience*, Joseph L. Sax, *Mountains without Handrails: Reflections on the National Parks*, and Bob R. O'Brien, *Our National Parks and the Search for Sustainability*.

Two essays in this section focus on wilderness, and the concept comes to us as part of the Judeo-Christian tradition. The word appears 246 times in the Old Testament of the Bible. Originally considered to be desert, worthless and without water, wilderness came to be thought of as a place for savage men and wild beasts, but also a place for solitude and sanctuary. A century and a half after the first farms had been planted along the Atlantic seaboard, Henry David Thoreau proclaimed in his 1851 lecture at the Lyceum in Concord, Massachusetts, "In wildness is the preservation of the world." But for a nation bent upon industrialization, his was a voice crying in the wilderness.

When the Civil War erupted and Republicans controlled Congress, they passed the 1862 Homestead Act, which was the realization of Thomas Jefferson's dream to provide for a nation of yeoman farmers. Any head of household could travel west and claim 160 acres if he or she lived on it for five years, but the West had neither the water nor deep enough soils to sustain agriculture without irrigation. Thousands of farm families failed, though pioneer museums across the West rarely tell that story. Much has been written in Western history about the end of the frontier in 1890. As the nation began to perceive the loss of public land and wild landscapes, a conservation movement emerged in the 1890s, followed by a broader-based environmental movement in the 1960s that focused not just on the value of public land for human uses, but also on the value of ecosystems. Wallace Stegner eloquently argued that the American character had been hewn out of wilderness. He explained that the frontier spirit had created America and that civilization was only an artifact hammered out of wilderness landscapes. Stegner called wilderness "the geography of hope," and in his famous 1960 wilderness letter he wrote, "Something will have gone out of us as a people if we ever let the remaining wilderness be destroyed."

In 1964 Congress passed the National Wilderness Act, one of the significant pieces of legislation coming from the Conservation Congress of President Lyndon B. Johnson. At last Americans had come to terms with our vanishing wild landscapes, and we sought to preserve small vestiges of the continent as it had existed when the Pilgrims arrived in 1620. Instead of carving up the entire public domain for private ownership, some of the land became U.S. Forest Service lands under the talented Gifford Pinchot, and other lands were designated national parks. What was left became, in 1946, the domain of the Bureau of Land Management, which is the only federal land management agency with citizen RACs, or Resource Advisory Councils. Designation of much of the public land that belongs to all Americans, and many thousands of acres of federally protected wilderness areas, can be attributed to President Theodore Roosevelt, who is one of my heroes.

In our bedroom we have two photos of strangers. In one image John Wesley Powell points off into the distance while a Ute friend looks on. In the second photo Teddy Roosevelt, president of the United States, sits in the morning sun in a cabin south of Silt, Colorado. He has Skip, an aspiring hunting dog, in his lap, and he is halfway through reading a book. The light glints off his spectacles. He wears dusty lace-up boots and an old hunting jacket. His work shirt is buttoned to the collar. The legs on his pants are frayed, and he is totally absorbed in his reading.

This photo of T. R. always draws my attention. Here was an Easterner from Manhattan and Oyster Bay, a Harvard graduate, a member of the New York legislature and later governor of New York who would

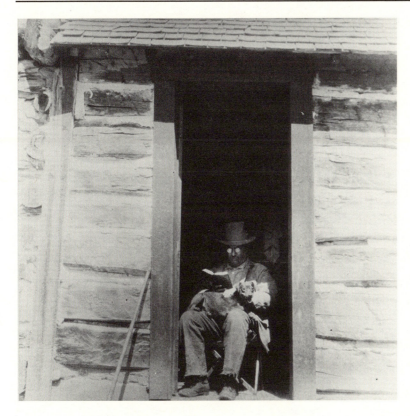

Figure 77. Teddy Roosevelt, the president of the United States, poses in his hunting clothes (note the frayed cuffs) south of Silt, Colorado, with "Skip," who became a White House dog. This undersized hunting dog became a favorite of Roosevelt during his 1905 hunting trip. Roosevelt took Skip back to live at the White House and the dog was a faithful companion of the president and his children for many years. Photo courtesy of the American Museum of Natural History, New York.

come to know the West unlike any other American president. Teddy hunted and fished across the United States, and he set aside more public land as national forests, national monuments and wildlife refuges than any president before or since.

Yes, Teddy made mistakes. He allowed the damming of the Hetch Hetchy River in Yosemite National Park, and he sacrificed the Owens Valley to Los Angeles, but this asthmatic weakling who once stated, "Aggressive fighting for the right is the noblest sport the world affords," also believed that America's future was utterly dependent upon natural resources. This old Rough Rider and Grand Canyon lion hunter would be appalled at many of today's politicians.

T. R. believed in corporate responsibility and in the proper administration of the public domain. Teddy demanded that the chief of the U.S. Forest Service, Gifford Pinchot, institute grazing fees on public lands and Fred M. Light from Snowmass, Colorado, contested it all the way to the Supreme Court, but the fees stuck. When Pinchot came out to explain the fee system to ranchers from Colorado's Western Slope, they were so angry that Pinchot never got off the back of the train in Glenwood Springs.

In 1909 Teddy argued to the nation's governors, "It is safe to say that the prosperity of our people depends on the energy and intelligence with which our natural resources are used." At the first national conservation conference he stated, "It is equally clear that those resources are the final basis of national power and perpetuity. Finally, it is ominously evident that those resources are in the course of rapid exhaustion." That was in 1909. What would Teddy think now?

I first saw this photo of him in an exhibit at the American Museum of Natural History in New York City. Other presidents have presidential libraries and museums, but T. R. has none. The American Museum honors him in its resplendent rotunda room and his ranch at Medora, North Dakota, is preserved, but Roosevelt's real legacy is the millions of acres of Western lands he saved from overzealous timber barons and cattle ranchers. I wish more presidents hunted deer and elk, read books in Colorado log cabins, and had frayed pants cuffs and dusty boots. It has been a century since T. R. hunted and fished in the White River National Forest of Colorado. I wish he would come back with his big stick and give his fellow politicians a good talking to. They need, we all need, his wisdom.

Theodore Roosevelt set aside millions of acres of public land that became national forests, and out of those forests Congress designated select roadless areas as wilderness areas. At present there are designated WSAs, or wilderness study areas, but they are in legal limbo and Congress has not acted on those lands in years. But we need wilderness. John Muir, that talented Scotsman who founded the Sierra Club, wrote in 1898, "Thousands of nerve-shaken, overly civilized people are beginning to find out that going to the mountains is going home, and that mountain parks and reservations are useful not only as fountains of timber and irrigating rivers, but as fountains of life."

We do not have enough acreage designated as wilderness. The percentage of wilderness in the lower 48 states actually equals the percentage of land that is paved. As a nation we have yet to adopt a land ethic, though Aldo Leopold referred to that in his classic *A Sand County Almanac*, which has become a bible for conservationists. Wilderness areas protect watersheds. They act as refuges and sanctuaries for humans and as genetic banks for flora and fauna. Federal wilderness areas are a small portion of the larger world of environmental and public history, but they inspire strong statements and political passions. Edward Abbey wrote in his classic *Desert Solitare*:

> We need wilderness whether or not we ever set foot in it. We need a refuge even though we may never need to go there.... Wilderness invokes nostalgia.... It means something lost and something still present, something remote and at the same time intimate, something buried in our blood and nerves and something beyond us and without limit.... But the love of wilderness is more than a hunger for what is always beyond reach; it is also an expression of loyalty to the earth, the earth which bore us and which sustains us, the only home we shall ever know, the only paradise we ever need—if only we had the eyes to see.... No, wilderness is not a luxury but a necessity of the human spirit, and as vital to our lives as water and good bread. A civilization which destroys what little remains of the wild, the spare, the original, is cutting itself off from its origins and betraying the principle of civilization itself.

In the book *Testimony*, edited by Stephen Trimble in defense of the Southern Utah Red Rocks Wilderness Act, many authors wrote eloquent words about our need for wild places. Rick Bass argued, "The unprotected wilderness of the West is one of our greatest strengths as a country. Another is our imagination, our tendency to think, rather than accept—to challenge, to ask why, and what if; to create, rather than to destroy. This questioning is a kind of wildness, a kind of strength, that many have said is peculiarly American.... We all know that what is rare is always valuable, and wilderness is our rarest and most imperiled resource of all."

In *Preserving Western History*, wilderness issues and the introduction of nonnative fish species are highlighted in Jeffrey Nichols's essay "These Waters Were All Virgin: Finis Mitchell and Wind River Wilderness, Wyoming." Finis horse-packed in thousands of young rainbow trout fingerlings, which have thrived in high mountain lakes where they were not native. What are the ethical issues of Mitchell's work in the twenty-first century, and did he irrevocably alter Wyoming wilderness? The concept of wilderness, an idea with deep meaning to thinkers like Aldo Leopold, Bob Marshall, and Olaus and Mardy Murie, finally coalesced into federal legislation in 1964 with congressional passage of the National Wilderness Act. Steve Schulte, author of a major biography on Congressman Wayne Aspinall, who for years fought against wilderness legislation, writes about wilderness preservation and natural landscapes "where man is a visitor and does not remain." Schulte sees wilderness legislation as a case study in Western public history.

Fire on the Mountain

Wildland Firefighter Tragedies and Firefighter Memorials

ANDREW GULLIFORD

When lightning strikes out of a western sky, the sound of rolling thunder bounces off boulders and rumbles deep down canyon walls. A snag on fire at midnight can become by noon a roaring blaze racing through dry timber, tall oak brush, or sweet-scented sage. Caused by lightning, extinguished by fire crews, western wildfire is a natural occurrence along the Rocky Mountains. A century ago a windborne wildfire could run its course, but now Westerners build houses adjacent to public lands. They build expensive homes in remote areas, and occasionally disaster strikes, as it did in the summer of 1994, when 14 firefighters died on a bony, rocky ridge near Storm King Mountain within view of an interstate highway and the Colorado River.

Twelve months later, concerned citizens from Glenwood Springs, Colorado, and donors from across the nation had contributed to a Storm King Memorial that represents a new community and environmental awareness in the American West. For the first time a western memorial has been created that is about heroism and tragedy and human losses to the forces of nature, but also about the natural place of fire in a western ecosystem. As late as the 1950s local communities erected monuments to commemorate conquest, western expansion, and Manifest Destiny. This may be the first western monument to reflect humility and the tragedy of losing young lives to a natural process.

As a public historian, I am fascinated with the process of memory becoming history and the symbolic meaning of monuments and memorials both to those groups who erect them and to the public, who often make pilgrimages to monuments as if to sacred ground. I wondered about the process of creating group consensus to build a monument and to dedicate a landscape to perpetuate memory. Why are some monuments erected and others not? How do local or national communities get involved, and how do monuments and memorials help forge and reinforce group identities? What can monument building teach us about the personal need of survivors to release grief cathartically and to ask metaphysical questions about life and death? What is this utterly human need to understand and remember? As a public historian, I considered these issues abstractly until July of 1994, when I was confronted with an enormous firefighting tragedy near my home in Colorado.[1]

On July 3, 1994, at the beginning of a dangerous wildfire season, lightning caused a small wildfire to ignite near Storm King Mountain on Bureau of Land Management (BLM) land in the Colorado River Valley. On July 4 a crew went in to contain the blaze. By July 5, when smokejumpers parachuted in to Storm King Mountain, 90 percent of available fire equipment and crews were already committed to other fires in the region. This would pose a problem when air shipments of fire retardant would become desperately needed.

On the afternoon of July 6 a fast-moving cold front caused the wind in South Canyon, below Storm King Mountain, to gust strongly enough to blow off hard hats worn by firefighters. Between 4 and 4:30 P.M., a fire blowup propelled flames uphill at 35 feet per second, and here, within two miles of Interstate 70, 14 firefighters died on Storm King Mountain as they tried to stop a fire that was burning perilously close to the town of Glenwood Springs. A small, lightning-caused fire had escalated into an intense firestorm traveling over 500 feet a minute, sucking up all oxygen in its path, and spewing a volcanolike mountain of smoke miles into the air. Within five hours the fire burned 2,115 acres.

The Storm King fire was one of the worst wildland firefighting accidents in the United States in 40 years. It made headlines around the world, and within the week television specials featured the lives of those young men and women who had died fighting a blowup—the most unpredictable type of wildfire that begins with a wall of superheated air and ends with a flame front in excess of 30 feet high. Their deaths deeply affected Coloradoans and all those who fight fires on public lands throughout the West. The accident stunned the citizens of Glenwood Springs, who vowed: "We will never forget."

Altogether, 32 people died during the 1994 wildland fire season, but the fact that the tragic deaths of the Storm King Fourteen occurred so close to the successful tourist and resort community of Glenwood Springs galvanized local citizens into action. Within 12 months volunteers created a memorial park for the 14 local deaths, an interpretive memorial trail, and an anniversary memorial event, which paid tribute to the families of those who died. Grateful citizens and firemen all over the United States contributed $135,000 in cash to the Storm King monument fund, a substantial amount in donated goods and services, and $425,000 in cash to a disaster fund for families of the 14.

Though there have been numerous wildfire firefighter fatalities since Congress created the Forest Service in 1905, the community response in Glenwood Springs, Colorado, is unprecedented. What explains the outpouring of public support? Why are these firefighters memorialized to the exclusion of others? What moves a community from observing an accidental tragedy to creating a public memorial? How did the creation of the "Storm King Fourteen Interpretive Trail and Memorial" coincide with other efforts to remember and memorialize firefighter deaths throughout the West?

Prineville, Oregon, erected statues symbolic of the Prineville Hotshots who died at Storm King. On the McCall Smokejumper Fire Base at McCall, Idaho, a memorial originated in 1993 was designed to be "simple, silent, realistic and useable." Situated away from public viewing, it is immediately adjacent to the path jumpers walk to receive a "spotters check" before boarding the plane for a fire call. According to Brad Sanders of the McCall Smokejumper Fund, "We wanted it to be comfortable and useable. A monument that smokejumpers can sit on while taking a break, lean on to tie their boots, or rest their helmet on while waiting for a spotters check." They thought that "new traditions may even develop around this monument, such as rubbing the life-size bronze of the original leather jump helmet for good luck prior to getting on the plane." Though planning began in 1993 to honor the 50th anniversary of the unit, after the Storm King fire two more names have been added to the memorial plaque—Jim Thrash and Roger Roth, both from McCall, who died on July 6, 1994.

This, then, is the story of wildfire tragedies and firefighter memorials in a study that describes human error and courage, desperation and valor, and an overwhelming community response to create a collective memory and sacred space from charred oak brush on a windswept mountainside consecrated by sudden, tragic death.

The first records of historical wildland firefighter fatalities began in 1910 with a horrible conflagration that torched 3 million acres in western Montana and Idaho, in which "thousands of people thought the world was coming to an end and for eighty-seven people it did."[2] Though the fire raged in the West, smoke and ashes obscured visibility as far away as the Atlantic Ocean. Survivors included a fire crew trapped with Edward Pulaski, who put a wet gunnysack around his head and led 42 men to safety in an abandoned mining tunnel. Once the men were inside the tunnel, a wall of intense heat outside ignited framing timbers in the mine, but under Pulaski's direction the men lived by lying flat at the bottom of the mine and keeping their noses and mouths to the ground. In Wallace, Idaho, monuments for firefighters who died in 1910 exist at Nine Mile Cemetery and at the West Fork of Placer Creek. At St. Maries, Idaho, Woodlawn Cemetery contains graves of some of the 1910 firefighters and a monument. In the War Eagle Tunnel a plaque commemorates Edward Pulaski's dramatic rescue.

For firefighters, Pulaski's name is synonymous with the tool he invented. Half hoe and half ax, the Pulaski is the basic firefighting implement used by hotshot crews who work on the ground to put a line around a fire to prevent flames from leaping into new fuel sources. Fire lines are as wide on the ground as one and a half times the height of the fuel, and under normal weather conditions once a fire line has encircled a wildfire, it will burn itself out. Then the crew mops up by burying any branches that are still smoldering. In the early days, and especially after the great fire season of 1910 (the most disastrous on record), standing orders called for putting out any wildfire that started, if possible, by 10 A.M. the following morning. Fire science was in its infancy, and the vagaries of fire behavior in canyons and in grasslands, with changing temperature, humidity, and wind, had not been studied.

Then came the Mann Gulch fire in 1949, 20 miles north of Helena, Montana, where 13 smokejumpers lost their lives in a fire blowup when a steep and peaceful canyon became a death trap. Before it was over, the fire had burned 4,500 acres and taken 450 men to control it. Fire defies gravity. Unlike any living thing in nature, it can run faster uphill. An updraft and fire whirls burst a hillside into a moving wall of flame 30 feet tall that caused the young Mann Gulch smokejumpers, most of them World War II veterans, to die. In *Young Men and Fire*, Norman Maclean wrote:

> As a fire up a hillside closes in, everything becomes a mode of exhaustion—fear, thirst, terror, a twitch in the flesh that still has a preference to live, all become simply exhaustion. So upon closer examination, burning to death on a mountain-side is dying at least three times . . . first, considerably ahead of the fire, you reach the verge of death in your boots and your legs; next, as you fail, you sink back in the region of strange gases and red and blue darts where there is no oxygen and here you die in your lungs; then you sink in prayer into the main fire that consumes, and if you are a Catholic about all that remains of you is your cross.[3]

Figure 78. A low stone wall and plaques on the ground represent the National Wildland Firefighter Memorial at the Smokejumpers' Base in Missoula, Montana, dedicated "in recognition of the brave men and women who have lost their lives fighting wildland fires throughout the United States, May 8, 1991." Photo in possession of the author.

Concrete crosses mark where the smokejumpers fell. Their average age was 20. A plaque commemorates their names and hometowns at Meriwether Campground in the Helena National Forest. A wayside exhibit along Interstate 90 also describes the fire.

For years there was no other monument to mark their passing or the significance their deaths had on changing firefighting policies. Historically, the Mann Gulch Fire is important because for the first time attention began to be paid to fire behavior. The Board of Review of the Mann Gulch Fire of August 5, 1949, met in Missoula on September 26–28 to assess what had happened and thus to begin formal attempts to research wildfire behavior in three national fire laboratories, including the Inter-Mountain Fire Science Laboratory adjacent to the smokejumpers' base in Missoula.

The foreman of the Mann Gulch crew, Wagner Dodge, survived by setting an escape fire in the grass, covering his face with a wet handkerchief, and lying down in the burnt-out area as flames from the blowout roared over him and superheated air literally lifted him off the ground. All firefighters now study the Mann Gulch Fire in the first training session every firefighter must take, and all wildland firefighters now learn about fire behavior in addition to how to use a Pulaski and

Figure 79. The devastation of the Storm King burn area is visible in this photo, taken the next spring after the fire. Photo by author, 1995.

when to deploy portable fire shelters to crawl into in case of a blowup. But it was not until 1991 and the centennial of the first U.S. Forest Reserves that family members who lost loved ones at Mann Gulch were able to have closure on this catastrophic event.

On May 8, 1991, at the Smokejumpers' Base in Missoula, which is the Aerial Fire Depot for Region I of the Forest Service, 500 visitors and 100 family members came together to dedicate an L-shaped granite wall built by jumpers and dedicated to wildland firefighters. Over $15,000 had been raised for this commemoration. The National Wildland Firefighters Memorial contains plaques with the names of those who died at Mann Gulch. Wayne Williams helped spearhead the memorial. He writes, "For a project, it is probably the most meaningful and emotional that I have ever worked on." He explains, "To contact surviving family members of Mann Gulch, I was not only apprehensive but also worried about stirring up past memories. As it turned out the families were very supportive of the project." Family members came from as far away as Brooklyn, New York, and Modesto, California, and Williams notes that in the process of organizing the event "we became close friends. I have received letters from the families expressing their thanks to all the people who have worked on this project, that the memorial finally put a positive end to the tragedy."[4]

One of the two survivors of the Mann Gulch Fire, Bob Sallee, spoke at the ceremonies and stated, "Smokejumping solidifies a courage that takes you through life. Nothing can ever be as difficult as stepping out that [airplane] door the first time . . . and participating with a crew of jumpers to build a fire line across the head of a fire before it blows is a study in the will to succeed." He concluded, "They were outstanding young men, selected from among the best, with proven courage, determined to succeed and dedicated to doing the job assigned. They gave their lives trying and this tribute is long overdue."[5] The Wildland Firefighters Memorial is toured by 30,000 to 40,000 visitors a year, who come to the visitor center at the Missoula Air Base to learn about wildland firefighting from tour guides who are smokejumpers.

Wayne Williams, a smokejumper himself, had helped to organize the successful Missoula memorial, and he relived the Mann Gulch fire many times as he spoke to family members who are still troubled years later on the deceased firefighters' birthdays. Two of the fallen young men were dating sisters, and both women came to the dedication. By an ironic twist of fate Wayne Williams was in Glenwood Springs on July 6, 1994, waiting to reinforce jumpers on the Storm King fire. When word came that shelters had been deployed and that there were probably fatalities on the mountain, he knew what to expect.

A blowup, "a catastrophic collision of fire, clouds, and winds," had occurred. With over 100 fires blazing in Colorado during the week of July 4, 1994, the Storm King fire had started out as just another lightning-caused ignition in a dangerously dry year. By 4 P.M. on July 6 wind gusts increased to 45 miles per hour, and the wind funneled up South Canyon of the Colorado River just as it had funneled up Mann Gulch on the Missouri River. Twelve-foot-high tinder-dry gambel oak brush exploded into flame as smokejumpers, hotshots from Prineville, Oregon, on only two hours of sleep, and two helitack crew members desperately sought shelter. Some firefighters heard the cry, "Get out! Get out!," on their portable radios and took the escape route to safety as they ran down the east side of Storm King Mountain to stand exhausted along the interstate highway.

On top along the west side of the ridge, just below the 8,000-foot crest, a few firefighters deployed their shelters. Others still carried their chain saws. One

Figure 80. In addition to smokejumpers and hotshot crew members, two helitack members died: Robert Browning and Richard Tyler. Granite crosses mark where they succumbed to heat and a lack of oxygen. Photo by author, 1995.

survivor was literally blown over the top of the ridge by the concussion of the firestorm. Four women and 10 men, two of Native American descent, most unmarried, a few with young children, will live forever on the mountainside. Through the dense smoke in the perilous updraft, airplanes tried to drop fire retardant on the reflective silver fire shelters, but for 14 it was too late. The top two firefighters died only 11 seconds from the ridge. Wristwatches melted.

Wayne Williams helped fly survivors off the mountain, and he made sure that the bodies were not disturbed until the investigating team arrived. Because of his experiences with the Mann Gulch families, for the next two weeks Williams manned an exclusive telephone hotline talking to and consoling family members. The deep grief process had begun again. In Glenwood Springs, news of the fatalities highlighted an emergency situation in which the fire still raged. As homeowners evacuated their houses in the eerie prolonged twilight of a deep orange sunset thickened by waves of smoke, news media from all over the country began calling. Barbara Bush from the Carbondale Fire/EMS/Rescue station wrote:

It was the most exhausting, miserable day of my life on a fire. I answered the phones. The universe knew only that something horrible had happened involving a wildfire on a mountain in Glenwood Springs. The bodies of 10 BLM firefighters had been found, badly burned, dead. So Glenwood Springs Fire Department was the number to call. Thursday morning, a mere fifteen hours since the explosion of a brush fire on a steep, tinder dry mountain—still many of the original 47 firefighters unaccounted for. And the phones rang . . . "My name is Tim Steel with a rural fire department in Arkansas, we've collected two hundred dollars for the families of the firefighters. Has a fund been started yet?" "I'm the fire chief in ___ Kentucky, and we will send you any equipment you need. You just call." "This is Marty at Doc Holiday's Restaurant in Glenwood Springs—free steak dinners and immediate service for any fire crews coming in." "My ranch is available for people being evacuated from their homes—hope they don't mind a few cows." And we would receive notification of another body found on Storm King Mountain.

And still the phones rang—and the roller coaster of emotions continued. "I own National Hose Company—you just call the Denver office and they will send you whatever you need immediately."

"My daughter is a firefighter for the BLM and she was being sent to Glenwood. Can you tell me if she's okay?"

"We're sending you a pile of sandwiches, and we made the cookies ourselves." But there is one man I'm looking for. There is a name that I want. I believe he is a salesman or may even own a fire suppressant/retardant company. It may be in South Carolina—all that I wrote on my notepad was the state—this is the man that announced to me over the phone, "If you had been using our fire retardant, those firefighters would not have died."

Firefighter Bush wrote, "I'll stay on the fire line next time. I'm not strong enough to answer phones."[6]

The community response continued to be overwhelming. Everyone in the Colorado River Valley felt touched by the tragedy of the fire because of its highly visible location along Interstate 70 and because so many residents know firefighters or have hiked or camped on nearby public lands. The fire united valley residents in compassion and in grief for young men and women they had never met. As the local and regional newspapers began to print biographies and photographs of the 14 who had died, everyone felt they knew them.

The blowup occurred on a Wednesday night. By Sunday afternoon the fire was under control and an impromptu memorial service drew hundreds of residents, weary firefighters, and concerned citizens to Two Rivers Park. A ministerial alliance organized four preachers to speak briefly on the nature of tragedy and accidental death. Most everyone wore purple in solidarity with those who had died. Red fire trucks and crews came from Denver, Grand Junction, Aspen, Vail, Eagle, Rifle, Leadville, Loveland, and other cities in a final tribute to their fallen comrades. Bureau of Land Management and U.S. Forest Service four-wheel-drive fire engines in red, yellow, and green joined the memorial parade for a total of 25 to 30 trucks.

After the ministers finished speaking and the audience tearfully sang "Amazing Grace," five helicopters flew overhead, including a large Sikorsky helitack copter that earlier in the week had been frantically dipping huge buckets into the Colorado River and carrying water up to the top of the mountain. As the helicopters flew overhead, in a symbolic aerial act the large Sikorsky broke off from formation and flew alone into the sky in what is termed the missing man formation to represent the loss or death of colleagues and friends.

Then on Tuesday, a week after they had died, the firefighters began the journey home. With a full police motorcade escort, 14 separate hearses drove the bodies to the Grand Junction airport, where friends of the firefighters loaded the coffins onto a C-47 flying boxcar for

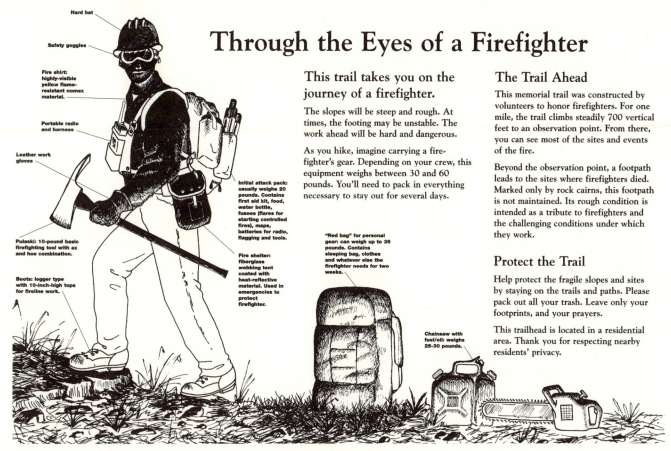

Figure 81. "Through the Eyes of a Firefighter" is artwork from a plaque along the hiking trail, which takes visitors high above Interstate 70 to where the Storm King Fourteen died. This is one of many excellent interpretive signs installed and maintained by the Glenwood Springs, Colorado, office of the Bureau of Land Management.

final interment in their hometowns. As the numbed citizens of Glenwood Springs began to slowly get on with their lives, they wore purple, and large purple wreaths and ribbons appeared along the freeway near South Canyon.

Mayor Bob Zanella organized a committee to plan a fitting memorial and anniversary of the tragedy so that families of the deceased would know that citizens of Glenwood Springs shared in their sorrow and would never forget. A Storm King Fourteen Committee was formed so that 14 Glenwood Springs residents might contact family members of the deceased firefighters to aid them in their grief and to get their comments and suggestions on a fitting memorial. After passage of a formal resolution by the city council, the committee met for two and a half hours each week from September to December.

Citizens volunteered to help build the memorial; others joined volunteer fire departments in the valley.

As soon as it was permitted, local residents began hiking up Storm King Mountain over scorched earth and between blackened branches. People wanted to know how it happened and where it happened. Family members began to arrive with the same desperate questions, and according to BLM Interpretive Planner Kathy Voth, "The Storm King 14 Memorial Trail was built by a community literally walking through the grieving process. It began as a footpath made by people hiking the mountain; families, friends, and local residents, attempting to understand what had happened." She explains, "When constructed, it was left steep and rough to provide visitors with the experience of a firefighter. The finished trail and interpretation harnesses what visitors were already doing, puts signs in natural rest stops, answers questions they were asking, and thus enhances their experience."[7]

Kathy Voth had been public affairs officer the night of the blowup, and she insisted that the trail be interpreted correctly as to the facts of the accident and the identities of the dead so that they would be remembered in the totality of their brief lives, not just as names on a plaque.

Voth explains, "Hundreds of visitors climbed the mountain to pay their respects and try to understand what had happened." She notes, "This trail is about remembering, about honoring our dead, and about honoring our living.... It was important to us that the trail continue to help people feel that personal connection, and that it provide them with information that would color future judgments about fires, firefighters and each other. Finally, we wanted the trail to remind firefighters everywhere of the dangers of their job, to encourage safety, and thus prevent future tragedies."[8]

The draft interpretive plan took only two weeks to write and then firefighters, administrators, and grieving families took months to review the text. Kathy worked intimately with those families, paring down their statements about their loved ones to fit the size constraints of the first interpretive panel, which features each firefighter's photograph and a brief biography. The trail goes for 1.5 miles up 700 vertical feet and reaches an observation point where granite crosses can be seen marking the exact spots where the firefighters died. Here "people stop and reflect. This is a place where people weep; for themselves, for what is lost, and for what still can be." Voth wrote:

There are many voices to listen to on this trail. There are the voices of the firefighters who lost their lives here. There are the voices of firefighters who continue the work. There is the voice of the trail, talking to you through your legs and lungs, saying, "This hurts, this is hard, this is very steep." There are the voices of the birds, the wind in the trees, the highway below. And then there is the silence. All are part of the experience, and part of the interpretation. The signs along this trail were designed so they would not overwhelm any of the other voices, but would become part of the choir. They were designed to fit in with their environment. Often, if someone whispers to you, you end up being quieter, and even whispering back. The signs were designed to be the whispers that would encourage visitors to be quieter, to pay more attention to everything around them.[9]

The interpretive trail is highly successful, but success comes with costs. Interpreter Kathy Voth had a difficult time editing the biographies of the Storm King Fourteen. She notes, "I struggled to put together just the right 160 words that would both satisfy their families and relay their special qualities to someone who wouldn't have the chance to know them." The stress of this work and meeting a tight one-year deadline caused Voth to take leave from her job and seek professional counseling. She helped to handle her grief by tying the firefighters' biographies to small sticks and one by one watching them float down the Colorado River. The parents of Don Mackey, one of the dead smokejumpers, buried their grief in hundreds of pounds of concrete.

Don Mackey emerged as a hero in the press when surviving firefighters related that smokejumper Mackey had left the safety of an area where they had eaten lunch to help the weary Prineville Hotshot crew, which included female firefighters. Mackey made the decision to go back to the fire line to make sure the others working in the flammable oak brush were aware that the fire had begun to spot on both sides of the gulch. His family was devastated by his death. In Mann Gulch the 13 smokejumper fatalities have been remembered by concrete crosses with brass name tags on the horizontal crossbar, but concrete deteriorates in western wind and weather.

Therefore the Mackey family requested granite crosses to mark where the Storm King Fourteen died.

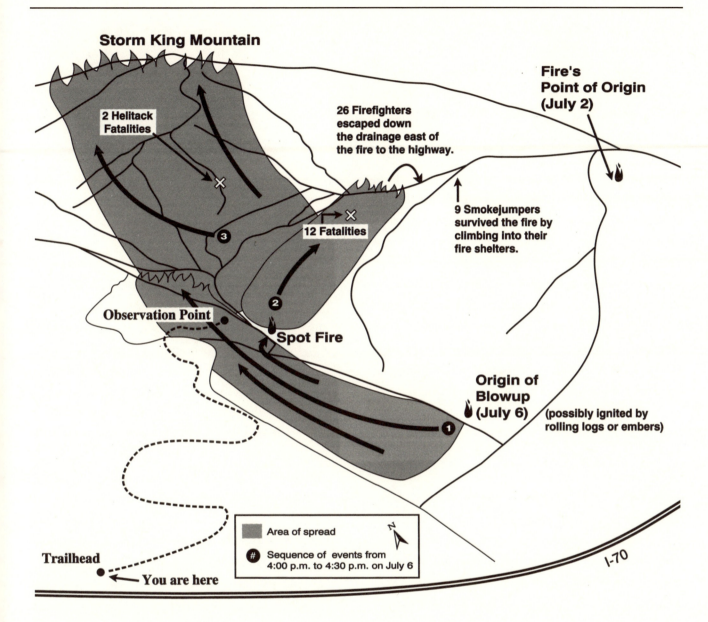

Figure 82. Graphic map of the trailhead and location both of where the fire "blew up" and what happened to firefighters, both those who died and those who survived, between 4:00 and 4:30 P.M. on July 6, 1994. The map is on a BLM plaque at the Storm King Trail site. Map from the Andrew Gulliford Collection, Center of Southwest Studies, Fort Lewis College, Colorado.

Bob Mackey, Don's father, designed and coordinated the stone cutting with a factory in Georgia, which then shipped the crosses to Montana for carving in Missoula. Then, with cement and water helicoptered in by the Bureau of Land Management, for eight days in April 1995, Bob, Tom, and Nadine Mackey and volunteers and cadets from the Air Force Academy in Colorado Springs dug three-foot holes in the mountainside to place rebar, cement, and the crosses. They finished their work on Easter Sunday.

Immediately visitors began leaving mementos at the crosses. For Terri Hagen, a young woman of Native American descent, Indian friends created a steel medicine wheel wind chime with six metal eagle feathers, four for each of the cardinal directions, one for the sky and one for the earth. Someone also left a wooden staff with a carved eagle's head as well as a tribute of red cloth. Two of the firefighters had been Native American, and seven of the others had Indian blood. Today on the mountainside the metal feathers gently tinkle in the wind as visitors approach the crosses from below.

By May 1995 the pilgrimages began in earnest with interested visitors as well as fire crews and firemen from all over the United States coming to Glenwood Springs to honor their fallen comrades. Division supervisors came, as did engine crews, managers, hotshot teams, and municipal firefighters from as far away as Newark, New Jersey. Active firefighting teams came from Colorado, Wyoming, Washington, Montana, Oregon, and Utah to pay their respects to the dead and to ponder their own vulnerability.

One hotshot crew from the Ashley National Forest near Vernal, Utah, had studied investigative reports, but they wanted to walk the terrain themselves to see what had happened. In their own forest, Firefighters Memorial Campground includes a plaque honoring three men who died in the Cart Creek fire on July 16, 1977. The older crew leader specifically wanted his young hotshots to walk the Storm King trail, to stand in front of the crosses, and to know in their bones what they could not know in their hearts—that they are mortal too. A few of the firefighters even paced themselves trying to run up the slope to simulate the Storm King Fourteen's attempt to escape, but they failed. The firestorm would have caught them too. And they said to each other, "They were the best. It could happen to us." At the start of the trail a seasoned firefighter from Wyoming wrote in the comment book, *If one person can learn from this and save someone's life, it'll be worth it.* Other visitors have written, *Rest in peace and thank you for giving your lives for such beauty.*

On July 6, 1995, formal ceremonies opened the Storm King Fourteen Memorial Trail and the bronze firefighter statues at Two Rivers Park. Around the statues are granite boulders with special plaques for each fallen firefighter that includes their photograph and name. Since that day people have come to look at the circle of boulders and to leave gifts and offerings. Fire crews who attended the memorial service left shirt patches, T-shirts, and caps as if to say, "They were one of ours." The gifts continue and are mailed back to the families.

Eighty local Colorado River Valley residents and other volunteers from across the United States worked for a year with the Mennonite Church to sew 14 Storm King quilts to give to the families of the firefighters who died. The family of smokejumper Jim Thrash called it "an incredible gesture of love."

On the first anniversary 150 family members and 4,000 visitors attended. The governor and other dignitaries spoke, as did family members. Some were eloquent, some were quiet, but all spoke of prayers and love and thanks. Amid calls for increased safety, hotshot crews in attendance received a standing ovation. The mother of the Indian firefighter Terri Hagen stated simply, "Her spirit is still here. It's still with us. Every bit of air and water. Each plant and animal. She is in the spirit world." Visitors were encouraged to share in the families' grief. One speaker stated, "When we lose a parent, we lose our past. When we lose a spouse, we lose our present. When we lose a child, we lose our future. Walk the trail and remember our children."[10]

What are the lessons from Storm King? The fatalities could have been avoided. Standing fire orders were not adhered to, and decision making collapsed. There were errors in judgment and confusion over who was in charge on the mountain, but at what personal price to families and friends should the truth be told? Who are we to speculate on the correctness or incorrectness of split-second life-or-death decisions made amid confusion brought about by heat, smoke, and exhaustion?

Those who survived dropped their equipment and deployed fire shelters or took the escape route when they were ordered to. Those who died included a few who were still carrying chain saws. Hotshot crew members and helitack crew members died, and so did the first smokejumpers since 1949.

If the Mann Gulch tragedy helped bring about a better understanding of fire behavior, perhaps the Storm King fire will stimulate better understanding of human behavior in dangerous and unforgiving conditions. Up on that mountain firefighters disregarded fuel behavior and were unaware of upcoming dangerous weather. They failed to establish adequate lookouts, safety zones, and safe escape routes and could not change escape strategies fast enough when a blowout occurred, sending a wall of flame 200 to 300 feet high. Norman Maclean wrote, "One risks one's life in fighting fire for a livelihood and that sometimes saving one's life depends entirely upon taking one's life in one's own hands and that at other times one's life and the lives of others must be put entirely into the hands of one boss—old lessons that through time have to be learned and relearned, only to be forgotten again."[11]

On Storm King those lessons were forgotten, but now perhaps they will be remembered because there is a statue in a park and a truly innovative memorial trail. Memorials serve to keep us from forgetting after the intensity of immediate events have faded. Two months after the fire a mud slide hurtling off the mountain buried Interstate 70 for 18 hours. Now grass has grown back, but it will be decades before Storm King will have mature trees. Anyone driving Interstate 70 can see the huge red scar.

What are the lessons of history? Longtime smokejumper and fire researcher Laird Robinson laments, "We're not real good at learning from our lessons, at learning from history. . . . What did Norman Maclean say? 'As long as there are young men and fire, there will be death.' I think so." The Storm King Fourteen Committee and citizens of Glenwood Springs have vowed, "We will never forget," but will we truly never forget? Or is forgetting as much a part of the human condition as remembering? Do we build monuments for the dead or for the living?

Fire crews from throughout the West and firefighters from throughout the nation will continue to visit Glenwood Springs and hike the interpretive trail. Hopefully the youngest of the firefighters will pause to think about what happened and why. On their pilgrimage they will learn some of the most important lessons that public history can teach about tragedy and compassion and the human need to remember. The living have remembered the dead and therefore the dead will

Figure 83. The granite marker at the site where Native American Terri Hagen died has offerings from other Native Americans, including a metal medicine wheel with metal eagle feathers. Photo by author, 1995.

go on living. A fire-scarred mountain is now a sacred place, and metal eagle feathers on a medicine wheel turn in the wind above granite crosses.

In July 2004 Glenwood Springs honored the tenth anniversary of the Storm King or South Canyon Fire. Once again Southern Ute Kenny Frost gave an invocation and local residents hosted the families of those who had lost loved ones. Everyone visited the memorials and had time to reflect. The U.S. Forest Service produced a special document that described the changes in federal firefighting policy since the Storm King Fire. Forest Stewardship Concepts, Ltd., produced a report on lessons learned from Storm King combined with the 2001 Thirtymile Fire in Washington and the 2002

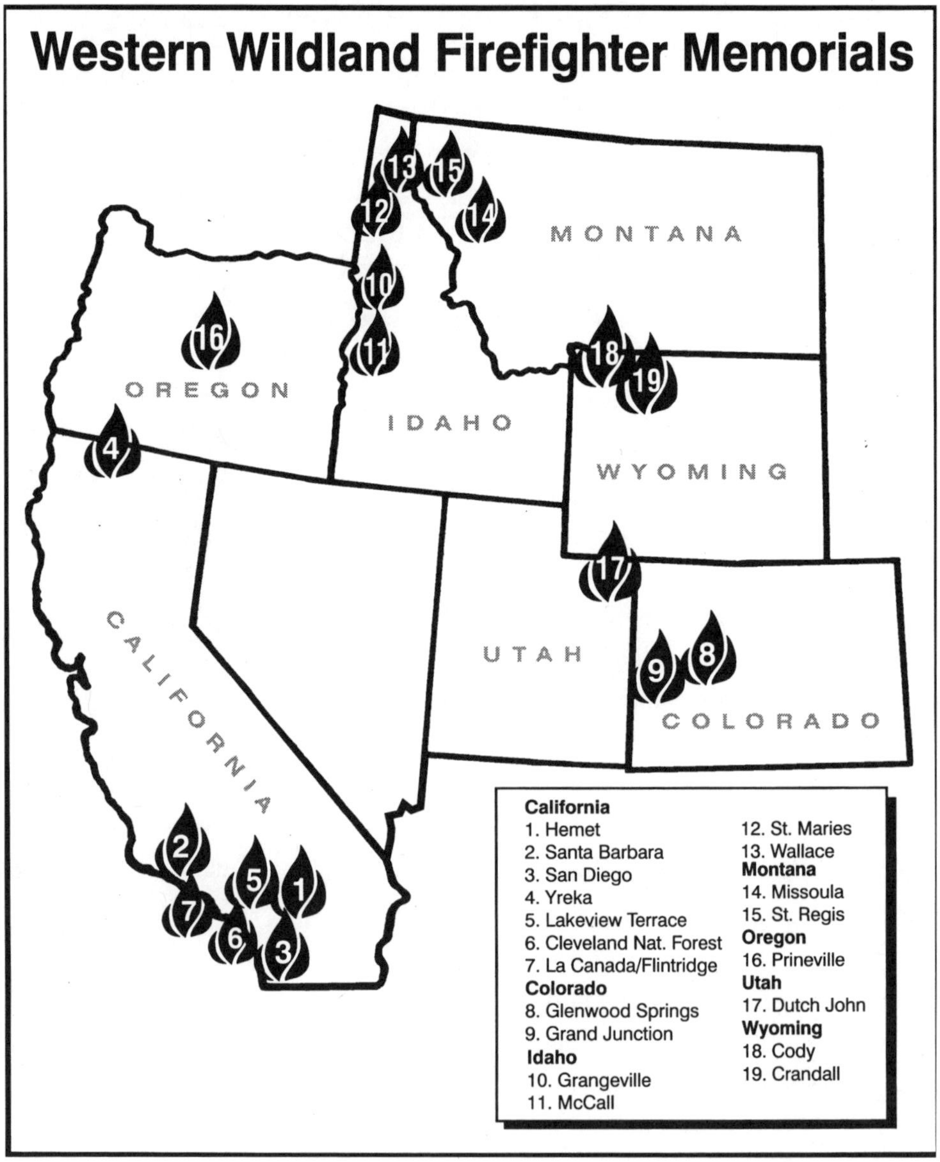
Western Wildland Firefighter Memorials
MONTANA
OREGON
IDAHO
WYOMING
UTAH
CALIFORNIA
COLORADO
California
1. Hemet
2. Santa Barbara
3. San Diego
4. Yreka
5. Lakeview Terrace
6. Cleveland Nat. Forest
7. La Canada/Flintridge
Colorado
8. Glenwood Springs
9. Grand Junction
Idaho
10. Grangeville
11. McCall
12. St. Maries
13. Wallace
Montana
14. Missoula
15. St. Regis
Oregon
16. Prineville
Utah
17. Dutch John
Wyoming
18. Cody
19. Crandall

Figure 84. Map of selected Western Wildland Firefighter Memorials. More research needs to be done to identify and document a century of wildland firefighter memorials across the American West. Map from the Andrew Gulliford Collection, Center of Southwest Studies, Fort Lewis College, Colorado.

Cramer Fire in Idaho, each of which produced casualties.[12] A second 10-year document came from the Office of the Inspector General from the Agriculture Department and for good reason: in the lethal 1994 fire season 32 young men and women lost their lives.[13]

Thanks to the Storm King Fire, agencies have learned the lessons of history, and some of their findings include more interagency cooperation when fighting fires and more opportunity for firefighters on the line to ask questions, seek clear directions, and take time to be safer. The aggressive, macho, "can-do" firefighter culture that existed in the twentieth century has evolved into a twenty-first-century culture with a heightened sense of safety and much better safety training, with posted fire lookouts secured by helitack bases. The goal now is to have a "passion for safety" that did not exist before. Firefighters can refuse assignments if they deem them too dangerous and not jeopardize their jobs or careers. More firefighting equipment is now available and the firefighter "watchout" signs have been revised so that young men and women on the line know that their safety comes first.

Firefighters have improved communication both among themselves and with dispatchers aware of swiftly changing weather conditions. Fire managers are more aware of potential threats, and leaders are held accountable after they have received improved leadership training. A direct result of the Storm King Fire is the new Red Book, or fire operations guide, and a Wildland Fire Lessons Learned Center in Arizona. Former White River National Forest supervisor Sonny La Salle believes that everyone should hike the trail on Storm King Mountain to understand what happened there. He argues, "Where memory fades, the opportunity increases for history to repeat itself. It's just imperative that people not let memory fade."[14] Public historians could not agree more.

New training techniques encourage better assimilation and teamwork, and group cohesion is encouraged so that firefighter crews are not split up. Team leaders are more aware of exhaustion and the need for rest both on a fire and between fires even during a busy fire season. There is also a better understanding of post–traumatic stress syndrome among firefighters. One of the Storm King survivors who went right back to work and did not take time to grieve later suffered because of it. Jailed because of a DUI, or a drunken driving charge, Brad Haugh wrote about trying "to force the South Canyon ghosts to leave me." He wrote in a personal letter three years after the fire, "I went to jail and while in detox was diagnosed with post–traumatic stress syndrome, survivor guilt syndrome, and self-destructive tendencies. . . . I thought I had it together, but the veil of denial had shaded my vision of reality."[15]

And what of the other firefighters who survived the inferno? On that fateful day Eric Hipke deployed his fire shelter near the others but then decided it was too dangerous to stay on the trail, and he began to run uphill, holding the shelter like a large aluminum shield. As he ran he felt a huge blast of hot air that severely burned his hands and upper arms before it blew him over the ridge and into the arms of other survivors, who helped him get down to the freeway and into a hospital. That was a terrifying experience, yet Eric Hipke still fights wildfires. In quieter moments he thinks about the granite crosses that mark where his comrades fell.

Notes

1. Adapted from the article "Fire on the Mountain: Tragic Death and Memorialization of the Storm King Fourteen," *Montana: The Magazine of Western History* (April 1997). See that article for more complete bibliographic citations.

2. Norman Maclean, *Young Men and Fire* (Chicago: University of Chicago Press, 1992), 23.

3. Ibid., 7.

4. Wayne Williams, Missoula Smokejumpers, to author, December 15, 1995, and telephone conversations in November 1995 and on January 19, 1996.

5. Transcript of Bob Sallee's notes from the National Wildland Firefighters Memorial Event in 1991 at the Smokejumpers' Base, Missoula. The event was videotaped by North Country Media Group, Great Falls, Montana. See also Staff Jenkins, ed., *Some of the Men of Mann Gulch* (San Luis Obispo, CA: 1993).

6. Discussion with firefighter Barbara Bush, Carbondale Fire/EMS/Rescue Station, Carbondale, CO, July 1994.

7. Kathy Voth, "Storm King Fourteen Memorial Trail Presentation to Manager's Core" (Rocky Mountain Interpretive Conference, June 1995).

8. Ibid.

9. Ibid.

10. Comments from Jill Hagen, mother of Terri Hagen, are available on videotape from the White River National Forest, Glenwood Springs, Colorado, from the first anniversary on July 6, 1995.

11. Maclean, *Young Men and Fire*, 220.

12. Safe Fire Programs & Forest Stewardship Concepts, "South Canyon Fire: Ten Year Review of the Effectiveness of Planned Actions," June 23, 2004. Another account is by John Maclean, Norman Maclean's son, who wrote *Fire on the Mountain*, but he does not offer footnotes or attribution for the many quotes or statements in his book, so it will be difficult for public historians to understand and utilize his sources.

13. See an entire week's worth of articles on the 10th anniversary of the Storm King Fire in the *Glenwood Springs Post Independent*, June 25–26, July 4, July 5, July 6, and July 7, 2004.

14. *Glenwood Springs Post Independent*, July 4, 2004, SK3.

15. Letter to author from wildland firefighter Brad Haugh, October 2, 1997.

Study Questions

1. Why was the Storm King Memorial built?
2. According to the author, why do people visit memorials like these?
3. Describe the Storm King monument. What elements does it combine?
4. Why is the Mann Gulch Fire so important to firefighters?
5. How is the trail itself (at the Storm King Memorial) a tribute to the firefighters?
6. Explain why the Storm King Fire was such an emotional time for the residents of Glenwood Springs.
7. In what way did building the monument help the residents of Glenwood Springs?
8. How are other fire crews using knowledge gained from the Storm King Fire?
9. What is the paradox of building a memorial?

Ecotourism and Western National Parks

A Case Study in Management to Protect Natural and Cultural Resources

Patrick Tierney

The United States has had a long, sometimes controversial, history of setting aside its most unique and valued natural and cultural resources and allowing visitation to these protected areas. Finding the balance between preservation and public use of protected areas is an arduous task. As former Yellowstone National Park superintendent Michael Finley said in 1999: "Finding the right balance is not as simple as use versus preservation; it is a more philosophical question of providing use that is consistent with preserving natural values."[1] Tourist activity and management paradigms have changed over the last century, and we now recognize that the well-intentioned actions of past managers have led to some of today's challenges. An ecosystem perspective, thorough scientific assessment, long-term planning, and plentiful public input into decision making is the wave of the future, which means managers of protected natural areas must stand firm against the whims of pseudoscience and political manipulation.[2]

This essay provides a historical perspective on two protected natural areas in the western United States, visitors to the parks, and local community interactions with them and it offers lessons we have learned since the first forest reserves and national parks were created in the late nineteenth century. The United States is blessed with a huge variety of parks and protected areas administered by federal, state, and local government organizations as well as a number of privately owned natural areas. These areas range from glaciated alpine peaks to tropical forests, to deep ocean trenches without light but teaming with life. This essay focuses on two federally managed protected areas to represent the range of natural resources in the West. I briefly explore their legislative mandates, resource base, management issues and paradigms, relationships with local communities and businesses, and finally, their visitation trends. Each park offers unique resources and perspectives. Yellowstone is considered a first-tier park, with mass tourism and international appeal, while Dinosaur National Monument is a second-tier park, with very significant natural and cultural resources but considerably less visitation and international recognition.

The volume, motives, and most popular activities of visitors to these protected areas have changed considerably over the last 120 years. There has been an overall shift from a few hardy explorers to millions of comfort-seeking excursionists. Legislation clearly requires protection of resources but also allows for public visitation and recreation uses. But levels and intensity of public use differ depending on resource capacity, legal mandates, and management assessments. The general public loves to visit parks and protected areas, but in some cases visitors are "loving the parks to death."

To protect the integrity of these natural areas and cope with the flood of visitors and demands of adjacent residents, management has had to limit access and activities by both local community residents and tourists. In some cases, however, local communities predate creation of the protected areas. So Congress and management have taken various types of actions either to remove residents or collaborate with them. In addition, federal agencies have not been able to meet the growing demands by visitors for services, ranging from educational talks to overnight accommodations. Legislation also allows for licensed providers to offer essential appropriate services in protected areas. So management has enlisted partnerships with mostly private companies and nonprofit organizations. The monetary impact of tourist services has become big business and grown to frequently be

Figure 85. As Old Faithful goes off and her steam and plume diminish, thousands of Yellowstone tourists each year "tour on" to other sites in the park. As at the Grand Canyon, over 95 percent of all Yellowstone visitors never get more than a mile and a half from an asphalt road. Photo by Andrew Gulliford, 2003.

the most important economic engine for communities surrounding protected areas. To understand protected areas and tourism, one most consider their relationship with local communities and tourist serving businesses.

Over the last 20 to 30 years a worldwide movement referred to as "ecotourism" or responsible tourism has arisen. In its pure form ecotourism seeks to address many of the concerns and inequalities of mass natural area tourism by minimizing impacts to resources, offering outstanding opportunities to learn about the resources and to enhance sustainable benefits to local communities. As well intentioned as this movement has been, history has shown it is only likely to succeed in protected areas that are well managed.

Yellowstone National Park, in the states of Wyoming, Idaho, and Montana, was established in 1872 and is the first and oldest national park in the world. The National Park Service (NPS) administers Yellowstone with a mandate to "promote and regulate the use of the . . . national parks . . . which purpose is to conserve the scenery and the natural and historic objects and the wild life therein and to provide for the enjoyment of the same in such manner and by such means as will leave them unimpaired for the enjoyment of future generations." Preserved within Yellowstone are Old Faithful Geyser and some 10,000 hot springs and geysers, an outstanding mountain wildland home of the grizzly bear and wolf, free-ranging herds of bison and elk and the core of the Greater Yellowstone Ecosystem, one of the largest intact temperate zone ecosystems remaining on the planet. It has been designated a World Heritage site. The park covers 2,219,791 acres and had an annual park budget of $27,122,000 and a total of 2,769,000 recreational visits in 2001.[4] Yellowstone has become an icon of the American park system, with popular activities including sightseeing by automobile, hiking, fishing, wildlife observation, and in winter cross-country skiing and snowmobiling. Hunting is prohibited in the park.

Dinosaur National Monument, in the states of Utah and Colorado, was created by a presidential proclamation in 1915 to initially protect an 80-acre parcel with a large concentration of dinosaur fossils and was enlarged in 1938, again by presidential proclamation, to 210,000 acres, which included the 2,500-foot-deep canyons of the Green and Yampa rivers. The enabling proclamation stated that the purpose of the monument was to provide protection and public enjoyment of these unique resources. The park has one of the world's largest concentrations of Jurassic-period dinosaur fossils, partially exposed and protected at a visitor center; it has many spectacular 1,000-year-old Indian rock art sites, and ecologically it covers intermediate elevations ranging from desert conditions to 9,000-foot alpine peaks. Over 329,000 recreation visits to the monument were made in 2001, with most of these people going to the dinosaur fossil bone quarry, while over 12,000 people a year raft or kayak the Green and Yampa rivers.[5] The following sections provide a historical perspective of the creation, uses, management issues, and lessons learned in these protected areas over the last 120 years.

Results

From the late 1800s through the 1920s, protected areas were characterized by exploratory expeditions, the first tourist arrivals, and the start of developing public facilities inside parks. Yellowstone was created in part to protect it from mining, development as a railroad corridor, logging, fur trapping, and wildlife exploitation. Initially the park had to be protected by the U.S. Army from poaching. Soon after, the National Park Service (NPS) took over management of the park and tourists started arriving, but even by 1900, much of the backcountry was unknown and received little public use. Trains and horse-drawn coaches provided access for adventurous travelers. The park's first superintendent, Stephen Mather, believed that in order to protect the park over the long term, he needed to solicit the support of wealthy patrons and increase the number of visitors. He hosted industrialists and secured funds and promises to jointly develop the park to bring more visitors as well as to protect it. To encourage visitation, the NPS undertook two actions that have had far-reaching implications. The first was artificially increasing populations of charismatic animal species, such as elk, through winter feeding and killing of predators, such as wolves.[6] Second, they built upscale lodges, visitor centers, and public facilities inside the protected area at the Old Faithful Geyser because few available public facilities existed outside the park and it was a long ride to the nearest town.

Dinosaur National Monument was created in 1915 to protect the rich deposits of dinosaur fossils from exploitation by both scientific institutions and museums as well as private entrepreneurs. Ranchers had established cattle and sheep operations in the canyon country of Dinosaur by the late 1800s. Fur trappers eliminated river otters and nearly did the same with beavers along the Green and Yampa rivers during the late 1800s and early 1900s. The Ute Indians, who had lived in the region prior to European American immigration, were pushed farther and farther back by settlers. U.S. Army troops built forts to protect settlers and later forced the Indians onto reservations. Major John Wesley Powell in 1869 was the first white man to conduct a scientific exploration of the Green River by boat. Tourist visitation to what was to become the park was almost nonexistent except for some hunting since the area was unknown to the general public and inaccessible.

The time from 1930 to 1950 for western protected areas was a period of national turmoil. A severe economic depression and a world war greatly reduced visitation, which rose dramatically in the 1950s in the era of two-week family vacations and long road trips in a station wagon. Yellowstone National Park saw the establishment of nearby interstate highways and "gateway" communities that started to provide tourist services and accommodations. Railroads and improved highways to parks reduced travel time significantly, thus allowing more Americans access. More visitor centers, campgrounds, and small villages were built within the park, and the first signs of resource deterioration due to recreation use started to appear. Animal species experienced die-offs, but recreation use, compared to current levels, was still quite low. Hunting of elk and deer had become very popular in areas surrounding the park. Despite laws prohibiting hunting in Yellowstone, hunting outside it impacted wildlife in the park due to wildlife migration and control of predators.

Figure 86. Each year dozens of raft trips on the Green River through Dinosaur National Monument begin at the Lodore Campground and the Canyon of Lodore, yet because of careful rules and regulations, the river never seems crowded. All motorized watercraft are banned, and visitors can experience silence, solitude, and darkness with vivid night skies. Photo by Andrew Gulliford, 2003.

The wolf and grizzly bear were eliminated by a combination of federal agents and ranching interests to minimize the loss of cattle and sheep. Management of grazing numbers inside and outside the park was begun, but little was known about its impacts on park resources. Stocking of nonnative trout began in several lakes and streams to provide a better recreational fishery for tourists.

Dinosaur National Monument was enlarged in 1938 to protect the 2,500-foot-deep canyons of the Green and Yampa rivers, thus making it one of the larger national parks in the West. To gather local support for the park expansion, the NPS had to allow existing grazing patterns but established a time frame to phase out grazing over a long period. A number of fish species native to the Green had evolved with natural river conditions of high, muddy spring flows and low, clear fall and winter flows, but development of western agriculture and urban areas required consistent water supplies. So in 1946 the U.S. Bureau of Reclamation first proposed the construction of two huge dams in the middle of the monument, which would have flooded almost all of the bottomland of the canyons. Since this would have set a precedent for dams within a national park and gutted the park, the proposal was controversial. Local residents and politicians almost unanimously supported the dams and reservoirs for their construction and mass-tourism job potential. The canyons were steep walled and inaccessible to vehicles except in a few places, so floating the rivers was the only practical means of seeing the river corridor. But only a few explorers had run the challenging rapids in the rivers, and recreational boating in the canyons was estimated to be less than 50 people in 1950. Improved road access and national publicity had increased visitation to the fossil bone quarry, but very few visited the park during the winter months.

The period from the 1950s to 1980 was an economic and environmental boom time in the United States. After World War II economic prosperity, public confidence in the future, and a population explosion occurred, leading to an expansionist political climate. Three key environmental laws passed at the federal level greatly influenced protected areas. In 1964 Congress passed the Wilderness Act and designated federal wilderness areas, which were to be managed so as to be untrammeled by man, without permanent improvements or human habitation; to preserve their natural conditions; and to offer outstanding opportunities for solitude and primitive recreation. Motorized travel was prohibited. The 1969 National Environmental Policy Act required full disclosure in advance of potential impacts on the environment and development of alternatives for all large federal projects. This provided the public with information and got them involved in the decision-making process. The

1973 Endangered Species Act required that federal agencies identify wildlife and plant species that were at risk of extinction to prohibit actions that would further reduce populations and so that steps could be taken that would increase these species' populations to sustainable levels. The three acts were backed by stiff penalties for failure to comply and were upheld and advanced by the courts.

This legislation reflected the growing awareness by the general public that our actions as a country and people were threatening the planet's health. Newspapers began covering proposals for public lands and protected areas. The number of protected areas and tourist visitation to them grew at a tremendous rate. Military surplus vehicles provided the first four-wheel-drive cars available to the public, which expanded accessible areas. This was the birth of the off-highway-vehicle (OHV) industry and sports. The number of river rafters, who at first used military-surplus life rafts, grew at exponential rates, as did the number of backpackers. This led protected area managers to establish the first programs for limited or rationing recreation use on rivers and in wilderness areas.

Federal agencies started inventorying and actively manipulating animal and range conditions in protected areas to reduce problems created by earlier policies or to use new scientific knowledge to encourage recovery of species. Even within national parks and wilderness areas, management interventions were used to "re-establish a balance between animal populations and their environment."[7] A national policy to put out all wildland fires was continued and expanded through the highly popular Smoky the Bear television campaign. Carrying-capacity studies began to appear for everything from animals to visitors. The Recreation Opportunity Spectrum (ROS) was developed, which provided guidance for an agency to control recreation use levels, activities, and support facilities in order to provide an optimum visitor experience and a wide range of recreational opportunities. The ROS system was used to assist managers to control use and identify appropriate development levels.

Yellowstone National Park during the period of 1950 to 1980 saw a rise in conflicts between resource protection in parks, land management actions outside the parks, and increasing visitor use. The news media and a concerned public were much more aware of protected area management proposals than ever before. The public demanded involvement in the planning process, and if they felt excluded, they relied on lawsuits to be heard. The NPS decided that grazing animal populations had exceeded the range capacity, and in 1961 they rounded up and killed elk and bison. But after several events the public outcry against the killing became so great it became a political issue and the NPS ceased the killing. Instead they started relying on live trapping and removal of animals or using hunters outside the park. Later the service shifted philosophies and policies so as to attempt to manage not just species, but ecosystems. Reseeding of rangeland and prescribed burning had their starts in Yellowstone during this period, and some of the first reintroductions of native predator species into the park began.

Thousands more Americans began to enjoy park wildlife from their cars or by backpacking in Yellowstone. Recreational use exploded in the park to the point where the NPS mandated backcountry camping permits. Different zones in the park were established, and some areas were designated Wilderness under provisions of the 1964 Wilderness Act. Firefighting in wilderness was limited because only nonmotorized means could be employed, resulting in more frequent and larger wildfires. Traffic jams occurred along roads where bears or large numbers of wildlife were easy to see. Drive-in campgrounds were full during the summer, and a reservation system was established. Black bears roamed the campgrounds at night, providing unintended entertainment for campers. Four-wheel-drive and OHV ownership increased, and visitation by snowmobile during the winter became more popular. The adjacent gateway communities increased their lodging and tourist-serving amenities, and jet airplane service was begun at renovated airports, some adjacent to the park.

The deep canyons of Dinosaur National Monument are at intermediate elevations, a long distance from the sources of the Green and Yampa rivers. This, together with the monument's remote setting, made it an ideal location, from an engineering standpoint, for the water storage reservoirs proposed in the late 1940s. Only at the last possible point in the legislative process in 1956 was a bill with funding for the Echo Park dam defeated; clearly it would be extremely difficult to build a dam inside a national park. This did not stop water development interests from building Flaming Gorge dam on the Green River, just 40 miles upstream from the monument in 1962. The dam drastically altered flows of the Green from a normal spring peak of about 25,000 cubic feet/second (cfs) to about 4,500 cfs, reduced naturally high sediment loads, and had other impacts on water parameters. This led to great reductions in the number of native fish in the park as well as changes in riparian vegetation through an invasion of exotic plants. Water development projects occurred on all large rivers in the Colorado River system. Finally the other major river in the park, the Yampa, was the last free-flowing river and lower-elevation aquatic ecosystem in the five-state basin.

In 1976 the Yampa was proposed as a National Wild and Scenic River, which would have prohibited large changes in water flows. But strong local opposition defeated the measure. Opponents wanted to build two dams just upstream from the park boundary to supply proposed power plants and oil refineries. Enough support seemed to exist to also dam the Yampa, but in 1978, the U.S. Fish and Wildlife Service declared four native fish species found in the Yampa to be threatened or endangered under the Endangered Species Act. This essentially stopped the proposed dams because they would have greatly altered stream flows and fish habitat. When the NPS attempted to file for permanent instream flow rights to maintain natural flows, the petition failed, and no permanent legal protection of water flows in the monument exists other than through the Endangered Species Act.

Simultaneously in Dinosaur, much of the cattle grazing was being eliminated because of time limitations

Figure 87. River runners stand in shallow water in Echo Park with Steamboat Rock in the background. If the dam had been built, all of Echo Park and both the Green and Yampa river canyons would have been flooded. Photo by Andrew Gulliford, 2003.

and bequest provisions in the original legislation. This led to significant increases in forage production for wildlife and reintroduced bighorn sheep herds increased. Another factor greatly impacting vegetation was the start of a prescribed burn policy, where some naturally caused fires were allowed to burn under certain safer conditions. It also called for the setting of fires to achieve resource enhancement goals in areas where fire was the only feasible means of restoring rangeland conditions altered by a combination of heavy grazing and fire suppression. The pesticide DDT was discovered to be the cause of depopulation of raptor bird species: in 1976 only one known pair of nesting peregrine falcons lived in the park. With funds through the Endangered Species Act, the park began an active peregrine recovery program.

Figure 88. River runner Amy Kendziorski experiences a microclimate in a side canyon on the Green River. Photo by Andrew Gulliford, 2003.

Recreation use at the Dinosaur Fossil Bone Quarry followed the pattern of steady growth seen in other western parks during this period. An exception was the explosion of commercial and private river rafting and kayaking on the two rivers. In 1954 river boating use was about 250 use days, but it increased to over 17,000 use days by 1972. The NPS observed numerous resource impacts from this swift increase in boating and imposed a moratorium on further increases in use until research could determine a sustainable carrying capacity for the river corridors. After a number of studies were conducted, including one on boater impacts by the author,[8] the park developed a river management plan that codified a permit system maintaining boater use levels at those in 1972. It also prohibited the use of motors on boats, thus requiring rafters to go at the speed of the current. Backpacking and multiday hiking, in contrast to river boating use, did not increase much in the park due to hot summer temperatures and a lack of trails and public demand. The typical visitor to the park spent about three hours visiting the fossil quarry and Indian rock art sites, except for river runners, who average three to five days in the park.

A continued economic boom until 2001 and an energy crisis, coupled with population migration to the West and coastal areas, has placed new demands on protected area managers. Clearly a more holistic ecosystem approach to protected area management exists. Armed with trend data on natural resources, such as air and water quality, wildlife, and even noise levels, managers are intervening and altering public use patterns to maintain the overall health of the area. An explosion in the ownership of recreational vehicles, ranging from four-wheel-drive all-terrain vehicles, mountain bikes, and jet skis to luxury motor homes, has occurred, forcing managers to often limit their use. New home development has accelerated, even around rural towns, to the point were parks and protected areas are the major source of open space along the coast and in metropolitan areas.

Tourism, especially nature-based tourism, has become the largest employer in many areas. Protected areas are normally the largest tourist attraction in a region, and decisions about park management and public access are of great concern to local communities. Conflicts between local communities and managers of protected areas, such as introduction of predators or limiting grazing and the number of cars that can enter a park, have caused considerable controversy. This has led to more political pressure being exerted on park managers by legislators and administrations in Washington and less discretion being given to park superintendents. Pressure is increasing to soften the Endangered Species Act, one of the most powerful legal tools managers have to maintain ecosystem integrity.

The last 20 years at Yellowstone National Park have seen the NPS increasingly taking an ecosystems conservation strategy, in which natural processes are allowed to take their course to the extent possible. But the park has changed from pre-European conditions, and the NPS has taken actions to restore health to the resources, including the reintroduction of wolves, protection of native fishes from hybridization, and the management of herbivore wildlife numbers. The NPS has established programs to control exotic wildlife, such as New Zealand mud snails and lake trout, that impact native species. Programs to control diseases in wildlife that affect species outside the park, such as whirling disease in trout, have been undertaken. The NPS has sought to locate or direct some new tourist-serving facilities to communities outside the park and in some cases, instead of replacing out-of-date public facilities within the park, it has relocated them outside it. Threats to the park from the outside continue, including a proposed open-pit gold mine, exploration of geothermal energy resources that scientists believe are linked to the park's geysers, and increased urbanization surrounding the park.

Yellowstone management has attempted to encourage the public, who still travels overwhelmingly by private automobile, to get out of their cars and use agency-provided public transportation at crowded attractions to reduce air pollution and then to explore the park on foot. The entrance fee has increased to $20 per vehicle. The NPS has had to struggle determining if and where popular new recreation activities, such as mountain biking, are appropriate. Tourists have generally become more mechanized and gear oriented, bringing long motor homes requiring electrical hookups, driving fast snowmobiles and OHVs, and using technical rock-climbing equipment. Total use at the park has remained relatively stable for the last 10 years at about 3 million recreation visits, but the timing and duration of these visits has changed. Winter use of the park by snowmobiles has increased rapidly and, according to the NPS, beyond the capacity of the park staff and facilities to accommodate it while protecting park resources.[9] Yellowstone staff have pro-

Figure 89. College students and college graduates train to get their water safety permits so they can run rivers in the West. Here boating guides pose at the Pot Creek 2 Campsite along the Green River. In Dinosaur National Monument all campsites are heavily regulated to ensure privacy and a quality outdoor experience. Photo by Andrew Gulliford, 2003.

posed a phaseout of snowmobiles and instead the use of public snow coaches, but this is politically very controversial and may not be implemented.

At Dinosaur National Monument, threats continue of a proposed dam just upstream of the park on the Yampa River. The NPS, the State of Colorado, The Nature Conservancy, and a local advisory board have attempted to find solutions to future water needs in the Yampa basin without damming the Yampa or greatly altering natural peak flows. The U.S. Fish and Wildlife Service has sponsored extensive research on endangered fish of the Yampa and Green rivers and has required changes in release patterns from Flaming Gorge dam, upstream on the Green; built a new endangered fish hatchery; started stocking the rivers with hatchery-raised native fish; and begun programs to reduce the number of nonnative fish that are predators of the native species. But with the current national political climate efforts have been renewed to dam the Yampa upstream of the park and severely impact the last free-flowing aquatic ecosystem in the Colorado River system.

Efforts to restore peregrine falcon numbers appear to have been successful, with 15 pairs of birds nesting in the park in 2001. In keeping with park management plans[10] prescribed burns have been done and natural fires left to burn out, restoring many acres from dense forest to native grasslands. But protecting some areas of the park by designating them as wilderness was extremely controversial and lacked strong local or even statewide support.[11] One of the most controversial issues centers around a private land inholding within the park and the grazing of the owners' livestock in the park. The ranch has such strong political and local community support to increase their grazing that two park superintendents who proposed reducing grazing in the park were forced to resign in the past 10 years.

During this period Dinosaur National Monument received funding for the first time to inventory Indian archaeological resources in the park, develop protection strategies, and fund an archaeological protection ranger. An outstanding and scientifically important set of archaeological resources has been discovered. Research suggests that areas in the park were occupied over 5,000 years ago. This funding has resulted in increased educational opportunities for visitors and enhanced protection of these cultural resources.

Recreation use at Dinosaur peaked in 1994 after the dinosaur adventure movie *Jurassic Park* came out and has declined since then. Visitation patterns to the Dinosaur Quarry, which has a very strong family orientation, have been affected by lengthening of the school year and competition from other, more well-known and accessible parks and resorts. However, demand continues to rise for whitewater boating. Currently there are about seven private permit applicants for each available launch date. The recreational boating use management system has been fine-tuned, which has stabilized

Figure 90. National Park Service river ranger on the Green River in Dinosaur National Monument. Photo by Andrew Gulliford, 2003.

resource impacts and kept use to about 12,000 boaters per year. Although specialized recreation activities such as rafting continue to increase in popularity, is the downturn in park visitation at Dinosaur and the stabilization of use at Yellowstone an indication of a trend toward declining overall tourism at parks? Will the NPS actually need to be more proactive in promoting visitation in the future, especially at second-tier parks, or is this trend a welcome relief from impacts to resources?

Conclusion

Tourists, local community decision makers, and park managers must incorporate the principles of true eco- and sustainable tourism into agency and concessionaire practices. For example, minimizing adverse visitor impacts, fighting mass tourism development projects inside parks, management through an ecosystem perspective, and sharing economic benefits with local communities by contracting with small, locally based park concessions are steps that need to be taken. But history has shown that the biggest threats to our national parks come from outside them, such as the proposed Yampa River dams, just upstream of the boundary in Dinosaur National Monument. As Stewart Udall, former U.S. Secretary of the Interior and a strong conservationist, stated: "It is incumbent upon the present generation to find the courage to protect our national and global natural resources for the children and the future health of our planet."[12] Only by tourists, local community decision makers, and park managers cooperating together can we continue to enjoy visiting our threatened national parks and overcome the seemingly huge obstacles to protecting them.

Notes

1. Yellowstone National Park, *State of the Park Report*, available at http://www.nps.gov/yell/stateofthepark.htm.

2. Charles F. Wilkinson and H. Michael Anderson, *Land and Resource Planning in the National Forests* (Colevo, CA: Island Press, 1987).

3. Martha Honey, *Ecotourism and Sustainable Development* (Covelo, CA: Island Press, 1999).

4. Yellowstone, *State of the Park Report*.

5. Ibid., Dinosaur National Monument Management Plan, Denver, CO, 1986.

6. Alston Chase, *Playing God in Yellowstone* (New York: Harcourt Brace Jovanovich, 1987).

7. National Park Service, press release, Yellowstone National Park, November 14, 1961.

8. Patrick T. Tierney, *Boater Impacts on Dinosaur National Monument* (master's thesis, Colorado State University, 1979).

9. Yellowstone National Park, press release, February 27, 2002, available at http://www.nps.gov/yell/press/0227.htm.

10. NPS, Dinosaur National Monument Management Plan.

11. Doug Goodman and Daniel McCool, *Contested Landscape* (Salt Lake City: University of Utah Press, 1999).

12. Stewart L. Udall, Patricia Nelson Limerick, Charles F. Wilkinson, John M. Volkman, and Willian Kittredge, *Beyond the Mythic West* (Salt Lake City: Peregrine Smith Books, 1990).

Study Questions

1. Overall, how has the nature of visitation to protected areas changed over time?

2. What did the National Park Service do to encourage visitation to Yellowstone National Park?

3. How did Yellowstone's increasing popularity eventually damage its wilderness?

4. How did the National Environmental Protection Act and the Endangered Species Act increase public support and visitation to national parks and other protected areas?

5. What are some methods the National Park Service used to protect Yellowstone National Park?

6. Ecologically, how did the Flaming Gorge dam affect Dinosaur National Monument?

7. What measures did the National Park Service take to protect Dinosaur National Monument?

8. What are some recent challenges affecting Dinosaur National Monument? In your opinion, does the future of the park look stable or unstable? Why or why not?

"These Waters Were All Virgin"

Finis Mitchell and Wind River Wilderness, Wyoming

Jeffrey Nichols

On a summer day in 1931, six horses plodded up a rough trail, each loaded with two milk cans full of water. In each can, a thousand inch-long trout sloshed beneath a layer of burlap. When the pack train reached the shore of a small alpine lake, Finis Mitchell unloaded the cans and tipped them into the cold mountain waters, and the tiny fish dispersed into the depths.

Those fish were entering a new world. Almost none of the hundreds of lakes that dot Wyoming's Wind River range had indigenous populations of trout. In Mitchell's words, "these waters were all virgin."[1] By his reckoning, Finis stocked two and a half million trout fingerlings in 314 lakes in the 1930s. He went on to hike, climb, photograph, fish, and guide others through the region for half a century. Finis set out to make himself the range's acknowledged expert, perhaps even a legend, and he succeeded. For many hikers and fishermen, Finis remains an inspiration, a kind of Johnny Appleseed in overalls who could still be found walking his beloved range decades after his good deed. By the 1970s, some called him the "Man of the Mountains" or even "Lord of the Winds." His trout stocking was one of the things of which he was most proud.[2]

Mitchell lived long enough to see, and sometimes influence, enormous changes in the management of public lands. Some environmentalists and fisheries biologists have become convinced that introduced fish have compromised the "natural" or "wild" qualities of lakes throughout the West, and fisheries managers confront a variety of dilemmas caused by the exotics. They view Mitchell's stocking as an unfortunate anachronism. Most people, however, accept or even celebrate the presence of the descendants of his fish. Many seem to have decided that those fish are both natural and wild.

The Wind River range in west-central Wyoming contains 23 peaks above 13,000 feet and is part of the Greater Yellowstone Ecosystem. On the Pacific side of the Continental Divide, the federally designated Bridger Wilderness contains most of the lakes Mitchell stocked. Nearly all of the waters of the Bridger are part of the Green River drainage, the largest tributary of the Colorado. The steep, rocky outlets of mountain lakes often formed waterfalls that blocked native fishes from migrating upstream into those waters.[3]

The range has a long human history as a commons, perhaps as much as 14,000 years' worth, although conditions are too harsh for large, permanent populations. Archaic Indian peoples hunted and gathered edible plants there, and Shoshone bands hunted, carved tools, and walked its passes.[4] Trappers found the region rich in beaver, and several of the famous 1830s rendezvous were held on the upper Green River. By the 1870s, a few white pioneers had settled north from the railroad line, and soon ranchers were grazing cattle and sheep in the openings, parks, and meadows of the range. Its vast watersheds received federal protection when President Theodore Roosevelt added much of the range to the Yellowstone Park Timber Land Reserve. The Winds had become one of the early pieces of the permanent public domain.[5]

Finis Mitchell's family joined the small influx of immigrants in 1906. Finis's father, Henry, traded his 40-acre Missouri farm for 160 acres in Wyoming, sight unseen. Henry, his wife, Fay, seven-year-old Mary, five-year-old Finis, and toddler Dennis confronted their patch of "sagebrush and sand and junk," and Fay Mitchell begged to go back home.[6] Finis wrote years later that the Winds were already exerting a strong pull upon him: "I prayed that father would win this argument. So I would get into those massive mountains."[7]

The Mitchells scratched a precarious living from

their land, which was too high, cold, and dry for most farming. On an elk hunt in 1909, Finis climbed his first mountain and gained a memorable look at ranks of snow-capped peaks. Nearly all of the alpine lakes he could see were barren of fish, but the lower waters already contained a mix of exotic and native species, including the only indigenous trout, the Colorado River cutthroat. A neighbor taught Finis to fish, and two lifelong obsessions—climbing and fishing—were born.[8]

Wyoming's officials had decided decades earlier to maximize the production of territorial waters, and the public eagerly joined in a consensus that lasted the better part of a century. The legislature created a Board of Fish Commissioners, which eventually became the Wyoming Game and Fish Department, or WGFD. The board reported in 1883 that "a majority of our streams are sterile of good fish, whilst a remainder in many places are nearly exhausted of a once bountiful supply." They concluded that managed fishing could boost Wyoming's immigration and its infant tourist economy.[9] The board decided to "plant" exotic species, including "sunfish, wall-eyed pike and trout, carp, brook trout and bass." Fish were a crop like corn or wheat to be nurtured in the "soil" of Wyoming's waters. The territory imported rainbow, brook, and lake trout, all native to North America, along with browns from Europe, and planted them in waters throughout the territory.[10]

The first known stocking in what became the Bridger Wilderness occurred in 1907, when cutthroat trout were planted in North Fork Lake.[11] When the state fish commissioner surveyed the Wind River mountain lakes in 1914, he reported 500 fishless lakes, although several of the larger lakes along the front already had "natural" (i.e., naturally reproducing) populations of cutthroat, brook, and rainbow trout.[12] Trout fry were brought to Rock Springs by railroad and transferred to private automobiles or trucks. Local ranchers and sportsmen drove them north, accompanied by United States Forest Service rangers, who supervised the planting.[13] The region got its own branch hatchery at Daniel, Wyoming, in 1917, and the local paper

Figure 91. The photo is of one bag limit of cutthroat trout where the bag limit is eight pounds. Since the big one was six pounds, the angler could fish for a second fish or two more pounds. Such fish are not common everyday catches but are found throughout the Wind River range. Courtesy Finis Mitchell Collection, American Heritage Center, University of Wyoming, 33-522012.

issued blanket appeals to anyone willing to retrieve fry and plant them in area waters.[14] One editor grumbled about the Winds' unused fishing potential: "Her mountain lakes are well-nigh numberless. Today many . . . streams are without trout, and the number of lakes without them is appaling [sic]. . . . Fish are as necessary as scenic attractions to lure the tourist."[15]

The Mitchell family benefited from this early stocking, but by 1915, Henry had abandoned his troubled farm and brought the family to Rock Springs, where he got a mining job. When Henry became ill, Finis had to leave school after the eighth grade to find work.[16] The Union Pacific Railroad hired him in 1923, and two years later he married Emma Nelson. When the Depression hit, Finis was laid off in 1930. A family friend suggested that he open a fish camp, so Finis, Emma, and Henry Mitchell obtained a Forest Service lease to establish a camp at Mud Lake in Big Sandy Openings, just inside the boundaries of Bridger National Forest.[17] Finis quickly found, however, that only five nearby lakes had native trout, so he and his father attempted a cumbersome stocking process. They caught 17 grown cutthroats in Big Sandy Lake and packed them to nearby fishless lakes. Two years later, Finis caught one of those emigrant trout: "He looked like you had blowed him up with a pump he was so fat."[18]

Figure 92. Fishing Gorge Lake is a great reward for the effort required to get to it. It has rainbow trout, which migrated downstream from both Seneca and Hobbs lakes. Then they swam downstream into Suicide Lake. Courtesy Finis Mitchell Collection, American Heritage Center, University of Wyoming, 7-551487.

Soon after that first stocking attempt, Walter Brewer, superintendent of the Daniel hatchery, came by the camp. Brewer offered to bring fry to the Mitchells if they would plant them. Brewer obviously believed that Wyoming citizens would benefit from better fishing, and the Mitchells needed to make a living. Neither questioned the impact of exotic fish on the existing lake ecosystems. Finis was in a well-established tradition of private citizens planting state-hatched fish into lakes on the federal domain.[19]

By Finis's oft-told count, over the next seven years he and his helpers planted 314 alpine lakes, mostly in the Big Sandy, East Fork, and Boulder Creek drainages above 9,000 feet. Many other local residents stocked area waters, including Finis's brother Dennis.[20] Finis wrote that the hatchery might bring him "rainbow, cutthroat, California golden, brook, or German brown" trout. His favorite, and the favorite of many fishermen for its beauty, rarity, and excellent taste, was the California golden, native only to the Kern River watershed.[21]

When the war brought better economic times in 1940, the railroad rehired Finis and the family moved back to Rock Springs, where Finis and Emma lived for (nearly) the rest of their lives. With a steady paycheck, the mountains ceased to be the means by which Finis made a living and became again a source of beauty, spiritual solace, and recreation. As soon as the snows melted, Finis headed north on virtually every weekend and vacation.[22] He meant to do more than just enjoy the scenery, however. In 1949, he wrote that "it has been my sole ambition since I retired from the fishing business in 1937, to master this most rugged and massive of all Rocky Mountain ranges." "Master" meant hiking every trail, climbing every mountain, and exploring (and fishing) every watershed until his knowledge of the place was encyclopedic.[23]

Finis's standing as a backcountry expert grew over the decades, thanks in part to his vigorous promotion of his favorite region (and by extension himself) as well as the growing public interest in outdoor recreation. By the early 1940s, he was presenting slide shows and giving talks to local groups. Invitations came from people he had met at the fish camp or on the trail. As his reputation spread, he addressed audiences across the country.[24] Trout stocking was an important element in his story. In the same 1949 letter in which he laid out his goals, Finis was already rehearsing the legend that he would repeat countless times: "Everyone knows . . . we packed out on pack horses some 2.5 million trout with which we stocked 314 individual lakes, and from these through connecting streams, another 700 became stocked."[25]

Finis became especially well known after 1975, when he published *Wind River Trails*, the first general guidebook to the region, which includes a short autobiography. The 1970s and 1980s brought magazine and newspaper profiles, an honorary Doctorate of Law from the University of Wyoming, and awards from the Environmental Protection Agency, the Izaak Walton League, the United States Forest Service, and the state legislatures of Wyoming and California.[26] Perhaps his proudest honor was the designation of "Mitchell Peak," a Wind River mountain Finis climbed many times.[27] Finis kept running totals of his Wind River experience. In 1987, he estimated that he had hiked 15,000 miles, climbed 276 peaks, and worn out 12 cameras taking 120,000 photographs.[28] In the 1980s, age finally began to catch up with him, and by the early 1990s, he was too frail for further hiking. Finis Mitchell died on November 13, 1995, one day before his 94th birthday.[29]

Finis had been aware from an early date of the possible failures of his stocking. His son remembers catching 200 fish in a single evening in 1945 from Middle Fork Lake, which Finis had planted with brook trout. "They were starving to death. . . . These high lakes don't produce food fast enough to support a big population."[30] Finis vowed "to lure enough anglers . . . to at least partially save the millions of accumulated trout which has [sic] resulted from my stockings."[31]

By then, fish biologists had determined that high-altitude stocking should be more carefully regulated. In 1935, James Simon called for "discretion" where food was scarce and suggested taking the various species' native habitat elevations into account: cutthroat and golden trout in the highest lakes; brook or cutthroat in the middle zone; and rainbow, cutthroat, or brook in the lower waters.[32] In 1940 Simon, now the state fisheries chief, declared that his agency would no longer allow private individuals like Finis Mitchell to plant fish: "Great losses have been suffered through improper planting. Both the Federal agencies and the Fish Department have allowed such losses through distributing fish to individuals who did not give them the proper care."[33] The Game and Fish Department began to hire fisheries biologists trained in environmental science and concerned with appropriate habitats for indigenous species instead of working solely for the largest-possible catch. The long tradition of volunteers planting exotic species in all waters no longer seemed the wisest course.[34]

The higher degree of federal protection afforded Wind River lakes strengthened the emphasis upon indigenous species. On February 9, 1931 (just months before Finis Mitchell planted his first hatchery fish), the secretary of agriculture established the Bridger Primitive Area. That meant preserving the land in its wild state by banning mechanized transport and limiting permanent structures. As a practical fact, the service's management changed little, since the region received so little human traffic. As the wilderness ideal gained currency around the middle of the century through the advocacy of Robert Marshall, Aldo Leopold, and others, some considered the Winds ideal candidates for a higher level of protection. In 1957, the regional forester proposed that the area be administratively reclassified as "wilderness." Among the "outstanding features" that the forester highlighted was its fine trout fishing. The secretary of agriculture accepted the recommendation in 1960 and designated the Bridger Wilderness. When Congress passed the landmark Wilderness Act four years later, the Bridger was one of the "instant" areas created because of its existing administrative status.[35]

In one important way, the Winds do not seem to fit the famous definition of "wilderness" written into the Wilderness Act, which reads in part: "An area where the earth and its community of life are untrammeled by man . . . which is protected and managed so as to preserve its natural conditions and which . . . generally appears to have been affected primarily by the forces of nature, with the imprint of man's work substantially unnoticeable."[36] The meanings of *natural* and *nature* are various, but the Wilderness Act clearly refers to nonhuman processes or aspects of the material world.

Figure 93. Left to right: Mount Lester, Wall Mountain, Fremont Peak, Harrower, and Knife Point. Finis Mitchell wrote late in life, "I seldom go to the Wind River Range to fish anymore. My aim is to climb all the peaks to show people what is actually theirs." Courtesy Finis Mitchell Collection, American Heritage Center, University of Wyoming, 34-572660.

Research ecologist Peter B. Landres and his collaborators have proposed a useful distinction between *wild*, which they equate with *untrammeled* (defined as "unimpeded, unhampered, uncontrolled, self-willed, and free") and *natural* (for which they suggest the synonyms *native*, *aboriginal*, *indigenous*, and *endemic*). The Wilderness Act assumes that wildernesses are both "wild" and "natural."[37] Finis Mitchell's stocking helps expose some of the complications inherent in that assumption.

Like virtually every other landscape, the Bridger Wilderness contains evidence of thousands of years of human use, such as Indian lithic sites, the remnants of small dams, and trappers' cabins. And several hundred lakes contain the imprints of the work of Finis Mitchell and others. The descendents of those planted trout can hardly be considered to "trammel" the entire wilderness, but some environmentalists and biologists believe they have hindered the free action of the community of life within individual lakes.

Trout are large, voracious, and opportunistic predators that can alter the ecology of a mountain lake. Finis wrote that the lakes he stocked were "just full of water lice, leaches [sic], fresh water shrimp, and that kind of stuff."[38] As he later discovered, however, some lakes lack sufficient food for an exploding trout population. James Simon wrote that "a lake with no fish present may appear to have good food until fish are introduced, then in a short time, this food supply diminishes, leaving the fish in a semi-starved condition."[39] Fish introductions can have consequences upon existing vertebrate and invertebrate communities. For instance, trout originally planted in the 1930s in Idaho and Washington have significantly lowered the densities of amphibians.[40] Although trout-prey relationships in Wind River lakes have not been intensively studied, specialists, including WGFD biologists, believe that larger-bodied individuals within each prey species have almost certainly declined.[41]

The various trout subspecies do not necessarily coexist well. Differences in spawning season or feeding habits can result in the dominance of one and the decline or complete elimination of another. Brook trout have especially thrived, as they can spawn heavily in conditions where other subspecies do less well. More importantly, brook trout eggs and fry were more easily available than those of other species and so more widely planted.[42] In one example, James Simon found golden trout succeeding in Clear Lake in 1934. Finis Mitchell reportedly planted brooks in that lake three years earlier; today only brooks are found.[43] Where native cutthroats compete with other trout, the latter often prove hardier. Finis admitted in 1985 that he had not understood the "disasters" that brook trout could cause and advocated poisoning the unwanted fish.[44]

Some subspecies get along *too* well, however. Goldens can interbreed with rainbows, for example, producing hybrids with reduced fertility. The widely stocked Yellowstone cutthroat can interbreed with native Colorado River cutthroats.[45] While none of the trout subspecies in Wind River lakes have been listed as endangered or threatened under the Endangered Species Act, Wyoming classifies the increasingly rare Colorado River cutthroat subspecies as "sensitive."[46] The WGFD also worries that another Finis could endanger the desirable imported golden trout population. The department suggested in 1980 that "some misguided person... with a large dishpan" could catch brooks from the East Fork River and transplant them into nearby lakes, wiping out the golden trout.[47]

These problems and the considerations of the Wilderness Act brought about a major change in the management of Bridger waters. The comprehensive 1978 Bridger Wilderness Fish Management Plan established the "natural or wildfish concept" as a management goal. The WGFD defines *wild* as "a naturally reproducing fishery" without further stocking.[48] By the mid-1990s, WGFD stocked only nine lakes on the Bridger, all with either golden or Colorado River cutthroat, and the agency no longer stocks fishless lakes. The official Wyoming fishing regulations brochure provides a toll-free number for fishermen to report illegal fish planting ("costly to both you and the fisheries resource").[49]

For a few people, however, the end of stocking is not enough. They believe that the presence of trout in Wind River lakes is unnatural and that if it were politically possible to do so, those fish should be removed.[50] Such removal, however, would entail further human manipulation of the lakes through poisoning or other methods, compromising the wildness of the region and possibly injuring other plant and animal species.[51]

Those who regret the stocking of Wind River lakes are almost certainly in the minority. Most people familiar with Finis's story take, at worst, a "what's done is done" attitude. Mitchell's actions, after all, were in a well-established tradition of developing fisheries in as many waters as possible, and he acted with the support of the WGFD, the United States Forest Service, and public opinion long before the Wind Rivers were designated wilderness. To those who protest the ecological damage wrought on the indigenous flora and fauna, Wyoming officials note that more than half of the lakes on the Bridger Wilderness are still fishless, just as "in their pristine state."[52] The plight of the fairy shrimp or the caddis fly has not yet received much attention.

Other people are much more enthusiastic about Finis's stocking. In the 1930s, stocking hundreds of lakes for a handful of hikers seemed quixotic, and as a dedicated backpacker, Finis Mitchell was unusual. Only 560 persons reportedly visited the Bridger Primitive Area in 1936, and fewer than 100 of those traveled on foot. By the 1970s, the boom in outdoor recreation made Finis virtually a prophet for the thousands who came to hike and fish the range.[53] Today about 300,000 people visit the Bridger Wilderness annually, probably half of whom carry a rod and reel. Fishing for trout in the glorious alpine scenery is one of the Wind's main attractions.[54]

Many people seem to have reached an unspoken consensus that Wind River fish are both "natural" and "wild" and thus in keeping with the Wilderness Act. By the time the area was designated "wilderness," many generations of fish had spawned, grown, and died since Finis's 1930s plantings, in many lakes without any further stocking. By Peter Landres's definition and the WGFD's classification, those descendants are indeed "natural," that is, native born. And the department has declared those fish to be "wild" under their policy of no further stocking; that is, no more human manipulation other than fishing. Finis himself drew a revealing distinction between Wind River lakes and the Flaming Gorge reservoir: "They keep dumping in more and more fish all the time [into Flaming Gorge].

And that's sort of a man-made condition. While this up here is a natural condition."⁵⁵

The consensus on Wind River trout has been a useful one: it helped Finis burnish his credentials as a conservationist, it helped wilderness advocates garner support for statutory protection, and it served to promote Wyoming fishing and tourism. In many ways, Finis Mitchell's long, multifaceted relationship with the Wind River mountains paralleled the nation's complicated relationship with wilderness. From an early age, Finis took much-needed food from the Winds to supplement his family's marginal farming, like millions of other Americans. At another desperate time, he manipulated the ecosystems of mountain lakes to make them provide him a livelihood and recreation for those to come, as many others had done in other waters. But throughout his life, the Winds also meant beauty, spiritual solace, and recreation. By 1964, enough Americans shared Finis's taste for the mountains to make them a "wilderness" in law, a wilderness that Mitchell had helped to create.

Notes

1. Finis Mitchell, *Wind River Trails* (Salt Lake City: Wasatch Publishers, 1975), 8.

2. See, for example, James R. Udall, "Finis Mitchell, Lord of the Winds," *Audubon* (July 1986): 72–88; Mitchell, *Wind River Trails*, 3.

3. Joe Kelsey, *Wyoming's Wind River Range* (Helena: American and World Geographic Publishing, 1988), 7–12, 32–35; Ron Remmick, "Managing the BWA Fisheries," n.p., 1994, copy in author's possession.

4. James R. Schoen, "Archeological Investigations in the High Country: Survey Results from the Bridger, Gros Ventre and Teton Wilderness Areas, Bridger-Teton National Forest," n.p., April 1998; copy in author's possession, 2; D. B. Shimkin, "Wind River Shoshone Ethnogeography," *Anthropological Records* 5, no. 4 (Berkeley and Los Angeles: University of California Press, 1947), 245–84.

5. Robert G. Rosenberg, *Wyoming's Last Frontier: Sublette County, Wyoming: A Settlement History* (Glendo, WY: High Plains Press, 1990), 17–41, 85–86; Dan Flores, *The Natural West: Environmental History in the Great Plains and Rocky Mountains* (Norman: University of Oklahoma Press, 2001), 119–22.

6. Finis Mitchell, interview by Mark Junge, July 3, 1989, Oral History 2010, tape recording, Wyoming State Archives, Cheyenne [hereafter cited as OH 2010]; Finis Mitchell, "My Life," a fragmentary manuscript transcribed by Sandra Snow, e-mail to author of July 16, 2002 [hereafter cited as Mitchell, "My Life"].

7. Mitchell, "My Life."

8. Mitchell, *Wind River Trails*, 6; OH 2010; and Mitchell, "My Life."

9. Quoted in Neal Blair, *The History of Wildlife Management in Wyoming* (Cheyenne: Wyoming Game and Fish Department, 1987), 22.

10. Ibid., 24, 30; Robert Henry Smith, "Rainbow Trout," in *Trout*, ed. Judith Stolz and Judith Schnell (Harrisburg, PA: Stackpole Books, 1991), 304–23; William A. Flick, "Brook Trout," in *Trout*, 196–207; Charles Harold Olver, "Lake Trout," in *Trout*, 286–99; and Robert A. Bachman, "Brown Trout," in *Trout*, 208–29.

11. Ralph Hudelson, Galen Boyer, and Jack McMillan, "High Mountain Lake and Stream Survey of the Bridger Wilderness Area: 1969–1975," Completion Report: D. J. Report F-1-R-8; F-1-R-9; F-1-R-10; F-1-R-11; F-1-R-12 (Cheyenne: Wyoming Game and Fish Department Fish Division, 1980) [hereafter cited as Hudelson, Boyer, and McMillan], c.

12. Robert W. Wiley, "Wyoming Fish Management, 1869–1993," administrative report for Wyoming Game and Fish Department Fish Division, n.p., July 1993, copy in author's possession, 5.

13. For examples of planting, see *Pinedale Roundup*, March 16, 1911, September 25, 1913, October 7, 1915.

14. *Pinedale Roundup*, April 25, 1924, September 30, 1926, August 9, 1928.

15. *Pinedale Roundup*, January 18, 1923.

16. William Mitchell (Finis's son), interview by author, July 16, 2002, Pinedale, tape recording, in author's possession.

17. Mitchell, *Wind River Trails*, 7; Rock Springs *Daily Rocket-Miner*, December 2, 1987; and OH 2010.

18. Udall, "Finis Mitchell," 79.

19. OH 2010; *Pinedale Roundup*, September 25, 1930, December 31, 1931.

20. Alta Faler (Dennis's daughter), personal communication with author, July 8, 2002; Anna Dew (Finis's daughter), interview by author, July 30, 2002, by telephone from Glendive, Montana, tape recording, in author's possession;

Irv Lozier interview; Mitchell, *Wind River Trails*, 81; and OH 2010.

21. Mitchell, *Wind River Trails*, 8; "Finis Mitchell records," n.p., ca. 1972, copy in author's possession [hereafter cited as "Finis Mitchell records"]; OH 2010; and Phil Pister, "Golden Trout," in *Trout*, 280–85.

22. OH 2010; William Mitchell interview; and Anna Dew interview.

23. *Pinedale Roundup*, March 3, 1949.

24. For example, see Superior Wisconsin *Evening Telegram*, September 28, 1979.

25. *Pinedale Roundup*, March 3, 1949.

26. Many of these honors hang in "Mitchell's Dining Room" in Western Wyoming Community College, Rock Springs.

27. Rock Springs *Daily Rocket-Miner*, August 13, 1975.

28. *Daily Rocket-Miner*, December 2, 1987.

29. *Pinedale Roundup*, November 23, 1995.

30. William Mitchell interview. See also "Finis Mitchell records"; OH 2010.

31. *Pinedale Roundup*, March 3, 1949.

32. James R. Simon, "A Survey of the Waters of the Wyoming National Forest," Department of Commerce, Bureau of Fisheries, n.p., April 1935, copy in author's possession, 11, 13.

33. Ibid., "Report of the Fish Division," in Robert Grieve, *Biennial Report of the Wyoming Game and Fish Commission, 1939–1940*, n.p., 32.

34. Blair, *History of Wildlife Management*, 77, 138; Wiley, "Wyoming Fish Management," 7–10; Fred Eiserman (fisheries biologist and Wyoming fisheries resource manager in the 1950s), interview by author, July 29, 2002, by telephone from Casper, tape recording, in author's possession; Tom Bell (former fisheries biologist in late 1940s), interview by author, July 29, 2002, by telephone from Lander, tape recording, in author's possession; and Mike Stone (Wyoming's Chief of Fisheries in 2002), personal communication with author, July 31, 2002.

35. Albert Wm. Collotzi, Don Bartschi, Glen Dunning, and Ralph Hudelson, "Bridger Wilderness Fish Management Plan," July 1978 (revised), 1–2 [hereafter cited as Collotzi et al.], 1–2.

36. Wilderness Act, *Statutes at Large*, 78, section 2 (c), 891.

37. Peter B. Landres et al., "Natural and Wildness: The Dilemma and Irony of Managing Wilderness," *USDA Forest Service Proceedings* RMRS-P-15-VOL-5, 2000, 377–81.

38. Mitchell, *Wind River Trails*, 8.

39. Simon, "Survey of the Waters of the Wyoming National Forest," 7, 12; O. H. Robertson, "An Ecological Study of Two High Mountain Trout Lakes in the Wind River Range, Wyoming," *Ecology* 28, no. 2 (April 1947): 97–98; and Hudelson, Boyer, and McMillan, Appendix A, 1.

40. David S. Pilliod and Charles R. Peterson, "Local and Landscape Effects of Introduced Trout on Amphibians in Historically Fishless Watersheds," *Ecosystems* 4 (2001): 322–33.

41. Kurt Nelson (WGFD fisheries biologist), interview by author, July 17, 2002, Pinedale, tape recording, in author's possession; Debra Patla, "Amphibians of the Bridger-Teton National Forest," Greater Yellowstone Ecosystem Amphibian Project, n.p., Herpetology Laboratory, Idaho State University, February 22, 2000, copy in author's possession.

42. Flick, "Brook Trout," 199–202.

43. Simon, "Survey of the Waters of the Wyoming National Forest," 10; "Finis Mitchell records"; and Rebecca Woods, *Walking the Winds: A Hiking and Fishing Guide to Wyoming's Wind River Range*, 2nd ed. (Jackson, WY: White Willow, 1998), 116.

44. *Pinedale Roundup*, September 19, 1985.

45. Robb F. Leary, "Why Not Stock?" in *Trout*, 346–50; Patrick C. Trotter, *Cutthroat: Native Trout of the West* (Boulder: Colorado Associated University Press, 1987), 248, 264.

46. Wyoming Game and Fish Department, "Wyoming Game and Fish Department Comprehensive Management and Enhancement Plan for Colorado River Cutthroat Trout in Wyoming," 1987; "Conservation Agreement and Strategy for Colorado River Cutthroat Trout (*Oncorhynchus clarki pleuriticus*) in the States of Colorado, Utah, and Wyoming," March 1999.

47. Hudelson, Boyer, and McMillan, 2.10.

48. Collotzi et al., 3; "Bridger Wilderness Action Plan and Implementation Schedule," March 1995, 23–25.

49. Remmick, "Managing the BWA Fisheries," 3; Wyoming Game and Fish Commission, "2002 through 2003 Wyoming Fishing Regulations," 17.

50. Remmick, "Managing the BWA Fisheries"; David Hohl (former recreation supervisor for the Bridger National Forest), personal communication with author, July 3, 2002; William Worf (board president of Wilderness Watch and former supervisor of the Bridger National Forest), interview by author, June 24, 2002, by telephone from Missoula, tape recording, in author's possession; and Kurt Nelson interview.

51. Landres et al., "Naturalness and Wildness," 377–81.

52. Remmick, "Managing the BWA Fisheries."

53. *Pinedale Roundup*, December 3, 1936; Roderick Frazier

Nash, *Wilderness and the American Mind*, 4th ed. (New Haven, CT: Yale University Press), 316–19.

54. Untitled draft history of Bridger-Teton National Forest, personal communication with author from James R. Schoen, July 10, 2002.

55. Finis Mitchell testimony, May 31, 1973, tape recording, Pinedale Resource Area MFP, Bureau of Land Management.

Study Questions

1. Why are environmentalists worried about stocking lakes with "exotic" species of fish?

2. Why did Wyoming's Board of Fish Commissioners decide to plant new species of fish in their lakes?

3. How did the guidebook *Wind River Trails* come to be written?

4. Why do the Wind River Mountains not seem to fit the definition of wilderness as defined in the Wilderness Act?

5. What are the differences among the different subspecies of trout, as mentioned in this essay? Why are these differences important?

6. What, if anything, is the answer presented in this essay to the problem of stocking fish in wilderness areas?

"Where Man Is a Visitor"

The Wilderness Act as a Case Study in Western Public History

Steven C. Schulte

On September 3, 1964, President Lyndon Johnson signed the Wilderness Act into law. Few pieces of legislation had ever faced such a long and torturous route to passage. The dream of a federal wilderness bill extended back to the 1920s, when then United States Forest Service ranger Aldo Leopold first convinced his bureaucratic masters to manage portions of the Gila National Forest as wilderness. While some federal land would be managed as de facto wilderness, advocates for wilderness wanted to expand the amount of wild land as well as to increase its level of protection. Sierra Club leader David Brower believed that by calling for a Wilderness Act, conservationists "wanted something that would give wilderness a stronger kind of protection."[1] Managing land as wilderness, without the protection of a strong federal statute, had made it subject to changing political winds, administrative caprice, and lack of systematic treatment.

Popular attitudes toward wilderness were changing throughout the United States in the post–World War II era as increasing numbers of urban Americans sought the solace of the great outdoors. Advocates believed that by establishing a national wilderness preservation system (NWPS), the nation would have a place to enjoy the outdoors, free from the works of man, for generations to come. As Wilderness Society leader Howard Zahniser phrased it, wilderness "perpetuates the choice that Americans have always had, the choice of going to the wilderness if they wish." Young people, especially, "should know the wilderness."[2]

While the movement for the Wilderness Act is a heroic story central to understanding the emergence of America's modern environmental movement, what is usually forgotten or discounted is the strenuous opposition to the bill that persisted until its passage in 1964. A balanced retelling of the wilderness movement must account for this opposition and interpret what it says about America's political and economic culture from World War II through the 1960s. Opponents like Congressman Wayne Aspinall (D-CO), who led the movement to reshape the bill more to the liking of traditional users of Western public lands, saw most early versions of the Wilderness Bill as threatening to the rural West's way of life. Aspinall and many other Westerners saw the land as a source of capital and never understood wilderness proponents' desire to "lock land up" as federally protected wilderness.

The Wilderness Act presents a particularly unique challenge to historians working in public history or in the realm of public policy. However, before assessing the dimensions of this challenge, it is imperative to briefly discuss what the Wilderness Act is and is not. The Wilderness Act created the National Wilderness Preservation System, initially an area of more than 9 million acres, with much more land slated to pass into the system after a review process. Additional parcels of land had to receive the backing of both houses of Congress and pass as a congressional bill. No land could be added by executive order or what many opponents feared would be administrative fiat. The act also allowed for many existing multiple-use activities upon wilderness lands. Mineral exploration in the wilderness system was allowed until 1984. Reservoirs and dams could still be permitted in wilderness areas if a president deemed it in the greater national interest. The Wilderness Act of 1964 was thus a compromise measure. It did not include as much initial land in the system as its proponents had originally hoped. Nor would it be easy to add additional wilderness parcels to the nation's wilderness system. On the other hand, opponents of the bill had doubted the need for such a bill in the first place. Many members of the federal public land management bureaucracy believed that much of the potential wilderness land was being managed as de facto wilderness, thus making this additional degree of legislative protection unnecessary.³

The Wilderness Act symbolized the tensions inherent in America's attitudes toward wild lands in the mid-twentieth century. It was both a great environmental landmark and a stirring testimony to America's ambivalence toward the land and wild things. However, it is rarely interpreted this way. Instead, it is usually cast as an unmitigated triumph for the environmental movement.

Some scholars see the bill as the real starting point for the 1960s and 1970s environmental movement. For the first time, this great industrial nation took stock of itself and decided to keep a portion of its lands free and undeveloped. As the act says, wilderness, in contrast with those areas where man and his works "dominate the landscape is hereby recognized as an area where the earth and its community of life are untrammeled by man, where man himself is a visitor who does not remain." Some modern commentators have assessed the bill as a disappointment, as too "watered down" and lacking in the crucial idealism that had given birth to the bill in the first place. It is challenging to find two people who agree on the bill's significance in part because its legacy is always changing. As America urbanized, it seemed to value its wild lands all the more. Significantly, even though only 9 million acres were originally included in the NWPS, the rigorous process for adding additional lands has allowed for the inclusion of more than 100 million federally protected acres today.⁴

The Wilderness Act and Public Historians

The many federal agencies who administer the nation's plethora of public land laws would benefit from an understanding of the historical circumstances surrounding the enactment and implementation of major land legislation. Far too often historical sites, museums, and even internal bureaucratic histories simply discuss the legislation as it actually passed Congress and ignore the context for the bill's passage.

This would be similar to a civil rights museum failing to address the larger nineteenth- and twentieth-century segregation context in an exhibit commemorating monumental bills like the Civil Rights Act of 1964 or the Voting Rights Act of 1965. In 1986, Richard E. Neustadt and Ernest R. May asserted that historical thinking benefited public policy makers in several concrete ways. An understanding of historical experience can offer policy makers a chance to make a better informed decision; understanding the circumstances surrounding the formulation of a public law can help contemporary officials understand what legislators and other pressure groups hoped to accomplish with the law's initial formulation.⁵ Public land officials who staff the agencies primary responsible for implementing the Wilderness Act, the United States Forest Service (USFS), National Park Service (NPS), and the Bureau of Land Management (BLM) understand the content of the Wilderness Act of 1964 but could better interpret the spirit of the law by understanding its rigorous route to passage and the legislative give-and-take involved in its formulation. Similarly, museum curators and interpretive park rangers working in the public land states of the American West could better bring the land's history to life with this knowledge.

How, then, do the Wilderness Act and public history intersect? What can knowledge of the Wilderness Act's complicated legacy offer to public historians in the American West? First, its route to passage needs to be assessed. In far too much of the historical literature, the passage of the Wilderness Act is trumpeted as only a great achievement for wilderness preservation. This is not incorrect, but it is somewhat misleading. A perceptive public historian should examine the rich strands of political culture that produced the law. Early drafts of the Wilderness Bill would have given unprecedented power to conservation laymen, professionals, and the president's executive caprice to craft a large and comprehensive wilderness system. The role of Congress was minimized. Instead of crafting bills creating wilderness areas, Congress could only pass bills objecting to specific areas already slated for inclusion by administrative fiat.⁶

The political backdrop for the introduction of the early wilderness legislation is also rich and interesting. In the late 1950s, the Wilderness Society, the Sierra Club, and other prominent organizations were energized following the defeat of a proposal to build two dams and reservoirs within Dinosaur National Monument in Colorado and Utah. For the first time, the power of the conservation movement had impacted the national political agenda. Dam builders, federal bureaucrats, and Western politicians now had to cope with this new force, soon to be called environmentalism, rooted in distant urban (and often eastern) locales. In the early 1960s, another development rebounded to the advantage of wilderness advocates. The new administration of President John F. Kennedy and his secretary of the interior, former Arizona congressman Stewart L. Udall, embraced the measure as part of their ambitious conservation program. The Kennedy administration was anxious to capitalize on the political potential of the postwar nation's conservation awareness.⁷

Because so much of the nation seemed to support the new conservation programs of both the Kennedy and Johnson administrations, the strong opposition to the Wilderness Bill is often forgotten. Not only was the opposition to the Wilderness Bill vigorous and vocal, it shaped the bill's ultimate form as much as the bill's original proponents had. Between 1956 and 1964, Congress devoted more time and effort to the Wilderness Bill than on any measure in American conservation history.⁸ Nine separate hearings were held on the bill, and it has been estimated that the original bill was rewritten and resubmitted to House and Senate committees at least 66 different times. The bill never faced huge obstacles in the Senate. With strong non-Western support and a cadre of liberal Westerners who supported conservation legislation, the bill passed the Senate several times before the House began to take the bill seriously. With the route to passage in the Senate assured, the national wilderness spotlight passed to the House of Representatives and the House Interior Committee, chaired by Colorado congressman Wayne N. Aspinall.⁹

Congressman Aspinall had a long record of opposition to certain types of conservation legislation. A tireless advocate of water resource development, Aspinall saw most preservation-minded conservation programs such as park creation or expansion or protection of scenic resources as a wasteful impediment to national progress. While he loved his home district's astounding mountain and desert vistas, this hard-nosed former schoolteacher and fruit grower never doubted that the land's natural resources should serve the economic needs of the people of his congressional district. The American West, to Aspinall, was a vast storehouse of raw materials. During his lengthy tenure in Congress, he would repeatedly attempt to open up the region's public lands to use—for the benefit of the nation and, of course, the individuals who lived and worked in the region. To Aspinall, conservation meant careful husbandry, not protection or isolation of resources. The Palisade, Colorado, congressman always regarded himself as a mainstream conservationist. This doctrine emphasized the wise use of resources as articulated by the Progressive Era' exponent of utilitarian conservation, Gifford Pinchot.¹⁰

Elected to Congress in 1948 from a House district that stretched from the Utah border to the central Colorado mountains and from the Wyoming border to New Mexico, Aspinall's huge territory was home to many timber and mining companies that felt threatened by the Wilderness Bill's potential to stymie access to natural resources on public lands. Aspinall became chairman of the House Interior and Insular Affairs Committee in 1959. Under his leadership, the House Interior and Insular Affair Committee would dominate congressional natural-resource policy reclamation and environmental policy for the next 14 years. No federal conservation law of any importance would pass Congress unless it first passed Wayne Aspinall's committee. With the Kennedy administration favoring

Figure 94. Trapper's Lake east of Meeker, Colorado, is considered the "cradle of American wilderness" because it was here that Arthur Carhart, a young landscape architect working for the U.S. Forest Service, decided that this landscape should remain pristine, though his seasonal job was to survey the lakeshore for summer cabin sites. No U.S. government official had ever suggested leaving a landscape alone before. Photo by Andrew Gulliford, 1994.

action on a wilderness bill and a growing national constituency supporting conservation legislation in general, Aspinall and other Western wilderness foes faced a precarious situation. Under mounting pressure to act, Aspinall made a determination to use his entrenched position as House Interior Committee chairman to slow the time frame for passing a wilderness bill and to reshape the legislation into a form that his district and much of the rural West could live with. From 1961 to 1964, Aspinall used every available parliamentary tactic at his disposal to slow wilderness consideration, redesign the bill, and gain major concessions for his position from wilderness advocates.

Aspinall initially promised to act upon the Wilderness Bill only after the Senate had passed it first and after the Outdoor Recreational Resources Review Commission (ORRRC) had made its recommendations. This tactic bought him several years. But by 1962, the Senate had passed its version of a wilderness bill and the influential ORRRC has reported its findings back to Congress, meeting its mandate set in the late 1950s to make recommendations about America's outdoor and recreational resources. Both the Senate's actions and the ORRRC's findings had raised expectations for Aspinall and the House to move constructively toward passing a wilderness bill.[11] Other events added to the pressure on Aspinall and the House of Representatives. In 1962 Rachel Carson published *Silent Spring*, a book that sensitized millions of Americans to the importance of environmental harmony. The same year President Kennedy hosted the White House Conference on Conservation, a meeting that helped to link his name ever more firmly with the growing environmental movement. Aspinall's next tactic was to work in committee during the fading months of the 87th Congress in 1962 to report a wilderness bill but one written by himself, favorable to Western resource users and totally unsatisfactory to most conservationists. Aspinall's action outraged David Brower of the Sierra Club, Howard Zahniser of the Wilderness Society, and scores of newspaper editors. The Colorado legislator appeared to be the principal obstacle between the desires of the American people and a wilderness bill.

While the larger nation was preoccupied with the growing civil rights crisis, in the American West, the wilderness battle burned almost as strong. By 1963, writer Paul Brooks in *Harper's Magazine* assaulted Aspinall's slowdown tactics in "Congressman Aspinall vs. The People of the United States". Brooks argued that one stubborn politician, Wayne Aspinall, represented large corporate interests that wanted easy access to public land resources. As a result, "our remaining wilderness" was gravely endangered. In April 1963,

Figure 95. A drawing of the Flat Tops Wilderness from Northern Ute cultural leader Clifford Duncan expresses Duncan's view of the Trapper's Lake area as a sacred place, which it is to Ute people. Arthur Carhart, who proposed to his supervisor that Trapper's Lake be left alone and pristine, may have been visited by a Ute spirit that caused a radical change in Carhart's thinking. All his life he spoke of the "voice of the wilderness," but a close reading of his journals in the Western History Collections at the Denver Public Library reveals that something profoundly moving happened to him on the shores of Trapper's Lake. Clifford Duncan and other Utes believe that a Ute spirit visited Carhart, who then advocated for wilderness protection of important landscapes within the U.S. Forest Service. Courtesy of the artist and the Center of Southwest Studies, Fort Lewis College.

Figure 96. Long known for its excellent trout fishing, a proud fly fisherman poses with his catch at Trapper's Lake, ca. 1920. Photo courtesy the Center of Southwest Studies, Fort Lewis College.

more pressure was focused on Aspinall and the House when the new 88th Congress approved the Senate's wilderness bill again by a wide margin.[12]

With pressure to act growing all the time, Aspinall laid out his requirements for cooperation with wilderness advocates: a bill that would "respect multiple purpose uses," but more importantly (and in contrast to the Senate's version), a bill that kept "affirmative Congressional action in future wilderness area establishment." Congress, not the president or some advisory board, would determine the status of future wilderness land parcels. To Aspinall these requirements were key. Without a wilderness bill that was friendly to existing public land uses, the West, where most of the wilderness lands would be, would face "the biggest land grab in history."[13]

Aspinall had made his demands. Wilderness advocates could either pare down their more environmentally friendly Senate bill or face more obstruction and

Figure 97. The Flat Tops Wilderness is clearly visible from this view of the Chinese Wall. An ancient Ute Indian trail takes visitors from the lake up into the higher reaches of the wilderness. Photo courtesy the Center of Southwest Studies, Fort Lewis College.

stalling from the House Interior Committee. By 1963, Aspinall had yet another idea that he hoped would rationalize the maze of laws that guided the nation's interaction with the public lands: the creation of a Public Land Law Review Commission to assess the hundreds of existing land laws and recommend changes and revisions to them. From this point forward, the fate of both the Wilderness Bill and the Public Land Law Review Commission would be intertwined. It is not an exaggeration to say that one of the prices Aspinall "charged" for action on wilderness legislation was the passage of a bill creating the Public Land Law Review Commission.

In 1964, both laws would pass Congress. Aspinall, because of his commanding position as chair of the Interior Committee, controlled the timing and content of both pieces of legislation. In early 1965 he would be named the chairman of the Public Land Law Review Commission. The Wilderness Act was hailed immediately as a victory for the emerging power of the environmental movement. While this is true to a degree, the Wilderness Act of 1964 provides stark testimony to the ability of a well-placed congressman to impose his vision on the West. The early drafts and Senate versions of the bill gave the advantage in access and use to recreational land users. In his years of stalling and revising, Aspinall redressed the philosophical balance in the bill toward multiple use and the traditional Western users of public lands. Aspinall's conduct throughout the long wilderness battle is best understood by sensing the outrage many Westerners have often felt when well-funded, urban, and eastern-based environmentalists have attempted to force their values on the peoples of the rural West. This sense of anger and outrage still animates the West from time to time, most notably whenever a president uses the power of the Antiquities Act of 1906 to create a national monument or, in a larger and more organized way, during the Sagebrush Rebellion of the late 1970s and early 1980s.

The Wilderness Act as a Living Law

While the context for the bill's passage is essential for those federal, state, and environmental organization bureaucrats working with the law, it is also important to examine how the law's significance has changed in the decades since its passage. Laws as significant and symbolic as the Wilderness Act take on new meanings over the decades. The mythology surrounding the Wilderness Act has already been addressed: it has been regarded as one of the first and greatest triumphs for America's nascent environmental movement. Contrary to the mythology, it was a product of great and careful compromise and, in final form, reflected the fears and needs of Western land users as much as those who wanted to lock up and preserve the land. Still, when the smoke cleared after the legislative battle, advocates of wilderness preservation could take heart that the United States had finally agreed to keep a portion of its lands substantially wild.[14]

Over the years, wilderness as a concept has taken on a stronger meaning than anyone connected with the original struggle for the act could have envisioned. An increasingly urban America has continued to look to wilderness for intellectual and physical sustenance. By the 1970s, issues relating to wilderness continued to inspire the American public. As historian Hal Rothman noted, "Wilderness had an iconographic meaning that gave it millions of armchair supporters."[15]

The original Wilderness Act set the parameters for defining wilderness. Over the years critics have charged that federal land-management agencies have used unreasonably strict or "purist" interpretations of the act to limit the number of new wilderness areas. Under the Wilderness Act, wilderness is defined as "an area of undeveloped federal land retaining its primeval character and influence . . . which generally appears to have been primarily affected by the forces of natures, with the imprint of man's work substantially unnoticeable." The definition, it should be noted, does not require an absolute primeval or pristine appearance, with no evidence of human activities. Obviously human imprints cannot dominate any land parcels being considered for inclusion in the National Wilderness Preservation System. The degree of wilderness purity thus remains a point of strong contention.[16]

A second development of recent note concerns land under the purview of the Bureau of Land Management. The original Wilderness Act directed both the United States Forest Service and the National Park Service to inventory lands under their jurisdiction for possible inclusion in the National Wilderness Preservation System. The BLM, the nation's largest federal landlord agency, was excluded from the original Wilderness Act. In part this was because the BLM had yet to have its ultimate mission clarified: was it merely a transitory holding agency that would ultimately sell the lands under its control? Might it have a permanent role in managing the 267 million acres of lands it controlled in the Western states and Alaska? In 1976 Congress enacted the Federal Land Policy and Management Act (FLPMA), the first comprehensive organic law to define the BLM's future role. Under Section 603, the FLPMA ordered the BLM to identify and inventory all the public lands having wilderness characteristics (as defined by the Wilderness Act) and study them for possible inclusion as wilderness: 27.5 million acres in 865 different areas were classified as Wilderness Study Areas (WSAs) deserving further wilderness consideration. The FLPMA required that the BLM manage the WSAs "so as not to impair the suitability of such areas for preservation as wilderness." The FLPMA also required that Congress complete studies of these lands and recommend further action on their status to the president by 1991. Since then, more than 5 million acres of BLM lands have become classified as wilderness, with more likely slated for inclusion as various WSAs gain public support for federal wilderness protection. Many of the present and future battles over the application of the Wilderness Act concern lands managed by the BLM.[17] Almost every time a land parcel is recommended for federal wilderness protection, familiar battle lines form reminiscent of the original 1950s–1960s struggle to pass the Wilderness Act.

As this case study of the Wilderness Act suggests, land managers, whether they are historians, interpretive rangers, or field personnel, can all benefit from a working historical knowledge of the legislation they are to uphold. History-based policy analysis is a crucial tool for land managers.[18] Understanding the legislation's historical backdrop aids in the understanding of the social, political, and economic contexts that spawned the legislation. Western politicians are frequently viewed as pork-barrel specialists, more interested in securing profit for companies or individuals who seek to exploit the public domain. This view is far too simplistic to be sustained by an examination of the historical record. The context for the passage of the law is also important to analyze. Without an understanding of how the Wilderness Bill started out and how it was refined, reshaped, and revised, a federal land manager would have little accurate understanding of the forces that ultimately made the bill possible. As Wayne Aspinall's behavior with the Wilderness Bill indicates, no more important question than one surrounding the future of his huge district's public lands could confront a politician from a public land state. The implication of wilderness or other public land legislation was rightly regarded by many Western politicians as one of economic life or death.

It is also necessary in the case of the Wilderness Act (or any other federal land law) to understand how the policy has been implemented over time and with what results. The Wilderness Act is best regarded as a compromise measure that blended the energy of the young 1960s environmental movement with the traditional political culture of the West. But in the case of the Wilderness Act of 1964, no matter what the deep struggles were that made the act possible, once passed, the act has become a key symbol of the nation's commitment to pristine preservation.

How, then, should the Wilderness Act be regarded on the occasion of its 40th anniversary? As a vital piece of environmental legislation, to be sure, yet like most pathbreaking pieces of legislation, like the Civil Rights or Voting Rights acts of the same era, it is a law filled with compromises. However, the compromises need not be regarded as absolute imperfections. Yet some politicians who helped shape and implement the act still look back on the final form of the bill with deep regret. Stewart L. Udall, who served as secretary of the interior for most of the 1960s, still sees it as a lost opportunity. To Udall, Congressman Wayne Aspinall's power to protect the prerogatives of traditional land users carried the day in the Wilderness Act. Aspinall used his powers as a committee chair at a time when Congress permitted chairs to act in ways that today would be either unlikely or unthinkable. To Udall, Aspinall not only watered the bill down, the bill became "less than half a loaf." On the other hand, some interpretations regard the bill as a great conservation achievement, but maybe more on a symbolic level. As one popular history wrote, the bill "put the nation foursquarely in the business of forever preserving substantial areas" of wild lands. Yet another saw the act as a "signal achievement" if only because the preservation of wilderness had become a national policy.[19]

Public history field workers should view this range of opinions about the Wilderness Act as only signposts for interpretation. Public historians should also emphasize to their various constituents that the real impact of the Wilderness Act will not be felt until much later in the present century. Most social indicators point to the growing popularity of wilderness areas. As more and more Americans crowd into urban

Figure 98. Wallace Stegner and others have argued that we need wilderness to preserve American character, individuality, and spirit. Aldo Leopold argued that we need wilderness to preserve "the primitive arts," such as hunting. Here deer hunters pose with their big bucks at the Rifle, Colorado, railroad depot, ca. 1920. Photo courtesy the Center of Southwest Studies, Fort Lewis College.

and suburban environments, wilderness will likely only increase in public use and visitation. Of course, it is possible, as is the case in many of our most popular national parks, to love something to death. It is likely that usage restrictions and increased regulations will need to be added to those wanting access to wilderness areas. On its 40th anniversary, the remaining framers of the Wilderness Act still should take solace in at least two major conclusions. Few laws in American history have been passed where the advocates and opponents were more philosophically apart from each other from the start of the debate over the bill in question—and where both sides had such a great impact on the bill's final outcome. Finally, the Wilderness Bill joins a selected group of federal laws that can truly be said to have reoriented the direction of American society, calling the old ways of wild land use and destruction into question. The fact that the law remains highly controversial but continues to work is a testimony to the farsightedness and careful nature of the decade-long wrangling that produced it.

Notes

1. David R. Brower, "Environmental Activist, Publicist, and Prophet," oral history conducted by Susan R. Schrepfer, Regional Oral History Office, Bancroft Library, University of California, Berkeley, 1974–78, 64.

2. Zahniser's testimony before Congress quoted in Steven C. Schulte, *Wayne Aspinall and the Shaping of the American West* (Boulder: University Press of Colorado, 2002), 155.

3. Schulte, *Wayne Aspinall*, 161; Roderick Nash, *Wilderness and the American Mind*, 3rd ed. (New Haven: Yale University Press, 1967), 226.

4. The Wilderness Society, *The Wilderness Act Handbook* (Springfield, VA: Goetz Printing, 1998), 7.

5. Richard E. Neustadt and Ernest E. May, *Thinking in Time: The Uses of History for Decision Makers* (New York: Free Press, 1986), xxii.

6. See the discussion of the early versions of the bill in Schulte, *Wayne Aspinall*, 116–27.

7. Ibid., 85.

8. This is Roderick Nash's assertion in *Wilderness and the American Mind*, 222.

9. The first Senate wilderness bill to pass cleared the chamber by a 78–8 margin on September 6, 1961. At this point, the House versions of the bill were still languishing in committee and would do so for some time yet.

10. Schulte, *Wayne Aspinall*, 53.

11. Richard Allan Baker, *Conservation Politics: The Senate Career of Clinton P. Anderson* (Albuquerque: University of New Mexico Press, 1985), 110–13.

12. Schulte, *Wayne Aspinall*, 144–45; see Paul Brooks, "Congressman Aspinall vs. the People of the United States," *Harper's Magazine* 226 (March 1963): 60–63.

13. The Washington, D.C., *Daily News*, July 19, 1963; Grand Junction (CO) *Daily Sentinel*, June 3, 1963.

14. Nash, *Wilderness and the American Mind*, 226.

15. Hal K. Rothman, *The Greening of a Nation?: Environmentalism in the United States Since 1945* (Fort Worth: Harcourt Brace, 1998), 128–29.

16. The Wilderness Society, *The Wilderness Act Handbook*, 29–30.

17. Ibid., 37–39.

18. David B. Mock, "History in the Public Arena," in *Public History: An Introduction*, ed. Barbara J. Howe and Emory L. Kemp (Malabar, FL: Krieger Publishing Company, 1986), 407–9.

19. Stewart Lee Udall interview with Steven C. Schulte, March 31 and April 1, 1998. Interview transcript in Steve Schulte's possession, Mesa State College, Grand Junction, CO; Kirkpatrick Sale, *The Green Revolution: The American Environmental Movement, 1962–1992* (New York: Hill and Wang, 1993), 15; Ted Steinberg, *Down to Earth: Nature's Role in American History* (New York: Oxford University Press, 2002), 243.

Study Questions

1. What did advocates of the national wilderness preservation system hope to establish?

2. Define *wilderness*, according to the Wilderness Act of 1964.

3. Describe the history behind the Wilderness Act.

4. Why did Congressman Aspinall delay the passage of the Wilderness Bill?

5. Without the Wilderness Bill, what would have happened to the available land in the American West?

6. Why was the BLM excluded from the Wilderness Act?

7. Why is it important for land managers to understand the history of the Wilderness Act?

Historic Preservation and Cultural Landscapes

Headnotes

Historic preservation in the United States begins with Anne Pamela Cunningham, a Southern belle who sought to save George Washington's Mount Vernon in 1853. By purchasing his property on the Potomac River, she hoped to unite the North and South in the preservation effort and prevent the Civil War. She failed to stop the war, but she did succeed in the nation's first effort to place private property in a public trust for preservation purposes. As America industrialized in the antebellum period, groups sponsored preservation efforts in New Orleans, Charleston, and Santa Fe, where a pueblo style of architecture came to dominate other styles. Early preservation legislation included the 1906 Antiquities Act, passed to preserve prehistoric sites and Native American ruins in the Southwest. In 1949 the National Trust for Historic Preservation was formed. In 1956, with passage of the Interstate Highway Act, Americans watched bulldozers destroy historic properties to create four-lane freeways. Citizens decided enough was enough. Urban renewal was not the panacea it claimed to be.

Ten years later, in 1966, Congress passed the National Historic Preservation Act (NHPA), which established the National Register of Historic Places and the office of the Keeper of the Register, who works for the National Park Service. The act also created SHPOs, or State Historic Preservation Officers. Since amendments to the law in 1990 there have also been THPOs, or Tribal Historic Preservation Officers. The goal of historic preservation is to use local and regional criteria to protect sites and structures significant to each part of the nation, and one way to achieve that goal is to use the Section 106 provision of the NHPA to identify, document, preserve, and protect sites that might be in danger because of the expenditure of federal funds for development or highway construction. Each federal agency has preservation responsibilities and obligations.

The Russian writer Nikolai Gogol wrote, "Architecture is the chronicle of the world. It speaks to us long after legends dies, long after poems and songs become silent." Relevant publications include *Vernacular Architecture Forum*, *CRM Journal*, and *Preservation*. Books on historic preservation continue to inform readers and students, including James Marston Fitch, *Historic Preservation*; William J. Murtagh, *Keeping Time: The History and Theory of Preservation in America*; Dell Upton and John Michael Vlach, eds. *Common Places: Readings in American Vernacular Architecture*; and Samuel N. Stokes et al., *Saving America's Countryside: A Guide to Rural Conservation*.

Historic preservation originally focused on the houses of Great White Men, but thanks to social history and other historical movements, preservation has broadened to include many other sites important to all Americans. Those sites need not be houses, great estates, or archaeological ruins. Historic sites can also be ranches, mining and industrial areas, historic highways, and auto routes. Heritage tourism is the process of utilizing local cultural resources as a draw for tourists to visit the West and experience authentic landscapes relatively unchanged by the passage of time. The scenic byway program represents successful heritage tourism that utilizes existing motels and lodging places along uncluttered two-lane asphalt roads. Route 66 represents one of the most famous scenic byways in the

West. As east-west traffic has moved to Interstate 40, the remaining sections of U.S. Route 66 and their vintage motels and cafés symbolize Americans' twentieth-century love affair with the open road.

This series of preservation essays in *Preserving Western History* begins with ranch preservation because so much of the Western landscape on private land is ranches, and many ranchers as well as environmentalists "would rather see a cow than a condo," though those options are fading fast. Across the West many ranches exhibit a high degree of historic integrity, with original buildings still standing. Ranching landscapes epitomize high-altitude farming and ranching through the early homestead period (1860s–90s) on into the settlement period (1900s–20s). These rural ranches across the Great Basin of Nevada or the eastern Montana plains are visual features of their communities and reminders of the area's agricultural roots. Many ranches succeeded by mixing farming and ranching and by acquiring land fronting a river or a stream with grazing much higher up on public land. Cattle or sheep moved to alpine meadows in the summer and returned to the home ranch for winter pasturage of alfalfa or grass hay. Depending upon the limited growing season and precipitation patterns, ranches frequently reused and recycled agricultural buildings, as exemplified by historical architect Ekaterini Vlahos and her essay "Colorado Ranch Preservation: The Twenty-First Century and the Changing American West." From a ranching family in historic Browns Park, Colorado, "Kat" Vlahos utilizes graduate students to help preserve ranching landscapes and to increase awareness of this endangered cultural resource. Across the intermountain West in beautiful, lush valleys laced by irrigation ditches and bordered by thick groves of aspen and Engelman spruce trees, the movement is toward condos and away from cows.

Western preservation issues unique to a long linear corridor are best represented by Route 66, also known as "The Mother Road." Architectural historian Peter Dedek writes "The Mother Road of Nostalgia: Preservation and Interpretation Along U.S. Route 66," which opened in 1932, closed two decades later, and is now a major two-lane tourist draw across eight states and 2,448 miles. Nicknamed the "Main Street of America," Route 66 presents unique preservation challenges in the West, and Dedek explains the difficulties of preserving a highway famous for its long distances and roadside cafés. Sprawling across three time zones from Chicago to Los Angeles, Route 66 represents a 2,400-mile linear folk museum of highway nostalgia with secondhand stores, junk shops, roadside cafés, and vintage 1950s automobiles. The National Park Service even sponsors a Route 66 Corridor Preservation Program that provides funding assistance to support the preservation, restoration, and rehabilitation of the significant and representative buildings, structures, and road segments along the eight-state route.

If Western history and public history are about American movement and mobility, they are also about a certain Western "look" in which historic architecture and 1950s popular television and films created a revival in false-front, clapboard buildings suitable for Kitty's saloon in the series *Gunsmoke* or the ranch buildings in *Bonanza*. Public historian Jay Price looks at thematic Western architecture and in his essay "Making the West Look Western: The Rise of the Old West Revival Architectural Style" argues for a distinctive commercial style of Western vernacular architecture based on false fronts, long porches, and vertical board-and-batten siding. He argues that the temporary rough-sawed wooden look of frontier towns has, more than a century later, become a style all its own. The issue of myth versus reality in Western history permeates this section of the book and is also a theme in historian Judy Morley's piece "Historic Preservation and the creation of Western Civic Identity: Case Studies in Albuquerque, Denver, and Seattle." Historic preservation student Kara Miyashima from the University of Colorado at Denver adds her own ethnic insights in the short essay "From Brothels to Buddhism: A Walking Tour of Denver's Red-Light District."

Mining architecture across the West represented vernacular forms and the use of indigenous materials in worker housing, boardinghouses, mills, assay offices, and railroad depots for small, localized narrow-gauge railroads. Architectural historian Doug Swaim views vernacular architecture as "place-related inflection of culture." John Brinckerhoff Jackson explains that vernacular architecture is "loyal to local forms" and "is not subject to fashion," which is why "the word *timeless* is much used in descriptions of vernacular building." Because miners and mining engineers migrated across the West and they were followed by troops of saloonkeepers, laborers, carpenters, and ladies of the night, a mining camp's first-phase architecture would be similar in Montana and Arizona. As the camp evolved into a mining district and wood frame buildings gave way to brick or even stone with cast-iron fronts brought in by steam trains, mining towns became highly urbanized and the streets of Silverton, Colorado, and Bisbee, Arizona, could have Queen Anne–style buildings identical to those in Denver. The classic study of this evolution is Duane Smith's *Rocky Mountain Mining Camps: The Urban Frontier*. But in the early stages of a mining area, when mining camps were mere villages near a stream or creek, vernacular architecture flourished with shacks, shanties, log cabins, and local adaptations to place seasoned by the cultural traditions of the builders. Howard Wight Marshall writes in his book *Folk Architecture in Little Dixie*, "The formal, exclusive architectural records list achievements and adventures in creativity. Behind this lie all the rest—the ordinary houses and their builders and users, whose intentions have long suggested the retention of accepted, normative models and the replication of traditional plans and concepts."

Historic preservation is not just about architecture. It is also about the historic communities that exist in remote places. Richard Moe, president of the National Trust for Historic Preservation, writes, "Small-town storefronts and battlefields, ancient ruins and roadside drive-ins, presidential estates and miners' shacks—they all tell America's story. They delight the eye and nourish the spirit. They help us know who we are and how we got here. They enrich our environment and our lives." He adds, "Reading history can't compare with the experience of walking through history, seeing in the bricks and boards of old buildings a tangible expression of the dreams and achievements of people long dead, an entryway into our nation's collective memory." To understand Western history and mining history is to spend time in remote mining camps listening to the wind rattle loose tin on an old cabin roof and to walk through towns whose golden age happened a century ago. Silverton, Colorado, in 1910 had 3,000 residents and was the hub of a booming mining area in the San Juan Mountains. Now 600 people live there year-round and 3,000 people reside in Hillside Cemetery. But thanks to historic preservation, the town may have a new lease on life.

Both the town itself and the Durango & Silverton Narrow Gauge Railroad are National Historic Landmarks as is the old Mayflower Mill, which crushed gold and silver ore through the 1980s. Heritage tourism is bringing new visitors, which is why Richard Moe believes, "We must keep teaching people that our heritage is too important to be hauled off to the landfill. We must keep sounding the alarm bell, alerting people to the threats that can let familiar landmarks go up in a cloud of smoke or collapse in a cloud of dust. Perhaps most important we must keep reminding ourselves that saving our historic treasures isn't someone else's responsibility."

For books focusing on mining and preservation, see Richard Francaviglia, *Hard Places: Reading the Landscape of America's Historic Mining Districts* and William and Beth Sagstetter, *The Mining Camps Speak*. Standard references for understanding American architectural styles include John J.-G. Blumenson, *Identifying American Architecture*, and S. Allen Chambers et al., *What Style Is It?* Readers interested in preserving mining history and heritage should consider joining both the Mining History Association and the National Trust for Historic Preservation as well as their local and state historical societies.

Case studies on mining architecture integrate heritage tourism, preservation, and a growing aesthetic about how to value industrial mining landscapes. Historian Eric Clements begins with "For Sale by

Owner: Western Tourism and Historic Preservation," followed by cultural geographer Richard Francaviglia, who is perhaps the dean of mining preservation. He integrates many examples of nineteenth-century mining communities in his essay "Boomtowns and Ghost Towns: Learning from the West's Preserved Historic Mining Landscapes." Another geographer, David Robertson, writes about Cokedale, Colorado, as a case study. Heritage tourism in the West usually focuses on the silver, copper, and gold mining regions of Aspen, Telluride, Park City, and Bisbee while little tourism occurs where coal was mined. Robertson argues that company-owned coal communities are a vital part of Western history and should also be an opportunity for heritage tourism. Historian James E. Fell concludes with an environmental twist to mining preservation with his analysis of the complicated interrelationships among environmental and preservation legislation in his essay "Old Mines, New Developments: Preservation, the Environment, and Public History in the Mining West."

Colorado Ranch Preservation

The Twenty-First Century and the Changing American West

Ekaterini Vlahos

It is not necessarily those lands which are the most fertile or most favored in climate that seem to me the happiest, but those in which a long struggle of adaptation between man and his environment has brought out the best qualities of both.
—T. S. Eliot, After Strange Gods

Western ranches are an imperative part of our landscape, both cultural and physical. These beautiful, historic compounds scattered across the western plains and mountains are direct links to our country's past and significant to its economic and ecological future. However, Western ranches are threatened with extinction by the same march of progress that once made them outposts of American culture. Examination of the cultural, economic, ecological, and aesthetic value of Western ranches is crucial to the successes and recent methods developed in ranch preservation.

When we think of the American West, our imaginations are swept away by idealized visions. Cowboys on horseback silhouetted against a wide sky. Broad vistas framing immense, unfenced rangelands. Homesteads nestled into idyllic, rolling landscapes. There is an undeniable pull to the notion of the American West as it was portrayed first by literature and later by Hollywood. "There is the thrill of the out-of-doors, men in action doing things of valor and whatnot that men dream of doing but never accomplish . . . it is easy for imaginative readers to place themselves in the roles of the heroes."[1]

But perhaps the Western hero that tugs at imaginations most is not the cowboy or the cowgirl; it is the

Figure 99. A classic Western ranch barn is the two-story log barn on the Dodo Ranch, north of New Castle, Colorado. Photo by Andrew Gulliford, ca. 1979.

Figure 100. This Silt Mesa, Colorado, barn shows the perfect proportions and symmetry of rural vernacular construction. Photo by Andrew Gulliford, ca. 1978.

landscape itself. The physical environment of the American West plays a pivotal role in its mythology. Every imagined gunfight or wagon train takes place on land where the natural and the man-made have freshly collided and grown together, where struggle and adaptation have etched themselves into the ground and pieced together buildings, homes, and lives. The landscape of the American West is its true towering hero. And unlike most heroes, it still exists in the modern world, embodied in the Western ranch.

Today, as in the past, the Western ranch is a living, dynamic cultural landscape. It can be viewed as buildings and corrals, barns and fences. But this misses the

Figure 101. Immigrants who came west brought with them their building traditions, and often the buildings have survived long after the immigrant groups have moved on. This two-story stone barn in Rio Blanco County, Colorado, in the Piceance Basin exhibits superb masonry techniques, especially in the tight corners. Photo by Andrew Gulliford, ca. 1980.

Figure 102. Many first-generation ranchers utilized hillsides and other elevations as much as possible to shelter crops and cattle, using bermed earth techniques as in this log shed and barn on Silt Mesa, Colorado. Photo by Andrew Gulliford, ca. 1978.

unique holistic nature of the Western ranch. These structures must be viewed as part of an entire landscape that is both physical and cultural. The vernacular cultural landscape shaped by ranching has evolved through utilization and occupancy. The topography reflects the physical, biological, ecological, and cultural makeup of everyday activities. The vernacular architecture, the common architectural language of a region, captures the character of the people who built the structures and live on the land. It is a tangible link to the first attempt at permanent settlement, an embodiment of the moral strength and will to live off the land in areas that had been viewed as remote and uninhabitable.

Similarly, the modern rancher is a direct connection back to the cowboys and cowgirls, the early pioneers who crossed the continent to a region where an essential adaptation to life took place. For the rancher, the immense outdoors is still a place of work, negotiated daily from sunrise to sunset. The house is a meeting spot, a place to eat and sleep after a long day on the open range. The barns are shelter for livestock, and the various outbuildings that contribute to the ranch complex are intended to serve the utilitarian needs of the ranchers to complete their daily venture. On a regular basis, the rancher has to understand the resources offered by the land and to bargain with the forces of the natural environment—climate, topography, flora and fauna. Over time, the built and natural environments have been transformed to reflect the necessities, cultural ideas, values, and life experiences of the rancher and his family.

In Dan Dagget's *Beyond the Rangeland Conflict—Toward a West That Works*, he highlights the potential of partnerships in creating sustainable ways of inhabiting the western land. The stories capture the unassuming fortitude ranch families have toward stewardship and preservation of their land and way of life. The traditional rancher, the land, the buildings, and agricultural structures are all icons, heroes of the American West. But they are quickly disappearing.

As a place and as a way of life, today the Western ranch is threatened by development, ownership change, economic viability, and natural forces. It is essential to understand the value of this culture and how it impacts and informs our future in the West. What is worth preserving? Is it a lifestyle that identifies the West? Is it a complex of structures that classify Western architecture? Is it the landscape that remains as open space or ranched land that continues to reflect markings carved into the land over time? The current challenges are understanding the forces that shaped the culture, ranches, and lands; interpreting their historical importance; and planning for their protection.

Figure 103. Near Lay, Colorado, and west of Craig, the Branson Ranch is an original homestead in Moffat County on some of the last land homesteaded in the West. Note the original log pioneer homestead and the wooden windmill astride the hand-dug well. Photo by Andrew Gulliford, ca. 1981.

Changing Landscapes

The Western landscape is undergoing drastic change, as is typified in the Front Range of Colorado. Like much of the American West, the intersection of the Great Plains and the Rocky Mountain foothills has long been a landscape dominated by agricultural properties and ranches surrounding smaller urban centers. These ranches and agricultural properties are typical of the integrated ecosystems of man-made and natural landscapes that have developed over generations in the American West, which, combined with Bureau of Land Management (BLM) open spaces leased for grazing, represent the largest parcels of land in the United States. Ranching has been and continues to be an important part of the cultural and ecological identity of the Rocky Mountain region.

However, large tracts of land surrounding cities like Denver and Colorado Springs proved ideal for urban development. By the 1990s, agricultural properties that once dominated the Front Range were sporadic islands, swallowed in a wave of urban housing expansion. And development continues as the population expands. Colorado has 4.8 million acres of threatened prime ranchland as identified by an American Farmland Trust report. This ranchland is rapidly being lost to subdivisions, malls, and resort development. Demand for housing and retail infrastructure is altering and ultimately threatening agricultural and cultural landscapes.

The greatest issue threatening the long-term viability of farming and ranching in the Rocky Mountain region is the loss of the land base. Because of the West's aridity, ranching traditionally requires large amounts of land so that cattle have sufficient forage for most of the year. Farming requires even terrain and a reliable source of irrigation water, usually found near major river floodplains, conditions that coincide with urban centers and areas of fast urban and suburban expansion.[2]

The loss of agricultural lands signifies the consumption of cultural landscapes, the destruction of historic structures, the development of economic pressures on surrounding ranchers through elevated land values, and ultimately, the loss of a lifestyle and history that define a critical part of the American West.

Pivotal in the changing landscape is the transformation in ranch ownership. Increasingly, ranchlands are owned not by traditional ranching families, but by government agencies, private landholders with little or no interest in ranching, and special-interest groups. The economic viability of ranching is no longer the driving force for purchasing the land, a fact that is bringing about a dramatic change in who owns modern ranchlands and why.

Government agencies, state and federal, are most often interested in the natural resources of the land

and water. Private landholders may be interested in acquiring the land for high-density residential development, sprawling 35-acre ranchettes, or solely for its recreational and aesthetic value. In contrast, special-interest groups normally purchase the large parcels for land and wildlife habitat conservation. This shift in the owners and intended uses of ranchlands directly affects not just the ranches themselves, but the entirety of the landscape of which they are an intrinsic part.

The Ranch Is Key to Western Preservation

In the face of widespread and drastic changes in the landscapes and people of the American West, preservation of the Western ranch is crucial to the preservation of the Western landscape in such tangible terms as the environment, history, economics, and, arguably just as tangible, the aesthetics of the American West.

Open lands typified by Western ranches are essential for maintaining a healthy environment. The large parcels of private open space offer valuable wildlife habitat, and the practice of ranching itself contributes to biodiversity of the natural environment. In fact, the ranch illustrates one of the more successful ways in which people dwell in Western lands.

> We have learned that grazing by livestock, when appropriately done, contributes to the disturbance that rangelands require. Perhaps we have come to the point where we measure land health premised on disturbance rather than just rest and realize there is no "balance of nature" but only a "flux of nature." Getting the disturbance patterns right is the challenge.[3]

In addition, the Western ranch represents our history in the region. It symbolizes an aspect of Western American culture that is vanishing at an astounding rate. We need to expand our understanding of preservation and look at these sites differently, both holistically and as unique systems.

Preservation of ranches goes beyond the structures. Various characteristics need to be taken into account when considering ranch preservation, including land uses and activities, patterns of spatial organization, cultural traditions, buildings, structures and objects, response to the natural environment, circulation patterns, and, ultimately, the history of the families that have lived off the land over time.[4] Taking into account these tangible preservation arguments, it is informative to examine how this preservation actually occurs. The following case studies highlight three recent preservation projects as well as how collaborative efforts can achieve positive preservation and conservation outcomes.

Case Study 1
Grassroots Preservation—A Way of Life—Routt County Successes

Agricultural properties in northwestern Colorado are excellent examples of ranches that reflect changing regional patterns in growth, economics, development, and agriculture. At the turn of the century, Routt County, in northwestern Colorado, was considered rugged and isolated. The first population increases began from about 1880 to 1900, when settlers were drawn to the region's mining opportunities and took up ranching as part of the Homestead Act (1862). Agriculture also promoted the establishment of small communities in the area, but heavy permanent settlement did not begin until 1909, in anticipation of the railroad. As mining proved ultimately unprofitable, settlers in the area fell back on agriculture.[5]

Many ranches in Routt County exist from original homesteading claims, passed down through generations that continue to work the land. These sites represent excellent examples of cultural landscapes and convey the early settlers' efforts to shape the environment for a specific use. The landscape dominates the built environment, and dynamic changes on the site reflect an evolution of ranching.

The ranches include both the land they are on and the complex structures of the ranch. The structures include a main ranch house—generally the original homestead house added to over time—a bunkhouse for ranch hands; a barn for cattle, sheep, horses, or hay; a smithy-blacksmith shop; a garage; various storage sheds; and other small outbuildings such as an outhouse, icehouse, and small cabin for teaching. Additional features on the site include corrals, fences, pens, hay stackers, wells, and pastures. As with most ranches, the complex of buildings generally evolved as needed rather than according to a master plan. Buildings were constructed to fill specific needs or were transported from other sites where they were no longer being used. Viewed holistically, the ranches of Routt County tell a story of the skills, technologies, and lifestyles of their occupants.

Many of the ranches near Steamboat Springs in Routt County are threatened today by urban growth, resort development, and changing economies, with a significant shift in ownership patterns. In a study of ranchland dynamics, the Center of the American West reports that the Routt County population grew almost 40 percent between 1990 and 2000, while the proportion of total county income derived from agriculture declined from 4.2 percent in 1990 to 0.8 percent in 2000.[6] This was due in large part to the growth of the Steamboat Springs ski resort economy and an influx of wealthy people with outside sources of income. Over 50 percent of ranchland is currently held by private owners who did not purchase the land specifically for ranching purposes.[7]

Still, there is a growing awareness and appreciation of the important role agriculture and ranches play in the culture and overall flavor of the region, even among tourists. Colorado State University Cooperative Extension points out a primary attraction to tourists coming to the area is that they can drive down country roads and see old barns and agricultural lands.[8] So in an interestingly circular twist, tourists' appreciation for the aesthetics of Routt County ranches may be instrumental in their preservation, which is necessary in part due to the growth of local tourism.

Preservation Program

In the late 1990s, a grassroots collaborative program was developed to preserve the traditional ranches of Routt County and respond to critical issues like deteriorating structure conditions due to age and weathering, increased property values, and decreased agricultural product profitability.[9] The impetus for this preservation program comes from a group of interested ranchers and locals who founded Historic Routt County! (HRC!), which is a nonprofit organization whose goal is to protect the character of Routt County's communities and rural areas by preserving its ranches and similar built environments.

The success of this program has been primarily dependent on a collaborative partnership between the local community and graduate students at the University of Colorado at Denver's College of Architecture and Planning. Through the program, ranchers and property owners receive surveys and inventories, nomination assistance, historic structure assessments, photographs, one-on-one technical assistance, grant facilitation, tax and other incentives, and preservation easement facilitation. At the same time, graduate students receive invaluable hands-on experience in preservation methodology. The key aspect of the program for ranchers is that it is incentive based and allows them to select the area of participation that best suits their needs. The program connects landowners to academics and students and preservationists to the landowners and community. Information is provided through educational programs, community outreach meetings, hands-on restoration workshops, lectures, and exhibits. Connection to the community is a key component to the program's success.

The goals and priorities of the communities involved in the preservation of the agricultural properties of Routt County include the development of a comprehensive plan to document and survey all possible ranches and agricultural properties. After initial survey and documentation, individual properties can be assessed for

Figure 104. The Medano Ranch Shed, a long, low log building, is perfectly adapted to the landscape as a vernacular structure. It would not catch the cold winter winds blowing across the 7,000-foot-high San Luis Valley. Photo courtesy State Historic Preservation Office, the Colorado Historical Society.

Figure 105. The nineteenth-century Trujillo Homestead House represented a powerful visual and cultural statement because of its height and because it was a clear break from traditional Hispanic one-story adobe dwellings. Photo courtesy State Historic Preservation Office, the Colorado Historical Society.

preservation needs and priorities, and the information can be forwarded to the owners. Additionally, designation of excellent individual buildings and districts will further involvement in preservation and increase pride among local historic property holders.[10]

The process ultimately allows for the local historic designation of as many ranch properties as possible, a primary goal of the pilot program. For many rural areas, it is a difficult and costly process to obtain the information needed to determine the viability of preserving their ranchland. This program eased the burden of such costs and provided the necessary information.

With the success of this program, the intent is to apply this mutually beneficial collaborative preservation model statewide. Additional partners that have contributed to the success of this type of program include the ranching community and property owners, the City of Steamboat Springs, the Yampa Valley Land Trust, and the Community Agriculture Alliance. As of 2003, 53 ranches have been surveyed. Through this collaborative preservation program, the University of Colorado at Denver is able to carry forward its mission to educate students in the process of preservation, including research, field studies, surveys, and information management. In turn, with the support of HRC!, the information is given to communities as a tool to nominate properties for historic designation and preservation as well as to create a useful database of the surveyed sites.

The collaborative effort promotes better understanding of the preservation process to students and rural communities alike and produces more efficient and thorough surveys and documentation with significance and integrity. Ranchers can use survey information to develop further preservation efforts such as tax incentives, easements, zoning, and land use control and to gather funds that aid in the conservation of historic areas.

Case Study 2
Ecoregions and Ranching—The Nature Conservancy—A Working Solution
The Medano-Zapata Ranch, San Luis Valley

The Medano-Zapata Ranch traces its origins to the beginnings of large-scale cattle raising in the San Luis Valley, a high valley in south-central Colorado. The broad valley is bordered by the rugged Sangre de Cristo Mountains and the equally imposing, if somewhat smaller, sand peaks of the Great Sand Dunes, formed over the millennia by wind and sand blowing across the valley floor. The Rio Grande is the main water outlet for the area, and the northern part of the valley lies within a closed basin. Herds of bison, distant ancestors to the original herds that roamed the valley floor, can still be seen today. Nestled along the Great Sand Dunes are two ranches that were combined into one of the great cattle ranches of Colorado. Their history is so interwoven that they are now referred to as one place, the Medano-Zapata Ranch. These ranches are rich in history, from prehistoric discoveries to ancient Native American hunting grounds to the development of cattle ranching.

The ranches represent early settlement and the evolution of cattle ranching in the San Luis Valley over the past 130 years, illustrating changing practices and the trend of consolidating smaller holdings into ever larger tracts. In 1862, the Homestead Act opened up a great deal of the valley to anyone willing to meet the challenge. In 1864, Teofilo Trujillo accepted the challenge and moved with his family to the Medano Springs area from Taos, New Mexico. He was the first permanent settler on the site, founding Zapata Ranch.

Medano Ranch similarly traces its beginnings to the range cattle industry of the 1870s, when two Ohio brothers brought large numbers of Texas cattle into the San Luis Valley.[11] In 1912, after a number of short-term owners, the 27,000-acre Medano Ranch was acquired by George W. Linger. Under the Linger family, the ranch became a fed-cattle operation and continued to expand. Members of the Linger family were prominent in Colorado cattle organizations and operated the ranch until 1947, during its peak.

The Medano ranch headquarters complex consists of a main ranch house to the north and buildings situated along the edges of the open ranch yard, roughly forming a square. Support facilities for the ranch workers are at the east end of the square, while animal facilities are to the west and south. A large corral area south of the buildings was considerably expanded after the purchase of the ranch by the Lingers. About 50 percent of the original structures are still at the Medano. The ranch

Figure 106. Historic ranching corrals need to be carefully studied and documented since ranchers today use portable metal fencing and gates. The Trujillo Homestead Corral is oriented north to south as are the Sangre de Cristo Mountains in the background. Photo courtesy State Historic Preservation Office, the Colorado Historical Society.

Figure 107. Historic photograph of the Medano Ranch Complex taken in 1912. Copyright The Linger Family photo collection.

was sold to The Nature Conservancy in 1998. It is still a working ranch with bison and cattle.

Preservation Program

Medano-Zapata Ranch is a good example of proactive preservation as well as how preservation and a continued ranching tradition can coexist in a symbiotic relationship. The owners of Medano-Zapata Ranch, aware of the pressures and threats to the continued preservation of the ranch, its land, and its culture, approached the state director of the nonprofit organization The Nature Conservancy (TNC) and asked for their assistance. The stated mission of TNC is to "preserve the plants, animals, and natural communities that represent the diversity of life on earth by protecting the lands and waters they need to survive," a goal TNC achieves through land acquisition, land management, and conservation funding. As of 2003, TNC has protected more than 116 million acres of land and waters worldwide.

Working with partners, the conservancy protects specific places where plant and animal species can survive for generations to come. TNC looks at entire ecosystems, places defined by climate, geography, and species instead of political boundaries. At each place, TNC uses a variety of strategies tailored to local circumstances. TNC recognizes that preserving the local way of life is integral to being successful in protecting natural communities. One way TNC does that is working with ranchers and farmers to keep agricultural land economically productive and ecologically healthy. The conservancy continually learns from those who have been excellent land stewards for generations.

The Nature Conservancy has purchased two ranches in Colorado, citing them as cultural landscapes that have a high historic profile to which local residents readily relate: Carpenter Ranch and Medano-Zapata Ranch. The ranches represent large land parcels with the biodiversity and complex ecosystems TNC seeks. The ranches are also historically and ecologically significant, creating a synergy and ideal opportunities for community engagement.

In the San Luis Valley, Medano-Zapata Ranch was a unique site of critical importance to biodiversity. Because of the scale of the property and the water rights involved, TNC determined that the conservancy should own this property. A total of 100,000 acres of ranchland has been preserved in perpetuity as open space and continues to exemplify the history of ranching in the state.

Case Study 3
Collaborative Efforts—Open Space— From Mining to Preservation
The Hayden Ranch, Lake County

Hayden Ranch was one of the earliest high-country ranches established in the northeastern portion of Lake County, Colorado. It greatly contributed to the growth and development of the area.

The history of the Hayden Ranch can be traced back to the earliest settlement period of the Arkansas River Valley, when the promise of striking it rich drew tens of thousands of prospectors to Leadville, perched high atop the very spine of the American Continent. From the earliest days, thousands of mules, horses, burros and oxen supplied the literal "horsepower" that provided transportation, hauled materials and powered the winches of the mighty mines. In the rarified environment above 10,000 feet, with a growing season of less than fifty days, feed for the livestock was in exceedingly short supply. To meet the demand, the hay meadows along the river bottom were homesteaded, irrigated, and harvested to provide the most elemental fuel of the mining boom.[12]

Early owners of Hayden Ranch had a considerable impact on the development of the Leadville area. Situated in the Upper Arkansas River Valley at the base of Mt. Elbert, Colorado's highest peak, Hayden Ranch produced the hay to support the area's livestock, mining industry horses, and mules. The ranch also served as stagecoach stop and railroad siding, employing many area residents. In addition, classes on the ranch offered an educational opportunity for the relatively isolated children of farm and ranch employees.

The ranch's architectural significance is reflected in the specialized function, and therefore form, of each building. Although some of the buildings lack individual architectural distinction, several of them are especially important as outstanding examples of their type. "Because of the small number of early lumbering complexes presently recorded and likely to be adequately recorded and identified through documentary research, each complex should be considered significant."[13] One of the most architecturally significant buildings is the large barn built over an unnamed tributary of the Arkansas River. This small creek provided the power to operate a 1918 sawmill and a stationary hay baler once inside the barn. Portions of the water wheel and belts still remain.

Closely related to the ranches and the open spaces that surround them, many areas in Lake County represent a critical hub for wildlife. Migration corridors, calving habitats, spawning beds, nesting sites, and foraging grounds for over 250 species reside within the county.

In 1997, Lake County received a shock. Approximately 7,000 acres of its historic ranchland, 11 percent of all privately held land in the county, went on the real estate market simultaneously. Faced with the parceling off of the Upper Arkansas River Valley's most scenic viewsheds, critical wildlife habitats, significant cultural resources, and recreational outlets, Lake County realized it had to act to preserve this important, sizable landmass. At the same time, Lake County was recovering from the collapse of its mining industry, with an over 80 percent loss in its assessed tax valuation, and had not yet transitioned from an economy fueled by natural resource extraction to one based on tourism and recreation. Economic realities were bearing down on the historic and natural landscapes of Lake County. Without the financial resources and staff to guide this transition on its own, thereby managing growth and preserving its important ecological and cultural resources, the county turned to a collaborative model of preservation. They formed the Lake County Open Space Initiative (LCOSI) partnership, which enlisted the cooperation of federal, state, and local agencies; municipalities; and organizations that share in the common goal of protection and stewardship of Lake County's land and water resources for open space, wildlife, historic preservation, smart growth, and outdoor recreation.

Preservation Program

Some 8,600 acres in total, or almost 13.5 square miles of land, have been incorporated into the Open Space Initiative, which preserves migration corridors and protects an island of critical habitat extending for six miles north and south along the river corridor. These acres also connect Forest Service lands on the east and west sides of the valley and provide control over six miles of class I waters along the headwaters of the Arkansas River. Due to the land's scarcity and the amazing diversity of wildlife species dependent upon it, much of it is classified as "lowland riparian habitat," the highest-priority habitat for Colorado Department of Wildlife (CDOW) acquisition, thereby maintaining the relative sanctity of the valley's wildlife habitat and movement corridors.

The stated primary objective of LCOSI is the protection and stewardship of land and water for wildlife. Land acquisitions have been prioritized to protect, preserve, and enhance wildlife habitat. Within those preserved areas, however, numerous ranch structures have also been and continue to be preserved through the program. Lake County and LCOSI are now pursuing smart growth and development strategies to replace the depleted tax base, proving a viable economic alternative to growth at any cost.

> Mounting evidence demonstrates that unrestricted growth harms rather than helps local economies. Analysis of economic consequences of residential development in rural areas has revealed that the outright purchase of open space can be less costly to taxpayers than allowing low-density development. A review of 47 case studies of the costs of residential development showed that low-density rural development demands between $1.02 to $3.25 in services for every dollar generated in taxes, while agricultural and open space provided an average surplus of 69 cents. The high costs of development of open space lands accrue because it is so expensive to provide services to remote locations. The implication for communities is that protecting open space and planning new growth becomes good fiscal and economic policy.[14]

Hayden Ranch, now the property of the City of Aurora, recently received Historic Landmark designation. Thanks to preservation efforts, over six miles of the

Arkansas River and 3,300 acres of land have been opened to the public for recreational use for the first time. The shifting of local economies based on natural resource extraction to those based on tourism and recreation, in conjunction with preservation efforts of historic landscapes and open space, is increasingly important in the American West. Western ranches represent a piece of the landscape whole, where the protection of wildlife habitat coincides with the preservation of historic and culturally significant man-made structures. The ranchlands viewed for recreational purposes support a high quality of life that is driving both population growth and job creation and highlights open vistas, clean water, outdoor recreation, and abundant wildlife.

Rural ranchlands in Colorado are diminishing at an alarming rate. The preservation, reuse, and interpretation of Hayden Ranch can help set a precedent to alert Coloradoans to the value that still remains in rural historic sites. Hayden Ranch has been an integral part of the history of Leadville and Lake County, and its preservation and reuse would benefit both the region and all Colorado.

The Necessity of Western Ranches, Preservation, and Understanding

There is a danger in ignoring the fading of Western ranches, our hero of the American West, into the graying of the past. With the passing of each ranch, we lose a piece of history, a link to our heritage and a connection to the land we take for granted. There is value, both tangible and intangible, in Western ranches. And we can preserve these priceless records of lives carved into the wild Western landscape either by setting them aside or by protecting their viability in the modern economic world. Here preservation is not only possible; it is imperative. The first tentative step of preservation is understanding. By studying ranches, we can hope to understand the forces that shaped them, the importance of their history, how to effectively preserve them, and, possibly, how they can better inform our own futures.

Notes

1. Walter Prescott Webb, *The Great Plains* (Texas: University of Texas Press, 1964), 465.

2. Leah Burgess, "Saving a Ranching Way of Life," *American Farmland* (fall 2002): 11.

3. Richard L. Knight, Wendell C. Gilgert, and Ed Marston, eds., *Ranching West of the 100th Meridian: Culture, Ecology, and Economics* (Washington, D.C.: Island Press, 2002), 17.

4. Linda Flint McClelland et al., *National Register Bulletin: Guidelines for Evaluating and Documenting Rural Historic Landscapes* (Washington, D.C.: U.S. Department of the Interior, National Park Services Cultural Resources, 1999), 15.

5. Laureen Lafferty Schaffer, *Agricultural Context of Routt County* (Denver: University of Colorado at Denver, College of Architecture and Planning, 2000), 5.

6. Bill Travis et al., *Ranchland Dynamics* (Boulder, CO: Center of the American West, 2003), http://www.centerwest.org/ranchlands.

7. Ibid.

8. R. G. Walsh et al., *Recreational Value of Ranch Open Space* (Fort Collins: Colorado State University, Department of Agricultural and Resource Economics, 1994), 8.

9. Ekaterini Vlahos, "Documenting and Saving the Historic Ranches of Colorado," *Vineyard: An Occasional Record of the National Park Service Historic Landscape Initiative* III, no. 1 (2001): 9–12.

10. Schaffer, *Agricultural Context of Routt County*, 58.

11. Thomas H. and R. Laurie Simmons, *Medano Ranch Architectural Inventory Form*, 5AL.301, Colorado Historical Society, Office of Archaeology and Historic Preservation, Denver.

12. State Historic Fund, Office of Archaeology and Historic Preservation, Colorado Historical Society, Denver, MC.SHF.R89 Site #5LK.1340.

13. Conlin Associates Resource Planners, *Lake County Open Space Initiative Ecosystem Management Plan, Public Review Draft*, Leadville, CO, 2003, http://www.coloradomtn.edu/lcosi/lcosi.htm.

14. University of Colorado, Boulder, Department of Geography, *Economic Values of Wildlife and Open Space Amenities*, 1999.

Study Questions

1. What part of the West holds the most charm, at least in the imagination?

2. Describe the ranchers' tie to the environment.

3. Recently, how have Western ranches been threatened? What is their greatest threat?

4. How has ranch ownership changed in the last decade or so?

5. How has ranching shaped the history of Routt County, how is it being threatened, and what steps are being taken to combat the problem(s)?

6. Describe briefly the "preservation program" for the Medano-Zapata Ranch.

7. What are some of the challenges in preserving the Hayden Ranch in Lake County?

8. How is the economy of the American West changing, and how is it possible to use this change to aid in the preservation of ranches?

The Mother Road of Nostalgia

Preservation and Interpretation Along U.S. Route 66

Peter Dedek

Figure 108. This is an eye-catching 1950s mock-up in Seligman, Arizona, where mannequins act out the nostalgic fantasies of twentieth-century American auto culture for both American and international tourists. Photo by author, 1998.

Route 66 is America's most famous highway. Many people in the United States and around the world view Route 66 as the primary symbol of American auto culture and auto-related landscapes from the 1920s to the 1970s.[1] Unlike most other long-distance pre-interstate U.S. highways, Route 66 currently enjoys a unique place in American popular culture because the road has earned a distinct, popular identity.

From 1927 to around 1956, Route 66 functioned as the primary and uninterrupted auto and truck route between Chicago and Los Angeles. After 1956, the highway experienced a subsequent period of continued heavy use and gradual decline that lasted until about 1970, by which time five interstate highways had replaced nearly the entire length of the route. In those early years of heavy use, Route 66 became forever fixed in the history and lore of the United States, particularly the West. Popular culture, such as John Steinbeck's 1939 novel *The Grapes of Wrath*, Bobby Troupe's 1946 lyrics "Get Your Kicks on Route 66," and the 1960–64 television show *Route 66* immortalized the highway, which earned names such as the "Mother Road," the "Main Street of America," and the "Will Rogers Highway."[2]

Much of the fame of Route 66 derives from myths of "wild Indians," the "Wild West," and the freedom and romance of the "open road." Because the road took travelers to California through the Southwest, a region already made popular by railroads in the late nineteenth and early twentieth centuries, Route 66 attracted a large number of tourists who saw the region as a "land of enchantment" that would offer them breathtaking scenery and exposure to exotic cultures.[3] Roadside merchants perpetuated the myth of the Southwest and worked to associate it with Route 66.

Despite its fame, Route 66 did not last forever. In 1984, the Arizona Department of Transportation completed the final bypass of old Route 66 by blasting a broad path around Williams, Arizona, the last remaining stretch of Route 66 still in use as the primary highway. A group of celebrities, including Bobby Troupe, gathered in downtown Williams to pronounce the highway dead in a funeral-like ceremony. Troupe sang "Route 66," which he had written nearly four decades earlier. During this ceremony, a state highway official whispered to Dennis Lund, the Kaibab National Forest Recreation officer: "I don't know why everyone's making such a fuss. Route 66 is like an old can of tuna—once you've used it up, you throw it away."[4]

Like this official, many people expected Route 66 to quickly fade from memory, now that the highway existed only as a series of mostly disused strips of eroding pavement stretching from Chicago to Los Angeles, lined by intermittent clusters of associated commercial structures, which were often crumbling into ruin. Without signs to direct would-be tourists, Route 66 existed only as a confusing jumble of local, sometimes dead-end roads.

With Route 66 out of business, most travelers

eagerly took to the new, efficient, and safer interstates. However, after an initial thrill at being able to drive long distances at high speeds without interruption, a small but growing number of motorists began to long for the "slower pace" of travel on old Route 66.⁵ The extensive land requirements of the new interstate highways, such as width, shallow grades, and long visibility lines, made a great deal of mountain blasting and valley fill-ins necessary, making the design of interstates far more intrusive on the landscape than Route 66. Interstates tended to cut through the contours of the land, while most portions of Route 66 had followed them, and interstates divided motorists from landscape with wider shoulders, uniform clear zones, and limited-access entrances and exits. Motorists discovered that, on an interstate, a family could travel from Chicago to Los Angeles and experience very little of the territory through which it passed, and by the 1980s, many vacationers began to miss old Route 66.

In retrospect, the often-crowded, narrow highway with its motley collection of vernacular roadside architecture and interesting cultural landscapes seemed quaint and humanizing compared to the massive, efficient, and impersonal interstates. For this and other reasons, hundreds of people who live near Route 66 and road enthusiasts from all over the world, especially Western Europe and Japan, began to form organizations to preserve and popularize the remnants of the historic route. By 1999, enthusiasts in Belgium, Canada, France, Japan, and the Netherlands had formed organizations dedicated to Route 66.⁶ Foreigners began to visit Route 66 on their vacations. Of the 530 reported visitors who stopped at Angel Delgadillo's Route 66 Visitor Center in Seligman, Arizona, in the first quarter of 1999, 208 came from foreign countries.⁷

To the ever increasing number of enthusiasts, the highway came to represent the eras in which it was active, particularly the 1930s and 1950s. Route 66 signified concepts such as flight, freedom, the delights of travel, coming of age, and other potent American archetypes such as a family vacation in the family automobile. Enthusiasts, who began working to keep the

Figure 109. Twin Arrows, Arizona. The symbols along Route 66 included references to local cultures. Photo by author, 1998.

memory of the road alive, often cited references to these ideas and images.⁸ Much of the Route 66 movement among Americans revolved around conservative nostalgia for the "good old days" of the 1950s, although some Route 66 enthusiasts expressed nostalgia for the social strife and rebellion of the 1930s and the 1960s.

Virtually every issue of *Route 66 Magazine*, a popular magazine published in Arizona, features accounts of remembered Route 66 experiences. Most articles involve recollections of a decade (usually the 1950s) that the authors consider to have been a simpler, "lost era," a more honest and innocent time. The consensus among most *Route 66 Magazine* authors is that the 1950s represent an age when life in America was pleasantly free of the complexities brought forth by the 1960s. These authors tend to downplay or completely

Figure 110. A symbol of Route 66 includes a large 1950s-style taillight and two chrome sixes at the Route 66 Monument in Tucumcari, New Mexico. The highway functions as a historic artifact of the Southwest and American auto culture. Photo by author, 1998.

Figure 111. Another preserved motel is the Arizona Motor Hotel ("cheap but clean") on the strip in Williams, Arizona. Photo by Andrew Gulliford, 2003.

ignore the undercurrents of the Cold War (including the shooting war in Korea), McCarthyism, racism, and labor strife that characterized life in the 1950s along with benign aspects such as drive-in restaurants and a low divorce rate. In a 1998 *Route 66 Magazine* article titled "Fifties Memories," writer Bob Moore recalls: "People had time for themselves and each other and our lives were not consumed with 'stuff.' Bad guys went to jail, always, and good guys got ahead. Everyone respected the President, even if we didn't agree with him. It was a comfortable time in America and some of us miss it very much."[9]

Other nostalgia writers offer alternative interpretations of the meanings of Route 66 and the decade of the 1950s. An article in *Route 66 Magazine* by Lou Delina interprets Route 66 from a less conservative political point of view and associates the highway with the defiant hoboism and restless travel of Jack Kerouac. Delina argues that the original Tod and Buzz of the 1960–64 television show *Route 66* were actually Jack Kerouac and Neal Cassady as Sal Paradise and his friend Dean Moriarty from Kerouac's novel *On the Road*. In Delina's view, *On the Road* and "the spirit of Route 66" "led to a revolution, a parting of the ways between the old guard and the new progressives, the so-called 'free thinkers.' This movement would manifest itself in the late 1960s." Here, instead of representing traditional values, Route 66 acted as a pathway for the Beat Generation, eventually leading to the cultural revolution of the late 1960s that Dansko and many other *Route 66 Magazine* contributors clearly disapprove of.[10]

Most enthusiasts, whether conservative or progressive, intimately familiar with Route 66 or with only a vague notion of Route 66, associate Route 66 with images, such as vintage cars and the open road. The following passage from a 1995 article published in *Esquire* expresses this popular sentiment:

You find yourself lumbering along a red-dirt road in a totally cherry '55 Cadillac and gazing dreamlike, trancelike [sic], out the thick glass windows. Route 66 is way behind you, and the sunset is melting into the car's huge, glossy hood. . . . The desert flatness and its cedar and sage give way to dramatic red buttes and cliffs.[11]

A 1998 tour book titled *Route 66 Mainstreet of America* cites additional common Route 66 themes:

The ride from Glenrio is as beautiful and vibrant as a Mexican tapestry—where copper colored cliffs and majestic mesas rise in brilliant contrast to clear desert skies. The roadside communities in this "Land of Enchantment" are steeped in desert culture, from souvenir shops peddling turquoise and silver trinkets, to ancient Indian Ruins, and lost cities.

This language could have come from a Fred Harvey railroad hotel promotional booklet written 70 years earlier.[12]

Much of the appeal of Route 66 lies in its sense of authenticity and place. One can still travel the often lonely stretches of road, meet genuine Route 66 personalities, stay in the same motels, and eat at the same restaurants, sometimes run by the same families, as the original tourists. The surviving segments constitute an American ruin. While Europe has castles and Roman aqueducts, the United States has the ruins of tourist courts, gas stations, and early viaducts.

Historic Route 66 presents visitors with a jumble of popular culture images and icons, many involving the automobile and the Southwest. The mix of cultural references associated with Route 66 has helped give the historic highway its appeal. While traveling the route, the contemporary traveler experiences architecture from various periods, images, and ruins that reflect multiple layers of memory, history, and myth.

Route 66 presents challenges to those who wish to preserve and interpret this historic transportation

Figure 112. Each year more Route 66 icons crumble. This is the ruins of the famous Club Cafe, Santa Rosa, New Mexico, demolished in 1998. Photo by author, 1998.

corridor. The most significant of these is that, in spite of their allure, many of the eclectic structures and buildings along the highway are endangered by neglect or demolition. In some cases, visitors see neglect as part of a structure's attractiveness. In addition, coordinating preservation professionals, enthusiasts, and members of communities along the historic 2,400-mile corridor, which passes through eight states, presents another preservation problem. Also, Route 66 possesses strong cultural meanings, making accurate historical interpretation problematic. Can these remnants be preserved while maintaining the corridor's free and open character? Would a high level of protection, such as converting Route 66 into a highly regulated linear park, remove all sense of place and authenticity? In order to preserve what is left of historic Route 66 enthusiasts and preservationists will have to set priorities for saving the highway, and public historians will have to formulate methods to present this highly symbolic historic highway to tourists and local residents.

In recent years, many significant Route 66 landmarks, such as the Club Cafe in Santa Rosa, New Mexico, and the Coral Court Motel (a property that was listed in the National Register) near St. Louis, Missouri, have been demolished. Many other historic Route 66 motels have fallen on hard times due to interstate highways and competition from chain motel operations. Historic road-related businesses often occupy large lots that make ideal sites for industrial parks, big box retail stores, or new chain motels.

A good first step in any effort to preserve road-related architecture is to perform a historic resource survey. Significant resource types along the highway include tourist courts and motels, cafés, gas stations, tourist attractions, Native American sites, and segments of the road itself. Systematic identification and documentation of these historic resource types allow preservationists to determine the most rare and significant properties and to target them for protection and restoration. Undertaking a historic resource survey helps a community create a preservation plan that will help them recognize which historic resources have value and should be reused as functional parts of modern life.[13] The Texas Historical Commission, in cooperation with the National Park Service, undertook an effort of this type in 2002. The project includes historical research into Route 66 sites and a complete survey of Route 66–related structures in Texas, which will result in a National Register multiple property nomination for historic Route 66 in Texas.[14]

Intact remnant segments of the Route 66 corridor should be surveyed and protected in a holistic manner that includes historic structures, original highway alignments, significant natural features, and prominent viewsheds. Those who complete the surveys need to pay careful attention to cultural landscapes, because the essential character and essence of Route 66 exists not only in individual structures such as gas stations and motels, but also in how these structures relate to one another, to the historic road, and to natural landscapes.

Without at least some of its original open landscape, a historic motel or historic roadside trading post is only a sad reminder of a lost and dead past. The surrounding context allows visitors and neighbors to appreciate a historic building's worth more fully and to better understand the value of preserving the property.

The secretary of the interior's Standards for the Treatment of Historic Properties with Guidelines for the Treatments of Cultural Landscapes defines a cultural landscape as:

> A geographic area (including both cultural and natural resources and the wildlife or domestic animals therein), associated with a historic event, activity, or person or exhibiting other cultural or aesthetic values. There are four general types of cultural landscapes, not mutually exclusive: historic sites, historic designed landscapes, historic vernacular landscapes, and ethnographic landscapes.[15]

Essentially, a cultural landscape consists of a geographic area, sometimes a linear corridor, where human activities have left identifiable and related traces on the natural terrain. A linear cultural landscape, Route 66 exhibits remnants of the many activities related to traveling by vehicle. Highway activities include servicing automobiles and trucks, spending a night, buying fuel, eating meals, buying souvenirs, and visiting natural attractions and cultural sites, with the resulting structures including service stations, motels, cafés, souvenir shops, and parks.

An example of the close relationship between historic significance and the natural landscape can be seen at Cozier Canyon on Route 66 in Arizona. In the last few years, a stone company has been quarrying the walls of the canyon. Although a natural formation, the canyon walls functioned as a landmark in the experience of driving old Route 66 through the area.[16]

Route 66 enthusiasts in Arizona oppose the quarrying, even though much of the rock will probably be used in environmentally friendly, water-saving landscape

Figure 113. The Blue Swallow Motel in Tucumcari, New Mexico, has a vintage neon sign. Route 66 landscapes often consist of strips of varied road-related buildings. Photo by author, 1998.

projects designed to replace chemical and water-consuming lawns throughout arid Arizona. Historian and Route 66 advocate Alfred Runte considers the removal of the rock an "abomination." "There are rocks all over the place," Runte said, "You don't have to use these rocks. This place should have been made a park years ago."[17] In addition, the quarrying played a role in Route 66 enthusiast Bob Waldmire's decision in 1998 to close his nearby Route 66 visitor center. "I can't handle living between two new rock quarry operations," said Waldmire, son of the inventor of the Cozy Dog, the first corn dog on a stick, developed on Route 66 in Springfield, Illinois, in 1949.[18] Although the quarrying impacts a natural feature, the destruction of the canyon is threatening the historic integrity of the Route 66 cultural landscape in the Hackberry, Arizona, area.

To interpret Route 66 in a meaningful way, the landscapes that evolved along Route 66, including natural and manmade elements, need to be preserved as a whole. If too much demolition or incompatible construction occurs, what remains of old Route 66 will have lost its context and will lose the magic that draws so many tourists from all over the world to the highway.

Listing the individual historic sites, districts, and cultural landscapes of Route 66 in the National Register of Historic Places can help ensure their protection. Listing provides formal recognition that a property is historic and guarantees that the history and historical significance of the property has been researched and documented. This recognition and recordation is particularly important for early-twentieth-century gas stations, motels, and restaurants, because the historical significance of these structures has not yet been widely accepted.

Some historic Route 66 properties, such as the U-Drop Inn Café in Shamrock, Texas, are listed in the National Register, and cities such as Amarillo, Texas, and Williams, Arizona, have established National Register districts along strips where Route 66 passes through town.[19] In addition, several abandoned alignments of old Route 66 that pass through the Kaibab National Forest near Williams, Arizona, have been listed in the National Register.[20] As of January 2001, at least 67 individual properties and districts directly associated with Route 66 were listed in the National Register.[21] Several Route 66 states, including New Mexico, Oklahoma, Texas, and Illinois, have completed National Register Multiple Property Listings for their segments of Route 66.[22]

National Register listing offers a property limited protection from federal undertakings under Section 106 of the National Historic Preservation Act of 1966.[23] While Section 106 can act as a useful tool to force an agency to negotiate and reduce any adverse effects of a project on a historic resource, the process rarely stops projects altogether. A stronger law designed to protect historic sites from transportation-related federal undertakings is Section 4(f) of the National Transportation Act. This provision requires an agency (usually a state highway department using federal transportation funds) to explore all "feasible and prudent" options to "minimize harm" to a historic property. As with Section 106, 4(f) defines a historic property as one listed or eligible for listing in the National Register. Because of the limitations of these regulations, preservationists cannot rely on them alone to save historic resources.[24]

Listing on the National Register has benefits in addition to Section 106 and Section 4(f). Designation and listing on the register makes owners of commercial properties eligible for a 20 percent federal tax credit if they rehabilitate their building in a historically sensitive manner. In many instances, the tax credit can make the difference between a profitable project and one that does not make money for investors.[25] National Register listing also makes road-related buildings owned by nonprofits, municipalities, and other government entities eligible for enhancement funding under TEA 21 (which replaced a former law called the Intermodal Surface Transportation Efficiency Act, or ISTEA). This program allocates federal highway monies for the rehabilitation of historic structures that are associated with transportation. At least one Route 66 building, the U-Drop Inn in Shamrock, Texas, has been awarded enhancement money.[26]

Another benefit of National Register listing is that it simplifies the creation of local historic districts. Municipalities can easily pass ordinances that designate any National Register districts within their jurisdiction as local historic districts.[27] Local historic districts provide much broader protection than National Register districts, because local districts regulate private demolition and rehabilitation activities, while National Register listing does not.

A number of preservation measures have been undertaken on Route 66, such as the recently restored Tower Station and U-Drop Inn building, a stunning architectural landmark built in 1936, which operates as a visitor and community center.[28] Visitor centers can be an excellent reuse for historic road-related buildings. However, the need for them is limited, and owners should find alternative economically viable uses.

An interesting adaptive use of a Route 66 structure can be found in Missouri, where a nonprofit group converted the abandoned 1929 Chain of Rocks Bridge across the Mississippi River into a pedestrian path and bikeway, which opened in 1999.[29] In another creative example of reuse, the Will Rogers Hotel, a historic multistory hotel on Route 66 in Claremore, Oklahoma, was rehabilitated in 1998 as affordable elderly housing using federal investment tax credits. In addition, private businesspeople have converted many nearby commercial structures along Claremore's Main Street into antique stores, creating an extensive antique shopping district.[30] The citizens of Amarillo, Texas, have also converted its Route 66 historic district into a shopping area for antiques and specialty items.

In addition to adaptive use, many historic motels, hotels, and cafés on Route 66 continue to be used for their historic purpose. Some, such as the El Rancho Hotel in Gallup, New Mexico, have been open for business since their construction. Motels such as this have been maintained and modified over the years but never rehabilitated. The Ariston Café in Litchfield, Illinois, a historic restaurant on Route 66, has remained intact and in operation since it opened decades ago. Other examples of continuous use include the Wigwam Motel in Holbrook, Arizona; Roy's Café & Motel in Amboy, California; and the Historic Route 66 (formerly Hull's) Motel in Williams, Arizona.

In addition to the preservation of individual properties, a large-scale preservation effort on Route 66 is currently under way: the Route 66 Corridor Act, which the U.S. Congress passed in 1999. The act calls for collaboration among Route 66 enthusiasts, State Historic Preservation Offices (SHPOs), and the National Park Service to work toward the designation and preservation of the Route 66 corridor. The act defines the Route 66 corridor as "lands owned by the Federal

Figure 114. Hull's Motel (ca. 1950) functions as the Historic Route 66 Motel in Williams, Arizona, and is an example of effective preservation on Route 66. Photo by author, 1998.

Government and lands owned by State or local government within the immediate vicinity of those portions of the highway formerly designated as United States Route 66, and private land within the immediate vicinity that is owned by persons or entities that are willing to participate in the programs authorized by this Act."[31] This definition ensures that private property rights will not be affected, reflecting the political climate in Washington, D.C., at the time the act was passed.

The Corridor Act authorized the National Park Service to perform the following actions: (1) enter into cooperative agreements for planning preservation, rehabilitation, and restoration related to the Route 66 corridor; (2) accept donations of funds, equipment, and supplies; (3) provide federal cost-share grants not to exceed 50 percent of the project cost; (4) provide technical assistance; and (5) coordinate, promote, and stimulate research on the Route 66 corridor. The act cites the Secretary of the Interior's Standards for Historic Preservation as the basis for all authorized rehabilitation work and offers federal assistance for local efforts.[32] For the Corridor Act to be successful, local citizens and governments must take the lead.

On February 24–25, 2000, representatives from the National Park Service (NPS), SHPO staff from states along the route, one Tribal Preservation Officer, representatives of the National Trust for Historic Preservation, and delegates from numerous Route 66 organizations met in Oklahoma City. The meeting focused on sharing ideas on how to implement the recently passed Corridor Act and how to determine the roles of government preservation professionals, community members, and Route 66 enthusiasts.

A key discussion at the meeting was how to identify and preserve the most significant resources for preservation and also how to interpret them.[33] According to Greg Smith, a representative of the Texas SHPO's History Programs Division who attended the meeting, the participants often disagreed, especially on the level of government involvement, although nearly everyone welcomed the federal funding included in the act. Many residents of Route 66 communities and Route 66 enthusiasts thought that the funds should be focused on specific sites along the highway. Enthusiasts tended to emphasize tourism, while the preservation professionals focused on cataloging and preserving historic properties.

Because Route 66 has the widest public support and the largest pool of enthusiasts of any American highway, the preservation of Route 66 will have a significant influence on efforts to save other historic, long-distance American highways. A combination of professionalism and enthusiasm will be required to successfully preserve and interpret Route 66. Tourism without strong preservation measures may facilitate the road's success as a tourist route by increasing traffic, but without legal protection, this may encourage new development and a resulting destruction of the highway's historic resources. Increased traffic may bring increased pressure to build tourist attractions, glitzy diners, and nonhistoric streamlined gas stations designed to mimic historic buildings. The "Route 66 Diner," a faux historic diner built in 1987 on Route 66 in Albuquerque, New Mexico, stands as an example of nonhistoric intrusions that reduce the integrity of Route 66 landscapes.

Another example of a loss of historical integrity on Route 66 is the historic Union Bus Depot in Lebanon, Missouri, which was unsympathetically rehabilitated and reused as a furniture store.[34] While its owners did recycle the building, this sort of rehabilitation removes many historic features, making the building nearly unrecognizable. Although carefully designed and marketed new businesses can enhance historic Route 66, care must be taken to ensure that people do not confuse these recent additions with historic sites and that the buildings retain enough historical integrity to be recognizable.

Also, without strong historical zoning, increased traffic may be an impetus for state departments of transportation to widen existing historic alignments and remove aging, narrow bridges, thus destroying characteristics that make the highway historic. A significant increase in traffic often raises safety issues on aging roads, and without specific protections for historic roads, safety usually prevails.[35]

Although increased tourism can have negative impacts on historic resources, effective preservation would be difficult without visitors to enjoy the sites. Much of the interest in Route 66 that drives preservation efforts at the local level arises because merchants in Route 66 communities view the road as a potential source of revenue from tourists. Without an economic incentive, many property owners might view historic regulations as merely an annoyance and may choose to circumvent the law in order to make a return on their property. Many towns along historic Route 66 are in need of economic revitalization. The fact that a famous road links them may be their best chance to tap into the tourist industry. Route 66 brings tourists to remote communities that they would probably never visit otherwise. However, in order to channel tourism so that visitation aids preservation rather than hurting it, communities need to develop comprehensive local preservation plans.

Preserving the corridor should be undertaken with Route 66 acting as the link and justification for a plethora of local efforts, with guidance and support from the SHPOs and the NPS. Many towns along Route 66 could adopt the National Trust for Historic Preservation's Main Street Program to assist local business owners in economic revitalization and historic preservation of commercial buildings.[36] Continued

Figure 115. The Union Bus Depot in Lebanon, Missouri, has lost the characteristics that make it a recognizable historic building. Photo by author, 1998.

occupation of historic structures by local businesses, adaptive-use projects, historic zoning, and historic districts are effective tools to protect historic structures.

Preserving and reusing historic Route 66 as a tour route should reflect an integrated effort by enthusiast groups, government agencies, and historians to relink communities, cultural landscapes, and layers of historic events into inclusive, historically accurate, exciting, and comprehensive stories. Auto tours can be engaging and effective tools for heritage education that promote meaningful leisure. To achieve this, public historians should interpret the history of Route 66 from a wide base of sources and interpret the points of view of a broad variety of participants.

Many of the individuals who currently operate visitor centers and museums along Route 66 can remember the road and the effects of major events, such as the Dust Bowl and World War II, and interpret its history firsthand. However, most of these people will stop their activities within the next decade, making it necessary for a new generation of historians and preservationists to step in and develop methods of interpreting Route 66 without the benefit of direct memory. This raises several questions: What can replace their direct memory, and can public historians fill this void? How can we interpret the history of a myth and chronicle nostalgia for realities that may never have existed?

Figure 116. Moonrise over Motel La Loma, Santa Rosa, New Mexico. The cryptic sign says the motel was founded by a World War II veteran. Photo by author, 1998.

In the case of Route 66, historical realities and historical myths should not be confused. Interpretation should relate what travelers on Route 66 actually experienced and not merely how nostalgic enthusiasts view historic Route 66. This means developing broad historical contexts within American history for historic sites and landscapes and placing individual memories and artifacts within those contexts.

Methods of interpretation include Route 66 museums, directional signs, wayside exhibits, guidebooks, guided tours, pamphlets about individual sites, annotated maps, and media presentations such as films, tapes, and radio broadcasts. Any interpretive materials should result from extensive historical research aided by eyewitness accounts of Americans who have used and continue to use the corridor.

Preserving and interpreting Route 66 will allow today's travelers to rediscover the remote American landscapes that many of their parents and grandparents discovered on their auto trips. A comprehensive tour route over historic pathways can provide an authentic alternative to relatively artificial environments such as Disney World in Florida or even historic Colonial Williamsburg, Virginia. The communities along Route 66 are living, changing places where layers of history from prehistoric Indian occupations to the present can be encountered and enjoyed.

Members of Route 66 communities and public historians should collaborate on preservation efforts and interpretive programs for historic Route 66 sites to accurately relate their historical significance. If done thoughtfully, this can be accomplished without diminishing the allure that Route 66 has for so many people. The highway functions both as a historic artifact and a living symbol of the Southwest and of American auto culture in the mid-twentieth century. The story of both the documented history and the lore of Route 66 should be told to visitors in a manner that is both interesting and accurate.

Notes

1. U.S. Department of Interior National Park Service, *Special Study—Route 66* (Washington, D.C., 1995), 2.

2. Michael Wallis, *Route 66: The Mother Road* (New York: St. Martin's Press, 1990); *Route 66 Magazine, in Memory of Bobby Troupe*, collector's edition (summer 1999); Jerry Richard, ed., "Well Known Song Added to Popularity of Route 66" and "Route 66 in Legend, Song, Film, TV Series, and History," *Route 66 News, Magazine and Newsletter for the Historic Route 66 Association of Arizona* (April 1990): 21.

3. New Mexico State Highway Department, "New Mexico Official Road Map" (Santa Fe: New Mexico State Highway Department, 1954). "The Land of Enchantment" is the state of New Mexico's slogan.

4. Teri A. Cleeland, "Route 66 Revisited," *Cultural Resource Management* 2 (1993): 15.

5. Michael Wallis, lecture, Route 66 Expo, Shamrock, Texas, September 1998.

6. The estimated membership of a selection of Route 66 associations includes The National Route 66 Federation: 1,700 members; the California Historic Route 66 Association: 300 members; Historic Route 66 Association of Arizona: 800 members; New Mexico Route 66 Association: 320 members; Old Route 66 Association of Texas: 143 members; Canadian Route 66 Association: 166 members; Norwegian Route 66 Association: 190 members. These estimates came from an Internet query made by the author, September 5, 2000.

7. *Route 66 News: The Quarterly Newsletter of the Historic Route 66 Association of Arizona* (winter 1999): 3. Of the 208 foreign visitors reported, 58 came from Germany and 38 from the United Kingdom.

8. Jayne Clark, "A Golden Road's Unlimited Devotion," *USA Today*, October 29, 2001, Internet. Available from www.usatoday.com/life/travel/leisure/2001/2001-06-29-route66.htm. Accessed December 21, 2001. Shawn Shepherd, "The Legacy of Route 66: Highways Always Have an Economic Impact, Positive and Negative; The Mother Road Transformed New Mexico," *New Mexico Business Journal*, Internet. Available from www.nmbiz.com/issues/01/Sep%2001. Accessed December 21, 2001. The Route 66 International Association Web Site, Internet. Available from www.rt66.com/~chs/help.html. Accessed December 21, 2001.

9. Bob Moore, "Fifties Memories," *Route 66 Magazine* (fall 1998): 50–51.

10. Lou Delina, "Kerouac & Cassady: Were These Free Spirits the Original Buzz & Tod?" *Route 66 Magazine* (winter 1995/96): 42–44.

11. Martha Sherrill, "55 Cadillac on Route 66: Tour Guide to Tad Pierson's America Dream Safari," *Esquire* (August 1995): 36.

12. D. Jeanene Tiner, *Route 66 Mainstreet of America* (Mesa, AZ: Terrell Publishing 1998), 17.

13. Anne Derry, H. Ward Jandi, Carol D. Shull, and Jan Thorman (rev. by Patricia L. Parker, 1985), *Guidelines for Local Surveys: A Basis for Preservation Planning*, National Register Bulletin 24 (Washington, D.C.: U.S. Department of Interior, National Park Service, 1977), 3.

14. Greg Smith, the National Register coordinator at the Texas Historical Commission and the author of this dissertation developed this plan in July 2001. The Texas Historical Commission is the State Historic Preservation Office of Texas.

15. Charles A. Birnbaum and Christine Capella Peters, *The Secretary of the Interior's Standards for the Treatment of Historic Properties with Guidelines for the Treatments of Cultural Landscapes*, National Park Service Cultural Resource Stewardship and Partnerships Heritage Preservation Services Historic Landscape Initiative (Washington, D.C.: U.S. Department of Interior 1995), 4.

16. David Knudson, "Director's Notes," *Route 66 Federation News* (summer 1998): 2.

17. Alfred Runte, quoted in "Canyons, Cozy Dogs, and the Meaning of the West," by Peter Fish, *Sunset* (December 19, 1998).

18. Bob Waldmire, quoted in "Canyons, Cozy Dogs, and the Meaning of the West," by Peter Fish, *Sunset* (December 19, 1998).

19. ARCHITEXAS, Architecture, Planning, and Historic Preservation, Inc., *Tower Station and U-Drop Inn, Shamrock, Texas: Historic Structure Report & Restoration Master Plan* (Dallas: ARCHITEXAS, 2000), 2.

20. Teri A. Cleeland, "Route 66 Revisited," *Cultural Resource Management* 16 (1993): 15–18.

21. An Internet search revealed that 67 sites associated with Route 66 have been individually listed in the National Register. Of these eight were in Arizona, one was in Illinois, 34 were in New Mexico, 23 were in Oklahoma, and one was in Texas. Property types listed included motels, gas stations, cafés, trading posts, auto dealerships, highway segments, bridges, a tire store, and a bakery. Internet. Available from www.amarillonet.com; accessed January 10, 2001.

22. Copies of these National Register Multiple Property Listings are available upon request from the respective State Historic Preservation Offices. They contain a statement of historic contexts and describe associated property types along Route 66 in detail.

23. Although properties deemed eligible for listing in the National Register by a State Historic Preservation Office receive the same protection as listed properties, listing removes any doubt that the property will be considered historic.

24. This statement is based on the author's experience working closely with Section 106 in Texas as an employee of the Texas Department of Transportation and at the Texas Historical Commission.

25. Olivia Fagerberg, Tax Credit coordinator, Texas Historical Commission, discussion with author, May 2000.

26. Mary Alice Robbins, "Area Towns Get in Proposal for Improvements," *Amarillo Globe-News*, January 26, 2000, Internet. Available from www.amarillonet.com. Accessed on September 21, 2000. Shamrock received $1,746,864 in federal funds to rehabilitate the tower station.

27. The city of San Antonio, Texas, has such an ordinance. The only shortcoming is that there has been opposition to the creation of new National Register districts by property owners, resulting in fewer districts in that city.

28. ARCHITEXAS, *Architecture, Planning, and Historic Preservation*, 3.

29. Gateway Trailnet, Internet. Available from www.cruisin66.com/stl/cor.html. Accessed on April 24, 2002. This is a nonprofit organization with 800 members that formed in 1996 to preserve the historic bridge.

30. Site visit by author, 1998.

31. U.S. Congress, Route 66 Corridor Preservation Act, Public Law 106–45, Historic Preservation 16 USC 461, H.R. 66 1999.

32. Ibid.

33. Gregory Smith and Carol Ahlgren, "Route 66 Revisited: Preserving the Mother Road," *SCA News* (winter 1999/2000): 3.

34. Historic postcard in author's collection.

35. This observation is based on the author's experiences working as an architectural historian for the Texas Department of Transportation.

36. Peter H. Brink, "Livable Communities and Historic Transportation Corridors," *Cultural Resource Management* 16, no. 11 (1993): 52–53.

Study Questions

1. How did the Route 66 help popularize the American West?

2. Compare the popularity of the new interstates to travelers' feelings about old Route 66.

3. Why does Route 66 cause Americans to feel so nostalgic? Why is it so appealing?

4. Describe some of the challenges associated with preserving what is left of Route 66.

5. Explain the concept of a cultural landscape. Why is Route 66 a cultural landscape?

6. What is the National Register of Historic Places (NRHP)? What are three benefits of being listed on the NRHP?

7. List four ways that places on Route 66 have been preserved, adapted, or kept consistent with their historical use.

8. Why is it so important to preserve the historical buildings along Route 66?

9. What are some ways to interpret Route 66 for tourists?

Making the West Look Western

The Rise of the Old West Revival Architectural Style

Jay Price

Tourists traveling the highways of the American West often encounter what look like vestiges of the "Old West" or "Wild West."[1] For example, along former Route 66, the traveler might stop at "Fort Courage," Arizona, where a full-scale "replica" of a wooden stockade fort stands next to a pancake house from the 1950s. Along the Arizona–New Mexico border, an immense, multistory building shaped like a tepee sits in a red rock canyon where travelers can purchase Indian jewelry and other souvenirs. Various other tepee (or "tipi" or "wigwam") structures dot the roadside from a wigwam village motel in Holbrook, Arizona, to Teepee Curios in Tucumcari, New Mexico.

Fictitious "Old West" buildings also cover the roadsides of the American West. Near Cubero, New Mexico, the motorist passes the remains of what looks like a Western town. Closer inspection reveals that it was really a cinder block structure with a wooden facade. Farther east, Amarillo, Texas, sports the Big Texan, a bright yellow Western-looking restaurant where hungry diners can get a free 72-oz. steak dinner provided they eat it in a given amount of time. Nor is Route 66 the only place where the motorist can find the Old West. Along Highway 54 in Kansas, travelers see the remains of Burketown in Greensburg, another Western-looking town whose wooden false fronts hide plywood and concrete. Just north of Lawrence, Kansas, Tipi Corner has stood since the 1930s as a local landmark.

"Old West Revival" is an apt description of this look. As the preceding structures demonstrate, popular culture holds a fairly consistent idea about what a "Western" town supposedly looked like. There are false-fronted buildings made out of rough, often unpainted wood. Side walls are covered in a crude board and batten or weathered clapboard siding. The front facade often has a shed roof porch with some simplified "Victorian"-looking details. The main entrance should have swinging doors. Decorative elements include wagon wheels, hitching posts, lassos, revolvers and shotguns, horse-riding equipment, and occasional "Indian" items. While not required, having a tepee or stockade wooden fort nearby reinforces the image. Lettering of signs has a familiar pattern with oversized and exaggerated serifs and a narrow/vertical appearance. Even certain words and names are part of the mystique. *Sheriff*, *ghost town*, *prospector*, and *gulch* evoke an image of a particular place and time. Establishments that serve food or alcohol are naturally going to be called "saloons"—even if the male-only domain of the original prototypes would have been anathema to modern family-style restaurants.

For nearly two decades, scholars have wrestled with the interplay among tourism, history, nostalgia, collective memory, and architectural revivals. Revival styles reflect the values and ideals of the builders and the owners.[2] For example, Alan Axelrod noted in his book *The Colonial Revival in America* that this style used elements and prototypes that symbolized a past dominated by faith, family, patriotism, and hard work. Its focus on domestic handcrafts made by skilled artisans evoked a time before the Victorian obsession with mass production. Axelrod observed that "in this country, colonial can be seen as a code word for anti- or non-Victorian, anti- or nonmodern."[3] There were also racial and ethnic reasons for using Colonial Revival. The style looked to a time when most of the white population of the United States came from British stock, a supposedly more "American" population that predated the influx of later immigrants from southern and eastern Europe.

Architectural historians have tended to place the heyday of the revival era from circa 1890 through the 1940s. The years after World War II fell simply into the eras of the "modern" and "postmodern," dominated by figures such as Frank Lloyd Wright and I. M. Pei. However, with a growing awareness that vernacular and commercial architecture is worth studying in its own right, it is becoming clear that the post–World War II era was not simply a bastion of form-follows-function modernism. Traditional Colonial Revival styles persisted and new revivals emerged. They just tended to be found in commercial structures or suburban houses rather than unique commissions from noted architects. Old West Revival has many of the same dynamics as earlier revival styles. It evokes a mythical past (one that often never existed), borrows and reinforces symbols that are common in the popular culture, and points to an era supposedly embracing values that should be emulated today. This style also reinforces a sense of national and regional identity by creating the basis of a supposedly "Western" look.

In contrast to earlier revivals, however, that showed up in domestic, commercial, public, and ecclesiastical buildings, Old West Revival emerged out of the commercial sector and stayed largely with that sector. Commercial needs even dictated the locations of the style. It was the look of the 1950s-era commercial strip, not the 1900s-era Main Street. The style was especially suited to businesses related to the tourist industry such as curio shops, motels, restaurants, and campgrounds. Moreover, this was a look communities developed if they were trying to cultivate a "Wild West" image as a tourist draw. It was architecture for boosterism. The look, however, reflected more than just business window dressing. As with many other revivals, the business community helped develop and promote a set of symbols for a region that was struggling to define its identity in connection with the tourist industry.

A Western Style Emerges

As with other revivals, Old West Revival borrowed images from actual prototypes, in this case structures found throughout the West. The irony was that there was nothing particularly Western about the original architecture. Buildings considered "Victorian" or

Figure 117. Many Western states have moved historic structures off their original sites and into "historic" villages, which ruins the buildings' historic context and makes the structures ineligible for the National Register of Historic Places. A notable exception is South Pass City, Wyoming, where the nineteenth-century false front buildings still exist on their original dirt streets close to the Oregon Trail. Photo by Andrew Gulliford, 1994.

simply "old-fashioned" in Maine or Virginia became identified as "Western" if they happened to be in Nevada or Colorado. The American West of the nineteenth century was a colonial society. Cultural, political, and economic ties connected with and supported the mother country. For Anglo-Americans that meant the eastern United States, whose architectural styles were themselves colonial-like adaptations of European models. Thus architecture in the American West tended to be "second-generation copies" of European forms.

As author C. Robert Haywood and others have pointed out, the goal of early town leaders was to develop their communities (and their investments) by encouraging growth, prosperity, and stability.[4] To make their communities look like good investments and good places to live, these businessmen and businesswomen tried, with the resources they had, to replicate the fashionable styles of the East. This became even easier once railroads worked their way across the region, bringing with them mass-produced details and materials. Wealth from mining, cattle, timber, agriculture, and commerce financed two- and three-story brick commercial structures, Second Empire– and Queen Anne–style mansions, and Gothic Revival

Figure 118. This authentic Western streetscape as it appeared in Silt, Colorado, in 1978 was dramatically altered by oil shale development in the 1980s. Photo by Andrew Gulliford, 1978.

churches. County seats built courthouses using classical and Romanesque revival elements. Ranch houses of the wealthiest cattle tycoons could look like miniature English castles or French chateaux. As Randolph Delahanty and A. Andrew McKinney have noted, "The Hollywood image of the wooden cowboy town is not *the* West, but only a part of a much more complex and architecturally rich region."[5]

Western towns certainly had their share of small, wooden, false-fronted buildings. Kingston Heath's contribution to the book *Images of an American Land: Vernacular Architecture in the Western United States* shows how the use of false fronts in Montana boomtowns represented attempts to re-create an urban feel in an otherwise sparsely inhabited region. Yet these structures represented vernacular buildings common throughout the United States well into the 1920s. Similar examples existed in any city in the country where there was a need for cheap housing or storefronts. One-story commercial stores with false fronts were typical of any small town of the nineteenth century, regardless of region. The wooden buildings of Colorado's mining communities often resembled those of the oil boomtowns or even military bases decades later. Small, wooden buildings with board and batten siding and false fronts were cheap and relatively easy to build, making them ideal for newly planted Western towns. They were the "prefabs" of their day: temporary shelters put up quickly until their owners could replace them with more substantial ones.

These communities had so many wooden vernacular structures because they were new, not because they were Western. Early photographs of newly founded "boomtowns" such as Wichita or Dodge City show main streets that look like the stereotypical wooden "Western" buildings. However, such photos often showed the very start of the town—within a year or two of founding. In a few years, if a town continued to grow and develop, those main streets often looked very different. Depending on the community, photographs taken of main streets five years after a town's founding often showed streetscapes indistinguishable from all but the very largest of Eastern cities. False-fronted wood structures still existed but often on the side streets or in areas developing outward from the central business district.[6]

The boom-and-bust cycle of Western economics favored some communities and ruined others. Towns that continued to grow and prosper usually kept up with the latest in architectural styles. By the twentieth century, bustling communities tore down their now-outdated Victorian-era buildings and replaced them with whatever style was fashionable elsewhere. Meanwhile, periodic fires had eliminated whole downtowns, encouraging places from Tombstone to Dodge City to rebuild out of brick or stone.

It was in the places that failed to grow that the process of architectural change stopped. Towns whose mines had played out, that got bypassed by railroads and roads, that lost out to rival communities could not afford to build new. As they languished, these smaller towns became time capsules. Their early buildings did not get replaced, embodying the look of their heyday. At first they appeared simply outdated. As the twentieth century wore on, however, these fading, sometimes dilapidated buildings gained a mystique as hallmarks to a bygone age. They became the embodiment of the West's earlier years.

Searching for a Western Look

Meanwhile, designers and architects in parts of the West started becoming interested in styles that represented their region. In an era when mass-produced sameness could be shipped worldwide, uniqueness started becoming an attractive quality for a place. Fairs and exhibitions, such as the 1893 Columbian Exhibition, prompted countries, states, and organizations to develop exhibits that showcased their unique features. In planning for these displays, architects from New England, the South, the Southwest, and California all began selecting images from existing historic structures to replicate in new buildings. Architects, promoters, and companies such as the Atchison, Topeka, and Santa Fe Railroad all borrowed languages from earlier styles and incorporated them, with varying success, into other buildings. The infant tourism industry was especially interested in promoting unique regional qualities to induce people to travel to things they could not find at home. This was also an era when activists began focusing on historic structures that were being lost to industrialization. Therefore, revival styles were a natural outgrowth of a society for whom national, ethnic, and regional identities—and their related symbols—were important issues. States such as California and New Mexico developed distinctive styles of architecture and design through these mediums.

In the early twentieth century, the closest style associated with the West was the Spanish-inspired look from California and the Southwest. Magazines such as *Sunset* actively promoted a Mediterranean or Mission style as western, although to such publications, California *was* the West. By the 1920s, the magazine featured a column called "the Home in the West" and usually discussed Mediterranean- and Spanish-inspired buildings that seemed classic yet modern. Meanwhile, stuccoed walls and tile roofs started appearing in places that the Spanish never settled. For example, the courthouse/city building for Maricopa County, Arizona (constructed 1928) and the city hall of Dodge City, Kansas (constructed 1929), were in a Spanish style. Whole communities such as Ajo, Arizona, used Spanish Colonial Revival motifs. There were even a few mining towns in the Southwest, such as Tyrone, New Mexico, that employed the style as a general look. When the mining ran out, Tyrone became a contradiction in imagery: a Spanish Colonial Revival–style ghost town. By the late 1920s and early 1930s, adaptations of this style merged with Art Moderne, Art Deco, and Pueblo Revival to form variants such as "Pueblo Deco."[7] Tile roofs—or at least sections of tile roofs—merged with stucco walls, simplified parapets, and arched windows to emulate what a "Southwestern" building supposedly looked like. Meanwhile, 1920s-era hotels and resorts, such as Santa Fe's La Fonda or the Jokake Inn outside of Phoenix, used pueblo motifs to create a distinctive image.

To an extent, Spanish Colonial, Pueblo Deco, and Southwestern styles reflected a Southwest with much more fluid boundaries than today. Wichita, Kansas, for example, proudly called itself "The Empire of the Southwest" and in the 1920s, boosters were very clear that the city's regional identity was connected to that region. Architecture reinforced this notion. In 1928, an article appeared in the *Wichita Eagle* about the rise in "Spanish style" houses in that city. The article quipped, "Perhaps the new way of thinking of Wichita as belonging to the Southwest instead of the Middle West is somewhat responsible for the increasing popularity of the Spanish type of structure."[8]

Yet the Mediterranean/Spanish/Pueblo styles were never fully convincing as a look for the entire West. Throughout the region, Tudor Revival and Colonial Revival were just as prevalent for public and civic buildings. For example the AT & SF Railway, the company whose Harvey Houses helped popularize the Pueblo and Spanish style in New Mexico, was just as likely to use English-inspired Tudor in places such as Kansas.

The lack of a regional architectural language for the interior West extended into the 1930s. New Deal architects were particularly interested in using regional architectural traditions in their works, resulting in Pueblo Revival schools and courthouses in New Mexico, Spanish/Mediterranean Revival–style projects in California, and Colonial Revival back east. When it came to the interior West, however, there was no indigenous style to borrow from. New Deal building in this region ranged from classical to modern, Colonial to Mediterranean. In a few cases, an architect or builder tried to create a "Western" theme to a structure by using designs from Native American art or incorporating figures of Native Americans, particularly the plains tribes. Dating from 1928, Wichita's North High School, for example, featured Indian portraits and buffalos among its decorations.[9]

Works Progress Administration guidebooks featured sections on architecture in each state but sometimes struggled to describe what was unique for the state. The guide to Kansas suggested that it was climate that shaped architecture, with a long section on the need for porches in the state.[10] The guide to Colorado noted in 1941 that "little today distinguishes the usual Colorado town or city from communities of comparable size anywhere in the West or Middle West."[11] The Oklahoma guide observed that "as he prospered, the Oklahoman was quick to adopt foreign types of architecture and mix one with another" but

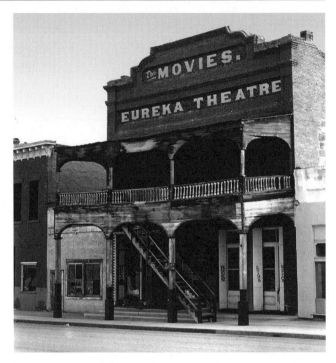

Figure 119. Old West Revival structures often include porches, but few are as ornate as this original two-story wooden porch on the brick Eureka Theatre in Eureka, Nevada, along U.S. Highway 50, accurately billed as "the loneliest highway in America." Photo by Andrew Gulliford, 1982.

did note that some tourist courts had walls of earth mixed with bitumen, musing that an "Oklahoma Adobe" look might be on the horizon.[12]

Developing a "Western" Architectural Language

The years from 1930 through the 1960s witnessed the development of Old West Revival as a look that represented the West as a whole rather than just the region settled by the Spanish. In part, this related to a growing awareness that the West had a regional identity. Sun Belt cities drew thousands of people to new lives in the deserts of the Southwest. Thousands more took advantage of decent roads, vacation time, and affordable automobile travel to visit the West and its attractions. The West already had a reputation as a place of natural beauty and exotic cultures. By World War II, a new quality to Western tourism had emerged as well: that it was the place of the "frontier" and the "Wild West," where cowboys and outlaws lived lives of romantic adventure. It was the place of rough boomtowns, where saloons, hitching posts, and six-shooters were supposedly still part of everyday life. The mythology that began with Buffalo Bill's Wild West Show, expanded through the dime novel, and was popularized through the movies, identified a historical past that could connect to modern American identity. Just as New England had developed an image centering on the small town and colonial experience, the South reveled in the legacy of the Civil War, and California connected itself to the Spanish era, "Western" and "Old West" started becoming one and the same. It allowed a region to tap into a white, Anglo-American heritage instead of the Spanish one. This was a white West with which large segments of the country could readily identify.

The West had qualities that went back to the mythical era of cattle drives and stagecoach robberies. One of the first guidebooks to Route 66 noted in 1946 that Erick, Oklahoma, "is the first town you encounter, going west, which has a true 'western' look, with its wide, sun-baked streets, frequent horsemen, occasional sidewalk awnings, and similar touches."[13] Las Vegas's early developers used the imagery of the Western gambler before they decided to promote a more glamorous look. Establishments were named the Golden Nugget, the Pioneer Club, and the Eldorado. There was even a "Helldorado" village, where original structures and re-creations recreated an Old West atmosphere. Meanwhile, towns such as Deadwood, South Dakota, and Tombstone, Arizona, both of which had started promoting their Western heritage as early the 1920s, mixed the myth of the Old West with the towns' actual histories.[14]

In the early twentieth century, tourism to the West was limited to the places accessible by rail and tended to center around two main regions: the Rocky Mountains and the desert Southwest. People visited to connect with stunning natural beauty, whether through fancy resorts or rugged dude ranches, or to experience exotic and romantic cultures of the Pueblo Indians and Spanish settlers. The development of the Old West as a place worth visiting in its own right was different from the nature and culture tourism of previous generations. It was more middle class, geared to the family vacation rather than the extended stay. It catered to a segment of the population little discussed in the literature on tourism: children. The ads alone are telling. While ads and articles in journals such as *Travel* showed mainly adults in European vacations, it was a rare Western-themed piece or ad that did not include some portrayal of children in cowboy hats. Often boys looked intently at a guide showing off a revolver. By visiting the Old West, families could connect with the world their children (and they as well) were very familiar with.[15]

The development of the Old West as a tourist destination increased the types of communities that could cater to the tourist industry. Desert towns in Arizona and Nevada that did not have the stunning natural scenery of the Rocky Mountains or the cultural heritage of Santa Fe found that they had something to promote. Magazines such as *Arizona Highways* and *Westways* regularly featured articles about picturesque old mining camps, old forts, and exotic ruins. Fading mining towns in Colorado and Montana had a new business to embrace once the mines closed. Plains states such as Nebraska, Kansas, and Oklahoma were not tourist destinations in the 1920s or 1930s but after World War II rediscovered (or in some cases manufactured) a Western heritage. By the 1950s, the ability to market a Western mystique allowed communities throughout the interior West such as Tombstone and Wickenburg in Arizona and Dodge City and Abilene in Kansas to tap into the business and supposed profits of tourism.

For these towns, image was as important as actual attractions. People visited the West to do more than just see things. They visited to experience a region, and by extension a nation, that supposedly was the product of hardy pioneers and rugged individuals who tamed a continent. The West was a sacred place, the crucible that authors such as Frederick Jackson Turner argued created the national identity. As Marguerite Shaffer has observed, "tourism . . . allowed white, native born middle- and upper-class Americans to escape the social and cultural confines of everyday life to liminal space where they could temporarily reimagine themselves as heroic or authentic figures."[16] As the mythology of the Western became quintessentially American, communities worked to turn that mythology into tangible, concrete forms. Events such as the Kansas Centennial celebration openly touted that connection. "Gunslingers, fast draw champions, can-can dancers, stage coaches, 'opery,' blacksmithy are all part of the Centennial atmosphere that is being created" quoted one article.[17] Starting in the 1940s, Old West Revival emerged as a way to reinforce this image.

Several trends came together to form the architectural language of Old West Revival, each influencing the others. Some of the first imagery clearly came from the works of Frederic Remington and Charles Russell as well as the illustrations for pulp Western novels. Architecturally, however, the first important trend was the development of commercial roadside architecture in the 1920s and 1930s. This was an era when businesses constructed fanciful buildings whose gaudy colors and unique designs captured the attention of the passing motorist. The point was to be readily identifiable from a distance so that drivers would slow down in time to pull off the road and visit. Examples ranged from mock icebergs in Albuquerque, New Mexico, to concrete whales in water parks in Oklahoma to statues of Paul Bunyan in Minnesota. These attractions transformed the American highway into a fantasyland filled with exotic places and sites. The mere act of driving allowed Americans to explore and become part of worlds that they read about in novels, listened to on the radio, and saw on the movie screen.

With its distinctive conical shape and suitability for colorful Native American designs, the tepee was a natural form for roadside entrepreneurs to copy. The man who helped popularize the artificial tepee was a Kentuckian named Frank Redford. According to legend, Redford first encountered conical roadside architecture at an ice cream stand in California that was shaped like a large ice cream cone. He then took the idea back to Kentucky, where he built "Wigwam Village" at Horse Cave, Kentucky, in 1933. It combined modern comfort with rustic, hickory furniture and an eclectic mixture of Apache, Navajo, and other Native American decorations with a distinctive, if contrived, look. By the 1940s, a "Wigwam Village" chain included 11 sites across the West, with those of Rialto, California, and Holbrook, Arizona, being the most famous. Although tepees appeared across the United States, they most commonly appeared in two regions: the upper plains states (Nebraska in particular) and along Route 66 in New Mexico, Arizona, and southern California. The latter concentration was in a region where the resident tribes did not even live in tepees, but such commercial architecture reflected a growing belief that there was a generic "Indian" look. As with New Deal–related buildings and earlier "Pueblo Deco," Pueblo and Plains Indian designs mixed with little regard to accuracy. Of course, historical accuracy was probably not paramount to someone who built concrete wigwams in regions where the real Native Americans built pueblos. What was important was that it looked "Indian," reinforcing the notion that Native Americans were a defining feature of the supposedly "Western" experience.[18]

A second trend was that of the dude ranch industry and the rise of a "ranch" look. Originally, dude ranches were working ranches that allowed guests to temporarily become part of the staff. By the 1920s, they had become a major part of the economy in the northern Rocky Mountains, enabling entrepreneurs in Montana and Wyoming to form the Dude Ranchers' Association. According to Lawrence Borne, the main era of dude ranching lasted into the 1950s. By then, such ranches had become a familiar part of the tourist landscape.

The buildings of the ranches, like the clothing and horseback riding, became standard images for the West. Ranches offered facilities that were usually comfortable with modern conveniences but promoted a simple, even rustic look. Some "dudes" lodged in existing ranch buildings, but many ranches constructed small cabins, often with shallow pitched roofs and front porches. Walls ranged from logs to board and batten to adobe,

Figure 120. Cerrillos, New Mexico, has a streetscape that is both historic and also modified to represent the nineteenth century. Movies played the biggest role in shaping global attitudes about what architecture looks "Western." Sometimes whole towns, such as Cerrillos, got makeovers to look Western enough for the movies. Photo by author.

depending on the region. The key, however, was that they looked like they were part of a working ranch instead of the tourist facilities that they were. Later on, motels were especially likely to borrow from dude ranch motifs, because they evoked images of relaxing on a ranch out west even if the motel was in a large city.

Although real ranch structures ranged from Victorian mansions to crude shacks, the ranches of California often served as a model for Western-themed architecture. In the 1940s and 1950s, builders adapted the long, low profiles, large, overhanging porches, earth tones, board and batten siding, and simple, wooden structural features with a minimum of detailing. Magazines such as *Sunset* began promoting the "ranch" house as the ideal American home, for reasons of comfort as much as nostalgia. In 1950, the editors of the magazine put out what was already the third printing of a book titled *Western Ranch Houses*, in which they mused that "most of us describe any one-story house with a low, close-to-the ground silhouette as a ranch house. . . . Wide, protected porches immediately suggest outdoor living—lazy summer afternoons, informal entertaining."[19] The book continues with a brief "history" of the ranch, connecting it to the Mexican/Anglo-American hybrids that developed along the coast of California. Even so, the authors were explicit that the ranch was a form of house, not a style. The plans in the book outlined several adaptations of this form, ranging from the white stucco and red tile of the Spanish Colonial Revival to the wooden shingles and board and batten siding that hearkened back to the period of Anglo settlement.[20]

The most important source for Old West Revival was Hollywood movies. Thanks to the movies, a distinctive, identifiable Western appearance developed. This look emerged for reasons of both cinematography and location. As several scholars of the genre have shown, the plot of the Western often hinged on characters interacting with nature and the "frontier." The world of the Western was meant to be the antithesis of everything urban and Eastern. The very roughness of the land and the characters gave the genre its edge. This type of setting lent itself to depicting towns as small, even token outposts of civilization

Figure 121. Old Cowtown in Wichita, Kansas, embodies the Old West Revival style. Sometimes museums placed historic structures next to re-creations that were supposed to "look Western." Old Cowtown Museum in Wichita, Kansas, set up in the 1950s, preserved several of the community's oldest structures. During the celebration of Kansas's centennial, the museum brought several structures on-site or constructed new buildings in the style that looked appropriate, often based on Hollywood imagery. The building on the left is the Empire House, dating from 1904. The large building on the right was originally a variety theater and dates from 1961. Photo by author.

surrounded by wilderness. Thus towns had a single main street, perfect for staging shoot-outs. Movies ignored most of the institutions that the Victorian West actually tried to promote such as ornate courthouses, fashionable schools, and substantial churches. In this mythology, the rough and the crude, not propriety and elegance, were "Western" qualities. Based on this image, one of the messages Old West Revival reinforced was an assertion of tough, rugged masculinity, when hardy pioneers and cowboys won the West. The Victorian elegance of the actual buildings seemed too feminine, Eastern, and effete to look really "Western."[21]

The locations of the Western movie and television show also contributed to the look. Essentially, there were two types of "Western" town in the movies: the frontier boomtown with wooden buildings and false fronts and the borderlands town with adobe and Mexican-inspired buildings, especially missions. More research needs to be done on the locations where most of these movies were shot and who developed them. Some movies used studio back lots, but many others used locations near Los Angeles. Some of the earliest films used California mining towns such as Bodie, California. These had once been prosperous or at least substantial towns but by the twentieth century had fallen on hard times. Buildings had become worn and dilapidated. Thus, some of the "roughness" associated with the Western may have been due to the fact that the locations for the films were in communities in decline.

By the 1930s, the Western look had become so well defined that movie lots became industries in their own right. Savvy investors purchased land around California and throughout the Southwest to develop into movie sets for Hollywood. Meanwhile, the leadership of movie lots such as Arizona's Old Tucson, California's Corriganville, and Knott's Berry Farm quickly found that the sets themselves were popular tourist attractions. Eventually, as rides and Western-themed paraphernalia catered to a generation of children reared on the Western, theme parks separate from the movie industry became big business. Some were large establishments, such as Frontierland at

Disneyland. However, there were scores of smaller parks with a Western or frontier theme. Using plywood and paint, these facilities attempted to recreate the "authentic" Old West, meaning, of course, the West as depicted in the movies.[22]

For all of the fake movie imagery that contributed to Old West Revival, however, there was an element of actual history. By the 1950s, communities throughout the West began to reassess the value of structures that had long been forgotten and neglected. It was a movement especially noticeable in small communities that had started looking to tourism as a profitable industry. By the late 1950s, for example, Tombstone, Arizona, had become a symbol of all that seemed to be Western. A town that had lost its status as the county seat and saw the mining industry fade seemed to discover a new source of wealth: its past. Four television shows: *Sheriff of Cochise*, *Wyatt Earp*, *Broken Arrow*, and *Tombstone Territory* were supposedly set in Tombstone. A speech at a 1950 local event noted that tourists "come here to see a show. They come to see part of the old West." This same speech encouraged local citizens to dress in Western-style outfits to reinforce that atmosphere.[23]

The attitude extended to architecture. In November 1949, a group of interested citizens formed the Tombstone Restoration Commission "so that the City of Tombstone may become a monument to the Old West." The commission also controlled future construction to match the 1880s style of the historic buildings. The town's image centered on the earliest years as a rough-and-tumble mining camp, a period that culminated in the now infamous shoot-out at the OK Corral on October 26, 1881. Its nickname, "the town too tough to die," conjured up images of gunfights, of cowboys and sheriffs, of the noose waiting for the outlaw who got caught. Tombstone embraced a macho toughness with Victorian elegance relegated to pseudobrothels. Nearly every business in the downtown district began to cater to the tourist trade by promoting the town's "Wild West" reputation, from stores selling Western merchandise to bars and diners that called themselves "saloons." In this surreal atmosphere, the past and present merged, as if Wyatt Earp might just appear out of the dusty desert to buy a cola and a Popsicle. Tombstone was just a more visible example of a trend that took place throughout the region: a gradual realization that much of the original architectural heritage was being lost to neglect and development.[24]

If historic preservation helped develop an awareness of Western architecture, a growing fascination with ghost towns reinforced it. Delahanty and McKinney suggest that "the West's contribution to the national mental landscape has been the ghost town—a string of places exploited and then abandoned when the main chance moved on somewhere else."[25] By the 1950s and 1960s, hundreds of mining towns throughout the West had fallen victim to the boom-and-bust economy of the region. Mines closed and workers left. Turn-of-the-century buildings that had served the community became abandoned and started falling into disrepair. The western landscape was dotted by dozens of towns whose wooden buildings needed paint and had started leaning against crumbling foundations. As more people visited and moved to the West, these ghost towns became popular places to visit. Guidebooks to ghost towns started appearing, complete with maps to lead the motorist to these romantic vestiges of the past. As one article put it, "The glory still lives of robust pioneer days when a man's calling card was the six-gun on his hip and there might always be a rich lode over the next hill."[26] The article went on to describe towns that dated from the turn of the twentieth century, when labor unrest was a greater issue than claim jumping. Even so, the ghost town craze allowed buildings from as late as the 1920s to be grandfathered into the Old West Revival style.

Small towns that were monuments to boom and bust could safely become among the most beloved symbols of the region because the big cities of the West were themselves booming and growing. Had the region faced harder economic times, the ghost town probably would not have seemed so romantic. When the Phelps Dodge Corporation closed its operations in Jerome, Arizona, in the 1950s, the community quickly retooled itself as "America's Largest Ghost City."

The city seemed to revel in its death, complete with an annual celebration called Spooks Homecoming. Throughout the West, communities found that economic death of one industry meant the emergence of another. Meanwhile, communities that did not have actual ghost towns, such as Los Angeles, could build replicas, such as Buena Park. At times, "ghost town" was simply a synonym for any Western town that looked old, regardless of habitation.[27]

By the late 1950s, these various trends had come together to create a common image for what a "Western" town should look like. Any Bugs Bunny or Wile E. Coyote cartoon set in the West featured stylized versions of rough, wooden, false-fronted buildings, testifying to the popularity of the image as a regional icon. Although the West had burgeoning cities suffering from suburban sprawl, the imagery of the region rested with the small, semi-abandoned towns whose architecture had survived from the late nineteenth century. What had been simply cheap buildings of Victorian society became icons of an era when cowboys and lawmen fought each other in saloons and dusty streets. Aging buildings that had endured years of neglect reinforced the supposed "wildness" of the Wild West, an image that would have horrified their original occupants.

For example, the museum at the Dalton Gang hideout in Meade, Kansas, featured rough, Old West Revival buildings in the twentieth century that look more "Western" than the Victorian-era vernacular house that the Daltons actually knew. Victorian gingerbread decorations did not seem tough enough to be linked to the Dalton Gang. Even more ironic was how communities that had never been part of the cattle era or mining booms embraced this look. Many towns in the interior West date from the 1880s and 1890s, well after the era of the stagecoach and the cattle drive. Many were railroad towns and agricultural centers. Yet by the 1950s, boosters in some of these towns tried to evoke a colorful and nostalgic past that never existed by playing into a Wild West mystique. Greensburg, Kansas, was one such community. It was founded in the late 1870s as a stop on the Santa Fe Railway and was never tied to the cattle trade as Abilene and Wichita had been. However, in the 1950s, a local restaurateur and collector named George Burke developed a theme park at the edge of town called "Burketown, U.S.A." Facades of a saloon, opera house, general store, and fire station hid structures that actually ranged from concrete block construction to Quonset huts. Exhibits were eclectic and included an array of horse-drawn vehicles and automobiles, ranging from a medicine show wagon to a 1913 Hudson Speedster. Burketown quickly became a point for town boosters to promote, with the world's largest hand-dug well and largest pallasite meteorite as local attractions. Old West Revival connected communities to a past shaped by cowboys and pioneers—even if that past was total fabrication. It helped reinforce a "Western" identity that communities could embrace and so opt out of the bland regional imagery of the Midwest.[28]

By the 1960s and 1970s, Old West Revival was an accepted look for Western buildings. The fad for rough wood became so intense in some places that people would go to ghost towns and take wood and other items for interior decorating. Meanwhile, convenience stores, restaurants, laundries, and gas stations around the country started imitating the look out of modern materials, a trend that continues to this day for any establishment that wants to evoke the image of the general store or the saloon. The tepee or wigwam was too unusual to be used for much beyond tourist-oriented architecture. However, the board and batten wall, false front, and rough porches of Old West Revival did manage to transcend their tourist industry origins and show up in businesses not connected with the motoring traveler. Even so, the look remains concentrated along highways and is still mainly commercial in nature.

Architecture for Boosterism

Old West Revival eventually became so established as "the" Western look that some communities did not

Figure 122. An offshoot of the movie ranch was the Western theme park. Burketown, in Greensburg, Kansas, was one of countless facilities where tourists could see "authentic" gunfights and participate in the mystique of the "Old West." Most of the buildings are made of plywood and concrete block and date from the 1960s. Photo by author.

feel their actual historic buildings looked "Western" enough. Structures that did not fit the image were either demolished or remodeled accordingly, as in the case of Dodge City, Kansas. Dodge City, sometimes called the "Poster Child of the West," provides a useful example of the development of Old West Revival. Dodge City began in the 1870s as a cattle town. Its Front Street sported the wooden false fronts typical of early boomtowns. However, within a decade, the downtown had developed the typical Victorian-era commercial structures found nationwide. For the next several decades, ornate brick facades dominated the downtown streetscape. As a railroad hub and center for a local ranching industry, there was little need to develop a unique look. Dodge City was not particularly interested in being associated with the 1870s Cowtown era. The community was always aware of its past but just as happy to talk about the present and future. By the 1910s, community leaders even promoted the modern sport of motorcycle racing as an attraction. Eventually, the town demolished an old school that had been built on Boot Hill (the cemetery that had been there was long gone and the bodies transferred to another cemetery by the 1880s) and constructed in its place a fashionable Spanish Colonial–style city hall in 1929.[29]

By the late 1930s, calls began to preserve some of Dodge City's Western-ness, especially after rumors started that the city commission was planning on leveling part of Boot Hill to create public tennis courts. Citizens began to develop symbols to recapture and reinforce the town's 1870s heritage. A local dentist, O. H. "Doc" Simpson, created a statue of a cowboy and then a yoke of oxen to go before the city hall. Simpson and the community Rotary Club then decided, partly as a prank, to re-create the cemetery on part of Boot Hill, a prank that lasted several years. Soon afterward, a former cattleman set up a curio shop nearby.[30]

Then Hollywood started promoting Dodge. In 1939, Warner Brothers held the premier of their movie *Dodge City* in the real namesake. The 10-day celebration brought stars and media attention from around the world, including Errol Flynn and Olivia de Havilland. The celebration was the first of what became the annual "Dodge City Days" celebration. Over the next two decades films and television shows, culminating in the series *Gunsmoke*, set their stories in Dodge City, bringing additional fame to the town.[31]

By the time Dodge City celebrated its 75th anniversary in 1947, the community's leaders were convinced that tourism was an important business to be in. Citizens and groups worked to provide attractions to visitors. As part of the celebration, the Junior Chamber of Commerce proposed an exhibit at Boot Hill, centering on a room-sized diorama of early Dodge City in miniature. The Jaycees ran the small museum on the hill for the next several years. By the 1950s, Dodge City had firmly identified itself as a "Western" town and looked for ways to reinforce that image. When the Cowboy Hall of Fame began looking for a suitable home for its facilities in 1955, Dodge City campaigned hard for the chance to build a shrine to the cowboy at the base of Boot Hill but failed.[32] Oklahoma City won the contest.

In Dodge City the Wild West image was too well established to be ruined by the loss of the Cowboy Hall of Fame. By 1958, a local pastor penned a tribute to the tune of the "Battle Hymn of the Republic":

Figure 123. Clearly, the Cowboy Cleaners can clean those cowboy duds. Western Revival architecture and popular culture meet in cowboy- and Western-themed establishments, which became common throughout the western United States by the 1950s. This dry-cleaning facility in Wichita, Kansas, is still in business. Photo by author.

> In the heart of Southwest Kansas,
> Where wild Western spirits ride—
> I have seen the ghosts of Wyatt,
> Masterson and Dillon stride,
> Through the dust, and smoke of Front street,
> Where the cheat and outlaw died.
> Boot Hill goes booming on!
> Glory to Dodge City's Marshals
> Praise the fearless frontier law men.
> Laud the famous Cowboy Capital
> Front Street goes marching on.[33]

Meanwhile, the Boot Hill Museum and Dodge City Jaycees embarked on the city's most ambitious attempt to showcase a Western past. They revived the idea of re-creating the first wooden buildings of Front Street. Since the real Front Street was still part of the commercial downtown, this rebuilt version had to be in a different location. The most popular site was at the base of Boot Hill, at a spot originally intended for the city tennis courts.

Actor Hugh O'Brian, who portrayed Wyatt Earp on television, dedicated the cornerstone of the new museum. In the shadow of the 1920s city hall, the community re-created the facades of 1870s Dodge City from historic photographs. The facades, however, covered what was otherwise a collection of modern cinder block structures. That did not deter the tourists to Boot Hill, who numbered over 370,000 in 1958 alone, making it the most popular tourist attraction in Kansas. A few years later, the museum expanded to the east, tripling the size of the former museum and cutting off Fourth Street. The buildings that had been there were torn down. The land not used for buildings was turned into a parking lot for visitors' cars. Original parts of the city's built history were erased so that a 1950s-era recreation of the Old West could again become the "real" Front Street.[34]

Eventually, the desire to re-create a Western look spread to the rest of the downtown. As tourism became increasingly important to Dodge City, the original downtown underwent a transformation. Turn-of-the-century buildings along the real Front Street fell to the wrecking crew to make more parking. The fronts of the buildings along former Chestnut Street that now faced the parking lot received portals out of rough wood. Meanwhile, Chestnut Street had become Wyatt Earp Avenue, while the next street back, Walnut Street, officially became "Gunsmoke Street" in honor of the television series (a series that, ironically, the local television station did not carry for several years).

Figure 124. A modern commercial street of fake nineteenth-century storefronts is seen at Bryce Canyon, Utah. The buildings are less than 20 years old. Photo by author.

In its attempt to look "Western," Dodge City ended up demolishing or altering a significant part of its real history. Businesses such as the Silver Spur Lodge, Vic's Lariat Café, and the Branding Iron Western wear store reinforced the image. Dodge City had tied its identity so closely to the image depicted in *Gunsmoke* that some in the 1970s wondered whether the tourist boom would survive once the series went off the air. In the years since, Dodge City continued to display the Old West—not just the West of the 1870s, but the revival of it from the 1930s through the 1970s.[35]

Concluding Thoughts

Hal Rothman once noted "in tourism, the very identity of place becomes its economic sustenance, and in that transformation is a complicated and paradoxical

Figure 125. The quick and the dead at the Boot Hill Cemetery in Dodge City, Kansas, would hardly recognize the massive arch and entrance to the Boot Hill Museum. Popular culture meets Western movies and the cinematic frontier. The Boot Hill Museum was a 1950s re-creation of Dodge City's 1870s-era Front Street. Situated at the base of Boot Hill, the museum's facades cover structures made out of concrete and other modern materials. Photo by author.

Figure 127. The Hogan Gift Shop east of Mesa Verde National Park has the standard Western cliché of large arrows next to tepees. The horse must be puzzled. Photo by Andrew Gulliford, 2002.

Figure 126. At the Arizona–New Mexico border tourists can buy phone cards and Native American music. The tepees are huge. A multistory "tepee" along Highway 40 is a curio shop. Photo by author.

situation for the people of that place."[36] Communities that embraced an identity tied to the "Old West" tried to reinforce that image through the use of "Old West Revival" styles—often at the expense of their actual architectural history. The creation of this revival, like other such revivals, involved selection of certain images of a romanticized past and adaptation of those images to modern needs. Its devotees transformed temporary and run-down buildings into emblems of an entire region. Abandoned mining communities, dude ranch architecture, and movie sets merged with actual historic preservation to create a composite image that is readily identifiable, even if contrived. As a result, the true history of the West—the story of a colonial society trying to adapt the latest architecture of the day—got overlooked. Victorian-era fronts received rough wood facades or stood in danger of being torn down because they did not look Western enough. Corporate mining towns from the Progressive Era became associated with cowboys and outlaws who lived three decades earlier. Towns that nineteenth-century boosters sought to make prosperous and respectable were transformed into arenas where shoot-outs happened on the hour for tourists.

Movies, tourist establishments, and historic preservation all contributed to the development of Old West Revival. Buildings provided communities with a sense of identity by connecting them to a mythical past. The look originated in the 1930s with specialized buildings and developed into a style that persisted into the 1960s and even today. The forms and images of Old West Revival have become so common that they go largely undetected, seeming so perfect a fit in the landscape that they mask a more complicated architectural story.

This raises an odd issue when it comes to historic preservation. Structures from the 1950s, such as those in the Old West Revival style, are starting to qualify as historic, given the 50-year rule that guides preservation

Figure 128. Tepees and roadside clutter sell just about everything at Fort Verde between Phoenix and Flagstaff. Photo by Andrew Gulliford, 1999.

policy. Old West Revival's historicity, however, does not come from the 1870s, 1880s, and 1890s that it supposedly imitates. Rather, it represents a fascination with the Wild West from the post–World War II era. Old West Revival may not be as fashionable or tasteful in the eyes of architectural historians as Mission or Pueblo Revival. To scholars such as Delahanty and McKinney, it seems fake and shallow, a contrived mythology at odds with real historic preservation. Yet preservation efforts along Route 66 already show that there is growing awareness of the built legacy of automobile tourism. Scholars of popular culture have a 30-year tradition of examining Western movies and the material culture they inspired. Perhaps the architectural form of the Western is now ready to become a legitimate part of the country's built legacy. Whether as "authentic" reproductions of the past or blatant fakery, Old West Revival deserves to be recognized as a legitimate part of American architectural and cultural history.

Notes

1. The terms "Old West" and "Wild West" will be used interchangeably in this essay to refer to the romanticized depiction of life in the late-nineteenth-century western United States.

2. See, for example, Shelley Baranowsky and Ellen Furlough, eds., *Being Elsewhere: Tourism, Consumer Culture, and Identity in Modern Europe and North America* (Ann Arbor: University of Michigan Press, 2001); Chris Wilson, *The Myth of Santa Fe: Creating a Modern Regional Tradition* (Albuquerque, University of New Mexico Press, 1997); John Bodnar, *Remaking America: Public Memory, Commemoration, and Patriotism* (Princeton: Princeton University Press, 1992); Michael Kammen, *In the Past Lane: Historical Perspectives on American Culture* (New York and Oxford: Oxford University Press, 1997), and *The Mystic Chords of Memory: The Transformation of Tradition in American Culture* (New York: Alfred A. Knopf, 1991); and David Thelan, "Memory and American History," *Journal of American History* 75 (March 1989): 1117–29.

3. Allen Axelrod, ed., *The Colonial Revival in America*, published for the Henry France du Pont Winterthur Museum (New York and London: Norton, 1985), 12.

4. Robert Haywood, *Victorian West: Class and Culture in Kansas Cattle Towns* (Lawrence: University Press of Kansas, 1991).

5. Randolph Delahanty and E. Andrew McKinney, *Preserving the West* (New York: Pantheon, 1985), 3.

6. Cathy Ambler, "Small Historic Sites in Kansas: Merging Artifactual Landscapes and Community Values," *Great Plains Quarterly* 15 (winter 1995): 33–48; Agnesa Lufkin Reeve, *From Hacienda to Bungalow: Northern New Mexico Houses, 1850–1912* (Albuquerque: University of New Mexico Press, 1988); and Thomas Carter, ed., *Images of an American Land* (Albuquerque: University of New Mexico Press, 1997).

7. Carla Breeze, *Pueblo Deco* (New York: Rizzoli, 1990).

8. "Something New in Home Building," *Wichita Beacon*, May 17, 1928. See also "Old West Lives On in Line and Figure," *Wichita Magazine* (October 1929): 8, 26. See Wilson, *Myth of Santa Fe*, 80–168, 232–310; Virginia L. Grattan, *Mary Colter: Builder Upon the Red Earth* (Grand Canyon, AZ: Grand Canyon Natural History Association, 1992); Carl D. Sheppard, *Creator of the Santa Fe Style: Issac Hamilton Rapp, Architect* (Albuquerque: University of New Mexico Press, 1988); Karen J. Weitze, *California's Mission Revival* (Santa Monica, CA: Hennessey and Ingalls, 1984); H. Roger Grant, *Kansas Depots* (Topeka: Kansas State Historical Society, 1990); and various editions of the "Home in the West" column in *Sunset Magazine*.

9. Breeze, *Pueblo Deco*; C. W. Short and R. Stanley Brown, *Public Buildings: Architecture Under the Public Works Administration, 1933–1939*, vol. I, reprint with new introduction by Richard Guy Wilson (New York: Da Capo Press,

1986); and David H. Sachs and George Ehrlich, *Guide to Kansas Architecture* (Lawrence: University Press of Kansas, 1996), 245.

10. Writers' Program of the Works Projects Administration, *The WPA Guide to 1930s Kansas*, reprint with new introduction by James R. Shortridge (Lawrence: University Press of Kansas, 1984), 153–58.

11. Writers' Program of the Works Projects Administration, *Colorado: A Guide to the Highest State* (New York: Hastings House, 1941), 78–82, quote from 79.

12. Writers' Program of the Works Projects Administration, *The WPA Guide to 1930s Oklahoma*, reprint with restored essay by Angie Debo and a new introduction by Anne Hodges Morgan (Lawrence: University Press of Kansas, 1986), 94–99, quote from page 95. See also Writers' Program, *Arizona: A State Guide*, (New York: Hastings House, 1940), 139–47; Writers Program, *The WPA Guide to 1930s New Mexico*, reprint, forward by Marc Simmons (Tucson: University of Arizona Press, 1989), 148–55; and Writers Program, *California: A Guide to the Golden State* (New York: Hastings House, 1942), 167–75.

13. Jack Rittenhouse, *A Guide Book to Route 66*, facsimile of the 1946 first ed. (Albuquerque: University of New Mexico Press, 1989), 61.

14. "Las Vegas: Gambling Pays the Bill for Unusual Fun—Whether or Not You Flirt with Lady Luck," *Travel* (March 1951): 18–21. See also Watson Parker, *Deadwood: The Golden Years* (Lincoln and London: University of Nebraska Press, 1981), 215–44, and Odie B. Faulk, *Tombstone: Myth and Reality* (New York: Oxford University Press, 1972), 186–209.

15. Marguerite S. Shaffer, *See America First: Tourism and National Identity, 1880–1940* (Washington: Smithsonian Institution Press, 2001); Hal Rothman, *Devil's Bargains: Tourism in the Twentieth-Century American West* (Lawrence: University Press of Kansas, 1998); Rothman, "Selling the Meaning of Place: Entrepreneurship, Tourism, and Community Transformation in the Twentieth-Century American West," *Pacific Historical Review* 65 (1996): 525–57; Scott Norris, ed., *Discovered Country: Tourism and Survival in the American West* (Albuquerque: Stone Ladder Press, 1994); Earl Pomeroy, *In Search of the Golden West: The Tourist in Western America* (Lincoln and London: University of Nebraska Press, 1957); Michael P. Malone and Richard W. Etulain, *The American West: A Twentieth Century History* (Lincoln and London: University of Nebraska Press, 1989); and Gerald D. Nash and Richard Etulain, eds., *The Twentieth Century West: Historical Interpretations* (Albuquerque: University of New Mexico Press, 1989).

16. Shaffer, *See America First*, 5.

17. "Kansas Centennial," *Travel* (January 1961): 28–31, 28.

18. Jan Jennings, ed., *Roadside America: The Automobile in Design and Culture* (Ames: Iowa State University Press, 1990), especially Keith A. Sculle, "Frank Redford's Village Chain," 125–35. For the larger context, see Karal Ann Marling, *The Colossus of Roads: Myth and Symbol Along the American Highway* (Minneapolis: University of Minnesota Press, 1984); Michael Wallis, *Route 66: The Mother Road* (New York: St. Martin's, 1990); Don J. Unser with photo editing by Louise Silver, *New Mexico Route 66 on Tour: Legendary Architecture from Glenrio to Gallup* (Santa Fe, Museum of New Mexico Press, 2001); John Ross, *Oklahoma Route 66* (Arcadia, OK: Ghost Town Press, 2001); and Warren James Belasco, *Americans on the Road: From Autocamp to Motel* (Cambridge, MA: MIT Press, 1981). At present, amateur enthusiasts, rather than academics, are at the forefront of remembering "wigwam"-themed architecture. See, for example, "Wigwam Nation," at www.dreamscape.com/dbporter/wigwam_nation.htm and "Wigwam Motels & Gas Stations" at www.netcolony.com/pets/agilitynut/wigwams.html.

19. Editorial staff of *Sunset Magazine*, *Western Ranch Houses*, 3rd printing (San Francisco: Lane Publishing, 1950), ix.

20. Ibid; Janet Ann Stewart, *Arizona Ranch Houses: Southern Territorial Styles, 1868–1900* (Tucson: University of Arizona Press and Arizona Historical Society, Tucson, 1974); Reeve, *From Hacienda to Bungalow*; Mary Anne Beecher, "The Motel in Builder's Literature and Architectural Publications," *Roadside America*, 115–24; "Dude Ranch Recreation," *Travel* (July 1955): 6–10; and Lawrence R. Borne, *Dude Ranching: A Complete History* (Albuquerque: University of New Mexico Press, 1983). For a discussion of the ranch look in modern decorating, see "Southwest Ranch Style," in Elmo Baca, *Southwest Expressions* (Lincolnwood, IL: Publications International, 1992).

21. Michael Coyne, *The Crowded Prairie: American National Identity in the Hollywood Western* (London and New York: I. B. Tauris Publishers, 1997); George N. Fenin and William K. Everson, *The Western: From Silents to the Seventies*, rev. ed. (New York: Grossman Publishers, 1973); Jim Hitt, *The American West from Fiction (1823–1976) into Film (1909–1986)* (Jefferson, NC, and London: McFarland & Company, 1990); Buck Rainey, *Western Gunslingers in Fact and on Film: Hollywood's Famous Lawmen and Outlaws* (Jefferson, NC, and London: McFarland & Company,

1998); Jane Tompkins, *West of Everything: The Inner Life of Westerns* (New York and Oxford: Oxford University Press, 1992); and "The West and the Western" edition of *Journal of the West* 29 (April 1999).

22. "Let's Explore a Byway . . . Through the San Fernando and Simi Valleys," *Westways* (December 1962): 13–16. Although Western movies are a very popular topic to historians and scholars of popular culture, the movie locations are surprisingly not. As with wigwam architecture, interest in the topic still rests largely with the general public rather than academe. Literature on Western movie locations is still largely in the form of guidebooks such as John A. Murray, *Cinema Southwest: An Illustrated Guide to the Movies and Their Locations* (Flagstaff, AZ: Northland Publishing, 2000). The web also is a useful source of basic information on Western movie locations; one of the best sites is Jerry L. Schneider's "Movie Making Locations Plus" at http://employees.oxy.edu/jerry/oldtucsn.htm.

23. Speech from Tombstone Restoration Commission (speaker unknown), December 21, 1950, Tombstone Courthouse State Historic Park.

24. State of Arizona, Arizona Corporation Commission, Articles of Incorporation of the Tombstone Restoration Commission, December 19, 1949, at Tombstone Courthouse State Historic Park. For an example in Arizona, see Harris J. Sorbin, editor/project director, "Florence Townsite, A. T.," Final Report of Florence Townsite Historic District Study, May 1977; *Arizona Preservation News*, editions from 1972–77; and George Lubick, "Forging Ties with the Past: Historic Preservation in Arizona," *Journal of the West* 24 (1985): 96–107, 100–1. For a regional context, see Elaine Freed, *Preserving the Great Plains and Rocky Mountains* (Albuquerque: University of New Mexico Press, 1992), and Delahanty and McKinney, *Preserving the West*.

25. Delahanty and McKinney, *Preserving the West*, 13.

26. "Ghost Towns," *Travel* (September 1960), 43–47.

27. "Historic Land," *The Jerome Chronicle* (summer 1999): 1–6; "Happy Birthday to the Jerome Historical Society," *The Jerome Chronicle* (spring 1988): 1–3; Jerome Historical Society, *News Bulletins* for 1955; and Minutes of the Jerome Historical Society, 1955–65; "Tumbledown Town with a Love of Life," *Arizona Highways* (May 1976): 40–45. See also "Ghost Town—with Crowds," *Travel* (November 1956): 29–31. See also, for example, Lambert Florin, *Western Ghost Towns* (Seattle, Superior Publishing Company, 1961), and *Ghost Town Album*, Second in the Western Ghost Town Series (Seattle, Superior Publishing Company, 1962); Stanley W. Paher, *Nevada Ghost Towns and Mining Camps* (Berkeley: Howell-North Books, 1970); and James E. and Barbara H. Sherman, maps by Don Percious, *Ghost Towns of Arizona* (Norman: University of Oklahoma Press, 1977).

28. "Welcome to Greensburg, Kansas," brochure printed by Freeman Studios in Berrian Springs, MI, 1967; at Kansas Heritage Center. "Rebuilt Cowtowns Showing Glimpses of Past," *Wichita Eagle and Beacon*, July 1, 1973, and "White Hats Winners (Natch) in 'Shoot-out' at Burketown," *Hutchinson News*, June 8, 1970.

29. Betty Bradock and Jeanie Covalt, *Dodge City: Cowboy Capital . . . Beautiful Bibulous Babylon . . . Queen of the Cowtowns . . . Wicked Little City . . . the Delectable Burg . . .* (Dodge City: Kansas Heritage Center, 1994); Frederick R. Young, *Dodge City: Up Through a Century in Story and Pictures* (Dodge City, KS: Boot Hill Museum, 1995).

30. "Awareness of History Comes Later to City," *Dodge City Globe* (DCG), March 6, 1971; "Begin Grading of Boot Hill," DCG, February 2, 1932; "Boot Hill Friends Rally," DCG, March 2, 1932; "Not to Level Boot Hill, the Commissioners Say," DCG, March 3, 1932; "Wild West Glamor Is State's Chief Tourist Lure," DCG, May 3, 1942; and "It's History vs. Tennis in New Boot Hill Battle," DGC, February 18, 1932.

31. "Dodge City Days Born Through Movie," DCG, July 25, 1991; "World Premier; 'Dodge City': The Day Hollywood Came to Town," DCG, December 31, 1999; and "Thousands Greet Starts at Film Fete," DCG, April 1, 1939.

32. Other cities competing for the site included Abilene, Kansas; Cheyenne, Wyoming; Denver, Colorado; Oklahoma City, Oklahoma; Las Vegas, New Mexico; Prescott, Arizona; and North Platte, Nebraska.

33. From the *Dodge City Daily Globe*, September 28, 1958.

34. "Early Day Relics Abound in Dodge City Boot Hill and Beeson Museums," DCG, June 16, 1957; "Tribute Paid to Wyatt Earp," DCG, January 27, 1958; "Expansion Plan Unveiled," DCG, January 31, 1958; "Replica, Museums, Markers: Tribute to Our Pioneer History," *High Plains Journal* (March 27, 1958); "Huge Crowd Sees 'Trail' Event," DCG September 27, 1958; "Boot Hill Replica Gives City State's Biggest Attraction," DCG, February 9, 1959; "Boot Hill Is Growing Thing," DCG, July 18, 1960; "Plans to Expand Front Street Replica," DCG, January 31, 1963; and "The Town 'Gunsmoke' Made Prosperous," *Grit*, October 8, 1972.

35. Timothy F. Wenzl, "*Discovering Dodge City's Landmarks* (copyright by the author, 1980); and "'Howdy': This Is Your Official Dodge City Greeter Guide," Kansas Centennial Edition (Dodge City, Hetzel Publishing Company, 1961). "Front Street's 3 Phases," *Plainsman* 7

(1961); and "Will the Ghost of Dodge Linger on Boot Hill?" *Topeka Daily Capital*, April 1, 1976.

36. Rothman, "Selling the Meaning of Place," 22–23.

Study Questions

1. What are the racial and ethnic reasons behind the Colonial Revival architectural style?

2. What architectural details and symbols characterize the Old West Revival style?

3. Why was the Old West Revival primarily commercial?

4. Why did Western builders and investors try to replicate the fashionable styles of the East?

5. How is the "Hollywood image of the wooden cowboy town" not truly representative of the West?

6. Why were Mediterranean- and Spanish-inspired buildings promoted as "typical" Western architecture?

7. How did tourism influence the Old West Revival?

8. How did the growing belief that there was a generic "Indian" look influence the Western revival?

9. What was the most important source of inspiration for the Old West Revival?

10. In what ways does use of Old West Revival styles damage or destroy actual architectural history?

Historic Preservation and the Creation of Western Civic Identity

Case Studies in Albuquerque, Denver, and Seattle

JUDY MATTIVI MORLEY

Once upon a time, in a century not so long ago, the downtown districts of western cities were delightful places. In southwestern cities, like Albuquerque, New Mexico, Hispanic villagers took siestas in the plaza, sold their wares at the trading post, and held colorful holiday festivals. In booming commercial cities like Denver and Seattle, mining and lumber barons built their mansions downtown, close to their offices in the financial district. Fashionable Victorian ladies strolled down wooden sidewalks while horses and carriages clopped along the litter-free street. Cities in the past were safer, cleaner, friendlier, simpler, more colorful, and more accessible.

Or so the city councils and tourism bureaus of western cities would have us believe. In the 40 years following World War II, city planners nationwide began designating portions of their downtowns as historic districts. The phenomenon of historic preservation hardly originated in the postwar era. Historic preservation began after the Civil War and was promoted mainly by individuals trying to preserve their cultural authority. Boston Brahmin descendents of wealthy textile merchants in the Northeast, progeny of Southern planters, and millionaires like John D. Rockefeller and Henry Ford helped to save landmarks they felt reflected and glorified America's heritage.[1]

While preservation had a tradition in the East, it was very limited in the West. The West's boom-and-bust economy promoted development, not preservation, and pre–World War II city planners had little regard for historic structures. The situation changed in the postwar period, however. Unprecedented growth stormed cities in the West after 1940, causing suburbs to eclipse downtowns and central business districts to decline. The traditional main street shopping areas stopped being the commercial centers of the region, and malls, banks, and grocery stores moved outside the city limits. As tax revenue in inner cities dwindled, residents, city councils, and urban planning boards began looking for ways to revitalize traditional commercial centers.

City and federal governments dealt with the declining fortunes of downtown by promoting urban renewal projects that bulldozed historic sections of the inner city to provide widened highways, parking lots, and nondescript office buildings. These projects usually used modern, national architectural styles, creating forbidding landscapes that favored cars over pedestrians. The standardized urban renewal styles tore down old buildings that were important to the city's history and robbed the area being "renewed" of anything that made it unique. Urban renewal did little to reverse the departure of residents and patrons from downtown.

As cities nationwide struggled with ways to revitalize the central business district, western cities faced the additional challenge of defining a civic identity. In American mythology, "western cities" was almost a contradiction in terms. Towns in the West meant small, clapboarded outposts complete with sheriffs, saloons, dusty streets, and tumbleweeds, like Tombstone, Arizona, or Dodge City, Kansas. Yet between 1950 and 1980, the West became the most urban region of the nation, containing more than half of the United States' fastest-growing cities. As western cities grew, they became more architecturally and culturally similar to the East. New residents, tourists, city planners, real estate developers, and politicians faced the problem of defining a regional identity in this time of rampant change. Although regional character is usually taken for granted, the postwar conditions caused newcomers to the urban West consciously to find something unique about their new hometowns. One tool western city planners and other activists used to create civic identities in the postwar period was historic preservation. Historic preservation rejuvenated ailing central business districts, attracted commerce to the city, promoted tourism, and established a unique civic identity. Yet the process of historic preservation transformed the district being preserved and, in the end, did not *preserve* history so much as *create* a civic identity.

While planners and newcomers to the West were trying to define civic identities, the field of historic preservation was changing. Traditionally, historic preservation was only something that wealthy old ladies did in their spare time. The first real historic preservation organization was the Mount Vernon Ladies' Association, founded in 1853 to save George Washington's home in Virginia. Until the 1940s, most of the people involved in historic preservation were not trained in city planning; instead, they were wealthy philanthropists and people doing the work as a community service. By the end of World War II, however, historic preservation moved into the city planning office, and young architects, mostly men trained to save old buildings, became professional preservationists.[2]

This new breed of preservation planners helped to shift the focus of historic preservation from single landmarks to historic districts. Historic landmarks prior to the 1930s were usually single buildings, like Mount Vernon or Independence Hall. A few districts, including Colonial Williamsburg, the French Quarter in New Orleans, and Charleston, South Carolina, sprang up in the 1930s, but they were the exception to the rule prior to World War II. The French Quarter and Charleston were also urban neighborhoods, designated as historic districts to protect property values and community spirit, not primarily to bring shoppers and tourists downtown. Colonial Williamsburg was a private project funded by John D. Rockefeller, Jr., to celebrate the roots of America's liberty and democracy.[3]

Although the first historic landmarks appeared in the East, the idea of historic districting became entrenched in city-planning policy in the West. Historic districts were different from landmarks in that districting preserved a group of old buildings that had little or no significance by themselves but taken together portrayed the ambience of the city. In Denver's Larimer Square, for example, no single building was associated with a famous person or event, but the block as a whole gave Denver visitors a sense of the city's early characteristics. Historic districts in the West were designed to revitalize inner cities, bringing people downtown on vacation or to shop and dine on weekends. Western historic districts had goals similar to urban renewal projects, but the major objective was to save the old buildings.[4]

Historic districting became prevalent in western cities because a number of factors converged in the region after World War II. Although none of those factors individually was unique to the West, the combination of all of the factors happened simultaneously in postwar western cities. First, the West experienced exponential population growth during the 1940s, 1950s, and 1960s. Albuquerque, New Mexico, for example, doubled its population between 1940 and 1950 and again between 1950 and 1960.[5] Most of the people moving to the West came from the Midwest and South and arrived to take advantage of newly created defense industry jobs. These people did not move into the inner cities, however. They moved to the suburbs, causing cities to sprawl farther and farther away from the historic downtowns. With the housing sprawl came commercial sprawl like strip malls, so new arrivals to a metropolitan area rarely went downtown—they could do their shopping, banking, dry cleaning, and marketing all on the outskirts of the city.

The sprawl changed traditional architectural patterns. Cookie-cutter subdivisions and standardized shopping malls used the same designs in Seattle as in Syracuse. The rapid growth and standardization of stores and offices overpowered most variations in regional style or building materials, enhancing Westerners' fear that their cities would turn into blighted, poverty-stricken no-man's-lands like industrial, eastern cities of the time.⁶ Urban renewal policies contributed to the problem of standardization, tearing down distinctive old landmarks and replacing them with nondescript, boxy cinder block buildings. Rather than giving people a reason to go downtown, urban renewal took away anything that might have been unique to that city.

The West also changed economically during the postwar period. World War II changed the West from a region dependent on investment from the East to the center of an urban-based, global economy. Traditionally "western" industries, like cattle ranching and gold mining, lost their relative importance in the West's economy. New industries, like computer chips, defense research laboratories, and tourism, became the mainstays of the West's economy.⁷ In Denver, for example, tourism surpassed mining as the state's third-largest industry, following manufacturing and agriculture. Revenue from tourism increased 418 percent between 1950 and 1968.⁸ National chains, especially grocery and department stores, took over niche markets that once had been controlled by local businesses. The shifting economy caused citizens of western cities to feel as if they were losing something that set them apart from the rest of the nation.

Tourism's relative economic importance came from western cities' position as starting points for outdoor adventures. The rise of skiing and other outdoor sports industries brought visitors west to take advantage of the natural landscape. Heritage tourism, meaning tourism based on a place's history, also became a popular form of vacation between 1950 and 1990. Americans frequently took their holidays to places that had some historical meaning, like Civil War battlefields, American Revolution sites, or gold rush ghost towns. As traditional industries declined, western cities depended more on tourists' dollars. To keep people in town longer before heading off to their desert or mountain adventures, city councils, chambers of commerce, and city planning boards tried to show off their city and promote their history for visitors.⁹

The years between 1950 and 1980 were also the era when the "Wild West" was the prevailing theme of popular culture. *Bonanza* and *Gunsmoke* ruled the television airwaves, and Western films with John Wayne, Jimmy Stewart, and later Clint Eastwood dominated theaters. When vacationers traveled to the West, they did not want to see a city that looked exactly like the one they had left in Pennsylvania or Iowa. They wanted to see something that looked like the movies and television shows they were watching. The need to fit tourists' expectations motivated historic preservation, as city councils and tourism bureaus, along with private citizens, rushed to save anything that looked "Western."¹⁰

To address the factors of growth, homogenization, economic change, and tourism potential, city planning commissions began to designate historic districts in their urban cores. Between 1955 and 1995, a wave of historic preservation ordinances swept western cities. Historic preservation ordinances generally dealt with both residential and commercial preservation, providing guidelines for renovating historic homes and establishing historic districts in commercial areas. Historic preservation presented an excellent strategy for revitalizing dilapidated commercial areas without sacrificing the historic character of the town. The laws creating historic districts only enforced the preservation of a building's exterior. The old blacksmith shop, for example, could be reborn as a bookstore or restaurant. The preserved districts revitalized inner cities, appealed to preservation-minded citizens, and offered city councils a level of control over the area that simple zoning could not give them.

In preserving the old downtown areas of cities, however, these groups actually created new landscapes and invented traditions that proved profitable for the city. Building renovations met the expectations of newcomers to the city and tourists coming to visit. Restorations generally reinforced an area's heritage, if not always remaining true to its history. In order to understand the subtle transformation that took place in western historic districts, it is important to understand

Figure 129. The Herman Blueher House, Albuquerque, ca. 1900. The Victorian structure with ornate architecture was typical of architecture around the United States at that time. Photo courtesy of Albuquerque Museum, 1978.50.73.

the distinction between *history* and *heritage*. *History* is a recounting of the events of the past. *Heritage* differs from *history* in that it celebrates only those aspects of history agreed upon and valued by a group, leaving out any problematic information. Thus *heritage* re-creates the past as a time of innocence and consensus. Heritage is mythic, using symbols rather than facts to explain the past. Some historians compare heritage to religious faith: people have no proof that the events occurred but accept them based on a feeling that they must be true. Historic preservation, then, created a heritage for a city, giving residents and visitors an identity based on a common sense of the past.[11]

Historic preservation created a common heritage and transformed the past in three western cities in the years following World War II.[12] Albuquerque, New Mexico, Denver, Colorado, and Seattle, Washington, all used historic preservation to re-create their history and turn their downtown historic districts into areas that could successfully be marketed to suburban residents and tourists alike. In Albuquerque's Old Town, historic preservation was an outgrowth of urban renewal. The City Commission tried to justify annexing the historic village of Old Town in 1949 by claiming they needed to upgrade the neighborhood. Old Town was founded in 1706 and grew slowly over the centuries. During the 1880s, railroad promoters planted a booming supply town, also called Albuquerque, two miles away. Despite the common name, the two towns grew separately through the first half of the twentieth century. Old Town remained a small village community, and parts of the neighborhood had dirt streets, no plumbing, and few city services like sewers or trash pickup. The City Commission argued that they needed to annex Old Town to update it, even though the residents of the neighborhood vehemently opposed becoming part of Albuquerque. The City Commission prevailed, however, and annexed Old Town, which was the first step to creating the historic district.

The motivation for creating a historic district in Old Town went well beyond providing services and updating the neighborhood, however. The City Commission wanted to create an identity for Albuquerque that distinguished the city from other growing Western towns, resonated with new residents, and took advantage of tourist traffic along Route 66. To do that, the City Commission created a historic zone in order to tightly control the architecture around Old Town's plaza and make sure that all new construction or renovations reflected the Pueblo Revival style for which New Mexico is known.

The irony of the creation of the historic district in Albuquerque, however, was that the district was not historically made out of adobe. At the end of the nineteenth century, two-story wooden Victorian houses, Queen Anne homes, and brick Italianate

Figure 130. The Herman Blueher House a century later. The gabled roof was removed, the exterior covered in stucco, and a portale built out to the street. Photo by author, 1999.

stores shared the plaza space with the adobe San Felipe church and a few adobe homes. During the 1920s and 1930s, private owners used stucco and adobe to change "Anglo"-looking buildings into structures that looked more like they belonged in New Mexico. It was the new, homogenized Old Town that became a historic district, not the truly diverse neighborhood of the nineteenth century. Today, if a resident wanted to restore a home to its Victorian roots, they would be in violation of the historic district ordinance. Thus, Old Town's historic district created an appropriate identity, downplaying its historic roots.

In Denver, opposition to urban renewal provided the impetus for the preservation of the city's first historic district, Larimer Square. Larimer Street had once been Denver's main street but after 1900 became a "skid row" area of vacant buildings, liquor stores, flophouses, and bums. By 1964, the Denver Urban Renewal Authority had condemned the entire street in order to build the ambitious Skyline Urban Renewal Project. Few people protested the destruction of Larimer Street, but one woman spearheaded the drive to "save" one block of it. Dana Crawford, a 30-something stay-at-home mother of four small boys, was looking for an investment opportunity and something to do with her time. She fought the city's proposed destruction of Larimer Street by forming a partnership with a few of the property owners and purchasing the

Figure 131. Denver's Larimer Street in 1905. The streetcar lines, power lines, and rutted and dirty streets show it to be part of a growing city. Photo courtesy of Western History Collections, Denver Public Library.

1400 block of Larimer. Her goal was to turn a profit by making "Larimer Square" into a retail shopping center, but she combined this profit motive with a sense of civic service. She wanted, she said, Denver's citizens to have someplace to celebrate their heritage as well as promote their "Wild West" identity. Larimer Square became an economic success, raising property values while maintaining the original structures on the block.

As Crawford promoted Larimer Square, however, she created a new identity for Denver. Her advertising messages and brochures reinvented the block as "the most famous street in the West," a dubious claim at

Figure 132. Larimer Square as it appeared in 1960. Photo courtesy of Western History Collections, Denver Public Library.

Figure 133. Larimer Square in 2002. Notice the almost rural atmosphere with street trees, benches, and the small-town-style banners across the street. Photo by author.

best. Yet Larimer Square's invented history gave Denver something that made it unique and helped to establish a "Wild West" identity that was lost to rapid urbanization and postwar growth. Larimer Square succeeded in revitalizing downtown where the Skyline Urban Renewal Project had not. Citizens wanted to come to Larimer Square to celebrate their heritage, and the block became host to festivals and events that attracted visitors from throughout the metropolitan area and the region.

Larimer Square proved to be so successful as a gathering place that city planners, some of them people who had opposed Dana Crawford's creation of Larimer Square, began talking about creating a new historic district in the adjacent warehouse district or lower downtown. Private developers, encouraged by Crawford's success, started the preservation efforts by rejuvenating the old warehouses. During the 1980s, Denver's mayor and planning department supported the creation of a mixed-use historic district out of the old warehouses. Almost 20 years later, this area became the Lower Downtown Historic District, or LoDo. By the year 2000, LoDo was the second-largest tourist attraction in Denver and home to the city's baseball stadium, Coors Field. LoDo became an ideal Denver neighborhood, creating a livable community and defining the city's identity, if not quite preserving the area's warehouse district history.

Seattle's preservation movement followed similar trends to those in Denver and Albuquerque. Seattle's oldest neighborhood, Pioneer Square, had also been a target for urban renewal bulldozers. Pioneer Square's historic fame came from the fact that it was the original "Skid Road," the place where the term "skid row" originated. Yesler Way, which borders Pioneer Square, was the hill where logs were "skidded" from the mountaintop to the sawmill, thus the street's nickname. Once the lumber industry declined, the road housed an abundance of single, unemployed men with nothing to do but drink. A local minister worried that the old road where logs skidded to the mill would become a place where souls "skidded straight to hell." The term "skid row" has ever after been used to designate run-down areas of town.

Pioneer Square witnessed a bit of a renaissance in the 1960s from private sources, thanks to architects and artists who restored the old buildings for offices and galleries. The biggest changes came when a reform-minded city council and mayor took office in 1970, however. The politicians made Pioneer Square Seattle's first historic district and tried to make it into a retail center and attraction similar to Denver's Larimer Square. Some groups in Seattle felt that the bums needed to stay in Pioneer Square, however, because they were there first and, after all, they were the districts' claim to fame. But the bums and the

Figure 134. Pioneer Square, Seattle, ca. 1900, when it was still the heart of Seattle. Photo courtesy of Manuscripts, Special Collections, University Archives, University of Washington Library, UW871.

tourists did not work well together, and Pioneer Square suffered. When King County Stadium, commonly called the Kingdome, went up on the edge of Pioneer Square, the crowds and traffic overwhelmed the district and, combined with the persistence of the bums, kept the area from becoming a viable retail center. The biggest factor in Pioneer Square's lackluster record, however, was that the proponents of the historic district could not decide which identity to promote. Some civic groups wanted to glorify the district as Seattle's birthplace, representing the booster idea of the "Seattle Spirit," while other groups wanted to save it as the original Skid Road. With no coherent identity, residents and tourists had no reason to come to Pioneer Square to celebrate Seattle's heritage.

Seattle's other downtown historic district had greater success, however. The Pike Place Market sits about a mile north of Pioneer Square and is constantly filled with shoppers, tourists, resident, and locals. The original market was a well-loved institution in Seattle, symbolizing the city's agrarian past and the working-class roots of its citizens. The preservation of Pike Place Market took place amid multiple proposals regarding what to do with the area. After World War

Figure 135. Pioneer Square Historic District, 2002. Notice the benches with little metal arms that discourage indigents from sleeping on them. Photo by author.

II, the market became a firetrap and an eyesore. Few farmers still sold their goods in the market, and most patrons were low-income pensioners who lived nearby and needed the access to cheap produce. By 1965, the city council and downtown business establishment wanted to tear down the market and erect luxury apartments, a hotel, and an upscale shopping area. After giving in to public pressure, the city council agreed to keep about one acre of the original market but still surround it with high-income skyscrapers.

Despite its run-down condition, a majority of Seattle residents wanted to preserve the market as it had always been, even if that meant keeping the seedy exterior and economically challenged residents. Led by architect Victor Steinbrueck, market supporters worked to get a citizen's initiative on the ballot to save the market, and in 1971 Seattle voters chose to keep all seven acres of the time-worn old landmark. The restoration of Pike Place Market did not exactly take visitors back in time, however. The Pike Place Market Preservation and Development Authority (PDA), the entity in charge of preserving the market, used government urban renewal money to do much of the revitalization work. Because the district depended on government funding, the PDA had to meet federal guidelines for urban renewal districts. Thus, the district ended up having more services for low-income residents than the market neighborhood had before preservation. Urban renewal funds also had to go to pay farmers to grow crops to sell in the market, since the economy around Puget Sound had changed so dramatically that there simply were not enough farmers to support the market. Despite the rhetoric that the market was saved as it had been in the first part of the twentieth century, it was really a creation of the funding realities of the late postwar period. Pike Place Market is a popular place for visitors, however, and the top tourist attraction in the Pacific Northwest.

In all three of these cities, historic preservation created tourist and entertainment districts out of former run-down urban neighborhoods. Although they brought people and money back downtown, these districts had their critics. Many observers pointed out that these areas were nothing like they had been in a previous century. Whereas Old Town, Albuquerque, was once a village-oriented community, historic preservation tore apart neighborhood ties and put political control in the hands of a far-off city board. Larimer Square was not part of the authentic fabric of Denver, but rather a shopping mall in old buildings, and Lower Downtown contained million-dollar lofts and restaurants targeting middle- and upper-class baseball fans rather than a diverse, mixed-use commercial area.

Pioneer Square, which retained more of its class and cultural diversity than any of the districts, was not successful commercially and failed to draw investment. And Pike Place Market, probably the most successful tourist district, had to create a government-controlled social and economic system to have enough farmers to sell goods.

Comparing historic districts to their historical antecedents is a futile endeavor, however. Of course these districts did not look as they did 100 years earlier. History is gone and cannot be replaced. The historic districts, however, did provide city planners and private developers in the 1950s and 1960s with viable redevelopment options. Historic districts usually succeeded where other urban renewal plans failed. They provided safe and clean areas for people to shop or dine. They allowed visitors to have a unique experience. Foremost, these districts created a unique identity for the city. Residents from the suburbs, newcomers moving to the city, and tourists visited the historic districts and were able to feel as if they were experiencing the city's heritage. By association, these non-natives could absorb part of the city's identity and make it their own. In this way, historic districts created identity, even if they failed to preserve history. Rather than taking a visitor back to the dirty, dusty past of a city, tourists and residents alike found a clean, well-marketed district, packaged for their enjoyment.

Notes

1. Mike Wallace, *Mickey Mouse History and Other Essays on American Memory* (Philadelphia: Temple University Press, 1996), 181–86.

2. Barbara J. Howe, "Women in Historic Preservation: The Legacy of Ann Pamela Cunningham," *The Public Historian* 12 (winter 1990): 31–61; Charles B. Hosmer, Jr., *Presence of the Past: A History of the Preservation Movement in the United States before Williamsburg* (New York: Putnam, 1965); Wallace, *Mickey Mouse History*, 181–86; and David Hamer, *History in Urban Places: The Historic Districts of the U.S.* (Columbus: Ohio State University Press, 1998), 102–7.

3. Wallace, *Mickey Mouse History*, 181–86.

4. Hamer, *History in Urban Places*, 1–5.

5. University of New Mexico Bureau of Business and Economic Research, "Population Profiles of Incorporated Places and Cities in New Mexico, 1910–2015," prepared for the New Mexico Department of Highways and Transportation, 1994.

6. John Findlay, *Magic Lands: Western Cityscapes and American Culture after 1940* (Berkeley: University of California Press, 1992), 2–5.

7. Gerald Nash, *The American West in the Twentieth Century: A Short History of an Urban Oasis* (Albuquerque: University of New Mexico Press, 1973), 234–41.

8. "Larimer Square Market Analysis, Mid-1969," in Larimer Square Associates Papers, Colorado Historical Society, Denver, CO.

9. Hal Rothman, *Devil's Bargains: Tourism in the Twentieth-Century American West* (Lawrence: University Press of Kansas, 2000).

10. Robert G. Athearn, *Mythic West in Twentieth Century America* (Lawrence: University Press of Kansas, 1986).

11. David Lowenthal, *Possessed by the Past: The Heritage Crusade and the Spoils of History* (New York: Free Press, 1996); and Michael Kammen, *Mystic Chords of Memory: The Transformation of Tradition in American Culture* (New York: Vintage Books, 1991).

12. See Judith Mattivi Morley, "Making History: Historic Preservation and the Creation of Western Civic Identity" (Ph.D. diss., University of New Mexico, 2002).

Study Questions

1. When did historic preservation begin and why?

2. What was one of the problems that came about when western cities started to grow? What was the "tool" used to solve this problem?

3. How did a "new breed" of preservation planners change historic preservation in the West?

4. How did making historical districts instead of historical landmarks enrich a city's heritage?

5. How did tourism and heritage tourism change the West?

6. Compare the meaning of history to that of heritage.

7. How did the City Commission change Albuquerque, New Mexico? In your opinion, was the change for the better or should it have been left alone?

8. What was the main problem for Seattle's Pioneer Square?

9. Compare the success of Pioneer Square to the Pike Place Market.

10. How do historic districts create identity?

From Brothels to Buddhism

A Walking Tour of Denver's Red-Light District

Kara Mariko Miyagishima

Trying to hook students and the general public on history, I've experimented with a tour of the most notorious red-light district in the Rockies. My walking tours of old Market Street in Denver also enabled me to talk about the Asian community there, who typically wound up on skid row, often snuggled up with the sisters of sin. In Denver, a stuccoed building sits at 1942 Market Street, which passersby may note for its carved bas-relief figures, including a busty madam atop the pediment and an eye-catching red neon sign in the window, Mattie's Red Light Lounge.

In the 1900s, feather boas, lace lingerie, sex, and booze once helped make this building a gold mine as "the House of Mirrors" for Madame Jennie Rogers. Jennie and her girls were classy businesswomen who made quite a profit from their luring endeavors. In 1910, Rogers's feisty competitor, Mattie Silks, purchased the House of Mirrors from her and inscribed her name, M. *Silks*, in the entry tiles at the front door. After Denver's progressive reformers shut down Mattie's and other Market Street joints in 1912, Mattie's old-time customers, still filled with pleasurable memories, returned to the doorstep of 1942 Market Street. Only a tiny sign in the window revealed the new owner, "Buddhist Temple of Denver." Instead of smelling cigar smoke and perfume drifting out of the windows, visitors smelled incense. Instead of seductive catcalls or the "professor" clinking on the piano, visitors heard children chanting the Buddhist sutra "Namu Amida Butsu."

Prostitutes were ostracized in society, and so were Asians. Most areas of Denver enforced either restrictive

Figure 137. Advertising for Mattie Silks. Courtesy of Tom Noel Collection.

Figure 138. Photo of a matronly Mattie Silks. Courtesy of Tom Noel Collection.

From Brothels to Buddhism / 339

Figure 139A (LEFT). Painting of Mattie Silks's bordello by Herndon Davis, 1940. Courtesy Denver Public Library. Figure 139B (RIGHT). House of Mirrors to the Tri-State Buddhist Temple to Mattie's Red Light Lounge and Dinner Theatre. What an evolution for a downtown Denver building! Note the irony of the adjacent police cruiser. Photo by Andrew Gulliford, 2003.

covenants or informal taboos against Asians. Most real estate outside of lower downtown had restrictions barring sale or lease to "people of color." On Market, Larimer, and Lawrence streets, also known as Denver's Skid Row between the 1890s and 1970s, all colors were acceptable. It is not a coincidence that Denver's Japanese first lived next to Hop Alley, where the Chinese community had once lived. The West Coast stigmatized Japanese and Chinese as the "yellow peril," a sentiment carried over to other western states. Even though the Japanese population was less than 1 percent of Denver's population (and still is), most whites categorized them with the Chinese, who were run out of Denver with the Anti-Chinese Riot of 1880.

In 1919, Denver's Japanese Buddhist community purchased the two-story, stone-faced structure at 1942 Market Street. It became a gathering place where Japanese could share in familiar conversation and food and also a community center where families lived, celebrated marriages, and celebrated Japanese festivals such as *hanamatsuri* (Cherry Blossom Festival) and *obon* for the dead. Children also attended Japanese language school or kendo practice.

1942 Market Street is a centerpiece of one of America's most successful historic districts—Lower Downtown Denver. Since its designation as the Lower Downtown Historic District in 1988 by the Denver Landmark Preservation Commission and the City of Denver, LoDo has evolved from Skid Row to an upscale neighborhood of million-dollar lofts, fancy restaurants, brewpubs, art galleries, and boutiques. The 25-block LoDo District, bordered by Coors Field (Home of the Colorado Rockies), the railroad tracks, and Cherry Creek, attracts innumerable tourists as well as locals to what has become Colorado's most popular amusement district. Quite appropriately, 1942 Market Street is once again a major amusement. The handsome Italianate edifice built in 1886 as the showplace brothel of Jennie Rogers, then of Mattie Silks, served as the Tri-State Buddhist Temple until 1947. After the Buddhists moved to a new temple two blocks away at 1947 Lawrence Street, the old temple became a warehouse, whose owners stripped it of its exterior stonework and handsome interior bird's-eye maple. New owners acquired 1942 during the 1990s and completed a $1.5 million restoration assisted by

$18,600 from the Colorado State Historical Society's State Historical Fund generated by taxes on restored casinos. Thanks to this extraordinary face-lift, the House of Mirrors is a classy cocktail lounge and restaurant. Also a minimuseum of whoredom, it capitalizes on heritage tourism.

Hookers and brothels may be glorified as the seamier, steamier, more provocative part of history, but it is also important to recognize that another community later inhabited this most notorious whorehouse. Today, as you enter Mattie's House of Mirrors restaurant, a glass case in the entryway displays a photograph of an elderly Japanese man and a child. Elegant old mirrors in the background, which once reflected shapely young women, reflect a tiny Japanese boy. He grew up in the temple, which became a home for Japanese newcomers or those passing through. Japanese grandmas I interviewed remember living in the old love parlors with entire families in one small bedroom. My auntie May Yoshihara, like many other Japanese brides, was married in the residence of "the brides of the multitudes." For Colorado's Japanese American community 1942 was their first anchor in an often hostile city. For them, it is vital to preserve this bordello to create continuity between generations future and past.

1942 Market Street carries with it a significance that goes beyond the stony facade, the black walnut staircase, the fancy mirrors, and the Buddhist statue and altar that were moved to the new temple. It is etched into the social memory of the Japanese American community, whose presence is still felt today in nearby Sakura Square and the new Tri-State Buddhist Temple at 1947 Lawrence Street, only two blocks away from where the Japanese first gathered in the House of Mirrors. Those mirrors reflect a subtle and little-known saga of Japanese Buddhists as well as the more blatant attractions of the scarlet sisters of perpetual indulgence.

Western Mining Landscapes: Case Studies

For Sale by Owner
Western Tourism and Historic Preservation

Eric L. Clements

At the beginning of the twentieth century, the American West made its living largely from resource extractive industries—agriculture, mining, lumbering, fishing. These produced raw materials sold to manufacturers and consumers, mostly outside the region. In the 50 years after the United States entered World War II, much of the region subsisted by hosting military research, manufacturing, testing, and training, demonstrating how much the West has changed in the last generation. New domestic and international economic realities, enhanced appreciation of environmental values, and the exhaustion of some resources have combined to curtail the extractive industries throughout much of the West. The end of the Cold War ended the need for much of the region's military infrastructure.

The West of the twenty-first century promises to be a region of urban centers devoted to high technology, light manufacturing, and service industries, freed of the specters of smelter smoke and atomic tests. This future may bode well for the urban centers, especially those of the Pacific states, but how will the small-town West of the interior make its living? As local mills and bases have closed, much of the West outside of urban areas has increasingly relied on tourism, selling either its wilderness or its history.

At first, the ecologically minded saw wilderness as both the spiritual and economic salvation of the West. But selling wilderness has its limits. Not everybody lives next to a Grand Canyon or a Yosemite Valley, after all. And those who do now often find themselves overwhelmed. By the year 2000 Grand Canyon National Park hosted about 5 million visitors annually. Every summer day an average of 6,000 private cars entered the park to fight over 1,500 parking spaces. The supervisor of the White River National Forest in central Colorado reported that the forest's 5 million visitor days in 1984 had grown to 12 million in 1999. She predicted 20 million visitor days in the forest by the year 2020.

Considering that number of visitors an impossible burden, federal officials discussed limiting visits in the White River National Forest. Their plan, consistent with contemporary values, deemphasized recreational use in favor of land and ecosystem stewardship. The economies of adjacent communities that had abandoned resource extraction depended on such recreational uses of the forest as four wheeling, snowmobiling, mountain biking, and skiing. Many residents of those towns were left none too happy with the Forest Service's proposed restrictions.

So what is left for the West to sell? Many places in the region subsist by selling history, but they face the same problem as those selling vistas: few communities have a nearby Little Bighorn or Mother Lode to draw upon. What most end up selling, therefore, is a mythic and symbolic West. Western historian Carlos Schwantes once observed that as Westerners were forced away from resource extraction or reliance on military expenditures, they convinced themselves that tourism is a nonpolluting industry and therefore a highly desirable economic activity in the post-industrial West. But Schwantes argues that tourism does pollute, and what it pollutes is history. Its eager sellers manipulate the West's heritage, converting it into a series of generic symbols that they can vend to visitors—the six-gun, the shady lady, the sombrero, the saguaro.

True, anyone's history can be manipulated for dramatic purposes. The popular history of the American West is famous for this sort of thing. Custer is always the last one left standing. But the corrosive phenomenon Schwantes identifies involves more than a little historical editing for narrative effect; it fundamentally disorients the region's past. Schwantes once reported seeing a sculpture of a saguaro cactus in the airport at Fairbanks, Alaska. You can purchase buffalo figurines in the curio shops at Tombstone, Arizona, hundreds of miles from where the buffalo roamed. Such gross biological distortions are matched by equally serious cultural and historical ones.

In this symbolic, generic, and salable version of Western history the complexities and unpleasantries of the region's experience are sanitized away. Consider Western violence. When discussing the mythic West with students, I use three vignettes of "frontier" violence: the Earp-Clanton feud in Tombstone, Arizona, which included the gunfight at the OK Corral in 1881; the Rock Springs, Wyoming, anti-Chinese riot of 1885, in which 28 Chinese residents were killed and $147,000 of Chinese property destroyed; and the 1905 bomb assassination in Caldwell, Idaho, of former Idaho governor Frank Steunenberg, apparently for his role in ending the Coeur d'Alene miners' strike of 1899.

Upon polling an audience following this discussion, you discover that everybody knows about the OK Corral fight, but only rarely has anyone heard of the Rock Springs riot or the Steunenberg assassination. One suspects that the reason for this is that the latter two incidents don't fit the generic image of Western violence. To serve the myth, even the gunfight at OK Corral is usually carefully cleaved away from the ambushes and assassinations that followed it. A serious examination reveals that the Earp-Clanton feud mostly fails to fit the popular formulation of lawmen and desperados dueling in dusty streets. In fact, the lessons one learns about frontier gunfighters' tactics from studying the doings in and around Tombstone aren't wholesome at all: jump 'em when you have the numbers; bushwhack 'em at night; shoot 'em in the back. Similarly, the moral composition of the feud—the really-bad guys against the not-so-bad guys—isn't very helpful either. We'll certainly have to clean it up before we try to sell it.

Daring duels between rugged individuals fit the forms of Western mythology. Bushwhack jobs, race riots, and bomb assassinations do not. No movie has ever been made about Harry Orchard, internationally famous in 1907 as Frank Steunenberg's confessed assassin. But Wyatt Earp, a victor in a local gang war that drew little outside attention initially, has been played by everyone from Ronald Reagan to Kevin Costner. In truth, the code of the duel was much more prevalent in the antebellum South than in the postbellum West. But shoot-outs are the generic and salable form of Western violence, facts notwithstanding.

An even harder problem is how to romanticize the normally difficult lives of the frontier West's prostitutes, a group composed largely of immigrant and minority women, whose lot in life consisted of great helpings of poverty, domestic violence, drug and alcohol addiction, venereal disease, homicide, and suicide. Still, somehow the "shady ladies" have also become a jovial part of Western legend, routinely celebrated at the region's tourist sites. One way to make this conversion is to euphemize it into palatability. Thus prostitutes become "sporting women" or "dance hall girls," the grim realities of their lives overlain with romantic connotations.

Another handy escape hatch is through the moral fable of the "hooker with the heart of gold," best formulated in what we can call the epidemic story. In this tale the prostitute plies her trade in the red-light district of some Western resource town, despised by community's genteel ladies. Then an epidemic strikes. At this point the town's "proper" women show their true colors, refusing to venture beyond their thresholds to come to the aid of the sickened miners (or cowboys or lumberjacks or sailors). These men are rescued from death by the ostracized "fallen" woman (or sometimes women), who ventures among them to render aid, revealing her own true character and rallying (and shaming) the town though her noble example.

I have, so far, found a basic served-in-the-epidemic story ascribed to three different prostitutes—Julia Bulette on the Comstock Lode, Nevada, Maggie Hall at Murray, Idaho, and another known as "Silverheels," at Alma in South Park, Colorado. So many epidemics in the West these days! In an improved version, the kindly prostitute catches the disease and dies, selflessly works herself to death treating those afflicted, or meets some other unjust and untimely end. Suddenly promoted from sinner to martyr, she is given "the largest funeral the town ever saw" as "the whole town turned out"—the alleged fates of Bulette and Hall.

Well, you might ask, what has any of this to do with historic preservation and preservationists? Were this creation of mythic symbols of the Wild West merely a question of personalities, it would remain purely a problem for historians. But the manipulation and commodification of the region's history to meet the expectations of its consumers intrudes upon the region's built environment as well. One of the better-known mythic symbols of the American West is the ghost town.

Politicians, historians, and the lay public have been arguing over the causes and meanings of Western ghost towns almost since they began to appear. While there have been spirited disagreements over these subjects, there is general consensus that the Western ghost town is powerfully symbolic of something. One author reports that the Midwestern farming state of Iowa has 2,205 abandoned settlements. Nobody cares. Iowa's ghost towns, though certainly important to that state's history, do not enter into Midwestern regional identity or the American national myth. In contrast, celebrating the Western ghost town is big business.

Under "ghost town," of course, we must include not only those communities that are actually defunct, but also those active towns that prosper to varying degrees by living off of romantic constructions of their former selves. By any standard of rational economics, many of these Tombstones and Tellurides—some of which are doing very nicely—should be dead.

There are certain qualifications necessary to enter this fraternity of the living dead; not every ghost town qualifies. Western ghost towns are not solely a product of the mining industry. Colorado has over 300 mining ghost towns—and over 200 agricultural ghost towns. But it is the mining ghost town that fascinates people. Few enthusiasts visit or eulogize dead farming towns. When discussing the mythic properties of the Western ghost town, historian Patricia Limerick wrote that one would have trouble finding a popular guide to the ghost towns of Massachusetts or Ohio. She might have added that it is almost as difficult to purchase a guide to the agricultural or lumbering ghost towns of the Old West.

Nor are we at all interested in the towns that developed to support the work of the mines. Mining sites often consisted of more than an individual town. A better unit of organization, the mining district, encompasses not only the place where ore is removed from the ground, but also the milling, smelting, and transportation centers that support that undertaking. Our fascination with the romance of the mining West does not extend to these sites, however. While Tombstone, Arizona, survives, all of the milling and transportation centers of the Tombstone District—Charleston, Millville, Fairbank, Contention City—have long since returned to the desert dust.

In truth, Tombstone subsists on its outlaw legends rather than its mining history. One can tour the town fairly extensively without learning that Tombstone began its life as the silver queen of the Southwest. In the 50 years after its mines shut down, the residents of Jerome, Arizona, also transformed their town. They organized a historical society, opened a museum, and gained the status of a state park and a National Historic Landmark. But as the years went by, the town also attracted artists and craftspeople, hosted music festivals, barbecues, and celebrations, started an historic homes tour, and for a few years sponsored an annual automobile race up the hill from the Verde Valley below. Jerome's transformation from heavy industry to retail sales is now so complete that a miner returning today would hardly recognize the place. Its current collection of curio and gift shops, antique dealers, art galleries, craft shops, confectioneries, coffeehouses, and cafés bears very little relation to the gritty, working-class town of a half century and more ago.

We might term the most extreme manifestation of this denial of history "mining camp chic." These are the towns like Aspen, Colorado, or Park City, Utah, so utterly transformed and gentrified that they scarcely acknowledge their industrial origins. They are now inhabited by wealthy celebrities who are usually horrified when someone suggests reopening a mine in the area. With only rare exceptions—Crested Butte, Colorado, and Red Lodge, Montana, being examples—mining camp chic never applies to former coal-mining towns, nor is there any strong urge to preserve such places. They are the forgotten ghosts of the mining West for several reasons. Coal is prosaic stuff, a commonplace, cheap commodity. The hard and dangerous conditions under which it was produced evoke Charles Dickens rather than Horace Tabor. Even the names associated with coal mining are sterile. Contrast the Smuggler Union or Camp Bird or Grand Central metal mines with the City no. 1 or Berwind no. 3. The names of coal towns could be similarly uninspired. CF&I Steel named its company coal towns on the Purgatoire River in station order west from Trinidad, Colorado: Primero, Segundo, Tercio, Cuatro, Quinto, Sexto.

These company towns often disappeared as soon as their usefulness ended, blotted out of existence on the orders of company officials far away. John Spratt, who grew up in the company coal town of Thurber, Texas, wrote that when its time came, "the reduction of Thurber was ruthless. The company ordered everything on the surface to be torn down or dug up." Phelps Dodge carried out the same treatment on its coal town of Dawson, New Mexico, once the largest company town in the West. When the dust settled, only a few houses, two smokestacks, and a cemetery remained.

Finally, the company towns in which coal was often mined have since become synonyms for exploitation, cockpits of class warfare. Contrast this to the "wide-open" metal mining bonanza camps, where—according to legend, at least—everyone had a chance to strike it rich. With these accumulated liabilities, Western coal towns cannot reflect the romantic luster of the bonanza camps. In short, they don't fit the Wild West formula. Hence there has been much less interest in preserving Western coal towns as such, although a number of them do survive uncelebrated.

So our ideal candidate for preservation stardom should really be an alpine or desert metal mining town, properly sanitized of its industrial origins. The best way to preserve such a mining landscape for commercial purposes is to minimize its actual history while promoting its symbolic adherence to the Western formulas customers desire. Bring on the gunfighters and the shady ladies!

The foremost practitioner of this approach has to be the aforementioned Tombstone, Arizona. In *Hard Places: Reading the Landscape of America's Historic Mining Districts*, historical geographer Richard Francaviglia writes that "townscapes such as Tombstone, Arizona, came to confuse popular imagery of television westerns with reality." During the glory days of the Western, Tombstone served as the setting for a number of movies and television series focused on the OK Corral gunfight or frontier Tombstone. Having seen the movie, many viewers wanted to see the "original"; having discovered their secret for success, Tombstone's merchants were loath to risk interrupting the flow of tourists' dollars. When preservationists suggested restoring the town to a more historically accurate image, away from its movie set appearance, they received a hostile reception from the local business community.

But the outstanding example of the manipulation of the built environment of a mining town to match the tastes of its tourists has to be Virginia City, Nevada. This largest and most famous town on the Comstock Lode was settled during the bonanza silver rush of 1859. Its first rush ended fairly quickly, replaced by another, more modest one in the late 1860s. The Comstock's "Big Bonanza" occurred in the mid-1870s, but this too played out by the 1880s. From there Virginia City began a genteel decline into its twentieth-century existence as a Victorian relic of the American frontier era.

But a fourth bonanza arrived in Virginia City's centennial year of 1959, in the form of the television Western of the same name. This NBC series, featuring the fictitious Cartwright family of Ben, Adam, Hoss, and Little Joe homesteading their Ponderosa Ranch, ran to 440 episodes over the next 15 years. Members of the family would ride into nearby Virginia City to confront weekly plot twists. The ranching supply town of Virginia City, Nevada, depicted in the television series was a board-and-batten-built, false-fronted creature constructed on level ground in proximity to the forests that gave the Cartwrights' ranch its name.

Unfortunately, the real Virginia City complicated the sale of the mythic West by being none of the above. Once they'd seen their town routed by fire a time or two, the sensible inhabitants of Western boomtowns gave up building structures out of wood and started using brick or adobe. So it was in Virginia City, whose central business district consists of the brick buildings erected after the town's great fire of October 1875. The town also shared another common characteristic of nineteenth-century mining camps—that of being situated in a fairly forbidding place. In Virginia City's case, this meant being dug into the steep side of Mount Davidson on the eastern slope of the Sierra Nevada at an elevation of over 6,300 feet.

Well, no matter. While they couldn't do anything about their town's altitude and gradient, Virginia City's merchants could certainly alter the architectural realities of their built environment to match those of the televised fiction. In *The Roar and the Silence: A History of Virginia City and the Comstock Lode*, Ronald James, the State of Nevada's Historic Preservation Officer, chronicles how Virginia City businesspersons changed the town's appearance in the 1960s to give the tourists the history that they wanted. Merchants simply paneled the facades of their brick buildings with rough cedar boards to make Virginia City look more authentic than Virginia City.

Figure 140. The Lace House, Black Hawk, Colorado, has been surrounded by a parking lot for local gambling casinos. Historic preservation and gaming was supposed to aid this nineteenth-century mining community, but instead it has utterly altered the fabric of the town. Photo by Andrew Gulliford, 2004.

With *Bonanza* now out of production for 30 years, the wooden facades have almost disappeared, but the town still hosts a Ponderosa Saloon and the wood-sheathed Bonanza Café, paying sober homage to Western characters and events that never existed. Of course, the *Bonanza* phenomenon is only the most spectacular instance of manipulating symbolic Western history for commercial gain in Virginia City. Down the street from the Ponderosa Saloon and the Bonanza Café lies a more conventional one: the Julia C. Bulette Saloon and Café . . . and Red Light Museum.

Can preservation prevail over commerce in these towns? Probably not, save in extraordinary cases. When large, international corporations brought casino gambling to Cripple Creek, Central City, and Black Hawk, Colorado, they crushed not only preservation projects but also the ideas and ideals of preservation itself. Usually when commerce meets preservation, money talks and history walks. It might seem foolish, therefore, to counsel people to stand in front of steamrollers, but as both a preservationist and a historian, I believe that preservationists are important both as guardians of our physical heritage and as agents in our historical discourse.

We certainly won't win all of the battles, perhaps not even most. But, often in cooperation with commercial

Figure 141. Behind the Lace House the mountainside has been gouged out and covered with concrete. The historic context for the Lace House has been destroyed, and the street it was on has become an entrance to a parking lot. Photo by Andrew Gulliford, 2004.

Figure 142. In Black Hawk, Colorado, all that remains of this historic commercial block is its facade, hence the phrase facadectomy. Photo by Andrew Gulliford, 2004.

interests, we can defend and preserve physical elements of our heritage and use them to interpret our history. Preservationists have the considerable advantage of being able to educate using tangible and authentic remnants of the past. People not interested in history from lectures and textbooks often find the authenticity of these sites and artifacts tremendously alluring.

A few years ago, while visiting the Edwardian monument to the victims of the Ludlow Massacre just north of Trinidad, Colorado, I was approached by another visitor, who asked, in a subdued voice, "Are you a brother?" He lost interest in me after I admitted that I was not a union member, but rather that strangest of creatures, a mining historian. He had impressed me more than I had him. He certainly could have learned the details of the Ludlow Massacre by reading some of the many books written about it. Instead, he chose to drive many miles from the nearest city in quest of something more than names and dates. He wanted to see it, to stand there, to feel it, to touch the past of his brothers.

That is the power of preservation and the privilege of preservationists. Working in the public interest for private and governmental agencies, professional and voluntary preservationists determine what to preserve, then acquire, protect, and interpret it. In the broadest sense, preservationists include anyone who works to retain or interpret evidence of our past—oral historians, archivists, records managers, artifact curators; even document editors and documentary filmmakers.

Even confining discussion to those who preserve the built environment still requires mention of an array of occupations and talents. Administrators such as State Historic Preservation Officers (SHPOs) oversee the budgets and operations of all of the historic properties held in trust by a particular state. They also cooperate with other agencies to plan the course of historic preservation and acquisition within a state. Cultural resource managers (CRM), who come from a dozen different specialties, oversee and operate individual sites of cultural or historic significance, while consultants and contract historians advise personnel at sites and agencies. Conservators and restorers combine theoretical knowledge of preservation's ideals and purposes with practical knowledge of traditional construction techniques to ensure that our historic built environment is properly maintained or restored. Educators and interpreters use their training and creativity to build the bridge between physical heritage and historical understanding.

In any of these careers, you will serve artifacts and structures as means to a much larger end. The places, the persons, the facts, the dates, the debates; all contribute to greater historical understanding. Each approach to the human past—be it through historical archaeology or oral history or the examination of the written record or the interpretation of the built environment—provides us with another tool that we can use to construct our understanding of our heritage. As a historian, you should embrace all of these different techniques; the more tools in your toolbox, the better the edifice you can build. Even the mythological Wild West of movie theaters and curio shops is valuable to us. Our legends tell us about ourselves, too. In whatever role you choose, your calling as a historic preservationist or public historian will be to help accurately interpret the past for the present and to preserve it for the future.

Study Questions

1. In what ways has the West changed since 1980?

2. How does tourism "pollute" history?

3. Why do the Rock Springs, Wyoming, anti-Chinese riot of 1885 and the assassination in Caldwell, Idaho, of former Idaho governor Frank Steunenberg fail to fit the accepted image of Western violence?

4. Why is the stark reality of Western prostitutes not as "palatable" as the myth of these women as dance hall girls?

5. What is the appeal of the Western mining ghost town over the agricultural ghost town?

6. Why are coal-mining ghost towns less romanticized than gold- and silver-mining towns?

7. In what way did the *Bonanza* series benefit or damage Virginia City, Nevada?

8. How can preservation prevail over commerce in historic mining towns?

9. How is the mythological Wild West of movie theaters and curio shops valuable to historians?

Boomtowns and Ghost Towns

Learning from the West's Preserved Historic Mining Landscapes

RICHARD FRANCAVIGLIA

The traveler on Colorado's "Scenic Highway of Legends," Highway 12 west of Trinidad, is awed by the rise of the Sangre de Cristo range's spectacular peaks opposite the deep valley of the South Fork of the Purgatoire River. Suddenly, as if by surprise, the highway plunges into Reilly Canyon, a small valley branded by the ruins of the mining industry. Here, amid the natural beauty of the Rockies, stands what is left of Cokedale. The town boomed in the early twentieth century as the thriving mining community produced coke to fuel the furnaces of the Colorado Fuel and Iron Company's steel mills. Today what remains of this enterprise is a National Register historic district.

Cokedale's site is very instructive on several levels. Behind a historic marker, a huge sinuous black gob pile marches down to the valley floor to join the remains of the town's buildings. Below is a magnificent row of abandoned coke ovens with graceful stone arches reminiscent of ancient Rome. Cokedale possesses its own transcendent beauty. Its artifacts complement the area's natural grandeur and add a haunting dimension to the scenery. One needs not wonder why "hard places" such as Cokedale sprang up in such remote locations across the United States. That is part of a long story in America's industrial development.[1] Rather, we should ask why—and how—former mining towns such as Cokedale wind up being preserved after their original reasons for being disappear.

If we doubt that mining towns have considerable staying power, we should consider Thurber, Texas. Thurber boomed from the 1880s to the 1920s in the semiarid country west of Fort Worth, where sandstone cuestas crown the brush-clad landscape. Here only a few buildings remain out of hundreds that once existed. Yet every June, hundreds return for the Thurber reunion. For several days, they rekindle memories of a long-gone time when coal was king. Even though only about 1 percent of Thurber's buildings remain, the town's mining industrial heritage is remembered in prose, poetry, and historical exhibits. Once again, we must ask why the Thurber town site possesses such enduring allure.

From Thurber, Texas, to Bodie, California, the West's landscape is dotted with places whose heydays passed in the early twentieth century—former mining towns that have not quite faded away, but instead remain preserved (in varying states of ruin) as sites on an ever-growing itinerary of historic tourist locations. "Visit Historic Cokedale" and "Take a Step Back into the Past" urges an attractive brochure prepared by the Cokedale Tourism Committee and the Colorado Center for Community Development. In Thurber, Texas, a new museum presents the industrial history of that town in particular and Texas in general. The activities of the Thurber Historical Association also present that town's industrial history. Looking at the Thurber town site today from a hill, that past seems safe as the place slumbers for about 360 days a year. A century ago, however, this very place would have been a hub of activity. In this essay, I would like to ask, and hopefully answer, some penetrating questions about such former mining locales where history is preserved, even celebrated: How much of the past do we really experience when visiting places such as Cokedale and Thurber? Is the past really preserved? How does Cokedale 2005 compare with Cokedale 1910? And how does Thurber in 2005 compare to Thurber in 1905? What elements of the landscape remain if preserved? What elements are gone but only preserved photographically or via historic markers? What elements are we encouraged to see? And what, we should always ask, has *not* been preserved?

Historical geographers like me are concerned with three major aspects of postindustrial locations. The first concern is *authenticity*, or how accurately preserved mining landscapes compare to historic imagery and historic descriptions. The second concern is *selectivity*: Why do only portions of the original landscape remain? Can lost features be added or re-created? The third concern, *utility*, determines the purposes these mining landscapes serve and how cultural/historical geographers or others concerned with the content of historic landscapes can utilize them. To address these concerns, we compare the touristic and preservation experience of the present with the past environment that once existed. By doing so, we see that places such as Cokedale and Thurber have multiple identities: historic, archaeological, pedagogical, and aesthetic.

We know that the Cokedale we view today is not—and can never be—the same boom community it was 100 years ago. Similarly, Thurber, most of which was sold off by the mining company when the mines closed in the late 1920s, will always only be a shadow of its former self. Yet many foundations and mining sites remain in Thurber even as the cactus and mesquite reclaim most of the site. In Thurber, as in Cokedale, markers and other clues help the visitor interpret the site. Thus, we must interpret both sites as postindustrial artifacts. Viewed in this way, places used by today's culture to explain the past serve many purposes, including educational, political, and aesthetic roles. Historical geographers have to reckon with our culture's need to preserve landscapes that become more interesting and attractive after they have failed. Two geographers have noted that "mining towns seem to be unusual, perhaps unique, among American settlements in being problems when they are booming but desirable when they have failed. . . . Americans have . . . remade into romantic sagas the histories of their early mining towns."[2]

These geographers are correct, but their observations must be placed in time. Mining landscapes preservation is a relatively recent phenomenon. Although a few visionaries began documenting and saving the physical heritage of mining towns as early as the turn of the twentieth century and more joined the cause later in the 1920s and the 1930s, it was the period following World War II that witnessed growing interest in our romanticized mining heritage. Before mining towns could be preserved or restored, however, Americans usually developed a romanticized vision of their place in history and nature. Merging prose, poetry, and art, they depicted the landscapes left in the wake of mining as grand ruins of great and exciting times. Among the most effective were Muriel Wolle's popular drawings and books. Her works on Colorado ghost towns defined the image for a generation of Americans, but they were not always so appreciated. Colorado, one contemporary 1880s observer described, "conjures up forsaken mining camps, ragged ravines and barren mountains, rocks, plains and precipices that go to make up a very uninviting view."[3]

Colorado, as noted above, became one of the earliest significant centers of mining landscape preservation efforts. By the 1930s, tourists had begun to discover the old mining ghost towns as writers and artists promoted them. This may partly explain why "mining towns" and "Western" are so closely linked in the public mind despite the fact that mining towns can be found in the East and upper Midwest.

Few writers have captured the sentiment of time and place better than the dean of popular historians, Lucius Beebe, and his partner, Charles Clegg, who wrote this ode to the Western mining landscape:

> The false fronts of once populous mining camps are good for a decade or so of Colorado winters at the most. The tailings and mine dumps are only a little more lasting and a few centuries will have eroded them past discerning to the most perceptive archaeologists. The elemental earth is quick to reclaim the cuts and fills of vanished railroads. Thus, while for a brief period the tangible souvenirs are at every hand, their impermanence is there also, implicit in the very nature of the society and its economics that mined the hillsides for precious metals. A rags-to-riches social emergence was not notably aware of its mortality. It didn't build for the ages.[4]

Descriptions such as these helped create a sense of urgency while generating an appreciation for the venerability of our mining landscapes. Beebe and Clegg were among the first to recognize the greatness of our mining heritage—even though this heritage was both ephemeral and pretentious. Landscapes of theatrical proportions displayed a montage of quickly built ornate sets emulating the high cultures of Europe and the East. Yet time's relentless march, together with the elements, underscored the vulnerability of this historic fabric while providing an almost perversely beautiful sense of desolation and decline. If every culture needs ruins to emphasize its past accomplishments and its relationship to nature, then our once prosperous mining towns are among the most powerful cultural symbols.

In my book about historic mining landscapes titled *Hard Places*, I showed that two very different motives lie at the roots of our fascination with history, and both affect how we perceive and preserve our mining towns. On the one hand, we need to recognize their former *greatness*, to show how, with limited technology, the miners dominated nature to win mineral riches. On the other, we need to venerate their *antiquity* by showing how this greatness fell to the hands of nature and time. Small wonder, then, that two types of mining town landscapes—boomtowns and ghost towns—are likely to be preserved for tourists to experience.

Ghost Town Preservation

Few places capture the imagination better than ghost towns, but historians continually debate the technical definition of just what constitutes a ghost town. Some insist that the place should be completely depopulated, although it must contain standing buildings or ruins. Others say that a few living hangers-on (perhaps 10 or fewer) may be permissible, as long as the town once had a much larger population. Others say that a true ghost town is a place where all aboveground signs of habitation, including buildings, have vanished. In that case, Cokedale (population 200) is a bit livelier ghost town than Thurber (population 16).

These distinctions are, of course, a bit academic. The public simply views a ghost town as a tangible but depopulated place inhabited only by memories of former occupants. Ghost towns imply former activity, perhaps even former greatness, as manifested in now decrepit buildings reclaimed by nature. We take an almost perverse interest in the aesthetics and symbolism of time marching into, and then overwhelming, such forlorn places. It gives them added power and pathos. Ghost towns certainly are instructional, for they depict risk taking, a revered trait in our culture. In creating the popular Knott's Berry Farm theme park in Orange County, California, in 1953, Walter Knott recognized the iconography. He was among the pioneers of a politically conservative school of educators creating mythical places to reaffirm the values of American greatness. Ghost Town was built anew in Los Angeles basin's fertile farmlands, but it depicted a wild and woolly, rough-hewn mining town main street wherein visitors could even pan for flecks of real gold. We are told:

> Ghost Town depicts an era in our nation's history when men were forging ahead and crossing new frontiers. Ghost Town also represents an era of free people who carved out their individual empires from a new land, asking only to work out their own salvation without hindrance. The people, the things, the buildings of Ghost Town are long dead, but the same pioneer spirit still lives on.[5]

Although Ghost Town was fictional, it was patterned after real places, such as the silver mining town of Calico, in California's Mojave Desert. Walter Knott, "a direct descendant of early day pioneers," recognized the deeply held American fascination with the past and capitalized on it. The real Calico itself, "site of one of the most spectacular silver strikes ever made in California," was one of the earliest resurrected ghost towns. In 1953, the public was told, "today the town-site, with its handful of ruins, is gradually being restored by the Knott family."[6] Calico emerged as one of the more popular booming ghost towns, an

Figure 143. Now a California state park, the forlorn site of Bodie is well preserved as a ghost town. Photo by author.

attraction not too far from the otherwise uneventful highway between Los Angeles and Las Vegas. Sequestered in the colorful, forlorn Mojave Desert hills that gave it its name, Calico became the liveliest of our mining ghost towns and one of the region's most successful tourism ventures. Even a recent fire that destroyed a portion of the town could not destroy this ghost. Most ghost towns are not as vibrant as Calico. Many, such as Ballarat in eastern California's Panamint Valley, are little more than historic markers standing near the melting adobe and splintered wooden walls of former buildings. Yet even those haunted sites draw great numbers of people.

The grandest, and most intact, of our mining ghosts is probably the silver-mining town of Bodie, California. Like all ghost towns, Bodie symbolizes our culture's desire to stop time at just the moment when nature is poised to erase it. Set in a sagebrush-covered, bowl-shaped valley in the high desert, Bodie was one of the roughest and most isolated boomtowns. Like most of its sister mining towns, Bodie had experienced devastating fires, one of which, in 1932, burned down half of the business district and further contributed to the town's forlorn quality. A watchman looked after the remains

Figure 144. A miner's home is preserved as a reminder of the past in Bodie, California, State Park. Photo by author.

of the town throughout the 1940s and 1950s, deterring souvenir hunters and scavengers. Private ownership by the wealthy Cain family guarded against Bodie's nearly sure fate of obliteration by scavengers.

Contrast Bodie with Columbia, the gold rush town in California's mother lode. Columbia is another state park, but this one attempts to capture the vibrant spirit of an active mining town; whereas Columbia is in a perpetual state of youth, Bodie is dead and proud of it. Since its opening as a state park in 1962, visitors to Bodie find themselves face-to-face with solitude. The town appears to be desolate and unoccupied. In reality, everything is carefully preserved in a state of arrested decay. Buildings lean at precarious angles, seemingly ready to topple with the next windstorm. They will not, however, for they are carefully propped up by hidden supports. However, things are not as peaceful here as they appear. Bodie's ghost is subject to serious disturbance, as mining companies have sought to begin mining anew right next to its sleeping corpse. Preservationists have resisted this effort, and there is a note of irony in that: after all, it was mining that helped create Bodie in the first place.

In Bodie itself, the preservation of the ghost town image finds man ironically resisting the elements and forestalling the inevitable. Such well-meaning efforts may sometimes miss their mark. Recognizing the extreme fire danger in Bodie, state park preservationists painted the buildings with a clear coating of fire retardant. To their chagrin, this treatment actually accelerated the deterioration of the wood that they were trying to protect! Nevertheless, the overall effect of the behind-the-scenes stabilization of ruin is stunning. Bodie has an artistic patina. The Standard Mill stands at the edge of town, its corrugated zinc metal sheathing burnished to a dull whitish blue. Dark basaltic rock foundations stand forlorn and geometrical. A hundred and twenty winters and summers have given the ramshackle wooden buildings a silvery golden hue. The gray-green sagebrush flourishes along with fat cattle grazing at the site. Left unattended, the elements and scavengers would reduce Bodie to an archaeological site in a matter of months. However, Bodie is preservation as theater, and its landscape is so provocative that the drama needs no "living history" actors, only a stage of deserted buildings to tell its story.

This preservation drama has been heightened recently with the National Historic Register's proposed nomination of the town and its mining-related landscape as a historic landmark—an action that the active Bodie Consolidated Mining Company opposed. In pursuing the nomination, mining preservationists recognized that the original boundaries did not include topographic features, such as ore dumps and tailings, which frame the historic town site. This is a reminder that historic preservation is no longer solely concerned with towns, but rather entire landscapes. This landscape includes mine dumps and even the hills surrounding the town. Therefore, historic preservationists believe Bodie's historic district should be expanded. Renewed mining activity adjacent to Bodie would, they claim, damage the feeling or ambiance of this historic mining town. This point, however, is of little concern to the present mining industry, which would just as soon mine the entire site, as their forebears would have done had they been able to extract silver and gold in low, but paying, quantities as can be done today.

Preservation of Boom Towns

Not all mining town sites are ghost towns. Often people remain behind to pursue new careers or retire in the places where mines have played out. Former mining community landscapes often convey a sense of the past that attracts visitors—a point not lost on merchants, who see their own potential gold mine in marketing the history. Consider, for example, Tombstone, Arizona, which was one of the earliest towns to capitalize on its mining-related boomtown heritage. A state park established at the historic Cochise County Courthouse (complete with its gallows) further encouraged visitation. The traveler on the way into town senses the spirit of the place when driving past Boot Hill and then arriving at a main street lined with false front buildings emblazoned with gaudy "Wild West" signs and fake porches.

By the 1960s, Tombstone had become a tourist town capitalizing on its bawdy, violent history as a frontier mining and cattle town. By the late 1970s, however, the historic preservation movement had matured to the point that two consultants were able to advise merchants to remove the fake Wild West trim and recover the right historical fabric. But the merchants resisted, saying in effect, "Why question success?" As the sophistication of tourists increases, they may be forced to reconsider this decision.

Hoping to capture some of Tombstone's tourist trade, nearby Bisbee launched into an aggressive marketing campaign in the early 1980s and continues to push tourism today. By promoting its copper-mining history, the "Queen of the Copper Camps" hoped to reverse the decline that followed the 1975 closing of its large open-pit copper mine. Not to be outdone by Tombstone, wags in Bisbee designed a sequel bumper sticker that, too, said something about the town's tenacity: "Bisbee: The Town Too Dumb to Die." Bisbee holds a rich historical legacy. Much of the downtown commercial core consists of buildings constructed prior to 1920. It is this historic downtown, as well as the mine tour, that draws thousands of visitors hungry for history. Bisbee has many touristic counterparts. Among them are the fabled Virginia City, Nevada; Virginia City, Montana; Park City, Utah; and Black Hawk and Central City in Colorado.

These types of revitalized mining towns are subject to intense development pressure as a result of tourism. Gambling is probably the most demanding of these, for it precipitates rapid commercial development, as in Central City, Colorado. Communities with preservation expertise (Deadwood, South Dakota) or with preservation ordinances (Jacksonville, Oregon) can mitigate the impact of tourism. Some mining towns, such as Aspen, Colorado, have been inundated by skiing tourism, losing much of their industrial character. Others, such as Park City, Utah, are trying to regain their historic character through participating in Certified Local Governments (CLG) programs jointly sponsored by the National Park Service (NPS) and the State Historic Preservation Offices (SHPO).

Preserving Company Town Landscapes

Another type of mining community—the company town—is increasingly experiencing preservation restoration. Some were based on copper mining, others on coal mining, but they all had one thing in common—nearly complete ownership of all property, and control of most activities, by a single corporation.

Company towns could be found coast to coast, from Pennsylvania's anthracite country all the way to the Cascade Mountain coal-mining town of Roslyn, Washington. Consider again Thurber, Texas, that classic coal-mining company town that went belly up in the 1920s. Like a number of company towns gone bust, the company tore down most of what had remained. Thurber now features a museum depicting the mining community's various historic phases. But the major attraction is the site itself, which now consists of less than a dozen historic buildings. A historic marker on New York Hill above Thurber identifies a few of the town's historic buildings; however, close scrutiny of historic photos reveals the town's complicated social geography. Thurber consisted of several ethnic neighborhoods, each occupied by Italians, Poles, Czechs, blacks, and Mexican Americans. Thurber provides tourists with an interesting blend of existing fragments and visually reconstructed history.

Its very ghost town status is part of that appeal, and historic glimpses of the ghost before its demise are available at the museum and in photographs posted in the town's two competing restaurants—the Smokestack and the New York Hill. Both restaurants, appropriately, are named after historic features. People are often amazed to learn that there are two factions in Thurber, each of which has a different idea of how history should be presented. This situation recently (2002) changed when a third interpreter of the town's history—the W. K. Gordon Center for Texas Industrial History—opened. This was applauded by some and resisted by others. One of the town's historians put it succinctly when he noted that, "I feel my heritage slipping away when [it is] left to outsider revisionists."[7]

Historic Preservation and the Landscape

If historic preservationists had their way, old housing and commercial buildings in mining towns would be restored or rehabilitated. Preservation, much of it done in accordance with the secretary of the interior's guidelines for rehabilitation, has given mining communities a distinctive, upscale preserved look. This

Figure 145. Large-scale mining-related structures like this head frame and ore bin at Butte, Montana, are important features in historic mining landscapes. Photo by author.

look confirms that preservation has become big business—and very popular. It has been so for nearly a generation: A Gallup Poll conducted for the Urban Land Institute in 1986 revealed that a majority of people support the objectives of historic preservation. "Retaining a sense of the past" was rated as the most important objective of historic preservation.[8] But historic preservation actually has two faces: the popular (or recreational/aesthetic) and the professional (or interpretative/educational). To the average person, historic preservation means saving and restoring historic buildings—usually historic homes and commercial buildings. To professionals, however, it is a process by which all historic properties (historic here includes both prehistoric archaeological and historic-architectural resources) are identified, evaluated, and protected. These may also include industrial structures and other features.

Here I would like to discuss the broader landscape associated with mining towns—not just the towns themselves, but all the other features that are associated with mining. Professional historic preservation involves rather mundane recordation of sites and structures that would or will normally be lost to progress or the elements. The professional preservationist's most effective role is determining the historic significance of resources and then providing this information to the public or private sector—which may or may not actively advocate actual preservation. If, for example, mining company officials have been informed by preservationists that a particular mine tipple is the last of its kind in the region, the owners are ideally expected to take that information into account when making decisions. The tipple might be saved on-site, relocated, or, at the least, recorded using professional preservation techniques such as those used by the Historic American Engineering Record (HAER) or the Historic American Buildings Survey (HABS).

Preservationists have another responsibility. They must also provide this information to public officials considering demolishing certain city-owned properties—such as an early miner's hall that later served as a community hall or a mining company office building that later served as city offices. When federal funds are involved in the project, the Section 106 process kicks in. Under this process, administrators are required to conduct a review to determine the proposed project's impact on historic properties. If the impact is negative, they must find ways to mitigate the adverse effects.

Preservationists face tough decisions in dealing with abandoned mining lands. What remains is often both historically interesting and extremely dangerous. Hazardous mine openings are understandably sealed up (sometimes with screens or grates). However, many other features, such as tipples and head frames, are often demolished because they pose tax liabilities. Different opinions exist as to what constitutes an unsound structure, but building inspectors not supportive of preservation almost always find them unsafe—especially when their superiors want the building or historic feature demolished.

The Preservation Process

The diverse mining locations that I have so far mentioned come under varied jurisdictions. Some are privately owned, some public, but all exist in the context of political jurisdiction. Historic preservation works at three levels: local, state, and national. Preserving mining landscapes reveals just how complicated the interrelationship among these levels can be. At the federal level, those who administer the National Register of Historic Places (the National Park Service of the U.S. Department of the Interior) review material from across the country and have a wider base of knowledge regarding what is historic. Sometimes it is the local residents who are the most ignorant about a particular mining-related feature's importance because they do not understand its context in relation to other properties nationwide: they may oversee a structure that is rare but be unaware of this. Then, too, local concerns about intrusions into personal freedom come into play. This is especially true for those whose interest in development or fear of large government leads them to reject information that puts a particular feature in a broader context. Yet properly informed and understanding locals are often the strongest and most knowledgeable preservation advocates.

Intermediate in the preservation process are the State Historic Preservation Offices, created by the 1966 Historic Preservation Act. The State Historic Preservation Officer, as appointed by the governor, is responsible for implementing the preservation program adopted by Congress. It is he or she who ultimately recommends National Register eligibility for historic resources. Preserving mining-related landscapes challenges the SHPO, however, because the state agencies responsible for stabilizing and reclaiming abandoned mine lands may not work closely with the SHPO. The task of educating all agencies involved with historic mining resources is formidable. Few public agencies want to be perceived as standing in the way of powerful mining interests that create jobs and fuel the local or regional economy. While not all states have addressed this issue, South Dakota's State Historic Preservation Agency took steps to reduce the problem by hosting a groundbreaking workshop on historic mining resources a generation ago. This 1987 meeting brought mining preservationists together from agencies across the country. In the last 15 years, numerous states, including Montana, have taken a stronger interest in preserving their mining-related heritages.

Both the strongest and weakest mining landscape preservation advocacy occurs at the federal level. The agencies' track records depend largely on the demography of their constituents. Agencies with little appreciation of mining heritage often represent either mining or environmental interests. Preservationists claim that the Office of Surface Mining (OSM) and the Environmental Protection Agency (EPA) have their own agendas and little or no awareness of historic resources and their preservation. One of the most sensitive issues in the early twenty-first century, hazardous site cleanup (some of them "Superfund" sites), involves areas such as Butte and Anaconda, Montana, which contain important historic resources. Then, too, the historic preservation activities of large agencies in the West, such as the Bureau of Land Management (BLM), are only now developing. The BLM administers huge areas but short staffing has kept that agency from fully addressing and protecting the historic resources of the lands they control.

As of this writing, the National Park Service has maintained the strongest interest in identifying and preserving significant historic mining-related resources. Recognizing that a comprehensive effort is needed to protect the historic resources of an aggressive industry that operates nationwide, the NPS initially hosted a conference in Death Valley in January 1989. The conference was aimed at increasing public-private sector understanding of the challenges involved in preserving mining-related features and landscapes. Summarized in an eight-part report by

Figure 146. The historic townscape of Austin, Nevada, is a remnant of aggressive mining activity in the Victorian West. Photo by author.

NPS mining historian Robert Spude,[9] the conference dealt with identifying, interpreting, and preserving mining features in the context of existing programs. The conference led to several resolutions, namely:

- Mining sites themselves, not just the legends and architecture of the mining frontier, must be looked at.
- Federal agencies must continue responsible management, and those that do not must be made accountable.
- Mining companies can continue their work while responding to public concerns and federal requirements.
- A national mining initiative, including congressional directives, is needed to identify and protect mining-related resources.

This conference helped lead to the creation of the Mining History Association (MHA), a nonprofit group concerned with interpretation of mining nationwide, though most of its members are Westerners and most of its annual meetings are held in the West.

The National Register and Mining Districts

Preservationists use the National Register of Historic Places as a yardstick to evaluate historic properties. The Keeper of the National Register in Washington, D.C., under NPS administration, maintains this historic listing. According to the NPS, "historic districts, sites, buildings, structures and objects that possess integrity of location, design, setting, materials, workmanship, feeling and association" may be listed on the register when they possess significant quality in American history, architecture, engineering, and culture. Listing on the register identifies a property's significance at either the local, state, or national level. After nearly 40 years, the register lists more than 75,000 historic properties. The list of several hundred mining-related resources reveals two major types: either very notable individual buildings or assemblages of historic resources. Almost all of them were more than 50 years old when listed.

Preservationists judge a historic property using one or more of the following questions:

- Is it associated with events that have made a significant contribution to the broad patterns of our history?

- Is it associated with the lives of persons significant in our past?
- Does it embody the distinctive characteristics of a type, period, or method of construction?
- Does it represent the work of a master or possess high artistic values?
- Does it represent a significant and distinguishable entity whose components may lack individual distinction?
- Has it yielded, or will it likely yield, information important to history or prehistory?

Using these criteria, one can see that mining communities possess a wide range of historic features associated with numerous themes, such as ethnic history, industrial history, and transportation history. However, given their cosmopolitan quality and their feverish productivity, most mining districts contain a wealth of features, making it difficult to select a boundary point where preservation begins or ends. To exacerbate the problem, new developments may have intruded on the site, causing one to question whether or not the mining district is still historic.

Public participation may also deter a site's chance at historic distinction. Local residents may or may not recognize the significance of their community's mining heritage. Property owners may care little for history, especially if it threatens their development options. A mining company might fear its property's listing on the National Register will hamstring its ability to further develop future mining operations. These fears, however, are unfounded: the National Register listing imposes no constraints on what an owner can do with private property. If changes prove detrimental to the historic property, it will simply be deleted from the list.

In parts of the arid West, abandoned mining features such as ore dumps may last hundreds, perhaps thousands, of years. They are especially visible because vegetation does not obscure them. But even here, change and attrition always poses problems for preservationists interested in historic mining districts. For example, abandoned mining-related topographic features that, over time, have further eroded or revegetated present a dilemma regarding their historic integrity. Placing a historic mining-related property or feature on the National Register involves an assessment of its present condition compared with its historic condition. How much of its *integrity*, to use the preservationists' jargon, remains? To determine this, historic features such as tailings piles and ore dumps can be compared with historical photographs. However, a value judgment is often required to determine how much change is acceptable before a feature loses its visual associative character or feeling. Historic preservation is, and is likely to remain, more art than science.

Historic Districts

Although individual buildings and features are listed on the National Register, there is greater tendency to think in terms of historic districts. An historic district is defined as a "geographically definable area—urban or rural, large or small—possessing a significant concentration, linkage or continuity of sites, buildings, structures and/or objects united by past events or aesthetically by plan or physical development."[10]

A historic district is largely a visual phenomenon. We know when we are in one because the place has a "feel" based on the presence of a significant number of historic buildings. There are few, or relatively few, modern intrusions even though modern uses such as bookstores and real estate agencies now occupy those historic buildings. The historic district in Jacksonville, Oregon, conveys this feeling of significance. The town prospered during the gold mining booms of the mid-nineteenth century. A preservationist tells us that "following a series of devastating fires, ordinances were passed that mandated the use of brick along the main street."[11] This contributes to the commercial district's sense of permanence. Following the closing of the mines, "fruit raising and a minimum of local commerce kept the settlement from becoming a ghost town, while poverty kept it from changing."

This condition enabled the town's historic architecture to survive into the middle 1960s, when "more than a hundred nineteenth century buildings in the town were placed on the National Register of Historic Places."[12]

These buildings epitomize the term *historic district*—an identifiable place that dates from a particular historic period. The commercial core or downtown area of Bisbee, Arizona, similarly displays a kind of historic architectural integrity. In Bisbee, more than 200 historic buildings are packed into a rugged canyon setting. With relatively little new construction and no vacant lots resulting from demolition, nothing spoils the general impression that one has stepped back in time. Preservationists originally placed the Bisbee historic district on the National Register in 1979. As is often the case, this first nomination identified the best of the historic resources. More recently, historic preservationists have expanded the Bisbee historic district to include other historic resources, including homes, that were overlooked in the earlier effort. It should be remembered that listing on the National Register can be a mixed blessing. The designation often attracts well-meaning development efforts that lead to a reconstructed postindustrial landscape at the expense of our historic understanding of the original mining landscape.

Multiple Resource Areas

Historic districts are the gems of the preservation world. More often, however, we visit historic mining districts where time has not stopped. Historic buildings, structures, and even districts may stand next to modern features that seem to compromise the location and historic character. Important features may have been removed to such an extent that the community or location does not possess the feel of a historic district. This does not mean, however, that the place is any less interesting. Even though its visible historic resources are scattered, the site may still have an important historic story to tell. A multiple resource area, then, displays a discontinuous distribution of important historic resources. Each resource plays a part in revealing the

Figure 147. In Central City, Colorado, preservationists found a rich historic resource that proved irresistible to the gaming industry. Photo by author.

history of the area. Looking carefully at such areas, one sees that they are actually interesting as historic districts because they permit us to see the impact that more recent developments—what some call progress—have had on the mining community.

That is just the feeling conveyed by the Tintic Mining District Multiple Resource Area in Utah. Here one sees an historic montage: in Eureka's once prosperous central business district the remnants of old Victorian bonanza buildings stand side by side with modern commercial buildings. There are gaping holes where historic buildings recently stood. Nevertheless, the district is a veritable museum of scattered engineering features, such as head frames, stamp mill sites, and ore bins. The Tintic Mining District's National Register nomination form states that the "primary significance of the historic resources

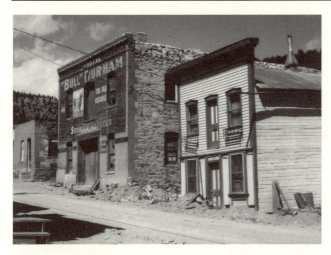

Figure 148. Before its recent resurrection as a gambling center, Black Hawk, Colorado, presented this serene picture of mining's past. Photo by author.

Figure 149. The ruins of adobe and galvanized sheathed metal buildings are about all that remains of the historic mining town of Gleeson, Arizona. Photo by author.

. . . is their value in the documentation of metal mining history, both on the state and national level."[13] A wide range of historic resources associated with numerous uses, from commercial to residential to engineering, abound in this area. Some historic resources are readily visible despite the intrusions. Others are archaeological in the sense that they are below ground level. The area is, in fact, rich in sites of historic archaeological significance. These sites, too, can tell us much about the location—provided that we have the ability to read them using methods that supplant those we rely on to interpret the visible landscape.

Vanishing Landscapes: The Historical Archaeology of Mining Districts

Not all historic mining landscapes look as though the clock stopped just after they were abandoned. Some have essentially vanished from view. Although we are most likely to know about the gems, such as Virginia City or Central City, which have many extant buildings and structures, another, more subtle landscape is associated with mining: the historic site where virtually nothing remains aboveground. Aurora, Nevada, fits this description. Whereas just 40 years ago, one could see the shells of abandoned buildings, the early twenty-first century reveals only a sagebrush-covered site. Does this make the location any less historic?

The answer, of course, is no—provided that we know how to read other, more subtle or hidden clues, such as eroding tailings piles, ore dumps, building foundations, and other below-ground works of man that nature is slowly reclaiming.

One of the most important and overlooked aspects of the National Register in evaluating historic resources is the *potential* of the property to yield information about the history or prehistory of a site. This brings us to the realm of historical archaeology, which is concerned with what the physical remains of fairly recent literate societies—such as the sites of mining towns—can tell us about the people who lived there. The physical record can be supplemented by the written records that were sometimes left by these people. In the case of the mining areas, the physical record can also tell us much about the processes that the

Figure 150. Mining leaves evocative landscapes in its wake, as evidenced in these eroded tailings near Virginia City, Nevada. Photo by author.

miners either did not understand well enough to document or chose not to write down at the time. Historical archaeologists are often concerned with the past housing patterns and commercial trade areas of mining areas. Their colleagues, interested in the heavier industrial features, such as smelting and ore concentration, are part of a related field called industrial archaeology.

Historical archaeologists have shed much light on mining landscapes. Their painstaking fieldwork often results in a wealth of information that is not otherwise visible in the landscape. In Nevada, historical archaeologist Ronald Reno has noted that "there are four major types of archaeological studies of mining camps: model, inventory, assessment and mitigation."[14] Reno states that a model based on a review of existing literature would predict distributions of cultural remains—what we might expect to find *before* fieldwork is completed. The process has three components or stages. *Inventory* includes all information that has been obtained from archaeological surveys. *Assessment* includes surveys of historic properties and historic significance completed for National Register nominations. *Mitigation* refers to work done in response to projects that are likely to disturb, perhaps destroy, a particular historic mining site. In the latter case, renewed mining activity is often an issue. In fact, Reno noted that "the real destruction caused by the shift from underground to open pit methods and the large scale of work required for companies to turn a profit is unprecedented in Nevada."[15]

Among the most important information revealed by historical archaeologists is patterns that express themselves on at least two levels: *vertically* on a social scale, where artifacts may be used to determine the social status of the artifact's user in the community, and *horizontally* on a geographic scale, where the actual spatial organization or layout of the community is determined. Historical archaeology fieldwork by Don Hardesty has helped clarify social and developmental conditions in several Nevada mining districts. Historical archaeology's value in answering important questions about the mining's impact on the landscape was underscored by a recent study that applied dendrochronology techniques (tree ring analysis) in the Cortez mining district of Nevada. Researchers determined that the tree ring records of historic and archaeological features, including stump and construction materials, provides an absolute chronology for the varying woodland use through time and for

Figure 151. Mining's impact includes huge features such as this leach dump near Ajo, Arizona, which are rarely preserved. Photo by author.

other human activities using piñon logs. These data provide details of the magnitude and history of deforestation unavailable in other lines of research.[16]

This is where historical archaeology and environmental history converge. The authors correlated the use of pine trees throughout the major time periods or phases of the mining district's development with the existing stands of vegetation through time. They concluded that "correlation of tree ring data with other data bases reveals changes in woodland use and structure to be mainly associated with mining activity" but that "the presence of old age trees indicates that the magnitude of the nineteenth century deforestation may have been less severe at Cortez than is claimed for other mining districts."[17]

Clearly, many of our vanished historic mining districts have the potential to yield an incredible amount of information about both the occupants and the environment. Yet our emphasis on the preserved or restored mining community/landscape obscures the fact that we may be able to learn as much from places with little aboveground remains. For every mining-related site on the National Register, there are dozens of others about which little or nothing is known.

Historic Landmarks Associated with Mining

The National Historic Landmarks (NHL) program focuses on sites of national significance that "commemorate and illustrate the history and culture of the United States." These properties are identified by a theme. Mining-related resources are included under two main categories: *westward expansion* and *business*. This is an interesting breakdown, for it reveals certain preconceptions about history, even among professionals. It tends to romanticize the westward movement or at least remove it from its context of Eastern financing. Moreover, it assumes that Western and Eastern mining activities were fundamentally different when, in fact, they were part of the same industrial system. It is largely the romance of the West that makes us think things were fundamentally different there. In reality, national and international forces fueled mining activities in both East and West. Yet the important factor of landscape means that the character of mining varied from east to west. In the West, a location's aridity might require certain adjustments and offer certain opportunities, as in the evaporative tailings ponds.

At any rate, only nationally significant, well-documented properties may qualify for listing as National Historic Landmarks. Therefore, this may be thought of as a refinement of the National Register program. Describing the process by which mining-related NHLs were selected in the early years of the program, NPS staff historian Robert Spude noted that "the historic sites and building inventory looked at over 100 mining sites and selected 17 as potential National Historic Landmarks.... Unfortunately, the NPS evaluation system reflected the popular view of looking only at the towns, rather than at the mines or mills," and "thus, significant mine structures or mills standing at the time were not recognized."[18] This oversight—a disregard for the engineering features of a mining district and a fascination with their residential or commercial architecture—remains a problem. It has certainly yielded a lopsided or distorted visual legacy in the preserved historic mining landscape. However, as it evolved, the National Historic Landmarks program has become more comprehensive and inclusive. Thus, Jacksonville, Oregon, is also listed as a National Historic Landmark under "westward expansion," as is the Bodie Historic District in California.

Conclusion

Mining landscapes are usually preserved or destroyed for economic reasons. However, this essay suggests that two other reasons come into play: *recreational* (often through private commercial ventures) and *educational* (often overseen by the public sector). In today's historic mining landscapes, we are either supposed to have fun or to learn something. In reality, of course, many preserved mining landscapes fall somewhere in between in intent and content. These are interactive landscapes. As we experience them using our leisure time, they often convey political/social agendas (for example, the virtues of private enterprise or the importance of labor organization) that we assimilate as consumers.

As with all historically contrived landscapes, preserved mining landscapes are complex. Many are not accurate; postindustrial (current) sentiments affect what is preserved. Preservation advocates operate using certain biases that result in selective preservation. Therefore, historical geographers need to approach any preserved mining landscape with a great deal of caution. At Jacksonville, we see our culture's attempt to make former mining landscapes more bucolic and idyllic than they ever were by obliterating the signs of gritty activity that once sustained the town. The mining landscape contains many messages, and the major lessons learned from preserving mining landscapes fit into several categories that correspond to cultural issues.

Man-Nature Reconciliation

At many restored or preserved mining camps, the most visible features of mining—the waste dumps and other unpleasant signs of environmental degradation—are often removed to present a scene of natural beauty that disguises the full extent of the former mining activity. If not actually removed, such features are often stabilized or revegetated. These actions reassure

Figure 152. Despite its historic significance, this huge slag dump at Anaconda, Montana, is considered more of an environmental problem than a historic resource. Photo by author.

us that man's activities are reversible, if not ephemeral. A case study of such reconciliation is found in Utah's Black Rock Canyon, where the Kennecott Copper Company has softened its impact.[19]

The Creation of Artifactual Symbols

A study of preserved mining landscapes reveals that certain features, such as head frames and ore-hauling equipment, come to symbolize mining activity and are preserved as landscape icons. Other less associative or poorly understood features, such as ore sampling equipment, may be considered too mundane to be preserved and therefore disappear. Whereas active mining landscapes contain features (machinery, buildings, and structures) that are associated with a full range of activities, usually only those that symbolize ore extraction and sometimes ore processing remain in preserved mining districts.

The Preservation of the Aesthetically Pleasing

While attempting to preserve the significant or valuable material culture associated with the past, historic landscapes inevitably satisfy aesthetic sensitivities. Thus, in preserved mining landscapes we find impressive (sometimes beautiful) features such as arched coke ovens and

Figure 153. Historic mining towns such as Virginia City, Nevada, present a rich array of historic architectural features. Photo by author.

attractive Victorian miners' homes being preserved. One rarely sees rows of shacks preserved. Rather, those that feature some trim or indications of architectural "style" remain. Likewise, the chaotic assemblages of discarded equipment characterizing active mining operations are reconstituted as "artifact gardens."

The Reinterpretation and Reaffirmation of Power

Active mining landscapes, especially company-owned towns, exhibit the strong role of owners and managers in decision making. Through selective preservation, power may be reinterpreted or reaffirmed. In Thurber, Texas, for example, the tension between labor and management in this former Texas & Pacific Coal Company town is nowhere apparent today—the company removed all of the miners' wooden homes years ago when it abandoned the town.[20] The one house that has been restored now sits near the base of New York Hill, a considerable distance from the few mining managers' homes that escaped the bulldozer.

The Reaffirmation of Gender

Active mining landscapes are "male" landscapes in that men shaped virtually all of the mining, trans-

Figure 154. The historic Fourth Ward School at Virginia City, Nevada, is one of the landmark buildings in the town's historic district. Photo by author.

portation, and settlement patterns. They remain so. Symbolically, tall smokestacks and erect head frames are among the most commonly preserved features in the mining landscape—as a look at Butte and Anaconda, Montana, reveals. Mining landscape preservationists are beginning to discover the important role of women in community life. Often, however, only the bawdy houses and homes of the mining managers (whose wives were influential in community affairs) are preserved and interpreted. We can expect that to change as an appreciation of the role of women in the life of mining towns grows.

In retrospect, a preserved mining landscape is a contradiction in terms, for active mining landscapes are in a constant state of flux and therefore are impossible to stabilize without compromising the integrity of the very process—mining—that created them. Those that are preserved are usually sanitized to satisfy health, safety, and aesthetic standards that simply did not exist when they were created. Nevertheless, preserved mining landscapes are important postindustrial artifacts that may tell us more about the way contemporary cultures reshape the past to meet the needs and values of the present than they do about the past.

Notes

1. Richard V. Francaviglia, *Hard Places: Reading the Landscape of America's Historic Mining Districts* (Iowa City: University of Iowa Press, 1991).

2. Thomas R. Vale and Geraldine R. Vale, *Western Images, Western Landscapes: Travels Along U.S. 89* (Tucson, AZ: University of Arizona Press, 1991), 48.

3. William Ralston Balch, *The Mines, the Miners, and Mining Interests of the United States in 1882* (Philadelphia: Mining Industrial Publishing Bureau, 1882), 769.

4. Lucius Beebe and Charles Clegg, *Narrow Gauge in the Rockies* (Berkeley, CA: Howell-North Press, 1958), 8.

5. Knott's Berry Farm, *Ghost Town and Calico Railway* (Buena Park, CA: Knott's Berry Farm, 1953), 59.

6. Ibid., 59.

7. Dianne Jennings, "Ghost Town Alive with Controversy," *The Dallas Morning News*, June 2, 2002 (as seen on Texas News web site http://www.txcn.com/texas-soughwest/stories/060202dntexthurber.a4d78.html.)

8. *A Gallup Study of Public Attitudes Towards Issues Facing Urban America*, 2 vols. (Washington, D.C.: Urban Land Institute, 1986).

9. Leo Barker and Anne E. Huston, *Death Valley to Deadwood; Kennecott to Cripple Creek—Proceedings of the Historic Mining Conference, January 23–27, 1989, Death Valley National Monument* (San Francisco: National Park Service, September 1990).

10. William Murtagh, *Keeping Time: The History and Theory of Preservation in America* (Pittstown, NJ: Main Street Press, 1988), 215.

11. Randolph Delahanty and Andrew McKinney, *Preserving the West* (New York: Pantheon, 1985), 123.

12. Ibid., 125.

13. Utah State Historical Society, Historic Preservation Office, Salt Lake City, Utah, National Register Nomination, Tintic Mining District.

14. Ronald Reno, "Archaeological Studies of Nevada Mining Camps" (paper presented at the Society for Historical Archaeology Annual Meeting, Reno, Nevada, January 1988).

15. Ibid., 2.

16. Eugene M. Hattori and Marna Ares Thompson, "Using Dendrochronology for Historical Reconstruction in the Cortez Mining District, North Central Nevada," *Historical Archaeology* 21, no. 2 (1987): 69–70.

17. Ibid., 71.

18. Robert Spude, Historic Mining Conference, *CRM Bulletin* 132, no. 4. (1990): 16–18.

19. See Zach Cononelos, ed., *The Man and His Mountains: The Paul Rokich Story* (Salt Lake City: Kennecott Utah Copper, 2002).

20. Richard Francaviglia, "Blake Diamonds and Vanishing Ruins: Reconstructing the Historic Landscape of Thurber, Texas," *Mining History 1994 Annual* 1, no. 1 (1994): 51–62.

Study Questions

1. How much of the past do we really experience when visiting places such as Cokedale and Thurber?

2. Explain why mining towns fail to tell the full story of their social history when only certain types of structures are preserved.

3. How do historic preservationists address the concerns of authenticity, selectivity, and utility of a mining landscape?

4. What has motivated people to preserve mining towns and mining landscapes?

5. How did Muriel Wolle influence the way we view Western mining towns?

6. Why did Colorado become one of the earliest significant centers of mining landscape preservation efforts?

7. Why did our once prosperous mining towns become powerful cultural symbols?

8. Why do we feel compelled to recognize the former greatness of mining towns or feel a need to venerate their antiquity?

9. How is Bodie, California, different from other preserved mining towns?

10. Why should historic preservation be concerned with entire landscapes and not merely with towns?

11. What are the professional preservationist's responsibilities to the public?

12. Define "historic integrity" as it pertains to a site.

13. How does a "multiple resource area" differ from a "historic district"?

14. In what ways can the most visible features of mining—the waste dumps and other signs of environmental degradation—contribute to the history of a site?

Cultural Landscape Preservation and Public History in Cokedale, Colorado

David Robertson

State Highway 12 runs west from Trinidad, Colorado, climbing into the foothills of the Sangre de Cristo Mountains. Eight miles west of Trinidad, the road tops a rise and the browns and greens of the piñon-speckled hills are interrupted by a wall of black coal waste. The highway parallels the ridge of mine spoil as it descends into the valley. On the south side of the highway lie two rows of crumbling coke ovens. In their ruin, the oven arches resemble an ancient Roman viaduct. To the north, at the base of the waste pile, a gravel road runs up the canyon. At this intersection sits a sign reading, "Cokedale—National Historic District." Cokedale was listed on the National Register in 1985. It stands as one of the best preserved company mining towns in the American West.

Built along Reilly Creek by the American Smelting and Refining Co. (ASARCO) in 1907, Cokedale lies hidden beneath a canopy of elm trees. Only after crossing the bridge that spans the creek does the town come into full view. A parking area marks the entrance to Cokedale. Here, pinned to a bulletin board, is a self-guided walking tour of the town; complimentary copies sit in a brochure holder.[1] The walking tour directs visitors north onto Spruce Street. To the left, a dozen cottages, uniform in design, string the dirt road. One is in disrepair and sits abandoned, but this is the exception: the majority of Cokedale's old company houses are well kept. The road curves and climbs up to Elm Street. At the junction, a road leads north to an elegantly restored schoolhouse, where, the brochure explains, the sons and daughters of three generations of miners once attended first to eighth grades. Elm Street is lined on both sides with cottages. Those to the west sit high on the canyon wall. Like all of the town's company-built houses, the modest cinder block structures have metal-clad roofs and are two rooms wide. All of the homes on Elm are occupied. Behind low fences lie carefully tended gardens. Beside the front doors of many are wood-cut signs bearing the names of the home's occupants.

Cokedale's town center lies at the south end of Elm Street. Here stand the community's largest structures: the company store, bath- and boardinghouses, the doctor's and superintendent's homes, and the mine office. All but the company store serve as homes. Next to the steps of the restored company store—known as the Gottlieb Mercantile when it functioned as bank, post office, and grocery store for mining-era residents—stands a sign declaring this the home of the Cokedale Mining Museum. The tour brochure points out that the mercantile was not a company store in the truest sense as miners were paid in cash, not scrip. All that remains of the walking tour is Cokedale's southern residential area. Sightseers are guided to the top of Church Street, where they find the Sacred Heart of Jesus and Mary Church, a structure that was built from two unused company houses in the 1930s. Backtracking down to Pine Street, the shady streetscape is a little less tidy than other areas of Cokedale, but most of the homes remain in good condition.

The walking tour returns to the town center; it takes approximately 30 minutes to complete. However, inquisitive visitors may, if visiting during the summer season, extend their stay with a visit of the miners' museum. Here a copy of *Cokedale 1907–1947: Anatomy of a Model Mining Community* can be purchased. Skimming through the community history, readers learn that Cokedale was a model mining camp. Allegedly, it was a harmonious place, run by a caring operator, and it differed from other company towns in the area, providing a higher quality of life. One also learns that Cokedale survived because it was a utopianlike company town, a place residents refused to abandon when its mines closed.[2]

Figure 155. Abandoned coke ovens at Cokedale, Colorado, convey the feeling of Roman ruins but are more recent remnants of industrial history. Photo by Richard Francaviglia.

This established public history is reinforced by the experience of strolling through Cokedale's preserved cultural landscape, where, as explained in the walking tour brochure, visitors can "take a step back into the past."[3] Indeed, if modern intrusions like the automobiles parked on Cokedale's streets can be ignored, it truly seems like one is walking through a living, early-twentieth-century company town. The community appears to have changed little in the course of nearly a century of habitation: it is orderly and pleasant. However, while its appearance supports perceptions of an idyllic, little-changed company town, what is actually experienced in Cokedale today, like what is read in its public history, is an incomplete story of the town's past.

In the early decades of the twentieth century more than three dozen company-owned mining communities dotted the mountain canyons of the Trinidad Coal Field.[4] Cokedale was the only company town in the area to survive mine closure, and, without question, it represents a remarkable historic resource. However, the town should not be considered a living history museum where time has stood still. Not evident in the preservation landscape is a sense of Cokedale's industrial heritage, the hardship residents faced during the mining era, and the community's struggle to survive following mine closure. These aspects of the town's past are underrepresented in Cokedale's public history texts and in the preserved cultural landscape. The reasons why are the focus of this essay, which explores the complex relationship between cultural landscape preservation and public history in Cokedale.

Cultural Landscape Preservation and Public History

Traditional approaches to historic preservation emphasize the protection of individual landmark structures. In contrast, cultural landscape preservation, a growing area of preservation scholarship, acknowledges the need to preserve a broader range of features. Described by Dolores Hayden, cultural landscape preservation advocates, "a broader approach to preservation, one more attuned to preserving the unique complexities of places as cultural resources, be they urban, suburban, or rural, built or natural, evolved or designed."[5] Explicitly recognized is the importance of preserving the landscape's vernacular elements: common buildings, structures, and landscape features such as working-class houses, community structures, and industrial sites.[6] Collectively, these landscape elements serve to interpret the social history of ordinary citizens.[7]

As such, cultural landscape preservation represents a powerful tool by which to convey public history.

The Cokedale Historic District stands as a case study in cultural landscape preservation. Historic district designation is one approach by which governments, organizations, and individuals can seek to protect and preserve cultural landscapes.[8] As defined by the National Register, a historic district is an area that possesses a significant concentration, linkage, or continuity of sites, buildings, structures, or objects united historically or aesthetically. Historic districts derive their importance from being unified entities, even though they may be composed of a wide variety of landscape elements.[9] Cokedale, for example, represents the best surviving example of a company coal-mining town in Colorado. Included within the boundaries of the historic district are a variety of vernacular landscape elements, including houses, community structures, and industrial features. All are considered contributing elements of the historic district because they are functionally related (they are original parts of a company town landscape), and together they transmit a sense of the community's history.

A two-way relationship exists between cultural landscape preservation and public history. As noted, cultural landscape preservation is an effective means by which to convey public history. In Cokedale, the community's company town origins are evoked by the preservation landscape. At the same time, however, public history can also influence preservation practice. The identification and protection of historically significant properties, and their interpretation, may be shaped by established public histories. This can occur, for example, in National Register nomination procedures. Nomination of historic properties requires justification of their historic significance (their importance to the history of a community) and identification of their historic context (the period, place, and events that created or influenced them).[10] A variety of primary and secondary research sources, including public history texts, are used for these purposes. Such use of public histories is not necessarily problematic.

However, if these sources contain significant biases, they may be passed on into preservation practice. Cokedale is a case in point. Its *National Register of Historic Places Inventory—Nomination Form* uses *Cokedale 1907–1947: Anatomy of a Model Mining Community* as its primary bibliographic reference. The source is used to justify the community's historical significance and explain its development and survival. As a result, this flawed public history has influenced the types of landscape features that have been preserved in Cokedale, reinforced perceptions that it stands as an intact company town, and shaped historical interpretation of the cultural landscape. In order to explain the shortcomings that exist in historical accounts of the community, and related deficiencies in preservation practice, it is first necessary to consider the regional history of the Trinidad Coal Field.[11]

The Trinidad Coal Field and Cokedale

Commercial coal mining began in southern Colorado in the 1870s. The Trinidad Coal Field contained a high-grade coking coal, a product that fueled the furnaces of steel mills in nearby Pueblo, Colorado, and metal smelters elsewhere in the West. Output of coal grew over the first four decades of the field's operation, and the mining industry brought dramatic changes to the area. Company-owned mining communities were built along expanding rail networks to the north of Trinidad, along the front range of the Sangre de Cristo Mountains, to the south up the Raton Pass toward New Mexico, and to the west along the Purgatoire River. The Colorado Fuel and Iron Co. (CF&I) built and operated the majority of these settlements. Cokedale was the only mining town operated by ASARCO. The district attracted a sizable number of Anglo and Hispanic workers from New Mexico and elsewhere in Colorado, but miners also came from farther afield. The two largest groups of foreign-born workers came from Mexico and Italy. Also present were first-generation Austro-Hungarians, Slavs, Poles, Greeks, Germans, English, Irish, Scottish, Canadian, and Japanese.[12]

Although it was Colorado's most productive coal-mining region, the Trinidad Coal Field is best remembered as the site of one of the bloodiest labor disputes in U.S. history. The coal miners' strike of 1913–14 was not the area's only instance of labor unrest, but in shaping the identity of the region's mining communities, the Great Coalfield War, as it has come to be known, was the most significant. Workers had numerous demands, the most important of which was union recognition; most were members of the United Mine Workers of America (UMWA). However, operators like the CF&I, the union's fiercest opponent, showed little interest in negotiation. Their first response was to evict union sympathizers from the company towns. The evicted workers and their families established tent colonies near the mouths of the canyons leading to the coal camps. The largest, at Ludlow Junction, housed more than 1,200 inhabitants.[13]

As the strike evolved, the company towns became guarded military zones. Hoping to quell tensions, the State of Colorado ordered the National Guard into the region in November 1913. Unfortunately, its occupation only amplified tensions. Siding with the coal companies, the National Guard facilitated the importation of strikebreakers, and a violent standoff ensued that came to a head on April 20, 1914 at the Ludlow tent colony. Shooting began in the morning, and by dusk the tent colony was ablaze. In the aftermath of the fire, the lifeless bodies of two women and 12 children were found in an earthen cellar beneath a burnt-out tent. The "Ludlow Massacre" sparked an armed rebellion in the field, but strikebreakers continued to be protected by government troops and production was maintained at most mines. By November 1914, with strike funds exhausted, the UMWA terminated the strike.[14]

None of the union's demands were achieved. However, while operators won the labor battle, they lost the propaganda war that surrounded it. The strike and Ludlow Massacre received widespread national press, much of which was critical of mine owners and their resistance to improving living and working conditions in the camps. John D. Rockefeller, Jr., principal shareholder and president of the CF&I, received especially harsh treatment. A series of highly publicized congressional investigations into the strike were also conducted that drew attention to the brutality of company control, publicity that bolstered the cause of workers. While life remained hard, living and working conditions improved in the wake of the strike and union organization was eventually permitted in the camps. The events of 1913–14 furthered growing public sentiment against the American company town, and the camps of the Trinidad field have been widely vilified by labor historians.[15]

Output of coal in the Trinidad field declined from the 1930s onward, and by the 1950s, the field was mostly played out. At its height (1910–20), more than 70 coal mines operated in the district; by the midpoint of the 1950s only seven remained. The high cost of underground mining, a general decline in the price of coal, and increased labor costs contributed to the field's decline. In some cases, buildings and mine equipment were moved to other camps. More commonly, structures were dismantled and salvaged by operators in an attempt to recover capital investments in town infrastructure. All of the company towns were demolished. Cokedale was the exception.[16]

Cokedale was developed to provide coking coal to ASARCO's El Paso copper smelter in south Texas. Operated by the Carbon Coal and Coke Co. (an ASARCO subsidiary), the town was sited on the west slope of Reilly Canyon, a mile from its entrance into the Purgatoire Valley. The town was carefully planned. Three rows of houses were built parallel to the creek. The top row (Elm Street) contained homes built for professional-class employees. A second group of houses, south of Elm along Pine and Maple streets, followed an arroyo into the west side of the canyon. Cokedale's public buildings were erected at the center of the community. The schoolhouse anchored the north end of town, and a community hall, icehouse, stable, and baseball field sat on the eastern margin. The company planted elm trees and maintained public spaces, giving the camp a pastoral atmosphere. ASARCO also enforced a uniform aesthetic standard, and residents were not permitted to change the appearance of their homes. ASARCO built 86 single-family cottages in Cokedale, 18 frame cottages, and two one-story and 20 two-story multiple-family duplexes. The modest housing units ranged in size from one to four bedrooms. All had coal-burning stoves, electricity, and drainless sinks. Only the top row of houses on Elm Street had indoor plumbing.[17]

Cokedale's mining and coking operation, one of the largest in the Trinidad area, was situated on the southern end of the community. An imposing powerhouse and washery-tipple complex lay on the western slope of the canyon. An aerial tramway ran across the valley, carrying washery waste to the tailings pile on the eastern slope. Cleaned coal was transported down valley by rail to the coke ovens: a double row of 350 beehive ovens built along the curve of Reilly Creek. Cokedale contained the largest set of ovens in the Trinidad district, begetting the community's name. Coal was initially extracted from two drift mines sunk close to the washery, but these proved inefficient and a third mine was opened at a site named Bon Carbo, nine miles up Reilly Canyon, in 1918. Workers and coal were transported to and from Bon Carbo on a spur of the Colorado and Rio Grande Railroad. The Bon Carbo mines remained in operation for close to 30 years before increased production costs and depressed coal prices resulted in their closure in 1947. ASARCO pulled out of Cokedale the same year.

Cokedale's Utopian Image

At the turn of the Twentieth Century, company controlled mining communities throughout the nation were plagued by intolerable working and living conditions. Substandard housing, disregard for sanitation, oppressive company control, company indifference to the safety of the workers, and limited opportunities for constructive social activity were widely prevalent. Cokedale, however, was an exception.[18]

The above excerpt comes from *Cokedale, 1907–1947: Anatomy of a Model Mining Community*, the town's most extensive and influential public history text.[19] Written by local historian Holly Barton, the work draws heavily on promotional literature produced at the time of the community's founding. In January 1907, for example, the *Trinidad Chronicle News* published an article titled "Riley [sic] Canon will be Model Camp of State." The article serves as the starting point in constructing Cokedale's idyllic image. The newspaper claimed that an unprecedented $1 million was being invested in the camp's construction. The town, it was detailed, would be equipped with every convenience; a "model camp" was being built, "where every man was to be paid a fair price for his hire."[20] Cokedale's status as a model mining camp has also been furthered by descriptions appearing in state coal reports and industry magazines. ASARCO, one report detailed, "has stepped out of the beaten track regarding houses for their workmen," making it "one of the prettiest mining camps in the state."[21]

Historians claim that Cokedale embodied the humanitarian concerns of Daniel Guggenheim, then president and director of ASARCO. This opinion is based on testimony Guggenheim gave at a hearing held by the U.S. Commission on Industrial Relations in 1916. Quoted in *Anatomy of a Model Mining Camp* as well as in other documents, including Cokedale's *National Register of Historic Places Inventory—Nomination Form*, Guggenheim stated:

> I do not think there can be too much legislation along humanitarian lines. Surely no man can be happy when he realizes the conditions of the workers. We must see that the worker not only gets sufficient wages but also gets some of the comforts and luxuries of life. I have always felt that way. I believe in the democratization of industry.[22]

Guggenheim serves as the benevolent founding figure of Cokedale, and his status, and that of the town, has been bolstered through contrast with the most villainized operator in the district, the CF&I's John D. Rockefeller, Jr. "If ASARCO's record in Colorado were judged from on high," writes one local historian, "it might have qualified for industrial sainthood. . . . If the verdict were delivered by a jury of Southern Colorado coal miners, the judgement would be simple and direct: 'Go straight to hell, Rockefeller! Thanks, Guggenheimer.'"[23]

Allegedly, Cokedale was different from other company towns in the Trinidad field. It was responsibly planned, offered modern homes rented to workers at the lowest-possible rates, and contained superior community facilities. Even the company store, the most reviled institution in the company towns, is portrayed as an exception. According to historians, ASARCO had no desire to expand its economic control by forcing employees to trade at the store: residents traded wherever they wanted, and scrip (a company coupon redeemable only at the company store) was never issued in lieu of cash on payday. In addition, it is believed that Guggenheim's concern for resident well-being created a harmonious and peaceful community. Conflict among the town's various ethnic groups was rare.[24]

ASARCO's concern for the well-being of its residents purportedly extended into the workplace. Historians have praised safety standards and the high wages paid in the Cokedale mines. The picture painted is that of a company caring for its workers, and this proved an effective antidote to unionization. *Anatomy of a Model Mining Community*, for example, claims that miners' grievances with the company were "few" and "insignificant" and that for most of Cokedale's 40 years of operation, miners had no need to unionize. The community, it is held, was the most fairly run in the area and was "unscathed" by labor disputes.[25]

The events surrounding mine closure are also an important part of Cokedale lore. It is believed that newly hired men familiar with union activities in other camps were responsible for the eventual organization of Cokedale late in its operation. Reportedly, unionization increased production costs and forced ASARCO to close operations in 1947.[26] Soon after, ASARCO sold its Cokedale property to a Denver salvaging firm: Florence Machinery and Supply Co. Allegedly, at ASARCO's request, the sale agreement included a provision that residents be allowed to purchase their homes. One historian writes: "When ASARCO closed its operations people envisioned another ghost camp . . . but ASARCO allowed what most companies wouldn't—the camp would remain if people wanted to buy their homes."[27] Ostensibly, residents expressed a willingness to stay and ASARCO made houses available for purchase. In 1948 residents incorporated the town.

The established public history is consistent: Cokedale was a paradise compared to other company towns—a model, utopianlike mining camp. Moreover, the story of its persistence is also tied to this perception. Cokedale's survival is attributed to the belief that the town was a desirable place to live and work. As a result, residents grew attached to the community and, with ASARCO's assistance, purchased their homes following mine closure. Even Cokedale's *National Register Historic Places Inventory—Nomination Form* cites a "cradle-to-grave sense of contentment" as the key contributor to the town's survival.[28]

A Reinterpretation of Public History

Cokedale's idyllic image does not stand close scrutiny. The community's story, as communicated in public history texts and in National Register historic district documents, lacks historical context and critical appraisal. "Model" company towns, for example, were being constructed across the U.S. industrial landscape in the early decades of the twentieth century. What distinguished these communities was the desire of operators to extend paternal control beyond the minimal architectural requirements of factories and mines. As was the case with Cokedale, these settlements were promoted as places where operators had an altruistic interest in the well-being of the worker. In extending paternalistic measures, however, model company towns were often oppressive places, and their construction was not undertaken for altruistic concerns.[29] For industrialists, the "model camp" label was a good public relations move, for at the turn of the twentieth century, company towns were increasingly being perceived as exploitive places. Moreover, model towns also served the economic interests of industry. An environmentalist philosophy underpinned their construction: operators believed that favorable living conditions and attractive communities would yield a loyal workforce and that company paternalism, operating in a designed environment, could be used to maintain control over labor.[30] In this context, it can be assumed that ASARCO's decision to build a state-of-the-art industrial settlement was guided by the belief that by subverting labor unrest and increasing worker productivity, expenditures in town infrastructure would prove to be a wise investment.[31]

Such critical dialogue is absent from historical interpretations of Cokedale. Instead, it is believed that the town embodied the humanitarian concerns of Daniel Guggenheim. His testimony to the U.S. Commission on Industrial Relations in 1916, held in the wake of the Ludlow Massacre, forms the basis for this belief. Unfortunately, not considered is that Guggenheim was ordered to appear at the hearing because of ASARCO's history of labor troubles and the notoriously poor conditions that existed at its smelters and mines. An astute businessman, Guggenheim was aware that the hearings provided an opportunity to sway public opinion of company operations. As has been detailed elsewhere, Guggenheim's stated concern for worker welfare was not representative of the company's practices.[32] However, more alarming in the use of this testimony is that Guggenheim made no mention of Cokedale at the hearing: a significant omission considering that he was asked to detail what measures the company had taken to improve living and working conditions at its facilities. In fact, no firm evidence has been put forward to suggest that Daniel Guggenheim had any direct involvement in the planning or operation of Cokedale.[33]

More than other claims made by historians, the notion that living conditions were of a higher standard in Cokedale holds the most truth. At the time of construction, Cokedale's housing was superior to that of adjacent camps. However, only in its early years were living conditions exceptional. Conditions in the camps of the Trinidad Coal Field did not remain constant over time. Generally, living conditions were deplorable at the time of the 1913–14 strike, but in its wake, public scrutiny forced operators to implement changes. The CF&I replaced dilapidated housing with structures comparable in design to those in Cokedale, and like ASARCO, it instituted community beautification programs. Virtually all of the camps operated elementary schools and provided recreational facilities. For most of Cokedale's operating lifespan, the town contained few amenities that were not available in other company towns.[34] It is also believed that ASARCO rented its houses to workers at lower rates, but an investigation of area housing conditions conducted in the 1920s shows that similar homes were being rented at identical rates elsewhere in the field: $2.00 a room per month.[35] Whether Cokedale's company store operated differently in terms of the use of scrip requires further investigation. In an interview conducted in 1978, for example, onetime miner Horace Hurtado confirmed that scrip was used as a means of pay early in the camp's operation.[36]

Division and conflict along ethnic and class lines was a common condition in the company towns, and Cokedale was no exception.[37] Census analysis reveals that the town's ethnic workforce was spatially segregated. Division existed between northern and southern residential districts. To the north, along Elm Street, lay 80 percent of Cokedale's Anglo-American-headed households. To the south, on Pine, Maple, and Church streets, were approximately 80 percent of the community's Italian- and 70 percent of its Hispanic-headed households. Ethnicity also played a role in the occupations held by residents. In 1920, 75 percent of miners—the largest occupational class in Cokedale and the lowest paid—were of Hispanic ancestry. Of the roughly 20 managerial positions in the camp, only two were held by non-Anglos. Because ASARCO assigned housing to its employees and jobs, it can be concluded that ethnic segregation and occupational discrimination were intentional. Moreover, documentary evidence and interviews conducted with long-time residents reveals that the company outwardly supported racist behavior and that the town was polarized along ethnic lines.[38]

ASARCO's labor policies also appear consistent with those of other operators. Cokedale miners suffered, as all in the district did, from dangerous working conditions and meager pay. In fact, *State Inspector of Coal Mines Annual Reports* show that fatality rates for Cokedale miners (one fatality per 148,000 tons of coal produced) were higher than those of the CF&I (one fatality per 244,000 tons). Moreover, Cokedale miners were paid for the amount of coal they dug, and in the 1910s a rate of 58 cents per ton was paid. According to state statistics, this was an average wage for the Trinidad field.[39] Also an important part of the town's mythology is the belief that Cokedale avoided the labor unrest of the 1913–14 strike. Again, evidence suggests otherwise: workers in Cokedale were organized during the dispute. At a United Mine Workers of America convention held during the strike, for example, Cokedale representative Tony Lamont detailed the oppressive conditions that existed in the camp:

> Every man is closely watched and if the guards suspect him of belonging to the organization, he is discharged. . . . The boss said he would have me fired because I was a member of the union, and I told him he was behind the times; that everyone was a union man now, but he notified the superintendent to give me my time.[40]

UMWA documents show that more than half of ASARCO's workforce was unionized during the dispute, and, like other camps, Cokedale also became a guarded military zone.[41] According to various accounts, the state militia joined company guardsmen in patrolling Cokedale. A fence was erected around the mining property, searchlights were installed on the washery, and a locomotive was stopped on the road to prohibit traffic in and out of the community.[42] Such measures belie the notion that Cokedale was a haven of labor peace.

Living and working conditions in Cokedale were not exceptional: in most respects it was a typical company town. What, then, can be said of the fact that it survived mine closure? Not documented in accounts of this period in the town's past is that the majority of Cokedale's residents left the community following mine closure. The town's population plummeted from approximately 850 to 200. Confirmed in interviews conducted with some of those that remained is that an attachment to community was an important motivation in their decision to stay. While life was hard, residents established long-term commitments to Cokedale. Indeed, research shows that strong attachments to place are common in North American mining communities and that mine closure is often a painful experience.[43] This suggests that the ties residents established to Cokedale may not have been unusual. In fact, some residents of other company towns in the Trinidad field also resisted eviction following mine closure. However, efforts to remain in other settlements failed because resident eviction and town demolition always followed mine closure.

Cokedale's survival is less romantic than has been portrayed. Quite simply, the town persisted because it was not completely demolished following mine closure. The nature of ASARCO's operations, and Cokedale's locational advantages, were contributing factors. Unlike the CF&I, ASARCO had no other operations in the Trinidad area where industrial and town infrastructure could be moved. Nor did the company need to maintain mineral rights in the area: it could no longer afford to supply its distant El Paso smelter with Colorado coke. As a result, ASARCO chose not to engage in a costly relocation or salvaging program. Instead, it sold the property outright to a local salvaging firm. When Florence Machinery and Supply Co. took control of Cokedale, it immediately began to dismantle the town. Valuable infrastructure, including mining equipment and municipal water pipes, was pulled up and sold. All of Cokedale's larger two-story homes were demolished and most residents were evicted. Of those remaining, many were employed in community demolition. They paid rent to the salvaging firm.

Contrary to popular belief, the future of Cokedale was in doubt during this period. No provision had been made by ASARCO in its sale agreement for residents to remain. However, Florence Machinery did eventually halt the town's demolition and remaining houses were made available for purchase. Florence Machinery recognized that more money could be made selling the houses that were left than tearing them down. Unlike other company towns, most of which were situated in remote mountain canyons, Cokedale was easily accessible by road to the city of Trinidad, where a market existed for affordable housing. Some longtime residents purchased homes, but many also moved into the community from Trinidad. More than other factors, it was a business decision made by Florence Machinery, based on Cokedale's favorable location, that facilitated its survival.

Public History and Cokedale's Preservation Landscape

Cokedale has been inaccurately depicted as an idyllic refuge set apart from other company towns in the Trinidad area. The following excerpt from its *National Register of Historic Places Inventory—Nomination Form* provides a final example:

> While most similar coal camps were dismantled as mines ceased operation, Cokedale continued to thrive.... The perception of the residents of Cokedale, and the entire Trinidad district, that the camp was a desirable place to live and work, coupled with a company philosophy differing from the theories prevalent in the area, created an environment in which Cokedale could remain intact.... The town remains the best example of an intact coal camp in Colorado.[44]

Clearly, public history texts played an important role in Cokedale's designation as a Historic District, and evidence also suggests that they have influenced cultural landscape preservation in problematic ways. Cokedale's image as a utopian company town has influenced the types of landscape features that have been preserved and, in turn, those that have been ignored. In fact, this accepted public history supports a false perception that Cokedale stands as an intact company town. It has also shaped landscape interpretation in ways that reinforce historical misperceptions.

Interest in preservation first emerged in Cokedale in 1976, when a group of residents organized the town's first reunion of old-timers. Held on the 69th anniversary of the community's founding, the reunion triggered interest in the town's heritage. Soon after, residents formed the Cokedale Historical Society, whose first order of business was to place a historical marker in the Commons Park. The Colorado State Historical Society then began exploring formal preservation initiatives. In 1984, the Cokedale Town Council consented to moving ahead with National Register nomination procedures. Within a year, Historic District nomination forms were completed. The town received National Register designation in 1985. It was hoped that Historic District status would raise local awareness of the importance of preservation. Many houses were being altered with building additions, and some structures were being lost to demolition and new construction. Although Historical District status did not halt these activities, it did facilitate significant restoration work and raise general awareness of the importance of cultural landscape preservation. However, not all elements of the cultural landscape received attention.

The most faithfully preserved features in Cokedale, and its most complete category of original structures, are its community buildings. Although direct involvement in preservation by the Town Council was limited by budget constraints, protection of several community buildings—the Gottlieb Mercantile and Cokedale School House—was facilitated through municipal

Figure 156. At Cokedale, Colorado, houses once occupied by miners are now the homes of retirees and solitude seekers. Photo by Richard Francaviglia.

ownership. In 1991, the mercantile was in a severe state of decay, and the Town Council formed a partnership with the Department of History at Abilene Christian University (ACU) to restore the building and create a miners' museum. Restoration grants were obtained from the Colorado Historical Society; labor was supplied by ACU students. Outside assistance was also used to restore the Cokedale School House. After considerable debate, the town sold the building to Christ of the Canyon's Ministries in 1989. Provisions in the sale agreement required the church to repair and restore the structure to its original condition. Today the mercantile and schoolhouse stand as Cokedale's most beautifully restored buildings. Efforts to preserve other community structures fell into the hands of individual property owners, several of whom seized the opportunity to preserve their historical character. The boardinghouse, bathhouse, superintendent's home, and mine office have been remodeled with relatively minor change to their exterior appearance. Only the doctor's home has been significantly altered by building additions.

More intrusive development and structure loss has occurred to Cokedale's housing stock. For example, 23 of 98 houses listed in Cokedale's *National Register of Historic Places Inventory—Nomination Form* were deemed "non-contributing" features of the historic district. Inappropriate development was the primary cause.[45] In fact, most of the cottages, originally lacking modern conveniences like indoor bathrooms, have been expanded. In addition, a substantial portion of Cokedale's original housing, all but one of its approximately 20 wood-framed, shared-housing structures, have been demolished (a single-story duplex remains—it serves as town hall). The crowded multiple-family homes, occupied mainly by lower-class Hispanic and Mexican residents, were demolished following mine closure. As a result, what remains of Cokedale's housing stock is only its more comfortable and better-built homes.

Cokedale's industrial infrastructure has received little attention. Most elements of the town's industrial heritage, landscape features that more than others stand as reminders of Cokedale's reason for being, have been demolished or lay in a state of decay. Although 10 industrial features were listed as contributing structures in its *National Register of Historic Places Inventory— Nomination Form*, none have received restoration work. This includes the substantial ruins of the coal washer and the coke ovens. The largest set of coke ovens in the Trinidad field, the features are deteriorating. At the time of their listing to the National Register in 1985, many of the beehive ovens had complete roofs; all have now collapsed. Moreover, since 1985, several of Cokedale's industrial structures, including the oil house and machine shop, have been demolished. Like most of the town's historical structures, Cokedale's industrial features lie on private land. Unlike the owners of community and residential buildings, however, the owners of Cokedale's industrial properties have not had a practical or perceived need to engage in preservation activities, nor have governmental organizations provided incentives to do so. Most of what remains of Cokedale's mining and coking operation, once the most dominant aspect of its cultural landscape, lies deteriorating behind barbed-wire fences and no-trespassing signs.

The claim that Cokedale represents an "intact" company town has clearly been overstated. While it retains most of its community structures, only a portion of its original housing stock remains. Furthermore, Cokedale's quiet and picturesque contemporary streetscape fails to convey historic conditions in the community. During the mining era the population of Cokedale was seven times greater than it is today (in 1910, Cokedale's population reached a high of 1,073; in 2000 it was 139).[46] The town was larger, more densely populated, and faster paced. In addition, the preservation landscape fails to convey the true nature of social life in Cokedale and the town's industrial heritage. Residents lived in a community fractured along ethnic and class lines and governed by restrictive company rule. Theirs was not a utopian existence. Moreover, Cokedale was an industrial place, a functional community that was built, first and foremost, for the efficient production of coal and coke. Not well reflected by the preservation landscape is the hardship of everyday life during the mining era. While historic photographs reveal the extent of industry's impress in Cokedale; its contemporary landscape reveals little of it.

Also not conveyed by the cultural landscape is the lengthy period of decline Cokedale experienced following mine closure. In fact, Cokedale's tidy and quaint contemporary appearance is the product of a relatively recent rejuvenation. Little evidence exists of the community's near death in the postmining era. Deindustrialization, a limited tax base, and a legacy of company paternalism posed serious challenges to the community's survival. From the 1950s through the 1970s, Cokedale deteriorated. Houses were abandoned, community infrastructure decayed, and the town's population dwindled. A heroic effort was required by a small group of residents to keep the town alive into the 1980s, when the processes of dereliction and population loss began to be reversed. Slowly, an improving regional economy, outside property investment, and rising awareness of the importance of preservation stimulated a rejuvenation.[47]

Cultural landscape preservation in Cokedale has failed to fully interpret the social history of its citizens. In large part, this is due to a flawed public history that dominates interpretations of Cokedale's past. Local historians have ignored the similarities that existed between Cokedale and adjacent company towns in the Trinidad Coal Field, and because their histories have guided preservation initiatives, so, too, does the preservation landscape. What one experiences in Cokedale today, like what is read in local histories, tells only part of the community's story. Attention has been paid to restoring Cokedale's impressive community structures and its quaint single-family houses, and publicly conveying their significance, because these features "fit" its image as an idyllic place. Likewise, the impression of "intactness" exists, because what remains standing in Cokedale is precisely what one would expect to see in a utopianlike company town: substantial community structures and comfortable homes.

Little attention has been devoted to the town's industrial infrastructure or the range of housing types that it once contained, because Cokedale's function as a company mining town has been poorly explored in public history. True, practical issues are also at play: generally, habitable structures have received restoration work; inhabitable structures have not. Telling, however, is that landscape features failing to fit Cokedale's utopian image have received virtually no historic interpretation. Although interpretative signs have been placed in front of most of its community structures (designating the original function of the buildings), no signs have been placed in industrial areas of the community or in the locations where the remains of shared housing structures are found. Not a single stop in Cokedale's historic walking tour is devoted to these features.[48] Other than the slag pile that is passed on the drive into Cokedale and a distant view of the coke ovens, visitors are left with little sense of the town's industrial past.

Like its accepted public history texts, the preservation landscape reflects an incomplete view of the past. As a result, opportunities to discover the complex story of life and landscape in Cokedale are being denied. While cultural landscape preservation is a powerful tool for conveying public history, it can also be influenced by it. In Cokedale, this two-way relationship has proved detrimental: visitors read that Cokedale was a utopian company town, and the preservation landscape seemingly confirms this. Fortunately, despite these problems, the town of Cokedale still conveys important aspects of its history. Enough original structures have been preserved, and enough retain original design elements, that the community retains a sense of its original streetscape. Cokedale's planned uniformity remains apparent, and there is no denying that residents lived modest, working-class lives. Moreover, if a timely reinterpretation of public history takes place, opportunities remain for preservation priorities to be refocused in productive ways.

Future visitors to Cokedale, for example, could be presented with a richer landscape experience, one that reflects a truer sense of life in the company towns of the Trinidad Coal Field. A turnout overlooking the coke ovens could be constructed on Highway 12. Restoration work aimed at arresting the decay of these landmark features, and an interpretive sign providing an overview of the industrial history of the region, would provide the historical context for understanding Cokedale's existence. In a revised walking tour, sightseers might be guided past Cokedale's uniform cottages and its domineering company store, where they would be told of ASARCO's economic rationale for constructing what was once considered a "model" company town. Near the end of Spruce Street, where the ghostly foundations of several of Cokedale's shared housing structures lie, the story of the town's near demolition following mine closure, and the circumstances surrounding its survival, could be explained. At the sites of other demolished multiple-housing units, and in the less affluent southern residential areas where most of the Italian, Mexican, and Hispanic workers lived, visitors could learn of Cokedale's ethnic communities and the social and physical divides that separated them.

Figure 157. The industrial legacy of Cokedale, Colorado, is evident in both the historic district signs and the huge culm pile at the edge of town. Photo by Richard Francaviglia.

Passing the houses on Elm Street, future visitors could be informed that this area was known as "Silk-Stockings Row," containing larger homes reserved for Cokedale's professional-class residents. Through thoughtful interpretation, the landscape might still convey its legacies of company paternalism. At the long-closed schoolhouse, a structure that was obviously built for a more populous community, visitors could be alerted to the former size and energy of Cokedale. Near the ruins of its mining and coal-processing facilities, the town's industrial function, and the gritty workaday world of its residents, could be highlighted. The enormous pile of coal tailings climbing the canyon wall opposite town, and the ruined foundations of the tipple and washery complex, reveal the extent of industrial operations that once existed in the community. The sites of Cokedale's original coal mines and the location of the weigh house, where the miners' loads of hand-dug coal were converted into meager amounts of pay, might also be identified. At these locales, the story of troubled labor relations in Cokedale could be persuasively conveyed.

A revised walking tour could conclude at a memorial, erected in the Commons Park, that would list the names of the 62 men known to have lost their lives in Cokedale's mines.[49] Situated in the heart of the community, such a miners' memorial would provide a somber reminder of the hardships of working life in the company towns of the Trinidad Coal Field, of which Cokedale was a representative rather than exceptional example.

Notes

1. "Cokedale: A Historic Coal Mining Camp," travel brochure and map, Cokedale Tourism Committee and the Colorado Center for Community Development, University of Colorado at Denver, n.d.

2. Holly Barton, *Cokedale, 1907–1947: Anatomy of a Model Mining Community* (privately published, 1976).

3. "Cokedale: A Historic Coal Mining Camp," n.d. In addition, preservation officials have noted that Cokedale stands largely unchanged from the mining era. See, for example, National Park Service, *National Register of Historic Places Inventory Nomination Form: Cokedale Historic District*, Washington D.C., 1985, and Colorado Office of Archaeology and Historic Preservation, Directory of Colorado State Register Properties, Las Animas County, Cokedale Historic District (http://www.coloradohistory-oahp.org/).

4. See, for example, James B. Allen, *The Company Town in the American West* (Norman: University of Oklahoma Press, 1966); John S. Garner, *The Company Town: Architecture and Society in the Early Industrial Age* (New York: Oxford University Press, 1992); and H. Lee Scamehorn, *Mill & Mine: The CF&I in the Twentieth Century* (Lincoln: University of Nebraska Press, 1992).

5. Dolores Hayden, "In Search of the American Cultural Landscape," foreword to *Preserving the Cultural Landscape in America*, ed. Arnold R. Alanen and Robert Z. Melnick (Baltimore: Johns Hopkins University Press: 2000), vii.

6. The industrial landscape's function as a historical resource is also central to the field of industrial preservation. See, for example, Robert B. Gordon and Patrick M. Malone, *The Texture of Industry: An Archaeological View of the Industrialization of North America* (New York: Oxford University Press, 1994), and Judith Alfrey and Tim Putnam, *The Industrial Heritage: Managing Resources and Uses* (New York: Routledge, 1992).

7. Dolores Hayden, *The Power of Place: Urban Landscapes as Public History* (Cambridge, MA: MIT Press, 1995); Arnold R. Alanen and Robert Z. Melnick, "Why Cultural Landscape Preservation?" in *Preserving the Cultural Landscape in America*, 5.

8. Arnold R. Alanen, "Considering the Ordinary: Vernacular Landscapes in Small Towns and Rural Areas," in *Preserving the Cultural Landscape in America*, 115.

9. National Park Service, *How to Define Categories of Historic Properties*, rev. ed., National Register Bulletin 15 (Washington, D.C., 2002).

10. National Park Service, *Researching a Historic Property*, rev. ed., National Register Bulletin 39 (Washington, D.C., 1998).

11. The author has produced a more extensive discussion of Cokedale that serves as the basis of this research. See David Robertson, "Enduring Places: Landscape Meaning, Community Persistence, and Preservation in the Historic Mining Town" (Ph.D. diss., University of Oklahoma, 2001).

12. Marius R. Campbell, "The Trinidad Coal Field, Colorado," in *Contributions to Economic Geology*, United States Geological Survey Bulletin 381 (Washington, D.C., 1910), 434–37; Sarah Deutsch, *No Separate Refuge: Culture, Class, and Gender on an Anglo-Hispanic Frontier in the American Southwest, 1880–1940* (New York: Oxford University Press, 1987); and Rick J. Clyne, *Coal People: Life in Southern Colorado's Company Towns, 1890–1930* (Denver: Colorado Historical Society, 1999).

13. The strike is discussed in detail by Barron B. Beshoar, *Out of the Depths: The Story of John R. Lawson, a Labor Leader* (Denver: Golden Bell Press, 1980); Priscilla Long, *Where the Sun Never Shines: A History of America's Bloody Coal Industry* (New York: Paragon House, 1989); and George S. McGovern and Leonard F. Guttridge, *The Great Coalfield War* (Boston: Houghton Mifflin, 1972).

14. Long, *Where the Sun Never Shines*, 281–82, 292–94. For further discussion of the Ludlow Massacre see Howard M. Gitelman, *Legacy of the Ludlow Massacre: A Chapter in American Industrial Relations* (Philadelphia: University of Pennsylvania Press, 1988), and Zeese Papanikolas, *Buried Unsung: Louis Tikas and the Ludlow Massacre* (Salt Lake City: University of Utah Press, 1982).

15. Long, *Where the Sun Never Shines*, 305–8, 320–23; Upton Sinclair, *King Coal* (New York: Macmillan, 1917);

The Coal War: A Sequel to King Coal (Boulder: Colorado Associated University Press, 1976); U.S. Commission on Industrial Relations, *Final Report and Testimony*, Senate Doc. 415, 64th Cong., 2d sess. (Washington, D.C., 1916); U.S. Congress, House Subcommittee on Mines and Mining, *Conditions in the Coal Mines of Colorado*, Pursuant to H.R. 387, 63rd Cong., 2d sess. (Washington, D.C., 1914).

16. Demolition of the company towns was also implemented by operators following mine closure in order to reduce property tax burdens. Lee Scamehorn, letter to author, June 27, 1999.

17. For a detailed analysis of town design and architecture see Gary L. Lindsey, "Creating Presence: The Early Twentieth Century Company Store in Three Coal Mining Towns in Southern Colorado" (master's thesis, Abilene Christian University, 1998).

18. Barton, *Cokedale, 1907–1947*, 1.

19. In addition to Barton's work, a 1993 family genealogy, *The Schafers of Cokedale: A Century in America*, written by onetime resident Rollie Schafer, deals with the history of the community. However, Schafer draws heavily on Barton's research. See Rollie Schafer, Jr., *The Schafers of Cokedale: A Century in America* (Trinidad, CO: privately published, 1993).

20. *Trinidad Chronicle News*, "Riley Canon Will Be Model Camp of State," January 15, 1907, 3.

21. W. B. Lloyd, "The Cokedale Mine," *Thirteenth Biennial Report of the State Coal Mine Inspector* (Denver, 1909), 152–56. The *Engineering and Mining Journal* also wrote a feature article that detailed mining and coking operations and civic features. The article exalted the community's cleanliness and systematic operation. Kenneth S. Guiterman, "Mining Coal in Southern Colorado," *The Engineering and Mining Journal* LXXXVII, no. 21 (1909): 1009–15.

22. Barton, *Cokedale, 1907–1947*; National Park Service, 1985. Guggenheim's original testimony appears in U.S. Commission on Industrial Relations, *Final Report and Testimony*, vol. 8, Senate Doc. 415, 64th Cong., 2d. sess. (Washington, D.C., 1916), 7559–79.

23. Schafer, *Schafers of Cokedale*, 41.

24. Barton, *Cokedale, 1907–1947*, 1, 30–70; Lindsey, "Creating Presence," 211–14; Schafer, *Schafers of Cokedale*, 48; Guiterman, "Mining Coal in Southern Colorado," 1015.

25. Barton, *Cokedale, 1907–1947*, 19, 17–18; Schafer, *Schafers of Cokedale*, 40, 57.

26. Barton, *Cokedale, 1907–1947*, 19–23; Schafer, *Schafers of Cokedale*, 91.

27. Patrick Donachy, *Coal, the Kingdom Below* (Trinidad, CO: Inkwell, 1983), 16.

28. National Park Service, 1985, 3.

29. For information on the "model" company town phenomena see John S. Garner, ed., *The Company Town: Architecture and Society in the Early Industrial Age* (New York: Oxford University Press, 1992), 4; Anne E. Mosher, 'Something Better Than the Best': Industrial Restructuring, George McMurtry and the Creation of the Model Industrial Town of Vandergrift, Pennsylvania, 1883–1901," *Annals of the Association of American Geographers* 85, no. 1 (1995): 84–107; and John S. Garner, *The Model Company Town: Urban Design through Private Enterprise in Nineteenth-Century New England* (Amherst: University of Massachusetts Press, 1984).

30. Mosher, "Something Better Than the Best," 86; Garner, *Company Town*, 4–5; and Long, *Where the Sun Never Shines*, 209–10, 248–49.

31. At the time of Cokedale's construction, the need for such measures was substantial. Poor conditions in neighboring camps were being investigated by the state in the wake of the field's first general strike, held in 1903–4. Furthermore, by 1907 labor interests in southern Colorado were reorganizing. With the more radical Industrial Workers of the World gaining a foothold in the area, incentive existed for operators such as ASARCO to minimize union activity.

32. Harvey O'Connor, *The Guggenheims: The Making of an American Dynasty* (New York: Covici Friede Publishers, 1937), 316–22.

33. Denver architect James Murdoch was responsible for the design of the camp. Prior to his Cokedale commission, Murdoch had been hired to design other Guggenheim developments. However, no information exists regarding what dialogue occurred, if any, between Murdoch and Daniel Guggenheim in the planning of Cokedale and in the ideology underpinning its design. See Lindsey, "Creating Presence," 216.

34. Long, *Where the Sun Never Shines*, 308–23; Scamehorn, *Mill & Mine*, 57–67.

35. Leifur Magnusson, "Company Housing in the Bituminous Coal Fields," *Monthly Labor Review* 10, no. 4 (1920): 215–22.

36. Interview transcript, Horace Hurtado, May 24, 1978, Eric Margolis Collection, 14-3, Archives, University of Colorado at Boulder Libraries.

37. See, for example, Deutsch, *No Separate Refuge*, 94–95, and Clyne, *Coal People*, 42–62.

38. Robertson, *Enduring Places*, 130–33. An active chapter of the Ku Klux Klan existed in Cokedale in the 1920s, and cross burnings were commonly held on company property. ASARCO also banned African Americans from employment. See Clyne, *Coal People*, 49.

39. *Report of the State Inspector of Coal Mines*, 1911 through 1929, Denver, Colorado; "Mining Prices Paid at the Various Coal Mines in Colorado, January 1, 1917," *Fourth Annual Report of the State Inspector of Coal Mines*, 1916, Denver, Colorado, 14–17.

40. Testimony of Tony Lamont, Edward Lawrence Doyle Collection, Western History Department, Denver Public Library, Folder 10, Envelope 9.

41. Edward Lawrence Doyle Collection, Western History Department, Denver Public Library, Folder 10, Envelope 9.

42. Hurtado, interview transcript; John Johnston, resident interview with author, Cokedale, CO, 1999.

43. See, for example, Ben Marsh, "Continuity and Decline in the Anthracite Coal Towns of Pennsylvania," *Annals of the Association of American Geographers* 77, no. 3 (1987): 337–52, and Kent C. Ryden, *Mapping the Invisible Landscape: Folklore, Writing, and the Sense of Place* (University of Iowa Press: Iowa City, 1993).

44. National Park Service, *National Register*, 4.

45. National Park Service, *National Register*, 4–5.

46. U.S. Bureau of the Census, *Thirteenth Census of the United States 1910, Colorado: Las Animas County* (Washington, D.C.); U.S. Bureau of the Census, *Twenty-second Census of the United States 2000, Colorado: Las Animas County* (Washington, D.C.).

47. Robertson, *Enduring Places*, 143–80.

48. The mine office is a highlighted stop on the walking tour, a structure now serving as a home. However, no features related directly to coal and coke production are pointed out other than in the brochure's introductory remarks.

49. *Report of the State Inspector of Coal Mines*, 1911 through 1929, Denver, CO.

Study Questions

1. What is the difference between a "company town" and other mining settlements?

2. What company built Cokedale, and what is the benefit of a company owning the town?

3. What is scrip, and what were the advantages to a company issuing this form of payment? What were the disadvantages to the miner?

4. What is cultural landscape preservation?

5. Why is it important to preserve the social history of ordinary citizens?

6. How can public history influence preservation practice?

7. What are the pitfalls of limiting background sources on historical interpretation?

8. What company owned the majority of settlements in the Trinidad Coal Field?

9. Why did coal companies oppose organized labor?

10. What were the differences between homes built for professional-class employees at Cokedale and homes for the miners?

11. How did Daniel Guggenheim's vision of a company town compare to John D. Rockefeller, Jr.'s? Did Cokedale correspond to Guggenheim's vision?

12. Why were the company stores the most reviled institution in the company towns?

Old Mines, New Developments

Preservation, the Environment, and Public History in the Mining West

James E. Fell, Jr.

The mining industry in the American West stretches back to the late 1840s, and in some cases even before, but the interest in preserving its heritage and concerns over its waste products are largely a late-twentieth-century phenomenon. They have combined, however, to create a renewed interest in the minerals enterprise of the region, and for different purposes: tourism, gambling, and environmental cleanup, along with the intrinsic interest in preserving the regional mining heritage, and that, in turn, has meant new roles and new opportunities for public historians involved in the different aspects of mining history.

In 1962, Rachel Carson, then a biologist with the U.S. Fish and Wildlife Service, published her controversial but highly influential book *Silent Spring*.[1] Based on a series of articles that appeared previously in the 1950s, it focused on widely used pesticides and their deleterious impact on various organisms. Though denounced by many in industry and other quarters, the book became an instant best seller and did more than anything else to galvanize, if not launch, the modern-day environmental movement. In the years that followed its publication, the Congress, state legislatures, and local governments passed significant, and often controversial, legislation and ordinances designed to clean up and protect the nation's land, water, and air. Environmentalism became one of the hallmarks of late-twentieth and early-twenty-first-century American life.

As Carson was developing her ideas and research on pesticides, the great postwar boom swept over the nation, creating an age of unprecedented growth and prosperity. Many urbanites fled traditional neighborhoods to enjoy what they perceived to be a better life in the booming new suburbs ringing older industrial cities. By the 1950s, it seemed to many Americans that the nation's inner cities had fallen into disuse, disrepair, and decay, and the population shift to suburbia only enhanced the ongoing deterioration in older urban areas. The result of those trends was urban renewal (which turned out to be anything but). Responding to congressional legislation, many cities developed urban renewal authorities that demolished innumerable old houses, business buildings, entire city blocks, even entire neighborhoods. As the destruction continued, however, it finally produced a public outcry calling for the preservation of the older fabric of American life, and the passage of the Interstate Highway Act led to further public outcries. The new superhighway builders often proved insensitive to cities, towns, and neighborhoods—plowing through innumerable old areas destroying homes, business buildings, entire neighborhoods, and traditional downtowns just like the urban renewal authorities. By the mid-1960s, the growing swell against this destruction contributed powerfully to the passage of the National Historic Preservation Act of 1966.

The opposition to demolition, coupled with the new Historic Preservation Act, contributed to the rise of public history and public historians. Not that they hadn't existed before—they had. But the idea of public history and the public historian was something of a new concept that began emerging with these new laws and the positive and deleterious impacts those laws had. Combined with the burgeoning environmental movement, they had a far-reaching impact on the remaining vestiges of the classic mining industry of the American West: its historians, mining regions, mining towns, and mining companies.

The Mining Industry

Though there were some antecedents in Spanish and Mexican times and even in the pre-Columbian era, for all practical purposes, the mining era in the West opened dramatically in January 1848, when James Marshall, a carpenter from New Jersey, discovered gold at Sutter's Mill on the American River in northern California. Marshall's find quickly touched off the California gold rush, mostly associated with the year 1849, though it began before and lasted later. California emerged as a great mining state. What was even more important, the rush set in motion the search for gold everywhere in the western United States. In the years to come, prospectors not only found the royal metal in many places, but also discovered silver, lead, copper, iron, zinc, and other metals. Those discoveries eventually led to finding more exotic metals like uranium, vanadium, and molybdenum, which had little use until the twentieth century. Prospectors also found coal, and so coal mining evolved almost simultaneously to provide fuel for homes, railroads, and industry (and metal mining itself) and to provide coke, which was used in the reduction of both iron and silver-lead ores.

Despite the powerful view that raising crops and grazing cattle prompted the settlement of the nineteenth-century West, as much as anything else, it was the minerals industry in all its forms that transformed the mountain and desert West and led to powerful streams of development. Though often left out of the settlement equation by a nation focused largely on farming, ranching, and their mythologies; by the dime novel and Hollywood West of the gunfighter; and by the public image that most mining consisted of independent prospectors panning for gold, the minerals industry that evolved in the late-nineteenth and early-twentieth-century West was one of the most advanced and technologically sophisticated in the world.

By the early- to mid-twentieth century, however, the bulk of the mining camps and mining towns that reflected the industry's early development had fallen on hard times. Rising costs, changing demand, and lower grades of mineral brought mining to an end in many quarters, and the heritage of the industry began to disappear. The seasons, the sun, and the snow destroyed many structures; fires ravaged old wooden buildings;

Figure 158. Historic mill near Marble, Colorado. Photo by Andrew Gulliford, 1981.

and industry people relocated buildings and machinery. The world wars and the Cold War prompted searches for scrap metal of every sort—and mining districts proved to be good locations to find just that; vandals destroyed what they could, and tourists carried off a lot of the rest—everything from ore cars for the front yard to tombstones for the mantelpiece. Older mining towns like Caribou, Colorado, simply disappeared. Newer communities like Goldfield, Nevada, just stood there in the desert: buildings shuttered, spaces empty, and structures abandoned.

As mining faded away, and thus the reason for being for so many towns, some communities managed to transform themselves into something else. Famous producers like Aspen, Breckenridge, Crested Butte, and Telluride in Colorado, along with Alta, Snowbird, and Park City in Utah, all reconstituted themselves as ski towns. That generated an even greater era of prosperity than mining had produced—so much so that the older heritage sometimes all but disappeared. Other communities, like Blackhawk, Central City, and Cripple Creek in Colorado, after lingering in the twilight for decades, eventually managed to remake themselves into gambling emporiums ("gaming" as the industry says)—as did innumerable old producers in Nevada, to a greater or lesser degree. Still others, like Virginia City or Tonopah in Nevada, or Silver City in New Mexico, or Butte in Montana, or Wallace in Idaho, or Bisbee in Arizona, and countless more focused on tourism and so presented themselves as what they were—mining towns. In looking at these developments broadly, tourism has probably been more important than anything else in preserving the old gold, silver, and copper producers—but not the coal producers. Mining coal and making coke, however important in industrialization, lack the glamour of gold rushes, silver strikes, and copper kings.

Historic preservation and public historians have made a significant impact on preserving the nation's mining heritage. And even the Western myth has helped in a circuitous way. Tourist dollars have helped preserve some buildings and neighborhoods even if the towns portray themselves as part of a West that wasn't.

Public History in Mining Regions

What should be the focus of public history and historic preservation in mining regions? Some individual sites and structures are worth preserving for their own intrinsic merit and for their particular associations—but most are not. As public historians focus on mining areas and as they consider the broad question of ore or coal production or the processing of ore and coal, they need to keep in mind that what is worth preserving is the mining region itself. Thus public historians need to focus on creating historic districts—the processing facilities, houses and business blocks, the transportation and distribution systems, the dumps and tailings, even the modern environmental remediation features. No matter how large, no matter how small, these structures and features once formed an integrated production unit, albeit one that has changed over time and continues to change.

Public historians have played important roles in creating historic districts, and as such, an ever larger number of mining areas have found their way into the National Register of Historic Places or onto individual state registers. Some, like Bisbee, Arizona, or Leadville, Colorado, or Butte, Montana, are internationally significant for their people, their production, their technology, and their impact on the development of a global industry. Others have a regional or stateside significance. Far more have local importance. But whatever the designation level, the key is in preserving what remains.

The boundaries of many historic districts have been controversial. Mining companies, various enterprises, government agencies, and private homeowners have opposed or supported what was included or excluded for a plethora of reasons. The most important objection has involved property rights or the perception of property rights. Many owners have opposed historic designation because they feared increased government regulation or a loss of control over what they own. Whether or not that view was accurate, the result was that in creating most districts, public historians found that politics and private interest influenced boundary decisions, and the outcome was that many districts excluded important properties.

Knowledge, professionalism, and sophistication within the preservation community has also had an impact on district boundaries. The public historians who created the first districts intuitively understood the significance of the towns, the mines, and the related structures and features, but they often lacked the knowledge and understanding of what to include in forming the first districts. The preservation movement was young and ideas of what to incorporate still forming. The architectural history of the nineteenth century focused largely on Victorian buildings outside the West and its mining towns. And to compound those problems, as the first preservation work began, the professional history of the minerals industry was itself in its infancy. There were few first-class professional histories to rely on, and so local folklore, "great man" icons, and inexpert studies provided the basis for selecting boundaries. Once again, the outcome was poor boundary definition.

We should not be too critical of these first preservationists—they were pioneers in the profession—and we need to remember that everything is political to a greater or lesser degree. And so in terms of mining districts, it's important to understand that boundary issues and boundary disputes are fluid, not static matters. These early problems of definition have meant that later public historians, possessed of greater knowledge and larger understanding, have fought to alter and generally enlarge historic districts. If the earlier boundaries tended to include only the important mines or the fashionable parts of towns or the properties of "great men," then later definitions, informed by broader knowledge and a more sophisticated understanding, have expanded older districts to include subjects often ignored in earlier times: ethnic neighborhoods, vernacular housing, industrial structures, and transportation features. Yet a key problem still remains with ore-processing facilities—so important but so little understood and thus often left out of district formation.

The classic era of mining in the West also evolved through Victorian times, and so the mining towns reflect the traditions of Victorian architecture and city planning (such as it was) in that era. This can become a problem in rehabilitating old structures or building on vacant lots in historic districts, given the powerful image of Hollywood's cattle towns as what once was. The myth again challenges the far more interesting reality.

Preservation Process and Problems

As historic preservation worked its way into the fabric of American life, it created jobs and opportunities for public historians—and that has certainly been true for those interested in mining history. Many sites and structures either lie on federal land or have been impacted by federally sponsored projects. Beyond writing National Register nominations, which garner diverse public interest, public historians have found work in different arenas. They have made eligibility assessments on properties for inclusion in the National Register, conducted surveys to find out what exactly remains, and developed contexts to serve as the overarching vehicle for assessments of mines, mining areas, and their role in a locality's development. Public historians in the mining field have thus become part of the ongoing planning process for the myriad of projects funded by the federal government in part or in full or of projects on the public lands.

A problem that arises for historians in mining areas is how to assess a site or property that is well preserved, but not associated with an important person or mining area. Many structures associated with important people, districts, or technologies have been lost in part because they were in areas where mining itself, or easy access, or tourist activity led to their loss. But sometimes in remote areas, a structure unimportant in itself but representative of an important process survives.

Another problem arises with the preservation of prosaic and radioactive sites. Coal mining in the West was very important, but when the mines closed, the companies demolished a great deal, more than in metal-mining areas. Most smelters and mills have disappeared—the surface structures were large, and few appreciated the significance of the technology. And in more recent times the West produced much of the nation's uranium for nuclear power and atomic bombs, but the environmental cleanup has destroyed many sites, including at least one, the smelter chimney at Durango, Colorado, listed in the National Register of Historic Places.

Finally, another problem arises where homes, buildings, and structures have largely disappeared. Little or no integrity may be left for the historian, but plenty may be left for the historical archaeologist. And so where one discipline leads into another is an important border area.

For public historians of mining, there have been different types of work. Many jobs have emerged in state preservation offices and with federal agencies, and that work has included National Register nominations, surveys, and eligibility assessments. Other jobs have included contract work with public and private entities and positions with cities, counties, and federal agencies. Finally, the advent of preservation has spurred the rise of consulting firms, sometimes one person in number and sometimes multiperson. Some of these proprietorships, partnerships, and small corporations have focused exclusively on mining areas—securing contracts for research and writing on a myriad of projects. More typical, however, is the enterprise that sees mining history and preservation as only one aspect of its services. Public historians have also found pro bono work, such as service on historic preservation boards at the state and local level.

The Lexicon

Public historians in mining history—like those in other fields—need to deal with a special lexicon, one unique in the industry and one little known outside it. A matte isn't something you put on the floor (though I've read that). You don't have dinner at a Wilfley table. You don't play cards at a card table. Cousin Jacks and Aunt Jennies don't refer to cousins named Jack or aunts named Jenny. A whim isn't a fast-passing thought. Coke is neither a lawful substance to drink nor an illegal substance to snort (I assume). A miner's canary isn't a bird, and a grizzly isn't a bear. Miner's consumption isn't tuberculosis (though I've read that, too). A tipple isn't a guy after too many drinks. A stamp isn't something you stick on an envelope. A raise isn't an increase in pay. And a shaft isn't a raw deal from the boss.

There are other specialized terms as well. We have adit, drag line, flotation, flume, stope, tailings, vug, and winze, to say nothing of stamp milling, double jacking, and hand steel, let alone the presence of tommyknockers. We could go on and on. The key is that any public historian—curator, preservationist, or environmentalist concerned with the minerals industry—must first learn a specialized language and then be able to interpret

Figure 159. Mining equipment and head frame near Mogollon, New Mexico. Photo by Andrew Gulliford, 1989.

that lexicon for the general public, which has little or no idea about the mining world aside from the belief that it involves panning for gold or a generic idea that a mine is something underground designed to retrieve gold and pollute the environment. This is a serious problem—the more technical the language, the less interest generally from the general public. The key is to find the right balance in discussion. Too much emphasis on technical detail will put a nontechnical audience to sleep, but too much simplification will seriously distort the interpretation of a site.

The Environment, Litigation, and the Public Historian

Since the 1970s and 1980s, the passage of national and state laws, coupled with local ordinances, has driven a significant cleanup of American's present and past industrial environment. The Environmental Protection Agency (EPA) has played a powerful, sometimes controversial role in many aspects of this effort. Innumerable environmental organizations have appeared to sponsor legislation, consult on cleanups, and develop reports on every conceivable subject. The minerals industry has been a key focus of the environmental movement, which has spawned innumerable opportunities for public historians.

Some people in mining claim—perhaps with some justification—that in recent years the principal output of American mines has been litigation. While that is an overstatement, it does reflect the immense impact of environmental legislation and litigation. A key piece of environmental legislation affecting the industry has been the Comprehensive Environmental Response, Compensation, and Liability Act (CERCLA) of 1980. This law placed a tax on the chemical and petroleum industries and gave the federal government the authority to respond to actual or potential releases of hazardous substances that might endanger either the environment or public health. From the tax emerged a superfund to provide the moneys for the cleanup of Superfund sites. Also from the law emerged the concept of liability for the cleanups and the remediation that would follow.

CERCLA spawned a massive amount of litigation in the minerals industry in the mid-1980s. The first efforts saw the Department of Justice, acting for the EPA, sue individuals and firms—everything from small property owners to major mining companies. State governments joined in the fray. A second wave of litigation involved the miners suing their insurance companies for the reimbursement of health costs. The mass of litigation resulted in a huge number of investigations that employed individuals in many disciplines, and because the litigation revolved around the course of events in the distant past, public historians played key roles in all phases of the process. To prove or disprove liability or to settle out of court, the government, the mining companies, and the insurers engaged historians for a myriad of research projects. These projects included the history of mining companies, mining districts, and mining towns; the development of technology that produced the dumps, tailings, slags, smoke, and other waste products; water quality over time; the roads and railroads used to move ore; and the railroads that used slags for ballast. The work also extended to individual mining people and the foundations or trusts they created. Often this work was very technical, requiring some historians to have at least some scientific background and/or work closely with geologists, geochemists, mining engineers, and other experts.

Some of the lawsuits threatened the viability of old giant international enterprises that once formed the heart of American mining. These entities included ASARCO, formed in 1899 as the American Smelting and Refining Company, and ARCO, once the Atlantic Richfield Oil Company, which had acquired the vast Anaconda copper properties in Butte, Montana. They also included railroads like the Denver & Rio Grande Western, which had acquired mining lands or run track over them, and the lawsuits involved various aspects of the modern ski industry that had evolved in older mining towns. They also involved individual citizens. The costs have been huge. In some cases, a few investigators have come to believe that the cost of the litigation exceeded the cost of the subsequent remediation.

The remediation efforts resulting from this litigation have also involved public historians. Rivers have been riprapped and rechanneled, water treatment plants built, cement culverts installed, tailings and dumps moved, and land covered and revegetated. In this effort, historians have found work in trying to determine what the landscape looked like when mining began since some efforts have gone into trying to re-create what once was to minimize the impact of the remediation itself. Historians have also researched and recorded sites before remediation, and they have attempted to direct the mediation itself to minimize its impact on the historic fabric of mining areas.

These efforts have actually propelled the mining industry into a new, unexpected phase. As the remediation has relocated tailings and dumps, demolished buildings, and created new structures and sites in the historic areas, it has created something that wasn't, but nonetheless reflective of mining's evolution. One of the best known of these new features is the so-called wedding cake on the east side of Leadville, Colorado. Here the different colors of tailings, dumps, and other waste products comingled in the environmental cleanup combine to create a giant mound that indeed resembles a wedding cake. But this is only one of many examples. New plastic pipes, cement culverts, and revegetated tailings piles are all prominent in mining areas and reflective of the cleanup. An important role for public historians is to record this work as it goes forward, obtain interviews, and monitor developments. These pioneering projects—whether or not they succeed—will eventually form part of the larger historic fabric in the overall evolution of the industry.

Controversies

The nature of this environmental work has sometimes led to conflicts between public historians committed to preservation and public historians committed to the environment. For many historians, preservationists, and museum professionals, the surviving mine dumps, tailings piles, slag piles, and other waste products and ruins reflect part of the historic fabric of the mining industry per se. For this group, these vestiges of times past constitute an essential part of what should be preserved—just as much as the houses, business blocks, churches, head frames, and mine buildings. Public historians in the environmental field, however, often see such waste products and the structures and technology that produced them as sources of dangerous heavy metals, water pollution, acid rain, and acid snow, and they also see them literally as eyesores on a beautiful landscape. This group wants to see these products removed and the land reclaimed and recovered, even restored to its original appearance in pre-mining times. The interpretation of what remains has split the historical community and landed historians on both sides of the political and legal battles that have ensued.

Some places, like Butte, Montana, and Leadville, Colorado, two of the great mining centers of the West, come to mind. Both have witnessed large environmental controversies, the result of a mining industry that unfolded over the course of well more than a century. The production was world class, the vestiges of the industry enormous, and the environmental litigation over the waste products very large. Both communities seemed reluctant to accept the fact that most mining had probably come to an end, at least for the foreseeable future, but as the economy began

Figure 160. Ore cars followed this track to dump ore into a mill, now abandoned, near Atlantic City, Wyoming, on land now historically interpreted by the Bureau of Land Management. Photo by Andrew Gulliford, 1994.

gradually shifting toward at least some tourism, the environmental remediation went hand in hand with this conversion. In the litigation that unfolded and in the settlements and remediation that developed, public historians played vital roles to all sides in researching some of the basic documents in the various cases.

In recent years, the remarkable evolution of the World Wide Web has again offered new opportunities for public historians. Developing web sites on mining in all its aspects has created fascinating challenges. As in museum work, there are problems of what to present and how to interpret. Yet the chance to develop something unique that can be used for many purposes for many years presents the opportunity to reach vast new audiences around the world. Inevitably, research on the web will substantially replace research in the archive. And so public historians in this new field of endeavor will make long-lasting contributions in many different ways.

Conclusion

Public historians of the mining West may work in preservation, museums, environmental fields, or web site development, and they will practice their profession in conjunction with other fields. But whatever their work, they need to think of the minerals industry as an industry central, not peripheral, to American development. They need to learn a special lexicon unique to mining itself. And they need to be able to interpret a complex, science-based industry to a public little acquainted with either science or mines and predisposed, if not committed, to believing in the mythology of the Old West.

Study Questions

1. How did the rise of an environmental consciousness and the destruction of decaying historical buildings lead to the National Historic Preservation Act of 1966?

2. What was the singular event that sparked the transformation and development of the West?

3. What are the advantages of preserving a mining region rather than simply a mine site or structure?

4. Why do some property owners oppose historic designation?

5. What are some of the problems mining site preservationists have to overcome?

6. Why is it important for a mining historian to understand terms used in the mining industry?

7. How did the Comprehensive Environmental Response, Compensation, and Liability Act of 1980 complicate mining preservation?

8. What contribution can the public historian provide in mining litigation and remediation?

9. Describe the conflicts that might arise between public historians committed to preservation and public historians committed to the environment.

Conclusion: A Past Presumed to Be Comfortable and Comfortably Past

Headnotes

Native New Mexican Dwight Pitcaithley, chief historian of the National Park Service, concludes *Preserving Western History* with his personal narrative about growing up near Carlsbad, New Mexico, and living with boosters and dreamers who sought to make the dry land bloom. Most of Western history is about boom and bust, and certainly Western public history needs to address the themes Dr. Pitcaithley raises in this essay. He also discusses evolving scholarship and the need "to engage the public in a discussion of new ways of looking at a past presumed to be comfortable, and comfortably past," while at the same time discussing fault lines in the historical profession and the goal for all of us to know our history.

Being Born Western and the Challenges of Public History

Dwight T. Pitcaithley

I keep a photograph of my grandmother in my office. It was taken during World War I, when she lived in New York. It is unlike other photographs of grandmothers I have seen. It is a posed photograph, and in it she is lying on her stomach on a dais. She is covered in a feathered costume, her knees are bent and ankles crossed. She is looking directly into the camera lens, her face resting on the palm of her left hand. My grandmother was a New York showgirl during the time of Florence Zeigfield. She married the stage manager for Howard Thurston, one of the leading magicians during the early decades of the twentieth century, but divorced him shortly after the birth of my mother in 1919. My grandmother was an actress who moved about the country from show to show, some owned by her second husband, some not; never living in one place for any length of time. Near the end of her life and in declining health, she moved in with my mother in Carlsbad, New Mexico, where she died in the mid-1980s.

On a blustery spring day, my mother and I drove into the Guadalupe Mountains west of town and scattered her ashes on a rough and rugged landscape distant in time and topography from her birth over 80 years before in Connecticut. I keep her photograph in my office partly as a conversation piece—"That's not really your grandmother!" visitors exclaim—and partly because it reminds me of the social mobility of the twentieth century and of the reasons I was born

Western. I grew up in Carlsbad, New Mexico, because my mother, who grew up in the show business world of her mother and father and stepfather, longed for the geographical roots a life on the road does not permit. When my father, also an actor, was drafted in 1942, they married and moved to Carlsbad, where he served as special services coordinator at the local army air base. Following the war, my father probably would have moved to California, where the film industry could have used character actors like him, but my mother would have none of it. She wanted roots, a permanent home, two children, a dog, and a fence; she wanted to be a teacher. She got all she wished for. My parents became a permanent part of the Pecos River valley in southeastern New Mexico.

So I grew up in that small Western town, shaped by its values, playing along the banks of the river, exploring the neighboring Guadalupe foothills, developing all of the geocentric beliefs teenagers in small, as well as large, places develop. I bought the idea of the rugged, Western individualist carving out societies in the hostile Western landscape. The West during that time was seen by its inhabitants as well as the rest of the country, thanks to Hollywood, through a lens that colored it at once romantic and different and wild and generally unconnected to the historical rhythms of the rest of the country. (Many years later, when my wife and I moved to Boston from Santa Fe, one of our neighbors came over to introduce herself. She asked where we were coming from, and when I answered, "New Mexico," she sighed and exclaimed, "Oh, how exotic!" In the New England financial corporation in which my wife worked, her fellow workers asked whether we still had trouble with "the Indians.")

After a failed college beginning as a music major and a three-year adventure with the U.S. Marine Corps, I became a historian of the American West and immersed myself in all of the comfortable narratives that characterized the study of the West during the late 1960s and early 1970s. I steeped myself in the scholarship of Ray Allen Billington and Thomas D. Clark as they echoed the theories of Frederick Jackson Turner. I

Figure 161. Pecos River flume, October 29, 1906. Photograph by W. J. Lubken. Courtesy National Archives.

learned that the West and the frontier were synonymous terms as the titles of the primary textbooks attested: *Frontier America: The Story of the Westward Movement* and *Westward Expansion: A History of the American Frontier*.[1] The West was about movement, of successive waves of explorers, traders and trappers, miners, ranchers using and subduing nature. The frontier West was "the meeting point between savagery and civilization," it was about rebirth and fluidity and simplicity.[2] Its characteristics, according to Ridge and Billington, could be described as "coarseness and strength combined with acuteness and inquisitiveness . . . that inventive turn of mind . . . that masterful grasp of material things," and perhaps most importantly, "that dominant individualism."[3] I uncritically accepted this interpretation of the West, although subconsciously I had a hard time placing my hometown in it. (It celebrated its 75th anniversary the year following my high school graduation.) During my formative years, Carlsbad was a mere three generations away from its founding and bore none of the characteristics I had learned to identify as Western.

And then, long after I received my degree and began an unplanned journey as a public historian, Patty Limerick and Richard White and Bill Cronon and others forced us to think differently about place and people and intersections in the West. What a slap in the

Figure 162. First National Bank Building—Carlsbad, New Mexico, from a contemporary photo. Courtesy National Archives.

Figure 163. First National Bank Building, Carlsbad, New Mexico, 1905. Courtesy National Archives.

face that was! They collectively turned Turner's frontier thesis on its head. They constructed different lenses by which one could observe the West. Suddenly, the place in which I grew up developed different meanings and I understood it more keenly than ever before.

During the 1950s, Carlsbad was a farm and ranch community, a mining town because of the nearby potash mines, and a tourist destination due to its proximity to Carlsbad Caverns National Park. Farming was a part of the town from its beginning during the 1880s, when Charles B. Eddy, James J. Hagerman, and Robert W. Tansill platted it and planned a sophisticated irrigation scheme by damming the Pecos River. (Pat Garrett, the Lincoln County sheriff who shot Billy the Kid, was also an early promoter.) The resulting dam and canal system included the largest masonry aqueduct in the United States in the form of a "flume" that carried the water over the Pecos River. The network was designated a National Historic Landmark in 1964. The irrigation system worked as planned until floods in 1893 and 1904 destroyed both the dam and the finances of its promoters. The enterprising entrepreneurs convinced the U.S. Bureau of Reclamation to take ownership of the system and rebuild it. So much for rugged individualism!

Through the resulting arrangement, the local irrigation district and its farmers turned control of the water system over to the bureau in return for a long-term buyout of government interests. (Final ownership of the district did not return to the local farmers until 1949.)[4] The town's agricultural future had been saved by the federal government. Indeed, it turns out that Carlsbad was largely shaped by the federal government from its beginning: first the irrigation system, then the promotion of the local cave system (designated a national monument in 1923 by President Harding), then the construction of a military base during World War II, and in recent years the development of a nuclear waste dump, euphemistically called a Waste Isolation Pilot Project (WIPP) by the U.S. Department of Energy.

I have spent my professional career as a public historian employed by the National Park Service. As a historian in Santa Fe, Boston, and presently Washington, D.C., I have been privileged to work with a wide variety of significant historic places on development, as well as interpretive, issues. I also have been able to watch as the agency evolved from a rather intellectually insular organization to one that embraces the rest of the historical profession, its scholars, and scholarship. Scholars of all kinds now participate in the development of interpretive plans and programs for parks. The National Park Service has formal cooperative agreements with the

Organization of American Historians, the National Council on Public History, and the Western History Association. This openness to changing interpretations of the past has also put it at the front lines of public discussions about history and historical revisionism and "political correctness."

Over the last 10 to 15 years, the National Park Service has revised its philosophy of interpretation and in the process embraced a much wider view of the past and of topics appropriate for interpretive programs. Part of this change was prompted by a congressional willingness to expand the National Park System by including parks such as Manzanar National Historic Site, Little Rock Central High School National Historic Site, Selma to Montgomery National Historic Trail, Washita Battlefield National Historic Site, and Sand Creek Massacre National Historic Site. All of these places, and others, require the National Park Service to develop interpretive programs that offer more than simple descriptions of events, more than "happy face" history. They demand that the agency say something meaningful about the place, the clash of personalities and philosophies, encourage a rethinking of assumed truths, and challenge the public to think more broadly about the legacy of these events in today's society.

The National Park Service has embraced this congressional challenge most notably by presenting the causes of the Civil War at its battlefield parks. (Beginning in 1989, Congress specifically directed the National Park Service to interpret the "causes and consequences" of the Civil War, something the service had avoided for almost 70 years.) For parks that traditionally limited their interpretive presentations to descriptions of the battles themselves, this expansion of interpretation posed challenges to park staffs and angered a public accustomed to avoiding causes when visiting these American shrines. The American public is most uncomfortable conversing about slavery in any setting, and having to confront this uncomfortable past at national battlefields clashed with the traditional manner in which battlefields were presented and, in many cases, with a public steeped in the Lost Cause version of the war, in which slavery was absent as a cause of the conflict. The managers of these special places, however, understood that without an understanding of the causes of secession and the resulting war, the battlefields could have no connection to the consequences of the war with which this country still struggles.

Using an evolving scholarship to engage the public in a discussion of new ways of looking at a past presumed to be comfortable, and comfortably past, is both challenging and necessary. And what better place to hold that discussion than at public places, in public parks? Presenting different views of history at public parks in the West presents delicious opportunities to engage the public on two fronts: the first relates to new ways of looking at traditional narratives of Western encounters and development, while the second offers the opportunity to talk about the work of historians and how they construct historical interpretations. The power of Western history makes this work easy and difficult at the same time: easy because many Western places and stories have become icons of America itself. (I recently had the opportunity to travel to Belgium with Douglas Scott—see Dr. Scott's essay earlier in this volume—and listen as he presented his Little Bighorn talk to a gathering of cultural resource specialists from the Belgium government. While his presentation and the ensuing discussion was handled through Flemish translators, it was clear that the recounting of this famous event in the American West held a special fascination to a transatlantic audience.) Our work is made difficult because any alteration of comfortable stories can and will lead to questions of ownership of history and accusations of revisionism. Both of these ideas, however, can constitute fruitful springboards into discussions about the nature of history and its usefulness in contemporary life.

My personal view of all this is that historians everywhere, public and academic, have an obligation to broaden public awareness about history and the role it should, and does, play in this democracy. Presenting history in and about the American West is filled with opportunities to teach history to a public eager to learn about the past, but unclear, or even hostile, about its relationship to the present. We are better equipped than ever to engage the public in this discussion but hampered by the odd notion that if we are read by large numbers of the public, we run the risk of being labeled "popular" historians and thereby deemed less scholarly.

The profession of history these days is, thus, challenged along several fault lines. The first separates historians from the public. Over the past century, historians have moved from being very much engaged with public issues to being considered "academic" and removed from public perceptions or discussions about the past and, at bottom, not relevant to an informed understanding of the past/present relationship. In a society in which current issues are shaped dramatically by past decisions (and what society is not?), we continue this separation at our peril. An understanding about how past circumstances have shaped contemporary life and values is critical to participating in public discussions and developing thoughtful plans that will shape the future. Because historians have withdrawn generally from public discourse, the public has grown to devalue their work and, more tragically, discount it when revisionist thinking clashes with traditionally comfortable versions of "truth." An additional and clearly related loss is any public knowledge or meaningful understanding of how historians work, how they mine evidence and develop interpretations of the past, and how their understanding of the past evolves with still further interpretations. Instead of being excited about revisionist interpretations, they feel threatened by them. "We have failed," writes the historian Leon Litwack, ". . . to communicate what we do to a larger audience—to a public that has long demonstrated an avid interest in history."[5]

The second fault line is within the profession itself, between "academic" historians and "public" historians. (We can hope that in the near future these distinctions will fade away and all historians will label themselves simply as historians.) Public history work is neither widely appreciated within the profession nor given the credit it deserves when tenure considerations are being made. Most public history work being done by non–public historians is being done by those faculty members who already have tenure and not by younger historians who continue to build traditional credits for their professional portfolio. Although great strides have been made over the last 15 years or so in bridging this gap, the issue of defining scholarship remains a thorny one.[6] Much remains to be done before the public nature of history has saturated even the most unreconstructed "academic" historian. To establish some sort of analogy, we might consider a scenario based on the medical profession. What if only those doctors who *taught* medicine were perceived at the top of their profession while all those who *practiced* medicine were deemed of only secondary importance? The latter, tenured medical professors would observe smugly, were only practicing medicine because they couldn't get a job teaching medicine! Is the importance of history in today's society any less than the importance of medicine?[7] John Gaddis uses a different analogy to make the same point. Social systems, he writes, "can hardy do without history as a discipline, because it's the means by which a culture sees beyond its own senses. It's the basis, across time, space, and scale, for a wider view. A collective historical consciousness, therefore, may be as much a prerequisite for a healthy well-rounded society as is the proper ecological balance for a healthy forest and a healthy planet."[8]

As one who considers all history to be public history, I consider the expansion of the public's perception of history to be a basic obligation of the historical profession. As one who speaks widely to public groups, I have found a useful tool in Patty Limerick's article, "A How-to Guide for the Academic Going Public."[9] With her usual thoughtfulness and good humor she provides an easy primer for those who are willing to venture forth into the uncertain and challenging seas of public history. My advice is, try it—you'll like it, and in all likelihood, it will make you a better historian.

The essays in this volume provide a wealth of subjects and issues relevant to Western history and

Westerners today. They examine a variety of topics from a variety of perspectives. Some of the subjects and approaches will be new even to the practitioners of public history; most will be new to a public still enamored with the traditional narratives of the grand Western American story. All in all, they provide grist for the public history mill. They *can* and *should* be used to foster expansive and vigorous discussions within the field about Western history and its relevance to us today. They *must* be used to prompt a vigorous discussion with the public about the past, the nature of history and the work of historians, and the role of history in civic education and engagement.

Patty Limerick is right: the "land of the American West isn't what it used to be."[10] It is more complex, more diverse, and much more interesting than it was when I first began exploring its history over three decades ago. It is also far more capable of teaching us things we need to know if we are to inhabit it with grace and sensitivity, manage its land with knowledge and wisdom, and build its communities with compassion and respect for all its citizens. Ben Nighthorse Campbell, earlier in this volume, expressed the view that Americans have the capacity to view their past honestly, take pride in their accomplishments, and admit and learn from their shortcomings. He concluded with the challenge that all of us "must recognize that we must constantly work to find ways to be better human beings." Knowing one's history is a fundamental beginning point in building better communities. This book gives us a rich and vibrant historical landscape with which to inform and challenge ourselves, engage the public, and plan for a better tomorrow.

Notes

1. Thomas D. Clark, *Frontier America: The Story of the Westward Movement* (1959; New York: Scribner, 1969), and Ray Allen Billington, *Westward Expansion: A History of the American Frontier* (1949; New York: Macmillan, 1969).

2. Martin Ridge and Ray Allen Billington, *America's Frontier Story: A Documentary History of Westward Expansion* (New York: Holt, Rinehart and Winston, 1969), 17–18.

3. Ibid., 23.

4. See Mark Hufstetler and Lon Johnson, *Watering the Land: The Turbulent History of the Carlsbad Irrigation District* (Denver: National Park Service, 1993).

5. Leon Litwack, "Beyond the Boundaries of the Academy," *History Matters!*, 8 (September 1995): 1.

6. The formation of the National Council on Public History during the late 1970s and the growth of 80 or so graduate programs in public history has done much to bring public history to the attention of university administrators. In addition, an ad hoc committee of the American Historical Association (AHA) produced a report in 1994 titled "Redefining Historical Scholarship" that fully incorporated pubic history work into the definition of historical scholarship for the purposes of tenure and promotion decisions; see "Redefining Historical Scholarship," *Perspectives* (March 1994). Unfortunately, this new definition was adopted neither by the board of the AHA nor any other historical organization. At this writing, however, the public history committee of the Organization of American Historians (OAH) is initiating efforts to revisit the formalization of the report by the boards of both the AHA and the OAH.

7. I am indebted to James Oliver Horton for sparking comparisons between the historical and medical professions.

8. John Lewis Gaddis, *The Landscape of History: How Historians Map the Past* (New York: Oxford University Press, 2002), 149.

9. Patricia Nelson Limerick, *Something in the Soil: Legacies and Reckonings in the New West* (New York: Norton, 2000), 323–32.

10. Ibid., p. 14.

Study Questions

1. Why was the West seen as "romantic and different and wild and generally unconnected to the historical rhythms of the rest of the country"?

2. What influenced the earlier views of Western history?

3. How did Patty Limerick, Richard White, and Bill Cronon change the romantic view of the West?

4. What is the definition of rugged individualism?

5. How did the federal government shape Carlsbad, and did this corroborate the idea of Western individualism?

6. In what ways has the National Park Service changed toward presenting history and working with historians?

7. What is meant by "historical revisionism"?

8. Should "political correctness" have a place in historical scholarship?

9. Why would the public prefer to avoid the root causes of the Civil War?

10. What is meant by the "Lost Cause" version of the Civil War?

11. How are traditional narratives of Western history different from progressive narratives? Are traditional narratives still relevant? If so, in what ways?

12. Why would a public eager to learn about the past be unclear, or even hostile, about history's relationship to the present?

13. What are the challenges for modern historians?

14. What are the obligations of both the public and the academic historian?

15. If "Americans have the capacity to view their past honestly," then why are they apprehensive of changes to their "comfortable stories" of the past?

Authors' Biographies

BEN NIGHTHORSE CAMPBELL has been an Olympic judo contestant, an award-winning jeweler, and a former congressman and U.S. Senator from Colorado who never lost in 10 elections though he switched his party allegiance from Democrat to Republican. A member of the Northern Cheyenne Tribe, Ben Nighthorse was elected to the Council of 44 Chiefs, which is the highest honor that can be bestowed upon a Northern Cheyenne. The honor is a lifetime commitment that comes with a variety of moral and community obligations.

FRED CHAPMAN is a professional archaeologist who has worked for over 20 years with the State of Wyoming's State Historic Preservation Office. He has been a staff archaeologist and Native American Liaison for Wyoming tribes including the Arapaho and Shoshone on the Wind River Reservation. He is also associated with the American Studies Graduate Program at the University of Wyoming where he teaches classes in anthropology.

ERIC L. CLEMENTS, an assistant professor of history and public history and assistant museum director at Southeast Missouri State University, grew up in Colorado. He received his master's degree in history with a museum studies certification from the University of Delaware and his doctorate in the history of the American West from Arizona State University. His particular interest is in the mining history of the West, with an emphasis on decline of mining communities and their resurgence in other forms. Clements's first book, *After the Boom in Tombstone and Jerome, Arizona: Decline in Western Resource Towns*, was published in 2003 by the University of Nevada Press.

PETER DEDEK is an assistant professor in interior design at Texas State University–San Marcos. He specializes in design history, historic preservation, and residential design. Dedek holds a master of arts in Interior Design from Cornell University in Ithaca, New York, and a doctor of arts in history with an emphasis in historic preservation from Middle Tennessee State University in Murfreesboro, Tennessee. His doctoral dissertation, *Journeys on the Mother Road: Interpreting the Cultural Significance of U.S. Route 66*, is currently being rewritten as a book.

PHILIP DUKE is a professor of anthropology at Fort Lewis College and co–principal investigator of the Colorado Coalfield War Archaeological Project. His research interests include public archaeology, repatriation issues, and Bronze Age archaeology of Greece. He is author of, among other publications, *Points in Time: Structure and Event in a Late Northern Plains Hunting Society*, and is co-editor of *Beyond Subsistence: Plains Archaeology and the Postprocessual Critique*.

JAMES E. FELL, Jr., holds an A.B. in chemistry from Colby College in Waterville, Maine, and an M.A. and Ph.D. in American history from the University of Colorado, Boulder. A leading historian of the minerals industry, he has authored or coauthored several books, including *Ores to Metals: The Rocky Mountain Smelting Industry*, and *Mining the Summit* (coauthor with Stanley Dempsey). He directed the National Register program for the Office of Archaeology and Historic Preservation at the Colorado Historical Society, served on the Colorado Historic Preservation Review Board, and has written a Colorado Mining Context for the Office of Archaeology and Historic Preservation as well. He teaches at the University of Colorado, Denver.

RICHARD FRANCAVIGLIA is a historian and geographer interested in the way environments change through time and how this change is depicted in maps, literature, museum exhibits, and popular culture. His background includes experience as a regional planner, historical resources consultant, college professor and administrator, and historic preservation program manager. He has written seven books, including *Believing in Place: A Spiritual Geography of the Great Basin* (2003); *The Cast Iron Forest: A Natural and Cultural History of the North American Cross Timbers* (2000); *Hard Places: Reading the Landscape of America's Historic Mining Districts* (1991); and *The Mormon Landscape: Existence, Creation and Perception of a Unique Image in the American West* (1978). He is currently director of the Center for Greater Southwestern Studies and the History of Cartography at the University of Texas at Arlington, where he is a professor of history and geography.

MARCIA TREMMEL GOLDSTEIN is a Ph.D. candidate at the University of Colorado at Boulder, whose research focuses on the history of Western women's suffrage and political activism. She has helped organize numerous public history projects for the Colorado Coalition for Women's History, including the Colorado Suffrage Centennial in 1993. She also curated, researched, and wrote the narrative for the online exhibit "This Shall Be the Land for Women: The Struggle for Western Women's Suffrage, 1860–1920," for the Women of the West Museum. Marcia is the author of a recent guide to women's history sites, *Denver Women in Their Places*, published by Historic Denver, Inc., in 2002.

ART GÓMEZ is a native of southwest Colorado and holds a Ph.D. in history from the University of New Mexico. A 23-year National Park Service employee, he is supervisory historian in the Intermountain Region, Santa Fe. His areas of specialization include Spanish Colonial, post–World War II American West, and environmental history. His most recent publications include *New Mexico: Images of a Land and Its People*, coauthored with landscape photographer Lucian Niemeyer (2004); *Forests Under Fire* (2003); *Quest for the Golden Circle* (repr. 2001); and *Chamizal National Memorial: Desert Island, Cultural Oasis* (forthcoming in 2005 from Texas A&M Press).

ANDREW GULLIFORD, formerly director of the Center of Southwest Studies at Fort Lewis College in Durango, Colorado, is now director of Special Projects at Fort Lewis College and a professor of Southwest Studies and history. He has written *America's Country Schools* (1984); *Boomtown Blues: Colorado Oil Shale* (1989); and *Sacred Objects and Sacred Places: Preserving Tribal Traditions* (2000). A former board member for the National Council on Public History, he currently serves on the National Register Review Board for Colorado and was appointed by the secretary of the interior to the Southwest Colorado Bureau of Land Management Resource Advisory Council. He has led Lewis and Clark tours in Oregon and Washington by cruise ship and in Montana by canoe and horseback, and he leads tours of national parks in the West for the Smithsonian Institution, National Geographic, and the National Trust for Historic Preservation.

WILLIAM W. GWALTNEY joined the National Park Service in 1977. He has served across the West at locations such as Bent's Old Fort near La Junta, Colorado; at Fort Davis in West Texas, and as superintendent at Fort Laramie in Eastern Wyoming. He made his first set of buckskins in 1973. Dr. Gwaltney is currently assistant regional director for Workforce Enhancement for the Rocky Mountain Region of the National Park Service in Denver. For the Park Service he consults nationwide on historical interpretation and museum planning related to African American history.

SARAH HORTON is currently writing a dissertation on the Santa Fe Fiesta for a Ph.D. in cultural anthropology at the University of New Mexico. She has presented papers on the issue of Spanish heritage and Hispano ties to a New Mexican homeland and has published "Maintaining Hispano Distinctiveness and Resisting Anglo Dominance in the Santa Fe Fiesta" in *Kiva: The Journal of Southwest Anthropology and History* (winter 2001).

JON HUNNER is the director of the Public History Program at New Mexico State University. In addition to teaching the regular courses in public history, he has created "Time Traveling through New Mexico's Past," an innovative living history program that transports students back to the Spanish Colonial period. Hunner also has published *Inventing Los Alamos: The Growth of an Atomic Community*, a social and cultural history of the birthplace of the Atomic Age.

JAN MacKELL is the archivist at the Cripple Creek District Museum in Cripple Creek, Colorado. She attended the University of Colorado at Colorado Springs for six years, studying humanities, communications, and history. MacKell has authored over 700 articles pertaining to Colorado in newspapers, magazines, and other periodicals. Since 2000, she has worked with Encore Video productions to write and produce a series of documentaries about Cripple Creek that currently air on Rocky Mountain PBS. In 2003 she published her first book, *Cripple Creek District: Last of Colorado's Gold Booms* with Arcadia Publishing. In 2004 her second book, *Brothels, Bordellos and Bad Girls: Prostitution in Colorado, 1860–1930*, was published through the University of New Mexico Press. From 1999 to 2004, MacKell served on the Historic Preservation Commission in Cripple Creek and remains an advocate for preserving the history of her city.

SALLY McBETH earned her doctorate in cultural anthropology from Washington State University in 1982. She is a professor of anthropology at the University of Northern Colorado in Greeley, where she has taught since 1990. McBeth authored *Ethnic Identity and the Boarding School Experience* (1983; University Press of America), coauthored *Essie's Story: The Life and Legacy of a Shoshone Teacher* (1998; University of Nebraska Press), and has contributed essays to numerous journals, edited collections, and encyclopedias.

RANDALL H. McGUIRE received his Ph.D. in anthropology from the University of Arizona in 1982. He is currently a professor of anthropology at Binghamton University, in Binghamton, New York. As an archaeologist his interests include reburial and repatriation, historical archaeology, and indigenous peoples of the Southwest United States and northwest México. His significant publications include "The Craft of Archaeology" (with Michael Shanks), *American Antiquity*, 1996; *A Marxist Archaeology*, Academic Press, 1992; and "Archaeology and the First Americans," *American Anthropologist* 1992.

KARA MARIKO MIYAGISHIMA earned her B.A. from the University of Colorado at Boulder in English and ethnic studies. She is currently pursuing her M.A. in U.S. history and public history at the University of Colorado at Denver and is completing a thesis on the Japanese in Colorado. Kara edited the 2003 UCD *Historical Studies Journal* and has studied abroad in Japan, Ecuador, and Mexico.

JUDY MATTIVI MORLEY received her Ph.D. from the University of New Mexico in 2002. Her dissertation, "Making History: Historic Preservation and the Creation of Western Civic Identity," examined the connection between historic preservation, city planning, tourism, and identity in post–World War II Western cities and is currently under contract with the University Press of Kansas. Dr. Morley is also the author of "Albuquerque, New Mexico, or Anywhere, USA?: Historic Preservation and the Construction of Western Civic Identity," published in the *New Mexico Historical Review*, April 1999. Dr. Morley currently teaches at Metropolitan State College of Denver and the University of Colorado at Denver and is the owner and president of Denver History Tours, LLC, which gives historically themed tours of Denver and the region.

JEFFREY NICHOLS is an assistant professor of history at Westminster College in Salt Lake City, Utah, and a former officer in the U.S. Navy. His research interests include the social history of the West in the late nineteenth and early twentieth century, environmental history, and women's history. His is the author of *Prostitution, Polygamy, and Power: Salt Lake City, 1847–1918* (University of Illinois, 2002).

THOMAS J. NOEL is a professor of history and director of Public History at the University of Colorado–Denver. He is a National Register Reviewer for Colorado and former chair of the Denver Landmark Preservation Commission. He teaches historic preservation and public history. Nicknamed "Dr. Colorado," Tom is the author of 30 books and the "Dr. Colorado" Saturday column for the *Denver Post–Rocky Mountain News*. He is currently working on *Landmarks Reborn: A Guide to Treasures Restored with the Colorado Historical Society's State Historical Fund*.

THOMAS PATIN is an associate professor of art history, Theory, and Criticism at Ohio University. His research deals with various forms of exhibition, display, and presentation. His dissertation, completed at the University of Washington, explores the history of the Museum of Modern Art, New York, and other aspects of museum history. His first paper on national parks, "The National Park as Museological Space," was presented in 1997 at the "People and Place: The Human Experience in Greater Yellowstone" conference, Yellowstone National Park, commemorating its 125th anniversary. In the summer of 2000 he worked at the Yellowstone Museum at Yellowstone National Park, consulting on museum collection, expansion, and planning.

DWIGHT T. PITCAITHLEY is the chief historian of the National Park Service. He began his career with the NPS as a seasonal laborer at Carlsbad Caverns National Park in 1963 and later served in Santa Fe, Boston, and Washington, D.C., before becoming chief historian in 1995. He has written *Let the River Be: A History of the Ozark's Buffalo River* (1987) and contributed chapters to a special issue of *The Public Historian*, "Public History and the Environment" (2004); *Myth, Memory, and the Making of the American Landscape* (2001); *Seeing and Being Seen: Tourism in the American West* (2001); *Past Meets Present* (1987); and *Public History: An Introduction* (1986). He was selected as a Woodrow Wilson Visiting Fellow in 2002, 2003, and 2005; appointed a Distinguished American Scholar by the Fulbright New Zealand board of directors in 2000; and in 1988 received the James Madison Prize from The Society for History in the Federal Government.

JAY M. PRICE, a native of Santa Fe, New Mexico, directs the Public History Program at Wichita State University. His publications include *Gateways to the Southwest: The Story of Arizona State Parks*. He has two books out by Arcadia Publishing: *Wichita, 1860–1930* and *Wichita's Legacy of Flight* with a forthcoming book on the El Dorado, Kansas, oil boom. His other writings include works on local history, the history of tourism, regional identity, and American sacred architecture. A member of the Kansas Humanities Council speakers' bureau, he has delivered the talks, "Reading Roadside Kansas," "Sacred Landscapes of Kansas," and "Building the Old West."

RAYMOND W. RAST is a Ph.D. student in the Department of History at the University of Washington, where he holds a Bank of America Graduate Fellowship. His dissertation examines the development of tourism in San Francisco and the rise of American Modernism between the 1870s and the 1910s. He maintains a strong interest in public history, and he is completing a National Historic Landmark Theme Study and Multiple Property Submission on César Chávez and the farmworkers' movement in the American West for the National Park Service. He has published articles on the preservation of historic blockhouses in the Pacific Northwest and the promotion of tourism in Yellowstone National Park during the late nineteenth century. He earned an M.A. in history from the University of New Mexico and a B.A. in history from Yale University.

PAUL E. RECKNER received his B.A. in anthropology from Temple University in 1994. After three years of work in cultural resource management in New York City, he entered the graduate program in the Department of Anthropology at the State University of New York at Binghamton. His master's thesis (1999) is titled "Meaning, Identity, and Class Struggle: A Practice Approach to Interpreting Clay Pipes from Urban Contexts in Late-Nineteenth- and Early-Twentieth-Century North America." He is currently a Ph.D. candidate at SUNY–Binghamton, and his dissertation project focuses on the interplay of solidarity, difference, and the materiality of social practice within the Ludlow Tent Colony community, Ludlow, Colorado, 1913–14. He presently works as a union organizer for the Teaching Assistants' Association, WFT/AFT Local #3200, at the University of Wisconsin–Madison.

DAVID ROBERTSON is an assistant professor in the Department of Geography at SUNY–Geneseo. He is a cultural/historical geographer whose research deals primarily with industrial culture and landscape. His Ph.D. dissertation (Oklahoma, 2001) explored issues of landscape meaning and community survival in three historic mining towns: Toluca, Illinois; Cokedale, Colorado; and Picher, Oklahoma. David has published articles in the *Journal of Cultural Geography*, the *Geographical Review*, and the *Journal of Illinois History*. He is currently engaged in research exploring the geography of the North American ghost town and the life and death of Centralia, Pennsylvania.

DEAN J. SAITTA is associate professor in the Department of Anthropology at the University of Denver and co–principal investigator of the Colorado Coalfield War Archaeological Project. He teaches courses in archaeology, evolutionary anthropology, and urban studies. He is coauthor of *Denver: An Archaeological History*.

STEVEN C. SCHULTE has been a professor of history at Mesa State College in Grand Junction, Colorado since 1989 after receiving his Ph.D. in history from the University of Wyoming in 1984. A specialist in Western American and environmental history, he is particularly interested in the region's water history. The author of *Wayne Aspinall and the Shaping of the American West* (University Press of Colorado, 2002), he is presently writing a book on how Colorado's Western Slope has fought to develop its water resources over the last 125 years.

DOUGLAS D. SCOTT is the Great Plains Team Leader with the National Park Service's Midwest Archaeological Center and holds a Ph.D. in anthropology from the University of Colorado–Boulder. He is also an adjunct professor at the University of Nebraska–Lincoln and in the forensic science master's program at Nebraska Wesleyan University. He has long-term research interests in the archaeology of the Great Plains and Rocky Mountain areas. Doug specializes in nineteenth-century military sites archaeology and forensic archaeology, with five books and over 100 monographs and articles published on those and related subjects. He is particularly noted for his expertise in battlefield archaeology and firearms identification. He was awarded the Department of the Interior's Distinguished Service Award for his innovative research in battlefield archaeology that started with his work at the Little Bighorn Battlefield National Monument.

LONN TAYLOR is a specialist in Southwestern U.S. history and culture. Formerly a curator at the Smithsonian's National Museum of American History, he was also the museum's historian for the Star-Spangled Banner Conservation Project. Mr. Taylor has held curatorial positions at the Museum of New Mexico, the American Folklife Center at the Library of Congress, the Dallas Historical Society, and the Winedale Historical Center in Austin, Texas. He has taught at Colorado College, the University of Texas at Austin, and Texas Christian University. A prolific writer, Mr. Taylor is the author of several books.

PATRICK TIERNEY received a Ph.D. in recreation resources with a concentration in tourism from Colorado State University in 1991. Currently he has a joint appointment in the Departments of Hospitality Management and Recreation-Leisure Studies at San Francisco State University, where he is a professor teaching classes in recreation, tourism, resort management, and eco-tourism. Patrick is also actively involved in tourism research, having completed tourism and ecotourism projects for the National Park Service, the Belize Tourist Board, U.S. Forest Service, Galapagos National Park, the country of Ecuador, and the California Division of Tourism. He is recipient of the 1997 Best Tourism Research Award from the California Division of Tourism, the 1991 Excellence in Research Award from the Commercial Recreation and Resort Association, as well as co-recipient of the 1990 Colorado Rural Tourism Achievement Award.

CARROLL VAN WEST is director of the Center for Historic Preservation at Middle Tennessee State University, director of the Tennessee Civil War National Heritage Area, and senior editor of the *Tennessee Historical Quarterly*. His books include *Capitalism on the Frontier: The Transformation of Billings and the Yellowstone Valley in the Nineteenth Century* (1993), *The New Deal Landscape of Tennessee* (2001), and *A History of Tennessee's Arts* (2004).

EKATERINI VLAHOS is an assistant professor in the Department of Architecture and Planning at the University of Colorado at Denver and a licensed architect. Her research focuses on the documentation, preservation, and interpretation of historic Colorado ranches as cultural landscapes. Her investigations emphasize understanding the development of the built environments of early Colorado settlements. She is a native of Colorado with family ties to ranching in the northwestern part of the state and is currently engaged in research exploring design within the context of historic vernacular landscapes as architectural solutions to sprawl in the West.

MARK WALKER is a Ph.D. candidate at Binghamton University, New York, working on the historical memory of Ludlow and its importance in the labor movement. He directed the field and lab work for the Colorado Coalfield War Archaeology Project from 1998–2001 and is currently at the Anthropological Studies Center of Sonoma State University in California.

JOSEPH WEIXELMAN graduated cum laude with a bachelor's degree in anthropology from the University of Colorado and has completed his doctorate in history at the University of New Mexico. After teaching social studies in high school, he began work on his graduate degrees, receiving his master's degree in history from Montana State University in 1992. In pursuit of his master's, Weixelman explored the Native American presence in Yellowstone National Park. The resulting paper, "Fear or Wonderment? Native Americans and the Geysers of Yellowstone National Park," was presented at the Fourth Biennial Science Conference on Greater Yellowstone in October 1997 and published in *Yellowstone Science* (fall 2001). Weixelman worked as a ranger at Mesa Verde National Park, Petroglyph National Monument, and Yellowstone National Park.

CHRISTINE WHITACRE, who has an M.A. in U.S. history from the University of Colorado–Denver, joined the National Park Service in 1989. She currently is serving as the NPS cultural resource specialist for the Rocky Mountains Cooperative Ecosystems Studies Unit (RM-CESU), headquartered at the University of Montana. Prior to moving to Montana, Christine worked at the NPS Intermountain Regional Office in Denver for nearly 15 years. The many and varied projects that she has been privileged to work on during her NPS career include the special resource studies for the Sand Creek Massacre National Historic Site (Colorado) and the Minuteman Missile National Historic Site (South Dakota); the "Clash of Cultures" theme study of trails associated with American Indian and U.S. Army conflict in the West; and technical assistance and research projects for several national parks, including Yellowstone, Grand Teton, Rocky Mountain National Park, and Colorado National Monument.

WILLIAM WROTH was curator of the Taylor Museum of the Colorado Springs Fine Arts Center from 1976 to 1983. Since that time he has served as guest curator for exhibitions at the Taylor Museum, the Museum of International Folk Art, the American Craft Museum, and other institutions. His primary interests are in the Hispanic and Native American cultures of the Southwest and Mexico, and he has long been concerned with the presentation of these cultures in the museum context. He is the author and editor of numerous works on Hispanic and Indian arts, including *Hispanic Crafts of the Southwest* (1977); *The Chapel of Our Lady of Talpa* (1979); *Christian Images in Hispanic New Mexico* (1982); *Images of Penance, Images of Mercy: Southwestern Santos in the Late Nineteenth Century* (1991); *The Mexican Sarape: A History* (1999); and *Ute Indian Arts and Culture from Prehistory to the New Millennium* (2000).

AMANDA ZEMAN is originally from Hanover, Pennsylvania. She earned a bachelor's degree in historic preservation from Goucher College and a master's degree in historic preservation planning from Cornell University. Amanda first joined the National Park Service in 2001, beginning her career at Grand Canyon National Park. In 2002, she transferred to Petrified Forest National Park, where she now serves as the park historic preservationist. During most of her career, Amanda has focused on vernacular and rustic park architecture, but much of her recent work deals with Mission 66. She also maintains and manages the List of Classified Structures database for Petrified Forest National Park and is working with park staff to establish a tribal consultation program.

List of Centers in the West

Arizona

Center for Sustainable Environments
Northern Arizona University
Hanley Hall, Bldg. 7, Box 5765
Flagstaff, AZ 86011-5765
Phone: (928) 523-6726
Fax: (928) 523-8223
Director: Gary Nabhan
URL: http://environment.nau.edu

Sonoran Institute
7650 E. Broadway, Suite 203
Tucson, AZ 85710
Phone: (520) 290-0828
Fax: (520) 290-0969
Executive Director: Luther Propst
URL: http://www.sonoran.org/

The Southwest Center
1052 North Highland Avenue
University of Arizona
Tucson, AZ 85721
Phone: (520) 621-2484
Fax: (520) 621-9922
Director: Joseph Wilder
URL: http://w3.arizona.edu/~swctr/index.html

Udall Center for Studies in Public Policy
The University of Arizona
803 East First Street
Tucson, AZ 85719
Tel: (520) 884-4393
Fax: (520) 884-4702
Director: Stephen Cornell
URL: http://udallcenter.arizona.edu/

Colorado

Center of the American West
University of Colorado–Boulder
Macky 229, 282 UCB
Boulder, CO 80309
Phone: (303) 492-4879
Fax: (303) 492-1671
Faculty Director & Chair: Patricia Nelson Limerick
Vice Chair: Charles F. Wilkinson
Executive Director: Tom Precourt
URL: http://www.centerwest.org

Center of Southwest Studies
Fort Lewis College
1000 Rim Drive
Durango, CO 81301-3999
Phone: (970) 247-7456
Fax: (970) 247-7422
URL: http://swcenter.fortlewis.edu/

The Hulbert Center for Southwest Studies
14 East Cache la Poudre
Colorado Springs, CO 80903
Phone: (719) 389-6649
Director: Victoria Levine
URL: http://www2.coloradocollege.edu/dept/SW/

Natural Resources Law Center
University of Colorado School of Law
Campus Box 401
Boulder, CO 80309-0401
Phone: (303) 492-1287
Fax: (303) 492-1297
Director: Jim Martin
URL: http://www.colorado.edu/Law/NRLC/

The Rocky Mountain Land Use Institute
2255 East Evans Avenue
Denver, CO 80208
Phone: (303) 871-6319
Fax: (303) 871-6051
Executive Director: Nancy E. Friedman
URL: http://www.law.du.edu/rmlui/

Idaho

The Andrus Center for Public Policy
PO Box 852
Boise, ID 83701
Tel: (208) 426-4218
Fax: (208) 426-4208
Chairman: Cecil D. Andrus
President: A. Wayne Mittleider
URL: http://andruscenter.org/

Policy Center for Western Public Lands
University of Idaho
Caldwell Research and Extension Center
16952 S. Tenth Avenue
Caldwell, ID 83607-8249
Phone: (208) 459-6365
Fax: (208) 454-7612
Director: Aaron Harp
URL: http://pacwpl.nmsu.edu/

Montana

Center for the Rocky Mountain West
Milwaukee Station, Second Floor
University of Montana
Missoula, MT 59812-3096
Phone: (406) 243-7700
Fax: (406) 243-7709
Director: Daniel Kemmis
URL: http://www.crmw.org

New Mexico

Center for Land Grant Studies
PO Box 342
Guadalupita, NM 87722
Phone: (505) 387-2738
URL: *http://www.southwestbooks.org/*

Center for Southwest Research
General Library
University of New Mexico
Albuquerque, NM 87131-1466
Phone: (505) 277-2857

Center for the Southwest
University of New Mexico
1104 Mesa Vista Hall
Albuquerque, New Mexico 87131-1181
Phone: (505) 277-7688
Fax: (505) 277-6023
Director: Virginia Scharff

National Hispanic Cultural Center
1701 4th Street SW
Albuquerque, NM 87102
Phone: (505) 766-9858
Fax: (505) 766-9665
Executive director: Katherine Archuleta
URL: http://www.hcfoundation.org/

Texas

Center for Greater Southwestern Studies
  and the History of Cartography
University of Texas at Arlington
Box 19497
Arlington, TX 76019-0497
Phone: (817) 272-3997
Fax: (817) 272-5797
Director: Richard Francaviglia
URL: http://www.uta.edu/southwesternstudies/

Center for the Study of the Southwest
601 University Dr.
San Marcos, TX 78666
Phone: (512) 245-2232
Fax: (512) 245-7462
Director: Mark Busby
URL: http://www.English.swt.edu/css/

The William P. Clements Center for Southwest Studies
Southern Methodist University
3225 University Avenue, Room 356
Box 750176
Dallas, TX 75275-0176
Phone: (214) 768-1233
Director: David Weber
URL: http://www.smu.edu/swcenter/

Utah

The American West Center
1901 E. South Campus Drive, Rm. 1023
University of Utah
Salt Lake City, UT 84112
Phone: (801) 581-7611
Fax: (801) 581-7612
Director: Daniel C. McCool
URL: http://www.amwest.utah.edu/

The Wallace Stegner Center
University of Utah College of Law
332 S. 1400 E. Front
Salt Lake City, UT 84112-0730
Phone: (801) 585-9695
Fax: (801) 581-6897
Director: Bob Keiter
Associate director: Keith Bartholomew
URL: http://www.law.utah.edu/Stegner/stegner.html

Washington

Center for Columbia River History
1109 E. 5th St.
Vancouver, WA 98661
Tel: (360) 258-3289
Fax: (360) 258-0030
URL: http://www.ccrh.org

Wyoming

American Heritage Center
University of Wyoming
PO Box 3924
Laramie, WY 82071
Phone: (307) 766-4114
Fax: (307) 766-5511
Director: Mark A. Greene
URL: http://ahc.uwyo.edu/

William D. Ruckelshaus Institute of Environment and Natural Resources
University of Wyoming
PO Box 3971
Laramie, WY 82071
Tel: (307) 766-5080
Fax: (307) 766-5099
Director: Harold Bergman
Assistant director: Diana Hulme
URL: http://www.uwyo.edu/ENR/IENR.HTM

Index

Page numbers in **bold type** indicate photographs or illustrations.

Abbey, Edward, 9, 235, 238
Adams, Robert, 89
adobe preservation, 103
Advisory Council on Historic Preservation, 148, 153–54
Albright, Horace, 134
Alfred P. Murrah Federal Building, 118
alien abduction theory, 138
Almodovar, Norma Jean, 229
altars: recreated, 147, 149–50; "repatriation" of reproductions, 152
Alvarado Hotel, 147
America's Country Schools (Gulliford), 4
American Association for State and Local History, 16, 48
American Association of University Women, 220
American Farmland Trust, 289
American Indian Religious Freedom Act, 123–24
American Places: Encounters with History (Leuchtenburg), 60
American Smelting and Refining Company (ASARCO), 368–74, 376, 386
Amfac, Inc., 148, 151, 153
Ammons, Elias, 35, 37
Anasazi Heritage Center, 56. See also Indians, Anasazi
Ancestral Puebloans, 134, 137, 138, 139, 193; and modern Pueblo Indians, 136
Anderson, Irving, 201
Anglo gentrification, 113
Annual Pearl's Follies, 227
Anthony, Scott, 177
Anthony, Susan B., 214, 220, 221
Antiquities Act of 1906, 123, 133, 215, 278, 283
Applegate, Frank, 94
Archaeological Resources and Protection Act, 124
archaeology, 17, 32, 40, 173. See also historical archaeology
Archibuque, Juan de, 91
architecture, 294, 314; for boosterism, 320–23; Colonial Revival, 310–11; gate entrance, **8**; geological formations which suggests, 67; Old West Revival, 310–28; Pueblo Revival, 313, 332; stone entrance, **8**; women and, 215
Archuleta, Ruben E., 89
Arizona: and deterrents to statehood, 89
Arlington National Cemetery, 119
Armitage, Susan, 195
Arnold, Sam, 11
art colonies, 98, 113
Arthur, Dolly, 231
artifact gardens, 363
artifacts, 61, 182–83, **183**; at Custer Battlefield National Monument, 27; four approaches to presentation of, 50–51; questions asked of, 62; repatriation of, 46, 149
Ashenhurst, Harold, 136
Aspinall, Wayne, 238, 272, 274–79
Association for Living History Farms and Museums, 16
Atchison, Topeka & Santa Fe Railway, 145, 146, 148, 313, 314, 320
The Atlas of the New West (Reibesame), 7
Aurora, Nev., 359
Austin, Nev., **356**
authenticity, 348; desire for, 1; determining, 151
Axelrod, Alan, 310
Aztec National Monument, 139

Bainbridge Island, Wash., 49; Nikkei Removal at, 74–88
Bainbridge Review, 80
Balolookong, 147
Bandelier National Monument, 134
barns, **287**, **288**
Barton, Clara, 214
Barton, Holly, 370
Bass, Rick, 238
Basso, Keith, 123, 211
battlefields: as ceremonial sites, 20; as monuments, 58
Battle of the Little Bighorn, 20–31; archaeological investigation and interpretation of, 23–30; cartridge cases, 24; excavations at, 28; field interpretation at, 27–28; ritual mutilation at, 25; valley fight map, **22**
Bauer, Erwin, 134
Baum, Henry Mason, 133
Baumier, Ellen, 229
Beckett, Anne, 125
Beebe, Lucius, 349–50
Benson, Susan, 3
Bent, Charles, 11
Bent, George, 179, 184
Bent, William, 11, 177
Bent's Old Fort, 6, 11, 14, 15
Benteen, Frederick, 21, 22
Berardinelli, Rick, 109
Berwind Coal Camp, 39; assemblages at, 40
Bethune, Frank, 24
Bierstadt, Albert, 163
Bighorn Medicine Wheel, 159–74, **161**, **162**
Big Medicine, Joe, 191
Big Medicine, Little Joe, 191
Billington, Ray Allen, 390
Birdsall, William, 131
Bisbee, Ariz., 353, 358, 383
Black Elk, 163
Black Hawk, Colo., **359**
Black Kettle, 175, 177, 189, 190, 194
Black Owl, George, 191
Blaunt, J. M., 111
Blue Swallow Motel, 303
Blumenson, John J.-G., 285
Bodie, Calif., 351–52
Bodnar, John, 38
Boggs, James, 172
Boggs, Rumalda, 216
Boime, Albert, 68
Bokides, Dessa, 89
Bonanza (TV series), 284, 331, 345
Bond, Anne, 178
Bonsall, Samuel, 176, 179
boomtowns, 348–65
Bootstrap Ranch, 8
bordellos, 226–33, 340, 342
Borne, Lawrence, 316
Bovey family, 58–59
Brackenridge, Henry, 203, 204
Brady, Mary, 197
Bray, Robert, 23
Brewer, Walter, 265
Bridger Wilderness, 263, 264, 266, 267
Bright Angel Lodge, 215
Brooks, Allyson, 75
Brooks, Paul, 275
Brower, David, 272, 275
Brown, Dee, 195
Brown, Hazel, 226
Brown, Joseph Epes, 51
Brown, Michael, 125
Brown, Molly, 214, 222
Browning, Robert, 243
Bryce Canyon, 67
Buckskinners, 11, 12, 14–15
Buffalo Bill, 222
Bulette, Julia, 197, 343
Bumgarner, Charlotte, 227
Bunsen Peak, 71
Bureau of Land Management (BLM), 7, 160, 232, 236, 273, 278; and firefighting, 247
Burke, George, 320
Bush, Barbara (firefighter), 243–44
Butler, Anne, 11, 196

Calhoun, Lieutenant, 25
Calico, Calif., 350–51
Cameahwait, 202, 208, 209
Camp Amache, **84**
Campbell, Ben Nighthorse, 126, 175, 184, 186, 394
Canyon de Chelly National Monument, 131

Carhart, Arthur, 275
Carmean, Kelli, 123
Carson, Josepha Jaramillo, 216
Carson, Kit, 216
Carson, Rachel, 235, 275, 381
Carver, George Washington, 59
Casa Grande, 130, 133
Casa Rinconada, 138
Cassady, Neal, 300
Catholicism, 110
Catt, Carrie Chapman, 220
cellars, 39
cement stucco, 103
Center of Southwest Studies, 5–6, 56
Center of the American West, 291
Cerillos, N. Mex., **317**
Chaco Canyon, 128, 129, 134, 137, 138
Chaco Culture National Historic Park, 124, 139
Chambers, S. Allen, 285
Chamizal National Memorial, 90, 117–22; lack of well-defined boundary, 118
Chandler, Milford, 207
Chaplin, Charlie, 227
Chapman, Fred, 126
Chapultepec Park, 120
Charbonneau, Jean Baptiste, 196, 201, 209
Charbonneau, Toussaint, 196, 201, 204, 208, 209
Charleston, S.C., 330
Chase, John, 35
chests, 91–96, **93**, **95**; three categories of, 93
Chicanos, 110–111
Chief Washakie, 209
Chivington, John M., 126, 175, 177, 178, 189, 190, 192, 194
Christianity: conversion of Pueblo Indians to, 106
churches: restoration of, 103–4
Churchill, Caroline Nichols, 214, 223
Cirillo, Dexter, 89
Civilian Conservation Corps (CCC), 71, 135, 172
Clark, Bonnie, 216
Clark, Thomas D., 390
Clark, William, 195
Clegg, Charles, 349–50
Clements, Eric, 285
Clinton, Bill, 175, 186
Club Cafe, **301**, 302
Coalition of Labor Union Women, 220
Cockeyed Liz, 197
Coconino National Forrest, 124
coke, coal, and steel, 32
Cokedale, Colo., 348, 349, 350, 366–80; industrial infrastructure, 375–76
Cold War, 58
Cole, Thomas, 129
Collier, John, Jr., 100
Collins, Judy, 217

colonia, 62
Colonial Williamsburg, 58, 59, 310, 330
Colorado Centennial-Bicentennial Commission, 4
Colorado Coalfield War, 18, 32–43; archaeological project, 38–41. *See also* Ludlow Massacre; strike of 1913–14
Colorado Endowment for the Humanities, 4, 41, 221
Colorado Fuel and Iron Company (CF&I), 33–34, 348, 368
Colorado Gold Rush, 176
Colorado Historical Society, 178, 194, 220, 340
Colorado History Group, 222
Colorado Industrial Plan, 38
Colorado Springs Fine Arts Center, 54
Colorado State Capital: Civil War monument at, 193, **194**
Colorado Suffrage Centennial, 214, 216–22
Colorado Woman Suffrage Association, 218, 220
Colter, Mary, 71, 126, 137, 145–49, 215, 216
Columbus, Christopher, 122
Cometsevah, Colleen, **191**
Cometsevah, Laird, 181–82, 184, **191**
company towns, 33, 353, 369
Confederates in the Attic (Horwitz), 11
Conforte, Joseph, 232
confraternities, 54
conquistadors, 89
The Conservation Fund, 186, 187
The Contested Plains (West), 6
Cooper, Bruce, 92
Copper Block, 228
copper mining, 7
Coral Court Motel, 302
Corbett, Katharine T., 195
Cordova Island, 121
Cornerstone Community Partnerships, 103–4
Cortés, Hernan, 107
Cowboy Hall of Fame, 322
Crawford, Dana, 333–34
cribs, **226**, 227
Cripple Creek, Colo., 35, 37, 197, 198, 226–27, 231, 345, 383
Crittenden, Lieutenant, 25
Cronon, William, 211, 390
Crowell, Claudia, **259**
Crumelle, Leonard, 210
cultural biases, 52
cultural heritage: natural wonders as part of, 66
cultural knowledge vs. scientific evidence, 184
cultural values, 52
Cunningham, Anne Pamela, 283

curators, 45; and conflicting values with museum visitors, 46
Cushing, Frank, 133
Custer, George Armstrong, 18, 21, 119; archaeological investigation of campsite of, 23; attitudes concerning, 20; map showing movement of, **21**
Custer's Last Stand. *See* Battle of Little Bighorn
"Custer's Last Stand" (print), **20**
Custer Battlefield Archaeological Project, 20, 27
Custer Battlefield Historical and Museum Association, 29
Custer Battlefield National Monument, 27, **30**. *See also* Little Bighorn Battlefield National Monument
cycloramas, 70, 72

Dagget, Dan, 288
Daniels, Roger, 76
Daniken, Erich von, 138
David, Susan, 106
Dawson, William F. and Tootie, 186, 190
Dean, Cecil A., 136
death cart, **99**
Death Pit, 37
"Death Special" armored car, 35
DeBaca, Vincent C., 89
De Bouzek, Jeannette, 109, 113
Dedek, Peter, 284
Deetz, James, 17, 18
DeHuff, John H., 113
Delahanty, Randolph, 312, 319, 325
Delgadillo, Angel, 299
Delina, Lou, 300
Demo, John, 60
Demosh, Mona, 195
Denver, Colo.: and Larimer Square, 333–34, **334**, 336; Market Street, 338–39
Desert Solitaire (Abbey), 235, 238
DeVere, Pearl, 231
Devil's Tower, 67, 160
DeWitt, John, 80, 82
Dinosaur National Monument, 254–61, **256**, 274
distinctiveness thesis, 111
Dodge, Wagner, 241
Dodge City, Kans., 321–23
Dodo family (of Old West), 5
Dora Moore School, 217
Dubrow, Gail, 75, 76, 79, 195
dude ranches, 316
Duke, Philip, 18
Duncan, Clifford, 275
Dye, Eva Emery, 205–7

Eagledale Ferry Dock, 75–88
Eagleton, Terry, 67
Earp, Wyatt, 319, 342

Earth First!, 67
Eastman, Charles, 207
Echo Park dam, 258
ecosystem disruption, 267
ecotourism, 235, 236, 253–62
Eddy, Charles B., 391
Edison, Thomas, 59
Eisenhower, Mamie Dowd, 217
El Camino Real, 97, 100
Ellis, Richard, 178
El Paso, Tex., 90, 97; and Juárez, Mex., 117–18
El Rancho de las Golondrinas, 102
El Tovar Hotel, 69, 70, 146
Endangered Species Act, 256, 258, 259
Enola Gay, 47
Ensley, Elizabeth, 221
environmental movement, 46, 381
Environmental Protection Agency (EPA), 75, 355, 385
epidemic story, 342–43
Erick, Okla., 315
ethnographic present, 51
Etulain, Richard, 195
Evans, John, 177, 189, 190, 192
Evans, Max, 197
excavations, 131, 133, 169; at Custer Battlefield National Monument, 27, 28; at Ludlow, Colo., 36, 39, 40; and recovery of human remains, 28, 29
exhibits: on agricultural history, 62; artifact driven rather than idea driven, 48; artifacts and planning of, 61; "Barelas a Travéz de Los Años: A Pictorial History of Barelas", 101; curated by indigenous community members, 53; and cycloramic exhibition technique, 71; desire of public for reinforcement of present understandings or biases, 47; "El Favor de Las Santos: The Retablo Collection of NMSU", 102; "Family and Faith", 53–54, 100; "Generations", 100; "Great Picture" convention, 69–72; on Hiroshima and the first atomic bomb (canceled), 47; "Images of Penance, Images of Mercy", 54; incorporating indigenous values and points of view into, 53; Indian and Hispanic arts in same, 55; "*Kodomo No Tame Ni*: For the Sake of the Children", 75; "La Luz: Contemporary Latino Art in the United States", 101; "Mountain — Family — Spirit: The Arts and Culture of the Ute Indians", 55; "Nuevo México Profundo: Rituals of an Indo-Hispano Homeland", 101; "Our Place in the West: Places, Pasts, and Images of the Yellowstone Valley, 1880 and 1940", 62; on plantation slavery (canceled), 47; "Prostitution and Deadwood's Badlands District", 231; "Sacred Land: Indian and Hispanic Cultures of the Southwest", 55; on Sigmund Freud (postponed), 47; traveling photo, 75; "Walk a Mile in Her Shoes", 217; "The West as America", 46; on Western women's suffrage, 218

Fell, James E., 286
Ferguson, Erna, 137
Finley, Michael, 253
Firestone, Harvey S., 59
First Mesa, 124, 125
Fishel, Leslie, 4
fish stocking, 264–66, 268
Fitch, James Marston, 283
Flaming Gorge dam, 258, 260
Flat Top Wilderness, **276**, **277**
Fleming, E. McClung, 61
Flynn Farm, 59
Ford, Henry, 45, 59
Forest Service, 165, 168, 273, 278
Forrest, Suzanne, 99
Forsythe, Scott, 176, 179–80
The Fort (restaurant), 11
Fort Berthold Reservation, 209
Fort Clatsop, 17
Fort Laramie National Historic Site, 61
Fort Lewis College, 5, 38, 56
Foster, Stephen, 59
Four Corners, 128, 137, 147
Fox, Richard, 27
Francaviglia, Richard, 285, 286, 344
Francis, Harris, 123
Francke, Paul, 169
Fred Harvey Company, 138, 145, 146, 147
Fred Harvey Indian Detours, 137
French Quarter, 330
Frisch, Michael, 79
frontier thesis, 57–58
Frost, Kenny, 249
fur trade, 11
Fur Trade Encampment, 13

Gaddis, John, 393
gambling, 383
Gandert, Miguel, 101
García, Fabián, 101
Garcia, Ignacio M., 97
Gardner Canyon, 71
Garrett, Pat, 391
Garrett, Ruby, 228
Gasquet-Orleans Road, 159
Gass, Patrick, 205, 209
Geary, Edward, 9
ghost towns, 319–20, 343, 348–65
Gibbon, John, 23
Gibbon Falls, 71
Giecek, Rudy, 228, 229
Gilman, Lance, 232

Gleeson, Ariz., **359**
Glen Canyon Dam, 67
Glenwood Springs, Colo., 237–52
Glory (film), 15
Gold, Aaron and Jake, 131
Goldstein, Marcia Tremmel, 196
Gómez, Art, 89
Gomez, Arthur R., 235
Gonzales, Phillip B., 111
Goodman, Jennifer, 195
Graham, Howard, 131
Grand Canyon, 67; and photo reconnaissance training, **154**; view from South Rim, **153**
Grand Canyon National Park, 49, 69, 145–58, 215, 341
Grand Canyon of the Yellowstone, 68, 71
Grand Canyon of the Yellowstone (Moran), 67, **67**, 69
Gray, Connie Walker, 75, 79, 80
Greasy Grass, 29
Greaves, Tom, 126
Greene, Jerome, 176, 182, 183
Greenfield Village, Mich., 45, 59
Greensburg, Kans., 320, **321**
Gregg, Josiah, 129
Grey, Zane, 134
Griffin, Gus and Ramona, 136
Griffith, James S., 89
Grosvenor, Gilbert S., 134
Guggenheim, Daniel, 370, 372
Gulliford, Andrew, 2, 5–6, 9, 123
Gunsmoke (TV series), 214, 284, 321, 323, 331
Gust, Sherri, 17
Guterson, David, 75
Gutierrez, Clemente, 91
Gutiérrez, Ramón, 107, 109
Guttridge, Leonard F., 36
Gwaltney, William, 2

Haertel, Kirstie, 78
Hagen, Terri, 247, 248; marker at death site, 249
Hagerman, James J., 391
Halaas, David, 180, 183
Hall, Maggie, 343
Hapiuk, William J., Jr., 151
Hardacre, Emma, 130
Hardesty, Donald, 18, 360
Harding, Warren G., 391
Hard Places (Francaviglia), 350
Harmonic Convergence, 124, 138
Harper, Ida Husted, 206
Harrison, William H., 133
Hart, Nathan, **190**
Harvey, Fred, 148, 215
Harvey Girls, 215
Harvey Houses, 146, 314
Harwood Foundation, 93

Haugh, Bob, 251
Hayden, Dolores, 367
Hayden, Ferdinand V., 67, 69
Hayes, Frank, 34, 38
Haywood, C. Robert, 311
Hearst, William Randolph, 215
Heart Mountain camp, **81**
Heath, Kingston, 312
Hebard, Grace Raymond, 206, 209
Hemenway, Mary, 133
Hemenway Expedition, 133
Henry, Patrick, 58
heritage tourism, 6, 283, 285, 286, 331
heritage vs. history, 3, 6, 332
Herman Blueher House, **332**
Hermit's Rest, 215
Hern, Harold and Lodi, 226
Hewett, Edgar Lee, 112, 133, 135, 136
Heye Foundation, 45
Hinton, Richard, 130
Hipke, Eric, 251
Hirsch, Jerrold, 100
Hispanic heritage and culture, 97–113
historians: academic vs. public, 393; and employment opportunities, 386; and visual illiteracy, 61. *See also* public historians
historical archaeology, 17–19, 182, 359–60; convergence with environmental history, 361
historic districts, 304, 330–31, 339, 357–58, 368, 374
Historic Preservation Act, 355
Historic Preservation Fund, 171
history: acceptable, 47; agricultural, 59; by association, 56, 60; challenges of the profession, 393; environmental, 235; ethnic, 193, 357; industrial, 357; invented, 334; living, 216; mixture of academic, public, and community, 74, 83; New Western, 32, 89, 214; oral, 79–80, 83, 101, 180–81, 207; real vs. faux, 323; social, 46, 61, 62, 211; transportation, 357; vernacular, 38; vs. heritage, 3, 6, 332. *See also* public history
History Center (Minn.), 62
history museums, 51; focus of, 46; four types of, 57
history trunk, 41
Hodge, Frederick, 207
Hodgson, Benjamin, 23
Hof, Dennis, 232–33
Hollywood movies, 317, 321
Holsinger, S. J., 133
Homestead Act, 236, 290
homestead houses, 6, **289**, **292**
Hoosava, Yvonne, 124, 125
Hopi Cultural Preservation Office, 149
Hopi House, 126, 145–48, 150, 152, 215; and repatriation, 153

Horton, Sarah, 89
Horwitz, Tony, 11
Hovenweep, 130
Howe, Sherman, 131
Huggard, Christopher J., 235
Hulkrantz, Äke, 207
Hull's Motel, 304, **305**
Hungate family, 177, 189
Hunner, Jon, 89
Hunt, Rebecca, 221
Huntley Project, 62
Hurtado, Albert L., 2
Hurtado, Horace, 372
Huyck, Heather, 216
Hyde, George, 179

"Impact Los Alamos", 101
Indian Arts and Crafts Act, 151
Indians: Anasazi, 126, 128–44, 192; Apache, 125; Arapaho, 6, 164, 175, 177, 178, 187, 194; Arikara, 209; arts and crafts of, 52, 151; and authenticity, 151; Aztec, 129; Bannock, 163, 164; Blackfeet, 160, 162, 164; Cheyenne, 6, 21, 23, 24, 25, 162, 164, 175, 177, 178, 181, 187, 192, 194; Comanche, 204, 207, 209, 211; conversion to Christianity, 106; Crow, **29**, 164, 172; dwelling ruins of, 67; Eastern Shoshone, 5, 165; Hidatsa, 204, 207, 208, 209–210, 211; historical treatment of, 192; Hopi, 124, 126, 128, 130, 135, 139, 151–52; Hupa, 159; Ioway, 59; Karok, 159; Kootenai-Salish, 164; Lakota, 23, 24, 25; Lemhi Shoshone, 208, 211; Mandan, 204, 209; Miwok, 123; and mythic threat of cultural extinction, 146; Navajo, 129, 139; Northern Arapaho, 165, 171, 208; Northern Cheyenne, 173; Plains Cree, 164; Pueblo, 106–116, 128, 133, 137–38, 193; scalping and mutilating of, 190; Shoshone, 123, 163, 164, 207, 263; Sioux, 21, 164, 211; Tolowa, 159; Toltec, 129; Ute, 6, 55, 123, 134; White River Ute, 6; Wind River Shoshone, 204, 205, 208–9, 211; Yakima, 204; Yurok, 159; Zuni, 50, 56, 125. *See also* Ancestral Puebloans; Native Americans
Ingersoll, Ernest, 130
In Small Things Forgotten: An Archaeology of Early American Life (Deetz), 18
International Sex Worker Foundation for Art, Culture and Education, 199, 229
internment camps, **78**; Japanese Americans relocated to, 74–88
Interstate Highway Act, 283, 381
invented traditions, 172
Ireland, Art, 180

irrigation, 62, 284, 391
Iwo Jima, 119

Jackson, Donald, 204
Jackson, Helen Hunt, 108, 216
Jackson, John Brinckerhoff, 285
Jackson, William Henry, 69, 130, 131
James, Ronald, 345
Jameson, Elizabeth, 195
Jameson, John H., Jr., 18
Jeep, Oddie, 136, 137
Jefferson, Thomas, 58, 119
Jefferson National Expansion Memorial, 120
Jensen, Billie Barnes, 219
Jerk Meat, 204, 209
Jerome, Ariz., 343
Johnson, Lon, 229
Johnson, Lyndon B., 236, 272
Johnson family (of New West), **5**
Jokake Inn, 313
Jones, Mary "Mother", 35, 36, 38
Juárez, Mex., 90; and El Paso, Tex., 117–18

Kabotie, Fred, 147
kachina dances, 124
Kammen, Michael, 193
Karzmiski, Ken, 17
Keeper of the National Register, 168, 283, 356
Kelleher, Michael, 1
Keller, Robert, 124
Kelly, Charles B., 136
Kelly, Klara Bonsack, 122
Kennecott Copper Corp., 7, 362
Kennedy, John F., 47, 120, 274, 275; eternal flame at grave of, 119
Kern, Richard H., 129
Kerouac, Jack, 300
Kessell, John, 89
Kidder, Alfred V., 135
King, Thomas F., 18, 160
King, W. L. Mackenzie, 38
kiosk, interpretive, 40
Kirkpatrick, David T., 18
Kirshen-Gimblett, Barbara, 66
Kline, Benjamin, 235
Knott, Elinore, 228
Knott, Walter, 350
Knott's Berry Farm, 350
Koshare Tours, 137
Kristof, Nicolas, 6
Kuwanwisiwma, Leigh, 125, 126

Lace House, **345**, **346**
Lacey, John, 133
La Conquistadora, 106, 107, 110, 112
La Fonda Hotel, 92, 313
La Garita cemetery, 103

La Gente: Hispano History and Life in Colorado (DeBaca), 89
Lamont, Tony, 373
Land of the Penitentes, Land of Tradition (Archuleta), 89
Landres, Peter B., 267, 268
landscapes: cultural, 173, 302; of Euro-American national identity, 162; interactive, 362; mining, **354**, 362; psychological, 161; spiritual, 161; as substitute for missing national tradition, 66; as Western hero, 287
Langford, Nathaniel, 71
La Posada Hotel, 215
La Purisima Mission, 17
La Salle, Sonny, 251
Las Vegas, Nev., 315
Lavender, David, 48
Lawson, John, 34
League of Women Voters, 220, 222
Lee, Martha, 138
Lee, Robert E., 119
Lee, Russell, 100
Lees, William, 178
Left Hand (Arapaho leader), 177
Legacy of Conquest (Limerick), 6
Leonard, Steve, 218
Leopold, Aldo, 238, 266, 272, 280
Leuchtenburg, William E., 60
Lewis and Clark Expedition, 161, 195–96, 200–213; campgrounds of, 17; use of mercury to treat venereal disease, 17
Library of Congress, 47
Light, Fred M., 237
lime plastering, 103
Limerick, Patricia, 1, 6, 159, 214, 218, 343, 390, 393, 394
Lincoln, Abraham, 119
Linderfelt, Karl, 37
Linger, George W., 293
Lisa, Manuel, 203
Little Bighorn Battlefield National Monument, 18, 20, 27, 119, 120
Litwack, Leon, 393
Living History Farms, 59, 60
LoDo District, 334, 339
Lookout Studio, 69
The Lore of New Mexico (Weigle and White), 89
Los Alamos National Laboratory, 101
Lovell, Charles, 102
Lowenthal, David, 193
Lowie, Robert, 207
Ludlow, Colo.: alcohol consumption, 40; assemblages at, 39; boarders in, 40; changes in household strategy, 40; funeral at, **37**; tent camp at, **33**; UMWA monument at, 40
Ludlow Massacre, 36–37, 346, 369, 372; annual memorial service at site of, 40. *See also* Colorado Coalfield War

Luján, Juana, 101
Lummis, Charles, 108
Luna, Soloman, 101
Lund, Dennis, 298
Luttig, John, 204

MacArthur, Douglas, 119
Machebeuf, Joseph, 222
MacKell, Jan, 198
Mackey, Don, 246–47
Maclean, Norman, 241, 249
Macomb Expedition, 129
Maestas, Monica, 110, 111
magisterial gaze, 68
Magoffin, Susan Shelby, 129, 216
Mammoth Hot Springs, 71
Mancos Canyon, 130, **132**
Manifest Destiny, 6, 45, 68, 129, 206, 251
Manitou Cliff Dwellings, 136
Mann Gulch fire, 241–48
Manzanar Relocation Center, 76–77
Marilley, Susan, 220
Marshall, Bob, 238, 266
Marshall, Howard Wright, 285
Marshall, James, 382
Martin, John, 22
Martinez, Jerome, 54
Martinez, Robert, 194
Mason, Charley, 131
Mason, John, 193
Mather, Stephen, 134, 255
Mattie's Red Light Lounge, 338
Mattson, Frank, 72
May, Ernest R., 272
Mayfield, Jack, 231
McBeth, Sally, 196
McClurg, Virginia, 133, 136, 215
McCrimmon, Dan, 14
McCutcheon, John T., 70
McDougall, Thomas, 21, 22
McElmo Canyon, 130
McGovern, George S., 36
McGuire, Randy, 18
McKinney, A. Andrew, 312, 319, 325
McLoyd, Charles, 131
Medicine Mountain Cultural Landscape, 166, 172
Meigs, John, 94
Merchant, Carolyn, 235
Meredith, Ellis, 218, 220, 221
Merriman, Nick, 32
Mesa Verde, 128, 135, 138
Mesa Verde National Park, 133, 139, 192, 193, 215
Mesilla, N. Mex., 103
Michoacán, Mex., 91, 95
Mickey Mouse History (Wallace), 3
Midwest Outdoor Museum Coordinating Committee, 16
Mining, 381–85; and litigation, 386; specialized language, 385

Mining Act of 1872, 160
Mining History Association, 285, 356
Minnesota Historical Society, 62
Mission 66, 71, 72
Mitchell, Finis, 263–71
Mitchell, W. J. T., 66–67
Miyashima, Kara, 284
model towns, 372
Moe, Richard, 285
Montana Historical Society, 61
Montaño, Mary, 89
Montezuma, 107, 129
Montezuma's Castle, 67
Montgomery, Charles, 89
Montgomery, Richard, 119
Monticello, 58
Moonlite Bunny Ranch, 232
Moore, Bob, 300
Moran, Thomas, 67, 68, 69, 130, 163
Morgan, Julia, 215
Morley, Judy, 284
Mormons, 169
Motel La Loma, **307**
Mountain State Legal Foundation, 167, 168
Mount Rushmore, 119, 120
Mount Shasta, 160, 171
Mount Vernon, 48, 58, 283, 330
Muir, John, 238
Muldoon, Dan, 14
Mullins, Paul, 39
Murie, Olaus and Mardy, 238
Murtagh, William J., 283
museum effect, 66
Museum of International Folk Art (MOIFA), 53, 100, 102; Hispanic Heritage Wing, 53, 54, 100; New Mexico Furniture History Project, 92; Spanish Colonial Arts Society Collection, 92, 94
museums, 45, 47; and accommodating community values, 52; Adams Museum, 231; Arizona State Museum, 56; Autry Museum of Western Heritage, 217; Brothel Art Museum, 231; Canadian Museum of Civilization, 45; Cokedale Mining Museum, 366; Cowtown Museum, 59, 60, **60**, **318**; Dalton Gang hideout, 320; and deification of early American heroes, 58; Denver Art Museum, 50; desire of public for exhibits which reinforce present understandings or biases, 47; development of regional, 46; District Museum (Cripple Creek), 231; Dumas Brothel, 198, 227, 228, 229, 231; as educational institutions communicating information, 50; El Museo Cultural de Santa Fe, 102–103; ethnographic, 51; Fanny Ann's Saloon and Restaurant, 226; Field Museum of Natural History, 146, 149; Graceland,

47; as halls of fame, 48; Heard Museum, 149; Holocaust Museum, 47; Jefferson National Expansion Memorial, 120; Julia C. Bulette Red Light Museum, 231, 345; Las Golondrinas Museum, 94; living history, 102; Mattie Silk's Restaurant, 226; Mesa Verde, 135; Millicent Rogers Museum, 93; and minority professionals, 48; Miss Hattie's Bordello, 231; Monte Carlo, 226; Museum of Indian Arts and Culture, 56; Museum of Man, 45; Museum of New Mexico, 106, 112; National Air and Space Museum, 46; National Museum of Art, 46; of natural history and anthropology, 51; New Mexico Farm and Ranch Heritage Museum, 100; Oasis Museum, 231; Old Homestead House Museum, 226, 227; Pioneer Bar, 226; Rancho Camulos Museum, 215–16; and reinforcement of dominant social views, 50; role of, 52; and shrine mentality, 58; Silver Nugget Museum, 231; Taylor Museum, 54, 55; Texas Schoolbook Depository, 47, 120; as vehicle for maintaining cultural superiority, 50; Wheelwright Museum, 56; Women of the West (WOW), 214, 216, 217. *See also* history museums; Museum of International Folk Art

Mustang Ranch, 232

Nadeau, Delia and Joseph, 228
Naranjo, Domingo, 107, 109
Nash, Roderick, 235
National Association for Interpretation, 16
National Council on Public History, 16, 392
National Environmental Policy Agency, 170
National Geographic, 134
National Hispanic Cultural Center, 56, 100, 101
National Historic Landmarks, 126, 285, 343, 361–62, 391; Bighorn Medicine Wheel, 159–73; Eagledale Ferry Dock, 74–88; M.E.J. Colter buildings, 145–55
National Historic Preservation Act, 1, 123, 145, 148, 149, 160, 167, 171, 283, 381; Section 106 of, 152–54, 159, 232, 283, 303–4, 354
national memorial concept, 118
National Park Service, 11, 27, 49, 120, 151, 175, 273, 283, 284, 302, 306, 355, 391; and concessionaires, 154; Death Valley conference, 355–56; and facing the uncomfortable past, 392; formation of, 134, 145; and Hispanic heritage, 99–100; and interpretative programs, 392; and living history demonstrations, 61; and misinterpretations, 128; and national memorials, 99–100; and nomination of Eagledale ferry landing for National Historic Landmark designation, 74–88; parks as museological institutions, 66; and preservation of Hispanic heritage, 100; and Route 66 Corridor Act, 305; and Sand Creek Massacre, 179–91; U.S.-Mexico Affairs Office, 100; and wilderness, 278; and Yellowstone National Park, 254–55
National Register of Historic Places, 76, 145, 159, 160, 171, 283, 303, 355
National Trails System, 100
National Trust for Historic Preservation, 4, 18, 103, 283, 285, 305, 306
National Wilderness Act, 236, 238
National Wilderness Preservation System, 272, 278
National Wildland Firefighter Memorial, 241, 242
Native American Graves Protection and Repatriation Act, 1, 124, 126, 138–39, 145, 148, 149, 151–55
Native Americans, 6; and national identity, 161; oral tradition of, 26; and religious freedom, 159; sacred sites/objects of, 152, 161. *See also* Indians
The Nature Conservancy, 292–94
Navajo National Monument, 134
Nelson, Emma, 264
Neustadt, Richard E., 272
Nevada City, Mont., 59
New Agers, 138; and damage to sacred sites, 124
Newberry, John S., 129, 131
New Mexico: and deterrents to statehood, 89, 133; and Hispanic population, 53; as oldest center of Latino culture in U.S., 98
New Mexico Endowment for the Humanities, 101
New Mexico State Monuments, 103
New Mexico State University, 102
New West, 6, 49, 159, 161
Next West, 6
Nichols, Jeffrey, 196, 238
Niederman, Sharon, 195
Nikkei community, 74–88
Noel, Tom, 126, 218, 219
Nordenskiöld, Gustaf, 131
Norris, Philetus, 71
North Dakota History Center, 61
Northern Pacific Railroad, 69, 71
Nostrand, Richard, 110; distinctiveness thesis of, 111
Nuevo Mexicanos, 98–104
Nusbaum, Aileen, 135
Nusbaum, Jesse, 135, 136, 137

Oakley, Annie, 214
O'Brien, Bob R., 236
Obsidian Cliff, 71
O'Donnell, I. D., 62
OK Corral, 342
Old Faithful Geyser, 68, **254**, 254
Old Oraibi, 146
Old West, 6, 315–23
Oñate, Juan de, 97, 106, 107
open spaces, 295–96
"The Opposition", 14
Orchard, Harry, 342
Ordway, John, 209
Organic Act, 145
Organization of American Historians, 16, 392
origin myths, 45
Ortiz, Frank V., 117, 122
overlooks, 68, 70, 71, 72

Palace of the Governors, 100, 102, 108
panoramas, moving, 70, 71, 72
Patin, Thomas, 49
Pecos Conference, 135
Pecos Pueblo, 129
Pedregone, Alcarita, 37
Penitente Brotherhood, 54, 55, 89
Peñuela, Marqués de, 112
petroglyphs, 147
Petrucci, Mary, 37
Phelps Dodge Corp., 6–7, 319, 344
pilgrimages, 168
Pinchot, Gifford, 236, 237, 274
Pinkley, Frank, 135
Pino, Peter, 138
Pioneer Village, 60, **60**
Pitcaithley, Dwight, 389
Pocahontas, 206
Poling-Kempes, Lesley, 195
Powell, John Wesley, 130, 236, 255
Prescott, William, 129
Presenting Archaeology to the Public: Digging for Truths (Jameson), 18
Presenting the Past (Benson), 3
preservation: of adobe structures, 103; and auto culture, 298–309; of bordellos, 196–99, 226–33; of historic buildings, 329–37; and landscape, 353–55; and Native Americans, 123–74; and NPS criteria, 77; of ranches, 283, 287–97; vs. development, 329; vs. public use, 253; of wilderness, 272–81; women and, 215
property rights, concerns about, 383
prostitution, 214–15, 226–33, 340, 342; ads for, **230**
Prowers, Amache Ochinee, 216
Prowers, John, 216
Prown, Jules David, 63
pseudoshrines, 124

public education, 32
The Public Historian (Hunner), 89
public historians, 215, 216; academic historians vs., 393; and preservation vs. environment, 387; working in teams, 1–2
public history, 1–4, 6, 16, 32, 83; defined, 1, 15; flawed, 376; Latino, 106
Pueblo Bonito, 133
Pueblo Pintado, 129
Pueblo Revolt of 1680, 106, 107, 109, 112
Pulaski, Edward, 240
Pulido, Lopez, 89

racial stratigraphy, 107, 113
racism, 80, 83, 110, 111, 165, 168, 373
ranches, 283, 287–97; as key to Western preservation, 290–96; ownership of, 289
Rankin, Jeannette, 217
Rast, Raymond, 49
Reagan, Ronald, 75, 342
Reckner, Paul, 18
Recreation Opportunity Spectrum, 257
Red Cherries, Mildred, 178
Redford, Frank, 316
Reed, John, 35, 38
reenactments, historical, 11; suffrage march, 221
reenactors, 14; in *Glory* (film), 15; as public historians, 2
Rehberger, Dean, 113
Remington, Frederic, 316
Rendezvous, 12–13, 263
Reno, Marcus, 21, 23, 24, 27
Reno, Ronald, 360
repatriation of cultural objects, 149; four-step process for, 150
retablos, 102
reverential gaze, 68
Reynolds, Minnie, 221
Rhodes, Arly, **191**
Rickey, Don, 23
Rickner, Thomas, 136
Ridge, Martin, 390
Riley, Glenda, 195
Ríos-Bustamante, Antonio, 111
Roberts, Alexa, 181
Robertson, David, 286
Robinson, Helen Ring, 35
Robinson, Laird, 249
Rockefeller, John D., Jr., 38, 58, 330, 369, 371
Rock Springs, Wyo., 342
Rodriguez, Richard, 97
Rodríguez, Sylvia, 98, 107
Rogers, Jennie, 198, 338, 339
Romanticism, 129
Romer, Roy, 222
Ronda, James, 211
Roosevelt, Franklin, 82

Roosevelt, Theodore, 133, 236–38, **237**, 263
Roth, Michael, 47
Roth, Roger, 240
Rothman, Hal, 235, 278, 323
Route 66, 283, 284, 298–309, 316, 332
Route 66 Corridor Act, 304–5
Routt County, Colo., 290–91
Roy, Cordell, 121
rugged individualism, 9
Rundell, Walter, 11
Runte, Alfred, 67, 236, 303
Russell, Charles, 316
Russell, Terry and Renny, 235

Sabin, Florence, 217
Sacagawea, 195–96, 200–213; controversy over name, 200–201; disputed date of death, 203; mythologization of, 205–6; roles in expedition, 201–3; statue of, **206**; and suffragist movement, 205–7
Sacajawea Cemetery, **204**
Sacajawea memorial, 211
Sacramento, Calif., 17
Sacred Objects and Sacred Places: Preserving Tribal Traditions (Gulliford), 5
sacred sites, 123, 124, 126, 145, 159, 160, 161, 170, 173
"The Sacred World of the Penitentes" (Pulido), 89
Sagebrush Rebellion, 161, 278
Sagstetter, William and Beth, 285
Saitta, Dean, 18
Sallee, Bob, 242
Sánchez, George, 98
Sanchez, Joseph, 100
A Sand County Almanac (Leopold), 238
Sand Creek Massacre, 175–94; site identification, 183–86; site map of, **185**
Sanders, Brad, 240
Sando, Joe, 128
San Juan River Ranch, 8
Santa Fe: reconquest of, 107
Santa Fe Archaeological Society, 133
Santa Fe Fiesta, 106–116; boycott by All Indian Pueblo Council, 108; and Fiesta Queen controversy, 110–111; as glorification of subjugation of Pueblo Indians, 109
Santa Fe style, 102, 113
Santa Fe Trail, 11, 129, 216
Santandér, Diego de, 101
santos, 53–54, 108
Sax, Joseph L., 236
Schablitsky, Julie, 18
Schlissel, Lilian, 195
schoolhouses, one-room, 4, **4**, 60
Schroeder, Pat, 218, 220, 222
Schulte, Steve, 238
Schultz, Peter, 17

Schuyler, Robert, 17
Schwantes, Carlos, 341–42
Scott, Douglas D., 18, 178, 182, 392
Seager, Joni, 195
Seattle, Wash.: and Pioneer Square, 334–36
Sena, José D., 113
Shabecoff, Philip, 235
Shados, Karyn, 229
Shaffer, Marguerite, 315
Shalako house blessing ceremonies, 124
Shaw, Anna Howard, 206
Sherman, William T., 180
Sherow, James E., 235
Shimkin, Demitri, 207
shrine mentality, 58
shrines, 126
Sierra Club, 67, 238, 274, 275
Silent Spring (Carson), 235, 275
Silks, Mattie, 198, 338, 339
Silver City Millie, 198
Silver Heels, 198
Silverheels, 343
Silverman, Lois, 214
Silver Reef, Utah, 17
Silverton, Colo., 285
Silvey, Sharnel, 232
Simms, S. C., 165
Simon, James, 266, 267
Simpson, James H., 129
Simpson, O. H. "Doc", 321
Sinclair, Upton, 35, 38
Sipapu, 147
Sitting Bull, 24
skiing, 381–82
Smith, Doug, 285
Smith, Frank, 117
Smith, Greg, 305
Smithsonian Institution, 11, 45, 46–47, 69
snake dances, 125
Snow Falliing on Cedars (Guterson), 75
Snyder, Frank, 37
Society for Historical Archaeology, 17
Soil Conservation Service, 180
Somerset County, Penn., 119
Something in the Soil: Legacies and Reckonings in the New West (Limerick), 1
Sorenson, Dirty Mouth Jean, 227
Southern Arizona Folk Arts (Griffith), 89
Southern Ute Cultural Center, 56
Southwestern Parks and Monuments, 29
Spain in the Southwest (Kessell), 89
Spanish American vs. Mexican American, 110–111
Spanish Colonial Arts Society, 102
Spanish conquest, 106, 107
Spanish heritage, 108, 110, 111
Spanish language, 97, 110
Spanish Market, 98, 102
Spence, Mark David, 124
"Spirit Warriors" (sculpture), 18
Spratt, John, 344

sprawl, 330
Spruce Tree House, 135, 136
Spude, Robert, **356**, 361
Stanton, Robert, 166
Star, Moses, Jr., **190**
State Historic Preservation Offices, 152, 153, 154, 160, 167, 173, 283, 306, 346, 355
Steele, Rufus, 67
Stefanco, Carolyn, 219, 220
Stegner, Wallace, 9, 236, 280
Steinbeck, John, 298
Steinbrueck, Victor, 336
Stephens, Douglas, 138
Steunenberg, Frank, 342
Stimson, Henry, 82
Stokes, Samuel N., 283
Stone, Lucy, 220, 221
Stone, Nat, 123
Storm King Mountain fire, 239, 243–45, **247**, 251
Stowe, Harriet Beecher, 216
strike of 1913–14, 33–34, 369; contemporary education concerning, 40–41; cost of militia bankrupts Colorado, 36; harassment of strikers, 35; and martial law, 35; place vs. space, 40; role of militia in, 35–36; role of Rockefeller in, 38; role of women and children, 35; and seven demands of coal miners, 34; strikebreakers, 33–35; and tent colonies, **34**, **34**, **35**, **36**; use of national brands, 39–40; weapons used by strikers, 36. *See also* Ludlow Massacre
Suffrage Association, 221
Summer Rain, Mary, 138
Swaim, Doug, 285
Sweeney, John, 40
Sweetgrass Hills, 160, 162–63, 171
Sweet Medicine, 163
Swidler, Nina, 123

Tabor, Baby Doe, 214
Tabor, Horace, 222
Takaki, Ronald, 76
Tallbull, William, 162
Tanaka, Stefan, 76
Tansill, Robert W., 391
Taylor, Lonn, 89
Taylor, Mike, 103
Taylor, Pat, 103
Taylor, Mary and J. Paul, 103
Teeuwen, Randall, 4
Terry, Alfred, 21, 23
Tetons, 68
Texas Historical Commission, 302
Thelen, David, 3
Theodore Roosevelt National Memorial, 119–20
Thomas, Craig, 166–67

Thrash, Jim, 240
Thurber, Tex., 348, 349, 350, 353, 363
Tierney, Patrick, 236
Tikas, Louis, 37
Tilden, Freeman, 136
Tintic Mining District, 358
Toahty, Robert, 181
Toll, Roger, 71
Tombstone, Ariz., 319, 342, 343, 344, 352
Tonto Cliff Dwellings, 134
Toothman, Stephanie, 75
Torrey Canyon Petroglyph District, 172
tourism, 6, 136, 169, 226, 253–54, 257, 261, 264, 291, 295, 311, 313, 330, 341, 381, 387; and Bisbee, Calif., 353; Calico, Calif. and, 351; and dams and reservoirs, 256; Dodge City and, 321–23; and economy, 1; and Fred Harvey, 137, 145–46; and Hispanic culture, 98, 108; and historic sites and museums, 57; as mainstay of economy, 331; at Medicine Wheel National Historic Landmark, 165; and movie lots, 318; and Route 66, 298, 302, 305, 306; and Santa Fe Fiesta, 106, 112; and theme parks, 318; Tombstone, Ariz. and, 344, 352; Virginia City, Nev. and, 345; and the Western look, 314–15. *See also* ecotourism; heritage tourism
Tower Falls, 68
Tower Falls and Sulphur Mountain (Moran), **68**
trade fairs, 12
Tradiciones Nuevomexicanos: Hispano Arts and Culture of New Mexico (Montaño), 89
Travelers' Rest, 15, 17–18
Tribal Historic Preservation Offices, 171, 283
Trimble, Stephen, 238
Trinidad Coal Field, 368–70
Tri-State Buddhist Temple, 338–40
Troupe, Bobby, 298
Trujillo, Teofilo, 293
Tubbs, Poker Alice, 231–32
Tunnel View overlook, **70**
Turek, Michael, 124
Turner, Christy, 193
Turner, Frederick Jackson, 9, 57, 315, 390
turnouts, 71, 72
Twain, Mark, 197
Twins, Lucien, **190**
Tyler, Richard, 243

Udall, Stewart, 261, 274, 279
U-Drop Inn Café, 303, 304
Union Bus Depot, 305, **306**
United Mine Workers, 18, 34, 38, 369, 373; monument at Ludlow, Colo., **41**
University of Denver, 38

University of New Mexico, 102
Upton, Dell, 283
urban renewal, 101, 329–36, 381
U.S. Bureau of Reclamation, 62, 391
USS *Arizona* Memorial, 118, 120
Ute Teachers Institute, 56
Ute Trail, 5
Utley, Robert, 121

Valdez, Juan de Jesús, 93
vandalism, 18
Vander, Judith, 207
Van West, Carroll, 48–49
Vargas, Diego de, 97, 107, 108, 112; Anglo portrayals of, 113
Vásquez, Carlos, 101
Venus Alley, 227, 228
Vietnam Veterans Memorial, 119
violence, 34, 35, 120, 342
Virginia City, Mont., 58–59
Virginia City, Nev., 344–45, **363**
vision quest structures, 163, **166**, 172
vista cuts, 71
visual illiteracy, 57, 61, 63
Vlach, John Michael, 283
Vlahos, Ekaterini, 284
Voth, Henry R., 146, 149, 151, 154
Voth, Kathy, 245–46

Wagner, Curly Bear, 162
Waldmire, Bob, 303
Waldo, Anna Lee, 195
Walker, Mark, 18
Wallace, Michael, 3
War Gods (Zuni figures), 50
Washburn Expedition, 67
Washington, George, 58, 119
Washington, John, 129
Washington Monument, 119
Watchtower, 69, 71, 145, 147, 148, 150, 152, 215; and repatriation, 153
water, 6, 7, 22–23, 62, 122, 181, 202, 235, 236, 244, 247, 256–60, 263–69, 274, 290, 293–96, 391
weaving, 6
Weber, David, 98
Weigle, Marta, 89
Weir, Thomas, 22
Weixelman, Joseph, 126
Welborn, Jesse, 37
Wellman, Judith, 76
West: demand for labor in, 82; and resource extraction, 6; as wonderland, 69. *See also* New West; Next West; Old West
West, Elliott, 6
Western Heritage Center, 62
Western Historical Quarterly, 2, 11, 16
Western History Association, 11, 16, 392
Western humor, 8

Western Wildlands Firefighter Memorials, 250
Wetherill, Alfred, 131, 136
Wetherill, Richard, 131
Whipple, T. K., 7
Whitacre, Christine, 126
White, Richard, 214, 390
Whitehouse, John, 209
Whiteley, Peter, 52
White River National Forest, 341
wilderness, 236–38, 272–81, 341
Wilderness Act, 256, 257, 266, 272, 277, 278, 279
Wilderness Area designation, 160
Wilderness Society, 274, 275
Wilderness Study Areas, 278–79
Wild Horse Casino, 227
Wilkinson, Charles, 6, 235
Willey, P., 24
Williams, Wayne, 242, 243
Wilson, Brian, 164
Wilson, Chris, 102, 112
Wilson, Woodrow, 37, 134
Wind River Reservation, 5, 165, 205, 207
Wind River Trails (Mitchell), 266
Winter Quarters (training program), 15
Winterthur Portfolio, 61
Wirth, Conrad, 72
Wolle, Muriel, 349
women, 195–233, 363–64
Women's Christian Temperance Union, 221
Women's Rights National Historic Park, 214, 220
Wood, Margaret, 40
Woodward, Walt and Milly, 80, 82
World Trade Center, 118, 119
Worster, Donald, 235
Wraith Falls, 71
Wright, Frank Lloyd, 215
Wright Brothers, 59
Wright Brothers National Memorial, 120
Wroth, William, 48
Wupatki National Monument, **128**, 138
Wycoff, Mike, 6
Wynkoop, Edward, 177
Wyoming Archaeological Society, 164
Wyoming Game and Fish Department, 264, 266, 268
Wyoming Sawmills, Inc., 167
Wyoming State Historic Preservation Office, 126
Wythe, George, 58

Yamada, Mitsuye, 74
Yard, Robert Sterling, 134
Yeibeichai songs, 135
Yellowstone Lake, 71
Yellowstone National Park, 49, 68, 69, 71, 128, 254, 257; and resource deterioration, 255; snowmobiles in, 260

Yosemite National Park, 70, *70*, 137
Yoshihara, May, 340
Young Women's Christian Association, 220
Yucca House, 130

Zahniser, Howard, 272, 275
Zakin, Susan, 235
Zanella, Bob, 245
Zarur, Elizabeth, 102
Zeaman, Amanda, 126
Zia Pueblo, 128, 138
Zion National Park, 49, 68, 70
Zion Tunnel, 70
Zuni, N. Mex., 124